DATE DUE ✓

Blackwell Handbook of Childhood Social Development

Blackwell Handbooks of Developmental Psychology

This outstanding series of handbooks provides a cutting-edge overview of classic research, current research, and future trends in developmental psychology.

- Each handbook draws together 25–30 newly commissioned chapters to provide a comprehensive overview of a subdiscipline of developmental psychology.
- The international team of contributors to each handbook have been specially chosen for their expertise and knowledge of each field.
- Each handbook is introduced and contextualized by leading figures in the field, lending coherence and authority to each volume

The *Blackwell Handbooks of Developmental Psychology* will provide an invaluable overview for advanced students of developmental psychology and for researchers as an authoritative definition of their chosen field.

Blackwell Handbook of Infant Development
Edited by Gavin Bremner and Alan Fogel

Blackwell Handbook of Childhood Cognitive Development
Edited by Usha Goswami

Blackwell Handbook of Childhood Social Development
Edited by Peter K. Smith and Craig H. Hart

Blackwell Handbook of Adolescence
Edited by Gerald Adams and Michael Berzonsky

Blackwell Handbook of Childhood Social Development

Edited by

Peter K. Smith and Craig H. Hart

Blackwell Publishers

Editorial Offices:
108 Cowley Road, Oxford OX4 1JF, UK
   Tel: +44 (0)1865 79110
350 Main Street, Malden, MA 02148-5018, USA
   Tel: +1 781 388 8250

Library of Congress Cataloging-in-Publication Data

Blackwell handbook of childhood social development / edited by Peter
K. Smith and Craig H. Hart.
      p. cm. — (Blackwell handbooks of developmental psychology)
Includes bibliographical references and index.
   ISBN 0–631–21752–5 (alk. paper)
   1. Developmental psychology—Social aspects.   2. Child psychology—
Social aspects.   I. Smith, Peter K.   II. Hart, Craig H., 1957–   III. Series.
   BF13.B565 2002
   305.231—dc21

                                                        2001003639

A catalogue record for this title is available from the British Library.

Typeset in 10.5 on 12.5 pt Garamond
by Ace Filmsetting Ltd, Frome, Somerset
Printed in Great Britain by T.J. International, Padstow, Cornwall

For further information on
Blackwell Publishers, visit our website:
www.blackwellpublishers.co.uk

Contents

List of Contributors

Maurissa Abecassis
Colby-Sawyer College, New Hampshire

Martyn Barrett
University of Surrey

Amy D. Bellmore
University of Connecticut

Kerry Bissaker
The Flinders University of South Australia

David F. Bjorklund
Florida Atlantic University

Bonnie Brinton
Brigham Young University, Provo, Utah

Eithne Buchanan-Barrow
University of Surrey

Eric S. Buhs
University of Illinois at Urbana-Champaign

Kim B. Burgess
University of Maryland

Jeremy Carpendale
Simon Fraser University, Vancouver

Sarah Caverly
George Manson University, Virginia

Antonius H. N. Cillessen
University of Connecticut

W. Andrew Collins
University of Minnesota

Robert J. Coplan
Carleton University, Ottawa

Maayan Davidov
University of Toronto

Susanne Denham
George Manson University, Virginia

Jessica Dennis
University of California at Riverside

Karen E. Diamond
Purdue University, W. Lafayette, Indiana

Judy Dunn
Institute of Psychiatry, University of London

Ada Fonzi
University of Florence

Mary L. Flyr
University of California at Riverside

Martin Fujiki
Brigham Young University, Provo, Utah

Susan Golombok
City University

Artin Goncu
University of Illinois at Chicago

Joan E. Grusec
University of Toronto

Sara Harkness
University of Connecticut

Craig H. Hart
Brigham Young University, Provo, Utah

Willard W. Hartup
University of Minnesota

Dale F. Hay
Cardiff University

Charles C. Helwig
University of Toronto

Sheryl A. Hemphill
University of Melbourne

Melissa Hines
City University, London

Carollee Howes
University of California at Los Angeles

Shelley Hymel
University of British Columbia

Jolena James
University of California at Los Angeles

Chris Jenks
Goldsmiths College, University of London

Colleen Killian
University of California at Riverside

Mina Kim
University of California at Riverside

Anita Kochanoff
George Manson University, Virginia

Emily Kouba
University of Illinois at Chicago

Gary W. Ladd
Arizona State University

Charlie Lewis
University of Lancaster

Leah Lundell
University of Toronto

Patricia McDougall
St. Thomas More College, University of Saskatchewan

David J. McDowell
University of California at Riverside

Jacqueline Mize
The Flinders University of South Australia

Alison Nash
State University of New York at New Platz

Tjeert Olthof
Utrecht University

Ross D. Parke
University of California at Riverside

Michelle B. Patt
University of Illinois at Chicago

Anthony D. Pellegrini
University of Minnesota

Alison Pike
University of Sussex

Yumee Rah
University of California at Riverside

Peter D. Renshaw
University of Queensland

Jacques F. Richard
University of Ottawa

Ken Rigby
University of South Australia

Kenneth H. Rubin
University of Maryland

Alan Russell
The Flinders University of South Australia

Ann Sanson
Australia Institute of Family Studies

Barry H. Schneider
University of Ottawa

Sandra D. Simpkins
University of California at Riverside

Diana Smart
University of Melbourne

Peter K. Smith
Goldsmiths College, London

Joan Stevenson-Hinde
University of Cambridge

Franca Tani
University of Florence

Fulvio Tassi
University of Florence

Giovanna Tomada
University of Florence

Wendy Troop
University of Illinois at Urbana-Champaign

Elliot Turiel
University of California at Berkeley

Marion K. Underwood
The University of Texas at Dallas

Tracy Vaillancourt
Mid-Sweden University and University of British Columbia

Karine Verschueren
Center for Developmental Psychology, Leuven, Belgium

Maria von Salisch
Freie Universität Berlin

Margaret Wild
University of California at Riverside

Introduction by the Editors

In this *Handbook* – one of the Blackwell's Handbook series, with companion volumes in other areas such as infant development, cognitive development, adolescent development – we have endeavored to bring together the scope and excitement of recent research in children's social development, with an accessibility and precision which will make the book not only a library resource, but also a real "handbook" – a volume for the individual student and researcher to have, consult, and be inspired by.

As editors, we feel very fortunate in the authors we were able to obtain. Of course, it is customary for editors to say this; but we feel we can say it "hand on heart." We really do have a collection of authors who are actively researching in their content areas and who have brought a truly high level of knowledge and expertise to their chapters.

When we, as editors, started planning this book, we had several specific aims in mind. First, we wished the book to have a wide scope within broad parameters consistent with the Blackwell series. This determined the relevant age range: We asked authors to concentrate on the post-infancy period, from about 3 years, through preadolescence; *not* material on infancy and adolescence, except in so far as it might be necessary for understanding or contextualizing the theories, methods, and findings of the research in childhood. Of course, a wide age range remains: the preschool (3 to 4 or 5 years), early school (5 to 7 years), and later elementary or middle school (8 to 11 years) periods.

Second, we asked for chapters at a certain level. This *Handbook* is not meant for beginners. Those persons who have not studied psychology or child development previously, will probably be better first reading a more introductory text (of which there are many, e.g., from Blackwell Publishers alone there are R. Schaffer, *Social Development*, 1996; K. Durkin, *Developmental Social Psychology*, 1995; or P. K. Smith, H. Cowie, & M. Blades, *Understanding Children's Development*, 3rd ed. 1998). The brief we gave authors was to give a clear and succinct account of work in their area, which would be suitable for anyone wishing to go beyond basic textbook coverage. This would include advanced undergraduates in psychology and behavioral sciences, postgraduates taking taught master's degrees or pursuing independent research, and teaching staff and researchers wishing for an authoritative update outside their immediate teaching/research area. The book should also be useful for those professionals now outside academic life – for example, educators, social workers, counselors, probation officers – who have had training in the behavioral sciences and retain an active interest in the implications of research for their professional practice.

Another aim we had was to get a geographical coverage of contributors. Much of the work in our domain comes from North America, especially the United States, but there are also very important contributions from the European countries, Australasia, Japan, and increasingly other countries in Asia, Africa, and South America. The child development field is truly developing into an international community. For example, both of us have been associated with the International Society for the Study of Behavioral Development (ISSBD) for many years, and have seen how it has grown and helped create an international research community. Part of the planning for this book took place at the meeting of the ISSBD in Beijing, China, in summer 2000, where many Chinese colleagues were able to participate. With one editor based in Europe and one in the United States, some spread of contributors was natural. Although the majority of our contributors do come from the United States, we also have authors from the United Kingdom, Canada, Australia, Italy, Belgium, and (at least for initial education) the Netherlands and Turkey. We would guess that in another decade, an equivalent *Handbook* could well have an even wider distribution of authorship.

Above all, we wanted chapters to be clear, succinct, but also interesting and challenging. In our letters of invitation we asked authors to "provide authoritative reviews of focused areas in social development, which both summarize existing knowledge, and highlight areas of debate and growing points in the discipline." We worked with authors, sometimes through several drafts, to try and ensure this was achieved. The reader will surely find these in the chapters that follow, and we highlight particular areas of debate and growing points in our short introductions to each section of the book.

The *Handbook* has 30 chapters, and 10 sections. The first section (one chapter) is an historical overview of psychological research in social development. This is followed by a section (four chapters) on major other disciplinary views – from genetics, evolution, anthropology, and sociology. The third section (four chapters) focuses on specific causal influences important for social development – temperament, sex, childcare, families, and peers. The next two sections are on major contexts for social development; first a section on the family (four chapters) and then a section on the peer group (four chapters). Four sections follow which cover particular areas of social development: social skills and social cognition (three chapters); play (two chapters); helping and moral reasoning (three chapters); and cooperation, competition, aggression, and bullying (three chapters). The final section is on children with special needs (two chapters).

We have enjoyed working with the authors, and Blackwell Publishers, in producing this *Handbook*. We hope that you will also enjoy reading it, and find it a useful and challenging resource whether for study, teaching, research, or professional practice.

Peter K. Smith, Craig H. Hart
June 2001

Part I

Historical Overview

This section has only one chapter, but it is a chapter which sets the scene for all that is to follow. W. Andrew Collins is in an excellent position to do this. He has worked for many years at the Institute of Child Development at the University of Minnesota, which was one of the pioneering sites of study of young children in North America. Much valuable work was done there from the 1920s onwards, including Mildred Parten's famous work on social participation in preschool children, which was based on her doctoral thesis at the Institute.

While all historical starting points and divisions are arbitrary, Collins justifiably takes a span of just over a century in his account, and follows Cairns (1998) in considering three periods: the emergent period (1890–1919); the middle period (1920–1946); and the modern period (1947–present). The emergent period really marks the beginning of any systematic interest in child (social) development, with baby diaries and some early empirical studies. The middle period saw both an injection of theory (for example from behaviorism and psychoanalysis), and a great increase in research, with the founding of child study centers and institutes, normative descriptions such as those of Gesell, and the development of methodologies such as experiments, observations, and questionnaires. The modern period has seen the decline of behaviorism but the rise of other theoretical views such as those of Piaget and Kohlberg, social learning theory and attachment theory, the testing of competing theories, the development of associated methodologies, and more sophisticated views of developmental processes and their contexts, and ways of envisaging and measuring causal influences in development.

The "modern period" that Collins describes is now a long one, over half a century. It may be that recent years have seen the beginnings of what future historians of science might see as a new period of research, as researchers take a step forward in theories, analytic procedures, and methodologies. Moving away from what (with the benefit of hindsight) seem rather sterile debates about "nature or nurture," or simple causal influences, developmental researchers now almost universally acknowledge the complex interaction of genetic and environmental influences, the multiply determined nature of developmental processes, and the need to develop stronger analytical procedures (such as multilevel analyses and structural equation modeling) to do justice to these complexities.

When caught up in current streams of research, it is easy to ignore the past of the discipline and how we have got to where we are. But in fact, the past may exert a strong influence on the parameters of our present thinking; also, we may learn something from the successes and failures of our predecessors. This chapter frames much of the content of this *Handbook*.

References

Cairns, R. B. (1998). The making of developmental psychology. In W. Damon (Series Ed.) & R. M. Lerner (Vol. Ed.), *Handbook of child psychology. Vol. 1: History and systems of developmental psychology* (pp. 25–105). New York: Wiley.

1

Historical Perspectives on Contemporary Research in Social Development

W. Andrew Collins

Research in social development began more than a century ago. Its roots are much older, springing from enduring philosophical traditions in Western thought, as well as from theory and research in other sciences such as biology and pedagogical studies (Cairns, 1998; Dewey, 1899; Hall, 1904). Only in the most general way, however, can these distal influences be discerned in the directions and concerns of social development research today. Much more visible are the intellectual currents within the social sciences themselves and themes arising from pressing social problems. The goal of this chapter is to detect those currents in this vital and increasingly diverse research enterprise.

The traditional purview of research in social development is "changes over time in the child's understanding of, attitudes toward, and actions with others" (Hartup, 1991, p. 253). Although the distinctness of social development as a subfield was not apparent in the early days of developmental psychology, questions of social behavior, attitudes, values, and personality have been central from the very earliest studies of psychological development. For example, Alfred Binet collaborated on early studies of physiological correlates of emotional changes, in addition to his work on perception, memory, and intellectual performance (Cairns, 1998); and G. Stanley Hall, often called the father of American psychology, studied ". . . the small child's activities and feelings, control of emotions and will . . .," as well as the development of the higher faculties, individual differences, and school processes and practices (White, 1992, p. 29).

Preparation of the chapter was supported partly by the Rodney S. Wallace Professorship for the Advancement of Teaching and Learning, University of Minnesota and a grant from the National Institute of Mental Health to Byron Egeland. The author gratefully acknowledges helpful information and comments from Willard W. Hartup, Brett Laursen, Ross D. Parke, Richard A. Weinberg, and Sheldon H. White.

The vitality of the field today is evident from this handbook and from the breadth and vigor of research described in its chapters. Yet no history of social development as a coherent field of inquiry has previously appeared. A number of useful historical accounts of particular research topics in the field exist (e.g., Eisenberg, in press; Hartup & Laursen, 1999; Maccoby, 1992a, b; Modell & Elder, in press), as do analyses of the contributions of influential researchers (e.g., Cairns, 1992; Emde, 1992; Grusec, 1992; Horowitz, 1992; White, 1992). One can discern much of the history of the field from these fragmentary accounts, especially when combined with historical accounts of the field of developmental psychology (Cairns, 1998) or social psychology (e.g., Jones, 1998). In addition, historical accounts that focus on institutions and organizations (e.g., Hartup, Johnson, & Weinberg, in press; Sears, 1975; Senn, 1975) illuminate historical changes in research topics and focal variables.

This chapter aims to distill from these disparate efforts an historical perspective on contemporary research on social development. The chapter is divided into three sections. The first section is a brief overview of historical trends in the study of social development, identifying significant shifts and transitions in the history of social development. The second part deals with major historical transformations in the field during the past century. These transformations further specify the contemporary significance of the trends outlined in the first section. The third and final section is an attempt to show how methodological issues are interwoven with the substantive concerns of social development researchers.

The Historical Flow

Few scholarly fields yield easily to simple chronological accounts. Social development is no exception. To establish some markers, however, I adopt Cairns' (1998) division of the first 100 years of developmental psychology into three periods, with slight adjustments for social development: emergence (roughly 1890 to 1919); the middle period of institutionalization and expansion (1920–1946), and the modern era (from 1947 to the present). The first part of this section characterizes advances in social development research during each of these periods. The second part deals with the impact of social and historical forces on successive eras of social development research.

Three periods of social development research

Emergence.   Interest in the phenomena of social development suffuses early accounts of childhood, from the writings of philosophers to the writings of diarists and social historians. So-called "baby diaries" are frequently mentioned examples (Darwin, 1877; Shinn, 1893–1899). Systematic scientific study began only in the final decade of the nineteenth century (Hartup, 1992; White, 1992). Among the early efforts were G. Stanley Hall's questionnaire studies focusing on ". . . (a) simple automatisms, instincts, and attitudes, (b) the small child's activities and feelings, (c) control of emotions and will, . . ." and the like (White, 1992, p. 29). In the same decade studies of peer collaboration (Triplett, 1897) and similarity between friends' attitudes and values (Barnes, 1896–1897, 1902–1903; Monroe, 1899) appeared. The interests of researchers in the early period, if not their methods and interpretations, are strikingly like the topics that preoccupy researchers at the beginning of the twenty-first century.

Middle period.   In its first three decades, the theoretical impetus in social development research was slight, at best. Researchers generally shared the view that "nascent social competences were . . . among the child's endowments, and the work of the scientist was to chart their unfolding" (Hartup, 1992, p. 107). This situation changed as views of psychological research shifted and as strong formal theories from other fields penetrated the study of social development. Virtually all of these impinging forces asserted that experience, not merely the unfolding of natural endowments, was an essential element in development. The most commanding figure in American psychology, John B. Watson, declared in "Psychology as the Behaviorist Views It" (1913) that learning alone accounted for development. Not only did this view challenge the suppositions underlying most work in the field up to that point, but Watson's insistence that psychologists must create an "objective experimental branch of natural science," characterized by "objectively collected, independently verifiable data" (Horowitz, 1992, pp. 361–362) implied considerable change in the conduct of social development research. Although much research continued in a normative-descriptive vein (e.g., Rheingold & Cook, 1975), theoretical issues were more explicit in the choice of variables and in writing in the field.

The shift from a maturationist orientation to an environmentalist one intensified as psychoanalytic propositions permeated the literature. Although of greatest interest to clinical and personality psychologists, Freud's ideas further pressed social developmentalists to consider socialization, or ". . . the processes through which the child is assimilated into society" (Hartup, 1992, p. 107; Maccoby, 1992a, b). Similar pressures emanated from sociological theories, such as symbolic interactionism (Cooley, 1909; Mead, 1934), that were concerned with how developmentally advanced individuals contribute to child growth and development. (Only much later did Vygotsky's ideas about the role of expert tutors in collaborative learning infiltrate Western developmental theory (Wertsch & Tulviste, 1992).) Learning theorists eventually assimilated these ideas, particularly those of Freud, into the first of a group of theories of socialization known as social learning theories (Miller & Dollard, 1941). The interest in socialization born in this period dominated social development research from the 1930s until the 1960s. Among its ramifications were an emphasis on parental influences and a relative neglect of interactions with peers, who were thought to lack the experience and authority to serve as socializing agents (Hartup, 1992).

The modern era.   The most recent sea change occurred with the renascence of structuralist ideas in the 1960s. Piaget's theory emphasized the significance of social processes and the role of the child as an active agent (Flavell, 1963). Without denying the role of authority figures in early development, Piaget (1932/1965) took the view that children most readily experienced the cognitive conflict necessary for developmental change when interacting with peers. Kohlberg's (1969) germinal chapter on stage and sequence further developed the notion of cognitive conflict as a necessary ingredient of movement from one stage to another and peers as ideal social resources for this process. Kohlberg's essay remains the major marker of a shift to theory encompassing both social environments and a child actively operating on those elements.

Piaget's and Kohlberg's writings gave rise to a new interest among social developmentalists in a normative-descriptive account of social-cognitive functioning (e.g., Barenboim, 1981; Selman, 1980). For many researchers, however, issues of socialization and the prediction of social behavior remained salient (e.g., Dunn, 1992; Harris, 1992). A further issue thus was to be joined: the possibility that the child's activity was central to the development of other aspects of social growth. Three current directions in the field have resulted from this impetus: (a) increasing interest in the ways in which children regulate their own behavior and emotions; (b) attention to biological processes in control and regulation; and (c) a conviction that the dyad is an essential unit of analysis in social development.

What is social development the development of? Historical determinants

As explanatory accounts fluctuated over the first century of social development research, the answer to the question "What is social development the development of?" changed with views of optimal outcomes. Early studies of children focused on qualities of independence, intelligence, honesty, and sociability largely because "wise commentators in America were certain" that these qualities represented the ideal culmination of development (Kagan, 1992, p. 992). In an era with little theoretical commitment, social values determined the typical set of outcome variables of interest in psychological research. One latter-day example of similarly value-driven preoccupations in the field are Western concerns with the self, which is of much less popular or scientific interest in countries with a more strongly collectivistic public value system (e.g., Markus & Kitayama, 1994).

As theoretical commitments to psychoanalytic theory and its offshoots became more common, other variables joined the group of initially dominant outcomes. The classic longitudinal studies of the 1920s and 1930s, for example, focused on social and mastery variables. Among these were dependence, independence, aggression to peers and parents, achievement, anxiety, and sociability. All have demonstrable connections to Freudian theory and the related shift to primary interest in parental socialization and children's social dispositions and control of emotions (Emde, 1992; Kagan, 1992). An interesting corollary is the implication of these assumptions for the parenting variables of interest. Kagan (1992) notes that, before World War II when most mothers stayed at home, concerns about childrearing problems tended toward fears about over-protectiveness, encouragement of dependency, and discouragement of age-appropriate independence. The psychodynamically influenced concerns with independence and emotional control accorded with typical rearing circumstances for middle-class American children in this case.

By the 1960s, a driving vision of the active child brought a further change in variables of common interest. Interest grew in children's concepts of self, others, and the interrelation of the two (Kohlberg, 1969; Selman, 1980) and in constructs such as intentions and causal attributions (e.g., Dodge, 1986; Eisenberg, in press). Increasing attention to biological processes and related constructs such as temperament led to greater focus on regulatory processes, including coping, inhibition, and attention (Eisenberg, in press; Kagan, 1992;

Rothbart & Bates, 1998). Research on social behavior gradually shifted attention to dyadic interactions as regulatory contexts, and constructs of relationship became more central. Instead of a primary focus on issues of dependence and anxiety, researchers also attended to sensitive responding by parents, signs of emotional security, measures of relationship quality, and the like (Hartup & Laursen, 1999; Thompson, 1998).

Parallel to these theoretical shifts were changes in economic and social patterns with extensive implications for children and child rearing. The preoccupation with parenting that assured independence and emotional control no longer seemed as relevant when half of the mothers in the United States were in the labor force. Public concerns shifted toward the prospect that children might not experience "quality care," that is, might experience insufficient parental affection and sensitivity to the child. Moreover, the concern extended to the possible ramifications of less supervision and monitoring of children; for example, problems of poor regulation and psychopathology became more salient among the public and researchers alike. The convergence of these changes in American family life and the re-orientation to attachment theory and behavioral regulation gave issues of attachment, the quality of out-of-home care, and the emotional life of the child considerable currency in social development research, as well as the public arena (Kagan, 1992).

Transformations in Social Development Research

The breadth of social development research today cannot be subsumed easily by a few common themes. Yet most of the activity in the field reflects four intellectual and empirical transformations during its first century. These encompass increasing interest in specifying developmental processes and intra-individual processes, understanding the nature and significance of the interpersonal context of development, understanding the dynamics of interpersonal experience, and recognizing the significance of variations in social contexts beyond the family for the development of social functioning.

Specifying developmental processes

The maturationist assumptions of researchers stemmed both from a naïve psychology of natural endowments and from an interest in the practical ramifications of "child study." Hall, though a committed scientist, believed a major value of the study of children was to gain insights that might eventually enhance their development, especially with respect to inculcating appropriate moral values (Cairns, 1998; White, 1992). Careful description was a useful first step. Despite Hall's training in experimental psychology in Germany, neither he nor any of the other early proponents of social development research investigated mechanisms of behavioral change.

Even in the middle period, researchers focused largely on description, although of a more rigorous kind than in the early period. This later work was motivated largely by substantial investment in research by funding agencies like the Laura Spelman Rockefeller Memorial and the Payne Fund, with the goal of improving the lives of children. Strong research contributions came from diverse sources during this period. Charlotte Bühler (1927, 1930) conducted compelling observational studies demonstrating the truly social nature of infants' behavior; Florence Goodenough (1929, 1931) studied children's emotional upset during testing and fears by children of different ages; and Mary Shirley (1931, 1933) published a three-volume report of the findings from one of the first short-term longitudinal studies of motor, intellectual, and personality development in the first two years of life.

In perhaps the most striking empirical advance of the period, two scholars of religion, Hugh Hartshorne and Mark May, working under the auspices of the Payne Fund, undertook a study of moral and ethical behavior by children. Quickly mastering the necessary methodological techniques, the two produced a mammoth series of experimental–observational studies showing that moral behavior was highly situation-specific (Hartshorne & May, 1928–1930). To the dismay of their funders, they also concluded that religious training and moral instruction made little difference in the actual behavior of children under conditions of temptation (Cairns, 1998).

These pioneering studies began to fill the need for a natural history phase of research on social behavior that the methodologically weaker studies of the early period had not provided. The newer research, however, offered few clues to developmental processes. The essential work of developing sound research methods pre-empted the energies needed for developing and testing theories (Cairns, 1998; White, in press). Bühler's (1931) survey of studies of social behavior in children, barely 35 years after the first published efforts, carried her judgment that these early studies failed because of "the lack of a systematic point of view" (1931, p. 392).

The search for developmental processes.   In neglecting theoretical development, social development researchers were falling behind other developmental psychologists. Developmentalists interested in intellectual growth had extended principles of conditioning to mental functioning (e.g., Mateer, 1918), but not until the 1920s and 1930s did the emergence of behaviorism and psychoanalytic theory move social development researchers past the level of description. With naïve maturationist views challenged by Watson's version of behaviorism and later other learning theories and by psychoanalytic concepts, the focus became rigorous testing of hypotheses about how changes occur in social behaviors, attitudes, and values.

The most theoretically innovative researchers in this period were Watson and Arnold Gesell. Watson's conviction that conditioning accounted for the acquisition of all behaviors from infancy onwards had aroused many social developmentalists to grapple with mechanisms of growth and change. Watson's own conditioning studies (e.g., Watson & Rayner, 1920) "were only demonstrational and would hardly deserve publication on their methodological merit" (Cairns, 1998, p. 67). Other able psychologists tested key implications of his ideas for infant behavior (e.g., Jones' (1931) rigorous demonstration of the counterconditioning of learned fear).

Gesell is best known for normative-descriptive studies of physical and mental growth (Cairns, 1998; Thelen & Adolph, 1992). Nevertheless, he wrote that human infants were endowed with a "pre-eminent sociality," or impulse to seek connection with others. Moreover, he regarded development as a transaction process: "Growth ... is a historical complex which reflects at every stage the past which it incorporates ... a continuous self-condition-ing process, rather than a drama controlled . ..." (Gesell, 1928, p. 357). Although he never offered a full-fledged theory of development, his speculative interpretations of his findings implied a developmental theory much like that of James Mark Baldwin (1897) before him and many more recent theorists. Neither Gesell nor subsequent scholars, however, have tested these ideas systematically (Cairns, 1998; Thelen & Adolph, 1992).

Not until the 1930s and 1940s did compelling theory-testing research appear in the literature. Up to that point the developmental predictions of psychoanalysis, although much discussed, had stimulated relatively few empirical efforts, and those few were largely unsuccessful (Sears, 1944). Just before World War II, however, a group of young psy-chologists at Yale synthesized these predictions with Hullian theory learning mechanisms. Soon organized as the Institute of Human Relations, they first tackled Freud's views on frustration and aggression, reconstruing aggression as a learned response to being thwarted in efforts to reach a goal (frustration) (Dollard, Miller, Doob, Mowrer, & Sears, 1939). Two members of the group then re-explained identification as imitation reinforced by the experience of similarity to a valued other (secondary reinforcement) (Miller & Dollard, 1941). The best known among the few longitudinal studies of the middle period incorpo-rated similar constructs to these pioneering process-oriented efforts (Baldwin, 1949; Kagan & Moss, 1962), as did other large-scale studies (e.g., Sears, Maccoby, & Levin, 1957; Sears, Rau, & Alpert, 1965; Sears, Whiting, Nowlis, & Sears, 1953) and laboratory experi-ments (e.g., Hartup, 1958; Hartup & Coates, 1967). The empirical fallout lasted for more than two decades.

The theoretical hybridizing of the Yale group proceeded in parallel to tests of predic-tions from other learning-theory formulations, such as operant learning (e.g., Gewirtz & Baer, 1958). An extensive body of findings accumulated around these behaviorist concep-tions of social processes, evident in Stevenson's (1965) influential review of social rein-forcement. By testing the theories that then occupied others in psychology, social development finally moved into the mainstream of the discipline (Cairns, 1998; White, in press).

The mechanistic core processes of social-learning theory, however, eventually quailed under accumulating evidence from infant studies, showing very early manifestations of abilities that had been assumed to result from conditioning, and from repeated findings that all children did not react to the same stimulus or the same reinforcers in the same way (Kagan, 1992; Maccoby, 1992a). Adaptations to these empirical findings by theorists like Bandura and Walter Mischel, among others, stimulated a search for processes that impli-cated intra-individual factors in behavioral and conceptual change. Following Bandura and Walters' (1963) classic volume on social learning and personality development, Mischel (1973) and Bandura (1986) each proposed a cognitive social-learning theory, in which such basic processes as reinforcement were reinterpreted as having informational, as well as emotional, significance (Grusec, 1992). In addition, Bandura (1977) advanced the idea that self-efficacy, or subjective beliefs about one's abilities in a domain, affect behavior and behavior change in that domain. These efforts were buttressed by the "cognitive revolu-tion" in psychology, with its focus on such processes as memory, attention, and inferential thought, and in particular by the influx of Piagetian theory (Flavell, 1963; Maccoby, 1992a).

Mediational processes in social development.   In search of processes, then, social development researchers moved toward change processes based on notions of structural re-organization of thought and action. Such ideas, though far from new in developmental psychology, were long forgotten, for the most part. James Mark Baldwin (1897) had proposed similar dynamic structural processes in his writing at the turn of the century, echoed in the thought of Dewey and Gesell, among others. Piaget's formulation fell on more fertile ground than the previous ones had.

Advanced primarily to account for intellectual development, Piaget's theory depicted the child as trying to reconcile an expectation, or cognitive schema, and incompatible information from the environment. The resulting intrapsychic conflict motivates the child to adapt the schema to the new experience, thus enlarging his or her capacity to grasp new instances. Development occurred as the child inevitably confronted and adapted to a wide range of experiences.

A social dimension was implicit in this formulation, because many of these conflict-inducing instances inevitably involved other persons. In contrast to the emphasis of learning theorists on parental socialization, Piaget gave special credence to interactions with peers. He reasoned that children encountering a discrepancy between their own schemas and the views of a parent would simply adopt the parent's view without undergoing cognitive change. With persons of equal power, children would be more likely to engage fully in the grappling with novelty that fostered cognitive growth. Piaget's explicit description of how and why children's action was essential to growth and especially the linking of this process to peer social interactions concretized the notion for researchers accustomed to the mechanistic accounts of social learning theorists. Kohlberg's (1969) classic essay elaborated the social ramifications, identifying equilibration following cognitive conflict as a fundamental process of social development.

The Piagetian–Kohlbergian account received most direct research attention in connection with stage-related hypotheses. But researchers working on a wide range of developmental problems today, some of them drawn from alternative theoretical models (e.g., information processing), invoke transactional accounts to explain the phenomena of social development. An example is formulations that invoke cognitive biases, such as the tendency to misattribute the causes of behavior in instances of provocation or failure, to account for behavior such as aggression (e.g., Dodge, 1986) or lack of persistence in difficult tasks (e.g., Dweck, 1986). Such cognitive biases result when children form schemas of events from repeated experiences that appear to confirm existing social scripts. In addition, homeostatic notions such as equilibration following conflict and transactional accounts of behavioral development suffuse the literature in fields such as parent–child relations, peer relations, stress and coping, and the development of prosocial behavior (e.g., Collins, 1995; Furman & Wehner, 1994; Gunnar, 1994). Regulatory mechanisms, whether intra-individual or contextual, occupy much of the intellectual energy in social development research at the beginning of a new century (Eisenberg, in press).

Expanded views of regulatory processes

Socialization, the dominant concern of social development research throughout the middle period, implies that individuals are "induced in some measure to conform to the ways of (their) society or of the particular groups to which (they) belong" (Clausen, 1968, p. 4). In social-learning formulations, regulation processes almost uniformly implied "other" regulation, whereas theories like Piaget's implied that children were collaborators in socialization. Moreover, research on language development and attachment implied that many developmental outcomes could not be explained by top-down influences; and studies of reinforcement and observational learning pointed to the likely variability in children's cognitive processing of, and inferences about, events, learning history, and other subjective intrusions into supposedly fixed, externally controlled processes (e.g., Grusec, 1992; Kagan, 1992; Maccoby, 1992a).

In the era of the active child, efforts to understand self-regulation focused on children's capacities for balancing internal and external demands to minimize disruptions of optimal functioning. Studies of regulation subsume diverse contexts, processes, and aspects of behavior and emotion. Among the salient topics have been attentional control and cognitive structuring of control tasks in delay of gratification (Mischel, 1984), coping strategies in stressful or anxiety-arousing conditions (Compas, 1987), and the relation between behavioral strategies and physiological "dampening" processes in response to stressors (Gunnar, 1994).

Closely related to the study of stressful circumstances is the burgeoning interest in children's regulation of their emotions. Able researchers in the middle period had conducted normative-descriptive research on emotional expressions, but had addressed questions of self-regulation only minimally. Yet evidence of self-regulation is abundant: children "manage" their emotional displays in accord with societal expectations and the demands of their parents (Saarni, 1990); and hormonal reactivity spikes under conditions of fear or novelty for some children, but typically returns to ambient levels following self-soothing activities of various kinds (Gunnar, 1994). Moreover, children vary in their typical emotion regulation, partly as a function of the socialization of emotion in families (Dunn, 1992; Eisenberg, in press).

Issues of self-regulation buttressed a growing renascence in the concept of temperament. The construct of temperament languished for three decades, partly because of political and popular resistance to implications of fixed qualities in individuals (Kagan, 1992) and partly because of inadequate measures of temperamental differences (Rothbart & Bates, 1998). With advanced instrumentation and sophisticated biological indicators, combined with behavioral profiles (Kagan, 1992), it is now more feasible to examine the regulatory patterns of infants and children who differ along common dimensions of temperament. Moreover, evidence is growing of interactions between temperament and socialization (Kochanska, 1993).

Interest in self-regulatory processes contributed, as well, to the resurgence of work on personality development after a long period of quiescence. Personality development had quavered under attacks from behaviorists (e.g., Mischel, 1968), but recent evidence from longitudinal studies and new techniques of combining research results across studies have provided stronger evidence of long-term continuity and change than previously was available (for reviews, see Caspi, 1998; Roberts & DelVecchio, 2000; Shiner, 1998).

Expanded units of social experience

The concept of an active child also fed a growing conviction that many of the most significant socializing experiences took place in interactions with others in which the child was an active partner. Sears (1951), in his presidential address to the American Psychological Association, had contended that "A diadic unit is essential if there is to be any conceptualization of the relationships between people . . ." (p. 479). Two decades later, Bell's (1968) article, "A Reinterpretation of the Direction of Effects in Studies of Socialization," and Rheingold's (1969) elegant essay, "The Social and Socializing Infant," again set forth the argument for child as well as parental effects. Another decade passed, however, before proposals for a science of relationships began to take hold in developmental and social psychology (Hinde, 1979; Kelley et al., 1983). New lines of research both bolstered the earlier argument for dyadic formulations and expanded the research directions in the area.

The dominant line of research stems from Bowlby's (1958) theory of attachment. Writing in reaction to earlier secondary-drive formulations (e.g., Freud, 1910/1957; Sears et al., 1957), Bowlby argued that initial bonds between infants and their caregivers result from evolved tendencies to maintain proximity to assure the infant's safety and survival. Such themes converged nicely with the interest in security as a social motive suggested by the discovery that young Rhesus monkeys deprived of social interaction sought contact comfort, rather than gravitating toward a source of food (Harlow & Zimmerman, 1959). Bowlby's (1969, 1973, 1980) theoretical works spurred systematic empirical studies of childhood attachment and numerous theoretical elaborations and refinements that continue unabated today.

Among the historically most important empirical sequelae of these activities are the following. First, the emergence of a bond between child and caregiver in the second half of the first year of life appears to be normative and universal (Ainsworth, 1967; Schaffer & Emerson, 1964). Second, both members of caregiver–child dyads contribute to these attachments (for recent reviews, see Marvin & Britner, 1999; Thompson, 1998). Third, the functional significance of attachment is underscored by evidence from non-human species that even minor deprivation of contact with responsive others results in abnormal neuro-anatomical structures and impaired endocrinological sensitivity related to stress and coping (e.g., Ginsberg, Hof, McKinney, & Morris, 1993). Studies of human children adopted from orphanages, some having impoverished opportunities for human interaction, also reveal neuro-hormonal sequelae of restricted social contact (Chisholm, 1998; Gunnar, 2001; Rutter et al., 1998). Fourth, research on the long-term significance of early attachments has yielded some compelling findings of continuity with relationships in childhood, adolescence, and adulthood, but many instances of null findings as well (for a review, see Thompson, 1999). Fifth, the process by which relationships are linked to behavior patterns at a much later time is thought to be one instance of the more general process of expectancies being applied to new situations. Few researchers now espouse a simple "early determinism" model, embracing instead multivariate accounts that acknowledge the some-times overlapping contributions of multiple kinds of dyads and that also attempt to ex-plain discontinuities (e.g., Belsky, Campbell, Cohn, & Moore, 1996; Weinfield, Sroufe, Egeland, & Carlson, 1999).

Studies of peer relations also rest heavily on assumptions of bidirectional influence and the dyad as a unit of analysis (Hartup & Laursen, 1999). A compelling example comes from findings that, when two toddlers or school-age children interact, the qualities of their interactions are a joint function of their respective early relationships (Pastor, 1981). Thus, ". . .it is not simply that children behave differently depending on the relationship histories of their partners, but that relationships with different partners themselves vary in quality" (Sroufe & Fleeson, 1986, p. 59).

Developmentalists face several unique challenges in research with dyadic units of analy-sis. One is that both developmental and power differentials contribute to the unique func-tioning of a dyad composed of individuals of different ages. Moreover, different rates of change in two partners of different ages make it difficult to determine which partner is contributing more to the ongoing adaptations between the two persons (Hartup & Laursen, 1991). A second challenge is that a bilateral perspective on change processes encourages a shift from viewing developmental outcomes only in terms of individual traits or habit patterns toward thinking of outcomes as competences for participating in social life (e.g., security, effective conflict resolution, commitment, involvement, hostility; see Furman, Brown, & Feiring, 1999; Maccoby, 1992a). Although contemporary researchers have achieved more compelling ways of specifying and analyzing relationships than had been true before 1980, scholars continue to grapple with questions of methods and statistical strategies appropriate for research with dyads (Reis, Collins, & Berscheid, 2001).

Incorporating contextual variations into social processes

The fourth and final transformation in social developmental concerns the significance of aspects of the contexts in which relationships and interactions occur. Until the 1970s, the term *environment* implied a range of sources of stimulation, from the proximal social mod-els or social reinforcers encountered by a child to unspecified sources of influence beyond a particular dyad. Psychological researchers were bent toward demonstrating generality in the effects of certain environmental influences, not appreciating the distinctions among them (Bronfenbrenner, 1979; Modell & Elder, in press).

An early challenge to this environment-neutral stance came from Kurt Lewin, who ar-gued that the individual's *psychological* environment, as opposed to the physical or objec-tively determined environment, was composed of both intra-individual forces and external ones (Lewin, 1931). Children's perceptions of the stimuli specified by the researcher had to be assessed and included in both design and statistical analysis. Both Lewin's conceptual prediction and his empirical findings (e.g., Lewin, Lippitt, & White, 1938) have influ-enced generations of research on effects of parenting behavior (Baldwin, 1949; Baumrind, 1973; Maccoby, 1992b), teachers' classroom behavior (e.g., Arnold, McWilliams, & Arnold, 1998), and the dynamics of peer groups (Hartup, 1992).

Lewin's emphasis on context has re-appeared in a variety of formulations in the ensuing decades. Bronfenbrenner's (1979) germinal volume, *The ecology of human development*, provided an organizing framework for diverse potential environmental influence, including those of historical period and cohort. In his now famous diagram of concentric levels, aspects of the environment of which the child did not have direct experience were pictured as distal, but possibilities for indirect influences were clearly apparent. Research examples of these indirect influences are increasingly familiar to developmentalists (see Elder, 1974; McLoyd, 1998). Another post-Lewinian manifestation came from developmental anthropologists' reminders of the centrality of the experienced, not the presumed, environment (e.g., Super & Harkness, 1986).

The impact of context is felt today not only in social development, but also in other subfields of developmental psychology and psychology generally. Many psychologists now believe that constructs should be labeled to specify the contexts to which they apply (Kagan, 1992). An example in social development is peer gender segregation (Maccoby, 1990), which refers specifically to the tendency for children to affiliate with same-gender peers *in mixed-gender settings*. Nevertheless, social developmentalists, like other psychologists, face continuing challenge in fully incorporating contexts into studies of development and developmental process (for recent critiques, see Elder, Modell, & Parke, 1993; Modell & Elder, in press).

The Search for Method

The earliest methods in social development research were observation and survey questionnaires. G. Stanley Hall's questionnaire method was purely descriptive research, similar in kind, though not in sophistication, to today's survey research. Only sporadically did the studies reported between 1890 and 1920 go beyond frequency counts of behaviors, attitudes, or values. Although description is an essential phase of any natural science, the early samples were too restricted and the administration too haphazard and error-ridden to serve this purpose for the emerging field of social development (Cairns, 1998; White, 1992). Early studies of children's social judgments (Schallenberger, 1894) and peer relations (Barnes, 1896–1897, 1902–1903; Monroe, 1899) were similarly descriptive and drawn from questionnaire responses. Observational and experimental methods were rare. One instance, however, was Triplett's (1897) report that children wound fishing reels faster when working with other children than when working alone. Not until the quest of 1930s' researchers for more rigorous descriptive studies did compelling observational work appear in the literature. Arrington's (1943) critical review of time-sampling methods revealed both the currency of observational strategies and the considerable progress toward a methodological canon (Smith & Connolly, 1972).

Charlotte Bühler (1927) led the way on controlled experimental observations of infants. She observed the babies of poor families at a milk station and concluded that interests in other babies were apparent by 6 months. Using clever methods such as the "baby party" she documented that 6-month-old infants incorporate simple coordinations into their social exchanges. Her advance in the study of infant social development was not matched for another 30 years.

Careful observational studies of nursery-school children in the United States, though, showed age-related patterns during early childhood. For example, coordinated interactions of many different kinds increased with age (e.g., Parten, 1932–1933); physical aggression increased and subsequently declined across ages (Goodenough, 1931); and verbal aggression initially increase with age, but then stabilized (Jersild & Markey, 1935). Similar methods also revealed that conflict instigation and management were moderated by children's relationships with one another (Green, 1933).

The social behavior of older children demanded still more innovative techniques. Group behavior, both normative and antisocial, was studied through participant observation (e.g., Thrasher, 1927). Field experiments, such as Lewin et al.'s (1938) classic work on group atmospheres, anticipated later equally classic studies of groups like the Robber's Cave experiment (Sherif, Harvey, White, Hood, & Sherif, 1961). Later, ethnographic studies expanded the study of individuals and groups in context (e.g., Bryant, 1985; Thorne, 1993). The most influential strategy to date has been comparing the behavior of children who vary in peer-group status. Sociometric methods, derived from Moreno's (1934) strategy for studying institutionalized adults, has undergone important refinements and has yielded significant clues to meaningful variations in social skills and behavior (e.g., Coie, Dodge, & Coppotelli, 1982).

Cairns (1998) has observed that, despite the relatively greater rigor of later studies, studies of peers relations in the middle period were scarcely more theoretically motivated. Only after 1960 were theoretically driven studies conducted extensively. Contemporary studies draw from a range of theoretical formulations, such as those of exchange theory, Sullivan's (1953) theory of interpersonal relations, attachment, and an array of newer formulations (Hartup & Laursen, 1999).

Work on parenting generally has trailed these efforts in sophistication, despite the longer history of sustained interest in, and the larger number of, studies of parental effects and child outcomes. Questionnaire studies and self-report inventories dominate research on parenting behavior even today. Observational studies (e.g., Forgatch & DeGarmo, 1999; Patterson, 1982) and laboratory analogs (e.g., Kuczynski, 1984; Parpal & Maccoby, 1985) are relatively rare. Reliance on self-report studies and correlational statistics has weakened the contributions of these studies. Collins, Maccoby, Steinberg, Hetherington, and Bornstein (2000) recently identified several more rigorous types of designs that have recently been used to specify parental contributions to social development. Among these are behavior-genetics designs augmented by specific measures of environment; studies distinguishing among children varying in genetically influenced predispositions in terms of their responses to different environmental conditions; experimental and quasi-experimental studies of change in children's behavior as a result of their exposure to parents' behavior, after controlling for children's initial characteristics; and research on interactions between parenting and nonfamilial environmental influences and contexts.

Technological changes underlie many methodological innovations of the modern era. Video recorders greatly facilitated progress in early studies of infant affect and mother–infant interaction (e.g., Cohn & Tronick, 1987). Digital and computer technologies, combined with video, have increased possibilities in observational and laboratory studies of social interaction in families and peers. Techniques to measure brain electrical activity, heart rate, blood pressure, muscle tension, cortisol, and blood chemistry have contributed to studies of temperament and are likely to be even more widely applied in the decade ahead (Eisenberg, in press; Kagan, 1992; Rothbart & Bates, 1998).

Many questions central to social development demand longitudinal research designs. Though more numerous in social development than in other subfields of developmental psychology, longitudinal studies were understandably rare in the first six decades of the history of social development. The exceptions were noteworthy for their scope and impact. The Berkeley and Oakland surveys (e.g., Clausen, 1993), Alfred Baldwin's study of parenting styles (e.g., Baldwin, 1949), and the Fels study (e.g., Kagan & Moss, 1962) all provided significant descriptive data on key constructs. The same can be said of pioneering short-term follow-ups of infants (e.g., Shirley, 1933). Today, the relatively numerous longitudinal efforts in the United States and Europe are all the more remarkable because of their size and scope. These efforts permit researchers to address heretofore intractable issues, such as the duration of the impact of significant social experiences, trajectories of change, the significance of timing of social experiences, and so forth (e.g., Sroufe, Carlson, & Shulman, 1993; also, see Magnusson, Bergman, Rudinger, & Torestad, 1991).

Conclusion

The development of social development research in its first century is a story of evolution, rather than revolution. Shifts of strategy and method are more apparent than shifts of interest or focal questions. The interests underlying the canonical work in the field are present today in more theoretically and methodologically sophisticated forms. The best work on parental influences today takes account of the nature of the child and the possibility of bidirectionality, as well as the strong likelihood of other socializing influences such as peers, schools, and the mass media (Collins et al., 2000). Research on peer relations acknowledges contextual effects and qualitative variations among peer companions, as well as child temperament, familial relationship history, and quantitative differences in the nature of the relationship. Studies of individual differences in behaviors (e.g., aggression) and behavioral orientations (e.g., gender) draw broadly on knowledge of social, biobehavioral, cognitive, and emotional processes to formulate hypotheses and interpret research results. The first century has been a promising start on the next one.

References

Ainsworth, D. D. S. (1967). *Infancy in Uganda: Infant care and the growth of love.* Baltimore: Johns Hopkins University.

Arnold, D. H., McWilliams, L., & Arnold, E. H. (1998). Teacher discipline and child misbehavior in day care: Untangling causality with correlational data. *Developmental Psychology, 34,* 267–287.

Arrington, R. E. (1943). Time sampling in studies of social behavior: A critical review of techniques and results with research suggestions. *Psychological Bulletin, 40,* 81–124.

Baldwin, A. (1949). The effect of home environment on nursery school behavior. *Child Development, 20,* 49–62.

Baldwin, J. M. (1897). *Social and ethical interpretations in mental development: A study in social psychology*. New York: Macmillan.

Bandura, A. (1977). *Social learning theory*. Morristown, NJ: General Learning Press.

Bandura, A. (1986). *Social foundations of thought and action: A social cognitive theory*. Englewood Cliffs, NJ: Prentice Hall.

Bandura, A., & Walters, R. H. (1963). *Social learning and personality development*. New York: Holt-Rinehart & Winston.

Barenboim, C. E. (1981). The development of person perception in childhood and adolescence: From behavioral comparisons to psychological constructs to psychological comparisons. *Child Development, 52*, 129–144.

Barnes, E. (1896–1897, 1902–1903). *Studies in education* (2 vols.). Philadelphia: Author.

Baumrind, D. (1973). The development of instrumental competence through socialization. In A. D. Pick (Ed.), *Minnesota symposium on child psychology, Vol. 7* (pp. 3–46). Minneapolis, MN: University of Minnesota Press.

Bell, R. Q. (1968). A reinterpretation of the direction of effects in studies of socialization. *Psychological Review, 75*, 81–95.

Belsky, J., Campbell, S. B., Cohn, J. F., & Moore, G. (1996). Instability of infant–parent attachment security. *Developmental Psychology, 32*, 921–924.

Bowlby, J. (1958). The nature of the child's tie to his mother. *International Journal of Psycho-Analysis, 39*, 350–373.

Bowlby, J. (1969). *Attachment and loss; Vol 1. Attachment*. New York: Basic Books.

Bowlby, J. (1973). *Attachment and loss: Vol. 2. Separation: Anxiety and anger*. New York: Basic Books.

Bowlby, J. (1980). *Attachment and loss: Vol. 3. Loss: Sadness and depression*. New York: Basic Books.

Bronfenbrenner, U. (1979). *The ecology of human development: Experiments by nature and design*. Cambridge, MA: Harvard University Press.

Bryant, B. (1985). The neighborhood walk: Sources of support in middle childhood. *Monographs of the Society for Research in Child Development, 50* (3, Serial No. 210).

Bühler, C. (1927). Die ersten soziale Verhaltungsweisen des Kindes. In *Soziologische und psychologische Studien über das erste Lebensjahr*. Jena: Fischer.

Bühler, C. (1930). *The first year of life*. New York: The John Day Company.

Bühler, C. (1931). The social behavior of the child. In C. Murchison (Ed.), *A handbook of child psychology* (pp. 374–416). Worcester, MA: Clark University Press.

Cairns, R. B. (1992). The making of developmental science: The contribution and intellectual heritage of James Mark Baldwin. *Developmental Psychology, 28*, 17–24.

Cairns, R. B. (1998). The making of developmental psychology. In W. Damon (Series Ed.) & R. M. Lerner (Vol. Ed.), *Handbook of child psychology. Vol. 1: History and systems of developmental psychology* (pp. 25–105). New York: Wiley.

Caspi, A. (1998). Personality development across the life course. In W. Damon (Series Ed.) & N. Eisenberg (Vol. Ed.), *Handbook of child psychology. Vol. 3: Social, emotional, and personality development* (pp. 311–388). New York: Wiley.

Chisholm, K. (1998). A three-year follow-up of attachment and indiscriminate friendliness in children adopted from Romanian orphanages. *Child Development, 69*, 1092–1106.

Clausen, J. A. (1968). Socialization as a concept and as a field of study. In J. A. Clausen (Ed.), *Socialization and society* (pp. 1–17). Boston: Little, Brown.

Clausen, J. A. (1993). *American lives: Looking back at the children of the Great Depression*. New York: Free Press.

Cohn, J. F., & Tronick, E. Z. (1987). Mother–infant face-to-face interaction: The sequence of dyadic states at 3, 6, and 9 months. *Developmental Psychology, 23*, 68–77.

Coie, J. D., Dodge, K. A., & Coppotelli, H. (1982). Dimensions and types of social status: A cross-age perspective. *Developmental Psychology, 18*, 557–570.

Collins, W. A. (1995). Relationships and development: Family adaptation to individual change. In S. Shulman (Ed.), *Close relationships and socioemotional development* (pp. 128–154). New York: Ablex.

Collins, W. A., Maccoby, E. E., Steinberg, L., Hetherington, E. M., & Bornstein, M. H. (2000). Contemporary research on parenting: The case for nature and nurture. *American Psychologist, 55*, 218–232.

Compas, B. (1987). Coping with stress during childhood and adolescence. *Psychological Bulletin, 101*, 393–403.

Cooley, C. H. (1909). *Social organization*. New York: Scribner.

Darwin, C. (1877). Biographical sketch of an infant. *Mind, 2*, 285–294.

Dewey, J. (1899). *The school and society*. Chicago: University of Chicago Press.

Dodge, K. A. (1986). A social information processing model of social competence in children. In M. Perlmutter (Ed.), *Minnesota symposia on child psychology, Vol. 18* (pp. 72–125). Hillsdale, NJ: Erlbaum.

Dollard, J., Miller, N. E., Doob, L. W., Mowrer, O. H., & Sears, R.R. (with Ford, C. S., Hovland, C. I., & Sollenberger, R. T.) (1939). *Frustration and aggression*. New Haven, CT: Yale University Press.

Dunn, J. (1992). Mindreading and social relationships. In M. Bennett (Ed.), *Developmental psychology: Achievements and prospects* (pp.72–88). Philadelphia: Psychology Press.

Dweck, C. (1986). Motivational processes affecting learning. *American Psychologist, 41*, 1040–1048.

Eisenberg, N. (in press). Emotion-related regulation and its relation to quality of social functioning. In W. W. Hartup & R. A. Weinberg (Eds.), *Child psychology in retrospect and prospect: The Minnesota symposia on child.psychology, Vol. 32*, Mahwah, NJ: Erlbaum.

Elder, G. H., Jr. (1974). *Children of the Great Depression: Social change and life experience*. Chicago: University of Chicago Press.

Elder, G. H., Jr., Modell, J., & Parke, R. D. (Eds.) (1993). *Children in time and place: Developmental and historical insights*. New York: Cambridge University Press.

Emde, R. N. (1992). Individual meaning and increasing complexity: Contributions of Sigmund Freud and Rene Spitz to developmental psychology. *Developmental Psychology, 28*, 347–359.

Flavell, J. H. (1963). *The developmental psychology of Jean Piaget*. Princeton, NJ: Van Nostrand.

Forgatch, M. S., & DeGarmo, D. S. (1999). Parenting through change: An effective prevention program for single mothers. *Journal of Consulting and Clinical Psychology, 67*, 711–724.

Freud, S. (1910/1957). The origin and development of psychoanalysis. *American Journal of Psychology, 21*, 181–218.

Furman, W., Brown, B. B., & Feiring, C. (Eds.) (1999). *The development of romantic relationships in adolescence*. New York: Cambridge University Press.

Furman, W., & Wehner, E. (1994). Romantic views: Toward a theory of adolescent romantic relationships. In R. Montemayor, G. R. Adams, & T. P. Gullotta (Eds.), *Personal relationship during adolescence* (pp. 168–195). Thousand Oaks, CA: Sage.

Gesell, A. (1928). *Infancy and human growth*. New York: Macmillan.

Gewirtz, J. L., & Baer, D. (1958). The effect of brief social deprivation on behaviors for a social reinforcer. *Journal of Abnormal and Social Psychology, 56*, 49–56.

Ginsberg, S. D., Hof, P. R., McKinney, W. T., & Morrison, J. H. (1993). Quantitative analysis of tuberoinfundibular tyrosine hydroxylase- and corticotropin-releasing-factor-immunoreactive neurons in monkeys raised with differential rearing conditions. *Experimental Neurology, 120*, 95–105.

Goodenough, F. L. (1929). The emotional behavior of young children during mental tests. *Journal of Juvenile Research, 13*, 204–219.

Goodenough, F. L. (1931). *Anger in young children.* Minneapolis, MN: University of Minnesota Press.

Green, E. H. (1933). Friendships and quarrels among preschool children. *Child Development, 4*, 237–252.

Grusec, J. E. (1992). Social learning theory and developmental psychology: The legacies of Robert Sears and Albert Bandura. *Developmental Psychology, 28*, 776–786.

Gunnar, M. (1994). Psychoendocrine studies of temperament and stress in early childhood: Expanding current models. In J. E. Bates & T. D. Wachs (Eds.), *Temperament: Individual differences at the interface of biology and behavior* (pp. 387–410). Hillsdale, NJ: Erlbaum.

Gunnar, M. (2001). Effects of early deprivation: Findings from orphanage-reared infants and children. In C. A. Nelson & M. Luciana (Eds.), *Handbook of developmental cognitive neuroscience* (pp. 617–630). Cambridge, MA: MIT Press.

Hall, G. S. (1904). *Adolescence: Its psychology and its relations to physiology, anthropology, sociology, sex, crime, religion, and education* (2 vols.). New York: Appleton.

Harlow, H. F., & Zimmerman, R. (1959). Affectional responses in the infant monkey. *Science, 130*, 421–432.

Harris, P. L. (1992). Acquiring the art of conversation: Children's developing conception of their conversation partner. In M. Bennett (Ed.), *Developmental psychology: Achievements and prospects* (pp. 89–105). Philadelphia: Psychology Press.

Hartshorne, H., & May, M. S. (1928–1930). *Studies in the nature of character* (3 vols.). New York: Macmillan.

Hartup, W. W. (1958). Nurturance and nurturance-withdrawal in relation to the dependency behavior of preschool children. *Child Development, 29*, 191–201.

Hartup, W. W. (1991). Social development and social psychology: Perspectives on interpersonal relationships. In J. H. Cantor, C. C. Spiker, & L. Lipsitt (Eds.), *Child behavior and development: Training for diversity* (pp. 1–33). Norwood, NJ: Ablex.

Hartup, W. W. (1992). Peer experience and its developmental significance. In M. Bennett (Ed*.), Developmental psychology: Achievements and prospects* (pp. 106–125). Philadelphia: Psychology Press.

Hartup, W. W., & Coates, B. (1967). Imitation of a peer as a function of reinforcement from the peer group and rewardingness of the model. *Child Development, 38*, 1003–1016.

Hartup, W. W., Johnson, A., & Weinberg, R. A. (in press). The Institute of Child Development: Pioneering in science and application. In W. W. Hartup & R. A. Weinberg (Eds.), *Child psychology in retrospect and prospect: The Minnesota symposia on child psychology, Vol. 32.* Mahwah, NJ: Erlbaum.

Hartup, W. W., & Laursen, B. (1991). Relationships as developmental contexts. In R. Cohen & A. W. Siegel (Eds.), Context and development (pp.253–279). Hillsdale, NJ: Erlbaum.

Hartup, W. W., & Laursen, B. (1999). Relationships as developmental contexts: Retrospective themes and contemporary issues. In W. A. Collins & B. Laursen (Eds.), *Relationships as developmental contexts: The Minnesota symposia on child psychology, Vol. 30* (pp. 13–35). Mahwah, NJ: Erlbaum.

Hinde, R. A. (1979). *Towards understanding relationships.* London: Academic Press.

Horowitz, F. D. (1992). John B. Watson's legacy: Learning and environment. *Developmental Psychology, 28*, 360–367.

Jersild, A. T., & Markey, F, U. (1935). *Conflicts between preschool children. Child Development Monographs No. 21.* New York: Columbia University Press.

Jones, E. E. (1998). Major developments in five decades of social psychology. In D. T. Gilbert, S. T.

Fiske, & G. Lindzey (Eds.), *The handbook of social psychology, Vol. 1* (pp. 3–57). New York: Oxford University Press.

Jones, M. C. (1931). The conditioning of children's emotions. In C. Murchison (Eds.), *A handbook of child psychology* (pp. 71–93). Worcester, MA: Clark University Press.

Kagan, J. (1992). Yesterday's premises, tomorrow's promises. *Developmental Psychology, 28*, 990–997.

Kagan, J., & Moss, H. A. (1962). *Birth to maturity, a study in psychological development.* New York: Wiley.

Kelley, H. H., Berscheid, E., Christensen, A., Harvey, J. H., Huston, T. L., Levinger, G., McClintock, E., Peplau, L. A., & Peterson, D. R. (Eds.). (1983). *Close relationships.* New York: Freeman.

Kochanska, G. (1993). Toward a synthesis of parental socialization and child temperament in early development of conscience. *Child Development, 64*, 325–347.

Kohlberg, L. (1969). Stage and sequence: The cognitive-developmental approach to socialization. In D. A. Goslin (Ed.), *Handbook of socialization theory and research* (pp. 347–480). Chicago: Rand McNally.

Kuczynski, L. (1984). Socialization goals and mother-child interaction: Strategies for long-term and short-term compliance. *Developmental Psychology, 20*, 1061–1073.

Lewin, K. (1931). Environmental forces in child behavior and development. In C. Murchison (Ed.), *A handbook of child psychology*, 2nd ed. (pp. 590–625). Worcester, MA: Clark University Press.

Lewin, K., Lippitt, R., & White, R. K. (1938). Patterns of aggressive behavior in experimentally created "social climates." *Journal of Social Psychology, 10*, 271–299.

Maccoby, E. E. (1990). Gender and relationships. *American Psychologist, 45*, 513–520.

Maccoby, E. E. (1992a). The role of parents in the socialization of children: An historical overview. *Developmental Psychology, 28*, 1006–1017.

Maccoby, E. E. (1992b). Trends in the study of socialization: Is there a Lewinian heritage? *Journal of Social Issues, 48*, 171–185.

Magnusson, D., Bergman, L. R., Rudinger, G., & Torestad, B. (1991). *Problems and methods in longitudinal research: Stability and change.* Cambridge, England: Cambridge University Press.

Markus, H., & Kitayama, S. (1994). A collective fear of the collective: Implications for selves and theories of selves. *Personality and Social Psychology Bulletin, 20*, 568–579.

Marvin, R., & Britner, P. (1999). Normative development: The ontogeny of attachment. In J. Cassidy & P. R. Shaver (Eds.), *Handbook of attachment: Theory, research, and clinical applications* (pp. 44–67). New York: Guilford Press.

Mateer, F. (1918). *Child behavior: A critical and experimental study of young children by the method of conditioned reflexes.* Boston: Badger.

McLoyd, V. C. (1998). Socioeconomic disadvantage and child development. *American Psychologist, 53*, 185–204.

Mead, G. H. (1934). *Mind, self, and society.* Chicago: University of Chicago Press.

Miller, N. E., & Dollard, J. (1941). *Social learning and imitation.* New York: McGraw-Hill.

Mischel, W. (1968). *Personality and assessment.* New York: Wiley.

Mischel, W. (1973). Toward a cognitive social learning reconceptualization of personality. *Psychological Review, 80*, 252–283.

Mischel, W. (1984). Convergences and challenges in the search for consistency. *American Psychologist, 39*, 351–364.

Modell, J., & Elder, G. H., Jr. (in press). Children develop in history: So what's new? In W. W. Hartup & R. A. Weinberg (Eds.), *Child psychology in retrospect and prospect: The Minnesota symposia on child* psychology, Vol. 32. Mahwah, NJ: Erlbaum.

Monroe, W. S. (1899). *Die Entwicklung des sozialen Bewusstseins der Kinder.* Berlin: Reuther & Reichard.

Moreno, J. L. (1934). *Who shall survive?* Washington, DC: Nervous and Mental Disease Publishing Company.

Parpal, M., & Maccoby, E. E. (1985). Maternal responsiveness and subsequent child compliance. *Child Development, 56,* 1326–1334.

Parten, M. B. (1932–1933). Social participation among preschool children. *Journal of Abnormal and Social Psychology, 27,* 243–269.

Pastor, D. (1981). The quality of mother–infant attachment and its relationship to toddlers' initial sociability with peers. *Developmental Psychology, 17,* 326–335.

Patterson, G. R. (1982). *Coercive family process.* Eugene, OR: Castalia Press.

Piaget, J. (1932/1965). *The moral judgment of the child.* New York: Free Press.

Reis, H. T., Collins, W. A., & Berscheid, E. (2001). The relationship context of human behavior and development. *Psychological Bulletin, 126,* 844–872.

Rheingold, H. (1969). The social and socializing infant. In D. A. Goslin (Ed.), *Handbook of socialization theory and research* (pp. 779–790). Chicago: Rand McNally.

Rheingold, H. L., & Cook, K. V. (1975). The contents of boys and girls rooms as an index of parents' behavior. *Child Development, 46,* 459–463.

Roberts, B. W., & DelVecchio, W. F. (2000). The rank-order consistency of personality traits from childhood to old age: A quantitative review of longitudinal studies. *American Psychologist, 126,* 3–25.

Rothbart, M. K., & Bates, J. E. (1998). Temperament. In W. Damon (Series Ed.) & N. Eisenberg (Vol. Ed.), *Handbook of child psychology. Vol. 3. Social, emotional, and personality development* (pp. 105–176). New York: Wiley.

Rutter, M., & English and Romanian Adoptees (ERA) study team. (1998). Developmental catch-up, and deficit, following adoption after severe global early privation. *Journal of Child Psychology and Psychiatry, 39,* 465–476.

Saarni, C. (1990). Emotional competence: How emotions and relationships become integrated. In R. A. Thompson (Ed.), *Socioemotional development. Nebraska symposia on motivation, Vol. 36* (pp. 115–181). Lincoln, NE: University of Nebraska Press.

Schaffer, H. R., & Emerson, P. E. (1964). The development of social attachments in infancy. *Monographs of the Society for Research in Child Development, 29* (3, Serial No. 94).

Schallenberger, M. E. (1894). A study of children's rights, as seen by themselves. *Pedagogical Seminary, 3,* 87–96.

Sears, R. R. (1944). Experimental analysis of psychoanalytic phenomena. In J. McV. Hunt (Ed.), *Personality and the behavior disorders, Vol. 1* (pp. 306–332). New York: Ronald Press.

Sears, R. R. (1951). A theoretical framework for personality and social behavior. *American Psychologist, 6,* 476–483.

Sears, R. R. (1975). Your ancients revisited: A history of child development. In E. M. Hetherington (Ed.), *Review of child development research, Vol. 5.* Chicago: University of Chicago.

Sears, R.R., Maccoby, E. E., & Levin, H. (1957). *Patterns of child rearing.* Evanston, IL: Row Peterson.

Sears, R. R., Rau, L., & Alpert, R. (1965). *Identification and child rearing.* Stanford, CA: Stanford University Press.

Sears, R. R., Whiting, J. W. M., Nowlis, V., & Sears, P. S. (1953). Some child-rearing antecedents of aggression and dependency in young children. *Genetic Psychology Monographs, 47,* 135–234.

Selman, R. (1980). *The growth of interpersonal understanding.* New York: Academic Press.

Senn, M. J. E. (1975). Insights on the child development movement in the United States. *Monographs of the Society for Research in Child Development, 40* (Serial No. 161).

Sherif, M., Harvey, O. J., White, B. J., Hood, W. R., & Sherif, C. W. (1961). *Intergroup conflict and cooperation: The Robbers Cave experiment.* Norman, OK: The University Book Exchange.

Shiner, R. (1998). How shall we speak of children's personalities in middle childhood? A preliminary taxonomy. *Psychological Bulletin, 124*, 308–332.

Shinn, M. (1893–1899). Notes on the development of a child. *University of California Publications, 1.*

Shinn, M. (1900). *Biography of a baby.* Boston: Houghton Mifflin.

Shirley, M. M. (1931). *The first two years. A study of twenty-five babies: Vol. 1. Postural and locomotor development.* Minneapolis: University of Minnesota Press.

Shirley, M. M. (1933). *The first two years. A study of twenty-five babies: Vol. 3. Personality manifestations.* Minneapolis: University of Minnesota Press.

Smith, P. K., & Connolly, K. (1972). Patterns of play and social interaction in pre-school children. In N. Blurton-Jones (Ed.), *Ethological studies of child behavior* (pp. 65–95). Cambridge, England: Cambridge University Press.

Sroufe, L. A., Carlson, E. A., & Shulman, S. (1993). Individuals in relationships: Development from infancy through adolescence. In D. C. Funder, R. D. Parke, C. Tomlinson-Keasey, & K. Widaman (Eds.), *Studying lives through time: Personality and development* (pp. 315–342). Washington, DC: American Psychological Association.

Sroufe, L. A., Egeland, B., & Carlson, E. A. (1999). One social world: The integrated development of parent-child and peer relationships. In W. A. Collins & B. Laursen (Eds.), *Relationships as developmental contexts: The Minnesota symposia on child psychology, Vol. 30* (pp. 241–261). Mahwah, NJ: Erlbaum.

Sroufe, L. A., & Fleeson, J. (1986). Attachment and the construction of relationships. In W. W. Hartup & Z. Rubin (Eds.), *Relationships and development* (pp. 51–71). Mahwah, NJ: Erlbaum.

Stevenson, H. W. (1965). Social reinforcement with children. In L. P. Lipsitt & C. C. Spiker (Eds.), *Advances in child development and behavior, Vol. 2* (pp.97–126). New York: Academic Press.

Sullivan, H. S. (1953). *The interpersonal theory of psychiatry.* New York: Norton.

Super, C., & Harkness, S. (1986). The developmental niche: A conceptualization at the interface of the child and culture. *International Journal of Behavioral Development, 9*, 545–570.

Thelen, E., & Adolph, K. E. (1992). Arnold L. Gesell: The paradox of nature and nurture. *Developmental Psychology, 28*, 368–380.

Thompson, R. A. (1998). Early sociopersonality development. In W. Damon (Series ed.), N. Eisenberg (Vol. Ed.), *The handbook of child psychology: Vol. 3. Social, emotional, and personality development* (pp. 25–104). New York: Wiley.

Thompson, R. A. (1999). Early attachment and later development. In J. Cassidy & P. R. Shaver (Eds.), *Handbook of attachment: Theory, research, and clinical applications* (pp. 265–286). New York: Guilford Press.

Thorne, B. (1993). *Gender play. Girls and boys in school.* New Brunswick, NJ: Rutgers University Press.

Thrasher, F. M. (1927). *The gang.* Chicago: University of Chicago Press.

Triplett, N. (1897). The dynamogenic factors in pacemaking and competition. *American Journal of Psychology, 9*, 507–533.

Watson, J. B. (1913). Psychology as the behaviorist views it. *Psychological Review, 20*, 158–177.

Watson, J. B., & Rayner, R. A. (1920). Conditional emotional reactions. *Journal of Experimental Psychology, 3*, 1–14.

Weinfield, N., Sroufe, L. A., Egeland, B., & Carlson, E. A. (1999). The nature of individual differences in infant-caregiver attachment. In J. Cassidy & P. R. Shaver (Eds.), *Handbook of attachment: Theory, research, and clinical applications* (pp. 68–88). New York: Guilford Press.

Wertsch, J. V., & Tulviste, P. (1992). L. S. Vygotsky and contemporary developmental psychology. *Developmental Psychology, 28*, 548–557.

White, S. H. (1992). G. Stanley Hall: From philosophy to developmental psychology. *Developmental Psychology*, *28*, 25–34.

White, S. H. (in press). Notes toward a philosophy of science for developmental science. In W. W. Hartup & R. A. Weinberg (Eds.), *Child psychology in retrospect and prospect: The Minnesota symposia on child psychology, Vol. 32*. Mahwah, NJ: Erlbaum.

Part II

Influences on Development: Disciplinary Views

Psychology forms a recognized discipline; and most of the contributors to the *Handbook* are developmental psychologists. However, child development is an interdisciplinary area. The Society for Research in Child Development, in the United States, has an explicitly interdisciplinary membership base. There are important traditions of child development research in other disciplines such as anthropology and sociology. In addition, disciplines such as genetics and evolutionary theory have important insights to provide. This section overviews these contributions to our understanding of childhood social development.

Alison Pike reviews the relevance of behavioral genetics for our understanding of social development. This area has grown radically over the last 10–15 years. The traditional methods of twin and adoption studies, refined and accumulating, indicate that there is a complex balance between genetic influences on particular characteristics, and shared and nonshared environmental influences. Some heritability influences are substantial. Also, in many areas the importance of nonshared environment appears to outweigh that of shared environment – a finding with an important impact on the balance of parental and peer influences, since parental influence has often been considered as largely shared environment so far as siblings are concerned (see also Chapter 9). These findings are often age-related. Pike looks critically at the methods and assumptions behind this work, highlighting the implications for developmental theories.

Another development that has featured strongly in the last 10–15 years has been the advent of "evolutionary psychology," and a realization that our evolutionary history may have important consequences for how individual psychological nature develops. Ideas of the importance of evolution for psychology do date back over a century (e.g., Stanley Hall), but only recently has a coherent research program been formulated. Evolutionary psychology emphasizes domain-specific aspects of human cognition and behavior, with these domain-specific mechanisms or modules having been selected during some hundreds of thousands of years, broadly described as the "environment of evolutionary adaptedness" and corresponding to a hunter-gatherer lifestyle. David Bjorklund and Anthony D. Pellegrini review the growing subfield of evolutionary developmental psychology, laying out its central tenets and giving examples of its application. Evolutionary developmental psychology places more emphasis on how domain-specific mechanisms, or modules, develop, and also allows for less specificity in some areas, in line with much thinking in cognitive development (e.g., Karmiloff-Smith, 1992).

Anthropology has a long tradition of studying children, though usually from the perspective of "socialization." Evolutionary perspectives have tended to be downplayed in cultural anthropology since the beginning of the twentieth century, with the influence of Boas, Benedict, and Mead (herself trained also as a child psychologist). Sara Harkness gives a clear historical account of trends in anthropological research on child rearing, from the early socialization work, through the "culture and personality" school, to multisite studies and cross-cultural comparisons such as Whiting's Six Culture Study. The more recent cultural–ecological models of Super and Harkness, and Weisner, are then described, and the theme of the "developmental niche" or "ecocultural niche" is explored. Harkness also critically reviews the area of cultural psychology, and especially the construct of "individualism and collectivism" which has been widely used but which may be much too simple to take us any further in understanding cultural differences.

Largely independent of both anthropological and psychological approaches, there has been a substantial current of research on child development from a sociological tradition. Over the last decade this has come together with some coherent viewpoints (e.g., James & Prout, 1990; Jenks, 1992) that challenge the conventional thinking of many psychologists. Chris Jenks sets out this "manifesto" at the start of his chapter. Seeing childhood as a "social construction" seems to take us a long way from the genetic and evolutionary perspectives of the chapters by Pike, and Bjorklund and Pellegrini. Nevertheless there may be some common ground. Both Jenks, and Bjorklund and Pellegrini, point out the conceptual limitations of an "adult-centered" view of child development. For the evolutionary theorist, some aspects of childhood are advantageous for childhood, not a preparation for adult life. For the sociologist, the world of children has its own intrinsic validity and the concept of "development" is subjected to a thoroughgoing critique; indeed the concept of "development" is itself socially constructed. While many psychologists may disagree with parts of the "manifesto" in this chapter, and may feel that some of the psychological examples given have already been surpassed, nevertheless there are profound issues raised here about the ways in which we perceive our domain and operate within it.

References

James, A., & Prout, A. (1990). *Constructing and reconstructing childhood.* Basingstoke, England: Falmer.

Jenks, C. (1992). *The sociology of childhood.* Aldershot, England: Gregg.

Karmiloff-Smith, A. (1992). *Beyond modularity.* Cambridge, MA: MIT Press.

2

Behavioral Genetics, Shared and Nonshared Environment

Alison Pike

Many of the chapters in this handbook consider the varied contexts that affect young children's lives (e.g., family environment, the school, peers, and the wider historical and cultural context). This chapter focuses on an individual-level factor that has pervasive effects for all children's development – genetics. Equally important, this chapter contains convincing evidence from behavioral genetic studies that children's environmental experiences do matter, but in somewhat unexpected ways. To appreciate the significance of findings and recent developments concerning nature and nurture, however, an understanding of behavioral genetic theory and methods is required. Therefore, the chapter begins with a brief explanation of these. Next, behavioral genetic results from selected areas of social development are considered; problem behaviors, self-concept, and parenting. The relative impact of shared versus nonshared environmental influences is then reviewed, followed by recent work considering parenting-adjustment associations within a behavioral genetic framework. The remainder of the chapter is devoted to the lively debate in recent years concerning the degree to which parents influence their children's social development.

Behavioral Genetic Theory

Behavioral genetics is the study of nature and nurture. The theory postulates that behavioral differences among individuals in a population are due both to genetic differences between people, and to differences in their environmental experiences. Specifically, behavioral geneticists explore the origins of individual differences (i.e., differences between people) in complex behaviors, such as social competence. It is as important to point out what behavioral genetics does *not* address, as well as what it does. For example, researchers may be interested in how, generally, children develop interpersonal skills. This is a question concerning normative development, and is not addressed by behavioral genetics. Similarly, many researchers are concerned with group differences (e.g., differences between children growing up in rural versus urban areas), and again traditional behavioral genetic methods cannot answer such questions. Instead, the focus is on individual differences. Continuing the example, behavioral geneticists would argue that an important question is why some children have difficulty getting along with peers, while others have no trouble. It is worth noting that individual differences, though often ignored in psychological research, or merely thought of as "error," are often of far greater magnitude than group differences.

Behavioral Genetic Methods

Due to space limitations, the following section is necessarily brief. For detailed treatments of the methods that are briefly described below, see Neale and Cardon (1992) and Plomin, DeFries, McClearn, and Rutter (1997).

Using behavioral genetic methods, variability for any given trait may be divided into three sources, heritability, shared environment, and nonshared environment. Heritability is defined as the amount of total variation in scores of a given trait that can be explained by genetic differences between people. For example, the heritability of social competence refers to the proportion of variation in scores of social competence originating from differences in people's genetic make-up. Shared environment refers to those environmental influences that are shared by siblings reared in the same family, and lead to sibling similarity (e.g., neighborhood, parental attitudes). On the other hand, nonshared environment refers to those aspects of the environment that are not shared by siblings, and lead to differences between siblings (e.g., siblings' different peer groups, birth order).

Although behavioral geneticists are beginning to identify specific genes that are associated with behavior, the classic methods are indirect quasi-experimental methods, such as twin and adoption studies. These methods estimate the relative contributions of genetic, shared, and nonshared environmental influence for a given trait or behavior. Studies in which family members (e.g., parents or siblings) are assessed provide indications of familial resemblance, but cannot disentangle this resemblance into its genetic and shared environmental sources.

Twin and adoption studies compare the similarity of family members of varying genetic relatedness, and estimate genetic and environmental contributions to specific traits. The twin method involves the comparison of resemblance between monozygotic (MZ) twin pairs and dizygotic (DZ) twin pairs. MZ twins are 100% genetically similar (they are "identical" genetically like clones), whereas DZ twins, like regular siblings, share only 50% (on average) of their segregating genes. Therefore, if genetic influence is important for a trait, MZ twins will be more similar than DZ twins. To the extent that twin similarity cannot be attributed to genetic factors, the shared environment is implicated. Finally, the extent to which MZ twins differ within pairs is accounted for by nonshared environmental factors.

Because identical twins are identical genetically and fraternal twins are 50% similar genetically, the difference in their correlations reflects half of the genetic effect and is doubled to estimate heritability. For example, MZ twins correlate about 0.90 for height, and DZ twins about 0.45. Here, the reference is to correlations, r, rather than r^2 (the measure of "variance explained"). The reason for this is that the covariance between relatives is of interest, rather than the degree to which, for example, the variance in Twin1 scores can be "explained" by Twin2 scores. Doubling the difference between these correlations yields a heritability estimate of 0.90 ($2(0.90 - 0.45) = 0.90$), suggesting substantial heritability for height. Shared environmental influence can be indirectly estimated from twin correlations by subtracting the heritability estimate from the MZ twin correlation. In this case the estimate is 0.0 ($0.90 - 0.90 = 0.0$). Nonshared environmental influence is estimated by subtracting the MZ twin correlation from 1.0 – yielding 0.10 in this case ($1.0 - 0.90 = 0.10$).

The other classic quantitative genetic design is the adoption design. Because adoptive siblings are unrelated genetically to other siblings in their adoptive family, the degree of similarity between these siblings is a direct index of shared environmental influences. That is, adoptive siblings do not share genes any more than pairs of randomly selected individuals, and so they only resemble one another more than random individuals would because of shared environmental reasons. Heritability can also be estimated using the adoption design. In this case, nonadoptive (biological) siblings share 50% of their genes, while adoptive siblings share 0% of their genes. The difference in correlations between biological siblings and adoptive siblings reflects half of the genetic effect and is doubled to estimate heritability. Biological siblings correlate about 0.45 for height, and adoptive siblings are uncorrelated, 0.00. Doubling the difference between these correlations yields a heritability estimate of 0.90 ($2(0.45 - 0.00) = 0.90$), again suggesting substantial heritability for height. Finally, in adoption studies, nonshared environment is estimated to be that which is "left over" after heritability and shared environment have been accounted for, that is, $1.0 - 0.90$ (heritability) $- 0.00$ (shared environment) $= 0.10$. Each design has its strengths and weaknesses; therefore it is the overall picture of results emerging from different studies that is important.

Behavioral Genetic Findings in Social Development

Due to space limitations, three selected areas of social development will be reviewed. The first area, behavior problems, is a relatively well-researched area that has been of interest to behavioral geneticists for some time. Behavior problems fit under the umbrella of "psychopathology," which, along with intelligence and personality, is one of the three major areas that have been of interest to behavioral geneticists. This is due to the fact that these are areas for which individual differences (rather than normative development) have been the focus, and these are often conceptualized as "outcomes" of genetic and environmental processes. The second area, self-concept, counter-balances the first by addressing a positive aspect of development. Far less work has been completed for positive as opposed to negative outcomes, thus the review of this topic represents a new avenue of research. Finally, the "nature of nurture" is explored through a review of parenting. This literature is at the heart of the gene–environment interface, and demonstrates how genetic influences may help explain children's roles in their own socialization.

Behavior problems

After intelligence, behavioral problems have probably been studied more extensively by behavioral geneticists than any other domain during childhood. This is due to the obvious societal importance in understanding their causes, and the present review will include a discussion of how these findings can illuminate and extend nongenetic studies and theories. This review will revolve around three issues: age trends, aggressive versus nonaggressive problem behaviors, and differences found between informants.

Results found for externalizing problems in preschool-aged children can be compared to those found during the middle-childhood period. Two studies have utilized parent reports of the Child Behavior Checklist (CBCL; Achenbach, 1991, 1992) to assess externalizing problems in twins approximately 3 years of age. Schmitz, Fulker, and Mrazek (1995) report moderate heritability (.34) and moderate shared environmental influence (.32), whilst van den Oord, Verhulst, and Boomsma (1996) report a much higher heritability estimate of .60, and a slightly lower shared environmental estimate of .20. The only ready explanation for this discrepancy (other than random fluctuations in sampling) is that the van den Oord study utilized average ratings from *both* parents, whereas Schmitz and colleagues utilized a single report from one parent. As will be elaborated in the discussion of informants, more reliable, composite measures of child behavior have the effect (as displayed here) of increasing the variance accounted for by genetic factors, and decreasing that accounted for by nonshared environmental factors, which includes measurement error. Support for the higher estimate of heritability is given via replication with a different parent-report instrument. This final study also involved 3-year-old twins, and again, reports of problematic behaviors were combined when completed by both parents (Deater-Deckard, 2000). Deater-Deckard reports a heritability of .59 and no shared environmental influence for the total problems score from the Strengths and Difficulties Questionnaire (SDQ; Goodman, 1997).

Genetically sensitive parent-report studies during the middle-childhood period have all utilized the CBCL. At this age, the subscales of aggression and delinquency together index externalizing problems. The study best poised to directly address the issue of whether the heritability of these problems increases or decreases over time is that of Schmitz and colleagues (1995), described above. This was a longitudinal study in which the twins were again assessed at seven and a half years of age. Over this five-year period, the heritability estimate for externalizing problems increased from .34 to .57, while the shared environmental effect decreased in magnitude from .32 to .22. In addition, the stability seen across the age span was due almost entirely to common genetic influences at both ages. No other longitudinal data has been used to address this issue, however, other extant results during middle childhood report higher estimates for genetic influence (e.g., Edelbrock, Rende, Plomin, & Thompson, 1995; Leve, Winebarger, Fagot, Reid, & Goldsmith, 1998). This increase in heritability remains speculative, however, given that the other studies of the preschool period indicated higher heritability estimates that are in line with estimates during middle childhood. Furthermore, cross-sectional analyses covering the age span from 5 through to 15 years uncovered no differences by age (Gjone, Stevenson, Sundet, & Eilertsen, 1996).

To summarize thus far; even during the early preschool period, it appears that genetic differences among children are partly responsible for the large individual differences seen in this domain. It should be emphasized, however, that heritability describes *what is* in a particular population at a particular time, rather than what *could be*. Therefore, if environmental factors within a population change (e.g., changes in discipline policy within the education system) then the relative impact of genes and environment will change. Beyond genetic influence, the moderate influence of siblings' shared environment underlines the utility of family-level intervention strategies (Gurman & Kniskern, 1980), and mirrors Patterson's reports of siblings' involvement in "coercive family processes" (Patterson, 1986).

Studies addressing the second issue, aggressive versus nonaggressive externalizing problems, have yielded quite consistent findings. Heritability is greater for aggressive problems, and nonaggressive problems yield higher shared environment estimates. A couple of recent replications will be reviewed. In a study of almost 200 twin pairs aged 7 to 11 years old, the parent-report aggressive behavior and delinquent behavior subscales from the CBCL were analyzed separately. Individual differences in aggressive behavior were substantially genetically influenced (.60), and shared environmental influences were modest (.15) and nonsignificant. The corresponding figures for delinquent behavior on the other hand were similar and moderate (.35 and .37, respectively). A report by Eley, Lichtenstein, and Stevenson (1999) is a particularly persuasive replication because it includes data from twin studies conducted in two countries (Britain and Sweden) yielding remarkably similar results. The heritability for aggressive behavior was estimated at .69 for the British sample and .70 for the Swedish sample, and shared environmental influences were negligible in both cases. In contrast, for non-aggressive antisocial behavior, shared environmental effects were significant and of moderate to substantial magnitude, and heritability estimates more moderate.

Finding moderate and significant shared environmental effects is unusual (see "Shared versus Nonshared Environmental Influences," below), and was first discussed for nonaggressive delinquent behavior by Rowe (1983). In this and subsequent work (Rowe, 1986), adolescent twins reported being "partners in crime" in terms of their delinquent acts. Thus, in addition to shared rearing experiences or parental attitudes being responsible for sibling similarity in this area, it appears that the twins are influencing one another. This is further supported by an adoption study for which the shared environmental component was more modest in magnitude, though significant (Deater-Deckard & Plomin, 1999).

This etiological distinction between aggressive and nonaggressive antisocial behavior is an excellent illustration of the contribution that behavioral genetic studies can make to theoretical issues in development. The distinction between adolescence-limited and life-course-persistent antisocial behavior put forward by Moffitt (1993) is supported by the differing origins of these behaviors. Aggressive behavior, mapping on to life-course-persistent antisocial behavior, is highly heritable and thus quite stable. Nonaggressive antisocial behavior, on the other hand, may be analogous to the adolescence-limited type, elicited by contextual cues particularly salient during the adolescent period, and bolstered by the findings of lower heritability and higher environmental contributions.

The final issue that will be considered is potential differences according to informant.

The studies reviewed above have relied on parental reports. A handful of studies have also utilized observational measures of child behavior, or parental interviews. In Deater-Deckard's study of 3-year-old twins, the children's difficult behavior was coded from videotaped observations of two 10-minute dyadic interactions with the primary caregiver, as well as via parental reports (Deater-Deckard, 2000). Heritability estimates were substantial for parent reports (.59), but nonexistent for the observational measure. Conversely, the shared environmental estimates were .00 and .25, respectively. There are several possible interpretations for this pattern of findings. First, the content of behaviors in the two measures was not identical. Deater-Deckard notes that, "observers were rating behaviors that were less severe in their consequences but parents were rating behaviors that were more extreme indicators of conduct problems" (p. 477). Second, the amount of time sampled (20 minutes) for the observational measure was a tiny fraction of the extensive experience that parents can call upon to answer questions about their child's behavior. Finally, observational interactions are "strong" situations. Perhaps questionnaire measures tap into more heritable, trait-like behavioral patterns of children, whereas the context of a specific parent–child interaction elicits consistency within families.

This finding is not restricted to the preschool period. A study conducted with 154 twin pairs between the ages of 6 to 11 years also compared observations of children's maladaptive behavior with parent reports (Leve et al., 1998). Two different coding systems were utilized for the observations, a global rating made by coders after watching the episode in total, and time-based sampling of discrete behaviors. The two systems yielded remarkably consistent results. Heritability estimates of .29 and .24, and shared environment estimates of .27 and .28 for the global and time-based coding, respectively. In contrast, parent reports of externalizing problems as indexed by the CBCL yielded a heritability estimate of .44, and a shared environment estimate of .41.

Finally, a systematic exploration of interview versus questionnaire data was conducted with a population-based sample of 8 to 16-years-old twins (Simonoff et al., 1995). The questionnaire measures indicated moderate heritability (.23–.34) and moderate shared environment (.25–.58). The interview measures yielded higher heritability results (.40–.73), and negligible shared environmental influences. Particularly striking were the differences between parental reports via questionnaire versus interview. The substantial shared environmental influence found for the questionnaire measures disappeared, suggesting that the questionnaire measures are subject to rater bias. That is, without the aid of an objective "filter," reporting biases (e.g., an optimistic outlook) may artificially inflate sibling similarity thereby inflating estimates of shared environmental influence.

This behavioral genetic evidence adds fuel to the debate regarding differences between informants. Lack of agreement between raters is often treated as error, and the argument is that composite measures (or latent variables) of behavior should be used because of their greater reliability and predictive power (e.g., Epstein, 1983). The counter-argument is that each reporter of a child's behavior has a unique, important perspective that should be examined in its own right. Children themselves, for example, may be in the best position to inform about their own internalizing problems, whereas parent and teacher reports may highlight potentially different frequencies of externalizing problems in contrasting contexts. Behavioral genetic evidence suggests that composite measures, and particularly latent variables of behavior, show higher heritability than do single informant measures (e.g.,

Simonoff et al., 1995; van den Oord et al., 1996). Is it thus fair to say that the more accurate the measurement, the more heritable will be the behavior in question? Instead, I would argue that assessments which index trait-like behavioral consistency across context are more genetically determined than more specific indices of behavior.

Self-Concept

Behavioral genetic research is in its infancy in the area of self-concept, with only two studies thus far concerning young children's understanding of their own personalities, strengths, and weaknesses. Participants in the first study (Pike, 1999) were 3.5-year-old twins. The challenge of assessing the self-conceptions of such young children was met by using a forced-choice puppet task (Eder, 1990). Factor analysis yielded two distinct, meaningful, and internally consistent dimensions, representing aggression/assertiveness (e.g., "Sometimes I like to tease people, and say mean things to them,","I think it would be fun to go down a slide head-first") and well-being (e.g., "I really like myself," "I have a best friend"). Both MZ and DZ twin correlations were similar and moderate across the board, apart from the MZ correlation for aggression/assertiveness that was modest in magnitude. This pattern of results indicated that genetic influence is *not* an important factor, that shared environment plays a moderate role, and that nonshared environmental factors are also important determinants of young children's self-conceptions at this age.

The second study involved adopted and nonadopted children at 9 and 10 years of age (Neiderhiser & McGuire, 1994). The Self-Perception Profile for Children (Harter, 1982) was utilized to assess behavior conduct, athletic competence, scholastic competence, physical appearance, social acceptance, and general self-worth. At age 9, over 80% of the variance for children's conceptions of their physical appearance was due to genetic factors, and approximately half of the variability for scholastic competence and general self-worth was also due to hereditary factors. The remaining domains were overwhelmingly influenced by nonshared environmental factors. These results were not, however, consistent at age 10. At this second time point only athletic competence and scholastic competence demonstrated considerable genetic influence, although nonshared environmental influence continued to prevail.

To summarize, the dominance of shared environmental factors in the preschool years suggests that parents or the family atmosphere plays a role in the early formation of children's understanding of their own personalities. This influence appears to decline by middle childhood, by which time those experiences unique to each child in a family (and perhaps emanating from outside the family) become paramount. Extreme caution is warranted, however, as both studies were based on relatively small sample sizes and await replication. These two studies also seem to be in line with an emerging trend that positive child outcomes demonstrate far less heritability than do negative outcomes. For example, in the Edelbrock and colleagues (1995) study described above, the competence scales from the CBCL indicated modest and nonsignificant genetic effects.

Parenting

During the past 15 years there has been a new wave of research that has subjected so-called "environmental" measures to behavioral genetic scrutiny. The majority of these studies have involved adolescents (see Plomin, 1994, for a review), and only the handful of studies concerning younger children will be reviewed here. In addition, this review is limited to child-based genetic designs (i.e., when the twins (or adoptees) are the children rather than the parents). Thus, any genetic influence found reflects heredity factors of the children, rather than the parents. Therefore, when genetic influence is detected on parenting, this indicates that parental behavior is in part shaped by genetically influenced characteristics of the child.

Braungart (1994) explored the parenting practices and more general home environment of preschool-aged children utilizing the adoption design, and avoiding subjective questionnaire measurement by employing home observations. Genetic analysis of a measure derived from the Home Observation for Measurement of the Environment (HOME; Caldwell & Bradley, 1978) was conducted. In contrast to studies of the HOME during infancy (Braungart, Fulker, Plomin, & DeFries, 1992), negligible heritability was demonstrated. This may be explained by inadequate psychometric properties of the scale at this age, an interpretation which is supported given that a more recent, systematic assessment of the family environment of young twins by Deater-Deckard (2000) yielded quite different results. The twin sample (n = 120 pairs) incorporated parent reports, information gained via interview, and observers' ratings of parent–child interactions. Parental reports of both positive and negative affect demonstrated genetic influence (.46 and .55, respectively), however, no heritability was shown for these domains as indexed by observers' ratings. Harsh discipline and control were also not heritable as assessed by interview and observation, respectively, however, observational ratings of parental responsiveness were substantially heritable (.49).

In a study of parenting during middle childhood, mother–child interactions were examined within the Colorado Adoption Study (CAP; DeFries, Plomin, & Fulker, 1994). The older and younger siblings were aged 7 and 4, respectively (Rende, Slomkowski, Stocker, Fulker, & Plomin, 1992). Four aspects of maternal behavior, control-intrusiveness, affection, attention, and responsiveness were coded from the videotaped interactions. Although maternal affection and responsiveness were not influenced by genetic factors, maternal control and attention were moderately and substantially genetically influenced, respectively. Utilizing the same CAP sample, a comparison of parental reports of warmth, control, and inconsistency of parenting were assessed when the children were 7 and 9 years old. Across both time points, heritability for warmth was quite substantial (.56 at age 7 and .40 at age 9). Control was consistent in showing no heritability across middle childhood, while inconsistency in parenting demonstrated no heritability at age 7, but was largely heritable by age 9 (.46). Finally, Deater-Deckard, Fulker, and Plomin (1999) compared child and parent reports of parenting during late childhood, again within the CAP sample. Parent reports of negativity and warmth were moderately heritable, whereas inconsistency demonstrated negligible genetic influence. According to the children, achievement orientation within the family was substantially influenced by genetic factors whereas family positivity was not significantly heritable.

From the extant evidence, it is difficult to draw overarching conclusions. Certainly parenting during both the preschool and middle childhood years shows some genetic influence, and this has been demonstrated via multiple informants. The presence of genetic influence on measures of the family environment is consistent with the idea that socialization is bidirectional. That is, when parents interact with their children, this interaction is affected by the child's behavior as well the parent's (Bell, 1968). There is, however, no clear pattern as to *which* dimensions are most heritable. This inconsistency may be due to differences in the degree to which measures index those parenting behaviors elicited by the child versus those that are more purely parent driven. Evidence for this distinction is provided by a small observational twin study by Lytton (1977, 1980). Future research following the Lytton tradition of detailed, time-sequenced coding of parent–child interactions with larger, representative samples would shed light on the exact nature of genetically influenced aspects of parent–child interaction.

Shared versus Nonshared Environmental Influences

Looking at behavioral genetic studies that have examined the traditional domains of personality, cognitive abilities, and psychopathology, it has been purported that genetic factors are important throughout psychology, and equally, that environmental factors are at least as important (Plomin & McClearn, 1993). Heritability rarely exceeds 50% and thus "environmentality" is rarely less than 50%. Somewhat surprisingly, summarizing across the lifespan, these same studies indicate that the environmental influence of primary importance is of the nonshared variety (Plomin & Daniels, 1987). That is, environmental factors that have the strongest effect are those which make siblings in the same family different from one another (Dunn & Plomin, 1990). This finding of the importance of nonshared environment has broad implications. Many global family factors such as the marital relationship, parental personality, neighborhood context, and socioeconomic status may not operate in the same way for all family members as has often been implied. For example, divorce is usually considered an event that is obviously shared by children in a family. However, the key issue might be each child's unique perception of, and reaction to, the divorce.

The balance of shared versus nonshared environmental influences does, however, change over the course of development. For the most widely studied area, cognitive abilities, extant findings converge on the conclusion that shared environmental factors are important during early childhood, and that these influences diminish across childhood and adolescence, becoming negligible by late adolescence (McCartney, Harris, & Bernieri, 1990). During this same period, heritability increases, and nonshared environmental influences remain quite constant (and are small in magnitude). This pattern of results mirrors the changing interaction patterns with family versus "external" influences (such as peers) across this period (Csikszentmihalyi & Larson, 1984). For the present purpose it is important to emphasize that differences between families *do* affect young children's cognitive abilities, a point that is sometimes neglected when emphasis is placed on findings for the adolescent period and beyond.

Behavioral genetic studies of the major areas of personality (e.g., extraversion and neu-roticism) that have used twins find that genetics accounts for approximately 50% of the phenotypic variance, and nonshared environmental factors explain the remainder of the variation between individuals (e.g., Eaves, Eysenck, & Martin, 1989; Loehlin & Nichols, 1976). Estimates of nonshared environmental influence from adoption studies are some-what higher, with estimates of genetic influence being correspondingly lower (e.g., Loehlin, Willerman, & Horn, 1987). The vast majority of this work, however, has involved the use of self-report questionnaires administered to adolescents or adults. For children, parental reports have been used, yielding odd results. Parents of fraternal twins tend to artificially contrast their twins' behavior such that DZ twin correlations are often "too low," or even negative (Plomin, Chipuer, & Loehlin, 1990). Support for this contrast effect comes from more objective measures of temperament/personality. For example, Saudino and Eaton (1991) demonstrated the usual "too low" DZ correlation for parental reports of activity level, whereas ratings from motion recorders yielded no such bias. The important point here is that throughout development, it is nonshared rather than shared environmental influences that dominate.

Psychopathology is a more diverse area of behavior for which broad statements cannot be applied. Still, for many disorders, including schizophrenia, autism, hyperactivity, and anorexia nervosa, nonshared environmental influence is substantial while shared environ-mental influence is negligible (Plomin, Chipuer, & Neiderhiser, 1994). Alcoholism may be an exception. As reviewed by McGue (1993), a number of adoption studies have found that being reared in an alcoholic family does increase a person's risk of becoming alcoholic. A recent review of behavioral genetic studies of depression concludes that MZ concord-ance for major depression is about .50, indicating that nonshared environmental influ-ences make a major contribution (Tsuang & Faraone, 1990). Genetic influence appears to account for the remaining variation, again indicating that the environmental variation is of the nonshared variety.

Relating Specific Aspects of the Environment to Children's Outcomes

Traditional behavioral genetic studies do not pinpoint *which* aspects of the environment are important, but do indicate that each child in a family should be considered separately, rather than assessing families as a unitary whole. Thus far, much of the work in trying to detect specific sources of nonshared environment has focused on differential parental treat-ment. That is, researchers have examined parents' distinct or differing behavior towards each of their children. Most of this work has used siblings rather than twins to detect differential treatment. For example, Dunn, Stocker, and Plomin (1990) found that older siblings receiving less affection from their mothers than their younger siblings also dis-played more internalizing problems (e.g., depression, social withdrawal) than did their younger siblings. In addition, older siblings who were the recipients of more maternal control demonstrated more internalizing and externalizing problems (e.g., aggressiveness, delinquency) than their younger siblings.

Sibling studies such as this cannot, however, address the direction of effects. It is often assumed that it is the parental behavior *causing* the differences in sibling behavior, but it could be that the children's behavior is in fact influencing parental behavior. In the example outlined above, it might be more plausible that it is the *children's* problem behaviors driving the maternal differential treatment, rather than the maternal differential treatment driving the children's problem behavior. One specific mechanism whereby children may be affecting their parents' behavior is via their genetically influenced traits.

Thus, as links between parental differential treatment and children's outcome have been found, it has become necessary to disentangle possible genetic sources of these associations. Because siblings differ genetically, relations between their environment and behavioral outcomes may be due to their genetic differences rather than to the parental differential treatment. Continuing the example above, it may be that *genetic* differences between siblings in families were the root of *both* the maternal differential treatment *and* the differences observed in the siblings' behavior problems. In order to study such a possibility, family environment measures (such as parental treatment), as well as children's outcome measures, must both be included within a genetically sensitive design.

For the purposes of this review, the single study of younger children that has utilized this approach will be presented (Deater-Deckard, 2000). Basic genetic analyses are univariate; they decompose observed variance of a single measure into genetic and environmental components. Bivariate genetic analysis focuses on the correlation between traits, decomposing this into its genetic and environmental components (see Figure 2.1), and can, for example, tell us whether a link between parental treatment and children's behavior is due to the nonshared environmental processes that Dunn and colleagues (1990) indicated, that is, differential parental treatment, or whether it is a common genetic component linking parental treatment and adolescent adjustment.

In the preschool twin study described above (Deater-Deckard, 2000), several moderate correlations emerged between parental behaviors and the children's behavior problems. For example, both parent report and observations of parental affect were associated with parent report and observations of the children's behavioral problems. Bivariate genetic analyses were then conducted for these associations to determine the degree of genetic versus environmental mediation. The pattern of results was clear. For parent-rated conduct problems, the lion's share of associations was due to genetic mediation. This finding suggests that genetically influenced traits of these children were being reflected not only in their behavioral difficulties, but also in the treatment elicited from their parents. This was in marked contrast to the results involving observations of child difficult behavior which were primarily due to shared environmental processes, whereby similarity in parental treatment was associated with similarity in sibling outcome.

Finally, a modest degree of nonshared environmental mediation was detected, in line with a previous utilization of this methodology with an adolescent sample (Pike, McGuire, Hetherington, Reiss, & Plomin, 1996). This modest amount of nonshared environmental mediation in no way discounts the wider importance of the nonshared environment. Any single bivariate association is a test for a *single* specific environmental process effective in the development of children's behavioral difficulties. It is sensible to believe that just as the specification of genetic influence involves multiple genes each with a small effect (Plomin & Rutter, 1998), the specification of environmental components of variance will be equally complex, involving a multitude of different factors, each of small effect.

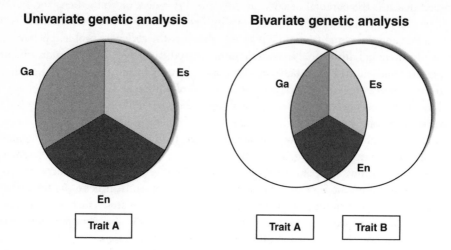

Figure 2.1   Univariate genetic analysis decomposes the variance of one trait into its genetic (Ga), shared environmental (Es), and nonshared environmental (En) components. Bivariate genetic analysis decomposes the covariance between two traits into its genetic (Ga), shared environmental (Es), and nonshared environmental (En) components.

It should be noted that finding evidence of genetic mediation suggests that nongenetic studies be interpreted with caution. Much of the developmental research relating parenting to children's adjustment is interpreted to mean that the parent's behavior is *causing* the child's behavior. The genetic findings suggest that this is not always the case. Instead, it is the children's genes that are reflected in both the parent's behavior and in the child's adjustment. In terms of process, it is quite plausible that a child's genetic propensities that lead to adjustment difficulties would also lead to displays of negativity from parents.

Socialization from a Behavioral Genetic Perspective

The seeming lack of communication between developmental psychologists (especially socialization researchers) and developmental behavioral geneticists is troubling (Goldsmith, 1993; Wachs, 1993). This can, in some measure, be attributed to the necessarily different methodologies employed by the two "camps." Behavioral genetic designs require the recruitment of quite large numbers of special families, often at the expense of more detailed assessments. This also does not (readily) allow some forms of data collection such as the assessment of peer relationships within the classroom context.

How can behavioral genetic findings such as those reviewed here inform socialization research? Estimates of genetic and environmental effects provide a useful roadmap in terms of where (and when) effective environmental factors are likely to occur. Finding differing etiologies across time highlights the likely location of potent socializing agents at different times during the life course. For example, as explained above, for intelligence shared environmental factors play a role in early and middle childhood, however, by the time of adolescence this effect has disappeared. I would argue, then, that familial factors should have an impact in the early years. If, however, familial factors (e.g., SES) are associated with IQ scores in late adolescence, behavioral genetic evidence suggests that this is likely to be a genetically mediated association.

Recently, behavioral genetic findings have been incorporated into two rather far-reaching theories concerning children's socialization. The first was put forward by Scarr in her presidential address to the Society for Research in Child Development in 1991 (Scarr, 1992). Scarr utilized behavioral genetic evidence to make the case that children's experiences are driven by their genetic propensities. That is, children are seen as active agents in their own socialization, and this active selection and creation of environmental experiences is genetically determined. Perhaps most controversially, Scarr made the claim that "average" parents are "good enough." Due to the lack of shared environmental influence found for most psychological traits, Scarr argued that within the species-normal range of environments, parents do not have a differential impact on their children's development. This idea runs counter to the traditional socialization theorists' claim that parents are the key socialization agents for young children, and Scarr's theory created lively debate and criticism (Baumrind, 1993, Jackson, 1993).

Scarr's theory received much attention; however, she is not the only behavioral geneticist to interpret lack of shared environmental influence as a lack of parental influence. For example, in his book *The Limits of Family Influence*, Rowe (1994) argues along the same lines, that a random allocation of children into families would not impact their developmental trajectories. These two authors emphasize the genetic link between parents and their children, but do not consider the impact of the nonshared environment. Firstly, a lack of shared environment does not necessitate that families are unimportant for children's development; parents may have a profound impact on their children, impacting each of their children in a unique, nonshared fashion. Secondly, although emphasizing the role of genetics on behavior, the nonshared environment is also of substantial magnitude for many domains, and these authors do not propose an alternative socialization agent for this role.

In her recent, well-publicized book, *The Nurture Assumption*, Judith Harris (1998) proposes that the peer group is this alternate socialization agent. Using behavioral genetic evidence, parents are deemed to be unimportant in determining individual differences in children's personality. Instead, it is children's genes that are responsible both for the way that parents respond to their children, and for children's personality characteristics. Genetic factors explain only half of the variance of personality development. The other half is due to environmental factors. As an alternative to parental environmental influence, Harris proposes that children's peers are the main source of these nonshared environmental influences. She argues that personality development is shaped through a process of peer imitation and pressure that encourages the child to conform to group rules. It is this environmental process that ultimately determines adult personality beyond hereditary influences.

What is not considered in Harris' thesis is that peer group characteristics, like parenting, might also be genetically influenced. That is, children are not randomly allocated to peer groups. Genetic factors might also influence the peer context experienced by children. An empirical test of this hypothesis measured adolescents' peer-group preferences for college orientation, delinquency, and popularity (Iervolino et al., 2000). Substantial genetic influence emerged for adolescents' self-reports of peer preference for college orientation and delinquency, with the remaining variance accounted for by nonshared environmental influences. For peer preference for popularity, genetic influence was not important and nearly all of the variance was due to nonshared environment. These results suggest that peers, at least peer preferences, may also show genetic mediation, as is the case for parenting. It remains to be seen, however, if these findings will also be true for younger children, or whether peer-group characteristics, like intelligence, show shared environmental influence at younger ages, this disappearing across development into adolescence.

Conclusion

Behavioral genetics has already made a sizeable contribution to many aspects of the social development literature. Such studies indicate that genetic factors are not only important for children's "outcomes," but also for "environmental" aspects such as parent–child interactions. Recent work at the heart of nature *and* nurture is combining the best of traditional socialization research with genetically sensitive designs. Emerging from such work are exciting, if controversial, new theoretical approaches to children's socialization.

References

Achenbach, T. M. (1991). *Manual for the Child Behavior Checklist /4-18 and 1991 Profile*. Burlington, VT: University of Vermont Department of Psychiatry.

Achenbach, T. M. (1992). *Manual for the Child Behavior Checklist /2-3 and 1992 Profile*. Burlington, VT: University of Vermont Department of Psychiatry.

Baumrind, D. (1993). The average expectable environment is not good enough: A response to Scarr. *Child Development, 64*, 1299–1317.

Bell, R. Q. (1968). A reinterpretation of the direction of effects in socialization. *Psychological Review, 75*, 81–95.

Braungart, J. M. (1994). Genetic influence on "environmental" measures. In J. C. DeFries, R. Plomin, & D. W. Fulker (Eds.), *Nature and nurture during middle childhood*. Cambridge, MA: Blackwell.

Braungart, J. M., Fulker, D. W., Plomin, R., & DeFries, J. C. (1992). Genetic influence of the home environment during infancy: A sibling adoption study of the HOME. *Developmental Psychology, 28*, 1048–1055.

Caldwell, B. M., & Bradley, R. H. (1978). *Home Observation for Measurement of the Environment*. Little Rock, AR: University of Arkansas.

Csikszentmihalyi, M., & Larson, R. (1984). *Being adolescent*. New York: Basic Books.

Deater-Deckard, K. (2000). Parenting and child behavioral adjustment in early childhood: A quantitative genetic approach to studying family processes. *Child Development, 71*, 468–484.

Deater-Deckard, K., Fulker, D. W., & Plomin, R. (1999). A genetic study of the family environment in the transition to early adolescence. *Journal of Child Psychology and Psychiatry, 40*, 769–776.

Deater-Deckard, K., & Plomin, R. (1999). An adoption study of the etiology of teacher and parent reports of externalizing behavior problems in middle childhood. *Child Development, 70,* 144–154.

DeFries, J. C., Plomin, R., & Fulker, D. W. (Eds.), (1994). *Nature and nurture in middle childhood.* Cambridge, MA: Blackwell.

Dunn, J., & Plomin, R. (1990). *Separate lives: Why siblings are so different.* New York: Basic Books.

Dunn, J. F., Stocker, C., & Plomin, R. (1990). Nonshared experiences within the family: Correlates of behavioral problems in middle childhood. *Development and Psychopathology, 2,* 113–126.

Eaves, L. J., Eysenck, H. J., & Martin, N. G. (1989). *Genes, culture and personality: An empirical approach.* London: Academic Press.

Edelbrock, C., Rende, R., Plomin, R., & Thompson, L. A. (1995). A twin study of competence and problem behavior in childhood and early adolescence. *Journal of Child Psychology and Psychiatry, 36,* 775–785.

Eder, R. A. (1990). Uncovering young children's psychological selves: Individual and developmental differences. *Child Development, 61,* 849–863.

Eley, T. C., Lichtenstein, P., & Stevenson, J. (1999). Sex differences in the etiology of aggressive and nonaggressive antisocial behavior: Results from two twin studies. *Child Development, 70,* 155–168.

Epstein, S. (1983). Aggregation and beyond: Some basic issues on the prediction of behavior. *Journal of Personality, 51,* 360–392.

Gjone, H., Stevenson, J., Sundet, J. M., & Eilertsen, D. E. (1996). Changes in heritability across increasing levels of behavior problems in young twins. *Behavior Genetics, 26,* 419–426.

Goldsmith, H. H. (1993). Nature–nurture issues in the behavioral genetics context: Overcoming barriers to communication. In R. Plomin & G. E. McClearn (Eds.), *Nature, nurture, and psychology* (pp. 99–120). Washington, DC: American Psychological Association.

Goodman, R. (1997). The Strengths and Difficulties Questionnaire: A research note. *Journal of Child Psychology and Psychiatry, 38,* 581–586.

Gurman, A. S., & Kniskern, D. P. (Eds.), (1980). *Handbook of family therapy.* New York: Brunner/Mazel.

Harris, J. R. (1998). *The nurture assumption.* New York: Free Press.

Harter, S. (1982). The perceived competence scale for children. *Child Development, 53,* 87–97.

Iervolino, A. C., Pike, A., Manke, B., Hewitt, J. K., DeFries, J. C., Reiss, D., Hetherington, E. M., & Plomin, R. (2000). *Genetic and Environmental Influences in Adolescent Peer Socialization: Evidence from Two Genetically Sensitive Designs.* Manuscript submitted for publication.

Jackson, J. F. (1993). Human behavioral genetics, Scarr's theory, and her views on interventions: A critical review and commentary on their implications for African American children. *Child Development, 64,* 1318–1332.

Leve, L. D., Winebarger, A. A., Fagot, B. I., Reid, J. B., & Goldsmith, H. H. (1998). Environmental and genetic variance in children's observed and reported maladaptive behavior. *Child Development, 69,* 1286–1298.

Loehlin, J. C., & Nichols, R. C. (1976). *Heredity, environment, and personality.* Austin, TX: University of Texas Press.

Loehlin, J. C., Willerman, L., & Horn, J. M. (1987). Personality resemblance between unwed mothers and their adopted-away offspring. *Journal of Personality and Social Psychology, 42,* 1089–1099.

Lytton, H. (1977). Do parents create or respond to differences in twins? *Developmental Psychology, 13,* 456–459.

Lytton, H. (1980). *Parent–child interaction: The socialization process observed in twin and singleton families.* New York: Plenum.

McCartney, K., Harris, M. J., & Bernieri, F. (1990). Growing up and growing apart: A developmental meta-analysis of twin studies. *Psychological Bulletin, 107,* 226–237.

McGue, M. (1993). From proteins to cognitions: The behavioral genetics of alcoholism. In R. Plomin & G. E. McClearn (Eds.), *Nature, nurture, and psychology* (pp. 245–268). Washington, DC: American Psychological Association.

Moffitt, T. E. (1993). Adolescence-limited and life-course-persistent antisocial behavior: A developmental taxonomy. *Psychological Review, 100,* 674–701.

Neale, M. C., & Cardon, L. R. (1992). *Methodology for genetic studies of twins and families.* Dordrecht, Netherlands: Kluwer.

Neiderhiser, J. M., & McGuire, S. (1994). Competence during middle childhood: Genetic and environmental influences and development. In J. C. DeFries, R. Plomin, & D. W. Fulker (Eds.), *Nature and nurture in middle childhood.* Cambridge, MA: Blackwell.

Patterson, G. R. (1986). Siblings: Fellow travelers in coercive family processes. *Advances in the Study of Aggression, 1,* 173–214.

Pike, A. (April, 1999). Preschoolers' self-concepts: A twin study. Paper presented at the biennial meeting of the Society for Research in Child Development, Albuquerque, NM.

Pike, A., McGuire, S., Hetherington, E. M., Reiss, D., & Plomin, R. (1996). Family environment and adolescent depressive symptoms and antisocial behavior: A multivariate genetic analysis. *Developmental Psychology, 32,* 590–603.

Plomin, R. (1994). *Genetics and experience: The interplay between nature and nurture.* Thousand Oaks, CA: Sage.

Plomin, R., Chipuer, H. M., & Loehlin, J. C. (1990). Behavioral genetics and personality. In L. A. Pervin (Ed.), *Handbook of personality: Theory and research* (pp. 225–243). New York: Guilford.

Plomin, R., Chipuer, H. M., & Neiderhiser, J. M. (1994). Behavioral genetic evidence for the importance of nonshared environment. In E. M. Hetherington, D. Reiss, & R. Plomin (Eds.), *Separate social worlds of siblings: Impact of nonshared environment on development* (pp. 1–31). Hillsdale, NJ: Erlbaum.

Plomin, R., & Daniels, D. (1987). Why are children in the same family so different from each other? *Behavioral and Brain Science, 10,* 1–16.

Plomin, R., DeFries, J. C., McClearn, G. E., & Rutter, M. (1997). *Behavioral genetics, 3rd ed.* New York: W. H. Freeman.

Plomin, R., & McClearn, G. E. (Eds.) (1993). *Nature, nurture, and psychology.* Washington, DC: American Psychological Association.

Plomin, R., & Rutter, M. (1998). Child development, molecular genetics, and what to do with genes once they are found. *Child Development, 69,* 1223–1242.

Rende, R. D., Slomkowski, C. L., Stocker, C., Fulker, D. W., & Plomin, R. (1992). Genetic and environmental influences on maternal and sibling interaction in middle childhood: A sibling adoption study. *Developmental Psychology, 28,* 484–490.

Rowe, D. C. (1983). Biometrical genetic models of self-reported delinquent behavior: A twin study. *Behavior Genetics, 13,* 473–489.

Rowe, D. C. (1986). Genetic and environmental components of antisocial behavior: A study of 265 twin pairs. *Criminology, 24,* 513–532.

Rowe, D. C. (1994). *The limits of family influence: Genes, experience, and behavior.* New York: Guilford.

Saudino, K. J., & Eaton, W. O. (1991). Infant temperament and genetics: An objective twin study of motor activity level. *Child Development, 62,* 1167–1174.

Scarr, S. (1992). Developmental theories for the 1990s: Development and individual differences. *Child Development, 63,* 1–19.

Schmitz, S., Fulker, D. W., & Mrazek, D. A. (1995). Problem behavior in early and middle childhood: An initial behavior genetic analysis. *Journal of Child Psychology and Psychiatry, 36,* 1443–1458.

Simonoff, E., Pickles, A., Hewitt, J., Silberg, J., Rutter, M., Loeber, R., Meyer, J., Neale, M., & Eaves, L. (1995). Multiple raters of disruptive child behavior: Using a genetic strategy to examine shared views and bias. *Behavior Genetics, 25,* 311–326.

Tsuang, M., & Faraone, S. D. (1990). *The genetics of mood disorders.* Baltimore: Johns Hopkins University Press.

van den Oord, E. J., Verhulst, F. C., & Boomsma, D. I. (1996). A genetic study of maternal and paternal ratings of problem behaviors in 3-year-old twins. *Journal of Abnormal Psychology, 105,* 349–357.

Wachs, T. D. (1993). The nature–nurture gap: What we have here is a failure to collaborate. In R. Plomin & G. E. McClearn (Eds.), *Nature, nurture, and psychology* (pp. 375–391). Washington, DC: American Psychological Association.

3

Evolutionary Perspectives on Social Development

David F. Bjorklund and Anthony D. Pellegrini

Evolutionary psychology is a relatively new discipline within psychology, growing out of the sociobiology movement of the 1970s and coming into its own in the 1990s (Buss, 1995; Tooby & Cosmides, 1992). However, developmental psychology had its origins in evolutionary thinking at the turn of the twentieth century (see Charlesworth, 1992), and many developmentalists, particularly those concerned with social development, have implicitly or explicitly incorporated the concepts of evolution into their theories (e.g., Bowlby, 1969; Hinde, 1980). Thus, the examination of social development from the perspective of the "new" discipline of evolutionary psychology should not involve a theoretical paradigm shift, as it seems to have required in "adult" psychology.

In the sections below, we first describe briefly the conditions under which humans evolved, and then introduce the basic concepts of evolutionary developmental psychology, taking our examples from the arena of social development. We then examine the concept of fitness, specifically as it relates to the development of social behavior. We next examine several aspects of social development from an evolutionary perspective. In the final section, we discuss briefly the benefits of an evolutionary perspective for social development.

Environment of Evolutionary Adaptedness

Evolutionary psychologists propose that *Homo sapiens'* unique intelligence (social and otherwise) evolved to solve adaptive problems faced by our hominid ancestors in the *environment of evolutionary adaptedness*. (*Hominids* refers to the class of bipedal (upright walking) animals that includes humans and our ancient ancestors.) During this time, which is usually conceived as spanning the Pleistocene period (from about 1.8 million years ago until about 10,000 years before present), our ancestors lived as nomadic hunters and gatherers. But our heritage and our cognitive and behavioral abilities extend further in the past. Modern humans last shared a common ancestor with chimpanzees (*Pan troglodytes)* about 5 to 7 million years ago. The earliest members of the hominid line were small-brained, bipedal animals (*Ardipithecus ramidus*, and *Australopithecus anamensis*) who lived in Africa. One group of australopithecines led to the *Homo* line, including *Homo habilis*, which gave way to *Homo ergaster* (or *Homo erectus)*. Although members of *Homo erectus* spread throughout Europe and Asia about 1.7 million years ago, modern humans apparently evolved in Africa, leaving about 100,000 years ago.

According to most paleoanthropologists, this new species replaced the aboriginal *Homo* species they encountered (e.g., *Neanderthals* in Europe, *Homo erectus* in Asia), either by killing or by out-competing them (Johanson & Edgar, 1996).

Based on analysis of the fossil and archeological records and examination of modern hunter–gatherer societies (see Johanson & Edgar, 1996; Mithen, 1996), our ancestors over the past 2 million years were surely a social species, likely living in groups of between 30 and 60 individuals. They made their living on the savannas of Africa gathering fruits, nuts, vegetables, and tubers (most likely the work of women), scavenging food left over from the kills of large predators, and hunting (most likely the work of men). For the first 4 or 5 years of life, children were most likely cared for almost exclusively by their mothers (as is the case in most mammals), although fathers likely provided protection and support in the form of food and other tangible resources for their children and their children's mothers. It is likely that some males had multiple "wives," whereas others had little or no access to females. In other words, ancient humans (as modern humans) were likely a marginally polygynous species, with males competing with one another for access to females, and females selecting males who could provide resources for themselves and their offspring. Females probably reached puberty in their late teens, with pregnancy following the cessation of nursing a previous child (likely every 3 to 5 years). Infant and childhood mortality were surely high, and, even for those who did make it to adulthood, life was relatively brief by contemporary standards, with few people living past 40 years. It was under these conditions that the modern human mind evolved.

Evolutionary Developmental Psychology

Evolutionary psychology takes the basic ideas developed by Charles Darwin (1859) and updated through the twentieth century and applies them to human behavior. It proposes that there is a true "human nature" – universal aspects of psychological functioning that have evolved to solve relatively specific problems our ancestors faced in the environment of evolutionary adaptedness. The central concept of Darwin's theory is *natural selection.* Darwin proposed that, in any generation, more offspring are born than will survive. Individuals vary in a host of features, and these features are heritable. Some of these features afford a better fit with the local environment than others, and individuals possessing these characteristics are more apt to survive, reproduce, and pass on these same features to their offspring than individuals not possessing these features. In other words, heritable variations in physical or psychological features of an individual interact with the environment, and, over many generations, change in frequency, resulting, eventually, in species-wide traits in the population. Thus, through the process of natural selection, adaptive changes in individuals, and eventually species, are brought about.

Evolutionary psychologists use natural selection to explain complex psychological functioning (Buss, 1995; Daly & Wilson, 1988; Tooby & Cosmides, 1992). However, evolutionary psychologists have focused mainly on adults. This is reasonable, because it is adults who do the reproducing, the *sine qua non* of Darwinian success. Yet, individuals must first survive infancy and childhood before they can reproduce, and we believe that psychological characteristics favorable to survival during the juvenile period are as, or more, important to the organism as are characteristics of the adult. Along these lines, several researchers have applied an explicitly developmental perspective to evolutionary thinking and formulated the subfield of *evolutionary developmental psychology* (Bjorklund, 1997a; Bjorklund & Pellegrini, 2000, 2002; Geary & Bjorklund, 2000), which is defined as "the study of the genetic and ecological mechanisms that govern the development of social and cognitive competencies common to all human beings and the epigenetic (gene–environment interactions) processes that adapt these competencies to local conditions" (Geary & Bjorklund, 2000, p. 57). Evolutionary developmental psychology assumes that, not only are behaviors and cognitions that characterize adults the product of selection pressures operating over the course of evolution, but so are characteristics of children's behaviors and minds. Evolutionary developmental psychology is concerned not only with universals – patterns that characterize all members of a species – but also with how *individuals* adapt their behavior to their particular life circumstances. Below we will articulate what we see as some of the concepts central to evolutionary developmental psychology, particularly as they are applied to social development.

Basic principles of evolutionary developmental psychology

1. *Evolutionary developmental psychology involves the expression of evolved, epigenetic programs, as described by the developmental systems approach.* Taking an evolutionary psychological approach requires that one make explicit one's stance on the nature/nurture issue. (In fact, we believe that taking a *developmental perspective*, of any type, also requires this.) Most developmentalists, we believe, would concur that the issue is not "how much" of any trait is due to nature and "how much" is due to nurture, but rather "how do nature and nurture interact to produce a particular pattern of development." But stating that biology and environment, broadly defined, interact, in and of itself, advances the argument very little. We must specify *how* biological and environmental factors interact. We believe that the *developmental systems approach* (e.g., Gottlieb, 1991, 1998) provides the most appropriate model for describing the nature of this interaction.

Central to the developmental systems approach is the concept of *epigenesis*, which Gottlieb (1991) defines as "the emergence of new structures and functions during the course of development" (p. 7). New structures do not arise fully formed, but are the result of the bidirectional relationship between all levels of biological and experiential factors, from the genetic through the cultural. "Experience," from this perspective, involves not only events exogenous to the individual but also self-produced activity, such as the firing of a nerve cell. Functioning at one level influences functioning at adjacent levels, with constant feedback between levels. This relationship can be expressed as follows:

genetic activity (DNA $\Leftrightarrow$ RNA $\Leftrightarrow$ proteins) $\Leftrightarrow$ structural maturation $\Leftrightarrow$ function, activity.

From this viewpoint, there are no simple genetic or experiential causes of behavior; all development is the product of epigenesis, with complex interactions occurring among multiple levels.

Evolved psychological mechanisms can be thought of as genetically coded "messages" that, following epigenetic rules, interact with the environment over time to produce behavior. Because the experiences of each individual are unique, this suggests that there should be substantial plasticity in development. Yet, there is much that is universal about the form and function of members of a species, despite this plasticity. The reason for this is that individuals inherit not only a species-typical genome, but also a species-typical environment, beginning with the prenatal environment. To the extent that individuals grow up in environments similar to those of their ancestors, development should follow a species-typical pattern.

Infants are not born as blank slates; evolution has prepared them to "expect" certain types of environments and to process some information more readily than others. Yet, it is the constant and bidirectional interaction between various levels of organization, which changes over the course of development, that produces behavior.

2. *There is need for an extended childhood to learn the complexities of human social communities.* Central to the application of evolutionary thinking to human development is the recognition that members of *Homo sapiens* have a life history in which they spend a disproportionate amount of time as pre-reproductives. Clearly there are costs to postponing reproduction. Until relatively recently, many children died before ever reaching puberty. From an evolutionary perspective, the benefits associated with an extended period of immaturity must have outweighed the costs. Those benefits can be seen in mastering the complexities of a human social community. A number of theorists have proposed that the single most potent pressure on human intellectual evolution was the need to cooperate and compete with conspecifics (e.g., Humphrey, 1976). As hominid social groups became more complex, individuals who could better understand their social world gained more of the benefits in terms of available mates and resources and passed those characteristics along to their offspring. The greater social complexity of hominid groups required a greater awareness of ourselves and the needs and motivations of others so that we could better understand, and perhaps manipulate, others. But there is much variability in human social life, necessitating a flexible intelligence to master the vagaries of group living. This requires not only a large brain, but also a long time to accomplish. It was the confluence of a large brain, social complexity, and an extended juvenile period that set the stage for the modern human mind.

3. *Many aspects of childhood serve to prepare the way for adulthood and were selected over the course of evolution. Many sex differences in social and cognitive abilities are good examples.* Evolutionary psychologists have, like social psychologists, been interested in sex

differences. The reproductive goals of men and women are similar (i.e., to get their genes into the next generation), but they are approached in different ways. This is because males and females invest differently in their offspring, with females of most species, including humans, investing more in their offspring than males. This differential investment in reproductive and parenting effort is captured by Triver's (1972) *parental investment theory*. The potential consequences of any copulation are substantially greater for women than for men. For women, conception can result in 9 months of pregnancy, and, until the recent advent of baby formula, 3 to 4 years of nursing. Men, unlike the vast majority of males of other mammalian species, do spend significant time caring for and interacting with their offspring, but still, in all cultures observed, spend significantly less time in such endeavors than women (see Geary, 2000). These basic differences in reproductive and parenting effort should have served as selective pressures for the evolution of different mating and childrearing strategies in men and women (Bjorklund & Shackelford, 1999). Although one's culture, a proximal mechanism, surely has a profound impact on such sex differences, evolved "strategies" are the distal mechanisms that interact with these differences in all societies. But importantly, these differences do not arise fully formed at adolescence, but develop gradually over childhood, with children adapting their gender-specific behavior to the local norm, based on evolved predispositions.

Sex differences in children's play provide good examples of precursors to (and thus preparations for) adult sex differences (Bjorklund & Pellegrini, 2000). (See chapters by Pellegrini and by Göncü, Patt, & Kouba, this volume, for more detailed discussions of children's play.) Boys and girls in all cultures, and indeed in many nonhuman mammalian species (e.g., Smith, 1982), segregate themselves by sex when there are enough children in the peer group to do so (Maccoby, 1998). One reason for this sex segregation is the way in which boys and girls play. For example, as early as age 3, boys engage in more rigorous rough-and-tumble play than girls (see Pellegrini & Smith, 1998), a pattern that is found in many nonhuman primates (Smith, 1982). One function proposed for rough-and-tumble play is preparation for adult fighting and hunting in males (Biben, 1998), based on the similarity between such play and adult behaviors. Girls, on the other hand, engage in more play parenting (i.e., doll play) than boys, a sex difference that is even found in some primates (Pryce, 1995). Girls' play is less often centered around physically based dominance relationships, a difference that has been viewed as an evolved tendency that relates to the fact that females are the primary caretakers for their offspring (e.g., Biben, 1998; Geary, 2000).

Another robust sex difference is in physical aggression (Maccoby, 1988). Males engage in more physical aggression than females in all cultures and at all ages, but the greatest consequence of this sex difference is seen in adolescence and young adulthood (Daly & Wilson, 1988). According to parental investment theory, the sex that invests more in offspring (females) is more selective in choosing a mate, and the sex that invests less in offspring (males) competes for access to the higher-investing sex. In humans, as in other mammalian species, there is substantial fitness variance between the sexes. Most mammalian females will find a mate, even if not a highly desirable one; in contrast, the fitness variance is larger for mammalian males, with many males being totally excluded from mating (Trivers, 1972). As a result, selection favored a male psychology that emphasized competitive risk (Daly & Wilson, 1988). Such risk taking, and the violence that can accompany it, peaks in adolescence and young adulthood, when males are entering the re-productive market. This is seen in deaths and injuries from automobile accidents as well as being victims and perpetrators of homicide (National Center for Health Statistics, 1999).

The proposal that sex differences in children's social behaviors serve as preparations for adulthood and are based upon evolved epigenetic rules, does not minimize the role of culture. These evolved "strategies" develop in interaction with children's physical and so-cial environment and can be viewed as biases that will lead children in the "right" direction (i.e., a form of adult behavior that has, over many generations, been associated with repro-ductive success). The strategies for complicated social behaviors that humans have evolved possess a substantial degree of plasticity. But the universality of these behaviors and the fact that many are also observed in nonhuman primates, suggest that they share a common evolved mechanism that requires a prolonged developmental period for their eventual ex-pression.

4. *There have been different selection pressures on organisms at different times in ontogeny, and some characteristics of infants and children were selected in evolution to serve an adaptive function at that time in development and not to prepare them for later adulthood.* Develop-ment is understandably thought of as being progressive, with earlier, immature forms of acting and thinking being replaced with later, more mature forms. Coupled with this rea-sonable idea is the notion that childhood is a preparation for adulthood. Early experience serves to organize the personality or the mind, setting the stage for later functioning. This, too, is a wholly reasonable argument, one we advocated for aspects of children's play above. However, we believe that many features of infancy and childhood have been selected in evolution to serve an adaptive function at that time in development only and not to pre-pare the child for later life (Bjorklund, 1997b).

One area of social-cognitive development that may be a candidate for the adaptive value of immaturity concerns young children's abilities to estimate their competence on a wide range of tasks. Young children are notorious overestimators of their own abilities. Pre-school and early school-age children think they are smarter, stronger, and generally more skilled than they really are (e.g., Bjorklund, Gaultney, & Green, 1993; Stipek, 1984). More specific to the social domain, preschoolers overestimate their own toughness, or dominance, in relation to the estimates of their peers (Sluckin & Smith, 1977). Bandura (1989) has postulated that the confidence people have in their competence in a particular domain affects which tasks they choose to perform and how long they persist at those tasks. Thus, children who think they are skilled in a domain are likely to attempt more challeng-ing tasks and stick at them longer than less optimistic children, and this, in turn, will influence how much they learn.

One area of particular importance for social development is that of imitation. Observa-tional learning is central to Bandura's (1989) theory of social cognitive development, and imitation is the best demonstration that observational learning has occurred. In research with preschoolers, Bjorklund and his colleagues (1993) reported that children overesti-mated their imitative attempts 56.9% of the time, believing that they were more compe-tent in their imitative attempts than the actually were; in contrast, underestimation was rare (5.1% of all occurrences). In a follow-up study, verbal ability was significantly related to 3- and 4-year-old children's meta-imitation (knowledge of their own imitation abili-ties), with children who overestimated more having higher verbal abilities than children who were more accurate at predicting their imitative attempts. The relation was reversed but nonsignificant for 5 year olds. Bjorklund et al. suggested that young children's immature metacognition permits them to imitate a broad range of behaviors without the knowledge that their attempts are inadequate. Thus, bright young children will continue to try a variety of different behaviors, unperturbed by the negative feedback that a more accurate perception of their abilities would provide. The central message we wish to make here is that many aspects of youth are adaptive for their own sake; they provide immediate rather than deferred advantages, and they should be evaluated not for their future benefits but for the function they serve children in the here-and-now.

5. *Most, but not all, evolved psychological mechanisms are domain-specific in nature.* Evolutionary psychologists propose that what has evolved are domain-specific information-processing programs, selected to deal with relatively specific types of problems that our ancestors would have faced in the environment of evolutionary adaptedness. Rather than seeing the human mind as consisting of a general-purpose processing mechanism that can be applied to a wide range of problems, evolutionary psychologists see the mind as consisting of a set of modules, each specialized to deal with a certain type of problem and relatively independent from other modules (Buss, 1995; Tooby & Cosmides, 1992). Within social psychology, domain-specific abilities have been hypothesized for attachment, hierarchical power, coalition groups, reciprocity, and mating (Bugental, 2000), as well as for theory of mind and other forms of social cognition (Geary, 2001), which we will discuss below.

6. *Evolved mechanisms are not always adaptive for contemporary people.* Just because some social, behavioral, or cognitive tendency was adaptive for our ancient ancestors does not mean that it continues to be adaptive for modern humans. Our penchant for sweet and fatty foods, highly adaptive in an environment when one could not be certain where the next meal was coming from, may be maladaptive today in our world of plenty. With respect to children, formal schooling represents a situation in which many of their evolved tendencies do not fit well with the demands of modern society. From the perspective of evolutionary psychology, much of what we teach children in school is "unnatural" in that teaching involves tasks never encountered by our ancestors (e.g., Pellegrini & Bjorklund, 1997).

Reading and higher mathematics may be the best examples of skills our ancestors never acquired, but the "unnaturalness" of school also extends to the social and behavioral realms. For example, most modern schools' emphasis on seat work and focusing attention for an extended period of time, may conflict with children's natural tendencies toward high activity and exploration, particularly in boys. This can be seen in the high incidence of attention-deficit/hyperactivity disorder (ADHD) among school children in some countries today (Jensen et al., 1997). Several researchers have suggested that many children diagnosed with ADHD may simply be highly active and playful youngsters who have a difficult time adjusting to the demands of school (Panksepp, 1998). Jensen et al. (1997) have suggested that the high levels of motor activity and constant switching of attentional focus in children diagnosed with ADHD may have been adaptive to our ancestors (and may still be in some environments today). Unfortunately, such behavior is in conflict with "proper" school conduct and is often treated with psychostimulant drugs that reduce hyperactivity, but may also reduce the desire and opportunity to play, which may, in turn, reduce neural and behavioral plasticity.

Fitness and the Development of Social Behavior

Although social developmentalists are concerned with a wide range of behaviors, most can be divided into two broad categories: prosocial and antagonistic, the latter including aggression and overt competition. Evolutionary psychologists have similarly been concerned with these two broad classes of social behavior, attempting to determine how these behaviors serve to benefit the reproductive success of those who engaged in them.

Any behavior has both costs and benefits to an individual, and if a behavior is associated with greater benefits relative to costs within a population, over many generations, it will be favored by natural selection. From this perspective, it is easy to see why aggression would be adaptive, especially when it is associated with low risks. When aggression "works" to secure mates or other resources more often than it fails, natural selection will favor those individuals who use it effectively. This does not make aggression inevitable; natural selection would not favor cases where costs associated with aggression outweighed benefits, for example, incurring a debilitating injury for the sake of securing a mate. But it does help us understand why aggression is so difficult to eliminate, especially in environments where resources go to the bold rather than the meek.

Although it is relatively easy to explain why aggression, in some contexts, should have benefits and be favored by natural selection, it is more difficult to explain the prevalence of prosocial behavior, particularly altruism, from an evolutionary perspective. Individuals who help others are incurring an immediate cost and no obvious immediate benefit. Given that modern evolutionary theory sees the individual, and not the group or the species, as the unit of selection, why should altruism flourish?

An initial explanation for altruism was provided by Hamilton's (1964) theory of *inclusive fitness*. Following Darwin, reproductive success is determined by how many children and grandchildren one produces. Inclusive fitness takes a gene's-eye view of evolution, however, and proposes that fitness is defined by how many copies of one's genes make it into future generations. For instance, a person enhances his or her inclusive fitness by fostering the success of genetic relatives such as siblings, children, grandchildren, nieces, and nephews.

But children (and adults) also behave prosocially with nonkin. Our ancestors likely lived in small groups that consisted of a high proportion of kin, but also many nonkin (Bowlby, 1969). As a result, groups comprised individuals with whom they shared not only genes, but also a social history as well as a social future, making cooperative relations between both kin and nonkin adaptive.

That social behavior tends to be cooperative among social actors who are familiar with each other and meet repeatedly, has been expressed in the theory of *reciprocal altruism* (Trivers, 1971). Costs associated with prosocial behaviors will be minimized, *quid pro quo*, by others reciprocating the good turn. Similarly, aggressive acts will be reciprocated. In this way, costs associated with cheating outweigh benefits when dealing with individuals in a stable social group. When actors are not related or familiar with each other, and when there is little chance of future interactions, individuals act in their own immediate self-interest. Such circumstances would reward deception and discount cooperation and altruism. In short, cooperating with kin and familiar conspecifics is favored by natural selection, because benefits outweigh costs. By extension, the ability to detect "deception" and "cheating" are important cognitive skills that probably evolved in response to such pressures (Humphrey, 1976).

Topics in Social Development from an Evolutionary Perspective

Evolutionary psychologists believe that all aspects of human functioning can be (perhaps *should be*) explained from the perspective of natural selection. There are some domains within social development, however, that have been analyzed extensively in terms of evolutionary theory, and we will describe briefly research for several of these topics.

Theory of mind

Perhaps the single most basic ability underlying human social interaction is the understanding that other people have knowledge and desires that may be different from one's own. *Theory of mind* has been used to reflect this knowledge. Most children develop an adult-like understanding of mind by 4 years of age (Perner, Leekam, & Wimmer, 1987; Wellman, 1990) as reflected by performance on *false-belief tasks*. In one version of the task, children are shown a box of candy. They are then asked what is inside the box, and they say "candy." The box is then opened and, instead of candy, they see that the box contains pencils. The pencils are then returned to the box and they are asked what their friend, who has not seen the pencils, will think is in the box. Most children 3.5 years of age and younger say "pencils," believing that their friend will know what they know. Interestingly, when asked what they originally thought was in the box, they say "pencils," seemingly forgetting their response from just seconds before. By age 4, most children answer these questions the way adults do.

Consistent with the domain-specificity perspective of evolutionary psychology, several researchers have proposed that theory of mind consists of a series of highly specialized modules that develop over the preschool years (Baron-Cohen, 1995; Leslie, 1994). For example, Baron-Cohen (1995) has proposed four separate interacting modules involved in theory of mind. For instance, the *intentionality detector* (ID) module permits one to infer that a moving object may have some intent toward him or her (e.g., it may bite me or groom me). The *eye-direction detector* (EDD) module serves to interpret eye gazes (if an organism's eyes are looking at something, that organism then *sees* that thing). These modules develop in infancy (by 9 months of age). The *shared-attention mechanisms* (SAM) module involves three-way interactions between the child, another person, and an object, so that if person A and person B are both looking at object C, they both see the same thing. This develops by about 18 months. The *theory of mind module* (TOMM) reflects "adult" understanding, and develops around 4 years of age.

The last two modules may be unique to humans. Although field research with chimpanzees indicate that they engage in some acts of social deception and cooperation, they may accomplish these feats without having a theory of mind, but relying instead on a well-developed learning ability that permits them to adjust their behavior as a consequence of previous interactions with other troop members (e.g., Povinelli & Eddy, 1996). In fact, some well-controlled laboratory research indicates that chimpanzees may not even possess the EDD module, for they frequently fail to recognize that an individual who is looking at an object possesses information that a blindfolded individual does not (Povinelli & Eddy, 1996). (But see research using a more natural competitive-food situation with conspecifics, Hare, Call, Agentta, & Tomasello, 2000; Hare, Call, & Tomasello 2001). Moreover, there is evidence that the principal deficit in high-functioning autistic people is related to theory of mind. Numerous studies have shown that high-functioning autistic children and adults are able to solve nonsocial problems relatively easily (comparable to an IQ-matched nonautistic sample), but more frequently fail similar problems presented in a social context (such as false-belief tasks) (see Baron-Cohen, 1995 for a review). What these individuals lack, presumably, are the SAM and TOMM modules, making the social lives of these people very different from those of others.

Although theory of mind develops at about the same time in most children around the world (e.g., Avis & Harris, 1991), the rate of its development is related to aspects of children's social environment. For example, both the number of adults and the number of older peers that a preschool child interacts with daily are positively related to their scores on false-belief tasks (Lewis et al., 1996). Similarly, children from larger families tend to pass false-belief tasks earlier than children from smaller families (Perner, Ruffman, & Leekam, 1994), although more recent research suggests that it is not family size, per se, that is so important but that the critical factor is having *older* siblings (Ruffman, Perner, Naito, Parkin, & Clements, 1998). There may be many reasons for the importance of interacting with older siblings, peers, and adults for theory-of-mind development. Among some that have been suggested are greater opportunities for discussions of mental states, managing social conflict, pretend play, and reasoning about social issues (e.g., Lewis et al., 1996; Ruffman et al., 1998; Smith, 1998). For example, Ruffman et al. argued that having older siblings stimulates fantasy play, which helps children represent "counterfactual states of affairs," a skill necessary for solving false-belief tasks. Cummins (1998) suggested an explanation based on dominance theory. Siblings are always competing for resources, with older sibs typically having the advantage because of their greater size and mental abilities. Younger children would be motivated to develop whatever latent talents they have to aid them in their social competition with their older sibs, and developing an understanding of the mind of your chief competitor sooner rather than later would certainly be to the younger sib's advantage. A similar argument can be made for interacting with older peers.

Although human children are clearly prepared to develop a theory of mind, something that seems not to be the case for any other species, they require a supportive social environment for these abilities to develop. Smith (1998) proposed a "theory-of-mind-acquisition-support system" analogous to what Bruner (1983) proposed for language acquisition. At this point in our evolutionary history, it seems that any "normal" human social environment will suffice. However, individual differences in children's social experiences, particularly over the infancy and early childhood years, may lead not only to differential rates of theory-of-mind development, but perhaps to different *types* of theory of mind, conducive to the type of environment (e.g., supportive, nonsupportive) in which children develop.

Alternative mating strategies in response to different life circumstances

One misconception many people have of evolutionary accounts of social behavior is that if some behavior "has evolved," it must be rigidly organized and not susceptible to modification. In actuality, evolutionary accounts propose that infants come into the world with predispositions to process certain classes of information in certain ways, but that different patterns of behaviors and thought will develop depending on a child's developmental history. Different patterns, however, should be generally predictable, based on what types of behaviors should produce (or should have produced in our environment of evolutionary adaptedness) adaptive outcomes.

Such differential patterns have been predicted and observed for adolescent behavior as a function of the nature or degree of parental support over childhood. For example, although secure attachment, with attentive parents who are responsive to infants' and young children's signals of physical and social needs, is viewed as optimal, it may not be the best-suited style of attachment in all environments. Different attachment styles may reflect different adaptive solutions to different environments, and insecure attachments, for example, should not automatically be viewed as less optimal than secure attachments. For instance, in comparison to children from low-stress, father-present homes, children from homes characterized by high stress, marital discord/father absence, inadequate resources, and harsh and inconsistent childcare, attain puberty earlier, form short-term and unstable pair bonds, invest relatively little in their own offspring, and tend to be noncompliant and aggressive (especially boys) (e.g., Belsky, Steinberg, & Draper, 1991; Kim, Smith, & Palermiti, 1997). Given the unpredictability of resources, this pattern of early maturation and adolescent promiscuity may lead to the greatest inclusive fitness and be the more prudent strategy than delaying reproduction and investing more in fewer offspring. The latter strategy may be most adaptive for children growing up in low-stress and stable environments. Thus, depending on the availability of resources, which is related to parental investment and spousal harmony, different patterns of socialization occur that result in differential investment in the next generation.

The effects of home environment on reproductive maturity tend to be greater in females (e.g., Kim et al., 1997), which would be expected given the greater investment in any offspring for females than for males. (Recall our earlier discussion of parental investment theory.) Other research, however, indicates that fast-developing girls from high-stress homes also had mothers who reached puberty early, indicating a possible genetic cause (Moffitt, Caspi, Belsky, & Silva, 1992). One interpretation of these findings is that, over many generations, maturation rates may be selected so that they are compatible (and confounded) with general aspects of the environment. For example, the mothers of fast-maturing daughters, too, grew up in unstable environments, making it difficult to untangle genetic from the environmental causation. Thus, we do not see evidence for the inheritance of maturation rate to be necessarily contradictory to an evolutionary psychological explanation for the phenomenon under study. Future research is needed, however, to determine how these factors interact.

Interacting with peers

Much research in social development has focused on peer interactions, and rightfully so, given the significant role that peers play in children's lives and in shaping their development. Harris (1995) has proposed that humans, and other primates, have inherited four evolutionary adaptations that underlie much of our social interactions with peers: (1) group affiliation and in-group favoritism; (2) fear of, and/or hostility toward, strangers; (3) within-group status seeking; and (4) the seeking and establishment of close dyadic relationships. Although these adaptations are found early in life, they nonetheless develop over childhood. Harris (1995), in her *group socialization theory*, further proposes that the peer group plays *the* critical role in socialization, with the effects of parents and teachers being filtered through the peer group. Although we do not mean to minimize the role that parents play in children's development (see Collins, Maccoby, Steinberg, Hetherington, & Bornstein, 2000), research has consistently documented the waning influence of the home environment on personality and intellectual development over the course of childhood (e.g., McCartney, Harris, & Bernieri, 1990). This makes good evolutionary sense, in that Harris proposes that, as they grow older, children will operate outside the home and compete and cooperate with agemates of their group. Becoming too well adapted to the home and too agreeable to the demands of one's parents is not (usually) conducive to one's inclusive fitness.

A thorough examination of peer relations from an evolutionary perspective is beyond the scope of this chapter. We will discuss briefly, however, the role of *social dominance* in children's groups.

Dominant individuals within a group have greater access to limited resources (be it food, mates, or toys in the case of children) and will use a variety of techniques to attain and maintain their preferred status (see Hawley, 1999). Dominance is usually expressed in terms of a hierarchy with transitive relations among individuals (e.g., if A is dominant relative to B and B is dominant relative to C, then A is dominant relative to C). Dominance in children's groups is often expressed in terms of aggressive behaviors, with more aggressive children being dominant relative to less aggressive ones (e.g., Vaughn & Waters, 1981). However, cooperative and other prosocial behaviors may also characterize high-status (i.e., dominant) children, depending on the context. In both children (e.g., Pellegrini & Bartini, 2001) and chimpanzees (e.g., de Waal, 1982), cooperative and reconciliatory strategies are used in situations where the dominant individual needs his or her subordinates and the subordinates are free to leave the group. That dominance includes both affiliation and agonistic behaviors is consistent with findings from both the period of early childhood and early adolescence, where dominance is positively and significantly correlated with popularity (Pellegrini & Bartini, 2001).

Dominance hierarchies serve to reduce antagonism within the group, distribute scarce resources, and focus division of labor. They are found at all ages in which children interact in groups, beginning during the toddler years (see Hawley, 1999). In the initial stages of group formation, children (particularly boys) attempt to establish leadership and gain access to resources via aggression (Strayer & Noel, 1986). Once dominance hierarchies are established, rates of aggression decrease and leaders use prosocial and cooperative strategies more frequently. This suggests that dominant children have a varied behavioral repertoire, which includes both cooperative and prosocial strategies as well as aggressive strategies. The data for both childhood and early adolescence suggests that in the initial phases of group formation dominant youngsters initially use aggression in effective and Machiavellian ways (e.g., to help friends) rather than indiscriminately and reactively. After this sort of dominance exhibition, the "winners" may use more cooperative and reconciliatory strategies. In this way "defeated" individuals" can be integrated into the alpha individual's group of possible allies (deWaal, 1982).

Cummins (1998) has argued that social reasoning grew out of the need to negotiate dominance hierarchies. The realities of life in a complex social group make dominance hierarchies necessary (at least in the absence of codified laws and police enforcement). The tendency to affiliate is strong and emerges early in childhood, and patterns of social dominance seem to be a necessary dimension of such affiliations. Children are well prepared for social relations, based both on inherited evolutionary adaptations and their species-typical experiences as infants. They require no formal instruction from adults to form groups and seem intuitively to understand and to learn quickly the reality of dominance hierarchies and how to live within them.

Evolution and Social Development

One cannot consider "human nature" independent of the social world in which people live and develop. Evolutionary psychology assumes that the human mind has been prepared by natural selection, operating over geological time, for life in a human group. But social complexity is not limited to adult interactions, it also characterizes the interactions of children. Moreover, because of the diversity of environments in which humans live, the complicated and often shifting nature of social alliances, and the need to both compete and cooperate with kin, familiar nonkin, and strangers, humans need a long apprenticeship to master the ways of their social world. Children, as well as adults, have been prepared by evolution to navigate these often stormy social waters. An evolutionary developmental perspective provides a broader framework (a "metatheory") for understanding children's social behaviors and permits us to ask new questions and to see development from a different vantage point. It also may provide insights to some contemporary social issues such as teenage pregnancy, bullying in schools, sibling rivalry, child abuse, and parent–child conflict, among others. Adopting evolutionary theory does not "reduce" humans to being "mere animals," but rather allows us to view our kind from a broader perspective and to gain a better appreciation for what it means to be human.

References

Avis, J., & Harris, P. L. (1991). Belief-desire reasoning among Baka children: Evidence for a universal conception of mind. *Child Development, 62*, 460–467.

Bandura, A. (1989). Social cognitive theory. In R. Vasta (Ed.), *Annals of child development*. Greenwich, CT: JAI Press.

Baron-Cohen, S. (1995). *Mindblindness: An essay on autism and theory of mind.* Cambridge, MA: MIT Press.

Belsky, J., Steinberg, L., & Draper, P. (1991). Childhood experience, interpersonal development, and reproductive strategy: An evolutionary theory of socialization. *Child Development, 62,* 647–670.

Biben, M. (1998). Squirrel monkey play fighting: Making a case for a cognitive training function for play. In M. Bekoff & J. A. Byers (Eds.), *Animal play* (pp. 161– 182). New York: Cambridge University Press.

Bjorklund, D. F. (1997a). In search of a metatheory for cognitive development (or, Piaget's dead and I don't feel so good myself). *Child Development, 68,* 142–146.

Bjorklund, D. F. (1997b). The role of immaturity in human development. *Psychological Bulletin, 122,* 153–169.

Bjorklund, D. F., Gaultney, J. F., & Green, B. L. (1993). "I watch therefore I can do:" The development of meta-imitation over the preschool years and the advantage of optimism in one's imitative skills. In R. Pasnak & M. L. Howe (Eds.), *Emerging themes in cognitive development, Vol. II: Competencies* (pp. 79–102). New York: Springer-Verlag.

Bjorklund, D. F., & Pellegrini, A. D. (2000). Child development and evolutionary psychology. *Child Development, 71,* 1687–1798.

Bjorklund, D. F., & Pellegrini, A. D. (2002). *The origins of human nature: Evolutionary developmental psychology.* Washington, DC: American Psychological Association.

Bjorklund, D. F., & Shackelford, T. K. (1999). Differences in parental investment contribute to important differences between men and women. *Current Directions in Psychological Science, 8,* 86–89.

Bowlby, J. (1969). *Attachment and loss: Vol. 1: Attachment.* London: Hogarth.

Bugental, D. B. (2000). Acquisition of the algorithms of social life: A domain-based approach. *Psychological Bulletin, 126,* 187–219.

Bruner, J. S. (1983). *Child's talk: Learning to use language.* New York: Norton.

Buss, D. M. (1995). Evolutionary psychology. *Psychological Inquiry, 6,* 1–30.

Charlesworth, W. R. (1992). Darwin and developmental psychology: Past and present. *Developmental Psychology, 28,* 5–16.

Collins, W. A., Maccoby, E. E., Steinberg, L., Hetherington, E. M., & Bornstein, M. H. (2000). Contemporary research on parenting: The case for nature and nurture. *American Psychologist, 55,* 218–232.

Cummins, D. D. (1998). Social norms and other minds: The evolutionary roots of higher cognition. In D. D. Cummins & C. Allen (Eds.), *The evolution of mind* (pp. 28–50). New York: Oxford University Press.

Daly, M., & Wilson, M. (1988). *Homicide.* New York: Aldine.

Darwin, C. (1859). *The origin of species.* New York: Modern Library.

de Waal, F. B. M. (1982). The integration of dominance and social bonding in primates. *Quarterly Review of Biology, 61,* 459–479.

Geary, D. C. (2000). Evolution and proximate expression of human parental investment. *Psychological Bulletin, 126,* 55–77.

Geary, D. C. (2001). Sexual selection and sex differences in social cognition. In A. V. McGillicuddy-DeLisi & R. DeLisi (Eds.), *Biology, society, and behavior: The development of sex differences in cognition* (pp. 23–53). Greenwich, CT: Ablex.

Geary, D. C., & Bjorklund, D. F. (2000). Evolutionary developmental psychology. *Child Development, 71,* 57–65.

Gottlieb, G. (1991). Experiential canalization of behavioral development: Theory. *Developmental Psychology, 27,* 4–13.

Gottlieb, G. (1998). Normally occurring environmental and behavioral influences on gene activity: From central dogma to probabilistic epigenesis. *Psychological Review, 105*, 792– 802.

Hamilton, W. D. (1964). The genetical theory of social behavior. *Journal of Theoretical Biology, 7*, 1–52.

Hare, B., Call, J., Agentta, B., & Tomasello, M. (2000). Chimpanzees know what conspecifics do and do not see. *Animal Behaviour, 59*, 771–785.

Hare, B., Call, J., & Tomasello, M. (2001). Do chimpanzees know what conspecifics know? *Animal Behaviour, 61*, 139–151.

Harris, J. R. (1995). Where is the child's environment? A group socialization theory of development. *Psychological Review, 102*, 458–489.

Hawley, P. A. (1999). The ontogenesis of social dominance: A strategy-based evolutionary perspective. *Developmental Review, 19*, 97–132.

Hinde, R. A. (1980). *Ethology*. London: Fontana.

Humphrey, N. K. (1976). The social function of intellect. In P. P. G. Bateson & R. A. Hinde (Eds.), *Growing points in ethology* (pp. 303–317). Cambridge, England: Cambridge University Press.

Jensen, P. S., Mrazek, D., Knapp, P. K., Steinberg, L., Pfeffer, C., Schwalter, J., & Shapiro, T. (1997). Evolution and revolution in child psychiatry: ADHD as a disorder of adaptation. *Journal of the American Academy of Child and Adolescent Psychiatry, 36*, 1672–1681.

Johanson, D., & Edgar, B. (1996). *From Lucy to language*. New York: Simon & Schuster.

Kim, K., Smith, P. K., & Palermiti, A. (1997). Conflict in childhood and reproductive development. *Evolution and Human Development, 18*, 109–142.

Leslie, A. (1994). ToMM, ToBY, and agency: Core architecture and domain specificity. In L. Hirschfeld & S. Gelman (Eds.), *Mapping the mind: Domain specificity in cognition and culture* (pp. 119–148). Cambridge, England: Cambridge University Press.

Lewis, C., Freeman, N. H., Kyriakidou, C., Maridaki-Kassotaki, K., & Berridge, D. M. (1996). Social influence on false belief access: Specific sibling influences or general apprenticeship? *Child Development, 67*, 2930–2947.

Maccoby, E. E. (1998). *The two sexes: Growing up apart, coming together*. Cambridge, MA: Harvard University Press.

McCartney, K., Harris, M. J., & Bernieri F. (1990). Growing up and growing apart: A development meta-analysis of twin studies. *Psychological Bulletin, 97*, 226–237.

Mithen, S. (1996). *The prehistory of the mind: The cognitive origins of art, religion and science*. London: Thames and Hudson.

Moffitt, T. E., Caspi, A., Belsky, J., & Silva, P. A. (1992). Childhood experience and the onset of menarche: A test of a sociobiological hypothesis. *Child Development, 63*, 47–58.

National Central for Health Statistics (1999). *Health, United States*. Hyattsville, MD.

Panksepp, J. (1998). Attention deficit hyperactivity disorders, psychostimulants, and intolerance of childhood playfulness: A tragedy in the making? *Current Directions in Psychological Science, 7*, 91–98.

Pellegrini, A. D., & Bartini, M. (2001). Dominance in early adolescent boys: Affiliative and aggressive dimensions and possible functions. *Merrill-Palmer Quarterly, 47*, 142–163.

Pellegrini, A. D., & Bjorklund, D. F. (1997). The role of recess in children's cognitive performance. *Educational Psychologist, 32*, 35–40.

Pellegrini, A. D., & Smith, P. K. (1998). Physical activity play: The nature and function of neglected aspect of play. *Child Development, 69*, 577–598.

Perner, J., Leekam, S. R., & Wimmer, H. (1987). Three-year-olds' difficulty with false belief: The case for a conceptual deficit. *British Journal of Developmental Psychology, 5*, 125–137.

Perner, J., Ruffman, T., & Leekam, S. R. (1994). Theory of mind is contagious: You catch it from your sibs. *Child Development, 67*, 1228–1238.

Povinelli, D. J., & Eddy, T. J. (1996). What young chimpanzees know about seeing. *Monographs of the Society for Research in Child Development (Vol. 61, No. 3, Serial No. 247).*

Pryce, C. R. (1995). Determinants of motherhood in human and nonhuman primates: A biosocial model. In C. R. Pryce, R. D. Martin, & D. Skuse (Eds.), *Motherhood in human and nonhuman primates: Biosocial determinants* (pp. 1–15). Basel, Switzerland: Karger.

Ruffman, T., Perner, J., Naito, M., Parkin, L., & Clements, W. A. (1998). Older (but not younger) siblings facilitate false belief understanding. *Developmental Psychology, 34,* 161–174.

Sluckin, A., & Smith, P. K. (1977). Two approaches to the concept of dominance in preschool children. *Child Development, 4,* 917–923.

Smith, P. K. (1982). Does play matter? Functional and evolutionary aspects of animal and human play. *Behavioral and Brain Sciences, 5,* 139–184.

Smith, P. K. (June, 1998). The theory of mind acquisition support system: Social origins of theory of mind. Paper presented at Hang Seng Conference on Evolution of Mind, Sheffield, UK.

Stipek, D. (1984). Young children's performance expectations: Logical analysis or wishful thinking? In J. G. Nicholls (Ed.), *Advances in motivation and achievement: Vol. 3. The development of achievement motivation* (pp. 33–56). Greenwich, CT: JAI Press.

Strayer, F. F., & Noel, J. M. (1986). The prosocial and antisocial functions of aggression. In C. Zahn-Waxler, E. M. Cummings, & R. Iannoti (Eds.), *Altruism and aggression* (pp. 107–131). New York: Cambridge University Press.

Tooby, J., & Cosmides, L. (1992). The psychological foundations of culture. In J. H. Barkow, L. Cosmides, & J. Tooby (Eds.), *The adapted mind: Evolutionary psychology and the generation of culture* (pp. 19–139). New York: Oxford University Press.

Trivers, R. L. (1971). The evolution of reciprocal altruism. *Quarterly Review of Biology, 46,* 35–57.

Trivers, R. L. (1972). Parental investment and sexual selection. In B. Campbell (Ed.), *Sexual selection and the descent of man* (pp. 136–179). New York: Aldine de Gruyter.

Vaughn, B. E., & Waters, E. (1981). Attention structure, sociometric status, and dominance: Inter-relations, behavioral correlates, and relationships to social competence. *Developmental Psychology, 17,* 275–288.

Wellman, H. M. (1990). *The child's theory of mind.* Cambridge, MA: MIT Press.

4

Culture and Social Development: Explanations and Evidence

Sara Harkness

For the human species, adaptability has been the key to success in a wide variety of different ecologies. From the icy coasts and plains of the arctic to the jungles and savannahs of the equator, we encounter families and communities of people living recognizably human, yet strikingly different, lifestyles. Nowhere is this plasticity more evident than in social development, as children grow and learn to be members of a myriad of different culturally organized milieux. How to explain the ways that culture shapes children's social development has been a central task of social anthropology, and more recently social and developmental psychology. This chapter will review selected frameworks for understanding how culture affects children's social development from early through middle childhood. Beginning with anthropological formulations of the early twentieth century, we will trace the historical progression of explanatory frameworks, including those that have emerged more recently within psychology. Since the measure of a theory's adequacy is its usefulness for understanding the reality it addresses, we will also consider the kinds of evidence associated with each model.

"Patterns of Culture": The Role of Childhood Socialization

Although anthropological studies of other, "primitive" cultures traditionally included chapters on family life including ceremonies related to birth and various developmental transitions, recognition of children's social development as adaptation to the culturally structured environment is first evident in the writings of Ruth Benedict and Margaret Mead, beginning in the 1920s. As Benedict wrote in her seminal work *Patterns of Culture*, first published in 1934:

The life-history of the individual is first and foremost an accommodation to the patterns and standards traditionally handed down in his community. From the moment of his birth the customs into which he is born shape his experience and behaviour. By the time he can talk, he is the little creature of his culture, and by the time he is grown and able to take part in its activities, its habits are his habits, its beliefs his beliefs, its impossibilities his impossibilities. Every child that is born into his group will share them with him, and no child born into one on the opposite side of the globe can ever achieve the thousandth part. There is no social problem it is more incumbent upon us to understand than this of the role of custom. Until we are intelligent as to its laws and varieties, the main complicating facts of human life must remain unintelligible (Benedict, 1934/1959, pp. 2–3).

By "custom," Benedict and Mead meant the practices of childcare that were part of the everyday fabric of life, not just the ceremonial events that had heretofore been the primary focus of anthropological research. In describing daily routines of 3 year olds in the Pacific society of Manus, Mead evokes the image of a morning outing in heavy dugout canoes:

Early in the morning the village is alive with canoes in which the elders sit sedately on the centre platforms while small children of three punt the canoes which are three or four times as long as the children are tall. At first glance this procession looks like either the crudest sort of display of adult prestige or a particularly conspicuous form of child labour. The father sits in casual state, a man of five feet nine or ten, weighing a hundred and fifty pounds. The canoe is long and heavy, dug out of a solid log; the unwieldy outrigger makes it difficult to steer. At the end of the long craft, perched precariously on the thin gunwales, his tiny brown feet curved tensely to keep his hold, stands a small brown baby, manfully straining at the six foot punt in his hands. He is so small that he looks more like an unobtrusive stern ornament than like the pilot of the lumbering craft. Slowly, with a great display of energy but not too much actual progress, the canoe moves through the village, among other canoes similarly manned by the merest tots. But this is neither child labour nor idle prestige hunting on the part of the parents. It is part of the whole system by which a child is encouraged to do his physical best (Mead, 1930/1966, p. 29).

Activities such as a daily outing with father in the family canoe, sleeping arrangements for the young child, and the organization of dinner were all customs that, in Mead and Benedict's thinking, were the bearers of cultural "messages" which the child would learn over and over in multiple contexts, distilling from these experiences the essence of what it meant to be a good member of his or her society. As Benedict pointed out in her analysis of Japanese culture and personality, written for the US government during World War II, these customs need not necessarily seem consistent over the lifespan. For example, she noted that although Japanese adults were expected to subordinate their own wishes for the good of the group, Japanese infants were highly indulged (Benedict, 1946). In this regard, the work of Mead and Benedict foreshadowed more recent recognition that what appear to be the "same" parenting practices may have different meanings and therefore different developmental consequences in varying cultural contexts. Mead and Benedict also presaged current research on culture and temperament in their recognition that the particular kinds of personal qualities encouraged by a given culture might not fit equally comfortably for all individuals. Mead proposed that "an individual whose temperament was incompatible with the type (or types) emphasized in the culture in which he was born and reared would be at a disadvantage – a disadvantage that was systematic and predictable for that culture" (Mead, 1972, p. 219); and Benedict (1934) went so far as to suggest that mental illness itself might be an extreme example of misfit between the individual and the demands of the cultural milieu.

In retrospect, the work of Mead and Benedict seems surprisingly modern, although some aspects of their theoretical approach were not fully developed. The "customs" they described constituted the informal education through which the lessons of the culture were implicitly taught and equally implicitly learned. Both parents and children were seen as active participants in this process, and individual differences among children and their families were documented along with description of the larger cultural patterns. The "patterns of culture" they proposed, in which certain themes were seen as general organizing principles of whole societies, resonate with the observation of "thematicity" in cultural models across a wide range of domains, as noted by today's cognitive anthropologists (Quinn & Holland, 1987). In contrast, explanations of culture and children's social development that dominated anthropology during the "culture and personality" era of the 1940s, 1950s, and 1960s, based largely on either Freudian psychology or social learning theory, now seem outdated. Nevertheless, this work led to some important advances in understanding of the relationships between culture and individual development.

"Culture and Personality": Monocultural and Cross-cultural Studies

Whereas Benedict introduced the idea of "patterns of culture" and Mead showed how children's life and development varied with the larger ethos of the parent society, anthropologists of the "culture and personality" school that followed (although there was some historical overlap) were concerned with finding psychological explanations for cultural variability. We should note that this work was focused not on understanding why childhood socialization practices vary across cultures, but rather how such practices might lead to culturally shared differences in adult personality and beliefs. Following traditional anthropological methods, much of this work was based on field research in a single society. Thus, Spiro (1953) suggested that beliefs in ghosts among the people of Ifaluk, a Pacific atoll, could be explained as the result of certain childhood experiences such as a daily cold-water bath and the abrupt transition from indulged infancy to relatively neglected toddlerhood, following the birth of the next child. Such experiences, Spiro hypothesized, might lead the child to "develop the hypothesis that their world is threatening and, therefore, predispose them to believe in these threatening ghosts" (p. 245). Although intriguing, such explanations tended to lose their persuasiveness when the relationship between particular childhood socialization practices and cultural belief systems was examined in other contexts, where exceptions often proved the rule. For example, many traditional societies, including those of sub-Saharan Africa, are characterized by an abrupt transition from infancy to toddlerhood, yet they do not have similar beliefs in the pervasive presence of ghosts as described for the Ifaluk (Harkness & Super, 1991).

The logical solution to this methodological problem was to seek wider samples of cultures with which to test relationships between childhood socialization practices and other aspects of the adult culture. Since individual anthropologists could not carry out fieldwork in more than a handful of cultures at best, it became necessary to rely on the pooled knowledge acquired over years of research by many investigators. The Human Relations Area Files (HRAF) provided such a resource by making available a vast archive of ethnographic information on over 200 societies, coded paragraph by paragraph into some 700 categories so that investigators interested in any particular topic could find the relevant information without having to search through the entire original document. There were complications, of course. Ethnographies were individual works whose content was dictated by the interests of the investigators and although there was a standard template of ethnographic topics, information on any given one might be scanty or altogether absent. Samples of cultures could not be drawn completely randomly around the world because relationships that held in one cultural area (for example, the Pacific islands) might not work the same way in other areas. Nevertheless, cross-cultural studies of childhood socialization using the HRAF provided some valuable new insights into the ways that culture and children's social development are linked (Whiting, 1976).

Notable in this literature is Barry, Child, and Bacon's (1959) analysis of the relationships between subsistence type and childhood socialization practices. Ethnographic studies of simple agricultural or peasant societies had repeatedly found that children were socialized for obedience and conformity to the rules of their society as mandated by elders. This observation seemed to support a general social evolutionary perspective in which egalitarianism and democracy gradually supercede more ancient authoritarian regimes. Research among technologically simpler and evolutionarily older cultures of hunter-gatherers such as the Kung San of the Kalahari, however, presented a rather different picture, in which parents were not particularly authoritarian and children were not especially industrious or obedient.

Barry, Child, and Bacon hypothesized that there is a functional relationship between particular kinds of societies as characterized by their mode of subsistence and the ways that children are socialized. Specifically, they suggested that in farming societies where "food accumulation" is necessary to tide the family over from one growing season to the next, children would be socialized to be responsible and obedient, to defer to the better judgment of their elders. In contrast, hunting and gathering societies in which food must be found on a daily basis would need individuals who could exercise initiative and imagination in the hunt or the search for wild vegetables; in such societies, the investigators suggested, children would be socialized toward achievement, self-reliance, and independence. The hypothesized relationships were found to be so reliable across a worldwide sample of cultures that the authors concluded that knowledge of the economy alone would be sufficient for predicting any given society's relative emphasis on socialization for compliance or assertiveness.

Much has been written about the inadequacies of both the "culture and personality" school and cross-cultural studies of that era (see Harkness, 1992), but this research left a vitally important legacy in the form of three principles. First, it established the fact that different parts of a culture are systematically linked, even though the mechanisms of that linkage may not be reducible to any single explanation. Second and more specifically, this research showed that there are consistent relationships between childhood socialization and the socioeconomic organization of the wider culture. Finally, research across a wide variety of cultures in different parts of the world also established the fact that features of childrearing, like linguistic features, can be essentially mapped onto different culture areas. Thus, armed with knowledge of both the way of life of the larger community and its place on a map of world cultures, today's researchers of culture and child development can approach any given new group with certain well-founded expectations about how children are likely to be brought up and how these patterns both support and recreate the parental culture.

Culture as a "Provider of Settings" for Children's Social Development: Multi-Site Ethnographic Studies

As Barry, Child, and Bacon's study illustrates, cross-cultural studies of culture and childhood socialization shed light on both the ways that culture shapes child development and how such development forms the basis for adult functioning. Further research, especially the work of John and Beatrice Whiting and their associates, produced a veritable harvest of new knowledge about children's social development in cultures around the world, including the home culture of the researchers. The explanatory framework for this research, known simply as the "Whiting model" after its originator John W. M. Whiting, posited that children's environments of learning and development are determined largely by the "maintenance systems" of their cultures such as social and political organization and principal means of subsistence. Mediating between the larger society and the child's own environment are parents' daily routines including women's workload (Whiting, 1977). Children, according to this view, are assigned to settings of socialization that stem naturally and inevitably from the necessities of their parents' daily lives as well as the cultural beliefs and values that permeate them.

This explanatory framework, first set out in the Six Culture Study (Whiting & Whiting, 1975) and further elaborated in B. Whiting and Carolyn Edwards' analysis of "children of different worlds" (Whiting & Edwards, 1988), guided analysis of ethnographic and psychosocial data collected using similar sampling and methods. Ultimately, the material on socialization and behavior of children in the first decade of life included a worldwide sampling of societies including five different ethnic groups in Kenya as well as one from Liberia, two communities in India, and sites in Mexico, the Philippines, Okinawa, and the United States. With indepth observations of children's social behavior with their parents, siblings, and others in these varied cultural settings, the researchers were able to analyze not only cultural differences among samples but also behavioral typologies related to culture, age, and gender.

Whiting and Edwards' analysis of mother and father involvement illustrates these features. Observations made at many different times of day show that in all cultures, children were with their mothers two to four times more frequently than with their fathers, and that children aged 6 to 10 were less frequently in the company of their mothers than younger children. In contrast, boys' time with their fathers increased with age in those cultures (particularly the Kenyan and Indian communities) where sons were expected to help out with male tasks such as cattle herding. Fathers' time with children seems to be mediated by several factors, among which the spousal relationship is particularly important. As Whiting and Edwards explain:

> The norms and rules pertaining to intimacy between husband and wife and their division of labor influence young children's contact with parents. In all our samples mothers have the primary responsibility for infant care, but the amount of paternal involvement varies widely. For example, in the Six Culture communities, participation of fathers in childcare is lowest in Khalapur (India) and Nyansongo (Kenya); many of these fathers actually sleep in different buildings from their wives and young children. Fathers are most involved with lap children [infants] and knee children [toddlers] in Tarong (Philippines) and Juxtlahuaca (Mexico), societies where fathers share a bed with their wives and children, and in Taira (Okinawa), where all the members of the household sleep side by side wrapped in their quilts (Whiting & Edwards, 1988, p. 62).

Sleeping arrangements such as those described above are important not only in terms of the actual opportunities for father–child contact they provide, but also because they index social relationships among various family members. The Kenyan samples, in which father involvement in care of young children was judged lowest, are typical of polygynous sub-Saharan societies in which marriages are arranged and the husband takes turns attending to each of his wives. In these societies, there is a strong division of social roles between men and women, and men are excluded from childbirth (except in emergencies) and prohibited from seeing their newborns for up to a month (Harkness & Super, 1991). The Rajputs of Khalapur, as described by Minturn (1993) in a later monograph, also construct very different worlds for men and women, in which husbands and wives have few opportunities for intimacy in the multigenerational extended family households. In contrast, fathers in more egalitarian societies with nuclear family households and greater sharing and intimacy between spouses are more involved in the care of young children. Father *presence*, as opposed to father involvement, however, is influenced by others factors such as the nature and location of fathers' work. U.S. fathers in the cross-cultural samples were generally employed outside the home, in contrast to the Kenyan fathers whose work was tied to their homesteads. In a comparison of these two groups of fathers, Harkness and Super (1992) found that fathers in these two widely differing settings were actually present in the lives of their young children about the same amount of time.

Mothers' behavior with their children, in Whiting and Edwards' analysis, was also shown to reflect the culturally organized reality of their own lives, which the authors defined in both pragmatic and symbolic terms. On the pragmatic side, women's workload, including such aspects as average family size and help with childcare in addition to the nature and amount of women's work, was found to be a powerful predictor of maternal behavior across cultures. On the symbolic side were mothers' cultural beliefs about the nature of the child and the roles of parents, or "parental ethnotheories" as Harkness and Super (1996) have called them. For example, Whiting and Edwards contrasted the fatalistic view of Indian parents that a child's destiny is "written on his brow" with the belief of the Orchard Town mothers that "their infant was a bundle of potentialities and that it was the task of the mother to assess these potentialities and to direct the training of the child so as to maximize them" (p. 91). Whiting and Edwards predicted that cultural variability in mothers' social behavior with their children would reflect the differences in both the pragmatic and symbolic domains.

Systematic observations of mothers and children across the Six Culture samples showed that maternal social behavior could be described in terms of the relative proportions of four basic types of behavior: nurturance (including actual caretaking as well as giving attention and emotional support); training (including teaching and assigning chores); controlling behavior (dominance intended to correct undesirable behavior); and sociability (including friendly conversation and physical affection). Three distinct maternal styles were evident.

The first, the "training mother," was found in all the sub-Saharan groups. These mothers, who labored hard on their farms and homesteads in addition to raising large families, taught their children early to be helpful and responsible. The second profile, the "controlling mother," was found in the two Indian samples as well as Mexico, Okinawa, and the Philippines. In these societies, men were the farmers whereas mothers provided support in the form of food preparation and housekeeping. Children were less needed to help out with basic economic activities although they were expected to be helpful when asked. On the other hand, children could also be a nuisance by virtue of their constant demands for attention and care, especially in the north Indian samples in which women were confined to their courtyards by the custom of *purdah*. Finally, the "sociable mother" profile was found only in the Orchard Town sample. Although controlling behavior was also high among these mothers, the addition of frequent social behavior with children made them distinctive. This behavioral profile is explained in terms of cultural beliefs – the desire to support children's individual development by teaching them from an early age – but also the social isolation of the mothers themselves. As Whiting and Edwards noted, these mothers were by far the most residentially isolated of all the samples. Lacking the company of other adults, the Orchard Town mothers turned to their children for companionship.

Children's behavior toward their mothers is shown by Whiting and Edwards to be the reciprocal of mothers' behavior toward them. Corresponding to the four most frequent maternal behaviors were a predictable set of child behaviors: maternal nurturance elicited children's dependent behavior; obedience or cooperation was the reciprocal of mothers' training behavior; dominance and aggression appeared (although not frequently) in response to mothers' controlling behavior; and mothers' sociability was matched by child sociability. Although all these behaviors were present across the samples and showed age-related changes, there were interesting differences in the ways and extent that they were expressed. For example, children's dependent behavior in the north Indian samples was characterized as "active, insistent, almost aggressive" (p. 142), a style attributed to their mothers' delayed and inconsistent responses to children's bids for care and attention, and related to both cultural values of interdependency and the immediate social ecology of these crowded Indian households. Children in the African samples were generally more compliant, corresponding to their mothers' training behavior. Finally, children in north India and Orchard Town, where mothers were most frequently controlling, showed the highest rates of dominance and aggression to their mothers.

The reciprocity between maternal and child behavior in the different cultural samples illustrates Whiting and Edwards' central focus on the "eliciting power of one's social partner" (p. 133). Children's social development, in their view, is the product of the social settings they inhabit and the people with whom they interact, including other children as well as their parents. Thus, children who were assigned to take care of younger siblings, as in the Kenyan samples, had more opportunity to learn nurturant behavior, whereas children who spent more time with peers, such as the children of Orchard Town once they reached school age, learned competitive and attention-seeking behaviors. Because the behaviors themselves were only observed in context, it is not possible to conclude that they became internalized as personality traits; but this research shows that at the very least they were well practiced.

In summary, the work of the Whitings and their associates, which altogether spanned over five decades, contributed both new ideas and new methods for the study of culture and children's social development. The Whitings' initial theoretical framework, in which children's learning environments are the product of a series of contextual factors from the most general to the most immediate, has often been mischaracterized as purely functionalist, lacking in recognition of cultural belief systems (Fiske, Kitayama, Markus, & Nisbett, 1998). On the contrary, the Whitings recognized the importance of meaning systems and, in a 1960 chapter for Mussen's *Handbook of Research Methods in Social Psychology* (Whiting & Whiting, 1960) stated that anthropologists' "unique contribution" to the study of human behavior was "in the formulation of the shared symbolic determinants of behavior, which, in our view, is the essential feature of the concept of culture" (Chasdi, 1994, p. 48). In B. Whiting's later work, as we have seen, the role of belief systems in parenting behavior becomes even more evident.

Cultural-Ecological Frameworks

Although *Children of Different Worlds* was published in 1988, it was the culmination of field research initiated in the 1950s. In the meantime, a new generation of theories was emerging, informed by the work of the Whitings but also shaped by the "cognitive revolution" and other developments across a broad spectrum of disciplines including linguistics, psychology, and ecology. Of particular relevance to children's social development are the cultural-ecological models developed by Charles Super and Sara Harkness, and by Thomas Weisner and his associates. Both of these models build upon the Whitings' idea of "settings" as a primary focus for the study of cultural effects on child development, in combination with other theoretical perspectives.

Culture and the child's developmental niche

The developmental niche as proposed by Super and Harkness "is a theoretical framework generated specifically to foster integration of concepts and findings from multiple disciplines concerned with the development of children in cultural context. . . Two overarching principles reflect its origins in social anthropology and developmental psychology: First, that a child's environment is organized in a nonarbitrary manner as part of a cultural system, including contingencies and variable flexibility, thematic repetitions, and systems of meaning; and second, that the child has an inborn disposition, including a particular constellation of temperament and skill potentials as well as species-specific potentials for growth, transformation, and the organization of experience into meaning. Both the environment and the individual are seen as open systems in the formal sense, that is, ones that participate in structured interchanges with external systems" (Super & Harkness, 1997, p. 26).

The developmental niche, thus, conceptualizes both the child and the environment as active and interactive systems. Taking the perspective of the child's place in this system, the niche is seen as consisting of three major components or subsystems: 1) The physical and social settings of the child's daily life; 2) Culturally regulated customs of childcare and rearing; and 3) The psychology of the caretakers, especially their cultural belief systems or "ethnotheories."

The developmental niche is further defined in terms of three corollaries. First, the three subsystems of the niche operate together as a system, with homeostatic mechanisms that promote consonance among them. This feature is the joint result of individual needs for reducing cognitive dissonance (as in a poor match between ideas and practice) and of the characteristic redundancy in cultural themes across domains. Second, each of the three subsystems of the niche is functionally embedded in other aspects of the larger ecology, making them open channels through which the niche can be altered from without. Thus, for example, the physical and social settings of children's lives are routinely altered by such things as seasonal changes and school vacation schedules; and they may be more profoundly altered by changes in the economy necessitating different patterns of parental employment. Third, as mentioned above, the child is conceptualized as an active contributor to his or her own developmental niche by virtue of temperament and other individual characteristics which modify parental decision making about daily routines as well as influencing social interaction directly.

From a methodological perspective, it is important that each of these subsystems represents a different kind of data, which can then be used to achieve convergent validity. For example, observational data on siblings' social interaction (physical and social settings) can form the basis for understanding customs regarding sibling care (customs and practices); interviews with parents about the meaning of everyday routines and practices can inform the investigator's interpretation of how parents think about children's roles in the family (psychology of the caretakers).

An example of coordination among the three subsystems of the developmental niche comes from a study of sleep and arousal in infants and young children in the Netherlands and the United States (Super et al., 1996). The samples in each cultural site were parents of children in several age groups from 6 months to 4.5 years (total n = 54 families). Parental interviews covering a wide range of topics related to child and family revealed that Dutch parents in the community of "Bloemenheim" (a fictitious name) were very concerned about the importance of a restful and regular schedule to support children's healthy development in infancy and childhood. This cultural belief also had the endorsement of the national well-child care system as communicated to parents through their local clinics, and had been formalized in the "three Rs" of good childcare: *rust* (rest), *regelmaat* (regularity), and *reinheid* (cleanliness). As the Dutch parents explained to their American interviewers, rest is important for children's growth, and an adequately restful and regular schedule is the foundation of the child's daytime behavior, promoting a calm yet cheerful and active disposition. In fact, the most frequent reason given for children's difficult behavior was disruption of this schedule by a late evening out or too much excitement.

A tabulation of themes in the Dutch parents' talk about this topic showed that by far the greatest emphasis was given to explaining the importance and consequences of rest and regularity; however, the parents did not experience establishing a regular schedule for sleep and eating as problematic. In contrast, American parents of same-age children from the Boston area emphasized different themes concerning the development of sleep. For these parents, biological maturation and individual differences were the prime determinants of children's sleep behavior. Many of these parents struggled with getting their children to sleep through the night, and (unlike the Dutch parents) had developed a repertoire of strategies to deal with night waking.

Data on daily routines of the children, based on parental diaries, showed that the Dutch children were actually sleeping more than the American children (at least as far as their parents could tell). The differences were quite dramatic, with a 2-hour average difference in total sleep per 24 hours at 6 months, diminishing to a still-noticeable 20-minute difference for children at 4.5 years of age. Furthermore, the Dutch children were consistently put to bed earlier and on a more regular schedule. Systematic behavior observations of the Dutch and American mothers and infants revealed a correspondence between ideas and action: the American mothers were more actively stimulating to their infants, talking to them and touching them more than the Dutch mothers. Finally, the infants themselves also showed differences in state of arousal during these observations, with the Dutch babies in a quiet alert state two thirds of the time and active alert one third, a pattern that was reversed for the American sample.

As this example illustrates, the developmental niche framework lends itself to systematic consideration of the ways in which the child's culturally structured environment of daily life can affect a wide range of issues in behavior and development. The social development of children is centrally involved in many of these, as it is through the child's experience in the social world that pathways of influence are established.

The ecocultural niche of children and families

The "ecocultural niche" construct, developed by Thomas Weisner and his associates (Weisner, 1984, 1996; Weisner, Gallimore, & Jordan, 1988), is closely related to the developmental niche – not surprisingly since both draw in part from the work of the Whitings. This model highlights the role of settings and routines of daily life as both the nexus of cultural transmission for children and families, and the measure of family adaptation to a variety of challenges. Settings are conceptualized as including the personnel present and their motivations, cultural scripts for conduct in the setting, the nature of tasks and activities in the settings, and the cultural goals and beliefs of the participants. In its emphasis on regularly occurring activities that are imbued with cultural meaning, the ecocultural niche framework draws also on sociocultural and activity theory in the tradition of Vygotsky (Cole, 1985; Rogoff, 1982; Wertsch, 1985).

The ecocultural niche framework has been used not only to study the effects of individual children's participation in cultural structured activity settings, but also the sustainability of daily routines for families. As Weisner, Matheson, and Bernheimer (1996) explain its application to a study of American families of developmentally delayed children: "Ecocultural theory proposes that the adaptive problem faced by families with children with delays is the same as that faced by all families: *constructing and sustaining a daily routine of life that has meaning for culture members, and that fits with the competencies of available members of the family and community* [original italics] (p. 504). The families in this study were broadly middle-class, and although there was variability in the age at which the child's delay was recognized, all families had recognized their child as delayed or possibly delayed by the time the child was three or four years of age. In answer to the question, "Is earlier recognition (and therefore intervention) better?" the authors provided evidence that within these first years of life, there was no developmental effect of earlier recognition. The reason, they suggest, is that all families in this sample already offered a protective environment to their children through their ongoing efforts to shape a sustainable and meaningful daily routine. For these middle-class American families, such routines already included parent–child play and book reading, activities that would be part of an early intervention program in any case.

A cultural mediational model of childcare

A third social-ecological framework is the "cultural mediational model" developed by Robert A. LeVine and used in a study of parenting and child development in a Gusii community of Kenya (LeVine et al., 1994). LeVine and his coauthors contrast their perspective to three other explanatory models that have been widely used in social science. The first model, the "biopsychological model," claims that childcare is overwhelmingly determined by species-specific characteristics. The second model, which they term "economic utility," has been typically used by demographers and economists to explain variations in childcare as they relate to socioeconomic conditions and birth and death rates. In the third type, the "semiotic models," it is assumed that cultural meaning systems guide and direct parental behavior. In contrast to all three of these often exclusionary models, the mediational model that informs these investigators' research is based on the premise that:

> . . . parent–child interaction begins with the universal hardware of child care, that is, innate capacities for communicating and responding, but the child is born in a social environment into which the local conventions of interpersonal communication and kin relationship have been preinstalled as scripts for interactive performance. In attempting to understand parental behavior, then, our first task is to find out what script is being followed and what each action means in terms of that script; later we can learn how performance based on this script represents a choice among organic and economic possibilities (pp. 20–21).

In this approach, the "cultural script" is defined with metaphorical reference to computer programming as a "highly directive software program, prescribing the content and sequence of interaction as well as the code for interpreting performance" (p. 21). As LeVine et al. point out, however, cultural scripts do not fully determine parental behavior; rather, they create central tendencies within populations. Parental behavior in any given instance is thus the joint product of cultural scripts that parents carry some version of in their heads, and the demands of their own situation. In their Gusii research, LeVine et al. concluded that the "cultural scripts" of parent–infant interaction are organized around the principle of ensuring the infant's survival in a traditionally high-risk situation; developmentally, this is superseded by a mandate to train the toddler and young child to be obedient and respectful. These cultural scripts, they suggest, were well adapted to bringing up children to take their place in the extended household economies of Gusii society, but they are not so well suited to prepare children for school. Nevertheless, a return visit to the community when the study children were 13 years old revealed that all who were not burdened with health or family problems were attending the local primary school. The authors suggest that their apparent success in adapting to school is an indication of developmental resiliency. We could also note that the school attended by these children was organized and taught by people who came from exactly the same background as the children themselves.

Research using social-ecological frameworks such as those reviewed here has produced a wealth of new knowledge about how children's development is shaped by their cultural environment. Although the primary focus of these studies varies widely, they include ethnographic as well as individual-level information on the social interface between child and culture. The researchers who have carried out this work have been trained in social anthropology or have worked closely with anthropologists; typically, they have had extensive experience of living and working in other cultures. These researchers have been interested in understanding the role of culture in human development, as well as the ways in which cultures are recreated and changed through the course of individual lives. In addition, they have been concerned with the adaptive significance of different styles of culturally organized parenting and related aspects of children's development.

In contrast to this research tradition which is rooted primarily in anthropology, the remaining two explanatory frameworks to be reviewed here come primarily from the disciplines of developmental and social psychology. Researchers from these backgrounds have been concerned with somewhat different theoretical challenges derived from the parameters of their own disciplines.

The Permeability of Culture and Psyche: Cultural Psychology

Beginning with William Kessen's (1979) conceptualization of the child-in-context as the proper unit of analysis for research in child development, an increasing number of developmental psychologists have argued against the premise that the child can be studied without regard for the circumstances of development. At the same time, Vygotsky's idea of the "zone of proximal development" (the difference between the child's performance on any given task alone and with help) has become influential as a way to conceptualize the role of the social context in children's learning (Vygotsky, 1978; Wertsch, 1985). The newly constituted discipline of cultural psychology takes a qualitative giant step further to assert that the person and the context cannot be considered as separate, distinct entities. As Rogoff, Baker-Sennett, Lacasa, and Goldsmith (1995) state:

> Our perspective discards the idea that the social world is external to the individual and that development consists of *acquiring* knowledge and skills. Rather, a person develops through

participation in an activity, changing to be involved in the situation at hand in ways that contribute both to the ongoing event and to the person's preparation for other involvement in other, similar events (p. 54).

In a similar vein, Fiske, Kitayama, Markus, and Nisbett (1998) argue that "psychological processes are culturally contingent," and that therefore scientific attention should be directed to "the dynamic mutual constitution of culture and psyche" (p. 915). As they explain:

> A premise underlying this work is that in order to participate in any social world, people must incorporate cultural models, meanings, and practices into their basic psychological processes. These psychological processes in turn constrain, reproduce, and transform the cultural system. So while each culture is constructed by the coordinated interaction of many psyches, these psyches are themselves oriented, structured, and motivated by the particular cultures in which they operate (pp. 915–916).

To date, studies of children using this approach have focused primarily on cognitive development, but this research entails observation of culturally structured practices and social interactions as they relate to learning school-related skills. The research methodology in these studies bears very close resemblance to traditional fine-grained ethnographic observation. For example, Rogoff et al. (1995) have analyzed an American Girl Scout cookie fund-raising project in relation to cognitive development, and Cole and his associates have studied children's activities in an after-school program as they reflect cognitive processes (Cole, 1996). In studies such as these, a major challenge has been to establish a way to cross-validate the observations of children's learning in particular contexts. In the most extreme version of this approach, this is an impossibility since the person and the context can never be separated. From this perspective, as argued by Shweder (1991), the only solution is for the research community to redefine its concept of "science." As he notes:

> A cultural psychology studies precisely those causal processes that go on because of our understanding of and involvement with them. It would seem to follow that the truths to be formulated in cultural psychology are typically going to be restricted in scope, because the causal processes they describe are likely to be imbedded or localized in particular intentional worlds (p. 106).

Many developmentalists, however, seek further evidence that what has been inferred from naturalistic observation can also be seen in other contexts, whether naturally occurring or constructed by the investigator. This challenge remains to be met, in part because it appears that some skills evident in particular contexts are not assimilated in such a way as to be available for use in other situations; and in part because the exercise of individual skills in a social context is often distributed among the participants in a seamless fashion (Super & Harkness, 1997).

Individual and Collectivism: A Transcultural Explanatory Framework

The premises of cultural psychology would seem to imply commitment to contextualism as a general explanatory framework: that is, human behavior, including children's social behavior, can only be understood in the context of its own unique historical moment. It is thus somewhat surprising that some proponents of cultural psychology have also suggested that a single duality, that of individualism (or independence) versus collectivism (or interdependence) can be used to capture the most important contrasts between different populations (Fiske et al., 1998; Triandis, 1988). In a recent review, Kagitçibasi (1997) has explored the question of why the Individualism–Collectivism (I–C) construct has become so popular among researchers. She suggests that its simplicity as a single dimension, and its close relationship to economic development at the national level, may make it attractive to social science researchers. This writer would add that the I–C construct also fits nicely into preexisting psychological or sociological research strategies in which a "social address" such as socioeconomic status is used as an independent variable without involving investigation of the construct itself in the particular research context.

The I–C construct has been put to good use by researchers such as Greenfield, Raeff, and others in their studies of differences between Latino (mainly Mexican) and Anglo children, parents, and teachers living in the United States (Greenfield, Quiroz, & Raeff, 2000; Raeff, Greenfield, & Quiroz, 2000). Even as this research has accumulated, however, its theoretical limitations are becoming increasingly evident. Several issues are of concern. First, the I–C construct can be used to build post-hoc explanations of a variety of behaviors, some of which may be inconsistent. For example, late weaning can be related either to a collectivistic orientation, as described for Korean mothers by Kim and Choi (1994), or to an individualistic orientation, in the context of American middle-class mothers' practice of letting the child decide when he/she is ready.

Second, the I-C dimension has been used to characterize both cultural groups and individuals. Although this might seem like a reasonable approach, it is necessary to distinguish between shared cultural values on the one hand and individual motivations on the other. Assuming that these two are the same leads to general statements such as the following contrast between North America or Europe and the rest of the world:

> This orientation [individualism] seems natural and obvious to investigators and subjects – in North America and Europe. These people share a set of implicit and unexamined cultural values and practices that emphasize individual rights, independence, self-determination, and freedom. But many other cultures – indeed, most – place a higher value on interdependence and fostering empathic connections with others . . . In these cultures, people gladly emulate their associates and are responsive to others' wishes in order to sustain smooth social relationships (Fiske et al., 1998, p. 919).

Although differences in cultural values can certainly be observed across different social groups, it is a mistake to assume that all individual members of any given society "gladly" follow its behavioral prescriptions. Indeed, one element that has not received adequate attention is how the position of an individual in relation to the group may influence that person's feelings about societal norms.

A third issue not yet sufficiently addressed within the I–C paradigm is the relationships among cultural values, socialization practices, and actual social development in children. For example, Fiske et al. (1998) argue that the European American custom of offering frequent praise and compliments to children promotes high self-esteem and independence from the group. Indeed, this hypothesized relationship is at the center of an American cultural model of good parenting. The actual data on rates of independent and dependent behavior from Whiting and Edwards' study (Whiting & Edwards, 1988), however, tell a different story: the American children had *higher* rates of dependent behavior than did children from all the other (mostly non-Western) cultural samples. Furthermore, current research by this writer comparing American parents with parents of six different Western societies has found that the American parents are most concerned about their children's self-esteem, suggesting that this is a problematic area of development for them.

A final weakness of the I–C framework is that it attempts to reduce all cultural variability to just two categories. It is significant in this regard that the framework was originally developed, and in fact still mainly rests, on comparative Asian–U.S. studies. Although earlier cross-cultural work has generated some transcultural themes, the I–C characterizations go much further in specifying multiple ways that the two kinds of cultures (or individuals) vary; and these do not all "travel well" across major culture areas. "Collectivism" in Asian societies does not really resemble "collectivism" in Africa or Latin America, and neither is "individualism" the same in the United States and in Europe (Harkness, Super, & van Tijen, 2000).

From the perspective of the research traditions reviewed earlier in this chapter, it seems that the rediscovery of culture within the discipline of psychology has led to some of the same formulations, and the same problems, that were experienced earlier in anthropology. The application of post-hoc explanations within the context of one or two societies is not unlike the problem of ethnographers' monocultural analyses that could not be generalized to other cultures. The application of a single framework at both the cultural and individual levels replicates the problems that led to the demise of the "culture and personality" school. The assumption of developmental consequences of certain value systems as instantiated in parenting behaviors reflects a continuing ethnocentrism that has always challenged cross-cultural research. Finally, the creation of two global categories for cultures and individuals is reminiscent of Ruth Benedict's "patterns of culture" which were soon shown to be overly simplistic even for the societies they were supposed to describe.

Conclusions: Explanations and Evidence

This chapter has reviewed a historical sequence of explanations of how culture and children's social development relate to each other. Along the way, we have seen evidence for the utility of these explanations for helping make sense of cross-cultural variability in children's social behavior and development. The evidence suggests several lessons for future researchers. First, explanations based on only one or two cultural samples are unlikely to hold up over a wider array of world cultures. Second, cultural differences are easy to recognize but difficult to categorize: most generalizations about beliefs or behavior in any given society turn out not to cover important facets of that society. Third, the prediction of future developmental outcomes based on the cultural structuring of child development at any given stage is perilous: until we understand more about the internal logic of specific cultural systems, we are likely to miss the mark. Finally, we should never assume that we have in hand all the relevant information about the cultural environment of children's development for any society, including our own. Even – and perhaps especially – for our own society, there are bound to be interesting surprises in store when we collect data on the environment of children's development that is as detailed and precise as what we collect on children themselves.

References

Barry, H. I., Child, I. L., & Bacon, M. K. (1959). Relations of child training to subsistence economy. *American Anthropologist, 61,* 51–63.

Benedict, R. (1934/1959). *Patterns of culture.* Boston: Houghton Mifflin.

Benedict, R. (1934). Anthropology and the abnormal. *Journal of General Psychology, 10,* 59–82.

Benedict, R. (1946). *The chrysanthemum and the sword: Patterns of Japanese culture.* Boston: Houghton Mifflin.

Chasdi, E. H. (1994). *Culture and human development: The selected papers of John Whiting.* New York: Cambridge University Press.

Cole, M. (1985). The zone of proximal development: Where culture and cognition create each other. In J. Wertsch (Ed.), *Culture, communication, and cognition* (pp. 146–161). New York: Cambridge University Press.

Cole, M. (1996). *Cultural psychology: A once and future discipline.* Cambridge, MA: Harvard University Press.

Fiske, A. P., Kitayama, S., Markus, H. R., & Nisbett, R. E. (1998). The cultural matrix of social psychology. In D. Gilbert, A. Fiske, & G. Lindzey (Eds.), *The handbook of social psychology, volume 2* (pp. 915–981). New York: McGraw Hill.

Greenfield, P. M., Quiroz, B., & Raeff, C. (2000). Cross-cultural conflict and harmony in the social construction of the child. In S. Harkness, C. Raeff, & C. M. Super (Eds.), *Variability in the social construction of the child* (pp. 75-92). San Francisco: Jossey-Bass.

Harkness, S. (1992). Human development in psychological anthropology. In T. Schwartz, G. M. White, & C. A. Lutz (Eds.), *New directions in psychological anthropology* (pp. 102–121). New York: Cambridge University Press.

Harkness, S., & Super, C. M. (1991). East Africa. In J. M. Hawes & R. Hiner (Eds.), *Children in comparative and international perspective: An international handbook and research guide* (pp. 217–239). New York: Greenwood.

Harkness, S. & Super, C. M. (1992). The cultural foundations of fathers' roles: Evidence from Kenya and the United States. In B. S. Hewlett (Ed.), *The father's role: Cultural and evolutionary perspectives* (pp. 191–211). New York: Aldine de Gruyter.

Harkness, S., & Super, C. M. (Eds.) (1996). *Parents' cultural belief systems: Their origins, expressions, and consequences.* New York: Guilford Press.

Harkness, S., Super, C. M., & van Tijen, N. (2000). Individualism and the "Western mind" reconsidered: American and Dutch parents' ethnotheories of the child. In S. Harkness, C. Raeff, & C. M. Super (Eds.), *Variability in the social construction of the child* (pp. 23–39). San Francisco: Jossey-Bass.

Kagitçibasi, C. (1997). Individualism and collectivism. In J. Berry, J. H. Sigall, & C.Kagitçibasi

(Eds.), *Handbook of cross-cultural psychology, volume 3: Social, behavioral, and applications* (pp. 1–49). Boston: Allyn and Bacon.

Kessen, W. (1979). The American child and other cultural inventions. *American Psychologist, 34,* 815–820.

Kim, U., & Choi, S.-H. (1994). Individualism, collectivism, and child development: A Korean perspective. In P. M. Greenfield & R. R. Cocking (Eds.), *Cross-cultural roots of minority child development* (pp. 227–257). Hillsdale, NJ: Erlbaum.

LeVine, R. A., Dixon, S., LeVine, S., Richman, A., Leiderman, P. H., Keefer, C. H., & Brazelton, T. B. (1994). *Child care and culture: Lessons from Africa.* Cambridge: Cambridge University Press.

Mead, M. (1930/1966). *Growing up in New Guinea: A comparative study of primitive education.* New York: William Morrow.

Mead, M. (1972). *Blackberry winter: My earlier years.* New York: Simon & Schuster.

Minturn, L. (1993). *Sita's daughters: Coming out of purdah.* New York: Oxford University Press.

Quinn, N., & Holland, D. (1987). Culture and cognition. In D. Holland & N. Quinn (Eds.), *Cultural models in language and thought* (pp. 3–42). Cambridge: Cambridge University Press.

Raeff, C. C., Greenfield, P. M., & Quiroz, B. (2000). Conceptualizing interpersonal relationships in the cultural contexts of individualism and collectivism. In S. Harkness, C. Raeff, & C. M. Super (Eds.), *Variability in the social construction of the child* (pp. 59–74). San Francisco: Jossey-Bass.

Rogoff, B. (1982). Integrating context and cognitive development. In M. E. Lamb & A. L. Brown (Eds.), *Advances in developmental psychology, volume 2* (pp. 125–170). Hillsdale, NJ: Erlbaum.

Rogoff, G., Baker-Sennett, J., Lacasa, P., & Goldsmith, D. (1995). Development through participation in sociocultural activity. In J. J. Goodnow, P. J. Miller, & F. Kessel (Eds.), *Cultural practices as contexts for development* (pp. 45–65). New Directions for Child Development, vol. 67. San Francisco: Jossey-Bass.

Shweder, R. A. (1991). *Thinking through cultures: Expeditions in cultural psychology.* Cambridge, MA: Harvard University Press.

Spiro, M. E. (1953). Ghosts: An anthropological inquiry into learning and perception. *Journal of Abnormal and Social Psychology, 48,* 376–382.

Super, C. M. & Harkness, S. (1997). The cultural structuring of child development. In J. W. Berry, P. Dasen, & T. S. Saraswathi (Eds.), *Handbook of cross-cultural psychology: Volume 2: Basic processes and human development* (pp. 1–39). Boston: Allyn & Bacon.

Super, C. M., Harkness, S., van Tijen, N., van der Vlugt, E., Fintelman, M., & Dijksltra, J. (1996). The three R's of Dutch childrearing and the socialization of infant arousal. In S.Harkness & C. M. Super (Eds.), *Parents' cultural belief systems: Their origins, expressions, and consequences* (pp. 447–466). New York: Guilford Press.

Triandis, H. C. (1988). Collectivism and individualism: A reconceptualization of a basic concept in cross-cultural psychology. In G. K. Verma & C. Bagley (Eds.), *Personality, attitudes, and cognitions* (pp. 60–95). London: Macmillan.

Vygotsky, L. S. (1978). *Mind in society.* Cambridge, MA: Harvard University Press.

Weisner, T. S. (1984). A cross-cultural perspective: Ecocultural niches of middle childhood. In A. Collins (Ed.), *The elementary school years: Understanding development during middle childhood* (pp. 335–369). Washington, DC: National Academy Press.

Weisner, T. (1996). Why ethnography should be the most important method in the study of human development. In A. Colby, R. Jessor, & R. Shweder (Eds.), *Ethnography and human development: Context and meaning in social inquiry* (pp. 305–324). Chicago: University of Chicago Press.

Weisner, T. S., Gallimore, R., & Jordan, C. (1988). Unpackaging cultural effects on classroom learning: Native Hawaiian peer assistance and child-generated activity. *Anthropology and Education Quarterly, 19,* 327–351.

Weisner, T. S., Matheson, C. C., & Bernheimer, L. P. (1996). American cultural models of early influence and parent recognition of developmental delays: Is earlier always better than later? In S. Harkness & C. M. Super (Eds.), *Parents' cultural belief systems: Their origins, expressions, and consequences* (pp. 496–532). New York: Guilford Press.

Wertsch, J. V. (1985). *Vygotsky and the social formation of mind.* Cambridge, MA: Harvard University Press.

Whiting, B. B. & Edwards, C. P. (1988). *Children of different worlds: The formation of social behavior.* Cambridge, MA: Harvard University Press.

Whiting, B. B. & Whiting, J. W. M. (1975). *The children of six cultures: A psychocultural analysis.* Cambridge, MA: Harvard University Press.

Whiting, J. W. M. (1976). The cross-cultural method. In E. H. Chasdi (Ed.), *Culture and human development: The selected papers of John Whiting* (pp. 76–88). New York: Cambridge University Press.

Whiting, J. W. M. (1977). A model for psychocultural research. In P. H. Leiderman, S. R. Tulkin, & A. Rosenfeld (Eds.), *Culture and infancy: Variations in the human experience* (pp.29–48). New York: Academic Press.

Whiting, J. W. M. & Whiting, B. B. (1960). Contributions of anthropology to the methods of studying child rearing. In P. H. Mussen (Ed.), *Handbook of research methods in child development* (pp. 918–944). New York: Wiley.

5

A Sociological Approach to Childhood Development

Chris Jenks

There are significant ways in which the positions taken by sociologists and developmental psychologists on the issue of child development diverge. Sociologists problematize the very idea of the child rather than treat it as a practical and prestated being with a relatively determined trajectory and certainly do not seek to offer advice concerning its appropriate mode of maturation. As I shall attempt here, sociology endeavors to realize the child as constituted socially, as a status of person which is comprised through a series of, often heterogeneous, images, representations, codes, and constructs. This is an increasingly popular perspective within contemporary childhood studies (James & Prout, 1990; Jenks, 1982/ 1992, 1989; Qvortrup, 1993; Stainton-Rogers, 1991).

Sociology is burgeoning in its innovative work in relation to children and in finding its way toward a concerted sociology of childhood and it still has a degree of exciting work to do. A major contribution consolidating such research was provided by James and Prout (1990) in a work that attempted to establish a new paradigm in our thinking. It is worthy of consideration here and I shall quote it in full, it can act as a manifesto in our subsequent considerations of the significance and relevance of sociological theory in our approach to development:

> . . . the key features of the paradigm:
> 1.   Childhood is understood as a social construction. As such it provides an interpretive frame for contextualising the early years of human life. Childhood, as distinct from biological immaturity, is neither a natural nor a universal feature of human groups but appears as a specific structural and cultural component of many societies.
> 2.   Childhood is a variable of social analysis. It can never be entirely divorced from other variables such as class, gender and ethnicity. Comparative and cross-cultural analysis reveals a variety of childhoods rather than a single or universal phenomenon.

3. Children's social relationships and cultures are worthy of study in their own right, independent of the perspective and concern of adults.
4. Children are and must be seen as active in the construction and determination of their own social lives, the lives of those around them and of the societies in which they live. Children are not just passive subjects of social structures and processes.
5. Ethnography is a particularly useful methodology for the study of childhood. It allows children a more direct voice and participation in the production of sociological data than is possible through experimental or survey styles of research.
6. Childhood is a phenomenon in relation to which the double hermeneutic of the social sciences is acutely present. That is to say, to proclaim a new paradigm of childhood sociology is also to engage in and respond to the process of reconstructing childhood. (James & Prout, 1990: pp. 8–9).

Such an approach, in this context, displays a variety of purposes. First, an attempt to displace the overwhelming claim made on childhood by the realm of commonsense reasoning – not that such reasoning is inferior or unsystematic but that it is conventional rather than disciplined (Garfinkel, 1967; Schutz, 1964). Commonsense reasoning serves to "naturalize" the child in each and any epoch, that is it treats children as both natural and universal and it thus disenables our understanding of the child's particularity and cultural difference within a particular historical context. Children, quite simply, are not always and everywhere the same thing, they are socially constructed and understood contextually – sociologists attend to this process of construction and also to this contextualization. Second, the approach indicates that the child, like other forms of being within our culture, is presenced through a variety of forms of discourse. These discourses are not necessarily competitive but neither is their complementarity inherent and a holistic view of the child does not arise from a liberal sense of varieties of interpretation or multiple realities. Rather, the identity of children or of a particular child varies within the political contexts of those forms of discourse – hence, the different kinds of "knowledge" of mother, teacher, pediatrician, social worker, educational psychologist, and juvenile magistrate, for example, do not live suspended in an egalitarian harmony. Hendrick (1990) has produced an instructive account of childhood constructions in Britain since 1800 through the analysis of a series of dominant forms of discourse, in which he includes the "romantic," "evangelical," "factory," "delinquent," "schooled," "psycho-medical," "welfare," "psychological," and the "family" as opposed to the "public" child – these languages have all provided for different modern lives of children.

Third, the approach intends to work out the parameters within which sociology, and thus its relation to understanding childhood, must originate – therefore I shall attempt to show sociology's conceptual limitations, and also its possibilities, as one form of discourse about childhood and the world. However, before I address sociology's conceptual base and therefore its different approach to the child let me firmly establish its difference from developmental psychology.

The Developmental Psychology Paradigm

In the everyday world the category of childhood is a totalizing concept, it concretely describes a community that at some time has everybody as its member. This is a community which is therefore relatively stable and wholly predictable in its structure but by definition only fleeting in its particular membership. Beyond this the category signifies a primary experience in the existential biography of each individual and thus inescapably derives its commonsense meanings, relevance, and relation not only from what it might currently be as a social status but also from how each and every individual, at some time, must have been. It is the only truly common experience of being human, infant mortality is no disqualification. Perhaps because of this seemingly all-encompassing character of the phenomenon as a social status and because of the essentially personal character of its particular articulation, commonsense thinking and everyday language in contemporary society are rife with notions concerning childhood. Being a child, having been a child, having children, and having continuously to relate to children are all experiences which contrive to render the category as "normal" and readily transform our attribution of it to the realm of the "natural" (as used to be the case with sex and race). Such understandings, within the collective awareness, are organized around the single most compelling metaphor of contemporary culture, that of "growth." Stemming from this, the physical signs of anatomical change that accompany childhood are taken to be indicators of a social transition, so that the conflation of the realms of the "natural" and the "social" is perpetually reinforced.

Developmental psychology is wholly predicated on the notion of childhood's "naturalness" and on the necessity, normality, and desirability of development and constructive change through "growth." Children are thus routinely constructed as partially rational, that is, in the process of becoming rational.

Perhaps the irony of the exclusion of the child through partial formulations of rationality is nowhere more fundamentally encountered than in the formative body of work generated by Piaget. It was Piaget who defined developmental psychology as follows:

> Developmental psychology can be described as the study of the development of mental functions, in as much as this development can provide an explanation, or at least a complete description, of their mechanisms in the finished state. In other words, developmental psychology consists of making use of child psychology in order to find the solution to general psychological problems (Piaget, 1972, p. 32).

However, as Burman has pointed out:

> Nowadays the status of developmental psychology is not clear. Some say that it is a perspective or an approach to investigating general psychological problems, rather than a particular domain or sub-discipline. According to this view we can address all major areas of psychology, such as memory, cognition, etc., from this perspective. The unit of development under investigation is also variable. We could be concerned with the development of a process, or a mechanism, rather than an individual. This is in marked contrast with the popular representations of developmental psychology which equate it with the practicalities of child development or, more recently, human development (Burman, 1994, p. 9).

Piaget's work on intelligence and child development has had a global impact on pediatric care and practice. Piaget's "genetic epistemology" seeks to provide a description of the structuring of thought and finally the rational principle of nature itself, all through a theory of learning. As such Piaget's overall project represents a significant contribution to philosophy as well. Following within the neo-Kantian tradition his ideas endeavor to conciliate the divergent epistemologies of empiricism and rationalism; the former conceiving of reality as being available in the form of synthetic truths discoverable through direct experience, and the latter viewing reality analytically through the action of pure reason alone. Kant, in his time, had transcended this dichotomy through the invocation of "synthetic a priori truths" that are the immanent conditions of understanding, not simply amenable to logical analysis. Piaget's categories of understanding in his scheme of conceptual development may be treated as being of the same order. His work meticulously constitutes a particular system of scientific rationality and presents it as being both natural and universal. However, as Archard (1993) stated:

> Piaget suggested that all children acquire cognitive competencies according to a universal sequence. Nevertheless, he has been criticised on two grounds. . . First, his ideal of adult cognitive competence is a peculiarly Western philosophical one. The goal of cognitive development is an ability to think about the world with the concepts and principles of Western logic. In particular Piaget was concerned to understand how the adult human comes to acquire the Kantian categories of space, time and causality. If adult cognitive competence is conceived in this way then there is no reason to think it conforms to the everyday abilities of even Western adults. Second, children arguably possess some crucial competencies long before Piaget says they do (Archard, 1993, pp. 65–66).

Within Piaget's system each stage of intellectual growth is characterized by a specific "schema" or well-defined pattern and sequence of physical and mental actions governing the child's orientation to the world. Thus the system has a rhythm and a calendar too. The development and transition from figurative to operative thought, through a sequence of stages contains an achievement ethic. That is to say that the sequencing depends upon the child's mastery and transcendence of the schemata at each stage. This implies a change in the child's relation to the world. This transition, the compulsive passage through schemata, is what Piaget refers to as a "decentering." The decentering of the child demonstrates a cumulative series of transformations: a change from solipsistic subjectivism to a realistic objectivity; a change from affective response to cognitive evaluation; and a movement from the disparate realm of value to the absolute realm of fact. The successful outcome of this developmental process is latterly typified and celebrated as "scientific rationality." This is the stage at which the child, now adult, becomes at one with the logical structure of the cosmos. At this point, where the child's matured thought provides membership of the "circle of science" the project of "genetic epistemology" has reached its fruition, it is complete.

Concretely, scientific rationality for Piaget is displayed through abstraction, generalization, logico-deductive process, mathematization, and cognitive operations. At the analytic level, however, this rationality reveals the intentional character of Piaget's theorizing and grounds his system in the same manner as did Parsons' transcendent "cultural values." Within Piaget's genetic epistemology, the process of socialization can be exposed as the analytic device by and through which the child is wrenched from the possibility of difference within the realm of value and integrated into the consensus that comprises the tyrannical realm of fact. Scientific rationality or adult intelligence is thus the recognition of difference grounded in unquestioned collectivity – we are returned to the irony contained within the original ontological question. The child is, once more, abandoned in theory. Real historically located children are subjected to the violence of a contemporary mode of scientific rationality, which reproduces itself, at the expense of their difference, beyond the context of situated social life. The "fact" of natural process overcomes the "value" of real social worlds. And the normality of actual children becomes scrutinized in terms of the norms predicted by developmental psychology. Rose (1990), commenting on the historical context of this oppressive tendency stated:

> Developmental psychology was made possible by the clinic and the nursery school. Such institutions had a vital role, for they enabled the observation of numbers of children of the same age, and of children of a number of different ages, by skilled psychological experts under controlled experimental, almost laboratory, conditions. Thus they simultaneously allowed for standardization and normalization – the collection of comparable information on a large number of subjects and its analysis in such a way as to construct norms. A developmental norm was a standard based upon the average abilities or performances of children of a certain age in a particular task or a specified activity. It thus not only presented a picture of what was *normal* for children of such an age, but also enabled the normality of any child to be assessed by comparison with this norm (Rose, 1990, p. 142).

Within Piaget's demonstrations of adult scientific rationality, the child is deemed to have appropriately adapted to the environment when she has achieved a balance between accommodation and assimilation. It would seem that the juggling with homeostasis is forever the child's burden! However, although from a critical analytic stance accommodation might be regarded as the source of the child's integration into the consensus reality, within the parameters of the original theory the process is treated as the locus of creativity and innovation – it is that aspect of the structuring of thought and being which is to be most highly valued. In contradistinction Piaget regards children's play as nonserious, trivial activity in as much as it displays an emphasis on assimilation over accommodation. Play is merely diverting fun or fantasy, it deflects the child from his true destiny and logical purpose within the scheme of rationality. The problem is that the criteria for what constitutes play need not equate with the rigorous, factual, demands of reality. Treating play in this manner, that is from the perspective of the rational and "serious" adult, Piaget is specifically undervaluing what might represent an important aspect of the expressive practices of the child and her world. Following Denzin (1982) and Stone (1965) I would argue that play is indeed an important component of the child's work as a social member. And I would argue further that play is instrumental in what Speier (1970) has designated the child's "acquisition of interactional competencies." Genetic epistemology willfully disregards, or perhaps just pays insufficient attention to, play in its urge to mathematize and thus render formal the "rational" cognitive practices of adult individuals in their collective lives.

By treating the growth process of the child's cognition as if it were impelled toward a prestated structure of adult rationality, Piaget is driven to concur with Levi-Bruhl's concept of the "primitive mentality" of the savage but in this instance in relation to the "prelogical" thought of the child. A further consequence of Piaget's conceptualization of the rational development of the child's "embryonic" mind as if it were a natural process, is that the critical part played by language in the articulation of mind and self is very much understated. Language is treated as a symbolic vehicle, which carries thought and assists in the growth of concepts and a semiotic system but it is not regarded as having a life in excess of these referential functions. Thus language, for Piaget, is insufficient in itself to bring about the mental operations that make concept formation possible. Language, then, helps in the selection, storage, and retrieval of information but it does not bring about the coordination of mental operations. This level of organization is conceptualized as taking place above language and in the domain of action. This is slightly confusing until we realize that action, for Piaget, is not action regarded as the performative conduct that generates social contexts, but rather a sense of action as that which is rationally governed within the a priori strictures of an idealist metaphysics. Language, for Piaget, itemizes the world and acts as a purely cognitive function. This is a position demonstrably confounded by Merleau-Ponty (1967) in his work on the existential and experiential generation and use of language by children – the classic example being the child's generation of a past tense in order to express the loss of uniqueness and total parental regard following the birth of a sibling; language here is not naming a state of affairs but expressing the emotion of jealousy. Merleau-Ponty's work serves to reunite the cognitive and the affective aspects of being which are so successfully sundered by Piaget; he stated:

> I pass to the fact that appeared to me to be worthy of mention . . . the relation that can be established between the development of intelligence (in particular, the acquisition of language) and the configuration of the individual's affective environment (Merleau-Ponty, 1964, p. 108).

I have attempted to explicate certain of the normative assumptions at the heart of developmental psychology which has held as the orthodoxy up until recent years and I might optimistically suggest that such conventional explanations have been successfully supplanted by feminist theories in relation to the family and what have come to be grouped as "social constructionists' views" of the child, possibly instigated by this author but subsequently titled and joined by significant company. We do not have a consensus view of the child in social theory: however, a spurious consensus is not necessarily a desirable goal. It is my intention to show that it is the different manners in which theoretical commitments are grounded that give rise to the diversity of views of childhood. At this point let us return to the conceptual bases of sociology.

The Conceptual Grounds of Sociological Thought

Although, in its various guises, sociology emerged as a critical response to the state of its culture and traditionally adopted a radical position in relation to the material constraints wrought through the progress of modernity, it was also, in origin, epistemologically imperialistic. Durkheim (1938) delineated sociology's peculiar realm of phenomena. He marked out their identifiable characteristics and the conceptual space that they occupied and he sought to devalue all other attempts to explain "social" reality (Hirst, 1975). Thus we arrive at a kernel idea for sociology, that of the "social structure"; it is from this concept that the discipline proceeds. Social structures appear to societal members as "facts" and as such have real and describable characteristics: they are typical, that is, they are a series of normal or taken for granted manifestations; further, they are constraining upon the actions of members either implicitly or explicitly; and finally they are, to some greater or lesser degree, independent of their individual will. As Durkheim put it:

> The proposition which states that social facts must be treated as things – the proposition which is at the very basis of our method – is among those which have stirred up the most opposition. It was deemed paradoxical and scandalous for us to assimilate to the realities of the external world the realities of the social world. This was singularly to misunderstand the meaning and effect of this assimilation, the object of which was not to reduce the higher forms of being to the level of lower ones but, on the contrary, to claim for the former a degree of reality at least equal to that which everyone accords the latter. Indeed, we do not say that social facts are material things, but that they are things just as are material things, although in a different way (Durkheim, 1982, p. 35).

The "social structure" then becomes the supra-individual source of causality in socio-logical explanations, whether it is experienced by members as a cognitive, moral, political, or economic orientation (Parsons, 1968). All sociological worlds seek to build in and analyze a series of constraints that work upon the individual and (however the particular perspec-tive places itself, within the debate over freewill versus determinism) there tends to be a primary commitment to treat the self as an epiphenomenon of the society (Cicourel, 1964; Dawe, 1970; Hollis, 1977; Wrong, 1961) and thus prey to apprehension in terms of epis-temological binaries. As O'Neill (1994) put it:

> The *tabula rasa* or clean-slate individual of liberal contract theory is as much a fiction as is its counterpart fiction of the many-headed monster state, or Leviathan. Each device serves to stampede thought into those forced alternatives of the under- or over-socialized individual (O'Neill, 1994, p. 54).

Sociology's tradition then makes little claim to provide a strong theory of the individual and this holds implications for our understanding of the child. Ironically the most con-temporary sociology of the late- or post-modern scene is even less secure in its explanations of self (Beck, 1992; Giddens, 1991). Thus despite the apparent cult of the individual and celebration of the ego in the latter part of the twentieth century, sociological analysis ap-pears increasingly unprepared to formulate the social identity of people, let alone the emer-gent identity of children.

The problems of structural causality, in relation to a study of the child, are further compounded by the fact that sociological systems of explanation are constructed in rela-tion to the conduct of typical rational "adult" members – children are largely theorized as states of pathology or inadequacy in relation to the prestated model of the actor. All soci-ologies, in their variety of forms, relate to the childhood experience through theories of socialization whether in relation to the institutional contexts of the family, the peer group, or the school. These three sites are regarded as the serious arenas wherein the child is most systematically exposed to concerted induction procedures. It is here that the child, within the social system, relates as a subordinate to the formalized strategies of constraint, control, inculcation, and patterning which will serve to transform his or her status into the tangible and intelligible form of an adult competent being.

> In sociological writings characterized as normative, the term socialization glosses the phe-
> nomenon of change from the birth of a child to maturity or old age. To observe that changes
> take place after birth is trivial, but the quasi-scientific use of the term socialization masks this
> triviality. In fact, the study of these changes as socialization is an expression of the sociolo-
> gists" common sense position in the world – that is, as adults. The notion of socialization
> leads to the theoretical formulations mirroring the adult view that children are incomplete
> adults (MacKay, 1973, p. 27).

A child's social, and ontological, purpose is therefore, it would seem, not to stay a child. Within this inexorable trajectory any signs of entrenchment or backtracking, like play for example, may be interpreted as indicators of a failure to "develop" (Piaget, 1977).

It is a further irony that were one to confront sociologists with the issue of "develop-ment" then their immediate frame of reference would be to consider the modes of transi-tion occurring between the structures of simple and complex societies (Frank, 1971). The concept of development, with relation to persons, is no part of a sociologist's vocabulary. Structures are sociologists' primary realities and the only organism that they might con-sider in a state of development is that, by analogy, of the society as a whole.

The Concept of Development

"Development," an essentially temporal notion, is the primary metaphor through which childhood is made intelligible, both in the everyday world and also within the specialist vocabularies of the sciences and agencies which lay claim to an understanding and servic-ing of that state of being. Thus, stemming from this root metaphor all empirical study, social policy, or remedial treatment in relation to the child tends to be longitudinal in character – the idea of time being left inviolable. Given "time" the child will change. More than this, development as the all-pervading source of the location of the child-as-other, has come to be realized as a wholly "natural" process in a manner that more than echoes the determinism of sociology's structural bias. Individuals are largely understood to be realiza-tions of what was biogenetically inherent, with perhaps a surface structure of personality, thought-style, or cognitive breadth being attributable to "nurture" – though even these finite provinces have been invaded by certain theories which sought to explain criminality, racial deficit, or insanity (writers such as Lombrosso; Jensen & Esyenck; Kraepelin). Fi-nally, development has certain resonances within the culture of modernity that enable the idea to be conflated with other axial contemporary social metaphors like "growth" and "progress." Within a post-Darwinian framework we are led to relate to development as necessary, inevitable and, essentially, for the good.

Let us now address these central elements in the concept of development. First, in relation to the issue of development as time, philosophers from Plato to the present day have grappled with the indeterminacy or experiential character of this dimension, yet most modern thinking appears locked within a Kantian sense of time as both external and quantitative (Hendricks & Hendricks, 1975). This in itself is a sociologically interesting phenomenon bound up with the scientism and mathematizing urge of contemporary society. However, what such mechanical diachronicity constrains and disfigures is the actual experience of time in social relations; as Durkheim asserted "A calendar expresses the rhythm of the collective activities, while at the same time its function is to assure their regularity" (Durkheim, 1968, p. 206). In everyday social life we are quite accustomed to the variability of the "time" experience; time spent with a lover is not comparable to time spent queuing in the supermarket. In similar fashion the existential experience of being a child seems to go on forever, the gap between Christmases seems unimaginable, bedtime is all too suddenly here, and "boring" time, doing usually what parents want to do, is interminable. Parallel with such interior sensation for the child, parents are unified in their sense that children "grow up so quickly" and are no sooner walking than they are asking to borrow the car!

Second, the "naturalizing" of development can be seen to obscure or mystify a set of criteria for change that might be implicit or grounded within a specific network of interests. Thus as examples, to have one's child designated as "advanced" in relation to Piagetian criteria may be a source of pride to a parent as it signifies rapid or special "natural" development; the criteria for such "development" remain, however, normative and unexplicated – the same parent might experience acute displeasure if their child were defined as "retarded" and thus relegated to an educational identity of a lesser status; the same covert criteria apply. It is often argued that natal induction, viewed as a critical stage of "development," is necessary for the benefit of the child but it would seem, in many cases, to relate wholly to the politics of hospital timetables. These examples are cited to demonstrate the "social" and embedded character of the "natural" experience of childhood.

Third, the conflation of development with ideas of growth and progress builds a competitive ethic into the process of development itself that supports the ideology of possessive individualism at the root of industrialized capitalist cultural formations. The dominant materialist reduction functions such that not only are mental and manual skills evaluated hierarchically and therefore stratified which, in turn, enables social stratification within the culture, but also manual/physical development is itself realized as internally competitive to generate further modes of stratification and ranking. There would appear to be a justified merit that stems from development. Such processes extend from the comparative parental talk at antenatal clinics, for example, "Is he crawling yet?'; "When did she start to walk?'; "Mine could talk at that age'; to the pinnacles of nationalistic projections in the form of the Olympic Games with collective physical prowess being measured by medal counts (and backward countries sometimes surprising advanced nations with their physical precocity). After all, success should accompany development – naturally!

What I am suggesting is that the concept of development does not signify a "natural" process – it does, however, make reference to a socially constructed sense of change pertaining to the young individual which is encoded within a series of benchmarks relevant to the topical or predominant form of discourse: which can relate to political engagement, moral and criminal responsibility, sexual consent, and patterns of consumption. Thus different codes move in and out of focus according to which aspect of the person we are attending to – in many senses there is a heterogeneity to these codes that resists the attempts to reduce them to the homogeneity of "naturalness".

The positive side of this deconstruction of the child experience into an assembly of signifying discourses is to explore certain possibilities within the social character of that encoding. While regarding childhood phenomenologically, in terms of the intentional constitutive practices that facilitate its recognizable form, it is not necessary to pursue such a tradition to the point of the child being wholly disembodied – as Merleau-Ponty (1967) and O'Neill (1973) have both, separately, argued – to do so deprives the child of an ontology.

A crucial aspect of childhood, and a sociological sense of "development," can be realized in terms of its "contingency." That is to say that childhood always speaks of a relationship, for example, adult–child, parent–child, teacher–child, etc. (Hambrook, 1987). As Ambert put it:

> The discussion is informed by a critical perspective viewing both childhood and parenting as social constructs that evolve with socio-historical changes. . . . discussion of parenting cannot be divorced from perspectives on the nature of childhood. . . . the nature of childhood is fluid, anchored as it is in the prevailing world views supporting societies and created by societies. In most societies, children and early adolescents are viewed within the context of the family. Consequently, as one cohort or one culture defines what childhood is, parenting is constructed, whether implicitly or explicitly (Ambert, 1994, pp. 530–531).

Also, whatever the general condition of childhood in society (treated violently, exploited, pornographized) it may be regarded as an index of the state of the wider social relation, the moral bond in society (Jenks, 1995; Hendrick, 1990).

The concept of development, then, might imply that the child's "becoming" is dependent upon the reference points or normative structures made conventional within the adults' world, but we need to pursue this idea further. In the obvious, cultural sense of the attribution, ascription, and assumption of meaning, all people "need" others in order to generate a meaningful environment for change, stasis, or whatever; quite simply, we cannot make sense alone. Any knowledge of self derives from an experience of collective constraint; and being and action, as opposed to being and behavior, is contingent upon the presence of and communication with "other." Adults, however, are assumed within social theory to operate with a degree of basic reciprocity of perspectives and interchangeability of standpoints in terms of the processes of meaning giving and meaning receiving (Parsons, 1964; Schutz, 1964). On top of this, adult relationships are subsequently stratified in terms of an unequal distribution of power.

The difference that is childhood may well be understood in terms of power (Holt, 1971; Illich, 1971; Postman & Weingarten, 1971), though this would be to treat the grounds of power as purely age-based (in the same way that Marxist feminism attempted to reduce the question of power to an issue of gender), neither argument is adequate nor sufficient. However, childhood might be more instructively theorized in terms of dependency. Children do practically have "need" of their parents and adult companions, a need that is a combination of the material, physical, emotional, and so on, but one that is always realized within particular sociohistorical, and cultural, settings. This understanding enables us to look toward the contexts of provision, instruction, and care in relation to a fundamental sociological analytic concept, that of "altruism." Thus the child–adult relation is, in one sense, expressive of "altruism," a dimension of sociality that is at odds with the dominant image of self and success within modernity, namely the ascendance of egoism (Durkheim, 1933). Perhaps, therefore, we should express the child–adult relation in multidimensional terms. As Gilligan et al. (1988) stated:

> The different parameters of the parent–child relationship – its inequality and its interdepend-ence or attachment – may ground different feelings which differentiate the dimension of inequality/equality and attachment/detachment that characterize all forms of human connec-tion. In contrast to a unitary moral vision and to the assumption that the opposite of the one is the many, these two dimensions of relationship provide coordinates for reimagining the self and remapping development. The two conceptions of responsibility, reflecting different im-ages of the self in relationship, correct an individualism that has been centered within a single interpretive framework (Gilligan et al., 1988, p. 5).

But I am not arguing that the altruism or care that the adult feels toward the child is itself a unitary or a "natural" feeling – no, rather I would suggest that it is a social construct. In one sense this construct might be viewed as the embodiment of the affective myth of romanticism that has given rise to the modern nuclear family, and perhaps we should add the "mother," as the center of all loving sensations – the instrumental accompaniment to the exaggeration and elevation of the autonomous cognitive ego that has followed in the wake of the enlightenment and assisted in the growth of science and capitalism (Williams, 1958). In fact, a feature of its time, no more and no less. Ambert (1994) was instructive in this context when she stated that:

> This linkage between what we conceive to be the nature of childhood and that of parenting is based less on the natural unavoidability of parents for children's survival and well-being as on society's structure and socioeconomic requisites, which not only place children in the context of family, but "parentalise" and, I will add, "maternalise" them. Thus, when one sees chil-dren, one "sees" parents. When one sees children who have problems, one looks for parents, especially mothers (Ambert, 1994, p. 530).

The sociological tradition would, however, attest to altruism as the very core of sociality. All sociologies spring from the Hobbesian problem of order and even if they attend to the conflictual character of social relations their basic commitment is to explain how societies hold together. In this latter sense altruism may be read as ideological, an appearance of care that disguises the true purpose of control. Here the social sense of dependency that accom-panies development takes on a sinister form, we have to shake ourselves free of the warm sense of sociality that holds together through spontaneous loving bonds. We are then con-fronted with a more cynical version of the idea, in fact the mechanisms of dependence that serve to sustain particular versions of the status quo. In this sense the development of the child may now instructively be viewed alongside the development of the Afro American in the United States or the Black South African, or indeed, the development of women's consciousness in Western Europe. Care, in this sense, itself becomes hegemonic (Gramsci,

1970). Dependence now becomes that feature of social structures which seeks to individualize guilt, pathologize the individual and which further militates to disguise the failures or shortcomings implicit within those very social structures. To this extent all societies demonstrate "dependence" through their members' adherence to drink, drugs, belief systems, or desires. Development through dependency then becomes an instrument in the processes of social and cultural reproduction (Bourdieu, 1977; Jenks, 1993).

Let us now look at certain aspects of the critical mode of social theorizing within sociology that would most systematically espouse this view. Althusser (1971) divides the mechanisms of control in modern societies into two forms, the repressive and the ideological state apparatuses. The latter contains all aspects of superstructure, the cognitive and transmissional aspects of culture, which serve to reproduce the existing oppressive structures of power and advantage without exposing naked aggression. Thus family life, patterns of socialization, schooling – all complementary contexts of a child's development, are realized as part of the deep structurally unconscious apparatuses whereby the going order is recharged, reaffirmed, and reconstituted. The education system, Althusser told us:

> . . . takes children from every class at infant school and then for years . . . it drums into them
> . . . a certain amount of know how wrapped up in the ruling ideology or simply the ruling
> ideology in its pure state. Each mass ejected en route is practically provided with the ideology
> which suits the role it has to fulfil in class society: the role of exploited, of the agent of repression or of the professional ideologist (Althusser, 1971, p. 147).

Marcuse (1965) has attended to the contemporary liberal *laissez-faire* adjustment to, and understanding of, the behavior of others; which we can clearly relate to the socialization process; that he regards as a "repressive tolerance." It might be likened to a cultural mannerism of acceptance that defuses critique, reaction, or change through its all-pervading quasi-approval. In an efficient, "caring" society childrearing and education liberates the individual into compliance. Marcuse stated that:

> A comfortable, smooth, reasonable, democratic unfreedom prevails in advanced industrial
> civilization, a token of technical progress (Marcuse, 1972, p. 16).

and sadly concluded that:

> To liberate the imagination so that it can be given all its means of expression presupposes the
> repression of much that is now free and that perpetuates a repressive society. And such reversal is not a matter of psychology or ethics but of politics . . . (*that is*) the practice in which
> the basic societal institutions are developed, defined, sustained, and changed. It is the practice
> of individuals no matter how organized they may be. Thus the question once again must be
> faced; how can the administered individuals – who have made their mutilation into their own
> liberties and satisfactions, and thus reproduced it on an enlarged scale – liberate themselves
> from themselves as well as from their masters? (Marcuse, 1972, p. 195).

An utterance redolent with critique of the contemporary adult–child relationship.

Bourdieu and Passeron (1977), whose work specifically addresses the process of social reproduction, demonstrated that there are intellectual fields of appraisal which surround any creative endeavor or unique form of expression and both render it meaningful and evaluate it in relation to existing patterns of social stratification. This can apply to the work of art but equally well to the performance of the developing child in significant social contexts like schools. Children, they argue, are differentially endowed with a "cultural capital" according to their original social milieu, their "habitus."

> It may be assumed that every individual owes to the type of schooling he has received a set of basic, deeply interiorised master-patterns on the basis of which he subsequently acquires other patterns, so that the system of patterns by which his thought is organised owes its specific character not only to the nature of the patterns constituting it but also to the frequency with which these are used and to the level of consciousness at which they operate, these properties being probably connected with the circumstances in which the most fundamental intellectual patterns were acquired (Bourdieu, 1967, pp. 192–193).

They are equipped with thought styles, manners, sensitivities, and patterns of relevance and relation that ensure a reproduction of their class position and the ideological framework that supports such a locus. Societies, it would seem, almost inevitably reproduce their structures of hierarchy and power through the processes of the development of self . . . "education serves to transform the cultural heritage into a common individual unconscious" (Bourdieu, 1967).

Finally, the work of Foucault (1977) offers us, at one level, a series of archaeologies of the strategies of control and oppression that have been exercised within modern Western culture. Thus when he informs us of the change and development in penology in Western Europe we find an historical transition from the excessive, explicit symbolic punishment of the seventeenth century to a gradually more subtle, implicit, and intrusive mode of discipline embodied in its finest modern form in Bentham's "panopticon" – the dream building, the rational correction machine. In this form, which we may parallel with the development of modern techniques of childrearing, absolute surveillance is the key. The developing individual, either within the context of criminal punishment or that of education, is to be watched, monitored, timetabled, regimented, and exposed. The private becomes more and more available to the public. Bodies and minds claim an allegiance to the social through dependency, guilt, and visibility.

Emerging from a different sociological perspective to the above the work of Bernstein (1971–73) has, for over two decades, provided a major source of inspiration for theory and research concerning childrearing, child development, and educational disadvantage. While apparently leaving the grounds of moral consensus within society intact he addresses the causes of differential educational achievement within the population of developing children. He was among the first to sophisticate the "educability" thesis beyond an explanation of child performance in relation to their particular constellations of positively or negatively oriented structural variables. Bernstein does not ignore the effect of social factors on a child's development but he shows how they become realized as world views and thus courses of action – in this sense he reveals his true concern being not with the issue of educability but rather with the complex relation between the social structure and the symbolic order. His central question is "how does our outside environment become transformed into modes of consciousness?" and this clearly provides a potentially dialectical view of development. Bernstein's analysis moves from the level of different types of community structure, through parental control variants, on to the linguistic realization of unique intent. Social stratification, however, remains the dominant implicit dimension.

What this brief summary of sociological theory relevant to child development aims at is not a summation of their central insights, all of which have been injured by the brevity of my exposition, but rather to show that even that large section of the discipline which is clearly critical of any existing form of social relations and thus dedicated to its change, even this body of work seems unable to mobilize the potentiality of the child as an agent of such change. The development of the child seems variously articulated as a process of entrapment. The newness and difference of childhood faces standardization and normalization. Thus all social influences on the developing child are presented and understood as structural constraints.

Sociological Models

During the 1960s in the United Kingdom, which was a time of full employment, economic expansion, growth in public provision, and a liberalizing of previously entrenched attitudes toward human behavior, education became viewed by government and populace alike as a crucial investment in the future collective good. The dominant ideology contained a strong sense of "human capital" that eventually blossomed into the "vocationalism" of the late 1980s and the 1990s. Schooling and university education expanded considerably and efforts were made to improve its quality also. This general attitude of the collective consciousness was reflected within sociology where the sociology of education became a burgeoning specialism. However, even within such a climate of progressive optimism the primary thesis was that, if ability is randomly distributed, how is it that educational achievement is socially distributed? Sociologists produced a plethora of studies which offered explanation in terms of such variables as family size, parental occupation, parental income, achievement motivation, immediate versus deferred gratification, peer group orientation, cultural deprivation, language use, and complexes of these (Banks, 1968; Halsey, Floud, & Anderson, 1961). Again, all of these variables were reducible to indices of social class, but more significantly at an analytic level, all are intelligible as contexts of non-willfulness. Even social theory that is critical seems to depotentiate the young through an intrinsically pessimistic vision. The becoming social actors, who are the developing child, are rendered passive receivers and perpetuators of the accidents of their historical moment. This is perhaps best epitomized in the irony of a study by Willis (1977) when he states that the reason that working-class children succumb to the social and cultural reproduction is because they are complicit in the processes, they are effectively active agents in their own lack of mobility.

> The difficult thing to explain about how middle class kids get middle class jobs is why the others let them. The difficult thing to explain about how working class kids get working class jobs is why they let themselves. It is much too facile simply to say that they have no choice . . . There is no obvious physical coercion and a degree of self direction (Willis, 1977, p. 1).

It would seem then that the social factors affecting development are such that they become internalized and expressed as matters of choice!

Development conceived of in these terms speaks not of an unfolding, a project of creativity and inspiration, in fact hardly of the individual child's biography at all. The child continues to be realized as an instance of a category and the concept of development only ever seems to depict the concerted and ultimately omnipotent violence of the social structure to which the individual inevitably succumbs. This is not to argue for the mobilization of the concrete child as a political force in response to these actual constraints as part of a "Children's Rights" movement, but rather to argue analytically for a more radical conception of the child as a vision and as a potential.

Development, though a dominant image in understanding the child, is only one way. Further it is that kind of concept which encourages the stance of looking backwards from within the sociological tradition. But sociology and its address of the child can occupy different spaces; let us take three possible examples. First, the child might be regarded historically, not as a series of evolutionary steps, but rather as a patterning of images that relate to different temporal contexts. In this way Aries (1973), the leading figure in a school of neo-enlightenment historians, looks at visual representations and fashion and shows the emergence of childhood within a particular group and within a particular epoch. History then, is not regarded as a description of a succession of events, rather it is seen as providing the moral grounds of current speech about the child. Second, the child can be approached comparatively, employing anthropological material. Here we might treat different childrearing practices as aspects of culture. Mead's (1954, 1971) work is instructive here in showing us how in different, yet contemporary, societies children assume far more autonomy and responsibility than is familiar within our own world.

> It may be said that where we are concerned with character formation – the process by which children learn to discipline impulses and structure their expectations of the behavior of others – this cross-cultural approach is very valuable. It provides insights into such subjects as conscience formation, the relative importance of different sanctioning systems, sin, shame and pride, and guilt, and into the relationship between independence training and achievement motivation (Mead, 1971, p. 219).

If nothing else, such an approach may serve to deflate much of the ethnocentrism that is inherent in a Western sense of maturation.

Finally a phenomenological perspective could enable us to gain insight into an existential and generative sense of sociality that emerges from within the consciousness of the child. Merleau-Ponty (1967), for example, has demonstrated the acquisition of new linguistic forms by the child, due not so much to teaching as to personal, and intentional, affective experience. And Rafky, developing a phenomenology of the child stated that:

> . . . the life-world the newborn enters contains more than objects and social institutions. It is also characterized by a complex of legitimations which explain and integrate the various action patterns of a group, a "matrix of all socially objectivated and subjectively real meanings; the entire historic society and the entire biography of the individual are seen as events taking place within this universe" [Berger & Luckmann]. In short, the individual has acquired a set or mode for interpreting the world meaningfully; he perceives it in an ordered and subjectively understandable frame of reference (Rafky, 1973, p. 43).

These three examples: the historical, the comparative, and the phenomenological, are suggestions for alternative and instructive approaches to the study of childhood; they do not in themselves constitute an exhaustive typology of programs for research into childhood.

References

Althusser, L. (1971). *Lenin and philosophy and other essays*. London: New Left Books.

Ambert, A.-M. (1994). An international perspective on parenting: Social change and social constructs. *Journal of Marriage and the Family, 56*, 529–560.

Archard, D. (1993). *Children: Rights and childhood*. London: Routledge.

Aries, P. (1973). *Centuries of childhood*. London: Cape.

Banks, O. (1968). *The sociology of education*. London: Batsford.

Bernstein, B. (1971–73). *Class, codes and control, volumes 1, 2 and 3*. London: Routledge & Kegan Paul.

Beck, U. (1992). *Risk society: Towards a new modernity*. London: Sage.

Bourdieu, P. (1967). Systems of education and systems of thought. *International Social Science Journal, 19*, 102–124.

Bourdieu, P. (1977). *Outline of a theory of practice*. Cambridge, England: Cambridge University Press.

Bourdieu, P., & Passeron, J. (1977). *Reproduction in education, society and culture*. London: Sage.

Burman, E. (1994). *Deconstructing developmental psychology*. London: Routledge.

Cicourel, A. (1964). *Method and measurement in sociology*. New York: Free Press.

Dawe, A. (1970). Two sociologies. *British Journal of Sociology, 21*, 207–218.

Denzin, N. (1982) The work of little children. In C. Jenks (Ed.), *The sociology of childhood*, pp.189–194. London: Batsford.

Durkheim, E. (1933). *The division of labor in society*. New York: Free Press.

Durkheim, E. (1938). *The rules of sociological method*. New York: Free Press.

Durkheim, E. (1968). *The elementary forms of the religious life*. London: Allen & Unwin.

Durkheim, E. (1982). *The rules of the sociological method* (Trans.W.Halls). London: Macmillan.

Foucault, M. (1977). *Discipline and punish*. London: Allen Lane.

Frank, G. (1971). *The sociology of development and the undevelopment of sociology*. London: Pluto Press.

Garfinkel, H. (1967). *Studies in ethnomethodology*. Englewood Cliffs, NJ: Prentice Hall.

Giddens, A. (1991). *Modernity and self-identity*. Cambridge, England: Polity Press.

Gilligan, C., Wood, J., & McLean Taylor, J. (1988). Mapping the moral domain: A contribution of women's thinking to psychological theory and education. Cambridge, MA: Harvard University Press.

Gramsci, A. (1970). *The modern prince and other writings*. New York: International Publishers.

Halsey, A., Floud, J., & Anderson, C. (1961) (Eds.). *Education, economy, and society*. Glencoe, IL: Free Press.

Hambrook, M. (1987). Accounts of the child–adult relationship in sociology: With special reference to the work of Piaget, Parsons and Freud. Unpublished M.Phil. thesis, University of London.

Hendrick, H. (1990). Constructions and reconstructions of British childhood: An interpretive survey, 1800 to the present, In A. James & A. Prout (Eds.), *Constructing and reconstructing childhood: Contemporary issues in the sociological study of childhood*, pp. 34–62. London: Falmer Press.

Hendricks, C., & Hendricks, J. (1975). Historical developments of the multiplicity of time and implications for the analysis of ageing. *The Human Context, 7*, 187–196.

Hirst, P. (1975). *Durkheim, Bernard and epistemology*. London: Routledge & Kegan Paul.

Hollis, M. (1977). *Models of man*. Cambridge, England: Cambridge University Press.

Holt, J. (1971). *Escape from childhood*. Harmondsworth, England: Penguin.

Illich, I. (1971). *Deschooling society*. London: Calder & Boyers.

James, A., & Prout, A. (1990) *Constructing and reconstructing childhood*. Basingstoke, England: Falmer.

Jenks, C. (1982, 1992). *The sociology of childhood*. London: Batsford and Aldershot, England: Gregg Revivals.

Jenks, C. (1989). Social theorizing and the child: Constraints and possibilities, In S. Doxiadis (Ed.), *Early influences shaping the individual*, pp. 43–103. NATO Advanced Study Workshop, London: Plenum Press.

Jenks, C. (1993). *Cultural reproduction*. London: Routledge.

Jenks, C. (1995) Child abuse in the postmodern context: An issue of social identity. *Childhood, 2*, 111–121.

MacKay, R. (1973). Conceptions of children and models of socialization. In H. P. Dreitzel (Ed.), *Recent sociology no.5 – Childhood and socialization*, pp. 27–43. New York: Macmillan.

Marcuse, H. (1972). Repressive tolerance, In R. Wolff, C. Barrington, & H. Marcuse (Eds.), *One-dimensional man*, pp.137–145. London: Abacus.

Mead, M. (1954). *Growing up in New Guinea*. Harmondsworth, England: Penguin.

Mead, M. (1971). Early childhood experience and later education in complex cultures. In M.Wax, S. Dimond, & F. O'Gearing (Eds.), Anthropological perspectives on education, pp. 219–240. New York: Basic Books.

Merleau-Ponty, M. (1967). *The primacy of perception*. Paris: Gallimard.

O'Neill, J. (1973). Embodiment and child development: A phenomenological approach. In H. P. Dreitzel (Ed.), *Recent sociology no. 5 – Childhood and socialization*, pp. 76–86. New York: Macmillan.

O'Neill, J. (1994). *The missing child in liberal theory*. Toronto: University of Toronto Press.

Parsons, T. (1964). *The social system*. New York: Free Press.

Parsons, T. (1968). *The structure of social action, volumes 1 and 2*. New York: Free Press.

Piaget, J. (1972). *Psychology and epistemology* (Trans. P.Wells). Harmondsworth, England: Penguin.

Piaget, J. (1977). *The language and thought of the child*. London: Routledge & Kegan Paul.

Postman, N., & Weingarten, C. (1977). *Teaching as a subversive activity*. Harmondsworth, England: Penguin.

Qvortrop, J. (1993). *Childhood as a social phenomenon*. Vienna: The European Centre.

Rafky, D. (1973). Phenomenology and socialization: Some comments on the assumptions underlying socialization theories. In H. P. Dreitzel (Ed.), *Recent sociology no. 5 – Childhood and socialization*, pp. 44–64. New York: Macmillan.

Rose, N. (1990). *Governing the soul*. London: Routledge.

Schutz, A. (1964). *Collected papers, volume 1*. The Hague: Martinus Nijhoff.

Speier, M. (1970). The everyday world of the child. In J. Douglas (Ed.), *Understanding everyday life*. London: Routledge & Kegan Paul.

Stainton-Rogers, M. (1991). *Child abuse and neglect*. Milton Keynes, England: Open University Press.

Stone, G. (1965). The play of little children. *Quest.4*, 27–38.

Williams, R. (1958). *Culture and society 1780–1950*. London: Chatto and Windus.

Willis, P. (1977). *Learning to labour*. London: Gower.

Wrong, D. (1961). The oversocialized conception of man in modern sociology. *American Sociological Review, 26*, 184–193.

Part III

Influences on Development: Causal Factors

Important causal influences in development cut across many or all particular areas (such as attachment, friendship, social cognition, play, helping, and aggression, all reviewed later). These include temperament and sex differences.

Temperament is an important dimension of individual difference in children that has origins in genetic factors and is evidenced from birth onwards, but continues to impact on development through the childhood years. Ann Sanson, Sheryl Hemphill, and Diana Smart review conceptualizations of temperament, its measurement and stability, and the interactional processes involved in its development. They then consider the role of temperament in important domains of social behavior: peer relationships, social competence, prosocial behavior, and aggression and oppositional behaviors. Although temperament is often seen as a biologically deterministic trait, the authors bring out the interactional context, and the importance of the "fit" between temperament and context in influencing developmental outcome.

Sex differences pervade social development. Their explanation provides a well-known battleground for genetic and environmental explanations, and several theories have been advanced for the explanation of the forms which sex differences take and how they develop. Susan Golombok and Melissa Hines first describe the development of sex differences, in areas such as gender identity, playmate preferences, and play styles. They then consider the theories, starting with biological explanations. The influences of hormonal factors are reviewed in expert and detailed fashion. Moving on to more psychological explanations, they consider social learning theory, cognitive theory, social cognitive theory, and the role of gender segregation. These different views are not necessarily in opposition, as clearly there are many influences at work. Both biological and psychological theories may also be consistent with an evolutionary perspective (see Chapter 3).

Families, and peers, provide important social contexts for development throughout childhood. Carollee Howes and Jolena James consider the development of social competence and socially interactive styles in terms of the influence of early caregivers – not only parents, but also childcare personnel. Race or ethnicity, and gender, are important mediating factors here. The authors review work on the influence of childcare settings and their quality on developmental, a theme that has been, and continues to be controversial, with important resonances in social policy regarding early childcare.

Howes and James highlight the role of adults on early social development, but do not neglect peer influences. Both adults, and peers in the sense of same or similar age children, can have powerful influences (and also siblings, see Chapter 13). The relative contribution of adults (particularly parents), and peers, has become particularly topical in the last decade. Following the work of behavior geneticists, who found that nonshared environmental factors often greatly exceeded shared environmental factors as contributors to development (see Chapter 2), Harris (1995) has advocated a "group socialization theory." This proposes that the main source of nonshared environment is the peer group, and that by middle childhood, peer influences greatly outweigh parent or family influences. Ross Parke, Sandra Simpkins, David McDowell, Mina Kim, Colleen Killian, Jessica Dennis, Mary L. Flyr, Margaret Wild, and Yumee Rah critically review this debate. While acknowledging the importance of genetics and of the peer group, they describe the very considerable range of ways in which parents may influence a child's development: not only through direct interaction, but via the managing or supervising of aspects such as playmate choice and opportunities, and the socioeconomic and cultural context of the family. Marital conflict may, unfortunately, also be an influence on children's development. The relative importance of parents and peers will continue to be debated, but this chapter illustrates the strong defense which the "family" side of the argument can mount (see also Hart, Newell, & Olsen, in press).

Many issues broached in this section are controversial, as already mentioned. Another relates to the definition of social competence and what is "adaptive" or "maladaptive" behavior. Both Sanson et al. (Chapter 6) and Howes and James (Chapter 8) label aggressive behavior as maladaptive, and/or socially incompetent. Not everyone would agree in labeling aggressive behaviors as maladaptive, since such behaviors may have individual advantage for the child exhibiting it; see, for example, Chapter 3, and also Sutton, Smith, and Swettenham (1999). However, they may be labeled maladaptive so far as the wider social network or society is concerned. In part this difference is just a matter of labeling, but in part it reflects a continuing, if recent, debate on the way we conceptualize child development (see also Chapter 5).

References

Harris, J. R. (1995). Where is the child's environment? A group socialization theory of development. *Psychological Review, 102*, 458–489.

Hart, C. H., Newell, L. D., & Olsen, S. F. (in press). Parenting skills and social/communicative competence in childhood. In J. O. Greene & B. R. Burleson (Eds.), *Handbook of communication and social interaction skills*. Mahwah, NJ: Erlbaum.

Sutton, J., Smith, P. K., & Swettenham, J. (1999). Socially undesirable need not be incompetent: A response to Crick and Dodge. *Social Development, 8*, 132–134.

6

Temperament and Social Development

Ann Sanson, Sheryl A. Hemphill, and Diana Smart

This chapter reviews the ways in which child temperament impacts upon aspects of social development. We start by providing some background on temperament as a construct, and theoretical propositions about the processes involved in temperament-development associations. We then review the research literature on the connections between temperament and peer relations, social competence and prosocial behavior, and problematic social behaviors. In concluding comments, we highlight areas in need of further research.

What is Temperament?

Historical background

Temperament refers to constitutionally based individual differences in behavioral style that are visible from early childhood. Ideas about temperament go back to ancient Greco-Roman times. However, interest in child temperament in modern times dates particularly to the pioneering work of Thomas and Chess in the New York Longitudinal Study (Thomas, Chess, Birch, Hertzig, & Korn, 1963). Responding to the prevailing environmentalism of the time, and drawing from clinical insights, they identified nine dimensions

Authors Sheryl Hemphill and Diana Smart have made equivalent contributions to this chapter; they are listed above in alphabetical order. Preparation of this chapter was partially supported by Australian Research Council Grant A79930720 to Ann Sanson and Ken Rubin, and National Health and Medical Research Council Grants 980627 and 9937433 to Ann Sanson and John Toumbourou. Direct inquiries to: Ann Sanson, Australian Institute of Family Studies, 300 Queen Street, Melbourne, Vic. 3000, Australia.

of temperament on which infants and young children could be seen to differ, and which impacted upon their subsequent psychosocial development. These were approach-withdrawal, adaptability, quality of mood, intensity of reaction, distractibility, persistence, rhythmicity or regularity, threshold of responsiveness, and activity.

Current conceptualizations of temperament

Following Thomas and Chess' groundbreaking work, their nine-dimensional structure of temperament became widely accepted, especially in clinical settings. However, a consensus is emerging that a smaller number of dimensions best represents the structure of temperament. These show considerable commonality across research studies (Rothbart & Bates, 1998). Three broad aspects of temperament are gaining wide acceptance. *Reactivity or negative emotionality* refers particularly to irritability, negative mood, inflexibility, and high-intensity negative reactions; it is sometimes differentiated into distress to limitations (irritability, anger) and distress to novelty (fearfulness). *Self-regulation* refers to the effortful control of attentional and emotional processes, and includes persistence, nondistractibility and emotional control. *Approach/withdrawal, inhibition or sociability* describes the tendency to approach novel situations and people, or conversely to withdraw and be wary. In this chapter, we focus on these broad aspects of temperament but where appropriate, also describe research on narrower band factors.

A number of researchers have used the categorization system, developed by Thomas and Chess, of "easy" and "difficult" clusters of children. "Difficult" children tended to be negative in mood, withdrawing, unadaptable, highly intense, and arhythmic, and Thomas et al. (1963) documented more troubled development for them. In later research these dimensions have not clustered together, and different researchers have tended to create their own definitions of "difficultness," resulting in problems in comparing studies. The "difficult" construct carries value-laden overtones, and ignores the fact that any temperament characteristic can be easy or difficult, depending on the demands of the situation. Use of these global categories also impedes progress in understanding the specific roles of particular temperament dimensions for specific aspects of development (Sanson & Rothbart, 1995). The "difficult" construct is thus relatively unhelpful in a research context. However, in the research to be reviewed, a multiplicity of temperament constructs have been used, ranging from "micro" aspects such as soothability or anger, to global conceptualizations such as "difficult" or "easy."

It is generally accepted that temperament is biologically based (see Rothbart & Bates, 1998 for review). There is some evidence of heritability, more for some aspects of temperament than others. Models from neuroscience and some specific psychobiological variables are being explored for their applicability to temperament research. However, more research is needed to fully specify the biological underpinnings of temperament.

Stability and change

If there was little or no stability of temperament over time, it would be hard to argue for its importance as a contributor to children's social development. Modest to moderate stability across age is typically found, with correlations ranging from .2 to .4 (see Slabach, Morrow, & Wachs, 1991). There are at least three explanations for the lack of higher stability estimates. First, even genetic underpinnings do not imply immutability, and some aspects of temperament appear to show considerable development with age. Secondly, temperament can only be assessed from its behavioral manifestations, which vary with age, making it difficult to ensure that the same underlying temperament constructs are assessed at each age. Thirdly and most significantly, correlational estimates of stability do not take into account measurement error. Using structural equation modeling (which corrects for attenuation of correlations due to measurement error) on data from the Australian Temperament Project (ATP) sample from infancy to 7–8 years, Pedlow, Sanson, Prior, and Oberklaid (1993) found considerably higher stability estimates, in the range of .7 to .8. Nevertheless, even at these levels of stability, there is still considerable room for change in children's temperament characteristics. Understanding the processes underlying these changes is an important current research question (see Sanson & Rothbart, 1995).

Measurement

There has been considerable debate about the measurement of temperament. Because temperament refers to the overall behavioral style of a child, rather than moment-by-moment behavior, primary caregivers who can observe the child across time and contexts have been considered appropriate informants, usually via parent-rated questionnaires. Findings of effects of such variables as maternal depression and stress on temperament ratings (e.g., Mednick, Hocevar, Schulsinger, & Baker, 1996) suggest a subjective element to maternal reports. However, there is also evidence of reasonable validity for parental ratings (Bates, Bayles, Bennett, Ridge, & Brown, 1991), and reports of convergence between parental ratings and observational measures (Allen & Prior, 1995; Kochanska, Murray, & Coy, 1997). More studies are now adopting observational measures, although these also have their limitations, being restricted in the time period and contexts in which observations can be made. While the controversies regarding measurement deserve more space than can be afforded here, it is generally agreed that the optimal solution at present is to use multiple measures of temperament (Rothbart & Bates, 1998). Few studies currently achieve this goal.

Theoretical Understandings of the Role of Temperament in Development

It is one thing to document associations between temperament and social development, and another to model and explain the developmental processes by which temperament has its effects. Here we briefly outline some processes by which temperament is likely to impact on social development.

Several broad categories of processes can be identified (see Rothbart & Bates, 1998 and Sanson & Prior, 1999 for fuller discussions). Firstly, temperament may have direct linear effects on social development. For example, an extreme ranking on a temperament dimension may be synonymous with a particular outcome (thus very high inhibition may be synonymous with social withdrawal). Another direct effect is when an extreme tempera-ment characteristic leads to or directly affects an outcome (e.g., very high reactivity may predispose a child to aggressive responses to frustration).

Indirect linear effects, or mediated effects, include those where a child's temperament affects the environment, which then impacts upon their adjustment. In general, children with different temperaments elicit different responses from people with whom they come in contact – a cheerful sociable child is likely to experience more positive responses from others than a moody withdrawing one; and a highly negative and reactive child might elicit punitive discipline practices from a parent, which in turn increase the child's risk for ag-gressive behavior. This history of differential reactions is then likely to impact on develop-mental outcome.

A third set of effects is interactional ones. Thomas and Chess (1977) proposed that "goodness of fit" explains the impact of temperament; that is, that particular temperament characteristics "fit" well with particular environments, and others "fit" poorly. Thus an active child in a cramped environment might do less well than the same child in a spacious environment where their activity could be channeled in safe and productive ways. In a related fashion, Rothbart and Bates (1998) note that temperament-by-temperament inter-actions are also plausible – for example, self-regulatory aspects of temperament might change the expression of other potentially problematic aspects of temperament (such as high activ-ity level), promoting competent outcomes. Although it has been difficult to operationalize goodness of fit (Paterson & Sanson, 1999), and findings of interactional effects are still relatively scant, it remains a popular theoretical model.

A more elaborated model is a transactional model (e.g., Cicchetti & Cohen, 1995) which posits that development is the outcome of a continuous interaction among intrinsic child characteristics and aspects of the environment. A child's health status, cognitive ca-pacities, and temperament, along with parent and family circumstances and the prevailing sociocultural context, all need to be taken into account in explaining and predicting devel-opmental pathways. In this model, temperament is often seen as a risk or protective factor.

There is widespread acceptance among researchers that interactional or transactional models best explain the developmental process. However, as Rothbart and Bates (1998) note, interactions have been easier to talk about than find, and there is currently most empirical support for linear additive effects. Limitations in methods and analysis strategies have undoubtedly restricted our capacity to uncover interactional effects, and recent ad-vances such as latent variable and trajectory analysis techniques may help establish their existence.

Conceptualization of Social Development

The term social development is broad, and we will not attempt a definition here. Rather, we will restrict our discussion to aspects of social development for which temperamental contributions have been most investigated. The measures of social behaviors considered here range widely, including peer nominations, observed behaviors, and ratings via checklists. We adopt an inclusive approach, to accommodate this heterogeneity. We will discuss research on both positive and problematic social developmental outcomes. As an organizational device, we make distinctions between different facets of social development, but acknowledge that the lines between these are often blurred.

The first area to be discussed is children's peer relations, with a particular emphasis on temperamental influences on the development of social withdrawal. We then turn to the development of positive social capacities, specifically the development of social skills, social competence, and prosocial behavior and cognitions. Finally, we address temperamental contributions to problematic social behaviors, such as aggression and oppositional behavior. Throughout the review we draw attention to age trends, as well as the influence of gender, social class, and culture, although as will be seen the research base in many cases is extremely sparse.

A note about methods: In this area of research, a recurring issue is the difficulty of clearly separating, both conceptually and methodologically, the predictive temperament factors from the social development outcomes. For example, wary behaviors and fearful affect in the face of novelty are commonly incorporated in measures of temperamental inhibition; however, they are also often part of the definition of social withdrawal. Further, if the same person (e.g., a parent or teacher) reports on both the presumed temperamental precursor and the social developmental outcome, it is likely that shared method variance accounts for some portion of any association found. These difficulties mean that findings of associations between temperament and social development do not necessarily reflect causal relationships, and may in some instances be inflated due to contamination of measures or shared method variance. While across-time associations derived from longitudinal methodology do not in themselves establish causal linkages, they do allow more confidence to be placed in interpretations.

We therefore focus our review on studies that meet at least one of two requirements: a longitudinal design, and the use of different informants or methods of data collection for the temperament and social development variables of interest.

The Role of Temperament in Peer Relations

Here we review research on the role of temperament in children's peer relations, including children's tendencies to withdraw from peers, to exhibit shyness or sociability in the company of peers, and their status within the peer group. Gender and cultural differences and research suggesting the importance of temperament-by-parenting interactions are reviewed. We do not comment on social class differences, as most studies have used middle-class samples, and we have not located any specifically addressing socioeconomic status (SES).

Most research in this area has focused on the role of temperamental inhibition in the development of social withdrawal. Inhibition is the disposition to be wary when encountering novel or challenging situations, whereas social withdrawal (or reticence) refers to consistent displays of solitary, onlooking, and unoccupied behaviors when with familiar or unfamiliar peers (Burgess, Rubin, Cheah, & Nelson, 2001). As noted above, some of the common indicators of inhibition overlap with those often ascribed to social withdrawal.

Preschoolers (3- to 4-year-olds)

Cross-sectional studies (e.g., Billman & McDevitt, 1980; Hinde, Tamplin, & Barrett, 1993), and longitudinal studies from infancy to preschool age, indicate that early inhibition is associated with social withdrawal or lack of peer interaction in preschool children (Kagan, Reznick, Clarke, Snidman, & Garcia-Coll, 1984; Sanson, 2000). Parker-Cohen and Bell (1988) found that children low on inhibition and high in activity showed, concurrently, higher levels of teacher-reported peer responsiveness. Task orientation (attentional self-regulation) and flexibility (positive mood, adaptability, and approach) have also been associated with more peer interaction (Keogh & Burstein, 1988), and highly persistent and active boys were found to be more socially interactive with peers, with boys low in persistence and activity having more negative interactions (Guralnick & Groom, 1990).

Early school age (5- to 7-year-olds)

Links have been found between toddler inhibition and observed social withdrawal at 5–7 years, especially when comparing groups of extremely inhibited or uninhibited toddlers (e.g., Kagan, 1988; Reznick et al., 1986). Gersten (1988) found that children identified as inhibited at 21 months spent less time interacting with peers and more time alone at kindergarten than uninhibited toddlers. Kochanska and Radke-Yarrow (1992) reported that "social inhibition" (inhibition to an unfamiliar adult) in toddlerhood predicted shy, socially withdrawn behavior with a peer at 5 years, while "nonsocial inhibition" (to an unfamiliar environment) was associated with less engagement in group play at 5 years, suggesting that different types of inhibition are associated with somewhat different peer relationship outcomes.

Concurrent relationships at this age have also been documented. For example, Skarpness and Carson (1986) found that 5–6-year-old children who showed less inhibition (by mother report) had more positive peer relations (by teacher report). Similarly, Stocker and Dunn (1990) reported that temperamentally sociable 5- to 10-year-olds were more popular with peers and had more positive relations with friends than less sociable children.

Later elementary school age (8- to 11-year-olds)

As with younger children, being inhibited as a toddler or preschooler has been associated with withdrawal from peers at 8–11 years (e.g., Eisenberg, Shepard, Fabes, Murphy, & Guthrie, 1998; Kagan, 1988). Temperamental dimensions other than inhibition have received little research attention, but some relationships have been found. For example, Kurdek and Lillie (1985) found that rejected children in grades 3 to 7 showed lower rhythmicity and poorer attention (both aspects of self-regulation).

Sex differences

Sex differences in this area have been somewhat neglected (Hinde et al., 1993). In one of few investigations, Skarpness and Carson (1986) found no sex differences in the links between mother-rated inhibition and teacher-rated withdrawal. However, Hinde et al. (1993) found that inhibited 4-year-old girls tended not to interact with peers, whereas for boys there was no relationship between inhibition and peer interaction. Sanson, Smart, Prior, and Oberklaid (1996) investigated the earlier temperament characteristics that differentiated children classified (on the basis of parent, teacher, and self-report) as having problematic, competent, or average peer relationships at 11–12 years. For boys but not girls, impersistence and poor task orientation (low self-regulation), assessed from 1–3 years on, differentiated the problem group from the other two groups. Higher irritability and inflexibility (reactivity), assessed between 1–3 and 9–10 years, more clearly discriminated the problem group of boys from the other groups than they did for girls.

In summary, there is suggestive evidence that temperament may have different implications for boys' and girls' peer relationships, although no clear-cut picture has yet emerged.

Cultural differences

Direct investigations of cultural differences in the links between temperament and peer relations are scant, generally focus on older children, and have almost exclusively considered Chinese and North American children. For example, Chen, Rubin, and Li (1995) found that peer-nominated inhibited 8–10-year-old Chinese children were more accepted by peers and scored higher on peer and teacher ratings of "honorship" and leadership than children identified as aggressive or average. Chen and colleagues argued that in China, unlike North America, inhibition is thought to reflect social maturity and understanding and is therefore viewed positively. Their findings clearly require replication and are somewhat inconsistent with recent findings regarding social withdrawal in younger Chinese children (Hart et al., 2000). However, they do suggest that temperament in itself is neither positive nor negative but that its effects can be mediated through cultural norms and belief systems.

The mediating role of culturally based parenting beliefs and behaviors was further demonstrated by Chen et al. (1998), where the pattern of correlations between observed toddler inhibition and self-reported parenting differed for Chinese and Canadian mothers. For example, for the Chinese sample, inhibition was positively correlated with maternal acceptance and encouragement of achievement, but in the Canadian sample the correlations were negative. These results again suggest that inhibition is desirable in China, and undesirable and problematic in Canada. Such cross-cultural comparisons, when extended across a wider age range and a broader range of cultures, promise to increase our understanding of how temperament works within a cultural context, through culture-specific parenting attitudes, expectations, and practices, to impact on social developmental outcomes.

Developmental models concerning links between temperament and peer relations

One of the most comprehensive models of the development of social withdrawal is Rubin and colleagues' "temple of doom" model (e.g., Rubin, LeMare, & Lollis, 1990; Rubin & Stewart, 1996). In this model, infant inhibition is considered a potential stressor to which, in the context of other family stressors, parents may react negatively (i.e., with insensitivity, overprotection and/or overcontrol), resulting in insecure parent–child attachment. Insecure children may then withdraw from the social environment, and eventually be rejected by peers. Here temperament is seen as a risk factor whose effect is mediated by the parental behavior elicited by it. Other aspects of temperament (e.g., reactivity, self-regulation) are not specifically addressed in this model.

Fox and Calkins (1993) have described a model that emphasizes the interaction between infant reactivity and regulation of affect, along with parental influences and parent–child interactions. Different child outcomes are postulated for particular combinations of reactivity and regulation; for example, infants who are high in both negative reactivity and fearfulness may become isolated and withdrawn from peers as early as 14 months of age (e.g., Kagan, Snidman, & Arcus, 1998). However, Fox and Calkins argue that parental support may alter the behavioral outcome. Strengths of this model are that it describes the role of two broad dimensions of temperament (reactivity and self-regulation) and recognizes the potential mediating influence of parents on children's outcomes.

Consistent with a transactional model of development, a growing body of literature investigates the influence of temperament-by-parenting interactions on children's peer relations. Some studies suggest that the association of inhibition with peer relationship difficulties occurs particularly in the context of an overprotective and controlling parent (e.g., Burgess et al., 2001).

Summary

To summarize, although most studies rely on concurrent data and there are many research gaps, there is increasing evidence of associations between early temperament and later peer relations (particularly social withdrawal). There is also evidence of differentiated paths from specific types of inhibition to particular types of peer relations. While few studies have investigated temperament dimensions other than inhibition, attentional self-regulation and reactivity also appear to be important contributors. To date, there is only suggestive evidence of sex differences in links between temperament and peer relations, but cultural differences in the role of inhibition suggest that temperament effects are likely to be mediated by parental and cultural expectations. Few studies have examined potential moderating and mediating variables, but promising developmental models attempt to explain the causal processes underlying the links between temperament and peer relations. Future development of these models will need to elaborate the influence of temperament-by-parenting interactions on children's peer relations.

Temperamental Contributions to Social Competence and Prosocial Behavior

Children's temperament characteristics have been shown to be related to skilled social behavior and to prosocial behavior and cognitions. Included here are reviews of studies assessing children's general levels of social competence and social skills, typically via check-lists; studies investigating specific behaviors observed during peer interactions; and research on prosocial outcomes including empathic capacities, conscience, sympathy, response to distress, and helping behaviors. Sex differences are discussed, but no studies addressing social class or cultural differences in the relationships of temperament to social competence and prosocial behavior have been located, other than those by Chen and colleagues previously discussed.

Preschoolers (3- to 4-year-olds)

Dunn and Cutting (1999) investigated concurrent linkages between 4-year-old children's temperament and the quality of their interactions with a friend. Negative emotionality was related to one aspect of peer interaction, "coordinated play" (e.g., agreeing with the other child's suggestion) which, while appearing socially competent, may reflect a more dependent interaction style. While the majority of studies have involved white, middle-class samples, Youngblade and Mulvihill (1998) used naturalistic observations of preschoolers from homeless families. Children who were active, soothable, or persistent more frequently displayed positive behaviors than emotional or shy children. In a concurrent observational study, Farver and Branstetter (1994) found children with an "easy" temperament profile gave more prosocial responses to peer distress than children who were "slow to warm up" or "difficult."

Some of the most illuminating work comes from Eisenberg and colleagues, focusing on the roles of reactivity/emotionality, self-regulation and their interaction. Eisenberg et al. (1993) found that a composite measure of social skills (parent, teacher, and observer report) was strongly predicted by low emotionality and high self-regulation capacities, with self-regulation being the more salient. Children who were both highly emotional and poorly regulated had lower social skills and sociometric status. Using naturalistic observation, Fabes et al. (1999) found that socially competent responding was associated with an aspect of self-regulation, "effortful control," only in high-intensity peer interaction contexts (e.g., energetic, stressful, wild or loud interactions). Hence, temperament seemed particularly relevant to social functioning in stressful social situations.

Eisenberg, Fabes, Guthrie, and Reiser (2000) propose that a moderate to high level of self-regulation is optimal for successful social functioning; thus negative emotionality, in the presence of optimum regulation, does not lead to low social competence. Extremely high regulation is argued to lead to overcontrolled and less socially skilled behavior. Low regulation is seen as a risk for externalizing behavior problems and low social competence, particularly when high negative emotionality is also present. Hence their model emphasizes the importance of temperament-by-temperament interactions, and points to the critical importance of regulation capacities. These specific and testable predictions provide a valuable direction for future research, although analysis strategies will need to take account of the hypothesized nonlinear relationships.

Early school age (5- to 7-year-olds)

The findings of Rothbart, Ahadi, and Hershey (1994) suggest complex and distinct relationships between components of negative emotionality and aspects of social behavior. Temperamental fear (unease, worry), sadness (lowered mood or energy), and effortful control were related to empathy, guilt, and shame. Aspects of negative affectivity reflecting irritability, such as anger or discomfort, were related to antisocial, but not prosocial, behaviors. These concurrent questionnaire-based data were corroborated by longitudinal data from infancy which were available for a subsample of the children. Attention regulation (persistence, akin to effortful control) was also a powerful predictor of parent- and teacher-rated social skills among a sample of 5-6-year-old Australian children, accounting for 24% of variance (Paterson & Sanson, 1999).

Kochanska and colleagues have investigated the role of temperament in conscience formation. Her model posits that experience of affect, guilt, and anxiety in response to transgression, and behavioral control (which enables the child to inhibit or suppress undesirable actions) contribute to conscience development (Kochanska, 1993). Thus the model emphasizes affective and self-regulatory aspects of temperament, as well as cognitive capacities, and argues that conscience emerges through a subtle, evolving interaction between the child's temperament and the parent's childrearing style.

Several studies provide support for the model. Connections between early school-age moral cognitions and behavior and toddler, preschool and concurrent inhibitory control were reported by Kochanska et al. (1997), leading to the conclusion that inhibitory control plays a critical role in conscience formation. Temperament-by-parenting interactions in the development of conscience have also been found (Kochanska 1997). For fearful children, a gentle style of maternal discipline in toddlerhood facilitated conscience development at preschool age. For fearless children, higher attachment security and higher maternal responsiveness in toddlerhood predicted later conscience. Additionally, fearful and fearless children differed in rate of conscience development, with fearful children apparently on a faster trajectory than fearless children. It seems that there are several pathways to conscience formation which relate differentially to child temperament and parenting style characteristics.

Later elementary school age (8- to 12-year-olds)

The contribution of concurrent and earlier temperament to social skills (combined parent, teacher, and child report) at 11–12 years was investigated by Prior, Sanson, Smart, and Oberklaid (2000). Concurrent parent and teacher reports of temperament explained 48% of the variance in social skills, with attentional self-regulation the most powerful predictor, and sociability and reactivity also contributing. Temperament data from 7–8 years of age explained 20%, and from 5–6 years 16%, of the variance in social competence at 11–12 years, with task orientation and flexibility (attentional and emotional self-regulation) being the most important predictors each time. Reports of temperament at 1–3 and 3–4 years also predicted significant, but modest, amounts of variance.

Temperament contributions to children's sympathetic capacities were explored by Murphy, Shepard, Eisenberg, Fabes, and Guthrie (1999). Negative correlations were found between teacher-reported sympathetic tendencies at 10–12 years and negative emotionality assessed concurrently and 2 and 4 years previously; and between negative emotionality and concurrent parent-reported sympathy. Positive correlations between regulation capacities and teacher- and parent-reported sympathy were found contemporaneously and 2 years earlier. Self-regulation capacities explained unique variance after controlling for the effects of negative emotionality, but the reverse was not true. Here again, the critical role of self-regulation capacities is evident.

Sex differences

Sex differences emerge in a number of studies. Among preschool-aged boys, high negative emotionality was related to poor social skills, and low emotionality to good skills. Among girls, high emotionality was again related to low social skills, but girls with moderate and low emotionality did not differ in social skills (Eisenberg et al., 1993). This suggests that high negative emotionality constitutes a risk for both boys and girls, whereas low negative emotionality is protective only for boys.

In a study of third through sixth graders, Eisenberg et al. (1996) found that girls received more prosocial nominations from peers and were more accepted, socially competent, and popular than boys. Analyses assessing direct relationships between individual temperament dimensions and prosocial peer nominations showed that high emotionality was negatively related to prosocial nominations for both sexes, although by parent report for girls and teacher report for boys. Attentional regulation was correlated with prosocial nominations, but only for boys. However, when the interactive effects of emotionality and attentional regulation on prosocial peer nominations were investigated, the effect of high emotionality was found to be moderated by levels of attention regulation, with sex differences again evident. Poorly regulated boys received lower prosocial nominations and highly regulated girls received higher nominations, regardless of level of emotionality. In contrast, higher emotionality was associated with lower prosocial nominations for boys with better self-regulation and for girls with poorer self-regulation. Overall, these results suggest the existence of complex sex differences in the relationships between aspects of temperament and social competence from the preschool age onwards, that may also be context-dependent.

Sex differences also feature in research on prosocial outcomes. Kochanska, DeVet, Goldman, Murray, and Putnam (1994), using a sample of children from 21 to 70 months, identified two higher order components of conscience, named Affective Discomfort and Moral Regulation/Vigilance. Girls had higher levels of Affective Discomfort, which was predicted by higher reactivity and focus/effortful control, but no temperament dimensions were predictive for boys. For both sexes, high focus/effortful control was associated with higher Moral Regulation/Vigilance. Reactivity among girls and impulsivity and sensation seeking among boys were related to lower levels of Moral Regulation/Vigilance.

Girls are consistently found to have higher levels of empathy, sympathy, and conscience than boys, and numerous sex differences are apparent in the connections between temperament and these aspects of functioning. Bryant (1987) found that emotional intensity and low soothability were related to higher empathy for girls, but not boys. The teacher-reported relationships found between negative emotionality, regulation, and sympathy described above (Murphy et al., 1999) were carried by significant results for girls but not boys, while connections between parent-reported regulation and sympathy were carried by significant results for boys and not girls. Clearly this is an area deserving more systematic investigation, from which the need for gender-specific models of pathways may emerge.

Summary

A small set of temperament dimensions are consistently associated with children's levels of social skills. Of particular relevance are negative emotionality or reactivity (particularly intensity, irritability, and mood), both emotional regulation (the ability to control emotional arousal) and attentional regulation (maintaining attention and following tasks through to completion) and approach/sociability.

For prosocial capacities, the temperament dimensions of importance include inhibition or shyness, emotionality, and self-regulation. Unlike the findings described in previous sections, here aspects of negative emotionality appear to contribute positively to a prosocial outcome. This alerts us to the fact that negative emotionality comprises two aspects: distress and fear reactions; and irritability and anger – the former appear implicated in the development of prosocial behavior, whereas the latter are associated with poor peer relations and, as will be seen later, in aggressive and acting-out behavior.

While the majority of findings suggest direct linear relationships between temperament and these outcomes, evidence is accumulating that temperament-by-parenting and temperament-by-temperament interactions are important contributors to the developmental processes involved.

Temperamental Influences on Maladaptive Social Behaviors

One of the most extensively researched issues in the temperament literature is the contribution of temperament to the development of socially maladaptive behaviors, particularly externalizing behavior problems (EBPs) such as aggression and oppositional behaviors. Given several recent reviews (e.g., Rothbart & Bates, 1998; Sanson & Prior, 1999), only highlights of this research will be presented, focusing particularly on longitudinal studies which allow stronger conclusions to be drawn about temporal and causal pathways. We also include findings from studies investigating temperament contributions to problematic social interactions, such as peer conflict and communication difficulties. Once again, there is an absence of studies on social class or cultural differences in the links between temperament and behavior problems.

Preschoolers (3- to 4-year-olds)

In a playground observational study, Billman and McDevitt (1980) found associations between parent- and teacher-reported temperament dimensions of activity level, intensity, distractibility, threshold, and rhythmicity and aspects of social behavior such as hitting, taking an object, and having an object taken away. Associations between a "difficult" temperament profile and EBPs have been consistently reported. ATP children with stable patterns of aggressive behavior from 3–4 to 7–8 years were consistently distinguished from transiently aggressive and nonaggressive groups on an easy–difficult temperament factor (Kingston & Prior, 1995). They also had poorer mother–child relationships, higher levels of sibling hostility, and harsher parenting practices. Similarly, the Bloomington Longitudinal Study revealed modest associations between temperamental "difficultness" (a combination of infant and toddler negative affectivity and attention-demanding characteristics) and EBPs at the preschool and middle childhood stages (Bates et al., 1991). Resistance to control and low manageability at 2 years were associated with conflicts with parents and parental management difficulties at the same age, and predictive of long-term EBPs for boys.

Individual temperament dimensions have also been linked to EBPs. Hagekull (1994) found that toddler impulsivity, activity, and negative emotionality were predictive of EBPs at 4 years. Oppositional behavior problems showed concurrent positive correlations with high emotionality, high activity, low persistence, and high sociability in a study by Webster-Stratton and Eyberg (1982). In this study, mothers of more difficult children were observed to be more negative and non-accepting when responding to their children, suggesting the presence of interactive processes.

Concurrent and longitudinal relationships between emotional regulation (observed expressiveness of negative emotions), and EBPs (combined parent and teacher report) were reported by Cole, Zahn-Waxler, Fox, Usher, and Welsh (1996). Children who were either inexpressive or highly expressive had more EBP symptoms at preschool age and two years later than did children with "modulated" expressiveness. Rubin, Coplan, Fox, and Calkins (1995) found emotional regulation capacities and social interaction styles combined to predict distinct patterns of externalizing and internalizing behavior problems. Poorly regulated children with high levels of social interaction (low regulation–high sociability) had more EBPs than high regulation–high sociability and average groups, while the low regulation–low sociability group had more internalizing problems than high regulation–low sociability and average groups. Thus emotional dysregulation may be a generalized risk factor for adjustment difficulties, the expression of which is affected by the presence of other more specific risk factors, such as social interaction skills.

Early school age (5-to 7-year-olds)

Several studies report longitudinal associations between a "difficult" temperament profile in toddlerhood or early childhood and school-age EBPs (e.g., Guerin, Gottfried, & Thomas, 1997; Maziade et al., 1990). More specific associations between temperament dimensions and EBPs are also evident. Parent-reported negative emotionality at 5 years was a substantial predictor of teacher-reported EBPs at 8 years, and a significant but relatively weak predictor of social behavior (Nelson, Martin, Hodge, Havill, & Kanphaus, 1999). In an ATP study investigating longitudinal predictors of early school-age hyperactive and/or aggressive problems, Sanson, Smart, Prior, and Oberklaid (1993) showed that the pure aggressive and comorbid hyperactive-aggressive groups had been less cooperative/manageable, more active/reactive and more irritable in infancy and toddlerhood, and more inflexible and impersistent in early childhood than those with only hyperactivity or neither problem. Other risk factors, including more negative parental perceptions of the child, larger family size, and more family stresses, also differentiated the groups.

Later elementary school age (8- to 12-year-olds)

Regulation capacities, particularly emotional regulation, and emotionality/reactivity are of importance for EBPs at this age. Wertleib, Weigel, Springer, and Feldstein (1987) found that negative mood, nonadaptability, activity, intensity, nonpersistence, and irregularity, were related to concurrent EBPs. Powerful prediction to concurrent EBPs was found by McClowry et al. (1993), particularly from negative reactivity but also from low persistence and maternal hassles. Children with oppositional or conduct disorder diagnoses were more likely to have "difficult" temperament characteristics such as low adaptability, distractibility and approach, and high intensity and negative mood (Maziade, 1989). In the ATP sample, boys with EBPs at 11–12 years had been consistently more irritable and inflexible in earlier years, while EBP girls had shown a similar but weaker pattern of differences on these factors (Sanson, Oberklaid, Prior, Amos, & Smart, 1996). Earlier low persistence was related to EBP outcomes for both boys and girls.

Sex differences

Given the large body of research on temperament-EBP connections, surprisingly few studies have explicitly investigated sex differences. As Sanson and Prior (1999) note, such research is impeded by the lower rates of EBPs among girls, the differential expression of EBPs across the sexes (e.g., physical vs. relational aggression), and the questionable applicability of the current methods of assessing EBPs for females. Nevertheless, some sex differences are apparent. Fabes, Shepard, Gurthrie, and Martin (1997) found that same-sex peer play escalated problem behavior among boys who had high arousal levels, whereas it decreased problem behavior for high-arousal girls. Sanson et al. (1996) found that inflexibility and irritability were stronger longitudinal predictors of EBPs for boys than girls, while low approach and high anxiety (often found to be precursors of internalizing problems) sometimes featured as predictors of EBPs for girls, but never for boys. In a study of sex differences in the longitudinal precursors of behavior problems at 7–8 years (combined internalizing and externalizing problems) and using temperament and other child and family variables as predictors, Prior, Smart, Sanson and Oberklaid (1993) found that temperamental inflexibility (principally tapping reactivity) was the most powerful predictor for both sexes. However, substantial sex differences were also noted. For boys, persistence at the earlier timepoints was important, whereas for girls, persistence was less salient, and parental use of punishment, low child centredness, and poorer maternal psychological functioning were powerful precursors.

Summary

In summary, the temperament dimensions which have been particularly implicated in the development of aggressive and oppositional behavior problems include: negative emotionality; aspects of reactivity such as inflexibility; low attention regulation capacities; and a "difficult" temperament profile. A notable trend from studies including both prosocial and maladaptive outcomes (e.g., Billman & McDevitt, 1980; Nelson et al., 1999) is the consistently stronger association of temperament characteristics to problematic, as compared with prosocial, outcomes. Again research has concentrated on investigating direct linear relationships, but mediated processes and temperament interactions are beginning to emerge.

Conclusion

This review has documented substantial relationships between temperament and social development. These include concurrent and across-time relationships, from very early to late childhood. It thus appears incontestable that these intrinsic differences between children are of consequence to their social development and should be incorporated into theoretical model building about the processes of social development.

Further, it is clear that there are differential relationships between specific aspects of temperament and particular social developmental outcomes. Inhibition appears to be central to peer relations, along with reactivity and attentional self-regulation. Attentional and emotional self-regulation emerged as important to social competence and prosocial capacities. Reactivity and attentional and emotional self-regulation appear the most salient temperamental contributors to externalizing behaviors.

In general, temperament traits regarded as problematic are associated with poorer social developmental outcomes, but interestingly, aspects of negative reactivity appear to enhance development of conscience, and the cross-cultural studies of Chen and colleagues indicate that the role of inhibition is moderated by culturally based beliefs about desirable child outcomes. These findings take us back to Thomas and Chess' notion of "goodness of fit" between a temperament attribute and the expectations of the particular social context, direct us away from simplistic ascriptions of temperament traits as "difficult," and indicate the inadequacy of global constructs like "difficult temperament."

One implication of the differential relationships between temperamental attributes and outcomes is that careful measurement of temperament is needed. Greater consensus and uniformity in the conceptualizations and operationalizations of temperament would facilitate interpretation of findings; given current understanding, the broadband dimensions of reactivity, self-regulation, and approach/withdrawal tendencies appear good candidates for an agreed framework. However, the data reviewed show that these constructs may also need to be decomposed; in the case of self-regulation, into attentional and emotional components; and in the case of negative reactivity, into fearful, anxious and angry, irritable affects. In each case, different implications for social development are apparent.

The difficulty of separating temperament measures from measures of developmental outcomes, especially but not solely in relation to internalizing problems like social withdrawal, suggests that the reliable and valid measurement of temperament remains a concern. Ad hoc approaches, such as relabeling measures originally designed to tap behavior as measures of temperament, is a problematic recent trend. Continued attention to measurement issues is needed.

Much research to date has relied on correlational analyses, often with concurrent data, with relatively little attention to the developmental processes involved. However, there are encouraging recent exceptions, such as the models of the development of social withdrawal, social competence, and conscience development described here. These models provide hypotheses which can be tested in future research, and are clear direction setters for future theorizing.

A feature of these models is that they posit interactive processes, either between temperament and parenting, or between different aspects of temperament. It is these interactive models which offer most hope for increased understanding of development, and also provide guidance for effective interventions which take the child, their parents, their social context and their interrelationships into account. Testing of these interactive models needs the application of sophisticated statistical modeling to elucidate potentially nonlinear interactive relationships between variables.

Gender differences in aspects of social development such as prosocial behavior and EBPs are pervasive, and the research reviewed suggests that different processes may link temperament and development in boys and girls. As yet, no clear picture of systematic differences in patterns of associations has emerged. The examination of gender differences in the role of temperament in paths to social development is a clear need for future research. Similarly, virtually no research has examined social class and culture as moderators of relationships between temperament and social development, but the little that does exist suggests that this will be a very fruitful area for future research.

Findings of temperamental contributions to development can sometimes be interpreted as a form of "biological determinism." However, the impact of temperament depends largely on its "fit" with the context, and findings of moderate stability over time indicate that it is not immutable. In taking temperament into account in attempts to optimize each child's social development, therefore, the tasks are to arrange the environment so as to maximize the "fit" between the child and the environment, to match parenting and educational practices to the characteristics of the child, and to help the child develop strategies to best manage their temperamental proclivities.

References

Allen, K., & Prior, M. (1995). Assessment of the validity of easy and difficult temperament through observed mother–child behaviours. *International Journal of Behavioural Development, 18*, 609–630.

Bates, J. E., Bayles, K., Bennett, D. S., Ridge, B., & Brown, M. M. (1991). Origins of externalizing behavior problems at eight years of age. In D. J. Pepler & K. H. Rubin (Eds.), *The development and treatment of childhood aggression* (pp. 93–121). Hillsdale, NJ: Erlbaum.

Billman, J., & McDevitt, S. C. (1980). Convergence of parent and observer ratings of temperament in observations of peer interaction in nursery school. *Child Development, 51*, 395–400.

Bryant, B. K. (1987). Mental health, temperament, family, and friends: Perspectives on children's empathy and social perspective taking. In N. Eisenberg & J. Strayer (Eds.), *Empathy and its development* (pp. 245–270). Cambridge, England: Cambridge University Press.

Burgess, K. B., Rubin, K. H., Cheah, C. S. L., & Nelson, L. J. (2001). Behavioral inhibition, social withdrawal, and parenting. In R. Crozier & L. Alden (Eds.), *International handbook of social anxiety* (pp. 137–159). New York: Wiley.

Chen, X., Hastings, P. D., Rubin, K. H., Chen, H., Cen, G., & Stewart, S. L. (1998). Child-rearing attitudes and behavioral inhibition in Chinese and Canadian toddlers: A cross-cultural study. *Developmental Psychology, 34*, 677–686.

Chen, X., Rubin, K. H., & Li, B. (1995). Social and school adjustment of shy and aggressive children in China. *Development and Psychopathology, 7*, 337–349.

Cicchetti, D., & Cohen, D. J. (1995). Perspectives on developmental psychopathology. In D. Cicchetti & D. J. Cohen (Eds.), *Developmental psychopathology: Volume 1. Theory and methods* (pp. 3–20). New York: Wiley.

Cole, P. M., Zahn-Waxler, C., Fox, N. A., Usher, B. A., & Welsh, J. D. (1996). Individual differences in emotion regulation and behavior problems in preschool children. *Journal of Abnormal Psychology, 105*, 518–529.

Dunn, J., & Cutting, A. L. (1999). Understanding others, and individual differences in friendship interactions in young children. *Social Development, 8*, 201–219.

Eisenberg, N., Fabes, R. A., Bernzweig, J., Karbon, M., Poulon, R., & Hanish, L. (1993). The relations of emotionality and regulation to preschoolers' social skills and sociometric status. *Child Development, 64*, 1418–1438.

Eisenberg, N., Fabes, R. A., Guthrie, I. K., & Reiser, N. (2000). Dispositional emotionality and regulation: Their role in predicting quality of social functioning. *Journal of Personality and Social Psychology, 78*, 136–157.

Eisenberg, N., Fabes, R. A., Karbon, R., Murphy, B. C., Wosinski, M., Polazzi, L., Carlo, G., & Juhnke, C. (1996). The relations of children's dispositional prosocial behavior to emotionality, regulation, and social functioning. *Child Development, 67*, 974–992.

Eisenberg, N., Shepard, S. A., Fabes, R. A., Murphy, B. C., & Guthrie, I. K. (1998). Shyness and children's emotionality, regulation, and coping: Contemporaneous, longitudinal, and across-context relations. *Child Development, 69*, 767–790.

Fabes, R. A., Eisenberg, N., Jones, S., Smith, M., Guthrie, I. K., Poulin, R., Shepard, S., & Friedman, J. (1999). Regulation, emotionality, and preschoolers' socially competent peer interactions. *Child Development, 70*, 432–442.

Fabes, R. A., Shepard, S., Guthrie I. K., & Martin, C. L. (1997). Roles of temperamental arousal and gender-segregated play in young children's social adjustment. *Developmental Psychology, 33*, 393–702.

Farver, J. A. M., & Branstetter, W. H. (1994). Preschoolers' prosocial responses to their peers' distress. *Developmental Psychology, 30*, 334–341.

Fox, N. A., & Calkins, S. D. (1993). Pathways to aggression and social withdrawal: Interactions among temperament, attachment, and regulation. In K. H. Rubin & J. B. Asendorpf (Eds.), *Social withdrawal, inhibition, and shyness in childhood* (pp. 81–100). Hillsdale, NJ: Erlbaum.

Gersten, M. (1988). Behavioral inhibition in the classroom. In J. S. Reznick (Ed.), *Perspectives on behavioral inhibition* (pp. 71–91). Chicago: University of Chicago Press.

Guerin, D. W., Gottfried, A. W., & Thomas, C. W. (1997). Difficult temperament and behavior problems: A longitudinal study from 1.5 to 12 years. *International Journal of Behavioral Development, 21*, 71-90.

Guralnick, M. J., & Groom, J. M. (1990). The correspondence between temperament and peer interactions for normally developing and mildly delayed preschool children. *Child: Care, Health and Development, 16*, 165–175.

Hagekull, B. (1994). Infant temperament and early childhood functioning: Possible relations to the five-factor model. In C. J. Halverson, Jr., G. A. Kohnstamm, & R. P. Martin (Eds.), *The developing structure of temperament and personality* (pp. 227–240). Hillsdale, NJ: Erlbaum.

Hart, C. H., Yang, C., Nelson, L. J., Robinson, C. C., Olsen, J. A., Nelson, D. A., Porter, C. L., Jin, S., Olsen, S. F., & Wu, P. (2000). Peer acceptance in early childhood and subtypes of socially withdrawn behavior in China, Russia and the United States. *International Journal of Behavioral Development, 24*, 73–81.

Hinde, R. A., Tamplin, A., & Barrett, J. (1993). Social isolation in 4-year-olds. *British Journal of Developmental Psychology, 11*, 211–236.

Kagan, J. (1988). The concept of behavioral inhibition to the unfamiliar. In J. S. Reznick (Ed.), *Perspectives on behavioral inhibition* (pp. 1–23). Chicago: University of Chicago Press.

Kagan, J., Reznick, J. S., Clarke, C., Snidman, N., & Garcia-Coll, C. (1984). Behavioral inhibition to the unfamiliar. *Child Development, 55*, 2215–2225.

Kagan, J., Snidman, N., & Arcus, D. (1998). Childhood derivatives of high and low reactivity in infancy. *Child Development, 69*, 1483–1493.

Keogh, B. K., & Burstein, N. D. (1988). Relationship of temperament to preschoolers' interactions with peers and teachers. *Exceptional Children, 54*, 456–461.

Kingston, L., & Prior, M. (1995). The development of patterns of stable, transient and school-age onset aggressive behavior in young children. *Journal of the American Academy of Child and Adolescent Psychiatry, 34*, 348–358.

Kochanska, G. (1993). Toward a synthesis of parental socialization and child temperament in early development of conscience. *Child Development, 64*, 325–347.

Kochanska, G. (1997). Multiple pathways to conscience for children with different temperaments: From toddlerhood to age 5. *Developmental Psychology, 33*, 228–240.

Kochanska, G., DeVet, K., Goldman, M., Murray, K., & Putnam, S. P. (1994). Maternal reports of conscience development and temperament in young children. *Child Development, 65*, 852–868.

Kochanska, G., Murray, K. T., & Coy, K. C. (1997). Inhibitory control as a contributor to conscience in childhood: From toddler to early school age. *Child Development, 67*, 490–507.

Kochanska, G., & Radke-Yarrow, M. (1992). Inhibition in toddlerhood and the dynamics of the child's interaction with an unfamiliar peer at age five. *Child Development, 63*, 325–335.

Kurdek. L., & Lillie, R. (1985). The relation between classroom social status and classmate likeability, compromising skill, temperament, and neighborhood social interactions. *Journal of Applied Developmental Psychology, 6*, 31–41.

Maziade, M. (1989). Should adverse temperament matter to the clinician? An empirically based answer. In G. A. Kohnstamm, J. E. Bates, & M. K. Rothbart (Eds.), *Temperament in childhood* (pp. 421–435). Chichester, England: Wiley.

Maziade, M., Caron, C., Cote, R., Merette, C., Bernier, H., Laplante, B., Boutin, P., & Thivierge, J. (1990). Psychiatric status of adolescents who had extreme temperaments at age seven. *American Journal of Psychiatry, 147*, 1531–1536.

McClowry, S. G., Giangrande, S. K., Tommasini, N. R., Clinton, W., Foreman, N. S., Lynch, K., & Ferketich, S. (1994). The effects of child temperament, maternal characteristics, and family circumstances on the maladjustment of school-age children. *Research in Nursing and Health, 17*, 25–35.

Mednick, B. R., Hocevar, D., Schulsinger, C., & Baker, R. L. (1996). Personality and demographic characteristics of mothers and their ratings of their 3- to 10-year-old children's temperament. *Merrill-Palmer Quarterly, 42*, 397–417.

Murphy, B. C., Shepard, S., Eisenberg, N., Fabes, R. A., & Guthrie, I. K. (1999). Contemporaneous and longitudinal prediction of dispositional sympathy to emotionality, regulation, and social functioning. *Journal of Early Adolescence, 19*, 66–97.

Nelson, B., Martin, R. P., Hodge, S., Havill, V., & Kanphaus, R. (1999). Modeling the prediction of elementary school adjustment from preschool temperament. *Personality and Individual Differences, 26*, 687–700.

Parker-Cohen, N. Y., & Bell, R. Q. (1988). The relationship between temperament and social adjustment to peers. *Early Childhood Research Quarterly, 3*, 179–192.

Paterson, G., & Sanson, A. (1999). The association of behavioural adjustment to temperament, parenting and family characteristics among 5-year-old children. *Social Development, 8*, 293–309.

Pedlow, R., Sanson, A., Prior, M., & Oberklaid, F. (1993). Stability of maternally reported temperament from infancy to 8 years. *Developmental Psychology, 29*, 998–1007.

Prior, M., Sanson, A., Smart, D., & Oberklaid, F. (2000). *Pathways from infancy to adolescence: The Australian Temperament Project: 1983–2000.* Melbourne, Australia: Australian Institute of Family Studies.

Prior, M., Smart, D. F., Sanson, A. V., & Oberklaid, F. (1993). Sex differences in psychological adjustment from infancy to eight years. *Journal of the American Academy of Child and Adolescent Psychiatry, 32*, 291–304.

Reznick, J. S., Kagan, J., Snidman, N., Gersten, M., Baak, K., & Rosenberg A. (1986). Inhibited and uninhibited children: A follow-up study. *Child Development, 57*, 660–680.

Rothbart, M. K., Ahadi, S. A., & Hershey, K. L. (1994). Temperament and social behavior in childhood. *Merrill-Palmer Quarterly, 40*, 21–39.

Rothbart, M. K., & Bates, J. E. (1998). Temperament. In W. Damon (Series Ed.), & N. Eisenberg (Vol. Ed.), *Handbook of child psychology: Volume 3. Social, emotional and, personality development,* 5th ed. (pp. 105–176). New York: Wiley.

Rubin, K. H., Coplan, R. J., Fox, N. A., & Calkins, S. D. (1995). Emotionality, emotion regulation, and preschoolers' social adaptation. *Development and Psychopathology, 7*, 49–62.

Rubin, K. H., LeMare, L. J., & Lollis, S. (1990). Social withdrawal in childhood: Developmental pathways to peer rejection. In S. R. Asher & J. D. Coie (Eds.), *Peer rejection in childhood* (pp. 217–249). New York: Cambridge University Press.

Rubin, K. H., & Stewart, S. L. (1996). Social withdrawal. In E. J. Mash & R. A. Barkley (Eds.), *Child psychopathology* (pp. 277–307). New York: Guilford Press.

Sanson, A. (2000, July). Temperament and social development in children. Keynote address at the 16th biennial meeting of the International Society for the Study of Behavioral Development, Beijing, China.

Sanson, A., Oberklaid, F., Prior, M., Amos, D., & Smart, D. (1996, August). Risk factors for 11–12 years olds' internalising and externalising behaviour problems. Paper presented at the International Society for the Study of Behavioural Development Conference, Quebec City, Canada.

Sanson, A., & Prior, M. (1999). Temperament and behavioral precursors to oppositional defiant disorder and conduct disorder. In H. C. Quay & A. E. Hogan (Eds.), *Handbook of disruptive behavior disorders* (pp. 397–417). New York: Kluwer /Plenum.

Sanson, A., & Rothbart, M. K. (1995). Child temperament and parenting. In M. H. Bornstein (Ed.), *Handbook of parenting: Volume 4. Applied and practical parenting* (pp. 299–321). Mahwah, NJ: Erlbaum.

Sanson, A. V., Smart, D. F., Prior, M., & Oberklaid, F. (1993). Precursors of hyperactivity and aggression. *Journal of the American Academy of Child and Adolescent Psychiatry, 32*, 1207–1216.

Sanson, A., Smart, D., Prior, M., & Oberklaid, F. (1996, August). Early characteristics of 11–12 year old children with competent, average and problematic peer relationships. Paper presented at the 26th International Congress of Psychology, Montreal, Canada.

Skarpness, L. R., & Carson, D. K. (1986). Temperament, communicative competence and the psychological adjustment of kindergarten children. *Psychological Reports, 59*, 1299–1306.

Slabach, E. H., Morrow, J., & Wachs, T. D. (1991). Questionnaire measurement of infant and child temperament: Current status and future directions. In J. Strelau & A. Angleitner (Eds.), *Explorations in temperament: International perspectives on theory and measurement* (pp. 205–234). New York: Plenum.

Stocker, C., & Dunn, J. (1990). Sibling relationships in childhood: Links with friendships and peer relationships. *British Journal of Developmental Psychology, 8*, 227–244.

Thomas, A., & Chess, S. (1977). *Temperament and development.* New York: Bruner/Mazel.

Thomas, A., Chess, S., Birch, H. G., Hertzig, M. E., & Korn, S. (1963). *Behavioral individuality in early childhood.* New York: New York University Press.

Webster-Stratton, C., & Eyberg, S. M. (1982). Child temperament: Relationship with child behavior problems and parent–child interactions. *Journal of Clinical Child Psychology, 11*,123–129.

Wertleib, D., Weigel, C., Springer, T., & Feldstein, M. (1987). Temperament as a moderator of children's stressful experiences. *American Journal of Orthopsychiatry, 57*, 234–245.

Youngblade, L. M., & Mulvihill, B. A. (1998). Individual differences in homeless preschoolers' social behavior. *Journal of Applied Developmental Psychology, 19*, 593–614.

7

Sex Differences in Social Behavior

Susan Golombok and Melissa Hines

From an early age, boys and girls can be easily distinguished according to their sex. While this is partly due to their appearance and the way in which their parents dress them and cut their hair, it is also because of the things that children do. Boys and girls like to play with different toys, prefer different games, and engage in different activities. Long before they reach school age it is possible to tell with a reasonable degree of accuracy whether a child is a boy or a girl simply on the basis of his or her behavior. This does not mean that all boys engage in male activities, or that all girls engage in female activities, all of the time. There is a great deal of overlap between the sexes with some girls being more "boyish" than the average boy and some boys behaving in a way that is more typical of a "girlish" girl. Although there is considerable variation in the behavior of children within each sex, it is generally more acceptable for girls to behave like boys than it is for boys to behave like girls. This may explain why the term "tomboy" used to describe masculine girls is often used endearingly whereas "sissy" is a much more derogatory term when applied to feminine boys.

What exactly are the differences in behavior shown by boys and girls? And how do these differences develop? These are the questions that will be addressed in this chapter. Firstly, sex differences in social behavior will be described from the preschool to the elementary school years. This will be followed by a consideration of the various theories that have been put forward to explain this phenomenon. The sections on biological theories draw from Collaer and Hines (1995) and Hines (2000) while those on psychological theories draw from Golombok and Fivush (1994). As we shall see, some theories have greater empirical support than others. Following Maccoby (1988), the terms "sex" and "gender" will be used interchangeably throughout the chapter without any assumption that "sex" implies biological causes or that "gender" results from socialization.

Preschool (3–4 Years)

Gender identity

By the time of their third birthday, children have generally developed a rudimentary sense of gender identity (Slaby & Frey, 1975). When asked "Are you a boy or a girl?" they will give the right answer. They can also correctly identify other people as male or female. But children of this age use physical appearance to make their judgments. A person with long hair who is wearing a skirt will be deemed female, and a short-haired person with a necktie will be seen as male, purely because of their external appearance. If these same people change their clothes and hairstyle to look like the other sex, children will report that their gender has changed as well.

At around 3 to 4 years of age, children develop gender stability, that is, they begin to recognize that gender does not change over time (Slaby & Frey, 1975). They realize that if they are a girl or a boy now then they used to be a girl baby or a boy baby, and that they will grow up to be a woman or a man. However, they still believe that children can change gender by changing their behavior; if a boy wears a dress, he can become a girl, and if a girl plays with guns, she can become a boy.

Toy preference

One of the most striking differences between boys and girls is their preference for different types of toys. This can be detected in 1 year olds (Snow, Jacklin, & Maccoby, 1983), and by 3 years of age, girls are much more likely than boys to play with dolls, dolls' houses, tea sets and other domestic toys whereas boys are most often to be found with toy guns, swords, cars, trains, and trucks (De Lucia, 1963; O'Brien & Huston, 1985; Sutton-Smith & Rosenberg, 1971).

Playmate preference

From as early as 3 years old, girls prefer other girls as playmates and boys prefer to play with boys (Maccoby & Jacklin, 1987). This phenomenon, known as "gender segregation," is not specific to particular nationalities or cultures. It can be seen in children's playgrounds around the world. Children's preference for same-sex playmates is a universal aspect of growing up (Whiting & Edwards, 1988). Gender segregation is most likely to occur when children are left to their own devices, especially when they are with others of a similar age, which suggests that it is children, not adults, who are driving this process. In an observational study of children in a daycare setting, LaFreniere, Strayor, and Gauthier (1984) found that the tendency for girls to play together became apparent at age 2. For boys, the preference for male playmates occurred slightly later but was clearly established at 3 years of age. Howes (1988) reported similar findings. Like LaFreniere et al. (1984), she observed children in daycare, and showed that 3 year olds were more likely to form new friendships with children of the same sex.

Play style

Differences in the play styles of boys and girls can also be seen from 3 years of age (Maccoby, 1998; Maccoby & Jacklin, 1987; Pitcher & Shultz, 1983). Boys tend to play in a more active, rough-and-tumble, and sometimes physically aggressive fashion than girls who tend to talk more to each other and be more nurturant than boys. When girls are aggressive this is more likely to take the form of behaviors intended to damage relationships such as exclusion from a circle of friends (Crick, Casas, & Mosher, 1997; McNeilly-Choque, Hart, Robinson, Nelson, & Olsen, 1996). Boys also like to play outdoors in large groups while girls are more often to be found in twos or threes indoors. Differences in the way in which boys and girls resolve conflict are also apparent from age 3. Whereas girls incline toward reaching a compromise, it is more common for boys to use physical force (Sheldon, 1990). In addition, pretend play differentiates the sexes with boys acting out heroic roles involving fighting and adventure, and girls preferring to be family characters or dressing up in feminine clothes.

Early School (5–7 Years)

Gender identity

It is not until the early school years that children attain gender constancy, the final stage of gender identity development (Slaby & Frey, 1975), and understand that gender is a fundamental aspect of a person's identity. They now realize that gender is constant across time and across all situations, and that however much someone wants to be the other sex, behaves like the other sex, and wears other-sex clothes, this simply cannot happen. The attainment of gender constancy is closely related to the conservation stage of cognitive development (Piaget, 1968). When Marcus and Overton (1978) administered both a conservation task and a gender constancy task to early school age children they found that children who could successfully complete the conservation task were more likely to pass the gender constancy task as well. There has been some controversy over the age at which children reach gender constancy, with different studies producing different findings depending on the assessment methods used (Emmerich, Goldman, Kirsh & Sharabany, 1977; Martin & Halverson, 1981; Zucker et al., 1999). Many children, it seems, do not reach the stage of gender constancy until the end of the early school years. It used to be thought that it was necessary for children to develop a full understanding of the gender concept before they would consistently engage in sex-typed behavior (Kohlberg, 1966) but the differences in toy, playmate, and activity preference shown by children as young as 3 years old clearly demonstrate that this is not the case.

Toy preference

The sex difference in toy preference that is apparent among preschool children continues to characterize the early school years. In a study of 3–5 year olds, Martin, Wood, and Little (1990) demonstrated a greater preference among boys for a car, an airplane, and a tool set and a greater preference among girls for a tea set, a doll, and a haircare set. Children in this study were also more likely to report that they preferred unfamiliar neutral items such as a pizza cutter and a hole puncher if presented to them as something that children of their sex really like. Similarly, when parents were asked to rate how often their children played with a selection of toys, differences between boys and girls were reported for guns, jewelry, tool sets, dolls, dolls' carriages, trains, cars, swords, and tea sets (Golombok & Rust, 1993).

Playmate preference

Gender segregation is an important feature of the early school years. Eleanor Maccoby and Carol Jacklin examined the playmate preferences of 100 children at 4.5 years old and again at 6.5 years (Maccoby & Jacklin, 1987). When first observed, the children were spending nearly three times as much time playing with same-sex peers than other-sex peers. By the second observation, only 2 years later, the amount of time spent playing with same-sex peers was more than 10 times greater than that spent with peers of the other sex. A similar increase in the preference for same-sex peers was demonstrated by Serbin, Powlishta, and Gulko (1993) when they compared children in kindergarten with children in the early school years. The process of gender segregation involves not only the preference for same-sex playmates but also the avoidance of playmates of the other sex as well.

Play style

As children move from preschool to the early school years, the play styles of boys and girls continue to diverge. Achieving dominance appears to be of particular importance to boys. In order to have status, boys need to be seen as "tough" (Maccoby, 1998). The way in which girls and boys communicate is also different. Girls talk to each other to form and strengthen relationships. Boys use language to give information, assert themselves, and command attention (Lever, 1976; Maccoby & Jacklin, 1987). Boys of this age like to play in large groups of other boys whereas girls prefer the company of one or two female friends. The nature of these relationships also differs between the sexes. Whereas girls' friendships are characterized by emotional and physical closeness, the friendships of boys are founded on shared activities and interests (Maccoby, 1998).

Elementary School (8–11 Years)

Toy preference

A study of letters to Santa Claus by elementary school children revealed a marked difference in the toys requested by boys and girls (Robinson & Morris, 1986). More than one quarter of the girls wanted a doll compared with less than 1% of the boys whereas almost half of the boys but less than 10% of the girls asked for some kind of vehicle. It seems that right until the end of elementary school boys and girls have a strong preference for sex-typed toys.

Playmate preference

The preference for same-sex peers is strongest among elementary school children. In reviewing the literature on relationships within the school environment, Maccoby (1998) reported that children's best friends are almost always the same sex as themselves. Furthermore, when observed during free time – in the playground, at lunch, or in the corridors – boys and girls are most likely to be found interacting with others of their own sex. Maccoby (1998) illustrates this with a description of behavior in the lunchroom: "In school lunchrooms, the children usually have a shared understanding that certain tables are 'girls' tables' and other tables are for boys. Very few instances are seen in which a child sits down next to a child of the other sex after emerging from the cafeteria line." A recent study of 8–11 year olds was particularly revealing. When Gray and Feldman (1997) investigated peer-group interaction at an ungraded school where boys and girls of all ages had the opportunity to mix, more than half of the children spent no time at all with children of the other sex. And from their examination of the peer preferences of children of different ages, Serbin et al. (1993) reported that 95% of elementary school children preferred same-sex peers. This is not just a Western phenomenon. The research of Whiting and Edwards (1988) shows that in India, Africa, South East Asia, and Central America, children of this age spend three quarters of their play time with peers of their own sex.

Play styles

In the elementary school years, much of boys' free time is spent in large groups of other boys playing competitive games. When Crombie and Desjardins (1993) observed boys and girls at play, they found that boys in large groups were involved in competition with other boys 50% of the time whereas this was true for girls in their smaller groups only 1% of the time. Girls spend most of their free time conversing with a female best friend, often sharing secrets or talking about mutual interests (Lever, 1976). Tannen (1990) examined the content of girls' and boys' conversations in a laboratory setting. The girls had long, intimate conversations. Boys, in contrast, found little to say and resorted to talking about finding something to do.

Theories attempting to explain the development of sex differences in toy preferences, play-mate preferences, gender identity, and play styles have been classified as biological or psychological. This distinction is somewhat misleading, because psychological processes have a biological basis and because biology and psychology influence one another. In addition, the theories discussed under these headings are not mutually exclusive. Nevertheless, to date, so-called biological and psychological research has proceeded largely separately, and so each will be discussed in turn.

Biological Explanations

Biological mechanisms underlying sexual development have been studied extensively in nonhuman mammals, and have been found to be similar for the genitalia, the brain, and behavior. These processes are summarized below, and discussed more fully in Collaer and Hines (1995), Goy and McEwen (1980), and Wilson, George, and Griffin (1981).

The primary and immediate biological determinants of sex differences are gonadal hormones. At conception, both genetically male (XY) and female (XX) mammals have the capacity to differentiate phenotypically as either males or females. In XY individuals, a region on the Y chromosome typically directs the primordial gonads (originally identical in males and females) to become testes. If this direction is not given, the gonads differentiate as ovaries.

The human testes differentiate at about week 6 of gestation and begin to produce hormones by about week 8. Testicular hormones then direct sexual differentiation of the internal and external genitalia, where receptors for these hormones are located. Testosterone causes the Wolffian ducts to develop into vas deferens, prostate, and seminal vesicles, while another testicular hormone causes Mullerian tissues, destined to become the uterus, fallopian tubes, and upper vagina, to regress. Testicular hormones also stimulate the external genitalia to become penis and scrotum. In the absence of these hormones, these tissues become the clitoris, labia, and lower vagina, the Wolffian ducts regress and the Mullerian organs develop.

Within the brain, similar processes occur, certainly in nonhuman mammals, and perhaps in humans as well. Like the genitalia, portions of the brain have receptors for testicular hormones. The same brain regions that contain hormone receptors typically show structural sex differences and regulate reproductive behaviors or other behaviors that show sex differences (i.e., differ for males and females of the species). Perhaps the best-known example is the sexually dimorphic nucleus of the pre-optic area (SDN-POA), a region that is larger in male than female rats (and some other species as well). Administering testosterone to genetic females during critical developmental periods increases the size of the nucleus. Similar hormonal effects on brain structure have been noted in other brain regions. In general, administering testosterone or its metabolites sculpts a more masculine-typical brain, while reducing these hormones sculpts a more feminine-typical brain.

Gonadal hormones also influence behavior. Genetic female rats treated with testosterone on the day of birth show increased male-typical sexual behavior, and decreased female-typical sexual behavior, as adults. Similarly, removing testosterone from developing males (by neonatal castration or treatment with anti-androgens) reduces male-typical behavior and increases female-typical behavior in adulthood. Hormones influence not only reproductive behaviors, but also other characteristics that show sex differences. In the rat, these include rough-and-tumble play, activity levels, and aggression. Hormonal influences are not limited to rats, but are seen in many species, including nonhuman primates. In the rhesus macaque, for instance, treating pregnant animals with testosterone produces female offspring who show increased rough-and-tumble (masculine-typical) play, increased masculine-typical sexual behavior, and decreased feminine-typical sexual behavior.

Two additional points regarding hormonal influences on brain development and behavior are relevant. First, hormones do not affect all aspects of sex-typical development in a uniform manner. For instance, hormones influence masculine-typical sexual behavior earlier than feminine-typical sexual behavior. The times of maximal effect are called critical periods, and they differ from one behavior to another. Thus, a brief hormonal perturbation can influence one sex-typical behavior without influencing others. In general, there is an overall critical period when hormones are influential and this corresponds to the time when testicular hormones are higher in developing males than females. In humans this is probably from about week 8 to 24 of gestation and from about the first to the sixth month postnatally. Second, the impact of hormones is graded. A developing organism does not become masculine when testicular hormones exceed a certain threshold and remain feminine otherwise. Instead, the amount of hormone corresponds to the amount of masculine-typical development. Therefore, small or moderate changes in hormones during development can move the organism along a male–female continuum, without causing it to become completely male or completely female. Thus, gradations in hormone levels during development could contribute to individual differences in sex-typical behavior within each sex as well as between the sexes.

Human development

Knowledge of mechanisms underlying sexual differentiation of the mammalian brain and behavior has come from experimental studies in species where hormones can be manipulated. Similar experiments are impossible in humans, because of ethical considerations. Therefore, information on the applicability of these animal models to human development has come from other sources. These include endocrine disorders of prenatal onset, and situations where women have been prescribed hormones during pregnancy. As might be expected, these sources are limited, and it is not possible to discuss the evidence in the age frames specified at the beginning of this chapter. However, where possible, data will be described in terms of the age groups for which they were gathered. In addition, because many studies have involved small numbers of subjects, sample sizes will be specified.

Toy preferences

Girls exposed prenatally to high levels of androgens (the major hormonal products of the testes) show increased preferences for masculine-typical toys. This conclusion is based largely on studies of girls with congenital adrenal hyperplasia (CAH), a genetic disorder involving deficiency in an enzyme (usually 21 hydroxylase) needed to produce cortisol. Because of the deficiency, feedback systems in the brain direct the adrenal glands to produce precursors to cortisol, including androgens. Genetic females with CAH almost always are born with ambiguous genitalia caused by elevated androgen prenatally. The clitoris is enlarged and the labia are partially fused to resemble a scrotum. The degree of virilization varies, ranging from essentially female-appearing genitalia, to genitalia that resemble those of a normal male. In the great majority of cases, diagnosis is made within the first few days or weeks of life, hormones are prescribed to regulate the postnatal hormonal environment, the genitalia are surgically feminized and the child is reared as a girl.

Despite these procedures, girls with CAH show alterations in their toy preferences (Berenbaum & Hines, 1992; Dittman et al., 1990; Ehrhardt & Baker, 1974; Ehrhardt, Epstein, & Money, 1968; Slijper, 1984). Studies have obtained information from questionnaires and interviews with the girls and their mothers, and from direct observation of toy choices in a playroom. Questionnaire and interview studies often combine information on toy choices with other behaviors, such as playmate and activity preferences. When toy choices are considered separately, conclusions are based on a few, or even a single, questionnaire or interview item. However, the observational study indicates that toy choices are altered when considered alone. In this study, 26 girls with CAH (ages 3 to 8 years) spent more time with toys typically preferred by boys (e.g., cars and trucks) and less time with toys typically preferred by girls (e.g., dolls) than did unaffected female relatives (Berenbaum & Hines, 1992).

The interpretability of data from CAH girls has been questioned because of their virilization at birth, and because their parents might treat them differently based on the knowledge that they were exposed to "masculinizing" hormones (Fausto-Sterling, 1992). However, the degree of genital virilization in individual girls does not correlate with the degree of alteration in their toy choices (Berenbaum & Hines, 1992), and interview and questionnaire data suggest that parents treat their CAH daughters as they would other girls (Berenbaum & Hines, 1992; Ehrhardt & Baker, 1974). Indeed, parents are advised by healthcare professionals to encourage feminine development in girls with CAH, and it would seem likely that they would do so.

The observational study of toy choices found no differences between 11 boys with CAH and unaffected boys. This finding, like that of increased masculine-typical toy preferences in CAH girls, is generally consistent with other studies of CAH children (Ehrhardt & Baker, 1974), and with data from studies of other species where adding testosterone to developing males does not typically enhance masculine-typical behavior.

Evidence regarding hormonal influences on toy choices has also come from situations where pregnant women were given hormones for medical reasons. One study involved 10 girls (ages 3 to 14 years) whose mothers were prescribed androgenic progestins during pregnancy (Money & Ehrhardt, 1972). Like girls with CAH, these girls were typically born with virilized genitalia, and surgically feminized during infancy. Sex assignment and rearing were female. Nevertheless, the hormone-exposed girls showed increased masculine-typical toy preferences.

Another study reported on 15 girls (ages 8 to 12 years) whose mothers were prescribed medroxyprogesterone acetate (MPA) during pregnancy. Because MPA counteracts the action of androgen, exposed girls might be expected to show enhanced feminine-typical behavior. The MPA-exposed girls did not differ from matched controls in interest in masculine-typical toys, but there was some evidence of reduced masculine-typical behavior on a composite variable called "tomboyism" (p = .06) and of increased interest in feminine-typical clothing (Ehrhardt, Grisanti, & Meyer-Bahlburg, 1977). MPA-exposed boys might be expected to be less masculine than other boys. Compared to matched controls, 13 MPA-exposed boys (ages 9 to 13 years) showed some reduction in masculine-typical play, but not specifically in toy choices (Meyer-Bahlberg, Feldman, Cohen, & Ehrhardt, 1988).

These studies of administered hormones assessed toy preferences using interviews and questionnaires. Typically, assessments were based on a small number of items in a questionnaire or interview assessing a range of sex-typical behaviors. In addition, exogenous hormone treatments differ from individual to individual and can be as brief as a few days or as long as several months. Thus, some children may not have been exposed to enough hormones to produce behavioral changes. Finally, regarding the studies of MPA, the authors note that effects might be hard to see in girls, because there is little scope for them to become more feminine, while for boys the testes might compensate for the small reduction in hormone levels likely to be produced by MPA. Thus, the studies of MPA-exposed children may have lacked the experimental power to detect hormonal influences on behavior.

Gender identity

Girls with CAH appear to show reduced feminine-typical gender identity or reduced satisfaction with the female gender role. This has been noted in four studies of girls with CAH ranging in age from 4 to 20 years. A total of 63 girls with CAH from three different regions of the United States and from the Netherlands participated in the studies and were compared to their unaffected sisters, as well as to matched controls and girls with other medical disorders. Data were collected using various methods, including interviews, paper and pencil questionnaires, and projective tests (Ehrhardt et al., 1968; Ehrhardt & Baker, 1974; Hurtig & Rosenthal, 1987; Slijper, 1984). A fifth study found that 2 of 18 girls with CAH met the criteria for a clinical diagnosis of gender identity disorder of childhood, as did 5 of 29 additional girls who had been exposed to high levels of androgen prenatally because of other endocrine disorders (Slijper, Drop, Molenaar, & de Muinck Keizer-Schrama, 1998). Two other studies (McGuire, Ryan & Omenn, 1975; Perlman, 1973), including 9 and 15 CAH girls respectively, found no significant alterations in gender identity. Given the small samples of CAH girls typically available for study, what might be more remarkable than one or two failures to find differences in gender identity is the relatively consistent evidence of an alteration in this fundamental aspect of a person's sense of self.

Studies of children exposed prenatally to progestins have generally not reported alterations in gender identity (Ehrhardt et al., 1977; Ehrhardt & Money, 1967; Meyer-Bahlburg et al., 1988). As was the case for toy choices, it is not possible to say whether this reflects a lack of an effect or a lack of power to detect effects. Boys with CAH also have not been found to show alterations in gender identity or satisfaction in the male gender role (Ehrhardt & Baker, 1974), a finding that is again consistent with predictions from animal models.

Playmate preferences

Playmate preferences also are altered in girls exposed to androgens prenatally. Three studies have reported that girls with CAH show reduced preferences for female playmates (Ehrhardt et al., 1968; Ehrhardt & Baker, 1974; Hines & Kaufman, 1994). The studies included a total of 58 CAH girls (ages 3 to 20 years) from three different regions of the United States who were compared to matched or sibling controls. The first two studies used interviews to assess playmate preferences along with other sex-typical behaviors. The third asked children to name their three favorite playmates and calculated the percentage of males. The 10 girls exposed to androgenic progestins who showed increased preferences for male-typical toys also reported increased preferences for male playmates (Money & Ehrhardt, 1972). Studies of MPA-exposed children have not found alterations in playmate preferences (Meyer-Bahlburg et al., 1988). It is again unclear whether this reflects a lack of an effect or a lack of experimental power. Boys with CAH do not show alterations in preferences for male playmates (Ehrhardt & Baker, 1974; Hines & Kaufman, 1994), again consistent with research in other species.

Play styles

Studies of hormone-exposed children have not looked at play styles in a manner comparable to that used in studies of other children. However, there is some information concerning aggression and rough-and-tumble play.

Reports on aggression following prenatal exposure to androgenic hormones do not present a clear picture. One study found that 22 women with CAH scored higher than matched controls on a questionnaire measure of "indirect aggression" (Helleday, Edman, Ritzen, & Siwers, 1993). A second study, also using questionnaires, presented a more complicated picture (Berenbaum & Resnick, 1997). Six groups of CAH individuals (3 female and 3 male) were compared to siblings of the same sex. One group of 18 female adolescents and adults with CAH reported more aggression than controls, but two other female samples (one including 11 adolescents and adults and the other 20 girls with CAH) did not. The different outcomes across the groups could relate to the age of participants, the specific questionnaire used to measure aggression, or sample size. There were no significant differences between males with and without CAH. Studies using interviews to assess fighting in girls with CAH have found no differences for a total of 32 girls (ages 4 to 20 years) from either siblings or matched controls (Ehrhardt et al., 1968; Ehrhardt & Baker, 1974). Finally, a questionnaire study found that 17 girls and 8 boys (ages 6 to 18 years) exposed to androgenic progestins prenatally showed increased tendencies to physical aggression in comparison to their unexposed siblings (Reinisch, 1981). Thus, some studies suggest an increase in aggression, as measured by questionnaires, following prenatal exposure to androgenic hormones, but this is not always the case. In addition, it is not clear whether hormone-related changes in questionnaire responses would translate into increased aggressive behavior, or if they would apply to children as well as adults. Therefore, it is not possible to say if the early hormone environment contributes to individual differences in aggressive play styles in children.

CAH girls have been reported to show high energy expenditure, and preferences for rough, active play, particularly in the context of "tomboyish" behavior (Ehrhardt et al., 1968; Ehrhardt & Baker, 1974). These studies included a total of 32 CAH girls (ages 4 to 20 years) compared to matched or sibling controls. Similar findings were reported for the 10 girls exposed to androgenic progestins prenatally (Ehrhardt & Money, 1967). A third study of 34 CAH girls (ages 11 to 41 years) found no differences from unaffected sisters in energy expenditure based on interview responses (Dittman et al., 1990). This study also found no differences in dominance or assertiveness in CAH versus control girls. Differences in assessment strategies could explain the different conclusions that might be drawn from these studies.

One study observed rough-and-tumble behavior in 20 girls with CAH (ages 3 to 8 years) and their unaffected relatives. Children played with a partner in a room containing toys selected to elicit rough-and-tumble play (e.g., a "Bobo" punching doll). Boys showed more rough-and-tumble play (e.g. hitting the "Bobo" doll, playfully hitting one another, wrestling), as found in prior studies using similar procedures (DiPietro, 1981; Maccoby, 1988). However, girls with CAH did not differ from control girls (Hines & Kaufman, 1994). These results contrast with data from female rats and rhesus macaques, where androgen exposure during development increases rough-and-tumble behavior (e.g., Goy & McEwen, 1980). Perhaps similar processes do not occur in humans. Alternatively, the testing situation might not have been adequate to detect effects. Most girls do not like rough-and-tumble play and most boys will not play rough with girls. Consequently, girls with CAH may have found that neither male nor female partners were interested in joining them in rough-and-tumble interactions (see Hines & Kaufman, 1994 for additional discussion).

Summary

Studies of girls exposed to high levels of androgen prenatally, because of the genetic disorder, CAH, suggest that they show more masculine-typical toy choices, gender identity, and playmate preferences. Some convergent evidence of hormonal influences on these behaviors has come from girls exposed to androgenic progestins. Alterations in play styles, including rough-and-tumble play and aggressive play, are less well established. The early hormone environment has generally not been found to influence gender development in boys. However, the most telling information, which would come from boys who were exposed to lower than normal levels of testicular hormones during development, is largely unavailable. Clearly, although findings from girls with CAH suggests that hormones can influence the development of children's gender-related behavior, further research is needed to fully understand the role of hormonal factors, particularly as they apply to normal development in both boys and girls.

Psychological Explanations

The psychological explanations discussed below have been organized according to theoretical approach as each theory has been applied to more than one aspect of gender development of interest in this chapter (gender identity, toy preference, playmate preference, and play style). The particular focus of each theoretical perspective will be highlighted where appropriate.

Social learning theory

The idea, founded in psychoanalytic theory, that children's gender development results from identification with the same-sex parent is a cornerstone of social learning theory. According to classic social learning theory, two mechanisms are at play: (i) the differential reinforcement of boys and girls and (ii) children's modeling of individuals of the same sex as themselves (Bandura, 1977; Mischel, 1966, 1970). Classic social learning theory posits that parents play a key role in the gender development of their children, both by differentially reinforcing their daughters and sons and by acting as models of sex-typed behavior. However, it is acknowledged that others such as teachers and peers, as well as images presented by the media, may also be influential.

The role of differential reinforcement in children's acquisition of sex-typed behavior has been widely investigated in an attempt to establish whether parents really treat their sons and daughters differently. In an influential review of the early studies, Maccoby and Jacklin (1974) concluded that there was little evidence that they do. In terms of the extent to which they allowed their sons and daughters to be independent, and the way in which they responded to their children's aggressive behavior, there was little evidence for the differential reinforcement of boys and girls. Nevertheless, there were some differences. Parents were found to reinforce their children for specifically sex-typed activities and interests such as doll play for girls and more active play for boys, and to discourage play that was associated with the other sex. A more recent review (Lytton & Romney, 1991) found a similar result. The only consistent differences to emerge between the treatment of boys and girls by parents were once again for sex-typed behaviors relating to toys, games, and activities.

Although Maccoby and Jacklin (1974) thought these differences to be of little significance, other researchers believe that the differential reinforcement of children's toy, game, and activity preferences does play a part in the acquisition of sex-typed behavior (Block, 1983; Lytton & Romney, 1991). From the moment of birth, parents treat their sons and daughters differently. They describe their newborn girls as soft and their newborn sons as strong (Rubin, Provenzano, & Luria, 1974), they give more physical stimulation to their male infants and talk more to their female infants (Moss, 1967; Parke & Sawin, 1980), they dress their girls in pink and their boys in blue (Shakin, Shakin, & Sternglanz, 1985), they give their daughters dolls and their sons cars and trucks (Rheingold & Cook, 1975), and they decorate their children's bedrooms according to their sex (Rheingold & Cook, 1975). The way in which parents interact with their infants is also guided by the child's gender. From as early as 1 year old, parents encourage their infants to play with sex-typed toys (Snow et al., 1983), a phenomenon that becomes even more marked during the toddler years (Fagot, 1978; Langlois & Downs, 1980), but seems to wane by the time they reach 5 years old (Fagot & Hagan, 1991). In addition, mothers are more likely to discuss emotions with their daughters than with their sons (Dunn, Bretherton, & Munn, 1987; Fivush, 1989).

It seems, therefore, that parents do treat their sons and daughters differently. But this does not mean that differential reinforcement by parents is responsible for the behavioral differences that are apparent between boys and girls. Parents might simply be reacting to the sex-typed behavior of their children rather than causing it. As already discussed, boys and girls may have a biologically based predisposition to behave in a sex-typed way. Most likely, differential reinforcement by parents not only produces sex-typed behavior in children but also operates by maximizing pre-existing behavioral differences between boys and girls.

Maccoby and Jacklin (1974) also examined the role of modeling in children's development of sex-typed behavior and concluded that the imitation of same-sex parents does not play a major part in this process. They argued that boys did not closely resemble their father, nor girls their mother, which would be expected if children imitated their same-sex parent more than their other-sex parent. Moreover, in observational studies, children did not necessarily imitate adults of the same sex as themselves. It is no longer thought that children learn sex-typed behavior simply by imitating individual same-sex models. Instead, it seems that children learn which behaviors are considered appropriate for boys, and which for girls, by observing large numbers of males and females and by noticing which behaviors are performed frequently by each sex. Children then model the behaviors that they consider appropriate for their sex (Perry & Bussey, 1979).

Children observe a wide variety of role models in their daily life, not just their parents. Friends, in particular, appear to be important role models. As already discussed, school-age boys and girls show a strong preference for same-sex peers (Maccoby, 1988). But it is gender stereotypes (widely held beliefs about the characteristics that are typical of males and females), rather than specific individuals, that seem to be most influential in the acquisition of sex-typed behavior. Gender stereotypes are pervasive in our society and children are aware of these stereotypes from as early as 2 years of age (Martin, 1991; Signorella, Bigler, & Liben, 1993; Stern & Karraker, 1989).

Cognitive theory

For cognitive theorists, the role of parents is a minor one. A central tenet of this approach is that children play an active part in their own development; they seek out for themselves information about gender and socialize themselves as male or female. Parents are viewed as simply one source of gender-related information. Early studies of cognitive processes focused on children's developing understanding of the concept of gender (see above). More recently, gender schema theorists have examined the way in which children organize knowledge about gender (Bem, 1981; Martin, 1989, 1991; Martin & Halverson, 1981). Gender schemas refer to organized bodies of knowledge about gender, and are functionally similar to gender stereotypes. Gender schemas influence the way in which we perceive and remember information about the world around us so that we pay greater attention to, and are more likely to remember, information that is in line with our gender schemas than opposing information.

An important step in gender understanding occurs when children can categorize themselves as belonging to one gender or the other. From as early as 2 to 3 years, soon after they begin to consistently label themselves and others as male or female, children organize information according to gender. If told that a person is male or female, they will make gender-related inferences about that person's behavior (Martin, 1989; Martin et al., 1990). For example, preschool children will say that boys like to play with cars and trains. Older children have a more complex understanding of gender and become more flexible in their understanding of gender stereotypes (Martin, 1993; Martin et al., 1990). Although they may know that boys in general like football, cars, and trains, and that girls in general prefer dolls and dressing up, they also come to understand there are many exceptions to the rule (Signorella et al., 1993). Thus it seems that gender stereotypes are more strongly held by younger than by older children.

There are differences between children in the extent to which they are gender schematized, that is, in the extent to which they organize, attend to, and remember information according to gender (Carter & Levy, 1988; Levy & Carter, 1989). Interestingly, however, children who are highly gender schematized are not necessarily more sex-typed in their behavior (Huston, 1985; Martin, 1991).

Social cognitive theory

Social cognitive theory draws upon both social learning theory and cognitive theories (Bandura, 1986; Bussey & Bandura, 1984, 1999). While same-sex modeling continues to be viewed as an important mechanism in the acquisition of sex-typed behavior, the processes involved are believed to involve complex cognitive skills rather that the direct incorporation of a model's characteristics and behavior. Social cognitive theorists stress the importance of social factors in influencing which behaviors are acquired. Thus behavior that is generally viewed as an other-sex activity, such as men's involvement in cooking, will be adopted in cultures where it is common for men to cook.

A major difference between social cognitive theory and the cognitive approach is the emphasis placed by social cognitive theorists on the mechanisms involved in the development of sex-typed behavior (Bussey & Bandura, 1999). Whereas cognitive theorists have focused on children's acquisition of knowledge about gender, social cognitive theorists are interested in the translation of gender knowledge into gender-related behavior. According to social cognitive theorists, a number of cognitive mechanisms are at work. Self-regulatory mechanisms in the form of both social sanctions and sanctions that children impose on themselves are believed to be operating; children do things that are valued and give them a sense of self-worth. Motivational mechanisms such as self-efficacy beliefs are also considered to be important. It is thought children are most likely to model behavior that they believe they can master. Although social cognitive theory provides a framework for examining the relationship between gender knowledge and gender role behavior, it is important to remember that existing research has failed to establish a consistent link between the two.

Gender segregation

Although psychological explanations of gender development have tended to focus on the individual, greater attention has been paid in recent years to group processes. Gender segregation – children's tendency to play with others of their own sex – is a striking aspect of gender development that occurs at the group rather than the individual level. Although there is evidence that biological, socialization, and cognitive mechanisms each play a part in this phenomenon, the most parsimonious explanation – that children segregate by gender due to behavioral compatibility with children of the same sex as themselves – incorporates all three approaches (Maccoby, 1988, 1990, 1998; Maccoby & Jacklin, 1987). Maccoby argues that children prefer to play with other children who have similar styles of interaction, and that this both creates and serves to preserve gender segregation. It is believed that girls begin to avoid boys because of boys' higher levels of physical activity and aggression, and boys begin to avoid girls because they find girls too sedentary. The differences in communication style between the sexes may also play a part. As we have already seen, boys are more dominant than girls. Girls tend to be more cooperative and may find it difficult to have their say. Thus girls may not wish to interact with boys because they see boys as too assertive, and boys may not wish to interact with girls because they find girls too quiet. Once formed, same-sex groups become even more differentiated in their styles of interaction. In this way, distinctive male and female cultures are established and maintained.

Summary

Gender development begins in the womb. Early in gestation hormones from the gonads mold the internal and external genitalia. These same hormones also may influence certain regions of the brain to develop in a more masculine-typical or feminine-typical manner. As a consequence, it is likely that we are each born with behavioral biases that can be enhanced or diminished by postnatal factors. Hormonal influences appear to play a role in children's gender development particularly in regard to sex-typical toy choices, playmate preferences, and gender identity. Hormonal influences on children's play styles are less well established.

From birth onwards, children are treated differently according to their sex. Although parents and others may simply be responding to differences in behavior that already exist between their daughters and sons, they may also be creating these differences. It seems likely that both processes are at work. In addition, children model behavior they consider to be appropriate for their sex. Although it used to be thought that gender constancy was necessary for modeling to occur, it is now believed that only a basic ability to label gender is required. The extent to which the various aspects of gender development discussed in this chapter (gender identity, toy preference, playmate preference, and play style) are interrelated, or develop independently of each other, remains uncertain. Although cognitive theorists have tended to argue that the ability to label gender, and knowledge of gender stereotypes, are essential for children to acquire sex-typed behavior, the sex differences in toy preference that are apparent from as early as 1 year old suggest that this is not the case. It does seem, however, that a child's knowledge of his or her own gender, but not necessarily of gender stereotypes, is associated with a greater preference for sex-typed behaviors. It is also important to remember that gender development does not occur in isolation from the child's social environment. As Eleanor Maccoby has so cogently pointed out, sex differences in social behavior are most apparent when children interact with each other.

Theorists operating from different perspectives have approached the analysis of gender development somewhat differently. To some, it is a unitary construct influenced uniformly by factors such as hormones or socialization. One contribution of recent research on hormonal influences is the realization that each aspect of gender-typical behavior may be influenced at different times and by different mechanisms. If so, it might be useful to conceptualize different sex-typical behaviors separately and evaluate the effects of different types of influences on each behavior considered alone. At present, data on toy choices are the most likely to provide an opportunity to do this. There is evidence that levels of androgenic hormones prenatally influence sex-typical toy choices. In addition, there is evidence that parents socialize children to show gender-typical toy choices, reinforcing them for playing with sex-appropriate toys. In fact, this is the one area of gender development where such differential reinforcement by parents has been established. Children also have been found to model the behavior of others of the same sex choosing neutral toys, and to express interest in toys that they have been told are for children of their own sex. Thus, sex-typical toys choices appear to be multidetermined, promoted by the prenatal hormone environment, as well as by several postnatal factors, including parental reinforcement, modeling, and gender labeling. In order to achieve a better understanding of sex differences in social behavior, it seems that an integration of biological and psychological explanations is required.

References

Bandura, A. (1977). *Social learning theory.* Englewood Cliffs, NJ: Prentice Hall.

Bandura, A. (1986). *Social foundations of thought and action: A social cognitive theory.* Englewood Cliffs, NJ: Prentice Hall.

Bem, S. (1981). Gender schema theory: A cognitive account of sex typing. *Psychological Review, 88,* 354–364.

Berenbaum, S. A., & Hines, M. (1992). Early androgens are related to childhood sex-typed toy preferences. *Psychological Science, 3,* 203–206.

Berenbaum, S. A., & Resnick, S. M. (1997). Early androgen effects on aggression in children and adults with congenital adrenal hyperplasia. *Psychoneuroendocrinology, 22,* 505–515.

Block, J. H. (1983). Differential premises arising from differential socialization of the sexes. *Child Development, 54,* 1335–1354.

Bussey, K., & Bandura, A. (1984). Influence of gender constancy and social power on sex-linked modeling. *Journal of Personality and Social Psychology, 47,* 1292–1302.

Bussey, K., & Bandura, A. (1999). Social cognitive theory of gender development and differentiation. *Psychological Review, 106,* 676–713.

Carter, D. B., & Levy, G. D. (1988). Cognitive aspects of early sex-role development: The influence of gender schemas on preschoolers' memories and preferences for sex-typed toys and activities.

Child Development, 59, 782–792.

Collaer, M. L., & Hines, M. (1995). Human behavioral sex differences: A role for gonadal hormones during early development? *Psychological Bulletin, 118,* 55–107.

Crick, N. R., Casas, J. F., & Mosher, M. (1997). Relational and overt aggression in preschool. *Developmental Psychology, 33,* 579–588.

Crombie, G., & Desjardins, M. J. (1993). *Predictors of gender: The relative importance of children's play, games and personality characteristics?* New Orleans: Society for Research in Child Development.

De Lucia, L. A. (1963). The toy preference test: A measure of sex role identification. *Child Development, 34,* 107–117.

DiPietro, J. A. (1981). Rough and tumble play: A function of gender. *Developmental Psychology, 17,* 50–58.

Dittman, R. W., Kappes, M. H., Kappes, M. E. Borger, D., Meyer-Bahlburg, H. F. L., Stegner, H., Willig, R. H., & Wallis, H. (1990). Congenital adrenal hyperplasia II. Gender-related behavior and attitudes in female salt-wasting and simple-virilizing patients. *Psychoneuroendocrinology, 15,* 401–420.

Dunn, J., Bretherton, I., & Munn, P. (1987). Conversations about feeling states between mothers and their young children. *Developmental Psychology, 23,* 132–139.

Ehrhardt, A. A., & Baker, S. W. (1974). Fetal androgens, human central nervous system differentiation and behavioral sex differences. In R. C. Friedman, R. M. Richart, & R. L. Vande Wiele (Eds.), *Sex differences in behavior* (pp. 33–51). New York: Wiley.

Ehrhardt, A. A., Epstein, R., & Money, J. (1968). Fetal androgens and female gender identity in the early-treated adrenogenital syndrome. *Johns Hopkins Medical Journal, 122,* 160–167.

Ehrhardt, A. A., Grisanti, G. C., & Meyer-Bahlburg, H. F. L. (1977). Prenatal exposure to medroxyprogesterone acetate (MPA) in girls. *Psychoneuroendocrinology, 2,* 391–398.

Ehrhardt, A. A., & Money, J. (1967). Progestin-induced hermaphroditism: IQ and psychosexual identity in a study of ten girls. *Journal of Sex Research, 3,* 83–100.

Emmerich, W., Goldman, K. S., Kirsh, B., & Sharabany, R. (1977). Evidence for a transitional phase in the development of gender constancy. *Child Development, 48,* 930–936.

Fagot, B. I. (1978). The influence of sex of child on parental reactions to toddler children. *Child Development, 49,* 459–465.

Fagot, B. I., & Hagan, R. (1991). Observations of parent reactions to sex-stereotyped behaviors. *Child Development, 62,* 617–628.

Fausto-Sterling, A. (1992). *Myths of gender.* New York: Basic Books.

Fivush, R. (1989). Exploring sex differences in the emotional content of mother–child conversations about the past. *Sex Roles, 20,* 675–691.

Golombok, S., & Fivush, R. (1994). *Gender development.* New York: Cambridge University Press.

Golombok, S., & Rust, J. (1993). The measurement of gender role behaviour in pre-school children: A research note. *Journal of Child Psychology and Psychiatry, 34,* 805–811.

Goy, R. W., & McEwen, B. S. (1980) *Sexual differentiation of the brain.* Cambridge, MA. MIT Press.

Gray, P., & Feldman, J. (1997). Patterns of age mixing and gender mixing among children and adolescents in at an ungraded school. *Merrill Palmer Quarterly, 42,* 67–86.

Helleday, J., Edman, G., Ritzen, E. M., & Siwers, B. (1993) Personality characteristics and platelet MAO activity in women with congenital adrenal hyperplasia (CAH). *Psychoneuroendocrinology, 18,* 343–354.

Hines, M. (2000). Gonadal hormones and sexual differentiation of human behavior: Effects on psychosexual and cognitive development. In A. Matsumoto (Ed.), *Sexual differentiation of the brain.* CRC Press.

Hines, M., & Kaufman, F. R. (1994). Androgen and the development of human sex-typical behavior: Rough-and-tumble play and sex of preferred playmates in children with congenital adrenal hyperplasia (CAH). *Child Development, 65,* 1042–1053.

Howes, C. (1988). Peer interaction among children. *Monographs of the Society for Research in Child Development, 53,* 1–92.

Hurtig, A. L., & Rosenthal, I. M. (1987). Psychological findings in early treated cases of female pseudohermaphroditism caused by virilizing congenital adrenal hyperplasia. *Archives of Sexual Behavior, 16,* 209–223.

Huston, A. (1985). The development of sex-typing: Themes from recent research. *Developmental Review, 5,* 1–17.

Kohlberg, L. (1966). A cognitive-developmental analysis of children's sex-role concepts and attitudes. In E. E. Maccoby (Ed.), *The development of sex differences.* Stanford, CA: Stanford University Press.

LaFreniere, P., Strayor, F., & Gauthier, R. (1984). The emergence of same-sex affiliative preference among preschool peers: A developmental/ethological perspective. *Child Development, 55,* 1958–1965.

Langlois, J. H., & Downs, A. C. (1980). Mothers, fathers, and peers as socialization agents of sex-typed play behaviors in young children. *Child Development, 51,* 1237–1247.

Lever, J. (1976). Sex differences in the games children play. *Social Problems, 23,* 478–487.

Levy, G. D., & Carter, D. B. (1989). Gender schema, gender constancy and gender role knowledge: The roles of cognitive factors in preschoolers' gender-role stereotypic attitudes. *Developmental Review, 25,* 444–449.

Lytton, H., & Romney, D. M. (1991). Parents' differential socialization of boys and girls: A meta-analysis. *Psychological Bulletin, 109,* 267–296.

Maccoby, E. E. (1988). Gender as a social category. *Developmental Psychology, 24,* 755–765.

Maccoby, E. E. (1990). Gender and relationships: A developmental account. *American Psychologist, 45,* 513–520.

Maccoby, E. E. (1998). *The two sexes: Growing up apart, coming together.* Cambridge, MA: Harvard University Press.

Maccoby, E. E., & Jacklin, C. N. (1974). *The psychology of sex differences.* Stanford, CA: Stanford University Press.

Maccoby, E. E., & Jacklin, C. N. (1987). Gender segregation in children. In H. W. Reece (Ed.), *Advances in child development and behavior.* New York: Academic Press.

Marcus, D. E., & Overton, W. F. (1978). The development of cognitive gender constancy and sex role preferences. *Child Development, 49,* 434–444.

Martin, C. L. (1989). Children's use of gender-related information in making social judgements. *Developmental Psychology, 25,* 80–88.

Martin, C. L. (1991). The role of cognition in understanding gender effects. In H. Reese (Ed.), *Advances in child development and behavior* (pp. 113–164). San Diego, CA: Academic Press.

Martin, C. L. (1993). New directions for assessing children's gender knowledge. *Developmental Review, 13,* 184–202.

Martin, C. L., & Halverson, C. (1981). A schematic processing model of sex typing and stereotyping in children. *Child Development, 52,* 1119–1134.

Martin, C. L., Wood, C. H., & Little, J. K. (1990). The development of gender stereotype components. *Child Development, 61,* 1891–1904.

McGuire, L. S., Ryan, K. O., & Omenn, G. S. (1975). Congenital adrenal hyperplasia. II. Cognitive and behavioral studies. *Behavior Genetics, 5,* 175–188.

McNeilly-Choque, M. K., Hart, C. H., Robinson, C. C., Nelson, L. J., & Olsen, S. F. (1996).

Overt and relational aggression on the playground: Correspondence among different inform-ants. *Journal of Research in Childhood Education, 11*, 47–67.

Meyer-Bahlburg, H. F. L., Feldman, J. F., Cohen, P., & Ehrhardt, A. A. (1988). Perinatal factors in the development of gender-related play behavior: Sex hormones versus pregnancy complica-tions. *Psychiatry, 51*, 260–271.

Mischel, W. (1966). A social learning view of sex differences in behavior. In E. E. Maccoby (Ed.), *The development of sex differences*. Stanford, CA: Stanford University Press.

Mischel, W. (1970). Sex-typing and socialization. In P. Mussen (Ed.), *Carmichael's manual of child psychology* (pp. 3-72). New York: Wiley.

Money, J., & Ehrhardt, A. A. (1972) *Man and woman, boy and girl. The differentiation and dimor-phism of gender identity from conception to maturity*. Baltimore: Johns Hopkins University Press.

Moss, H. A. (1967). Sex, age, and the state as determinants of mother-infant interaction. *Merrill-Palmer Quarterly, 13*, 19–36.

O'Brien, M., & Huston, A. C. (1985). Development of sex-typed play behavior in toddlers. *Devel-opmental Psychology, 21*, 866–871.

Parke, R. D., & Sawin, D. B. (1980). The family in early infancy: Social interactional and attitudinal analyses. In F. Pedersen (Ed.), *The father–infant relationship: Observational studies in a family context*. New York: Praeger.

Perlman, S. M. (1973). Cognitive abilities of children with hormone abnormalities. Screening by psychoeducational tests. *Journal of Learning Disabilities, 6*, 21–29.

Perry, D. G., & Bussey, K. (1979). The social learning theory of sex difference: Imitation is alive and well. *Journal of Personality and Social Psychology, 37*, 1699–1712.

Piaget, J. (1968). *On the development of memory and identity*. Worcester, MA, Clark University Press.

Pitcher, E. G., & Shultz, L. H. (1983). *Boys and girls at play: The development of sex roles*. South Hadley, MA: Bergin and Garvey.

Reinisch, J. M. (1981). Prenatal exposure to synthetic progestins increases potential for aggression in humans. *Science, 211*, 1171–1173.

Rheingold, H. L., & Cook, K. V. (1975). The content of boys' and girls' rooms as an index of parents' behavior. *Child Development, 46*, 459–463.

Robinson, C. C., & Morris, J. T. (1986). The gender-stereotyped nature of Christmas toys received by 36-, 48-, and 60-month old children: A comparison between requested and nonrequested toys. *Sex Roles, 15*, 21–32.

Rubin, J. Z., Provenzano, F. J., & Luria, Z. (1974). The eye of the beholder: Parents' views on sex of newborns. *American Journal of Orthopsychiatry, 44*, 512–519.

Serbin, L. A., Powlishta, K. K., & Gulko, J. (1993). The development of sex typing in middle childhood. *Monographs of the Society for Research in Child Development, 58*, 1-74.

Shakin, M., Shakin, D., & Sternglanz, S. H. (1985). Infant clothing: Sex labelling for strangers. *Sex Roles, 12*, 955–963.

Sheldon, A. (1990). Pickle fights: Gendered talk in preschool disputes. *Discourse Processes, 13*, 5–31.

Signorella, M. L., Bigler, R. S., & Liben, L. S. (1993). Developmental differences in children's gender schemata about others: A meta-analytic review. *Developmental Review, 13*, 106–126.

Slaby, R. G., & Frey, K. S. (1975). Development of gender constancy and selective attention to same-sex models. *Child Development, 46*, 849–856.

Slijper, F. M. E. (1984). Androgens and gender role behaviour in girls with congenital adrenal hyperplasia (CAH). *Progress in Brain Research, 61*, 417–422.

Slijper, F. M. E., Drop, S. L. S., Molenaar, J. C., & de Muinck Keizer-Schrama, S. M. P. F. (1998). Long-term psychological evaluation of intersex children. *Archives of Sexual Behavior, 27*, 125–144.

Snow, M. E., Jacklin, C. N., & Maccoby, E. E. (1983). Sex-of-child differences in father–child interaction at one year of age. *Child Development, 49*, 227–232.

Stern, M., & Karraker, K. H. (1989). Sex stereotyping of infants: A review of gender labelling studies. *Sex Roles, 20*, 501–522.

Sutton-Smith, B., & Rosenberg. B. G. (1971). Sixty years of historical change in the game preferences of American children. In R. E. Herron and D. Sutton-Smith (Eds.), *Child's play*. New York: Wiley.

Tannen, D. (1990). Gender differences in topical coherence: Creating involvement in best friend's talk. *Discourse Processes, 13*, 73–90.

Whiting, B. B., & Edwards, C. P. (1988). *Children of different worlds: The formation of social behavior*. Cambridge, MA: Harvard University Press.

Wilson, J. D., George, F. W., & Griffin, J. E. (1981). The hormonal control of sexual development. *Science, 211*, 1278–1284.

Zucker, K. J., Bradley, S. J. Kulsis, M., Pecore, K., Birkenfeld, A., Doering, R. W., Mitchell, J. N., & Wild, J. (1999). Gender constancy judgements in children with gender identity disorder: Evidence for a developmental lag. *Archives of Sexual Behavior, 28*, 475–502.

8

Children's Social Development within the Socialization Context of Childcare and Early Childhood Education

Carollee Howes and Jolena James

Introduction

From our point of view, children's social development can best be understood as embedded within relationships with significant adults and peers and that these social relationships are embedded within larger contexts of social setting, culture, and societal organizations (Howes, 2000a). In more particularistic terms, we argue that 3-year-old Jenna's skillful (or maladaptive) play with her peer can be interpreted and explained only when we know that she is playing with Marissa, who has been her best friend since both girls were toddler age, and that she has a secure attachment relationship with her caregiver, Renna. Jenna's play can be even better interpreted when we add the information that both she and Renna are African American, that Marissa is Latino, and that the girls are playing in the Good Start Childcare Center, a well-funded full-day program that provides services to teen moms who are in school. We also believe that to fully understand Jenna's play competence it helps to understand that Jenna, an African-American girl from a poor family, is an "other" with regard to the dominant society that accords highest status to white males from affluent families. Because of this status as an other, Jenna will need to acquire social interactive styles within her extended family of grandmother, aunts, and cousins that are distinct from patterns or styles of interaction within the dominant society, and she will need to understand social cues for when to employ the different sets of patterns (James, 2000).

Social competence

Despite this emphasis on culture and society we are not arguing for a relativistic definition of social competence. We start from the premise that children (regardless of race, class, or home language) will develop social competence, but that the display of social competence and the processes of becoming socially competent may be different. Our definition of social competence is drawn from the peer relations literature, but is extended to include adult–child interactions and relationship (Howes, 1988a). Social competence is defined as behavior that reflects successful social functioning. To be successful, children must be both effective in meeting their own social goals with others and be sensitive to social communications from others so that their partners also are effective in meeting social goals. Both social interaction skills and positive relationships are included in the definition. Social incompetence or maladaptive social development is defined by relationships that are mistrustful, and by behavior that disregards the reciprocal nature of social interaction and relationships. One maladaptive category of social behavior is aggression or bullying which may achieve the actor's social goals but not the partner's. Another type of maladaptive category of social behavior includes avoidance, withdrawal, or passive acquiescence which does not achieve the child's social goals and may (or may not) achieve the partner's.

Social interactive style

In our work we use the term social interactive style to denote patterns of interaction that are particular to individuals who share a race or ethnic identity or home language. For example, in certain communities titles are important when children address an adult. Adults are either addressed as Mr., Mrs., Miss, Auntie, Uncle, etc. followed by their family name or first name. It is not uncommon to hear a child call a caregiver by her first name, but preface it with Miss. "Miss Helen, can I play with this?" In other communities, however, it is quite appropriate for children to address an adult by her first name only. In the African-American community, tone and eye expression are especially important in understanding social interactions. Mrs. Pettaway, a favorite among her 4 year olds, is helping the children needlepoint. Deondre is clearly frustrated and communicates this with his face as he continues to work on his project. Mrs. Pettaway calls to him, but he continues to fumble with his artwork. She then says, "Boy, get over here," in a sassy, but humorous manner. Deondre immediately breaks out in a smile and approaches her. While we do not want to imply that this is typical of all African-American caregivers, the tone and language of the interaction could be misunderstood outside of the African-American community. The caregiver plays with a harsh statement, but softens it so it becomes an endearment.

Another example lies in the Latino community's use of terms of endearments. It not uncommon to hear a caregiver say to a Spanish speaking toddler, "¿Papi qué quieres?" (Little father, what do you want?) or "Mami, ven acá" (Little mother, come here). The language used in these social interactions carries with it the feeling of warmth and nurturance.

Social interactive styles can be socially competent or maladaptive. We observed Jesse taunting his peer Lucia as he attempts to take her truck. In a loud assertive voice, Lucia says, "No Jesse!" instead of hitting him. Lucia, in a "use-your-words" childcare program, is exhibiting socially competent behavior. Now, if Jesse were her caregiver and Lucia was supposed to have put the truck away 5 minutes ago, Lucia's loud voice would be socially maladaptive. Or if Jesse was teen parent Lucia's one-year-old child, Lucia's loud voice would be extreme and would be considered inappropriate. The interpretation of all these interactions depends on the context. As stated above, children must learn when and where to employ one style over another. The same behavior can be considered socially competent in one context and socially maladaptive in another. When Deondre rolls his eyes in an attempt to ignore his playmate's verbal directive, we rate Deondre as socially competent. If Deondre were to roll his eyes at Mrs. Pettaway, an adult, in an attempt to disobey her instructions, we would rate his behavior maladaptive.

Development and social competence

Because we are developmental psychologists we are interested in the development of social competence across time as well as context. Therefore, we assume that as children develop, their capacities for communication, cognition, and memory, social interaction patterns become more complex. Over time, children come to behave as if each participant is a social actor and that social actions between partners can be coordinated and communicated. With further development, children incorporate symbols and shared meanings into the interaction patterns(Howes, 1983, 1985, 1988, 1996; Howes & Tonyan, 1999; Howes, Unger, & Seidner, 1989).

As much of our work is rooted in attachment theory (Bowlby, 1969), we also assume that over time children develop internal working models of their significant relationships with adults and with peers. To reach this understanding, we construe Bowlby's attachment theory as applicable to other-than-child-mother attachment relationships (Howes, 1996, 1999). According to this reinterpretation of attachment theory, relationships, whether attachment or playmate relationships, develop through multiple and recursive interactive experiences. Recursive interactions are well-scripted social exchanges which are repeated many times with only slight variation (Bretherton, 1985). Examples include child–adult interaction around naptime or repeated toddler-age peer run-and-chase games. From these recursive interactions, the infant or young child internalizes a set of fundamental social expectations about the behavioral dispositions of the partner (Bowlby, 1969). These expectations form the basis for an internal working model of a particular relationship. Therefore, through repeated experiences of social and social pretend play with a significant adult or peer partner, a child forms an internal representation of an attachment or a playmate or friendship relationship. It is important to note that both the structure and content of experiences interacting with a partner are part of the child's representation of the partner. Children who engage in more complex interactions are more likely to recognize the partner as a social other and construct a relationship. Furthermore, the content and context of the interaction is likely to influence the quality of the resulting relationship.

Childcare

In this chapter we apply this framework of social development embedded within relationships which are located within social settings, culture, and societal organizations to the social setting of childcare and early childhood education. Childcare and early childhood education is an awkward term which we will shorten to childcare. By this term we mean any regular arrangement of care provided for children by adults other than parent figures. The functions of these care arrangements always includes keeping children safe from physical harm and optimally includes providing a context for enhancing social and/or cognitive development. The adults who provide care in these settings may be grandmothers, neighbors, nannies, or teachers. Because the parents directly or indirectly communicate to their children that these other-than-mother adults are to keep them safe, these adults function (well or not so well) as attachment figures (Howes, 1999). Most, but not all, of the children in childcare are cared for in the presence of peers. In some settings, peers tend to be same-age nonrelatives, in other less formal arrangements, peers may be mixed-age and may be siblings or cousins. Thus, in terms of opportunities for experiences with adults and peers, childcare can be considered a socialization context for social development.

Childcare settings, according to our framework, are embedded within culture and societal organizations and, therefore, we begin a review of research examining this embeddedness. We will address the following questions: How do family markers of race, class, and home language influence the selection of childcare, the experiences within childcare of children and the continuity and discontinuities with home? How does the placement of the childcare setting within race, class, and home language culture and societal organizations influence process and interactions within childcare? And how does gender organize childcare experiences?

In the subsequent section we will examine the empirical basis for childcare as a socialization context for social development. We will briefly touch on the debate around childcare as a risk for the development of social incompetence, or as an opportunity or an intervention to enhance social competence. We will then move inside and past this debate to examine structural variations within childcare settings and issues of stability and change in childcare arrangements as influential to the development of social competence.

The final section of the chapter will focus on understanding the within-childcare socialization context. We propose a model that incorporates key dimensions for understanding processes of socialization within childcare: the peer group; caregiver–child relationships; children's dispositions and relationship history; and classroom climate.

Childcare, Culture, and Society

Within this section we will explore relations among childcare, culture, and society. The first issues to be explored are class (measured by family income), race, and ethnicity of children. The class, race, and ethnicity of children's families influence the selection of childcare settings for children. As a result most, but not all, childcare settings are homogeneous in class, race, and ethnicity of children and staff. What does this mean for the socialization experiences of children within the settings? And are there continuities or discontinuities between socialization experiences rooted in class, race, and ethnicity at childcare and at home? We then turn to the issue of gender and explore how children's experiences in childcare are organized by gender.

Class, race, and ethnicity

Selection of childcare. Our expanded definition of childcare, care by someone other than parents, means that in the United States the majority of preschool children are experiencing childcare. In 1995 approximately 43% of 3-year-old and 70% of 4-year old children in the United States were enrolled in a center-based or formal childcare arrangement (Statistics, 1996). Estimates of the proportion of children enrolled in informal, unregulated childcare arrangements are more difficult to obtain. Census data from the early 1990s suggest that at least 20–30% of preschool children were cared for in informal or unregulated childcare – approximately 25% by a nonparent relative in or out of the child's home; 5% by a nonrelative in the child's home and 20% by an unrelated provider not in the child's home (Lamb, 1998). Two events in the mid-1990s influenced childcare usage. The passage of new welfare legislation means that more parents are required to transition off welfare into the workforce. Early reports suggest that most of the children affected by this legislation are enrolled in informal, unregulated care (National Center for Children in Poverty, 2000). As well, many states have passed initiatives to offer preschool services to 4-year-old children in the year before they enter kindergarten (Clifford & Early, 1999).

The particular care arrangements of children are influenced by parental employment patterns as well as family income and race and by the availability of care (Fuller, Halloway, & Liang, 1996; Holloway, Rambaud, Fuller, & Eggers-Pierola, 1995; Lamb, 1998; Phillips, Voran, Kister, Howes, & Whitebook , 1994; Singer, Fuller, Keiley, & Wolf, 1998). Children of higher income parents and children of very low income parents are most likely to be in formal center-based care. Lower income working parents are more likely to use informal care because they are less likely to be income eligible for subsidized center-based care and cannot afford to pay for unsubsidized care and/or they work swing or night shifts so that one parent is always home. High income families with unemployed mothers have traditionally used part time center-based care for preschool-age children. Low income families with unemployed parents before welfare reform typically used Head Start and other income-eligibility-based center care. As much of this care has been part time, many of income-eligible children are now either unable to use this care as their parents transition off welfare or they are enrolled in a patchwork of childcare arrangements to cover the hours of parental work.

Many studies find patterns of childcare usage linked to racial, ethnic, and home language characteristics of families. For example, Latino families, especially families in which Spanish is spoken in the home, are under-enrolled in formal care even when the mother is working (Fuller et al., 1996). While factors such as family choices or language issues may explain this pattern, when researchers map organized childcare availability onto family ethnicity, it appears that some of this variability in ethnicity is due to variability in supply of formal childcare (Singer et al., 1998).

Class, race, and ethnic socialization within childcare

Between 1988 and the present, four large-scale observational studies have been or are being conducted on representative samples of childcare in the United States. The Childcare Staffing Study (Whitebook, Howes, & Phillips, 1990) and the Cost Quality and Outcome Study (Helburn, 1995) focused on center care.. The Family and Relative Care Study (Kontos, Howes, Shinn, & Galinsky, 1995) observed in regulated family childcare homes and unregulated relative and nonrelative home-based childcare. The NICHD Early Childhood Research Network (NICHD, 1996) observed in a variety of childcare settings. From these studies a picture of a race, class, and ethnically segregated childcare system in the United States emerges. Most (but not all) children attend childcare in settings that are homogeneous in terms of children's family income level, race, and ethnic backgrounds. This means that to the extent that social interaction styles are rooted in class, race, and ethnicity (Coll et al., 1996; Coll & Magnuson, 1999), children do not experience discontinuity between home and childcare peer group social interaction styles.

It also means that we might expect children's experiences of interactions with peers within or between childcare to vary by the class, race, and ethnicity of the enrolled children. That is, for example, we might expect children in Head Start programs to have different patterns of social interactive styles than, for example, children in half-day preschool programs in affluent suburbs. Vaughn and colleagues (Bost, Vaughn, Washington, Cielinski, & Bradbard, 1998; Vaughn et al., 2000) in a series of carefully constructed studies have been testing this hypothesis. They report that despite differences in interactive styles, social competency as indexed by sociometric status, socially skilled interactions, social dominance, and reciprocated friendship are similarly interrelated constructs for children enrolled in predominantly African-American Head Start programs and for children from the dominant culture. This brings us back to the critical distinction between social interaction style and social competence discussed in the introduction: socially competent children vary in social interactive style.

What about the race, ethnicity and class of caregivers?   Adult caregivers in childcare vary in their own class and/or race and ethnicity, and therefore in their social interaction style. Exploration of the four large childcare databases described above suggests that most children are similar to their caregivers as well as peers in childcare in terms of race and ethnicity. While childcare caregivers generally are better educated than other women workers, they are paid far less than similarly educated workers which makes childcare workers' class position ambiguous (Whitebook, 1999). One line of research suggests that to the extent that adult caregivers in childcare settings are exposed to formal education and training in early childhood education, they may adopt values and/or social interactive styles that are associated with White middle-class interactive styles (Lubeck, 1985, 1996). If so, discontinuities between home and school social interactive styles may make it difficult for children (and their parents) (Baker, Terry, Bridger, & Winsor, 1997; Wang & Gordon, 1994). Instead of feeling safe, children may feel out of place, unwanted, or not sure about how to behave and whom to trust.

As part of a larger project that explores race, ethnicity, and childcare quality we have conducted case studies on 12 center-based childcare programs that are respected in their communities for providing services to families and children who are low income and predominantly children of color. We were interested in examining the very specific ways that children spend their time during the day, and the interactions they had with adults and peers. We wanted to know who the staff was that was working with the children specifically, what motivated them to become caregivers, and what were their attitudes toward working with families. We wanted to look at the mission and focus of each center. In line with the need to capture content inside of context, we incorporated a mixed-method approach by interviewing staff and observing and participating in the classrooms of these centers.

Seventy staff members (66 women; 59 teaching staff) participated in this study. 40% of the program directors were African American, 30% Latino, and 30% White. 55% of the teaching staff were Latino, 26% African American. The others were White, Asian or biracial. All of the teaching staff was highly educated in child development: 83% of the directors had MA or Ph.D. degrees; 55% of the head caregivers had BA degrees; and 79% of the assistants had AA degrees.

From our ethnographic work seven different categories of program philosophy emerged, ranging from providing a safe environment and positive trusting social relationships, through helping young children understand and appreciate differences based on race, gender, or disability, to providing academic preparation for school. We created, based on staff interviews, categories of caregivers' motivation to teach. Caregivers who report being motivated for the community see themselves as self-consciously involving themselves in their work in order to transform their own community into a community of which they wish to be a part. In contrast, caregivers that are motivated for the children gain little for themselves because their efforts are always for the children, children not necessarily from the caregiver's "heritage" community, but children from all communities. Caregivers of every ethnic, racial, and educational background subscribed to each of the program philosophies and motivations to teach.

Using our observational data, we examined differences in caregivers' behaviors with the children based on caregiver ethnicity, educational background, motivation to teach, and program mission (Howes & Ritchie, in preparation). We found that while an association between ethnicity and educational background existed, teaching motivation and program missions better explained the differences in behaviors.

These findings suggest that while socialization for social development within childcare is embedded within race and ethnicity, individual variations in motivation to teach and to provide services for children are equally important to consider. Having said this there were again subtle stylistic differences particular to race and ethnicity. For example, African-American caregivers invoked the construct of other-mothers, the notion that women who are not children's biological parents are responsible for the well-being of children who are not otherwise receiving adequate care and attention. While Latino caregivers talked about creating an extended family that took care of women and the children associated with them.

Gender

Childcare settings, of course, include both girls and boys at a period in development important for the acquisition of gendered behavior styles. Adult caregivers in childcare settings vary in their use of gender as an organizing category within the program. In two of our case study programs children as young as 2 years old must form lines based on gender, and be careful not to use the bathroom of the opposite sex. In one of these programs, girls and boys wear different uniforms, and the girls are in skirts or jumpers. And in another the roles in a preliteracy activity involving acting out fairy tales are carefully assigned to the appropriate gender children. This is in dramatic contrast to another program that has fully implemented the National Association for the Education of Young Children's Anti-Bias Curriculum (Derman-Sparks, 1989) and actively corrects children and adults who consciously or inadvertently attempt to impose traditional sex role behaviors on children as well as highlights when children or adults behave outside of predetermined roles. Yet another program delights in its well-equipped dramatic play area and energetically encourages girls to pretend to be plumbers and boys to take care of the babies.

Maccoby (1998) argues that the peer group has a more powerful socializing effect on gender than adults, either parents or caregivers. She analyzes large bodies of biological, psychological, anthropological, and sociological evidence to conclude that children, by age 3, separate into gender-segregated peer groups. Within these peer groups children develop the social behaviors and interaction styles specific to their gender. This suggests that children's experiences in childcare are gender specific, that because children are spending their childcare daytime hours in childcare they have multiple opportunities for socialization by same-gender peers in gender-segregated groups.

Gender segregation appears to influence the style rather than the competence of peer play. There are well-established differences in the content of the play of boys and girls (Maccoby, 1984). However, consistent with the lack of racial and ethnic differences in the competence of peer play, there appear to be few gender differences in the competence of children's peer play (Howes, 1980, 1988; Howes & Matheson, 1992). Girls and boys of the same age engage in structurally similar play, although the social interaction style and content may differ. For example, both a game of mother, sister, and baby among girls, and a game of the day the tigers ate the village among boys are very likely to be rated as competent social pretend play.

Gender socialization within segregated peer groups does not entirely negate the role of the adult values in the organization of experiences in childcare. If the adults in the childcare setting encourage the girls to use the tool bench, make airplanes, and run frantically around the yard being women pilots, they are acknowledging that girls are active, powerful, and able to do anything. If instead, caregivers ignore or covertly encourage the boys to rule the play yard and block corner, the girls' group will have a different repertoire of self-images. Thus caregivers can support or actively disconfirm traditional gender socialization.

In this section of the chapter we have argued that because childcare is embedded within a larger society which is organized by class, race, ethnicity, and gender, children's experiences in childcare are as well. Because childcare programs tend to be economically and racially segregated, children in childcare will acquire social interactive styles specific to these segregated environments. We have further argued that these differences in social interactive style are not associated with social competence.

Childcare as a Particularly Efficacious or Detrimental Context for Social Development

The social institution of childcare as we have defined it is rooted in two somewhat contradictory traditions. Prior to the dramatic increase in workforce participation of middle and upper income women in the 1970s, preschools and nursery schools were considered educational experiences. Half-day programs either served as intervention programs for children of lower income families or enrichment social experiences for children of affluent families. Daycare was a social service for the children of women who had to work. Full-day center-based programs and informal care by relatives and neighbors provided primarily custodial care. Beginning in the 1970s these two functions began to merge so that childcare provided both a caregiving and an educational function. Research on the social experiences of children in childcare and the influence of these experiences on children's social competence also began to flourish in the 1970s (Rubenstein & Howes, 1979; Ruopp et al., 1979). By the end of the decade an important review article concluded that although the full range of childcare setting had not been studied, preschool-age childcare did not appear to be detrimental to children's social development (Belsky & Steinberg, 1978).

This researchers' consensus began to break down beginning in 1986 with a series of reports in the popular media and research literature suggesting that childcare might adversely affect infant–parent attachment and related aspects of social development (Belsky, 1988). There were at least two parts to this argument. One part suggested that the experience of being enrolled in childcare as infants would interfere with the construction of secure parent–child attachment relationships. The theoretical and methodological explanations necessary for the full discussion of this issue are beyond the scope of this chapter. For a full review see Lamb (1998). The conclusion of Lamb's review and the large NICHD childcare study (NICHD, 1997) is that most infant–mother attachments are not adversely affected by childcare enrollment.

The second part of Belsky's argument is that the experience of childcare will negatively influence the development of significant dimensions of social competence: compliance with parents and childcare providers; relations with peers; and behavior problems (Bates et al., 1994). These issues are germane to this chapter and will be reviewed in some detail. Again there are both theoretical and methodological issues within this argument. Belsky (1988) grounded his argument within attachment theory. Children with insecure child–mother attachments are expected to be less socially competent as older children than children with secure child–mother attachments. But more recent evidence suggests the strength of this relation is more modest than previously assumed (Thompson, 1999). Furthermore, there is increasing evidence that children's attachment relationships with someone other than the mother, most notably in children attending childcare their relationship with the childcare provider, shape children's social competence (Howes, 1999; Lamb, 1998; Thompson, 1999).

Some of the methodological issues inherent in this controversy lead us back to issues of social competence versus social style. For example, how do we understand and measure compliance? When is compliance autonomy and when is it defiance? What are the most important outcomes to measure in the area of peer relations – cooperation and friendship or aggression – and how should they be measured?

However, the most substantive methodological issue concerns the mediating variables of family environment and childcare quality. When family environment is considered, the simple main effect of childcare is not influential in understanding the development of children's social competence (Lamb, 1998; NICHD, 1998). That is, childcare enrollment appears to have little or no direct effect on the development of children's social competence when the influences of family are taken into consideration. However, when childcare quality is used as a mediator it does appear to have an effect, although not as large an effect as that of family influences (McCartney & Rosenthal, 2000).

Defining childcare quality

There is general agreement among researchers that childcare quality can be defined and reliably measured (Abbott-Shim, Lambert, & McCarty, 2000; Kontos et al., 1995; Lamb, 1998; NICHD, 1996). Whether parents agree with researchers' definition of childcare quality is a matter of some debate. See reviews by Lamb (1998) and by Dahlberg et al. (1999). However, parents and researchers agree that good childcare provides children with warm and positive relationships with childcare providers, a safe and healthy environment, and opportunities for children to learn (Hofferth, Shauman, Henke, & West, 1998; Kontos et al., 1995). As discussed in the introduction, childcare can take many forms. However, the markers of quality remain stable across these forms, except for informal or unregulated care which is generally lower in quality than regulated or formal care (Hofferth et al., 1998; Kontos et al., 1995).

Researchers have identified two dimensions of childcare quality: process and structure. Process quality captures the day-to-day experiences of children in childcare. The cornerstone of process quality is the relationship between the provider and children. Children whose childcare providers give them ample verbal and cognitive stimulation and generous amounts of individualized attention perform better on a wide range of assessments of social development (Howes, 1999; Peisner-Feinberg et al., in press). Stable providers are essential for development of these trusting and positive provider–child relationships. More stable providers engage in more appropriate, attentive, and engaged interactions with the children in their care (Raikes, 1993; Whitebook et al., 1990). Children who do not have stability and consistency in regards to their providers are more aggressive and less skilled with peers (Howes & Hamilton, 1993).

Structural dimensions of childcare are features that predict warm, sensitive, and stimulating adult–child interactions (Phillipsen, Burchinal, Howes, & Cryer, 1997; NICHD, 1996). Across all of the comprehensive research linking structural dimensions of childcare to childcare quality and to children's optimal outcomes, three dimensions emerge as most predictive: childcare providers' compensation, education and specialized training, and adult:child ratio (Abbott-Shim, Lambert, & McCarty, 2000; Helburn,1995; Kontos et al.,

1995; NICHD, 1996; Phillips, Mekos, Scarr, McCartney, & Abbott-Shim, in press; Ruopp et al., 1979; Whitebook et al., 1990). Childcare adults with higher levels of compensation, with more advanced education and specialized training in child development, who work with smaller groups of children are most often found in settings with higher quality ratings, are more effective with children, and are associated with more optimal child development outcomes in children.

Influences of childcare quality on social development

The positive effects of childcare quality on virtually every facet of children's development are one of the most consistent findings in developmental science. The effects of childcare quality on children's development are only about half as large as those associated with family environments, but emerge repeatedly in study after study and are consistent across children of every ethnicity and every language group. Some (but not all) research suggests that high quality care, especially center-based care, is particularly beneficial for low-income families (Burchinal, Ramey, Reid, & Jaccard, 1995; Caughty, DiPetro, & Strobine, 1994; Hart et al., 1998). All of the research that we report has controlled for family background effects. This means that researchers first accounted for family influences and then looked at the influences of childcare. The findings are consistent across all forms of childcare, but it is extremely important to understand that the positive influences of childcare on children's development are only found when the childcare is high quality.

Children enrolled in high quality childcare are more likely as toddlers and preschoolers to cooperate and comply with their mothers and childcare providers (Field, Masi, Holdstein, Perry, & Park, 1988; Howes & Olenick, 1986; NICHD, 1998; Phillips, McCartney, & Scarr, 1987). Children enrolled in high quality childcare as infants and toddlers are more likely as older children to cooperate with caregivers, and in the eyes of caregivers and parents, to have fewer behavior problems. In the longest-studied children, these findings persist into adolescence (Andersson, 1989, 1992; Field, 1991; Howes, 1988b, 1990; Howes, Hamilton, & Phillipsen, 1998).

Children enrolled in high quality childcare as toddlers and preschoolers are more socially competent with peers and less likely to be aggressive or withdrawn from peers as young children (Deater-Deckard, Pinkerton, & Scarr, 1996; Harper & Huie, 1985; Holloway & Reichert-Erickson, 1989; Howes, 1990; Howes, Matheson, & Hamilton, 1994; Howes, Phillips, & Whitebook, 1992; Kontos, Hsu, & Dunn, 1994; Lamb et al., 1988; NICHD Early Childcare Network, in press; Phillips et al., 1987). Children enrolled in high quality childcare as toddlers and preschoolers are more socially competent with peers and less likely to be aggressive or withdrawn from peers into adolescence (oldest children studied) (Andersson, 1989, 1992; Howes, 2000b; Pianta & Nimetz, 1991).

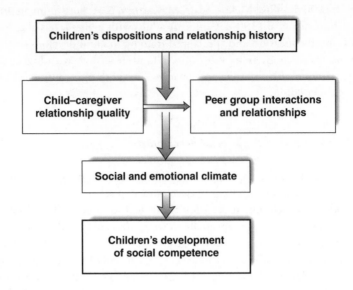

Figure 8.1   A model for understanding processes of socialization within childcare.

Process Model for Understanding the Within-Childcare Socialization Context

In the most comprehensive and recent review of the influences of childcare on children's development, Lamb (1998, p. 116) concludes that " . . . the global indices of quality that have served a generation of researchers and regulators so well must now yield center stage to a generation of more refined measures and concepts that allow practitioners to determine whether and how specific practices have the desired effects on children's learning and development." In the final section of this chapter we contribute to this effort by proposing a model that incorporates key dimensions for understanding processes of socialization within childcare: the peer group; caregiver–child relationships; children's dispositions and relationship history; and social and emotional climate.) The conceptual pathways between these dimensions are in Figure 8.1.

Children's dispositions and relationship history

We make two assumptions in the first section of this model. The first assumption is that children enter childcare with a relationship history and dispositions that are consistent (or inconsistent) with positive social interactions and relationships. The second assumption is that both dispositions and relationship history will contribute to the construction of positive child–caregiver relationships and to positive peer-group interactions and relationships. The specific dispositions that we are interested in are dispositions towards regulation of emotions and impulses. Children who are able to strike a balance between their own desires and interests and those of the other children and caregivers are the children who are able to regulate and control their emotions and impulses (Eisenberg et al., 1997; Fabes et al., 1999; Rothbart, Ahadi, & Hershey, 1994). If children have these dispositions or are helped to develop them within childcare they are more likely to engage in harmonious interactions with others and to develop positive relationships with others (Howes & Ritchie, in press).

Attachment theory suggests that children come to childcare with an attachment organization that functions as a working model of adult–child relationships (Bowlby, 1969). Children use their working model as a map or blueprint for ways to engage with new caregivers. Therefore, when children encounter a new caregiver, they tend to act towards this new adult in ways that are consistent with their prior relationship history, their working model. This means that children will act towards a new teacher in ways that may have been adaptive in the past, but will not, particularly in the childcare environment, lead to a positive relationship (Sroufe, 1983). Children with maladaptive prior attachment histories may "set the caregiver up" for replicating distrustful, insecure relationships. These models for relationships may come from home or from prior childcare experiences (Howes & Ritchie, in press).

Child–caregiver relationship quality

There is now a large body of evidence on the validity of assessing attachment relationships between children and teachers, identifying and examining antecedents of different qualities of relationships between children and their teachers and examining the concurrent and long-term correlates of different relationship qualities and children's social competence. In brief, the findings of these studies suggest that child–caregiver attachment relationship quality can be reliably and validly assessed, that similar processes are implicated in the formation of child–alternative caregiver attachment and child–mother attachment relationships of different qualities, and that child–alternative caregiver attachment security predicts social competence in the long and short term (Howes, 1999). Children with more positive child–caregiver relationships appear more able to make use of the learning opportunities available in childcare (Howes & Smith, 1995), and construct more positive peer relationships in childcare and as older children (Howes et al., 1994, 1998; Howes & Tonyan, 2000).

Peer group interactions and relationships

The development of children's peer relations may be semi-independent of their relationships with adults (Hay, 1985). This argument is based in part on the premise that the construction of social interaction with a peer is different than with an adult. Peers, unlike adults, are not particularly more knowledgeable or skillful in social interaction than the infant or toddler. But, to their advantage, peers share interests in activities that adults generally do not. Most adults quickly tire of games like run-chase or jumping off a step.

There is evidence that with more time in a particular peer group children do become more socially skillful at interactions and friendships (Howes, 1988a).

The perspective that peer relations are primarily constructed within peer groups is not necessarily at odds with an attachment theory perspective. It is possible that early adult–child attachment relationships serve to orient children towards or away from the peer group. Children with secure adult–child attachment relationships would perceive peers as potentially fun and interesting social partners, enter into peer play, and with experience become socially skilled. Children with insecure adult–child attachments would perceive peers as hostile or threatening and withdraw from or aggress towards peers. Once a child has withdrawn from peers or has constructed antagonistic patterns of interaction and relationships, it may be especially difficult to develop alternative behaviors with peers (Howes & Phillipsen, 1998). Unlike some sensitive adults who can understand that what appear to be maladaptive behaviors are instead based on mistrust; peers may perceive the potential peer partner as unpleasant and to be avoided. A skillful adult can work to disconfirm a child's hostile or withdrawing behavior. A peer is more likely to react in ways that maintain the maladaptive sequences.

Social and emotional climate

The positive or mistrustful nature of child–caregiver relationships and interactions and the positive or maladaptive nature of peer interactions and relationships contribute to the social and emotional climate of the childcare setting. Imagine a childcare setting in which most of the interactions were harmonious and respectful, in which children and adults worked together on projects, in which a child who was distressed or frustrated was comforted and helped, and in which laughter and other expressions of positive affect predominated. Contrast this with a childcare setting in which children were ridiculed for being different, talked to and touched in a harsh rejecting manner, competed rather than helped each other, and the general tone included mistrust and anger. The development of social competence would be to take different paths in these two extremes. Because childcare is ultimately an experience of "living" within a group, it is insufficient to understand the development of a child's social competence as isolated from the group. One piece of evidence that supports the importance of the social and emotional climate of childcare is an analysis of the Cost Quality and Outcome database that finds that climate in preschool childcare centers in addition to child–caregiver relationship quality and children's dispositions predicted peer relations in second grade (Howes, 2000b).

Closing Thoughts

It remains for future researchers to continue the program of studies that would confirm (or disconfirm) this or other models of socialization within childcare. In this chapter we have argued that socialization for the development of social competence (or maladaption) in childcare occurs within a society organized by class, race, ethnicity, and gender. Therefore childcare as a setting for socialization cannot be disentangled from these organizers and children are socialized into social interaction styles that are embedded within class, race, ethnicity, and gender. We have further argued that childcare per se cannot be considered an environment that is either detrimental to or enhancing of social development. We presented evidence that childcare quality does influence social development (although not independently of the influences of family environments). And finally we proposed that future research on socialization within childcare attend to multiple dimensions of variation within childcare.

References

Abbott-Shim, A., Lambert, R., & McCarty, F. (2000). Structural model of Head Start classroom quality. *Early Childhood Research Quarterly, 15*, 115–134.

Andersson, B. (1989). Effects of public day care: A longitudinal study. *Child Development, 60*, 857–866.

Andersson, B. (1992). Effects of day care on cognitive and socioemotional competence of thirteen-year-old Swedish school children. *Child Development, 63*, 20–36.

Baker, J. A., Terry, T., Bridger, R., & Winsor, A. (1997). Schools as caring communities: A relational approach to school reform. *School Psychology Review, 26*, 576–588.

Bates, J. E., Marvinney, D., Kelly, T., Dodge, K. A., Bennett, D. S., & Pettit, G. S. (1994). Childcare history and kindergarten adjustment. *Developmental Psychology, 30*, 690–700.

Belsky, J. (1988). The effects of infant care reconsidered. *Early Childhood Research Quarterly, 3*, 235–272.

Belsky, J., & Steinberg, L. (1978). The effects of daycare. *Child Development, 49*, 929–949.

Bost, K. K., Vaughn, B. E., Washington, W. N., Cielinski, K. L., & Bradbard, M. (1998). Social competence, social support, and attachment: Demarcation of construct domains, measurement, and paths of influence for preschool children attending Head Start. *Child Development, 69*, 192–218.

Bowlby, J. (1969). *Attachment and loss. Vol. 1: Attachment.* London: Hogarth.

Bretherton, I. (1985). Attachment theory: Retrospect and prospect. *Monographs of the Society for Research in Child Development, 50*, 3–35.

Burchinal. M. R., Ramey, S. L., Reid, M. K., & Jaccard, J. (1995). Early childcare experiences and their association with family and child characteristics during middle childhood. *Early Childhood Research Quarterly, 10*, 33–61.

Caughty, M., DiPetro, J., & Strobine, D. M. (1994). Day care participation as a protective factor in the cognitive development of low income children. *Child Development, 65*, 457 – 471.

Clifford, R. M., & Early, D. (1999). Almost a million children in school before kindergarten: Who is responsible for early childhood services? *Young Children, 54*, 48–51.

Coll, C. G., Lamberty, G., Jenkins, R., McAdoo, H. P., Cunic, K., Wasik, B., & Garcia, H.V. (1996). An integrative model for the study of developmental competencies in minority children. *Child Development, 67*, 1891–1914.

Coll, C. G., & Magnuson, K. (1999). Cultural differences as sources of developmental vulnerabilities and resources. In J. Shankoff & S. Meisels (Eds.), *Handbook of early childhood intervention.* Cambridge, England: Cambridge University Press.

Dahlberg, G., Moss, P., & Pence, A. (1999). *Beyond quality in early childhood education and care: Postmodern perspectives.* London: Falmer Press.

Deater-Deckard, K., Pinkerton, R., & Scarr, S. (1996). Childcare quality and children's behavioral development: A four-year longitudinal study. *Journal of Child Psychology and Psychiatry, 37,* 937–948.

Derman-Sparks, L. (1989). *Antibias curriculum tools for empowering young people.* Washington, DC: National Association for the Education of Young Children.

Eisenberg, N. A., Gutherie, I. K., Fabes, R. A., Reiser, M., Murphy, B. C., Holgren, R., Maszk, P., & Losoya, S. (1997). The relations of regulation and emotionality to resiliency and competent social functioning in elementary age children. *Child Development, 68,* 295–311.

Fabes, R. A., Eisenberg, N., Jones, S., Smith, M., Guthrie, I., Poulin, R., Shepard, S., & Friedman, J. (1999). Regulation emotionality and preschoolers' socially competent peer interactions. *Child Development, 70,* 432–442.

Field, T. (1991). Quality infant day care and grade school behavior and performance. *Child Development, 62,* 863–670.

Field, T., Masi, W., Goldstein, S., Perry, S., & Park, S. (1988). Infant childcare facilitates preschool social behavior. *Early Childhood Research Quarterly, 10,* 341–359.

Fuller, B., Halloway, S. D., et al. (1996). Family selection of childcare centers: The influence of household support, ethnicity, and parental practices. *Child Development, 67,* 3320–3337.

Harper, L., & Huie, K. (1985). The effects of prior group experience, age, and familiarity on quality and organization of preschool social relationships. *Child Development, 56,* 704–717.

Hart, C. H., Burts, D. C., Durland, M., Charlesworth, R., DeWolf, M., & Fleege, P. O. (1998). Stress behaviors and activity-type participation of preschoolers in more and less developmentally appropriate classrooms: SES and sex differences. *Journal of Research in Childhood Education, 12,* 176–196.

Hay, D. (1985). Learning to form relationships in infancy: Parallel attainments with parents and peers. *Developmental Review, 5,* 122–161.

Helburn, S. (1995). *Cost Quality and Outcome Study Final Report.* University of Colorado at Denver.

Hofferth, S. L., Shauman, K. A., Henke, R. R., & West, J. (June, 1998). *Characteristics of children's early care and education programs: Data from the 1995 National Household Education Survey (NCES 98–128).* Washington, DC: U.S. Department of Education.

Holloway, S., & Reichert-Erickson, M. (1989). Childcare quality, family structure, and maternal expectations: Relationship to preschool children's peer relations. *Journal of Applied Developmental Psychology, 10,* 281–298.

Holloway, S. D., Rambaud, M. F., Fuller, B., & Eggers-Pierola, C. (1995). What is appropriate practice at home and in childcare? Low income mothers' views on preparing their children for school. *Early Childhood Research Quarterly, 10,* 451–473.

Howes, C. (1980). Peer play scale as an index of complexity of peer interaction. *Developmental Psychology, 16,* 371–372.

Howes, C. (1983). Caregiver behavior in center and family daycare. *Journal of Applied Developmental Psychology, 3,* 99–107.

Howes, C. (1985). Sharing fantasy: Social pretend play in toddlers. *Child Development, 56,* 1253–1258.

Howes, C. (1988a). Peer interaction in young children. *Monograph of the Society for Research in Child Development no. 217, 53(1).*

Howes, C. (1988b). Relations between early childcare and schooling. *Developmental Psychology, 24,* 53–57.

Howes, C. (1990). Can the age of entry into childcare and the quality of childcare predict adjustment in kindergarten? *Developmental Psychology, 26,* 292–303.

Howes, C. (1996). The earliest friendships. The company they keep: Friendships in childhood and adolescence. In W. M. Bukowski, A. F. Newcomb, & W. W. Hartup (Eds.), (pp. 66–86).

New York: Cambridge University Press.

Howes, C. (1999). Attachment relationships in the context of multiple caregivers. In J. Cassidy & P. R. Shaver (Eds.), (671–687), *Handbook of attachment theory and research*. New York: Guilford Press.

Howes, C. (2000a). Social development: The family and attachment relationships of infants and toddlers. Research into practice. In D. Cryer & T. Harms (Eds.), *Infants and toddlers in out-of-home care* (pp. 87–113). Baltimore: Brookes.

Howes, C. (2000b). Social-emotional classroom climate in childcare child–teacher relationships and children's second grade peer relations. *Social Development, 9,* 194–204.

Howes, C., & Hamilton, C. E. (1993). The changing experience of childcare: Changes in teachers and in teacher–child relationships and children's social competence with peers. *Early Childhood Research Quarterly, 8,* 15–32.

Howes, C., Hamilton, C. E., & Phillipsen, L. (1998). Stability and continuity of child–caregiver and child–peer relationships. *Child Development, 69,* 418–426.

Howes, C., & Matheson, C. C. (1992). Sequences in the development of competent play with peers: Social and social pretend play. *Developmental Psychology, 28,* 961–974.

Howes, C., Matheson, C. C., & Hamilton, C. E. (1994). Maternal, teacher and childcare history correlates of children's relationships with peers. *Child Development, 65,* 264–272.

Howes, C., & Olenick, M. (1986). Family and childcare influences on toddler compliance. *Child Development, 57,* 202–216.

Howes, C., Phillips, D. A., & Whitebook, M. (1992). Thresholds of quality in childcare centers and children's social and emotional development. *Child Development, 63,* 449–460.

Howes, C., & Phillipsen, L. C. (1998). Continuity in children's relations with peers. *Social Development, 7,* 340–349.

Howes, C., & Ritchie, (in preparation). Beyond quality: Childcare practices in programs for children with difficult life circumstances.

Howes, C., & Ritchie, S (in press). Teachers and children: Constructing relationships to enhance learning and positive classroom climate.New York: Teachers College Press.

Howes, C., & Smith, E. (1995). Relations among childcare quality, teacher behavior children's play activities, emotional security, and cognitive activity in childcare. *Early Childhood Research Quarterly, 10,* 381–404.

Howes, C., & Tonyan, H. (1999). Peer relations. In L. Balter & C. S. Tamis-LeMonda (Eds.), *Child psychology: A handbook of contemporary issues*. Philadelphia: Psychology Press.

Howes, C., & Tonyan H. (2000). Links between adult and peer relations across four developmental periods. In K. A. Kerns, J. M. Contreras, & A. M. Neal-Barnett (Eds.), *Family and peers: Linking two social worlds* (pp. 85–114). Westport, CT: Praeger .

Howes, C., Unger, O., & Seidner, L. (1989). Social pretend play in toddlers: Social pretend play forms and parallels with solitary pretense. *Child Development, 60,* 132.

James, J. O. (2000). To be young, black, and female. Masters Thesis submitted to the Department of Education. University of California Los Angeles.

Kontos, S. (1992). *Family childcare: Out of the shadows and into the limelight*. Washington, DC: National Association for the Education of Young Children.

Kontos, S., Howes, C., Shinn, M., & Galinsky, E. (1995). *Quality in family childcare and relative care*. New York: Teachers College Press.

Kontos, S., Hsu, H.-C., & Dunn, L. (1994). Children's cognitive and social competence in childcare centers and family childcare homes. *Journal of Applied Developmental Psychology, 15,* 87–111.

Lamb, M. E. (1998). Nonparental childcare: Context quality and correlates. In I. E. Siegel & K. A. Renninger (Eds.), *Handbook of child psychology, vol. 4, Child psychology in practice*. New York: Wiley.

Lamb, M., Hwang, C., Bookstein, F., Brober, A., Hult, G., & Frodi, A., (1988). Determinants of social competence in Swedish preschoolers. *Developmental Psychology, 24*, 58–70.

Lubeck, S. (1985). *The sandbox society: Early education in Black and White America.* London: Fulmer Press.

Lubeck, S. (1996). Deconstructing "Child Development knowledge" and "teacher preparation." *Early Childhood Research Quarterly, 11*, 147–167.

Maccoby, E. E. (1984). Socialization and developmental change. *Developmental Psychology, 55*, 317–328.

Maccoby, E. E. (1998). *The two sexes: Growing up apart; coming together.* Cambridge, MA: Harvard University Press.

McCartney, K., & Rosenthal, R. (2000). Effect size, practical importance, and social policy for children. *Child Development, 71*, 173–180.

National Center for Children in Poverty (2000). *Scant increases after welfare reform.* New York: National Center for Children in Poverty.

NICHD Early Childcare Research Network (1996). Characteristics of infant childcare: Factors contributing to positive caregiving. *Early Childhood Research Quarterly, 11*, 269–306.

NICHD Early Childcare Research Network (1998). Early childcare and self-control, compliance, and problem behavior at 24 and 36 months. *Child Development, 69*, 1143–1168.

NICHD Early Childcare Research Network (1997). The effects of infant childcare on infant–mother attachment security: Results of the NICHD Study of Early Childcare. *Child Development, 68*, 860–879.

NICHD Early Childcare Research Network (1998). Relations between family predictors and child outcomes: Are they weaker for children in childcare? *Developmental Psychology, 34*, 1119–1128.

Peisener-Feinberg, E., Burchinal, M., Clifford, R., Culkin, M., Howes, C., & Kagan, S. L. (in press). The children from the Cost Quality and Outcome Study go to school. *Child Development.*

Phillips, D. McCartney, K., & Scarr, S. (1987). Childcare quality and children's social development. *Developmental Psychology, 23*, 537–543.

Phillips, D., Mekos, D., Scarr, S., McCartney, K., & Abbott-Shim, M. (in press). Within and beyond the classroom door: Assessing quality in childcare centers. *Early Childhood Research Quarterly.*

Phillips, D. A., Voran, M., Kister, E., Howes, C., & Whitebook, M. (1994). Childcare for children in poverty: Opportunity or inequity. *Child Development, 65*, 472–492.

Phillipsen, L. C., Burchinal, M. R., Howes, C., & Cryer, D. (1997). The prediction of process quality from structural features of child care. *Early Childhood Research Quarterly, 12*, 281–303.

Pianta, R. C., & Nimetz, S. (1991). Relations between children and teachers. *Journal of Applied Developmental Psychology, 12*, 379–393.

Raikes, H. (1993). Relationship duration in infant care. Time with a high ability teacher and infant–teacher attachment. *Early Childhood Research Quarterly, 8*, 309–325.

Rothbart, M. K., Ahadi, S. A., & Hershey, K. L. (1994). Temperament and social behavior in childhood. *Merrill-Palmer Quarterly, 40*, 21–39.

Rubenstein, J., & Howes, C. (1979). Caregiving and infant behavior in daycare and homes. *Developmental Psychology, 15*, 1–24.

Ruopp, R., Travers, J., Glantz, F., & Coelen, C. (1979). *Children at the center: Final results of the national day care study.* Cambridge, MA: Abt Associates.

Singer, J. D., Fuller, B., Keiley, M. K., & Wolf, A. (1998). Early childcare selection variation by geographic location, maternal characteristics, and family structure. *Developmental Psychology, 34*, 1129–1144.

Sroufe, L. A. (1983). Infant-caregiving attachment and patterns of maladaptation in preschool: The roots of maladaptation and competence. In M. Permutter (Ed.), *Minnesota Symposium on Child Psychology, vol. 16* (pp. 41–81). Hillsdale, NJ: Erlbaum.

Statistics, U.S.D.o.E.N.C.f.E. (1996). *National household educational survey of 1995.* Washington, DC: U.S. Department of Education.

Thompson, R. A. (1999). Early attachment and later development. In J. Cassidy & P. R. Shaver (Eds.), *Handbook of attachment* (pp. 265–287). New York: Guilford Press.

Vaughn, B., Azria, M., Krzysik, L., Caya, L., Boost, K., Newell, W., & Kazura, K. (2000). Friendship and social competence in a sample of preschool children attending Head Start. *Developmental Psychology, 36,* 326–338.

Wang, M. C., & Gordon, E. W. (1994). *Educational resilience in inner-city America: Challenges and prospects.* Hillsdale, NJ: Erlbaum.

Whitebook, M. (1999). Childcare workers: High demand, low wages. *Annals of the American Academy,* 146–141.

Whitebook, M., Howes, C., & Phillips, D. (1990). *Who cares? Childcare teachers and the quality of care in America.* Final Report of the National Childcare Staffing Study.

9

Relative Contributions of Families and Peers to Children's Social Development

Ross D. Parke, Sandra D. Simpkins, David J. McDowell, Mina Kim, Colleen Killian, Jessica Dennis, Mary L. Flyr, Margaret Wild, and Yumee Rah

Families have traditionally been viewed as the major socialization agency for the development of children's social behavior. Under the influence of Freudian theory and subsequently Bowlby's fusion of psychoanalytic and ethological approaches, the mother–child relationship has remained a prominent cornerstone of children's social development. In recent decades, our views of the socialization process have changed in a variety of ways. First, our limited view of the mother–child dyad as central to the socialization process has been replaced by a recognition of the family as a social system in which fathers, siblings, and the marital relationship are all viewed as playing important roles in children's social development (Parke & Buriel, 1998). Second, it is increasingly recognized that socialization is a multifaceted process which includes a variety of influential agents beyond the family, such as extended families, adult mentors, formal and informal support systems, and children's peers and friends. Of particular interest is the role of families and peers in the socialization matrix. Several views concerning the relative importance of family and peers as well as the degree of linkage between these two social systems have been suggested over the last several decades. As Hartup (1979) has noted in his classic formulation, children's relationships with peers are viewed as either independent of family relationships or interdependent social systems. Those who take the "independent" view argue that peer and family systems develop separately and each perform unique functions in the socialization process (e.g., Harlow, 1958). More recently some writers (e.g., Harris, 1995, 1998, 2000) have extended the independence argument and proposed that parents have little influence on children's behavior beyond a biological or genetic contribution. Alternatively, Harris argues that the peer group is largely responsible for socialization of children's social behavior.

(See the recent exchange between Vandell (2000) and Harris (2000) for more detail on the current status of the issue.)

In contrast to the independence view of the nature of family and peer relationships, others argue that family and peer systems mutually influence each other in the course of childhood socialization. Conceptualization of the nature of the linkage has varied. Historically, family and peer systems have been viewed as conflictful, with the framing of the family–peer linkage issue in terms of "parents versus peers" (Youniss & Smollar, 1985). Evidence in support of this view has been limited and instead considerable support for continuity between parental values and attitudes largely discredited this viewpoint (Douvan & Adelson, 1966). Instead, most recent accounts and the perspective which guides this chapter suggest that families and peers both play important roles in children's social development and recognize the interdependence between these two social systems. It is further assumed that the nature of family–peer relationships varies across development periods as well as across different family types and ecological, historical, and cultural contexts. Finally, recent advances in this area in uncovering the mechanisms or processes by which those two systems are linked will be briefly examined. Our goal is to provide a contemporary and balanced perspective on the roles played by both family and peers in children's social development.

Genes versus Parents and Peers: The Wrong Question

Several writers have downplayed the influence of parents on children's social development (Harris, 1995, 1998, 2000; Rowe, 1994; Scarr, 1992) and instead have argued that heredity accounts for a sizeable amount of the variance in children's development. Indeed, behavior geneticists have provided a much-needed corrective to the earlier and simplistic view that the environment alone, including parents and peers were the major influence on social development. At the same time, the finding of behavior genetics that "heredity rarely accounts for as much as 50% of the variation among individuals in a particular population" (Collins, Maccoby, Steinberg, Hetherington, & Bornstein, 2000, p. 228) leaves half of the variance due to environmental effects or gene X environment interactions. Ironically, our best evidence to date that the environment matters comes from behavior genetic studies. However, there are major problems with the additive approach which assumes that genetic and environmental influences operate independently but together account for the variance in outcomes. As Collins et al. (2000) note, in their critique of research on the role of nature versus nurture in our studies of socialization, recent models have adopted a variety of more sophisticated assumptions and designs to reflect the reality that "the expression of heritable traits depends strongly on experience, including specific parental behaviors, as well as predispositions and age-related factors in the child" (Collins et al., 2000, p. 228). This contemporary look in behavior genetics research is leading to new designs which permit the estimation of gene X environment effects in which the operation of genetic predispositions are conditional on the type of environment, including parenting, to which the child is exposed (Reiss, Neiderhiser, Hetherington, & Plomin, 2000).

Studies of the role of temperament, a genetically determined individual difference, in children's development have illustrated the conditional nature of genetically based predispositions. While a difficult temperament in infancy is sometimes associated with the development of insecure infant–mother attachment, this link is most evident when social support available to the mothers is limited (Crockenberg, 1981). When maternal social support was high, there were no differences in the quality of the infant–mother attachment relationship for difficult and easy infants. Since this early study, evidence has mounted in support of this interactive view of temperament. For example, several researchers have found that difficult temperament predicts long-term behavior outcomes, such as externalizing problems; however, additional parental influences are evident beyond the effects of temperament (Bates, Pettit, & Dodge, 1995). Other studies have found moderating effects of parenting on temperament–behavior links (Bates, Pettit, Dodge, & Ridge, 1998; Rothbart & Bates, 1998). Moreover, as Vandell (2000) has recently argued, difference in parental treatment is "not driven solely by children's genetic differences . . . Children in the same family can have very different experiences as a function of changes in family circumstances related to parents employment, divorce, relocations, illness, separation, and death" (p. 702). These arguments are consistent with the conditional view of parenting, and underscore the importance of environmental factors as moderators of the interplay between genetic factors and parenting. In sum, parenting remains an important influence on children's social development (Parke & Buriel, 1998), although it is increasingly recognized that genetic factors interact with parenting styles to achieve these effects (Hart, 1999; Vandell, 2000).

Just as parents remain important agents of socialization, ample evidence (see Rubin, Bukowski, & Parker, 1998) suggests that peers play an important role in social development – after controlling for parental effects. A variety of social and academic outcomes are forecast by the quality of children's peer relationships in early childhood (Parker & Asher, 1987). Moreover in the study of social relationships distinctions have often been made among different relationship units of analysis, including dyads and groups. It is assumed that friendship based on a reciprocal relationship between two individuals makes a distinctive and unique contribution to children's social adaptation, which is different from measures of peer-group acceptance or experience in peer-group contexts. Recent efforts to limit peer influence to group-level effects (Harris, 1995, 2000) are inconsistent with the accumulating body of evidence which demonstrates that friendships have important influences on children's social adaptation over time (Hartup & Stevens, 1997; Newcomb & Bagwell, 1995). Moreover, different types of peer relationships, such as companions, friends, and teammates serve different functions in development (Krappman, 1992; Vandell, 2000) a view that stands in sharp contrast to Harris (1995, 2000) who argues that peer-group level experience is the major socialization influence. Just as parenting interacts with genetic/biological variables, a similar argument can be made in the case of peers (Vandell, 2000). Recent evidence suggests that the choices of particular peers, and activities and the timing of entry into these activities are likely to be biologically as well as socially mediated. As Vandell (2000) recently noted, interpretation of the direction of effects in these studies is difficult to establish. Indeed much of the research on the peer group as a central socialization force "suffers from the same challenges of gene–environment correlations that confront parenting researchers. Children actively select some peer groups and not others on the basis of their interests and proclivities" (Vandell, 2000, p. 704). Indeed the move toward longitudinal and experimental studies has been motivated, in part, by attempts to clarify the nature of these gene–environment correlations.

An example will illustrate this interplay between genetically influenced processes and social variables in shaping children's social development and recent attempts to disentangle gene–environment relationships. Just as the parent research has shown, a conditional model that implicates both environmental and biological/genetic influences emerges as the best account of the available data. Infants with difficult temperament are more likely to be rejected by peers (Bates, Bayles, Bennett, Ridge, & Brown, 1991), while inhibited infants are more likely to be socially withdrawn in early and middle childhood (Calkins & Fox, 1992). In sum, in the case of both parents and peers, the impact of these socializing agents are best understood by recognizing their interplay with biological/genetic determined child characteristics.

Parents versus Peers or Parents and Peers

Just as genetic factors do not operate alone, our view is that parents and peers operate together in the socialization process. In contrast to Harris (1995, 1998, 2000) who argues that the peer group is the major environmental socializing force in children's development, and parents play a minor role in this process, we argue that parents and a variety of types of peer relationships, including friendships, matter in the socialization process. Second, rather than peers functioning independently of parents, we argue that parents play a major role in shaping the timing of entry into peer contexts, the nature and frequency of peer contacts and the quality of peer activities. Moreover, the links between these two systems is transactional with parents affecting their children's peer contacts and experiences, which in turn, modify parent–child relationships, which subsequently further modify peer relationships (Hart, Olsen, Robinson, & Mandleco, 1997).

Parental Influence on Children's Peer Relationships: A Tripartite Model

There are many ways in which parents have been found to influence their children's relationships with peers. We propose that there are three different paths that lead to variations in children's peer relationships. These three paths include parent–child interaction, parents' direct advice concerning peer relationships, and parents' regulation of children's peer activities and access to peers.

Parent–child interaction and the parent–child relationship

Parent–child interaction has a long history in the area of developmental psychology. Research in this area is based on the notion that face-to-face interactions between children and parents may afford children the opportunity to learn social skills that are necessary for successful peer relationships (see Parke & O'Neil, 1997, for a fuller description). This research has shown that controlling parent interactional styles are related to negative social outcomes for children and that warm interactional styles are related to positive social outcomes. Recent studies found that children of mothers who interact more positively or are more responsive and engaging with their children were more socially accepted by peers (Harrist, Pettit, Dodge, & Bates, 1994; Hart, Ladd, & Burleson, 1990; Putallaz, 1987). Pettit and Harrist (1993) observed positive and negative maternal interactional styles during a family meal and found positive peer outcomes for the children whose mothers were more sensitive and negative peer outcomes whose mothers were more intrusive. Similarly, parents who exhibit negative affect, who are over-controlling, and who are more distant in their interactions have children that are less accepted by peers or socially skilled (e.g., Carson & Parke, 1996; Hart, DeWolf, & Burts, 1992; McDowell & Parke, 2000; Olsen et al., in press).

Studies of child–parent attachment have provided evidence that the quality of attachment is linked with the quality of children's peer relationships. When a child is provided with sensitive and contingently responsive caregiving from his/her primary caregivers in infancy a secure attachment is formed within a relationship between infant and caregiver (Sroufe, Carlson, & Shulman, 1993), which leads to the child being more positive and competent in later peer relationships.

As these studies underscore, the nature of parent–child interactional history and the parent–child relationship are linked to variations in the quality of peer relationships – further evidence of the interdependence of these two social systems. Moreover, subsequent outcomes, which have often been attributed to peer influences, clearly have their origins in early parenting practices and family-based relationships. In fact, disentangling the interplay between these two systems may be a false goal, since in reality the two systems mutually influence each other across development and operate together in accounting for socialization outcomes.

Research in this area has moved beyond the description of links between the two domains. In the most recent stage, the focus has been on the processes mediating the relations between parent–child interactions and/or relationships and peer outcomes. A variety of processes have been proposed including affect management skills (e.g., emotional encoding/decoding; emotional understanding; emotional regulation), attention regulatory mechanisms, and cognitive representational models.

Children learn more than specific affective expressions, such as anger or sadness or joy, in the family. They learn a cluster of processes associated with the understanding and regulation of affective displays, which we term "affect management skills" (Parke, Cassidy, Burks, Carson, & Boyum, 1992). It is assumed that these skills are acquired during the course of parent–child interaction, and are available to the child for use in other relationships. Moreover, it is assumed that these skills play a mediating role between family and peer relationships.

Evidence suggests that children's emotional encoding and decoding skills (see Hubbard & Coie, 1994, for review) are related to their social competence with peers. Other evidence suggests that children's emotional understanding (e.g., causes of emotion; appropriate reaction to emotions) is also related to peer competence (Cassidy, Parke, Butovsky, &

Braungart, 1992; Denham, 1998). It is assumed that these skills are acquired in the course of parent–child play. Through physically playful interaction with their parents, especially fathers, children may be learning how to use emotional signals to regulate the social behavior of others.

Emotional regulation has also been suggested as a potential link between family and peer contexts. For example, parental comforting of children when they experience negative emotion has been linked with constructive anger reactions (Eisenberg & Fabes, 1994). Several studies have suggested that parental willingness to discuss emotions with their children is related to children's awareness and understanding of others' emotions (Denham, 1998; Dunn & Brown, 1994; Gottman, Katz, & Hooven, 1997).

In concert with emotion regulation, attentional regulatory processes have come to be viewed as an additional mechanism through which familial socialization experiences might influence the development of children's social competence. These processes include the ability to attend to relevant cues, to sustain attention, to refocus attention through such processes as cognitive distraction and cognitive restructuring, and other efforts to reduce the level of emotional arousal (Denham, 1998). Attentional processes are thought to organize experience and to play a central role in cognitive and social development beginning early in infancy (Rothbart & Bates, 1998). Thus, Wilson (1999) aptly considers attention regulatory processes as a "shuttle" linking emotion regulation and social cognitive processes because attentional processes organize both cognitive and emotional responses, and thus, influence the socialization of relationship competence. In support of direct influences, Eisenberg, Fabes, Bernzweig, Karbon, Poulin, and Hanish (1993) found that children who were low in attentional regulation were also low in social competence.

A third mechanism has been championed by both attachment and social processing theorists namely cognitive representational models of social relationships (see Parke & O'Neil, 2000 and Sroufe & Fleeson, 1986, for reviews). According to attachment theorists the early experience with the parent is incorporated into the child's internal working models of the self, the parent, and the parent–child relationship, and these models are carried forward into the individual's social representations and behavior in subsequent interpersonal settings, including peer contexts (Ainsworth, 1989; Sroufe & Fleeson, 1986). Indeed, attachment is related to interpersonal cognition or representations that are applied to challenges in peer relationships (e.g., Cassidy, Kirsh, Scolton, & Parke, 1996; Rabiner, Keane, & MacKinnon-Lewis, 1993; Suess, 1987). Suess (1987) found that insecurely attached children displayed more unrealistic or hostile/negative biases in judging intentions of children involved in hypothetical mishaps with peers. Cassidy et al. (1996) found that greater perceived rejection by both mothers and fathers was associated with greater perceived hostile intent by peers. These studies provide evidence that the quality of attachment may have direct or indirect influences on later mental representations with respect to peers (see also McDowell, Parke, & Spitzer, in press).

Parent as advisor, instructor, and consultant

Parents' direct advice concerning children's peer relationships represents a second path of influence. It is assumed that parents influence children's peer relationships by providing direct instruction about the appropriate ways of maintaining social relationships. Work in this area has indicated that different qualities of parental advice giving are related to variations in children's social competence. For example, young children have been found to play more cooperatively and exhibit more turn taking when an adult is facilitating than when playing alone (Bhavnagri & Parke, 1991). Similarly, Finnie and Russell (1988) examined the types of advice mothers gave during their children's attempts at group entry. Children of mothers who facilitated preschoolers' entry into a play situation by use of more group-oriented advice strategies were more socially competent. When examining mothers' advice to hypothetical vignettes, Finnie and Russell (1988) found that more skillful responses (more rule-oriented and positive) were related to children being more socially accepted (see also Russell & Finnie, 1990). Mize, Pettit, Laird, and Lindsey (1993) found that children whose mothers offered more positive solutions to peer dilemmas were rated as more socially competent by teachers. Furthermore, these researchers found mothers' explicit advice giving predicted social competence more than simply discussing peer situations.

While prior work with younger children has generally found positive relations between both positive style and clear and explicit content of advice giving, several theorists (Ladd, 1992; Parke, Burks, Carson, Neville, & Boyum, 1994) suggest that the impact of advice giving may change across development. As children develop a future orientation, parents are likely to try to keep their children from being influenced by peers by talking to them about the future consequences of their behavior (Mounts, 2000). In the early years of development, parents may use advice giving as a socializing tactic to help children acquire the skills necessary for adequate social adaptation to peers. However, both parents and children may regard explicit parental advice as less necessary and/or less appropriate as children develop adequate social skills. Instead, by middle childhood, provision of advice would be expected to be used by parents for remediational goals in which the advice giving would be highest in the case of poor socially functioning children. Work in our own lab has supported this notion. Specifically, when parents offered more advice and more specific advice about peer dilemmas, children were rated as less positive and more negative by teachers and peers (McDowell, Parke, & Wang, in press).

There is a shift in recent research toward an integrated approach to these topics. As Grusec and Goodnow (1994) suggest, both style and content need to be considered together in determining the impact of parental advice giving on children's peer outcomes. The combined impact of these two aspects of parental advice giving is beginning to achieve recognition. In their study of 3–5-year-old children, Mize and Pettit (1997) found that maternal information giving and guidance (content) predicted over and above mothers' warmth and responsiveness (style) to children's peer acceptance (as rated by teachers) during a play interaction context. In our own work we have found similar results showing that the style and content of parental advice play nonoverlapping roles in children's peer relationships (McDowell, Parke, & Wang, in press). This second pathway through which parents influence children's peer relationships provides further evidence in support of our argument that family and peer systems are interdependent.

Beyond parent–child interaction and advice giving: Parents as social managers and social supervisors

Parents influence their children's social relationships not only through their direct interactions with their children. They also function as managers of their children's social lives (Hartup, 1979; Parke, 1978) and serve as regulators of opportunities for social contact with extra-familial social partners. Although peer influence increases as children develop (Rubin et al., 1998), parents continue to play an important regulatory role as gatekeeper and monitor of children's social choices and social contacts throughout middle childhood and into adolescence. This view stands in marked contrast to some claims (Harris, 1998) that parental influence over peer-group activities does not extend beyond preadolescence.

Parental monitoring.   One way in which parents can affect their children's social relationships is through monitoring of their children's social activities. This form of management is particularly evident as children move into middle childhood and later is associated with the relative shift in importance of family and peers as sources of influence on social relationships. Monitoring refers to a range of activities, including the supervision of children's choice of social settings, activities, and friends. Parents of delinquent and antisocial children engaged in less monitoring and supervision of their children's activities, and less control of their sons' choice of friends, than parents of nondelinquent children (Patterson & Stouthamer-Loeber, 1984).

It is unlikely that parental discipline, interaction, and monitoring are independent. In support of this view, Dishion (1990) found that *both* inconsistent, negative, and punitive discipline and low parental supervision and monitoring were related to emergence of antisocial behavior, which, in turn, was linked with rejection by peers. Similarly, Steinberg (1986) found that children in grades 6 to 9, especially girls who are on their own after school, are more susceptible to peer pressure to engage in antisocial activity (e.g., vandalism, cheating, stealing) than are their adult-supervised peers. In addition, children of parents who were high in their use of authoritative parenting practices were less susceptible to peer pressure in the absence of monitoring, in nonsupervised contexts. Developmental shifts may be important, because younger children are less likely to be left unsupervised than older children; moreover, it is likely that direct supervision is more common among younger children, whereas distal supervision is more evident among older children. Finally, recent work (O'Neil, Parke, & McDowell, 2001) suggests that monitoring and limitation of children's activities are, in part, determined by parental perceptions of neighborhood quality. When parents perceive the neighborhood to be of poor quality, they increase their level of supervision and limit their children's activities which, in turn, leads to higher social competence. This suggests a new direction for future research, namely the determinants of different levels of parental monitoring and supervision.

Play rules.   Rarely have researchers explored the relation between play rules for children and children's peer relationships. Simpkins and Parke (in press) explored the relations between the number of parental play rules and sixth-grade children's loneliness, depression, and friendship quality. Boys whose parents had fewer play rules reported lower levels of depression and more conflict in their best friendship. Boys' loneliness and positive qualities in their best friendships was not significantly predicted by paternal play rules, nor were girls' outcomes significantly correlated with the number of parental play rules (see also Furstenberg, Cook, Eccles, Elder, & Sameroff, 1999).

Parents as social mediators of social contact.   Parents manage children's peer relationships by arranging for their children to interact with peers. Children's contact with peers after school can occur through informal play contacts with children or formal after-school activities (e.g., team sports). Informal contacts occur when parents and/or children arrange time to play with peers outside of school. During these contacts, children can practice and learn new social skills and behaviors with peers. This also provides children with a nonschool context in which to form and develop peer relationships. Parents who initiated at least one contact had children with a larger range of playmates and more companions with whom they had frequent contact (Kerns, Cole, & Andrews, 1998; Ladd & Golter, 1988; Ladd & Hart, 1992). In addition, boys were more liked and less rejected by peers if parents initiated at least one informal play contact (Ladd & Golter, 1988). Furthermore, parents who initiated a larger number of play contacts had children who had higher prosocial behavior and spent less time exhibiting nonsocial behavior in school (Ladd & Hart, 1992).

As with informal play contacts, children can spend their time after school with peers during formal activities. Bryant (1985) found that 10 year olds enrolled in formal activities were more likely to have better perspective-taking skills, which are helpful in children's peer relationships. Similarly, Pettit, Laird, Bates, and Dodge (1997) examined the relations between adult-supervised activities (e.g., music lessons, church, scouts, and youth groups) in first and third grade and children's peer relationships in sixth grade. Girls' activities in first grade were curvilinearly related to their grade point average (GPA) in sixth grade. Further, girls' activities during third grade were related curvilinearly to sixth-grade externalizing behaviors. These curvilinear patterns for girls indicated that an average number of activities was related to a higher GPA and fewer externalizing behaviors while a low or high number of activities was related to poorer outcomes. Boys' activities in first grade were not significantly related to sixth-grade outcomes. In third grade, boys with more activities showed more externalizing behaviors in sixth grade.

Parents' social networks as a source of potential peer contacts for children.   Cochran and Brassard (1979) have proposed that parents' social networks can influence children's cognitive and social development. Parents' networks may influence children's social adjustment by providing opportunities for social interaction with the children of their parents' network members. Children's contact with peers would be facilitated by the presence of potential play partners among the offspring of parents' network members. Cochran and his colleagues (Cochran, Larner, Riley, Gunnarson, & Henderson., 1990) have provided support for the overlap between parent and child social networks. They found that 30% to 44% of 6-year-old children's social networks were also included in the parents' networks.

The overlap between parents' and children's networks is also a form of social integration (Coleman & Hoffer, 1987). With high social integration or social capital (Coleman, 1988), parents' goals for their children's development or management of their behavior can be carried out through parents' network members. Thus, parents who have larger networks have more adults that can help their children's development through several pathways. First, parents and children have more social support. Second, parents are better able to control or regulate problem behavior by having other parents guide their children's behavior when they are not present. Third, other parents can encourage prosocial behavior and parents' values when they are not present. Another way these two networks may be linked was proposed by Coleman (1990), who argued that when both parents and their children are acquainted with other parents and their children, they form network closure. According to Coleman, when network closure exists, there are likely to be more shared values and more social control over their offspring, which, in turn, would be related to better social outcomes. Darling, Steinberg, Gringlas, and Dornbusch (1995) found that social integration (as indexed by network closure) and value consensus were related to adolescent social and academic outcomes. Specifically, adolescents who reported high degrees of contact among their parents, friends, and their friends' parents, as well as high levels of interaction with nonfamily adults, were less deviant and higher in academic achievement than their peers who were less socially integrated.

Other studies suggest that the quality of adult social networks relates to children's social behavior (e.g., Melson, Ladd, & Hsu, 1993; Uhlendorff, 2000). In an Australian study, Homel, Burns, and Goodnow (1987) found positive relations between the number of "dependable" friends that parents report and 11-year-old children's self-rated happiness, the number of regular playmates, and maternal ratings of children's social skills. Recently, Simpkins, O'Neil, Lee, Parke, and Wang (under review) extended this work by showing a relation between parents' enjoyment of friends in their network and peer ratings of social competence. The more parents enjoyed their friends, the less the child was disliked and perceived as aggressive by peers. Moreover, the more contact that parents had with relatives, the less disliked children were by their peers. Finally, these investigators found that maternal and paternal social networks have distinctive links to children's social relationships. Fathers who rated their networks as less enjoyable had children who were more aggressive and more disliked by peers, whereas the less contact that mothers had with their friends, the higher teachers rated their children on avoidance of interaction with other children.

Finally the quality of the relationship that adults develop with friends in their social network is an important correlate of their children's friendship quality, Doyle and Markiewicz (1996) found that mothers who reported having supportive friends had children who experienced more closeness with their best friend. Or, if mothers felt less secure about their best friendship or rated their friends as interesting, their own children were more likely to have a best friend. The findings concerning the links between lack of mothers' security about their friendships is consistent with earlier work on maternal recollections of their childhood peer experiences. In this work, Putallaz, Costanzo, and Smith (1991) found that mothers who had anxious peer relations as children had children who were more socially competent, which supports a compensatory model of parenting. More recently, Simpkins and Parke (2001) found that the quality of both maternal and paternal friendships was related to children's friendship quality. However, the quality of the parents' best friendship was a better predictor of daughters' friendships, while both the quality of the parents' best friendship and breadth of their social network were predictive of sons' friendships. As these studies illustrate, the quality and scope of adult friendships and social networks are important correlates not just of children's peer competence but of their friendship qualities as well. Finally, these findings suggest that the parental correlates of dyadic friendship qualities may, in fact, be different than the correlates of sociometric studies or other measures of peer-group experience.

In sum, parents serve as regulators of children's peer interactions and relationships. Peers are influential in children's development but some of the variance in outcomes is clearly the product of earlier and concurrent parental managerial strategies.

The Interplay Across Pathways

It is critical to remember that these three sets of parental strategies do not operate separately (Parke & O'Neil, 2000). The work of Dishion, Poulin, and Skaggs, (2000) illustrates the ways in which these separate parental strategies (i.e., parental childrearing practices, parental management) often operate together. In addition, this work illustrates how family factors influence children's behavior, which over development leads to different peer-group choices. Clearly, the nature of family–peer linkages needs to be considered from a developmental perspective. Children who associate with antisocial peers are more likely to engage in antisocial behavior; while it is common to blame the peer group for this increased deviant activity, the Patterson et al. (1989) research suggests that earlier family conditions modify the likelihood of associating with deviant peers. Poor monitoring as well as coercive/authoritarian childrearing practices in early childhood lead to aggressive behavior and poor school performance in middle childhood. In adolescence when there is more autonomy in the choice of peers, youth from these dysfunctional homes are more likely to choose antisocial peers, which, in turn, increases the rate of deviant activity. "Even when selection effects are controlled, much of what appears to be peer influence is actually the end result of familial influence at an earlier point in the child's development" (Collins et al., 2000, p. 228).

Marital Conflict and Children's Social Relationships

The relationship between the marital relationships and children's peer competence has a very recent history in the social development literature. Two perspectives are found: a direct and indirect effects models of the relations between marital conflict and children's peer relationships.

Marital discord can have an indirect influence on children's adjustment through changes in the quality of parenting (Fauber & Long, 1991). Affective changes in the quality of the parent–child relationship, lack of emotional availability, and adoption of less optimal parenting styles have been implicated as mechanisms through which marital discord disrupts parenting processes. Several studies (Cowan, Cowan, Schulz, & Heming, 1994; Katz & Kahen, 1993) have found that marital conflict is linked with poor parenting, which, in turn, is related to poor social adjustment on the children. Other work has focused on the specific processes by which the marital relationship itself directly influences children's immediate functioning and long-term adjustment. More frequent interparental conflict and more intense or violent forms of conflict are not only particularly disturbing to children but are also associated with externalizing and internalizing problems. Grych, Seid, and Fincham (1992), for example, found that children who were exposed to an audiotaped analog of marital interaction responded with distress, shame, and self-blame to intensely angry adult exchanges. Conflict which was child-related in content was more likely than conflict involving other content to be associated with behavior problems in children (Grych & Fincham, 1993). Exposure to unresolved conflict, has been found to be associated with negative affect and poor coping responses in children (Cummings, Ballard, El-Sheikh, & Lake, 1991). In addition, Katz and Gottman (1993) found that couples who exhibited a hostile style of resolving conflict had children who tended to be described by teachers as exhibiting antisocial characteristics. When husbands were angry and emotionally distant while resolving marital conflict, children were described by teachers as anxious and socially withdrawn. Finally, children from divorced and remarried families are more likely to experience internalizing and externalizing problems and difficulties with peers (Amato & Keith, 1991 Hetherington, Bridges, & Insabella, 1998).

Conflict is inevitable in most parental relationships and is not detrimental to children's functioning under all circumstances. Disagreements that are extremely intense and involve threat to the child are likely to be more disturbing to the child. When conflict is expressed constructively, is moderate in degree, is expressed in the context of a warm and supportive family environment, and shows evidence of resolution, children may learn valuable lessons regarding how to negotiate conflict and resolve disagreements (Davies & Cummings, 1994).

Siblings as a Socialization Context for Peer Relationships

Children's experiences with siblings provide a context in which interaction patterns and social understanding skills may generalize to relationships with other children (McCoy, Brody, & Stoneman, 1994). According to Stocker and Dunn (1990), interactions with siblings provide a setting in which children "develop social understanding skills which may enable them to form particularly close relationships with a child of their choice, a close friend." Unfortunately, a somewhat inconsistent picture of the connections between children's patterns of interacting with siblings and patterns of interacting with peers is evident (see Parke & O'Neil, 1997, for a review of this work). There is modest evidence of a straightforward "carry-over" of interaction styles between children's relationships with siblings and peers. Hetherington (1988) found that when relationships with their siblings were described as hostile and alienated as opposed to warm and compassionate, children had poorer peer relationships and other behavior problems. Others report little evidence of a carry-over effect between siblings and peers. Abramovitch, Corter, Pepler, and Stanhope (1986), found little evidence that patterns of sibling interaction were related to the interaction styles of children with a friend. Older siblings are more likely to assume dominant roles such as managers of activities and teachers during the course of their interactions with siblings; whereas, the same children were more likely to adopt an equalitarian style during interactions with friends.

Finally, the sibling relationship may play a role in compensating for other problematic relationships by providing an alternative context for experiencing satisfying social relationships and protecting children from the development of adjustment difficulties. East and Rook (1992) found that children who were socially isolated in their peer relationships were buffered from adjustment problems when they reported positive relationships with a favorite sibling.

Although our theories have emphasized the carry-over from sibling relationships to peer relationships, the direction of influence from peers to family is evident as well. Kramer and Gottman (1992) examined the role that positive relationships with peers plays in children's adaptation to the birth of a new sibling. They found that children who displayed a more positive interaction style with a best friend and who were better able to manage conflict and negative affect, behaved more positively toward their new sibling at both 6 months and 14 months.

Factors Altering the Relative Impact of Family and Peer Systems

A variety of moderators of the relative impact of families and peers on children's social adaptation have been identified, including social class and culture.

Social class, poverty, and job loss

Families who come from impoverished socio-economic backgrounds are more likely to experience a number of stressors, which, in turn, could affect their children's social relationships with peers. In addition to economic stressors, low-income families are more likely to experience such stressful events as medical problems, overcrowding in the home or a large family size, parental psychopathology, parental criminality and/or imprisonment, marital discord, and divorce (Duncan, Brooks-Gunn, & Klebanov, 1994; Hetherington, Bridges, & Insabella, 1998). Some have proposed that having any one of these stressors may not put a child at great risk for developing adjustment problems, but instead, it is the accumulation of many of such stressors that increases the likelihood of maladjustment (Rutter, 1987; Sameroff, Bartko, Baldwin, Baldwin, & Seifer, 1998). Shaw and Emery (1988) found that the number of family-level stressors a child had experienced was related negatively to the child's perceived social competence.

Poverty has its effect on children adjustment through both indirect and direct pathways. The link between family stressors and child adjustment may be mediated indirectly by parental behavior. Acute stress has been found to be associated with maternal depression which is related to increasingly poor discipline, which, in turn, is related to increases in child deviancy, including poor peer relations (Conger, Patterson, & Ge, 1995). Other researchers have investigated the direct linkage between social disadvantage and child outcomes. Patterson, Vaden, Griesler, and Kupersmidt (1991) have found that children from low-income homes have fewer friendships than children from middle-income homes both in and out of school. The largest difference between low-income and middle-income children was for friendship activities in the home. Children from poor families may have homes that are not well equipped for children and their playmates and parents may not encourage their children to bring friends home. Furthermore, these low-income children were also more likely to experience social isolation. Thus, economic disadvantage may decrease their opportunities for peer companionship and hamper their opportunities for learning many of the social skills necessary to maintain positive peer relations.

Poverty is not the only route through which children and families are affected by economic factors. Even economically viable families suffer unemployment, and employment instability, which leads to financial stress. Economic hardship is often associated with subjective feeling of stress on the part of parents, which in turn, has been found to be associated with increased depression (Brody & Flor, 1997; Conger & Elder, 1994) and decreased self-esteem (Brody & Flor, 1997). Stressed and depressed parents are more hostile and tense and less warm and nurturant (Brody & Flor, 1997; Conger & Elder, 1994), and less likely to follow regular family routines (Brody & Flor, 1997). Disruptions in parenting can increase children's adjustment problems including difficulties in peer relations, such as fewer close friendships and less perceived support from friends (Conger, Patterson, & Ge, 1995).

Cultural differences in family and peer influence

An issue that has generated considerable interest is the variability in children's development across cultures as well as between and within cultural subgroups within the same country. Two issues are of interest, namely the relative influence of parents and peers in different cultures and the nature of family–peer linkages across cultures. The relative impact of parents and peers varies across cultures. In a classic study of Russian and American children, Bronfenbrenner (1970) found that Russian children were more likely to follow parental rules when with their peers than American children who exhibited a greater tendency to deviate from parental rules when with their peers. More recently, Chen, Greenberger, Lester, Dong, and Guo (1998) found that peer influences were stronger correlates of misconduct among European and Chinese Americans than among Chinese and Taiwanese adolescents.

In spite of overall differences in the relative contribution of peers and families to children's social outcomes, numerous studies report that the nature of the parental and peer correlates of children's social competence are similar. In the Chen et al. (1998) study for example, family relationships (parent–offspring conflict, parental warmth, and parental monitoring) as well as peer sanctions (peer approval/disapproval of misconduct) were related to child misconduct in similar ways across European and Chinese American and Chinese groups.

Others have reported similar relations between parental practices and children's peer relationships. In a study based in China, Chen and Rubin (1994) reported that authoritarian parenting and punitive disciplinary practices were linked with childhood aggression and peer rejection; on the other hand, parental warmth and authoritative parenting predicted social competence, which, in turn, predicted peer acceptance. However, as Chen,

Rubin, and Li (1994) found, the correlates of peer acceptance among Chinese children shift across development. While shyness is positively correlated with peer acceptance among 8–10 year olds, this same characteristic is associated with rejection when displayed by adolescents (Chen, Rubin, Li, & Li, 1999). Other work suggests that the domains in which behavior is exhibited is also important to understanding cross-cultural differences. Chinese-Canadian children who were competitive in academic tasks were well liked, but disliked if the domain was athletics. The reverse was true for non-Asian Canadian children (Udvari, Schneider, Labovitz, & Tassi, 1995). Studies of Russian parents reveal a similar pattern. Children of punitive, authoritarian mothers in combination with less responsive fathers display more reactive overt and relational aggression (Hart et al., 2000).

In terms of parental management, similarities and differences across cultures were evident as well (Hart et al., 1998). In Russia, China, and the United States, parental initiating and arranging decreases as children develop. In all three countries, mothers who initiate more peer contacts had children who were more accepted by peers. However, Chinese children were given more autonomy in their initiating activities with peers. Mothers in all cultures were more likely to arrange peer contacts if their children were perceived by teachers as less socially competent. Parental monitoring has similar positive effects on children's misconduct in a variety of cultures, including Denmark (Arnett & Balle-Jensen, 1993), England (Belson, 1975), China (Chen et al., 1998), and Australia (Feldman, Rosenthal, Mont-Reynaud, & Leung, 1991).

Across a variety of cultures, the relative influence of families and peers on children's social behavior may differ but the family processes (e.g., child rearing; advice giving, monitoring) or peer processes (e.g., association with deviant peers) by which these socialization agents achieve their influence are similar.

Conclusions and Remaining Questions

As we have argued in this chapter, both families and peers play significant roles in children's social development. Rather than viewing these two social systems as independent, they function in an interdependent fashion throughout development. Even though the relative balance between peer and family influence shifts across development, with peers playing a larger role as children move from childhood to adolescence, earlier parental childrearing, advice-giving, and managerial practices as well as through concurrent parental efforts to influence and shape their adolescent's social choices, families continue to play an important role.

There are many issues that are still not well understood and these remain challenges for our field. First, although the general outlines of the links between family and peer systems are coming into focus, many details of this picture are still blurry. Of particular concern is the need to increase our understanding of the specific family subsystem experiences and processes, which are related to different aspects of peer relationships, such as friendships, peer groups, and social acceptance. While attachment and close intimate family ties may be more clearly linked to friendships, another form of close relationships than acceptance by peers (Youngblade & Belsky 1992), group-level aspects of family life such as cohesiveness and organization may be more closely tied to children's ability to function in the peer group rather than in close dyadic relationships.

Second, the multidirectionality of influence is often included in our models but less often empirically evaluated (Hart et al., 1997). This concept of multidirectionality can take several forms. Within the family itself, the interplay among the subsystems needs more attention. As noted above, the mutual influence among parenting, marriage and sibling relationships needs more attention, instead of assuming that the direction of influence is usually singular (e.g., from marital interaction to parenting). Even when these subsystem links are more clearly understood, the assumption remains that the direction of influence flows from the family to extra-familial relationships. Although there is considerable evidence that extra-familial social friends and social networks have an impact on parent–child relationships (Belsky, 1984), we rarely explore this issue with children. What is the impact of children's extra-familial relationships with friends, peers, and relatives on their family relationships? As has been found in several studies, for example, children's relationships with peers/friends can influence their adjustment to a new sibling (Kramer & Gottman, 1992) and their relationships with their parents (Repetti, 1996).

Third, a developmental analysis of these issues is clearly needed. As other research suggests (Collins & Russell, 1991), the direction of influence between parent and child is more balanced across development, as issues of autonomy become of more central importance to the child and adolescent. Even fundamental descriptive data concerning the ways in which different interactive strategies or managerial processes shift across development are lacking at this point. More importantly, the ways in which the family strategies (e.g., as interactive partner, manager, or direct tutor) relate to social relational competence at different points in the child's development merit investigation.

Finally, our focus in this chapter has been on families and peers but many other socialization influences such as the mass media, the school, and religious institutions play important roles in social development of children. By locating family and peer influences in the larger matrix of socialization forces, we will develop a richer understanding of children's social development. Through a deeper and more textured appreciation of the relative roles of various socialization agents we will be able to develop more effective guidelines for prevention and intervention programs on behalf of children with social problems.

References

Abramovitch, R., Corter, C., Peper, D. J., & Stanhope, L. (1986). Sibling interaction and peer interaction: A final follow-up and a comparison. *Child Development, 57,* 217–229.

Ainsworth, M. S. (1989). Attachments beyond infancy. *American Psychologist, 44,* 709–716.

Amato, R. R., & Keith, B. (1991). Parental divorce and the well being of children: A meta-analysis. *Psychological Bulletin, 110,* 26–46.

Arnett, J., & Balle-Jensen, L. (1993). Cultural bases of risk behavior: Danish adolescents. *Child Development, 64,* 1842–1855.

Bates, J., Bayles, K., Bennett, D. S., Ridge, B., & Brown, M. M. (1991). Origins of externalizing problems at eight years of age. In E. J. Pepler & K. H. Rubin (Eds.), *The development and treatment of childhood aggression* (pp. 197–216). New York: Academic Press.

Bates, J., Pettit, G., & Dodge, K. (1995). Family and child factors in stability and change in children's aggressiveness in elementary school. In J. McCord (Ed.), *Coercion and punishment in long-term perspectives* (pp. 124–138), New York: Cambridge University Press.

Bates, J. E., Pettit, G. S., Dodge, K. A., & Ridge, B. (1998). Interaction of temperamental resistance to control and restrictive parenting in the development of externalizing behavior. *Developmental Psychology, 34,* 982–995.

Belsky, J. (1984). Determinants of parenting: A process model. *Child Development, 55,* 83–96.

Belson, W. A. (1975). *Juvenile theft: The causal factors.* London: Harper & Row.

Bhavnagri, N. P., & Parke, R. D. (1991). Parents as direct facilitators of children's peer relationships: Effects of age of child and sex of parent. *Journal of Social and Personal Relationships, 8,* 423–440.

Brody, G. H., & Flor, D. L. (1997). Maternal psychological functioning, family processes, and child adjustment in rural, single-parent, African American families. *Developmental Psychology, 33,* 1000–1011.

Bronfenbrenner, U. (1970). *Two worlds of childhood: US and USSR.* New York: Russell Sage Foundation.

Bryant, B. (1995). The neighborhood walk: Sources of support in middle childhood. *Monographs of the Society for Research in Child Development, 50* (Serial # 210).

Calkins, S. D., & Fox, N. A. (1992). Relations among infant temperament, security of attachment and behavioral inhibition at twenty-five months. *Child Development, 63,* 1456–1472.

Carson, J., & Parke, R. D. (1996). Reciprocal negative affect in parent–child interactions and children's peer competency. *Child Development, 67,* 2217–2226.

Cassidy, J., Kirsh, S. J., Scolton, K. L., & Parke, R. D. (1996). Attachment and representations of peer relationships. *Developmental Psychology, 32,* 892–904.

Cassidy, J., Parke, R. D., Butovsky, L., & Braungart, J. (1992). Family–peer connections: The roles of emotional expressiveness within the family and children's understanding of emotions. *Child Development, 63,* 603–618.

Chen, C., Greenberger, E., Lester, J., Dong, Q., & Guo, M. (1998). A cross-cultural study of family and peer correlates of adolescent misconduct. *Developmental Psychology, 34,* 770–781.

Chen, X., & Rubin, K. H. (1994). Family conditions, parental acceptance, and social competence and aggression in Chinese children. *Social Development, 3,* 269–290.

Chen, X., Rubin, K. H., & Li, B. (1994). Social and school adjustment of shy and aggressive children in China. *Development and Psychopathology, 7,* 337–349.

Chen, X., Rubin, K. H., Li, B., & Li, D. (1999). Adolescent outcomes of social functioning in Chinese children. *International Journal of Behavioral Development, 23,* 199–223.

Cochran, M. M., & Brassard, J. A. (1979). Child development and personal social networks. *Child Development, 50,* 601–616.

Cochran, M., Larner, M., Riley, D., Gunnarson, L., & Henderson, C. (1990) *Extending families: The social networks of parents and their children.* New York: Cambridge University Press.

Coleman, J. (1988). Social capital in the creation of human capital. *American Journal of Sociology, 94,* 95–120.

Coleman, J. (1990). *Foundations of social theory.* Cambridge, MA: Harvard University Press.

Coleman, J., & Hoffer, T. (1987). *Public and private high school: The impact of communities.* New York: Basic Books.

Collins, W. A., Maccoby, E. E., Steinberg, L., Hetherington, E. M., & Bornstein, M. H. (2000). Contemporary research on parenting: The case for nature and nurture. *American Psychologist, 55,* 218–232.

Collins, W. A., & Russell, A. (1991). Mother–child and father–child and adolescence: Relationships in middle childhood. A developmental analysis. *Developmental Review, 11,* 99–136.

Conger, R. D., & Elder, G. H. Jr. (1994). *Families in troubled times.* New York: De Gruyter.

Conger, R. D., Patterson, G. R., & Ge, X. (1995). It takes two to replicate: A mediational model for the impact of parent's stress on adolescent adjustment. *Child Development, 66,* 80-97.

Cowan, C. P., Cowan, P. A., Schulz, M., & Heming, G. (1994) Prebirth to preschool family factors predicting children's adaptation to kindergarten. In R. D. Parke & S. G. Kellam (Eds.), *Exploring family relationships with other social contexts: Advances in family research, Vol. 4* (pp. 75–114). Hillsdale, NJ: Erlbaum.

Crockenberg, S. (1981). Infant irritability, other responsiveness and social support influences on the security of infant–mother attachment. *Child Development, 52,* 857–865.

Cummings, E. M., Ballard, M., El-Sheikh, M., & Lake, M. (1991). Resolutions and children's responses to interadult anger. *Developmental Psychology, 27,* 940–950.

Darling, N, Steinberg, L. Gringlas, B., & Dornbusch, S. (1995). Community influences on adolescent achievement and deviance: A test of the functional community hypothesis, Unpublished manuscript, Temple University, Philadelphia, PA.

Davies, P. T., & Cummings, E. M. (1994). Marital conflict and child adjustment: An emotional security hypothesis. *Psychological Bulletin, 116,* 387–411.

Denham, S. (1998.) *Emotional development in young children.* New York: Guilford Press.

Dishion, T. (1990). Peer context of troublesome behavior in children and adolescents. In P.E. Leone (Ed.), U*nderstanding troubled and troubling youth: A multidisciplinary perspective* (pp. 128–153). Beverly Hills, CA: Sage.

Dishion, T. J., Poulin, F., & Skaggs, N. M. (2000). The ecology of premature autonomy in adolescence: Biological and social influences. In K. A. Kerns, J. M. Contreras, & A. M. Neal-Barnett (Eds.), *Family & peers: Linking two social worlds* (pp. 27–46). Westport, CT: Praeger.

Douvan, E., & Adelson, J. (1966). *The adolescent experience.* New York: Wiley.

Doyle, A. B. & Markiewiez, D. (1996). Parents' interpersonal relationships and children's friendships. In W. M. Bukowski, A. F. Newcomb, & W. W. Hartup (Eds.), *The company they keep: Friendship in childhood and adolescence* (pp. 115–136). New York: Cambridge University Press.

Duncan, G. J., Brooks-Gunn, J., & Klebanov, P. K. (1994). Economic deprivation and early childhood development. *Child Development, 65,* 296–318.

Dunn, J., & Brown, J. R. (1994). Affect expression in the family: Children's understanding of emotions and their interactions with others. *Merrill-Palmer quarterly, 40,* 120–137.

East, P. L., & Rook, D. S. (1992). Compensatory patterns of support among children's peer relationships: A test using school friends and nonschool friends, and siblings. *Developmental Psychology, 28,* 163–172.

Eisenberg, N., & Fabes, R.A. (1994). Mothers' reactions to children's negative emotions: Relations to children's temperament and anger behavior. *Merrill-Palmer Quarterly, 40,* 138–156.

Eisenberg, N., Fabes, R.A., Bernzweig, J., Karbon, M., Poulin, R., & Hanish, L. (1993). The relations of emotionality and regulation to preschoolers' social skills and sociometric status. *Child Development, 64,* 1418–1438.

Fauber, R. L., & Long, N. (1991). The role of the family in child psychotherapy. *Journal of Consulting and Clinical Psychology, 59,* 813–820.

Feldman, S., Rosenthal, D. A., Mont-Reynaud, R., & Leung, K. (1991) Ain't misbehavin': Adolescent values and family environments as correlates of misconduct in Australia, Hong Kong, and the United States. *Journal of Research on Adolescence, 1,* 109–134.

Finnie, V., & Russell, A. (1998) Preschool children's social status and their mothers' behavior and knowledge in the supervisory role. *Developmental Psychology, 24,* 789–801.

Furstenberg, F. F., Jr., Cook, T. D., Eccles, J., Elder, G. G., Jr., & Sameroff, A. (1999). *Managing to make it: Urban families and adolescent success.* Chicago: University of Chicago Press.

Gottman, J. M., Katz, L. F., & Hooven, C. (1997). *Meta-emotion: How families communicate emotionally.* Mahwah, NJ: Erlbaum.

Grusec, J. E., & Goodnow, J. J. (1994). Impact of personal discipline methods on the child's internalization of values: A reconceptualization of current points of view. *Developmental Psychology, 30,* 4–19.

Grych, J. H., & Fincham, F. D. (1993). Marital conflict and children's adjustment: A cognitive-contextual framework. *Psychological Bulletin, 108,* 267–290.

Grych, J. H., Seid, M., & Ficham, F. D. (1992). Assessing marital conflict from the child's perspective: The Children's Perception of Interparental Conflict Scale. *Child Development, 63,* 558–572.

Harlow, H. F. (1958). The nature of love. *American Psychologist, 13,* 673–685.

Harris, J. R. (1995). Where is the child's environment? A group socialization theory of development. *Psychological Review. 102,* 458–489.

Harris, J. R. (1998). *The nurture assumption.* New York: Free Press.

Harris, J. R. (2000). Socialization, personality development, & the child's environment: Comment on Vandell (2000). *Developmental Psychology, 36,* 711–723.

Harrist, A. W., Pettit, G. S., Dodge, K. A., & Bates, J. E. (1994). Dyadic synchrony in mother–child interaction: Relations with children's subsequent kindergarten adjustment. *Family Relations, 43,* 417–424.

Hart, C. H. (1999). *Combating the myth that parents don't matter.* Paper presented at the World Congress of Families II, Geneva, Switzerland.

Hart, C. H., DeWolf, M. D., & Burts, D. C. (1992). Linkages among preschoolers' playground behavior, outcome expectations, and parental disciplinary strategies. *Early Education and Development, 3,* 265–283.

Hart, C. H., Ladd, G. W., & Burleson B. R. (1990). Children's expectations of the outcomes of social strategies: Relations with sociometric status and maternal disciplinary styles. *Child Development, 61,* 127–137.

Hart, C. H., Nelson, D. A., Robinson, C. C., Olsen, S. F., McNeilly-Choque, M. K., Porter, C. L., & McKee, T. R. (2000). Russian parenting styles and family processes: Linkages with subtypes of victimization and aggression. In K. A. Kerns, J. M. Contreras, & A. M. Neal-Barnett (Eds.), *Family & peers: Linking two social worlds* (pp. 47–84). Westport, CT: Praeger.

Hart, C. H., Olsen, S. F., Robinson, C., & Mandleco, B. L. (1997). The development of social and communicative competence in childhood: Review and a model of personal, familial, and extra familial processes. In B. R. Burleson (Ed.), *Communication yearbook, Vol. 20* (pp. 305–373). Thousand Oaks, CA: Sage.

Hart, C. H., Yang, C., Nelson, D. A., Jin, S., Bazarskaya, N., Nelson, L., Wu, S., & Wu, P. (1998). Peer contact patterns, parenting practices, and preschoolers' social competence in China, Russia, and the United States. In P. T. Slee & K. Rigby (Eds.), *Children's peer relations* (pp. 3–30). London: Routledge.

Hartup, W. W. (1979). The social worlds of childhood. *American Psychologist, 34,* 944–949.

Hartup, W. W., & Stevens, N. (1997). Friendships and adaptation in the life course. *Psychological Bulletin, 121,* 335–370.

Hetherington, E. M. (1988). Parents, children, and siblings: Six years after divorce. In R. A. Hinde & J. Stevenson-Hinde (Eds.), *Relationships within families: Mutual influences* (pp. 311–331). Oxford, England: Oxford University Press.

Hetherington, E. M., Bridges, M., & Insabella, G. M. (1998). What matters? What does not? Five perspectives on the association between marital transitions and children's adjustment. *American Psychologist, 53,* 167–184.

Homel, R., Burns, A., & Goodnow, J. (1987). Parental social networks and child development. *Journal of Social and Personal Relationships, 4,* 159–177.

Hubbard, J. A., & Coie, J. D. (1994). Emotional correlates of social competence in children's peer relationships. *Merrill-Palmer Quarterly, 40,* 1–20.

Katz, L. F., & Gottman, J. M. (1993). Patterns of marital conflict predict children's internalizing and externalizing behavior. *Developmental Psychology, 29,* 940–950.

Katz, L. F., & Kahen, V. (1993). Marital interaction patterns and children's externalizing and internalizing behaviors: The search for mechanisms. Paper presented at the Biennial Meeting of the Society for Research in Child Development, New Orleans.

Kerns, K.A., Cole, A. K., & Andrews, P. B. (1998). Attachment security, parent peer management practices, and peer relationships in preschoolers. *Merrill-Palmer Quarterly, 44,* 504–522.

Kramer, L., & Gottman, J. M. (1992). Becoming a sibling – with a little help from my friends. *Developmental Psychology, 28,* 685–699.

Krappman, L. (1992). The development of manifold social relationships among children. In A. E. Awhagen & M. Von Salisch (Eds.), *Interpersonal relationships* (pp. 37–58). Goettingen: Hagrete.

Ladd, G. W. (1992). Themes and theories: Perspectives on processes in family-peer relationships. In R. D. Parke & G. W. Ladd (Eds.), *Family–peer relationships: Modes of linkage*. Hillsdale, NJ: Erlbaum.

Ladd, G. W., & Golter, B. S. (1988). Parents' management of preschoolers' peer relations: Is it related to children's social competence? *Developmental Psychology, 24,* 109–117.

Ladd, G. W., & Hart, C. H. (1992). Creating informal play opportunities: Are parents' and preschoolers' initiations related to children's competence with peers? *Developmental Psychology, 28,* 1179–1187.

McCoy, J. K., Brody, G. H., & Stoneman, Z. (1994). A longitudinal analysis of sibling relationships as mediators of the link between family processes and youths' best friendships. *Family Relations, 43,* 400–408.

McDowell, D. J., & Parke, R. D. (2000). Differential knowledge of display rules for positive and negative emotions: Influence for parents, influence on peers. *Social Development, 9,* 415–432.

McDowell, D. J., Parke, R. D., & Spitzer, S. (in press). Parent and child cognitive representations of social situations and children's social competence. *Social Development.*

McDowell, D. J., Parke, R. D. & Wang, S. J. (in press). Differences between mothers' and fathers' advice giving style and content: Relations with social competence and internalizing behavior in middle childhood. *Merrill-Palmer Quarterly.*

Melson, G. F., Ladd, G. W., & Hsu, H. (1993). Maternal support networks, maternal cognitions, and young children's social and cognitive development. *Child Development, 64,* 1401–1417.

Mize, J., & Pettit, G. S. (1997). Mothers' social coaching, mother–child relationship style, and children's peer competence: Is the medium the message? *Child Development, 68,* 312–332.

Mize, J., Petitt, G. S., Laird, R. D., & Lindsey, E. (1993, April). Mothers' coaching of social skills and children's peer competence: Independent contributions of substance and style. Paper presented at the biennial meeting of the Society for Research in Child Development, New Orleans.

Mounts, N. S. (2000). Parental management of adolescent peer relationships: What are its effects on friend selection? In K. A. Kerns, J. M. Contreras, & A. M. Neal-Barnett (Eds.), *Family & peers: Linking two social worlds* (pp. 169–194). Westport, CT: Praeger.

Newcomb, M. A. F., & Bagwell, C. L. (1995). Children's friendship relations: A meta-analytic review. *Psychological Bulletin, 117,* 306–347.

Olsen, S. F., Yang, C., Hart, C. H., Robinson, C. C., Wu, P., Nelson, D. A., Nelson, L. J., Jin, S., & Wo, J. (in press). Maternal psychological control and preschool children's behavioral outcomes in China, Russia, and the United States. In B. K. Barber (Ed.), *Intrusive parenting: how psychological control affects children and adolescents*. Washington, DC: American Psychological Association.

O'Neil, R., Parke, R. D., & McDowell, D. J. (2001). Objective and subjective features of children's neighborhoods: Relations to parental regulatory strategies and children's social competence. *Journal of Applied Developmental Psychology, 22*, 135–155.

Parke, R. D. (1978). Children's home environments: Social and cognitive effects. In I. Altman & J. R. Wohlwill (Eds.), *Children and the environment* New York: Plenum.

Parke, R. D., & Buriel, R. (1998). Socialization in the family: Ecological and ethnic perspectives. In W. Damon (Series Ed.) & N. Eisenberg (Vol. Ed.), *Handbook of child psychology. Vol. 3, Social, emotional, and personality development* (5th ed., pp. 463–552). New York: Wiley.

Parke, R. D., Burks, V. M., Carson, J. L., Neville, B., & Boyum, L. A. (1994). Family–peer relationships: A tripartite model. In R. D. Parke & S. G. Kellam (Eds.), *Exploring family relationships with other social contexts.* Hillsdale, NJ: Erlbaum.

Parke, R. D., Cassidy, J., Burks, V. M., Carson , J., & Boyum, L. (1992) Familial contributions to peer competence among young children: The role of interactive processes. In R. D. Parke & G. Ladd (Eds.), *Family–peer relationships: Modes of linkage* (pp. 107–134). Hillsdale, NJ: Erlbaum.

Parke, R. D., & O'Neil, R. (1997). The influence of significant others on learning about relationships. In S. Duck (Ed.), *The handbook of personal relationships,* 2nd ed. (pp. 29–60). New York: Wiley

Parke, R. D., & O'Neil, R. (2000). The influence of significant others on learning about relationships: From family to friends. In R. Mills & S. Duck (Eds.), *The developmental psychology of personal relationships.* London: Wiley.

Parker, J., & Asher, S. (1987). Peer acceptance and later personal adjustment: Are low accepted children at risk? *Psychological Bulletin, 102,* 357–389.

Patterson, G. R., De Barshyshe, B., & Ramsey, R. (1989). A developmental perspective on antisocial behavior. *American Psychologist, 44,* 329–335.

Patterson, G. R., & Stouthamer-Loeber, M. (1984). The correlation of family management and delinquency. *Child development, 55,* 1299–1307.

Patterson, C. J., Vaden, N. A., Griesler, P. C., & Kupersmidt, J. B. (1991). Income level, gender, ethnicity, and household composition as predictors of children's peer companionship outside of school. *Journal of Applied Developmental Psychology, 12,* 447–465.

Pettit, G. S., & Harrist, A. W. (1993). Children's aggressive and socially unskilled playground behavior with peers: Origins in early family relations. In C. H. Hart (Ed.), *Children on playgrounds: Research perspectives and applications.* Albany, NY: State University of New York Press.

Pettit, G. S., Laird, R. D., Bates J. C., & Dodge, K. A. (1997). Patterns of after-school care in middle childhood: Risk factors and developmental outcomes. *Merrill-Palmer Quarterly, 43,* 515–530.

Putallaz, M. (1987). Maternal behavior and sociometric status. *Child Development, 58,* 324–340.

Putallaz, M., Costanzo, P. R., & Smith, R. B. (1991). Maternal recollections of childhood peer relationships: Implications for their children's social competence. *Journal of Social and Personal Relationships, 8,* 403–422.

Rabiner, D. L., Keane, S. P., & MacKinnon-Lewis, C. (1993). Child beliefs about familiar and unfamiliar peers in relation to their sociometric status. *Developmental Psychology, 29,* 236–243.

Reiss, D., Neiderhiser, J. M., Hetherington, E. M., & Plomin, R. (2000). *The relationship code.* Cambridge, MA: Harvard University Press.

Repetti, R. (1996). The effects of perceived social and academic failure experiences on school-age children's subsequent interactions with parents. *Child Development, 67,* 1467–1482.

Rothbart, M., & Bates, J. (1998). Temperament. In W. Damon (Series Ed.) & N. Eisenberg (Vol. Ed.), *Handbook of child psychology: Vol. 3, Social, emotional, and personality development* (pp. 105–176). New York: Wiley.

Rowe, D. (1994). *The limits of family influence: Genes, experience, and behavior.* New York: Guilford Press.

Rubin, K., Bukowski, W., & Parker, J. (1998). Peer interaction, relationships and groups. In W. Damon (Series Ed.) & N. Eisenberg, (Vol. Ed.), *Handbook of Child Psychology: Vol. 3, Social, emotional, and personality development* (pp. 619–700). New York: Wiley.

Russell A., & Finnie, V. (1990). Preschool children's social status and maternal instructions to assist group entry. *Developmental Psychology, 26,* 603–611.

Rutter, M. (1987). Psycholsocial resilience and protective mechanisms. *American Journal of Orthopsychiatry, 57,* 316–331.

Sameroff, A. J., Bartko, W. T., Baldwin, A., Baldwin, C., & Seifer, R. (1998). Family and social influences on the development of child competence. In M. Lewis & C. Feiring (Eds.), *Children and families at risk* (pp. 161–185). Hillsdale, NJ: Erlbaum.

Scarr, S. (1992). Developmental theories for the 1990s: Developmental and individual differences. *Child Development, 62,* 1–19.

Shaw, D. S., & Emery, R. E. (1988). Chronic family adversity and school-age children's adjustment. *Journal of the American Academy of Child & Adolescent Psychiatry, 27,* 200–206.

Simpkins, S. D., O'Neil, R., Lee, J., & Parke, R. D. (under review). The relation between parent and children's social networks and children's peer acceptance.

Simpkins, S. D., & Parke, R. D. (2001). The relations between parental friendships and children's friendships: Self-reports and observational analysis. *Child Development, 72,* 569–582.

Simpkins, S. D., & Parke, R. D. (in press). Maternal monitoring and rules as correlates of children's social adjustment. *Merrill-Palmer Quarterly.*

Sroufe, L. A., Carlson, E., & Shulman, S. (1993). The development of individuals in relationships. In D.C. Funder, R. D. Parke, C. Tomlinson-Keasey, & K. Widaman (Eds.), *Studying lives through time: Approaches to personality and development.* Washington, DC: American Psychological Association.

Sroufe, L. A., & Fleeson, J. (1986). Attachment and the construction of relationships. In W. W. Hartup & Z. Rubin (Eds.), *Relationships and development* (pp. 51–72). Hillsdale, NJ: Erlbaum.

Steinberg, L. (1986). Latchkey children and susceptibility to peer pressure: An ecological analysis. *Developmental Psychology, 22,* 433–439.

Stocker, C., & Dunn, J. (1990). Sibling relationships in childhood: Links with friendship and peer relationships. *British Journal of Developmental Psychology, 8,* 227–244.

Suess, G. L. (1987). Consequences of early attachment experiences on competence in preschool. Unpublished doctoral dissertation, University of Regensburg, Germany.

Udvari, S., Schneider, B. H., Labovitz, G., & Tassi, F. (1995, August). *A multidimensional view of competition in relation to children's peer relations.* Paper presented at the meeting of the American Psychological Association, New York.

Uhlendorff, H. (2000). Parents' and children's friendship networks. *Journal of Family Issues, 21,* 191–204.

Vandell, D. L. (2000). Parents, peer groups, and other socializing influences, *Developmental Psychology, 36,* 699–710.

Wilson, B. J. (1999). Entry behavior and emotion regulation abilities of developmentally delayed boys. *Developmental Psychology, 35,* 214–223.

Youngblade, L., & Belsky, J. (1992). Parent–child antecedents of five-year-olds' close friendships: A longitudinal analysis. *Developmental Psychology, 28,* 700–713.

Youniss, J., & Smollar, J. (1985). *Adolescent relations with mothers, fathers, and friends.* Chicago: University of Chicago Press.

Part IV

The Family Context

Research suggests that a host of variables contribute to the social development of young children. These include individual biologically based genetic and temperament factors (e.g., Chapters 2 and 6) as well as more distal extra-familial influences, including the peer group, schools, media, and culture. Parenting and family interactions are factors proximal to children that combine with individual and extra-familial influences in ways that are linked to childhood social competencies. Although peers and other extra-familial influences become increasingly important across early and middle childhood, parents and siblings continue to constitute a major portion of a child's social milieu in many parts of the world (see Hart, Olsen, Robinson, & Mandleco, 1997).

The focus of this section is on mechanisms in the proximal family environment that are germane to parenting and sibling interactions. How family structures mirror the ebb and flow of societal change in the extra-familial environment is also covered, particularly with regard to explicating how family members interact with one another in varying family contexts.

Parent–child attachment relationships have been the subject of serious inquiry for many decades. Joan Stevenson-Hinde and Karine Verschueren review the historical development of this work, beginning with John Bowlby's ethological framework. They overview attachment quality and the conceptual and methodological issues associated with studying patterns of attachment that are linked to varying parent–child interaction styles. In line with recent meta-analytic approaches (Schneider, Atkinson, & Tardif, 2001), the authors link different attachment indices to children's social competence, behavior disorders, and peer acceptance. Future directions for this line of research are clearly charted (e.g., connecting social cognitive and verbal capacities to attachment indices). This chapter is a must read for those interested in moving the field forward in this area.

Because parents provide a critical environment for children's social development, it is important to consider ways that parent–child relationships are different from other kinds of close relationships. Alan Russell, Jackie Mize, and Kerry Bissaker take on this challenge by examining levels of complexity regarding individual characteristics that parents and children bring to the relationship and then delineating parent–child relationships from interactions. They show how relationships comprise many interactions that have different features. A helpful scheme for organizing dimensions of parent–child relationships is explicated, emphasizing vertical and horizontal distinctions that parents can make when adjusting to varying childrearing contexts (e.g., disciplinary vs. power sharing contexts). The authors also address how parent–child relationships are bi-directional and co-constructed, with the child assuming an active role in the process. They explicate ways that individual characteristics, including the sex and personality of parents and children, impact parent–child relationships across development. Russell and his colleagues conclude by carefully considering ways that extra-familial neighborhood, social, ethnic, and cultural factors impact on parent–child relationships.

With the exception of countries like mainland China, where the one-child policy is associated with parents encouraging child contact with cousins as substitute siblings (Hart et al., 1998), Judy Dunn notes that the majority of children in Europe and the United States grow up with biological siblings. She reviews systematic research on relationships of brothers and sisters in family interaction. A wealth of information is provided concerning why there is so much variation in how siblings get along. Siblings can be sources of stress or of support to one another, depending on a variety of factors. These factors can include child temperament, relative age, family size, birth order, and security of attachments to, and relationships with, parents. Linkages between the worlds of siblings and peers are also explicated, highlighting evidence for consistency across sibling and peer contexts as well as compensatory patterns. Finally, the question that has puzzled parents throughout the ages is addressed: Why are siblings so often different from one another?

Dale Hay and Alison Nash provide an insightful discussion of children's social development in different family arrangements (e.g., single parents, nuclear family structures, communal childrearing, extended family arrangements). How family members interact with one another and foster social competencies are likely associated with different family structures; however, Hay and Nash show that there is little solid evidence for this claim. Most studies comparing child outcomes in different family arrangements are weakened by serious methodological and theoretical limitations that diminish our ability to reach any firm conclusions. For example, many studies do not distinguish two-parent families where the parents are married and those where the parents' relationship has not been legalized. Despite the limited state of scholarship, the authors carefully synthesize existing research on different family arrangements by utilizing five organizing perspectives: the attachment model, the parenting model, the nuclear family model, the family systems model, and the social networks model. Findings from research on different family types such as never-married mothers, divorced families, nuclear families, same-sex parent families, stepparent families, cohabiting and married parent families, are presented with an eye towards understanding how these different family arrangements may affect children. The message is that children's social development in the context of the multitude of family arrangements that exist in the world today is in dire need of further investigation.

References

Hart, C. H., Olsen, S. F., Robinson, C., & Mandleco, B. L. (1997). The development of social and communicative competence in childhood: Review and a model of personal, familial, and extra-familial processes. In B. R. Burleson (Ed.), *Communication yearbook 20* (pp. 305–373). Thousand Oaks, CA: Sage.

Hart, C. H., Yang, C., Nelson, D., Jin, S., Bazarskaya, N., Nelson, L., Wu, X., & Wu, P. (1998). Peer contact patterns, parenting practices, and preschoolers' social competence in China, Russia, and the United States. In P. Slee & K. Rigby (Eds.), *Peer relations amongst children: Current issues and future directions* (pp. 1–30). London: Routledge.

Schneider, B. H., Atkinson, L., & Tardif, C. (2001). Child–parent attachment and children's peer relationships: A quantitative review. *Developmental Psychology, 37*, 86–100.

10

Attachment in Childhood

Joan Stevenson-Hinde and Karine Verschueren

Ever since Mary Ainsworth's original work (e.g., Ainsworth, Blehar, Waters, & Wall, 1978), the bulk of attachment research has concerned behavioral assessments of attachment patterns in infancy. Our focus here is on ways of assessing attachment beyond infancy, from ages 2.5 to 11 years. Observational and representational procedures will be considered, with respect to both validation and implications for development and psychopathology. But first, these procedures must be set within the context of attachment theory.

An Ethological Perspective

In a retrospective paper, John Bowlby described how his early clinical observations pointed to the adverse effects of separation and loss of a mother figure. This led him to ask, "If the disruption of a child's relationship with mother-figure in the early years creates much distress and anxiety, what is so special about the relationship that has been disrupted?" (1991a, p. 303). The prevailing answer was that bond formation stemmed from the association of mother with the provision of food, thereby satisfying a primary need. But, in Bowlby's view, this "cupboard love theory" (1991a, p. 303) was insufficient. Impressed by the phenomenon of imprinting in animals, Bowlby looked to ethology to provide a scientific framework.

Within ethology, the occurrence of species-characteristic behavior patterns suggests that such behavior may have been selected for during the course of evolution. Bowlby applied this thinking to attachment behavior, which he defined as any form of behavior, which attains or maintains proximity to a caregiver in times of need or stress. He argued that individuals who exhibited attachment behavior would have been more apt to survive and leave offspring, who in turn would reproduce (i.e., would have increased their "inclusive fitness"), compared with those who did not show attachment behavior. Selection for attachment behavior could not have happened without a similar pressure on its complement, caregiving behavior. "During the course of time, the biologically given strategy of attachment in the young has evolved in parallel with the complementary parental strategy of responsive caregiving – the one presumes the other" (Bowlby, 1991b, p. 293).

Taking an ethological perspective a step further, Bowlby suggested that attachment behavior reflects the operation of a distinct control system in its own right, not dependent upon prior association with any other motivational system such as hunger. A behavior system is "distinguished on the basis of common causation . . . [and is] usually found to subserve a particular biological function" (Baerends, 1976, pp. 731–733). Bowlby postulated a function of protection from harm, "by keeping him or her in touch with one or more caregivers" (1991a, p. 306). Activation of a fear behavior system leads to activation of the attachment behavior system; attachment behavior leads to proximity to caregiver, which in turn deactivates the fear system, enabling activation of an exploratory or social system (e.g., Bowlby, 1982; see also Greenberg & Marvin, 1982).

Bowlby realized that an evolutionary argument could provide insight into behavior which otherwise appeared abnormal, including the "irrational fears of childhood." The tendency to fear unfamiliar situations, darkness, or separation is "to be regarded as a natural disposition of man. . . . that stays with him in some degree from infancy to old age. . . . Thus it is not the presence of this tendency in childhood or later life that is pathological; pathology is indicated either when the tendency is apparently absent or when fear is aroused with unusual readiness and intensity" (Bowlby, 1973, p. 84). In one of his final contributions Bowlby wrote, "Once we postulate the presence within the organism of an attachment behavioural system regarded as the product of evolution and having protection as its biological function, many of the puzzles that have perplexed students of human relationships are found to be soluble. . . . an urge to keep proximity or accessibility to someone seen as stronger or wiser, and who if responsive is deeply loved, comes to be recognised as an integral part of human nature and as having a vital role to play in life. Not only does its effective operation bring with it a strong feeling of security and contentment, but its temporary or long-term frustration causes acute or chronic anxiety and discontent. When seen in this light, the urge to keep proximity is to be respected, valued, and nurtured as making for potential strength, instead of being looked down upon, as so often hitherto, as a sign of inherent weakness" (Bowlby, 1991b, p. 293).

Development of an Inferred Attachment Bond and Internal Working Models

As attachment behavior develops, it forms the basis for an inferred attachment bond. Bowlby described particular phases of its development: pre-attachment (from birth to about 2 months), involving signaling without discriminating one person from another; attachment-in-the-making (2–6 months) where signals become directed to particular persons; clear-cut attachment (0.5–4 years) with locomotion and goal-corrected behavior; and finally a goal-corrected partnership (4 years onwards) with perspective taking, communication skills, and sharing mutual plans. Although additional attachments may develop throughout life, early attachments endure.

Furthermore, Bowlby (1973) postulated that attachment relationships must become internalized. Internal working models may be defined as "'operable' models of self and attachment partner, based on their joint relationship history. They serve to regulate, interpret, and predict both the attachment figure's and the self's attachment-related behavior, thoughts, and feelings" (Bretherton & Munholland, 1999, p. 89). This definition reflects Bowlby's view of the complementary nature of an internal working model, representing both sides of the relationship. "A working model of self as valued and competent, according to this view, is constructed in the context of a working model of parents as emotionally available, but also as supportive of exploratory activities. Conversely, a working model of self as devalued and incompetent is the counterpart of a working model of parents as rejecting or ignoring of attachment behavior and/or interfering with exploration" (Bretherton & Munholland, 1999, p. 91).

The Quality of Attachment

So far, we have been presenting concepts that are applicable to all humans. But what is *not* common to all individuals is the *quality* of attachment, first assessed by Mary Ainsworth in her "strange situation procedure" (Ainsworth et al., 1978). This is a series of short episodes involving mother and a stranger, in which the child's attachment behavior system is activated by the unfamiliarity of the situation and by mother leaving. The return of mother allows one to see how the child organizes his attachment behavior to her. Ainsworth identified three patterns: Avoidant, Secure, and Ambivalent. A Secure pattern has been associated with antecedent interactions with a "sensitively responsive" mother, as found in Mary Ainsworth's pioneering Baltimore study and subsequently in other studies (see the meta-analysis by DeWolff & van IJzendoorn, 1997). The insecure patterns have been associated with different maternal styles, including Avoidance with rejection, Ambivalence with inconsistency, and Disorganization (described by Main & Solomon, 1990; Solomon & George, 1999) with fear.

As for which pattern of attachment is desirable, Bowlby was concerned with what might be called "psychological desiderata" (Hinde & Stevenson-Hinde, 1991). Making an analogy with "physical well-being," Bowlby argued that "psychological well-being" had an absolute meaning, involving security of attachment. Research has supported this view, with security associated with self-reliance and efficacy, as opposed to dependency, anxiety, or anger. Insecure patterns are not seen as pathological in themselves, but rather as risk factors for pathology, while security is viewed as a protective factor (reviewed in Weinfield, Sroufe, Egeland, & Carlson, 1999).

In addition to behavioral assessments of attachment quality, once children reach Bowlby's "goal-corrected partnership" stage, their verbal behavior may be used to index representations of attachment. Here, we shall outline behavioral and representational approaches to assessing attachment in children aged 2.5 to 11 years. From the above, it follows that assessment of the quality of the attachment bond requires activation of the attachment behavior system, and different methods do this to different degrees. The brilliance of the

strange situation procedure is that it actually involves separation from the attachment figure, with a built-in method of preventing too much stress, through curtailing an episode if
that should happen. Representational methods typically require thinking about separation
issues or other distress-provoking situations, while a Q-sort based on unstructured home
observations typically involves little stress.

The Attachment Q-sort (AQS)

The AQS consists of 90 items, with many reflecting secure-base behavior. Each item is
sorted into one of nine piles, according to how characteristic it is of that particular child.
Sorts by observers are based on several home visits, totaling several hours. The correlation
between an individual's Q-sort and a criterion Q-sort of a theoretically secure child (Waters, 1995; Waters & Deane, 1985) provides a security score, ranging from −1 to +1. Such
scoring does not make distinctions among the insecure children. While inter-observer reliability tends to be high, relations with other attachment measures are far from clear (see
Solomon & George, 1999). A lack of congruence between the Q-sort and a strange situation is not surprising, in view of the very differing contexts. Whereas the home puts little
stress on the child or indeed the mother, the strange situation may activate both the child's
attachment behavior and mother's caregiving behavior, thereby providing a window for
observing particularly salient interactions.

Nevertheless, the Q-sort procedure is efficient, with the advantage of avoiding both a
laboratory visit and extensive training of coders. Although additional savings may be achieved
by asking parents to do the Q-sort, there is evidence that attachment figures may not be
well placed to judge their child's attachment behavior toward them (van IJzendoorn,
Vereijken, & Riksen-Walraven, in press). For example in a sample of 2.5 year olds, mothers of children classed *Secure* in a strange situation provided security scores which were
significantly *lower* than observer ratings of security based on behavior in the strange situation. This could happen with sensitive mothers who reported openly, without being de-
fensive. Within the *insecure* groups, mothers Q-sorted their children significantly *higher*,
or more secure, than observers. Furthermore, mothers of Avoidant and Controlling children Q-sorted them above the observed security-score mean of the whole sample, while
mothers of Ambivalent children sorted them well below the mean (Stevenson-Hinde &
Shouldice, 1990). "It is likely that these sorting biases reflect the same maternal information-processing biases that are believed to be causal factors in the development of the different types of attachment relationships" (Solomon & George, 1999, p. 309).

Strange Situations

Mary Ainsworth's Strange Situation procedure for 12–18 month olds (Ainsworth et al.,
1978) has been applied to children beyond infancy, either in its original form or with
modifications. Coding systems for older children are reviewed by Solomon and George

(1999): the Cassidy–Marvin system (1992) for 2.5 to 4.5 year olds, Crittenden's Preschool Assessment of Attachment (1994), and the Main–Cassidy system (1988) for 5 to 6 year olds. The Cassidy–Marvin system falls coherently between the Ainsworth system for infants (12–18 months) and the Main–Cassidy system for 5 to 6 year olds (see George & Solomon, 1999, Table 14.3). Within these three systems, patterns of attachment and rating scales (security and avoidance) carry similar meanings, but the precise behaviors involved differ in that they are age-appropriate. Because of their coherence with each other and with the original Ainsworth system, the Cassidy–Marvin and the Main–Cassidy systems will be the focus of the following sections.

The Cassidy–Marvin (C–M) System for 2.5 to 4.5 Year Olds

The Cassidy–Marvin (C–M) system reflects a collaborative effort among a number of laboratories. Hosted by the Seattle node of the MacArthur Network on the Transition from Infancy to Early Childhood, the group met over several years, with Mark Greenberg as its leader and guidance from Mary Ainsworth as well as Mary Main. The coding emphasis is upon reunion episodes and how a child organizes his or her behavior to mother following the stress of separation. In brief, a Secure child greets mother's return with full gaze and positive affect. Interactions are calm, while also intimate and indicative of a special relationship. The two main insecure patterns may be contrasted with this, and indeed, with each other. Whereas the Avoidant child shows minimal responses and maintains a polite neutrality, the Ambivalent child emphasizes dependence on mother, with angry/whiny resistance and/or immature behavior. Within the age range of the C–M system, or from infancy to the Main–Cassidy system at 6 years, one may see a transition from the Disorganized pattern, reflecting confusion and apprehension (see Main & Solomon, 1990), to the Controlling pattern, reflecting a developmentally unnatural effort to reduce uncertainty by taking charge. Such children appear confident, but in a brittle, anxious way (Cassidy & Marvin, 1992; Main & Cassidy, 1988).

Inter-coder reliability has ranged from 75% to 92% (Solomon & George, 1999). Stability was 66% from infancy to preschool (Cassidy, Berlin, & Belsky, 1990), and 72% from 2.5 to 4.5 years for the three main classifications (A, B, & C: Stevenson-Hinde & Shouldice, 1993). Table 10.1 lists publications involving the C–M system, arranged under headings which may be seen as reflecting various forms of validity.

Attachment-related indices

Relations have been found between results from the C–M system and representational methods – the Attachment Story Completion Task (Bretherton, Ridgeway, & Cassidy, 1990) and the Separation Anxiety Test (Shouldice & Stevenson-Hinde, 1992) – as well as with reported knowledge of self and mother (Pipp, Easterbrooks, & Harmon, 1992). However, correspondences with the Q-sort did not occur. When mothers completed the Q-sort, there no significant differences in Q-sort scores according to C–M patterns of

Table 10.1   Publications Using the Cassidy and Marvin (C–M) Coding System for 2.5 to 4.5 Year Olds in Relation to Various Topics

Attachment-related indices

Bretherton, Ridgway, & Cassidy (1990)	3 year olds: C–M & story completion
Pipp, Easterbrooks, & Harmon (1992)	1 to 3 year olds: C–M & knowledge of self and mother
Shouldice & Stevenson-Hinde (1992)	4.5 year olds: C–M & SAT
Stevenson-Hinde & Shouldice (1990)	2.5 year olds: C–M & Attachment Q-sort by mothers

Aspects of caregiving

M/C interactions

Achermann, Dinneen, & Stevenson-Hinde (1991)	2.5 year olds: C–M & observed maternal style while clearing up (in lab)
Barnett, Kidwell, & Ho Leung (1998)	4 year olds: C–M & parenting style
Marvin & Brittner (1995)	Preschool: C–M and parental caregiving patterns in the strange situation
NICHD Early Child Care Research Network (2001)	Infancy to 3 years: Ainsworth, C–M, and maternal sensitivity
Stevenson-Hinde & Shouldice (1995)	4.5 year olds: C–M & maternal interactions (in home and lab) & maternal self-reports

Maternal psychosocial problems

DeMulder & Radke-Yarrow (1991)	Ainsworth for 15–30 months; C–M for >30 months: Affectively ill vs. well mothers
Easterbrooks, Davidson & Chazan (1993)	School age: C–M, psychosocial risk, and behavior problems
Manassis, Bradley, Goldberg, Hood & Swinson (1994)	Ainsworth for ages 18–23 months, $n = 5$; C–M for ages 24–59 months, $n = 15$: Anxiety disordered mothers
Marvin & Pianta (1996)	Children with cerebral palsy, 14–54 months old; Ainsworth coding for 5 locomotor infants; C–M for 34 locomotor preschoolers; & special system for 31 non-locomotor infants/preschoolers: Mothers' non-resolution of child's diagnosis associated with insecure attachment

Maltreatment

Cicchetti & Barnett (1991)	Preschoolers: C–M & maltreatment

Adoption

Marcovitch, Goldberg, Gold, Washington, Wasson, Krekewich, & Handley-Derry (1997)	Behavioral problems in Romanian children adopted in Ontario. C–M at 3-5 years: Adoptees ($n=44$) differed significantly from normals ($n=38$): Controlling/other most common; none were Avoidant

Aspects of child
Temperament

Stevenson-Hinde (2000)	Shyness in the context of close relationships [overview]
Stevenson-Hinde & Marshall (1999)	4.5 year olds: C–M, behavioral inhibition (BI) & heart period (sampled selected for low, medium, high BI)
Stevenson-Hinde & Shouldice (1990)	2.5 year olds: C–M & BI (unselected sample)
Stevenson-Hinde & Shouldice (1993)	2.5 & 4.5 years: C–M & BI (unselected, longitudinal sample)
Vaughn, Stevenson-Hinde, Waters, Kotsaftis, Lefever, Shouldice, Trudel, & Belsky (1992)	Infancy & early childhood: C–M, temperament, Q-sort

Interactions with others

Booth, Rose-Krasnor, McKinnon, & Rubin (1994)	C–M at 3 years: Predicting social adjustment in middle childhood
Turner (1991)	4.5-year-olds: C–M & peer-peer interactions
Turner (1993)	4.5-year-olds: C–M & interactions with adults in preschool

Behavior problems

DeKlyen (1996)	Preschoolers (normal vs. clinic-referred): C–M & behavior disorders
DeKlyen, Speltz, & Greenberg (1998)	Preschoolers: C–M & positive and negative parenting
Goldberg (1991)	Preschool: C–M and behavior problems in normal, at risk, and clinic samples
Greenberg (1999)	Attachment and psychopathology in childhood
Greenberg, DeKlyen, Speltz, & Endriga (1997)	Preschool: C–M & externalizing psychopathology
Greenberg, Speltz, DeKlyen, & Endriga (1991)	Preschool: C–M in children with and without externalizing behavior problems
Moss, Rousseau, Parent, St.-Laurent, & Saintonge (1998)	5–7 year olds: used C–M and Main & Cassidy in combination – maternal reported stress, mother–child interaction, and behavior problems
Speltz, DeKlyen, & Greenberg (1999)	Preschool: C–M in boys with early onset conduct problems
Speltz, DeKlyen, Greenberg, & Dryden (1995)	Preschool: C–M & Oppositional Defiant Disorder

attachment. However, the discrepancies between the two systems occurred in predictable ways (see above), which lent support to the C–M system (Stevenson-Hinde & Shouldice, 1990).

Aspects of caregiving

Reflecting infancy studies, various indices of maternal sensitivity have been associated with security. The studies listed under Caregiving (Table 10.1) indicate that within the C–M system security has been associated with the following parental interactions: mothers' constructive involvement in a free-play situation, and in a clear-up task a high proportion of positive statements and a low proportion of control statements, but of those a high proportion with positive tone (at 2.5 years: Achermann, Dinneen, & Stevenson-Hinde, 1991); and in a low-income sample, caregivers as warm and accepting, less controlling and less apt to use corporal punishment (at 4–5 years: Barnett, Kidwell, & Leung, 1998). Security has been associated with maternal positive mood, meshing, enjoyment of child, and being relaxed in home observations; and with monitoring, planning, affirming, and providing a sensitive framework in a laboratory joint task (3.5 to 4.5 years: Stevenson-Hinde & Shouldice, 1995). In a particularly large sample (NICHD, 2001; $N = 1060$) of variables involving aspects of childcare, family, mother, and child, the strongest predictor of attachment security at 3 years was maternal sensitivity. Furthermore, from 15 months (Ainsworth coding) to 36 months (C–M coding), a change from *secure to insecure*, compared with stably secure, was associated with less sensitive mothering at 24 and 36 months. The least sensitive mothering at 24 and 36 months was associated with *stable insecurity*. Thus, validation for the C–M system is adequate with respect to linking maternal style with security. However, similar validation for fathers is lacking.

Concerning the further question, of whether the differing patterns of insecurity are associated with different caregiver styles, a simple answer is unlikely to be forthcoming. A coherent picture emerges only when both the context and the type of measure are noted. For example, correspondences with each pattern of attachment did emerge with observational measures in a stressful setting, when Marvin and Brittner (1995) observed mothers' behavior upon reunion in the strange situation. However, in a nonstressful home setting, mothers of Avoidant children did *not* differ significantly from mothers of Secure children (although their mean scores did differ by more than a standard deviation in the expected direction). In a more demanding joint task in the laboratory, mothers of Avoidant children did tend to withdraw, in terms of monitoring and planning significantly less than all other groups. Furthermore they showed possible idealization, in terms of reporting themselves in a significantly better light than all other mothers on three temperament scales and a depression scale. In contrast, mothers of Ambivalent children rated themselves as significantly the most depressed and anxious and the least satisfied with their marriages, and their interactions at home were the least positive, particularly in ratings of low meshing with child. Like mothers of Ambivalent children, mothers of Controlling children also had low positive interactions at home. And like mothers of Avoidant children, mothers of Controlling children rated themselves in a good light – least irritable and anxious – while in the laboratory joint task they affirmed least, enjoyed the task least, and provided the least sensitive framework (Stevenson-Hinde & Shouldice, 1995). Further observations of maternal style are needed, particularly regarding the clinically interesting Disorganized/Controlling category, where a lead has been given by infancy research (see Hesse, 1999a, 1999b; Lyons-Ruth & Jacobvitz, 1999).

Consistent with infancy studies (see meta-analyses by van IJzendoorn, Goldberg, Kroonenberg, & Frenkel, 1992; van IJzendoorn, Schuengel, & Bakermans-Kranenburg, 1999), the Disorganized/Controlling category in preschoolers has been associated with maternal problems. Insecurity, particularly Disorganization, has been associated with clinical diagnoses of maternal depression (DeMulder & Radke-Yarrow, 1991) and anxiety (Manassis, Bradley, Goldberg, Hood, & Swinson, 1994), as well as psychosocial risk (Easterbrooks, Davidson, & Chazan, 1993) and maltreatment (Cicchetti & Barnett, 1991).

Turning to adoption, and bearing in mind the caveat that an attachment bond may still be in the making and not fully formed, the C–M system has been used with Rumanian adoptees, aged 3–5 years. Controlling/Insecure-other patterns were most common, and none were Avoidant (Marcovitch et al., 1997).

Aspects of the child

With studies focusing on characteristics of the child, relations have been found between a child's behavioral inhibition (BI) and an Ambivalent pattern (reviewed in Stevenson-Hinde, 2000). Furthermore, attachment status informs the relation between BI and autonomic functioning. That is, only Secure children showed the predicted relation between high BI and high heart rate (Stevenson-Hinde & Marshall, 1999). For an overview of attachment and temperament, see Vaughn & Bost (1999).

With peers, security has been associated with social adjustment (Booth, Rose-Krasnor, McKinnon, & Rubin (1994). With 4.5 year olds, insecurity was associated with dependent behavior in playgroup. However, of more interest was an interaction effect, with *insecure girls* showing the most positive expressive behavior and compliance, and the least assertive and controlling behavior; while *insecure boys* showed the least positive behavior and compliance but the most attention-getting, assertive, controlling and aggressive behavior, thereby reflecting sexual stereotypes (Turner, 1991, 1993).

In infancy, attachment has been related to both acting out and withdrawal behavior with peers, with a suggestion that an Avoidant pattern is associated with the former and an Ambivalent pattern with the latter. However, when Disorganization has been assessed, this proved to be the primary predictor of problem behavior with peers (reviewed in Lyons-Ruth & Jacobvitz, 1999). Similarly with 5–7 year olds, Moss et al. (1998) concluded: "Controlling/other children were most at risk for both externalizing and internalizing problems across both age periods" (p. 1390). Furthermore, Greenberg and colleagues found a high incidence of controlling and insecure-other attachment patterns in clinic samples of 4–6 year olds, including boys with oppositional defiant disorder (see references in Table 10.1). After reviewing results from normal, at-risk, and clinic samples, Goldberg concludes that "as we move along a continuum of risk to clear diagnosis, the likelihood of secure attachment decreases and the likelihood of disorganized, controlling, and insecure-other attachment increases" (1991, p. 190). She goes on to suggest that "further differentiation within these categories based on clinic samples may prove to be more useful than are the normatively derived classification schemes" (p. 190).

Table 10.2   Publications Using the Main–Cassidy (M–C) Coding System for 6 Year Olds in Relation to Various Topics

Attachment-related indices

Cassidy (1988)	6 year olds: M–C & self-perceptions
Jacobsen, Edelstein, & Hofmann (1994)	Attachment in childhood and cognitive functioning in childhood and adolescence
Slough & Greenberg (1990)	5 year olds: Representations of separation from parents
Solomon, George, & DeJong (1995)	6 year olds: M–C & evidence of disorganized representational strategies and aggression at home and at school

Aspects of caregiving

George & Solomon (1996)	Representational models of relationships: Links between caregiving and attachment

Interactions with others

Cassidy, Kirsh, Scolton, & Parke (1996)	6 year olds: M–C & representations of peer relationships
Cohn (1990)	6 year olds: M–C & social competence in school
Wartner, Grossmann, Fremmer-Bombik, & Suess (1994)	6 year olds: M–C predictability from infancy and implications for preschool behavior

The Main–Cassidy (M–C) System for 6 Year Olds

Inter-coder reliability has ranged from 70% to 82% (references in Table 10.2; George & Solomon, 1999). Stability for the ABC classification was 84% over one month (Cassidy, 1990; Main & Cassidy, 1988). From infancy to 6 years stability was 82% with mothers in samples from two different countries (Main & Cassidy, 1988; Wartner, Grossmann, Fremmer-Bombik, & Suess, 1994), and 62% with fathers (Main & Cassidy, 1988).

Attachment-related indices

In a structured doll-play situation designed to arouse the attachment behavior system, agreement was 79% between resulting classifications and classifications based on the M–C system (Solomon, George, & DeJong, 1995). Although agreement between the systems was very high for the Secure, Ambivalent, and Controlling groups, it was lower for the Avoidant group. Indeed, it is worth noting that Avoidant children may be particularly difficult to distinguish from Secure children on tasks that rely solely on verbal behavior. With pictures of attachment-related events, a high level of agreement with the M–C system has also been found (Jacobsen, Edelstein, & Hofmann, 1994; Slough & Greenberg, 1990). And with measures of the self, Secure children on the M–C system were more open about themselves and about their feelings of vulnerability than insecure children (Cassidy, 1988).

Aspects of caregiving

Children who had been classed as Disorganized on the M–C system tended to depict themselves as frightened and the caregiver as frightening (Solomon et al., 1995). As in infancy, controlling/disorganized behavior has been associated with unresolved loss or trauma in mothers. Such mothers adopt a helpless stance, failing to provide reassurance to the child, or fearful of the child or of her own loss of control (George & Solomon, 1996; Greenberg, Speltz, DeKlyen, & Endriga, 1991).

Interactions with others

Finally, links have been found between a Secure M–C classification and social competence and peer acceptance in school (Cohn, 1990; Wartner et al., 1994). Results for boys were compatible with those found in playgroup with the C–M system (Turner, 1991, 1993). That is, insecure boys (but not girls) were less well liked by peers and teachers, perceived as more aggressive by peers, and by teachers as having more behavior problems and being less competent (Cohn, 1990). Finally, Cassidy, Kirsh, Scolton, and Parke (1996) found that Secure children had more positive representations of peers' feelings than did insecure children.

Representational Procedures

As Mary Ainsworth asserted, "Attachment is organized within the individual, and we must infer its nature from whatever clues that are available to us, whether these be how the individual behaves or what he says about what he is thinking, feeling, or intending" (1990, p 469). In infancy, the clues to attachment quality are necessarily behavioral. However, from the early preschool years on, children are increasingly capable of using symbols in the form of actions, images, or words to reveal their internalized experiences with attachment figures and resulting expectations about these relationships. Thus not surprisingly, in attachment research beyond infancy, observational assessments of attachment were soon complemented by the so-called "representational" assessments.

Representational attachment measures involve procedures in which attachment security is assessed in the absence of the actual attachment figure, thereby making use of the child's representational or symbolic capacities. A variety of attachment-related tasks can be used – such as making a family drawing, responding to a photograph of the family, etc. However, the most widely used representational assessments rely on the child's verbal communication about attachment-related issues, commonly referred to as "attachment narratives." Two kinds of narrative assessments will be discussed below: attachment doll-play procedures and picture-response procedures. These cover the age range from 3 to about 8 years.

Narrative attachment measures for older children are also being developed (e.g., Wright, Binney, & Smith, 1995).

Attachment Doll-play procedures: Overview of Measures

In the doll-play procedures, children are asked to use a doll family and some props to complete a set of standardized attachment-related story beginnings. The children are requested to enact and verbalize what happens, and are systematically probed for further clarification if needed. On the basis of their enactment of each story and their verbal responses, both transcribed in detail, the quality of the children's representations of attachment relationships is inferred. The underlying assumption is that the quality of attachment is revealed in the pattern of communication about attachment-related issues, that is, in the content and structure, or the "what" and "how" of the narratives (Bretherton, 1990; Bretherton et al., 1990).

In the past decade, several doll-play methods have been developed. Table 10.3 gives a chronological overview of the different published assessments for preschoolers and young school-age children. As can be seen, the number of attachment-related stories varies from four to six across procedures. Moreover, the range of scenarios presented is variable. Stories about fear- or distress-provoking situations (e.g., child being afraid in bed at night) are presented in all procedures. In addition, most procedures include one or more separation and reunion situations, for example, the parents depart for a trip and then return (Bretherton et al., 1990; Oppenheim, 1997; Solomon et al., 1995), or the child is lost while shopping with the parent (Green, Stanley, Smith, & Goldwyn, 2000). Two assessments include potentially conflictual and other emotionally charged parent–child interactions, which may be relevant for children in the phase of the "goal-corrected partnership" (Cassidy, 1988; Verschueren, Marcoen, & Schoefs, 1996). Some procedures assess the overall representation of attachment to both parents (Bretherton et al., 1990; Solomon et al., 1995). Others focus on the representations of specific attachment relationships – mother and/or father (Cassidy, 1988; Green et al., 2000; Verschueren et al., 1996). Oppenheim's (1997) doll-play task includes stories dealing with mother alone, as well as stories dealing with both parents together.

In most coding systems (with two exceptions), two criteria for security are – more or less – explicitly used. The criteria are based on theoretical ideas about the content and structure of working models of attachment relationships (Bretherton, 1990), on research using picture-based procedures, and on the inspection of subsamples of transcripts. The two criteria can be labeled: (1) emotional openness in sharing one's narratives with others; and (2) emotional tone (positive or negative) of the interactions presented, including the constructiveness of the story resolution. In addition to a secure category with narratives characterized by emotional openness and positive tone, two different insecure categories arise: (1) stories characterized by avoidance or a lack of emotional openness; and (2) stories characterized by negative emotional tone, with hostile, violent, bizarre interactions, and a destructive ending or no resolution at all. This latter insecure category is labeled differently across systems, but the key characteristics are the same. Oppenheim (1997) uses similar criteria, but only uses scores and no classifications. Two other coding systems were devel-

Table 10.3   Chronological Overview of Attachment Doll-Play Procedures for 3 to 7 Year Olds

Authors	Assessment	Age (years)	Stories	Coding system
Cassidy (1986, 1988)	Incomplete stories with doll family	6	6 attachment stories (using only mother)	3 categories: secure, avoidant, & bizarre/negative (or hostile/negative)
Bretherton et al. (1990) (Page & Bretherton, 1994)	Attachment story completion task	3	5 attachment stories (using mother & father together)	3 categories: secure, avoidant, & disorganized (also labeled ambivalent)
Solomon et al. (1995)	Separation-reunion story completion task	6	4 attachment stories from Bretherton et al. (using mother & father together)	4 categories (based on 2 stories): confident, frightened, casual, & busy
Verschueren et al. (1996)	Attachment story completion task	4–6	5 attachment stories (adapted from Cassidy & Bretherton et al.) (using mother or father separately)	3 categories: secure, avoidant, & bizarre/ambivalent
Oppenheim (1997)	Attachment doll-play interview	3–5	6 attachment stories (some using only mother; some using both parents)	No categories. Scores for: emotional openness, constructive solution, & positive emotional tone
Green et al. (2000)	Manchester child attachment story task	5–7	5 attachment stories (using 1 parent)	4 categories: secure, avoidant ambivalent, & cannot classify; and a superordinate category: disorganized

oped somewhat differently. Solomon et al.'s (1995) system is derived empirically, based on the inspection of protocols of 6 year olds who were known to be classified as A, B, C, or D in the M–C observation system. Thus, these authors made a distinction between four categories. Green et al.'s (2000) system draws on concepts and methods from attachment research in infancy and in adulthood. It includes four main categories (A, B, C, and Cannot Classify), a superordinate D category, as well as various ratings of narrative coherence similar to the ratings from the Adult Attachment Interview.

Attachment Doll-play Procedures: Overview of Empirical Results

Inter-coder reliability was not reported in the Bretherton et al. (1990) study, but was satisfying in all other studies. The percentage agreement ranged from 71 to 88%. Cassidy (1988) investigated the test–retest reliability for one story. Stability of classification was 73% over a 1-month period. Green et al. (2000) report a stability of 77% for the ABC classification over a 5- to 8-month period.

Theoretically predicted associations with attachment quality as concurrently assessed by observational assessments (C–M or M–C observation systems), were established in three studies (Bretherton et al., 1990; Cassidy, 1988; Solomon et al., 1995, see above). In addition, Bretherton and her colleagues (1990) found significant associations with attachment quality in infancy as measured in the Strange Situation. Oppenheim (1997) examined the connection between preschoolers' responses to his doll-play interview and their separation–reunion behavior toward their mother in a small, new classroom setting. He found that both positive emotional tone and more emotional openness in the stories were related to more classroom exploration in the preseparation period, and less contact maintenance with mother when she returned.

Evidence for a connection with parent–child interactions observed in the home or in theoretically relevant laboratory situations other than separation–reunion situations, is not available yet. Connections with self-reported family functioning are reported in two studies. Bretherton et al. (1990) found that mothers' self-reported marital satisfaction, family cohesion, and family adaptability were positively related to the children's attachment security as measured by the doll-play procedure one year later. Verschueren (1996) reported a positive connection between kindergartners' attachment security, measured via doll play, and parents' self-reported encouragement of the children's independence. Interestingly, the quality of the child–father attachment representation was only related to autonomy encouragement (reported) by the father, whereas the quality of the child–mother attachment representation was only related to autonomy encouragement (reported) by the mother. Connections with self-reported parental warmth were, however, not significant.

Associations with socioemotional functioning have been investigated in three studies. In a study with 6 year olds, Cassidy (1988) found a positive connection between the security of the child–mother attachment representation, assessed via doll play, and the quality of self as indexed by the Puppet Interview. Oppenheim (1997) found that preschoolers' emotional openness and positive emotional tone in the doll-play interview were related in the predicted way to teacher ratings of behavioral self-esteem and quality of attention seeking.

In a study with 5 year olds, Verschueren and Marcoen (1999) examined the associations between representations of attachment to mother and to father, representations of self, and several aspects of socioemotional functioning (teacher ratings of school adjustment, social competence with peers, anxious/withdrawn behavior, etc.). The predicted connections were largely found. Surprisingly however, differential effects of attachment to mother and to father were revealed. The children's positiveness of self, as measured by the Puppet Interview, was most strongly predicted by the quality of attachment to mother, whereas their degree of anxious/withdrawn behavioral problems were most strongly predicted by the quality of attachment to father. Moreover, the insecure children who told bizarre, hostile, disorganized stories showed most signs of maladaptation. In two studies, such insecure attachment stories were found to be related to the Controlling (D) observational pattern in the M–C system (Cassidy, 1988; Solomon et al., 1995).

Picture Response Procedures: Overview of Measures

Another type of representational assessment makes use of photographs depicting parent–child separations. Most of these picture-response procedures are based on Klagsbrun and Bowlby's modification of Hansburg's Separation Anxiety Test – the SAT (Bohlin, Hagekull, & Rydell, 2000; Fonagy, Redfern, & Charman, 1997; Kaplan, 1987, cited in Solomon & George, 1999; Main et al., 1985; Shouldice & Stevenson-Hinde, 1992; Slough & Greenberg, 1990; Verschueren & Marcoen, 2000). Some researchers constructed and validated their own separation pictures (Jacobsen, Edelstein, & Hofmann, 1994; Wright et al., 1995).

The Klagsbrun–Bowlby modification of the SAT is developed for 4- to 7-year-old children. It comprises pictures of three parent–child separations considered to be mild (e.g., mother putting child in bed), and three parent–child separations considered to be severe (e.g., parents departing for a 2-week vacation). Each picture is introduced in a standardized way. Next the children are asked how the child in the picture might feel, why he or she might feel that way, and what this hypothetical child might do. In Slough and Greenberg's (1990) Seattle version of the SAT, the children are also requested to describe their own feelings and coping behavior, if they were to be confronted with these separations.

To code the children's responses to the SAT, several schemes have been developed. In Kaplan and Main's system (Main et al., 1985), the emotional openness and the constructiveness of the coping responses are rated. Kaplan (1987, cited in Solomon & George, 1999) later constructed a four-category system based on the same two criteria. Jacobsen et al. (1994) successfully applied this classification system and labeled the four categories as: secure, avoidant, ambivalent, and disorganized. The most widely used system is the Seattle scoring scheme developed by Slough and Greenberg (1990). Based on a 21-category system, three summary scores are computed: (a) the ability to express vulnerability in the context of severe separations; (b) the ability to express self-confidence in the context of mild separations; and (c) the degree of avoidance in discussing separations. Secure children are assumed to score high on the first two measures, and low on the third. These scales and/or scales based on the Seattle category system are used in the studies of Bohlin et al. (2000), Fonagy et al. (1997), Verschueren and Marcoen (2000), and Wright et al. (1995).

Picture Response Procedures: Overview of Empirical Results

Inter-rater reliability of the SAT coding systems (if reported) was satisfactory. Test–retest reliability was examined in one study by Wright et al. (1995). In a small clinical sample of 15 children, they found positive but very low test–retest correlations (between .12 and .39). However, the respondents in this study were older (8–12 years), and a self-constructed set of pictures was administered.

In several studies theoretically predicted concurrent relations were found between responses to the SAT and attachment quality as assessed by an observational measure (C–M or M–C system: Main et al., 1985; Shouldice & Stevenson-Hinde, 1992; Slough & Greenberg, 1990). Moreover, concurrent connections with security scores based on an attachment story completion task were found, even when controlling for the children's verbal competence (Verschueren & Marcoen, 2000). Relations with the Strange Situation classification at age 1 were found in two studies using the Kaplan coding scheme (Jacobsen et al., 1994; Kaplan, 1987, in Solomon & George, 1999). No such association was found by Bohlin et al. (2000). Again however, the respondents in this study were older (8–9 years).

Very few studies investigated the associations with parent–child interactions in contexts other than separation–reunion situations. Slough and Greenberg (1990) reported a significant association with mother affect ratings (p. 82), but the way these ratings were gathered is not described. Verschueren (1996) found a connection between an overall security score based on the Seattle system, and the self-reported encouragement of independence by mother and by father. As for the story completions, connections with self-reported parental warmth were not significant.

Verschueren and Marcoen (2000) examined the connection between children's responses to the SAT and aspects of their socioemotional functioning. Results showed a positive association between children's overall security score on the SAT and their popularity, prosocial behavior, and global school adjustment as seen by the teacher. Moreover, higher overall security scores were related to a more positive representation of self as indexed by the Puppet Interview. In a study with 8 year olds, Bohlin et al. (2000) found significant concurrent associations between this SAT overall security score and popularity and social initiative-withdrawal as evaluated by parents, teachers, and observers. In a sample of 3 to 6 year olds, Fonagy and colleagues (1997) concluded that attachment security as assessed by the SAT significantly predicted children's social-cognitive capacities, specifically their belief-desire reasoning ability. In two longitudinal studies, significant connections were found between security of attachment representations at age 7 and later performance on reasoning tasks (Jacobsen et al., 1994), attention-participation and security about self according to the teacher, and grade point average in school (Jacobsen & Hofmann, 1997), even when controlling for differences in intelligence. Finally, as compared with a nonclinical control group, children in a clinical group had more difficulty in discussing feelings about separations openly and in expressing feelings of vulnerability in the context of severe separations (Wright et al., 1995).

Conclusion

Thus with strange situation classifications from infancy to about 7 years, a coherent picture is emerging. In addition to interobserver reliability and reasonable stability over time, classifications have been related in predictable ways to other indices of attachment, aspects of caregiving including maltreatment, interactions with peers, and behavior disorders.

The picture emerging with representational assessments is somewhat less coherent, partly due to the use of various procedures and coding schemes. Overall, however, results are very encouraging. Inter-rater reliability and test–retest reliability are generally adequate, and connections with concurrent and antecedent strange situation classifications were found in several studies from different research groups. Research on the connection with children's socioemotional functioning is growing and provides considerable evidence for the construct validity of the representational attachment measures. Up to now, research on the relation with caregiving or parent–child interactions assessed at home or in relevant laboratory situations (besides separation–reunion situations) is scarce. Examining how patterns of narratives are related to patterns of caregiving remains an important task for future studies.

Current Issues and Future Directions

Now that predictable differences have been found between Secure versus Insecure groups over this age range, the next challenge is to make further distinctions in antecedents and outcome among the Insecure categories (Avoidant, Ambivalent, Disorganized/Controlling, and Insecure-other). Unfortunately for research purposes (but not for child development), about two-thirds of a normative sample tend to be classed as Secure. Thus, sample selection for more Insecure children is needed within community samples, as well as further work with clinical samples. We should be open to the possibility of additional categories emerging as clinical samples are explored further.

We should caution that coding strange situation procedures requires extensive training. Furthermore with the C–M and M–C systems, training workshops are held only on an ad hoc basis rather than routinely as with the infancy system. Assessment would be greatly helped by organizing routine training sessions, encompassing the age range of both the C–M and M–C systems. This would require making an explicit link between the two systems, with a single coding manual for ages 2.5 to 7 years, perhaps with age-appropriate sections.

Regarding the representational attachment measures, several issues remain to be addressed. Firstly, more attention should be given to establishing connections with patterns of caregiving as observed in the home or the laboratory. However, the relations between parenting style and children's attachment representations need not be perfect. They are likely to be moderated by child characteristics (e.g. meta-cognitive or social-cognitive capacities) and/or correcting experiences within the larger network of attachment relationships (Verschueren & Marcoen, 1999). Examining such interactive effects of caregiving experiences and child characteristics on the quality of attachment representations as indexed by narrative measures is a prominent task for further research.

Secondly, research should focus more on relations with cognitive and social-cognitive development. To what degree are the patterns of verbal communication about attachment-related issues related to children's verbal and cognitive capacities in general? And to what degree are attachment representations related to other aspects of social cognition? Although significant connections are to be expected (e.g., Meins, 1997; van IJzendoorn, Dijkstra, & Bus, 1995), relations should not be too high in order to support the discriminant validity (Green et al., 2000; Verschueren & Marcoen, 1999).

Thirdly, the number of insecure response patterns that may be distinguished is still unclear. All classification systems comprise at least two insecure patterns. Some systems include an additional third insecure category (corresponding to the C-observational category). Whether such a further differentiation within insecure patterns is necessary or desirable, remains an open question (e.g., given the very small proportion of these "C-narratives" found by Green et al., 2000, and Jacobsen et al., 1994). In each case, the number of meaningfully distinguishable categories may vary across developmental periods and types of assessment, and need not fixed be a priori in order to match patterns in infancy.

This leads us to a final important challenge for the future. In contrast to the observational assessments, diversity among representational measures has been much larger. This is especially true for the doll-play assessments. This "intellectual freedom" certainly has advantages, especially in an early stage of instrument development. However, in order to make significant progress in the future, researchers with expertise in doll-play assessments may want to collaborate in developing a standardized doll-play assessment, clearly rooted in theory and research on the normative development of attachment in children, and combining the strong elements of existing measures. This kind of collaborative effort may provide the best guarantee for the systematic examination of remaining questions.

References

Achermann, J., Dinneen, E., & Stevenson-Hinde, J. (1991). Clearing up at 2.5 years. *British Journal of Developmental Psychology, 9,* 365–376.

Ainsworth, M. D. S. (1990). Some considerations regarding theory and assessment relevant to attachments beyond infancy. In M. T. Greenberg, D. Cicchetti, & E. M. Cummings (Eds.), *Attachment in the preschool years: Theory, research and intervention* (pp. 463–488). Chicago: University of Chicago Press.

Ainsworth, M. D. S., Blehar, M. C., Waters, E., & Wall, S. (1978). *Patterns of attachment.* Hillsdale, NJ: Erlbaum.

Baerends, G. P. (1976). The functional organization of behaviour. *Animal Behaviour, 24,* 726–738.

Barnett, D., Kidwell, S. L., & Ho Leung, K. (1998). Parenting and preschooler attachment among low-income urban African American families. *Child Development, 69,* 1657–1671.

Bohlin, G., Hagekull, B., & Rydell, A.-M. (2000). Attachment and social functioning: A longitudinal study from infancy to middle childhood. *Social Development, 9,* 24–39.

Booth, C. L., Rose-Krasnor, L., McKinnon, J. A., & Rubin, K. H. (1994). Predicting social adjustment in middle childhood: The role of preschool attachment security and maternal style. *Social Development, 3,* 189–204.

Bowlby, J. (1973). *Attachment and loss, Vol 2: Separation, anxiety and anger.* London: Hogarth Press.

Bowlby, J. (1982). *Attachment and loss, Vol 1: Attachment,* 2nd ed. London: Hogarth Press.

Bowlby, J. (1991a). Ethological light on psychoanalytical problems. In P. Bateson (Ed.), *Development and integration of behaviour* (pp. 301–313). Cambridge, England: Cambridge University Press.

Bowlby, J. (1991b). Postscript. In C. M. Parkes, J. Stevenson-Hinde, & P. Marris (Eds.), *Attachment across the life cycle* (pp. 293–297). London: Routledge.

Bretherton, I. (1990). Open communication and internal working models: Their role in attachment relationships. In R. A. Thompson (Ed.), *Socioemotional development. Nebraska symposium on motivation, Vol. 36* (pp. 57–114). Lincoln, NE: University of Nebraska Press.

Bretherton, I., & Munholland, K. A. (1999). Internal working models in attachment relationships: A construct revisited. In J. Cassidy & P. R. Shaver (Eds.), *Handbook of attachment: Theory, research, and clinical applications* (pp. 89–111). New York: Guilford Press.

Bretherton, I., Ridgeway, D., & Cassidy, J. (1990). Assessing internal working models of the attachment relationship: An attachment story completion task for 3-year-olds. In M. T. Greenberg, D. Cicchetti, & E. M. Cummings (Eds.), *Attachment in the preschool years: Theory, research and intervention* (pp. 273–308). Chicago: University of Chicago Press.

Cassidy, J. (1986). Attachment and the self at age six. Unpublished doctoral dissertation, University of Virginia.

Cassidy, J. (1988). The self as related to child–mother attachment at six. *Child Development, 59,* 121–134.

Cassidy, J. (1990). Theoretical and methodological considerations in the study of attachment and the self in young children. In M. T. Greenberg, D. Cicchetti, & E. M. Cummings (Eds.), *Attachment in the preschool years: Theory, research and intervention* (pp. 87–119). Chicago: University of Chicago Press.

Cassidy, J., Berlin, L., & Belsky, J. (1990, April). *Attachment organization at age 3: Antecedent and concurrent correlates.* Paper presented at the biennial meeting of the International Conference on Infant Studies, Montreal.

Cassidy, J., Kirsh, S. J., Scolton, K. L., & Parke, R. D. (1996). Attachment and representations of peer relationships. *Developmental Psychology, 32,* 892–904.

Cassidy, J., & Marvin, R. S. (1992). *Attachment organization in preschool children: Procedures and coding manual* (4th ed.). Unpublished manuscript, MacArthur Working Group on Attachment, Seattle, WA.

Cicchetti, D., & Barnett, D. (1991). Attachment organization in maltreated preschoolers. *Development and Psychopathology, 3,* 397–411.

Cohn, D. (1990). Child–mother attachment in six-year-olds and social competence in school. *Child Development, 61,* 152–162.

Crittenden, P. (1994). *Preschool Assessment of Attachment* (2nd ed.). Unpublished manuscript, Family Relations Institute, Miami, FL.

DeKlyen, M. (1996). Disruptive behavior disorders and intergenerational attachment patterns: A comparison of normal and clinic-referred preschoolers and their mothers. *Journal of Consulting and Clinical Psychology, 64,* 357–365.

DeKlyen, M., Speltz, M. L., & Greenberg, M. T. (1998). Fathering and early onset conduct problems: Positive and negative parenting, father-son attachment, and the marital context. *Clinical Child and Family Psychology Review, 1,* 3–21.

DeMulder, E. K., & Radke-Yarrow, M. (1991). Attachment with affectively ill and well mothers: Concurrent behavioral correlates. *Development and Psychopathology, 3,* 227–242.

DeWolff, M. S., & van IJzendoorn, M. H. (1997). Sensitivity and attachment: A meta-analysis on parental antecedents of infant attachment. *Child Development, 68,* 571–591.

Easterbrooks, M. A., Davidson, C. E., & Chazan, R. (1993). Psychosocial risk, attachment, and behavior problems among school-aged children. *Development and Psychopathology, 5,* 389–402.

Fonagy, P., Redfern, S., & Charman, T. (1997). The relationship between belief-desire reasoning and a projective measure of attachment security (SAT). *British Journal of Developmental Psychology, 15,* 51–61.

George, C., & Solomon, J. (1996). Representational models of relationships: Links between caregiving and attachment. *Infant Mental Health Journal, 17,* 198–216.

Goldberg, S. (1991). Attachment and childhood behavior problems in normal, at-risk, and clinical samples. In L. Atkinson & K. J. Zucker (Eds.), *Attachment and psychopathology* (pp. 171–195). New York: Guilford Press.

Green, J. M., Stanley, C., Smith, V., & Goldwyn, R. (2000). A new method of evaluating attachment representations in young school age children: The Manchester Child Attachment Story Task. *Attachment and Human Development, 2,* 48–70.

Greenberg, M. T. (1999). Attachment and psychopathology in childhood. In J. Cassidy & P. Shaver, (Eds.), *Handbook of attachment* (pp. 469–496). New York: Guilford Press.

Greenberg, M. T., DeKlyen, M., Speltz M. A., & Endriga, M. C. (1997). The role of attachment processes in externalizing psychopathology in young children. In L. Atkinson & K. J. Zucker (Eds.), *Attachment and psychopathology* (pp. 196–222). New York: Guilford Press.

Greenberg, M. T., & Marvin, R. S. (1982). Reactions of preschool children to an adult stranger: A behavioral systems approach. *Child Development, 53,* 481–490.

Greenberg, M. T., Speltz M. A., DeKlyen, M., & Endriga, M.C. (1991). Attachment security in preschoolers with and without externalizing behavior problems: A replication. *Development and Psychopathology, 3,* 413–430.

Hesse, E. (1999a). The Adult Attachment Interview. In J. Cassidy & P. R. Shaver (Eds.), *Handbook of attachment: Theory, research, and clinical applications* (pp. 395–433). New York: Guilford Press.

Hesse, E. (1999b). Unclassifiable and disorganized responses in the Adult Attachment Interview and in the Infant Strange Situation Procedure. Doctoral Dissertation, University of Leiden, The Netherlands.

Hinde, R. A., & Stevenson-Hinde, J. (1991). Perspectives on attachment. In C. M. Parkes, J. Stevenson-Hinde, & P. Marris (Eds.), *Attachment across the life cycle* (pp. 52–65). London: Routledge.

Jacobsen, T., Edelstein, W., & Hofmann, V. (1994). A longitudinal study of the relation between representations of attachment in childhood and cognitive functioning in childhood and adolescence. *Developmental Psychology, 30,* 112–124.

Jacobsen, T., & Hofmann, V. (1997). Children's attachment representations: Longitudinal relations to school behavior and academic competency in middle childhood and adolescence. *Developmental Psychology, 33,* 703–710.

Lyons-Ruth, K., & Jacobvitz, D. (1999). Attachment disorganization: Unresolved loss, relational violence, and lapses in behavioral and attentional strategies. In J. Cassidy & P. Shaver (Eds.), *Handbook of attachment* (pp. 520–554). New York: Guilford Press.

Main, M. (1991). Metacognitive knowledge, metacognitive monitoring, and singular (coherent) versus multiple models of attachment. Findings and directions for future research. In C. M. Parkes, J. Stevenson-Hinde, & P. Marris (Eds.), *Attachment across the life cycle* (pp. 127–159). London: Routledge.

Main, M., & Cassidy, J. (1988). Categories of response to reunion with the parent at age six: Predictable from infant attachment classifications and stable over a 1-month period. *Developmental Psychology, 24,* 415–526.

Main, M., Kaplan, N., & Cassidy, J. (1985). Security in infancy, childhood, and adulthood: a move to the level of representations. In I. Bretherton & E. Waters (Eds.), Growing points in attachment theory and research. *Monographs of the Society for Research in Child Development, 50* (1-2, Serial No. 209), 66–104.

Main, M., & Solomon, J. (1990). Procedures for identifying infants as disorganized/disoriented during the Ainsworth strange situation. In M. T. Greenberg, D. Cicchetti, & E. M. Cummings (Eds.), *Attachment in the preschool years* (pp. 121–160). Chicago: University of Chicago Press.

Manassis, K., Bradley, S., Goldberg, S., Hood, J., & Swinson, R. P. (1994). Attachment in mothers with anxiety disorders and their children. *Journal of the American Academy of Child and Adolescent Psychiatry, 33*, 1106–1113.

Marcovitch, S., Goldberg, S., Gold, A., Washington, J., Wasson, C., Krekewich, K., & Handley-Derry, M. (1997). Determinants of behavioral problems in Romanian children adopted in Ontario. *International Journal of Behavioral Development, 20*, 17–31.

Marvin, R. S., & Brittner, P. A. (1995). Classification system for parental caregiving patterns in the preschool strange situation. Coding Manual, University of Virginia.

Marvin, R. S., & Pianta, R. C. (1996). Mothers' reactions to their child's diagnosis: Relations with security of attachment. *Journal of Clinical Child Psychology, 25*, 436–445.

Meins, E. (1997). *Security of attachment and the social development of cognition.* Hove, England: Psychology Press.

Moss, E., Rousseau, D. R., Parent, S., St.-Laurent, D., & Saintonge, J. (1998). Correlates of attachment at school age: Maternal reported stress, mother–child interaction, and behavior problems. *Child Development, 69*, 1390–1405.

NICHD Early Child Care Research Network. (2001). Child-care and family predictors of preschool attachment and stability from infancy. *Developmental Psychology, 37*, 847–862.

Oppenheim, D. (1997). The Attachment Doll-play Interview for preschoolers. *International Journal of Behavioral Development, 20*, 681–697.

Page, T., & Bretherton, I. (1994). *Preschoolers' coping with parental divorce as reflected in their family narratives.* Poster presented at the Biennial Meetings of the International Society for the Study of Behavioral Development, Amsterdam.

Pipp, S., Easterbrooks, M. A., & Harmon, R. J. (1992). The relation between attachment and knowledge of self and mother in one- to three-year-old infants. *Child Development, 63*, 738–750.

Shouldice, A., & Stevenson-Hinde, J. (1992). Coping with security distress: The Separation Anxiety Test and attachment classification at 4.5 years. *Journal of Child Psychology & Psychiatry, 33*, 331–348.

Slough, N., & Greenberg, M. (1990). Five-year olds' representations of separation from parents: Responses from the perspective of self and other. In I. Bretherton & M. W. Watson (Eds.), *New directions for child development: No. 48. Children's perspectives on the family* (pp. 67–84). San Francisco: Jossey-Bass.

Solomon, J., & George, C. (1999). The measurement of attachment security in infancy and childhood. In J. Cassidy & P. R. Shaver (Eds.), *Handbook of attachment: Theory, research, and clinical applications* (pp.287–316). New York: Guilford Press.

Solomon, J., George, C., & DeJong, A. (1995). Children classified as controlling at age six: Evidence of disorganized representational strategies and aggression at home and at school. *Development and Psychopathology, 7*, 447–463.

Speltz, M. L., DeKlyen, M., & Greenberg, M. T. (1999). Attachment in boys with early onset conduct problems. *Development and Psychopathology, 11*, 269–285.

Speltz, M. L., DeKlyen, M., Greenberg, M. T., & Dryden, M. (1995). Clinic referral for Oppositional Defiant Disorder: Relative significance of attachment and behavioral variables. *Journal of Abnormal Child Psychology, 23*, 487–507.

Stevenson-Hinde, J. (2000). Shyness in the context of close relationships. In W. R. Crozier (Ed.), *Shyness: Development, consolidation, and change* (pp. 88-102). London: Routledge.

Stevenson-Hinde, J., & Marshall, P. J. (1999). Behavioral inhibition, heart period, and respiratory sinus arrhythmia: An attachment perspective. *Child Development, 70*, 805–816.

Stevenson-Hinde, J., & Shouldice, A. (1990). Fear and attachment in 2.5-year-olds. *British Journal of Developmental Psychology, 8,* 319–333.

Stevenson-Hinde, J., & Shouldice, A. (1993). Wariness to strangers: A behavior systems perspective revisited. In K. H. Rubin & J. Asendorpf (Eds.), *Social withdrawal, inhibition, and shyness in childhood* (pp. 101–116). Hillsdale, NJ: Erlbaum.

Stevenson-Hinde, J. & Shouldice, A. (1995). Maternal interactions and self-reports related to attachment classifications at 4.5 years. *Child Development, 66,* 583–596.

Turner, P. J. (1991). Relations between attachment, gender, and behavior with peers in preschool. *Child Development, 62,* 1475–1488.

Turner, P. J. (1993). Attachment to mother and behaviour with adults in preschool. *British Journal of Developmental Psychology, 11,* 75–89.

van IJzendoorn, M. H., Goldberg, S., Kroonenberg, P. M., & Frenkel, O. J. (1992). The relative effects of maternal and child problems on the quality of attachment: A meta-analysis of attachment in clinical samples. *Child Development, 63,* 840–858.

van Ijzendoorn, M. H., Schuengel, C., & Bakermans-Kranenburg, M. J. (1999). Disorganized attachment in early childhood: Meta-analysis of precursors, concomitants, and sequelae. *Development and Psychopathology, 11,* 225–249.

van IJzendoorn, M. H., Vereijken, C. M. J. L., & Riksen-Walraven, M. J. M. A. (in press). Is the Attachment Q-sort a valid measure of attachment security in young children? In B. E. Vaughn & E. Waters (Eds.), *Patterns of secure base behavior: Q-sort perspectives on attachment and caregiving.* Hillsdale, NJ: Erlbaum.

Vaughn, B. E. & Bost, K. K. (1999). Attachment and temperament: Redundant, independent, or interacting influences on interpersonal adaptation and personality development? In J. Cassidy & P. R. Shaver (Eds.), *Handbook of attachment: Theory, research, and clinical applications* (pp. 198–225). New York: Guilford Press.

Vaughn, B. E., Stevenson-Hinde, J., Waters, E., Kotsaftis, A., Lefever, G. B., Shouldice, A., Trudel, M., & Belsky, J. (1992). Attachment security and temperament in infancy and early childhood: Some conceptual clarifications. *Developmental Psychology, 28,* 463–473.

Verschueren, K. (1996). Een veilige gehechtheid, een positief zelf ? Representaties van gehechtheidsrelaties en van het zelf en sociaal-emotionele competentie bij kleuters [A secure attachment, a positive self? Representations of attachment relationships and of the self and socioemotional competence in kindergartners]. Unpublished doctoral dissertation, Center for Developmental Psychology, Catholic University Leuven.

Verschueren, K. & Marcoen, A. (1999). Representations of self and socioemotional competence in kindergartners: Differential and combined effects of attachment to mother and to father. *Child Development, 70,* 183-201.

Verschueren, K., & Marcoen, A. (2000). Correlates of the overall attachment representation in five-year-olds as assessed by the Separation Anxiety Test. Manuscript in preparation.

Verschueren, K., Marcoen, A., & Schoefs, V. (1996). The internal working model of the self, attachment, and competence in five-year-olds. *Child Development, 67,* 2493–2511.

Wartner, U. G., Grossmann, K., Fremmer-Bombik, E., & Suess, G. (1994). Attachment patterns at age six in south Germany: Predictability from infancy and implications for preschool behavior. *Child Development, 65,* 1014–1027.

Waters, E. (1995). The Attachment Q-Set. In E. Waters, B. E. Vaughn, G. Posada, & K. Kondo-Ikemura (Eds.), Caregiving, cultural, and cognitive perspectives on secure-base behavior and working models. *Monographs of the Society for Research in Child Development, 60* (2-3, Serial No. 244), 247–254.

Waters, E., & Deane, K. (1985). Defining and assessing individual differences in attachment relationships: Q-methodology and the organization of behavior in infancy and early childhood. In

I. Bretherton & E. Waters (Eds.), Growing points of attachment theory and research. *Monographs of the Society for Research in Child Development, 50* (1-2, Serial No. 209), 41–65.

Weinfield, N. S., Sroufe, L. A., Egeland, B., & Carlson, E.A. (1999). The nature of individual differences in infant–caregiver attachment. In J. Cassidy & P. R. Shaver (Eds.), *Handbook of attachment: Theory, research, and clinical applications* (pp. 68–88). New York: Guilford Press.

Wright, J. C., Binney, V., & Smith, P. K. (1995). Security of attachment in 8–12-year-olds: A revised version of the Separation Anxiety Test, its psychometric properties and clinical interpretation. *Journal of Child Psychology and Psychiatry, 36,* 757–774.

11

Parent–Child Relationships

Alan Russell, Jacqueline Mize, and Kerry Bissaker

Relationships between parents and children are among the many close relationships that individuals experience throughout their life. Parent–child relationships are important because they are central to the lives of both parents and children, and provide one of the most important environments in which children develop as individuals and as functioning members of their culture (Hartup & Laursen, 1991).

In this chapter, we discuss special features of parent–child relationships against other kinds of close relationship. Consideration is given to issues of definition and conceptualization, especially about the core elements and dimensions of parent–child relationships. Included is a discussion of the distinction between interactions and relationships. Influences of the broader social context on parent–child relationships are outlined. The focus throughout is mainly on parent–child relationships from early childhood (about 3–4 years of age) through middle childhood (to about 12 years of age). Special attention is given to the child's contribution to parent–child relationships. Emphasis is placed on the active role of children, and therefore of parent–child relationships as bidirectional and co-constructed. Another emphasis in the chapter is on the diversity of parent–child relationships.

Throughout the chapter, the need to examine parent–child relationships at different levels is recognized. Dialectic tensions between personal/individual, interpersonal, and social or systems orientations have been noted (Levinger, 1994). This means that when discussing parent–child relationships, attention must be directed to the individuals as participants in the relationship, to the interpersonal aspects of the relationship, and to the broader social context and systems that influence parent–child relationships.

Some *themes* we develop are: (a) the definition and core dimensions of parent–child relationships remain in dispute, (b) parent–child relationships need to be seen as co-constructed, with due acknowledgment of the active role of children in this process, (c) the middle childhood period provides for a number of important developments in parent–child relationships, and (d) diversity is a strong feature of parent–child relationships.

Definitional Matters

Relationships

At the most basic definitional level there are issues such as "what is a personal relationship?" (e.g., Duck, Acitelli, Manke, & West, 1999), and "what are close relationships?". These definitional issues help in efforts to better understand parent–child relationships (Hinde, 1987, 1997). Included in Hinde's work has been an attempt to separate interactions and relationships, and to provide an overall model for the analysis and understanding of relationships.

Hinde's analysis of relationships.   Hinde's analysis of relationships has been widely used in research on parent–child relationships. He argued that "a relationship involves a series of interactions over time between two individuals known to each other" (Hinde, 1987, p. 24). In turn, interactions involve a series of specific interchanges. Hinde's definition is part of a perspective that sees relationships as dialectically linked with interactions. Therefore, relationships comprise interactions, and two-way processes link relationships and interactions, so that interactions are in turn influenced by relationships.

Hinde's (1997) model of relationships was used to provide a structure for the present chapter. In this model, not only are relationships dialectically related to interactions, but interactions and relationships in turn arise out of psychological processes within individuals. Further, relationships influence and are influenced by the groups and broader society in which the individuals participate. Finally, relationships are influenced by the sociocultural structure of beliefs, values, and institutions, and by characteristics of the physical environment.

Hinde's model directs attention to the influence of characteristics and processes within individuals, in this case features of both parents and children. This suggests a consideration of how personal beliefs, values, and attitudes impact on parent–child relationships. It also directs attention to characteristics such as sex (parent and child), parent illness, such as depression, and child temperament and child disabilities as contributors to relationships.

Second, Hinde's model emphasizes the link between interactions and relationships. Although there has been general acceptance of the relationships/interactions distinction in research on parent–child relationships, there is a need for greater clarity on this matter. Researchers will often claim they are assessing parent–child relationships, but in fact study interactions only, and do not address issues about the extent to which or in what ways parent–child relationships are more than the sum of interactions.

This raises questions about what comprises relationships that could be over and above interactions. Relationships appear to be more global and long lasting than interactions, and relationships are usually defined and influenced by more than just the particular interactions. Features such as beliefs, values, commitment, goals, affect, and expectations are important in describing and understanding parent–child relationships. These features are not readily examined through specific observed interactions.

Interactions and interchanges occur at specific points in time. In contrast, relationships involve a past, present, and future. A passing comment to a stranger walking her dog is an interaction, but by itself, this interaction is not part of a relationship. In the case of parents and children, interactions comprise individual elements in a continual flow of exchanges over time. Furthermore, each of the interactions, when considered alone, will have a specific theme or focus, for example, about the child's bedtime, or about their day at school. The relationship comprises large numbers of interactions, with different features or themes.

The research and theoretical literature on parent–child relationships appears to have directed little attention to questions about how interactions influence relationships and in turn how relationships influence interactions. Hinde (1997) emphasized the role of cognitive and affective process in the move from interactions to relationships, including expectations of relationships and interactions, and affective responses to interactions. For example, a harsh exchange and disagreement between parent and child in relationship terms needs to be seen in the context of expectations that the parent and child have of each other, their satisfaction with the relationship, and their affective response to the interaction (as well as to prior interactions of a similar kind). Researchers often include measures of both interactions and relationships, but then do not examine the link between these two levels of social complexity (e.g., Colpin, Demyttenaere, & Vandemeulebroecke, 1995).

In addition to factors at the levels of (a) psychological processes and individual behavior and (b) interactions and relationships, Hinde's (1997) model emphasizes a third level, (c) that included groups and society. It is at this level that ethnic and cultural influences are apparent as well as the ecological context such as the neighborhood. Throughout the chapter, factors at all three of these levels are discussed.

Before turning to an examination of parent–child relationships per se, two other areas of debate in the literature are helpful to consider in order to better understand these relationships. They are the nature of close relationships and the difference between "parenting" and "parent–child relationships."

Close relationships

Central among children's close relationships are those with their parent/s, and in understanding these relationships, it is helpful to consider in what ways this close relationship might differ from other close relationships.

Close relationships are associated with participants having strong influence on one another over an extended time period and in multiple ways (Berscheid & Peplau, 1983). Parent–child relationships display many of the core characteristics of close relationships. For example, they are relatively enduring, extending over time even without propinquity, usually have strong elements of emotional involvement and commitment, with mutual influence a powerful component of the relationship.

Although features of parent–child relationships overlap those of other close relationships, such as in the roles of affection and conflict, parent–child relationships have been argued to contain a number of unique characteristics (Maccoby, 1999). For example, Maccoby (1999) argued that parent–child relationships are not typical of "exchange" relationships because what children offer to their parents could not balance what parents provide. Further, they are not typical of "communal relationships" (Mills & Clark, 1994) because children typically do not take responsibility for their parents' welfare and young children have a limited capacity to understand their parents' needs. Nevertheless, there are some communal elements in parent–child relationships, as shown in interactions that involve mutuality or synchrony.

Overall, it can be seen that parent–child relationships contain some elements of other types of close relationships. However, parent–child relationships are unique in a number of ways. The uniqueness appears to be especially associated with the level of commitment and obligation, in a relationship that contains aspects of asymmetry, but also where the child has considerable power. This matter of asymmetry and power will be revisited below in the discussion of dimensions of parent–child relationships.

Parenting versus parent–child relationships

Recent writing on parent–child relationships (e.g., Maccoby, 1999; Mills & Grusec, 1988) has emphasized the need to separate parenting per se from parent–child relationships. When parenting is the focus, attention is directed to matters such as parenting practices and styles (Darling & Steinberg, 1993). Linked to styles, for example, is the discussion of different parenting patterns, such as authoritative, authoritarian, and permissive parenting (Baumrind, 1967, 1971). Parenting classified using one or other of these patterns might also be described in terms of the type of relationship that the parent has with the child. For example, an authoritarian parent would likely have a relationship with his/her child that involved demanding and controlling behavior from the parent. However, the child could either respond to this with compliance or with resistance. Therefore, once the child's side is considered, the overall relationship could be one of demandingness and compliance or of demandingness plus resistance and conflict. The point is that parenting considers mainly the parents' side of the equation, and if relationships are to be examined, then both parent and child need to be taken into account.

The importance of considering both the parent and child sides of relationships is also evident from the literature that deals with socialization. For example, Bugental and Goodnow (1998) as well as Parke and Buriel (1998) have much to say about parent–child relationships, but both chapters are written from a socialization perspective. In considering the family's role in socialization, parent–child relationships are central, but much of the emphasis is on the effects on the child of the relationship or of parents' behavior, goals, etc. That is, socialization focuses on parent's roles in influencing child behavior and development rather than on relationships per se.

Dimensions of Parent–Child Relationships

Parent–child relationships are complex and multidimensional. They vary over time, differ from the perspective of the parent and of the child, and differ from one situation to another, and so on. Depending on one's theoretical perspective, there are many ways to describe the central features or dimensions of parent–child relationships. For example, discussions of family relationships (e.g., Noller & Fitzpatrick, 1993) typically cover areas such as affection, conflict, and power and control. When other close relationships are discussed (e.g., Canary & Emmers-Sommer, 1997), intimacy and control have been given special treatment. Duck (1992) emphasized communication, including verbal and non-verbal communication, as central elements in a relationship.

Hodges, Finnegan, and Perry (1999) raised connectedness/closeness and independence (autonomy) as major issues in parent–child relationships. Some of the key dimensions that Hinde (1997) highlighted include matters of reciprocity versus complementarity, conflict and power, and closeness. The discussion of closeness covered satisfaction and commitment.

Maccoby (1999) discussed important questions about the conceptualization of parent–child relationships in terms of intra-individual differences. The notion here is that within the overall parent–child relationship there are likely to be differences according to the context or domain of the interactions. For example, if the domain pertains to discipline, one set of "rules" or relationship qualities will be apparent. On the other hand, if the context is one of play and games, then another set of relationship characteristics will be appropriate. Contexts differ and the roles of parent and child are multiple. Thus, there are multiple parent–child relationships rather than *the* parent–child relationship.

A helpful scheme for examining the different dimensions of relationships is provided by the vertical/horizontal distinction (Hartup, 1989; Kochanska, 1992; Kuczynski, 1997; Russell, Pettit, & Mize, 1998). The same distinction can be drawn in terms of relationships qualities that display asymmetry versus symmetry (Hinde, 1997). Parent–child relationships have generally been assumed to be vertical. This is because parents have been considered to have greater knowledge and power than children. Accordingly, it is expected that parent–child relationships will be asymmetrical and complementary. In contrast, horizontal relationships are said to occur when there is reasonable equality between the partners (such as between peers), and therefore display symmetrical qualities. For example, Bugental and Goodnow (1998) quoted Youniss, McLellan, and Strouse (1994) in saying that "Peer relationships are marked by use of symmetrical reciprocity and guided by the overarching principle of cooperation by equals" (p. 102) and then contrasted this with the so-called unilateral authority or power asymmetry that is more characteristic of adult–child relationships.

The traditional view, therefore, is that parent–child relationships are typically vertical, asymmetrical, and complementary. There are two principle ways in which these vertical qualities are apparent. The first concerns relationships or components of relationships where parents are directive or controlling with their children. For example where parents instruct, correct, teach, or discipline their children. When these matters are the focus of the parent–child relationship, indeed parents and children are in complementary or asymmetrical roles. However, complementarity also can occur when parents are nurturing and supportive. Therefore, child-centered behavior, such as parents attempting to facilitate the interests and wishes of the child, also involve complementary and different roles. In this case, parents are being nurturant and the child is the recipient of the nurturance.

In contrast to a stress on complementary roles, recent writings have drawn attention to the possibility that parent–child relationships can contain more peer-like qualities (Bigelow, Tesson, & Lewko, 1996; Bugental & Goodnow, 1998; Kuczynski, 1997; Russell et al., 1998). In doing so, equality rather than complementarity is emphasized. Features of parent–child relationships such as mutuality, synchrony, power sharing, and reciprocity become the focus. Terms generally used to characterize horizontal relationships are egalitarian, cooperative, symmetrical, fair, and collaborative. Throughout childhood, horizontal qualities such as these are increasingly evident, as children make greater contributions to relationships with parents. Two examples of horizontal qualities are power sharing and reciprocity.

Reciprocity, according to Hinde (1979), occurs when participants show similar behavior, either simultaneously or alternatively. Reciprocity has been described as a fundamental feature of human relationships (Gouldner, 1960; MacDonald, 1996), including parent–child relationships. By middle childhood, children are likely to reciprocate both positive and negative moods and behavior from parents. Children have power to accept or reject parental behavior and efforts at socialization or relationship formation. Some of this acceptance and rejection can be best conceived in terms of children displaying reciprocity.

Reciprocity between parents and children involving negative behavior and relationship qualities is likely to be associated with difficulties in the relationship. On the other hand, a system involving positive reciprocity and mutual cooperation has been argued to be a foundation for successful socialization (Kochanska, 1997). Maccoby (1992) and Kochanska (1997) described this system as a mutually binding, reciprocal, and mutually responsive relationship (Kochanska, 1997, p. 94).

Shared power is an especially significant indication of horizontal qualities in parent–child relationships. Child development from early through middle childhood means that parent–child relationships increasingly are open to possibilities for shared power. Shared power occurs, for example, when parent and child cooperate, negotiate, make joint decisions, argue about rules and then reach a compromise, and when they collaborate. To some extent "shared power" occurs because parents give up some of their power. Nevertheless, significant amounts of power also reside with the child in parent–child relationships. Mutuality is one way in which shared power has been investigated. For example, Lindsey, Mize, and Pettit (1997) studied mutuality in terms of the relative balance during parent–child play of (a) parent and initiations and (b) compliance to the other's initiations.

Clearly, there are a number of perspectives on the central dimensions of parent–child relationships. Dimensions to do with affection and closeness as well as control appear to be widely acknowledged. The vertical/horizontal distinction appears to provide helpful strategies for analyzing parent–child relationships. Nevertheless, while there is some consensus about the definition and core dimensions of parent–child relationships, much remains in dispute. This is an area of active debate and research.

Parent–Child Relationships as Bidirectional and Co-constructed

Although Bell argued strongly for an active role for children in socialization as long ago as 1968, recent authors continue to find it necessary to make the case for child effects, bidirectionality, or co-construction in relationships. Kuczynski and Lollis (in press), Kuczynski, Marshall, and Schell (1997), and Lollis and Kuczynski (1997), for example, recently proposed that research on parent–child relationships has been constrained by a set of assumptions connected to what they called a "unilateral model of parent–child rela-tions." In this model, there are assumptions that (a) influence flows from the parent to the child, (b) parents are considered active agents and children as passive, (c) parents and children are separate interacting individuals rather than connected through their relation-ship, and (d) there is an asymmetry in power, with most of the power residing in the parent. They attacked each of these assumptions. Their alternative model is based on equal agency, bidirectional causality, parent–child interactions occurring within a relationship context, and power as interdependent asymmetry. Similar arguments were developed by Mills and Grusec (1988).

At a conceptual level it is easy to make a case for parent and child effects, with relation-ships being jointly constructed. However, empirically it is more difficult to describe and measure the separate effects of parents and children or to articulate the processes and steps involved in the co-construction of relationships (A. Russell & G. Russell, 1992). One of the factors contributing to the empirical difficulties arises from the role of cognitive proc-esses. For example, if a child is shy and parents undertake attempts to support the child's social endeavors, this might be described as a child effect (the parents are responding to the child's shyness). However, not all parents will respond in this way in Western cultures, and in other cultures shyness could be seen as not problematic. Clearly, parental perceptions and beliefs about children and shyness are implicated in their behavior and the type of relationship they develop with their child. When the role of parental cognitions is taken into account, the matter of who is shaping the relationship (the parent or the child) in-creases in complexity. The complexity is multiplied when child cognitions are added to the equation.

Current research should pay more attention to notions of bidirectionality and co-con-struction. There is a need for more sophisticated models of the way in which relationships are co-constructed over time. That is, we need to move beyond the finding that children have an impact on parents, and more to evidence about the construction of parent–child relationships using principles such as bidirectionality and co-construction.

When parent–child relationships are considered to be bidirectional or co-constructed, attention is drawn to (a) how characteristics of both parents and children contribute to the relationships and (b) the processes through which relationships are formed and maintained. In the present chapter, the role of individual attributes will be illustrated through a discus-sion of child characteristics in terms of sex and features such as ADHD, and parent charac-teristics such as sex and personality. Included is a discussion of how developmental changes in middle childhood have an impact on parent–child relationships.

Child characteristics: ADHD

Conclusions that parent–child relationships are bidirectional and co-constructed have of-ten been drawn when the focus is on how child characteristics influence parent behavior and the relationship. A good example is provided by children with attention deficit hyper-activity disorder (ADHD). These children may exhibit overt behaviors including impulsivity and aggression, or more covert behaviors of stealing and property destruction with a mid-point of this overt-covert continuum being noncompliance lying (Hinshaw, Zuppan,

Simmel, Nigg, & Melnick 1997). Viewpoints differ about whether such behaviors are the result of inappropriate parenting, or whether difficulties in parenting and parent–child relationships arise from the behavior and characteristics of the child (Miller, Cowan, Cowan, Hetherington, & Clingempeel, 1993).

The middle-ground possibility is that relationships between parent and children with ADHD are bidirectional. This is shown in the coercive cycles that are evident in interactions between children with ADHD and their parents (Anderson, Hinshaw, & Simmell 1994; DeKlyen, Biernbaum, Speltz, & Greenberg, 1998). For instance, there is evidence that boys with ADHD are more noncompliant and controlling of their parents than their nonproblem peers. In turn, parents of boys with ADHD are more controlling and critical than the parents of nonproblem boys (Pelham et al., 1997). Along these lines, Pelham et al. (1997, p. 414) noted the importance of considering the "role of children's behavior in a reciprocal, transactional family system" citing several studies that indicate the "distressing effects that defiant child behavior has on immediate reactions and long term functioning of parents." Parents rated interactions with such children as being significantly unpleasant, resulting in feelings of inadequacy, anxiety, depression, and hostility. One mother reported: "My experience as a parent with him was one of being totally inept and frustrated, not knowing what to do for this child. It was not a happy experience" (Paltin, 1993, p. 225).

The role of child behavior is shown by the results of Anderson, Lytton, and Romney (1986) suggesting that mothers' behavior was influenced by the child's characteristics. Barkley's (1989) results also support this conclusion, where it was found that harsh and punitive parenting practices diminished significantly when the behavior of the child with ADHD was bought under control with medication. However, as Anderson et al. (1994, p. 249) suggest, "the acute shift in parental style induced by medication does not rule out the possibility that the child's negative, externalizing behaviors while unmedicated may have been shaped by parental coercion in earlier interactions."

The research on children with ADHD provides evidence of apparent child effects on parents. When this is combined with findings such as those dealing with cycles of coercion, there is support for conclusions about the co-constructed nature of parent–child relationships.

Relationships with boys and girls

Among the individual characteristics often assumed to have an impact on parent–child relationships is the child's sex. Research (Russell & Saebel, 1997) and theoretical treatments such as psychoanalytic theory (Chodorow, 1978; Washburn, 1994) have highlighted differences in parents' relationships with boys and girls. In an analysis of 116 studies containing both mothers and fathers and boys and girls as subjects that were published in four leading developmental journals over a 4-year period, Russell and Saebel (1997) noted that 36 studies reported some sex-of-child differences in relationships. This suggests that differences in relationships with sons and daughters are relatively prominent in the research. Supporting this, in a meta-analysis of mothers' language behavior with boys and with girls, Leaper, Anderson, and Sanders (1998) outlined evidence of greater amounts of talk with girls than with boys and more supportive speech with girls than with boys. This result was interpreted as consistent with a greater emphasis by parents on verbal interaction and affiliation with daughters than with sons and points to differences in the qualities of relationships with boys and with girls, partly along the lines of gender expectations.

A conclusion that there are some differences in parent–son and parent–daughter relationships should not be taken to imply that this arises simply because parents are responding to differences in the characteristics (e.g., behavior or personality) of boys and girls. This type of difference could also arise from parental expectations and socialization goals.

Child development and parent–child relationships

Parent–child relationships evolve and change throughout childhood (Ambert, 1997; Collins & Russell, 1991; Maccoby, 1984), partly as a consequence of, and in response to, child development. Selman (1980), Ambert (1997), and Collins, Harris, and Susman (1995) provide accounts of some of the developmental changes during this period that impact on parent–child relationships.

Selman (1980) set out a developmental framework for children's understanding of relationships, including stages in conceptions of parent–child relationships. From early childhood through middle childhood, for example, it would be expected that children might move from Stage 1 through to Stages 2 and 3. In Stage 1, children identify with parental views and opinions and they accept parental knowledge. Parents are viewed as "knowing best." In Stage 2 children conceive of parental advice as guidelines rather than as an absolute authority. Reciprocal feelings now define love between parent and child, and there is an appreciation of the other's intentions. There is an awareness of the quality of the emotional tie between parent and child. In Stage 3, children are able to take a third-party perspective and consequently better appreciate the complexities of the parental role. Children in this stage consider that it is important that parents foster psychological competence and maturity, and they expect parents to provide for self-esteem and to help with psychological concerns. These children also are sensitive to parents' psychological needs and are expected to show respect. Therefore, in this stage children appreciate the needs of parents to be respected and acknowledged as a source of authority, and become aware of differences in the needs and expectations of parents and children. They also gain a sense of fairness and are sensitive to whether they believe they are being treated fairly.

Selman's analysis of developmental changes has a number of implications for parent–child relationships. The move away from acceptance of parental authority, for example, opens the way for areas of dispute between parents and children, with a need for a better appreciation of each other's viewpoint and the use of perspective taking skills. Smetana (1989) showed that by about ages 11 and 12 there were a number of issues that generated conflict between parents and children. These included matters such as homework, not getting along with others (such as siblings), and choice or timing of activities (e.g., how much time is spent on the telephone or watching TV). This illustrates that by late middle childhood parent–child relationships typically incorporate aspects of dispute and negotiation. Children's conception of fairness, albeit limited, also becomes a source of dispute and negotiation, for example about how they are treated in the relationship, especially vis-à-vis siblings. Throughout middle childhood, reciprocity is a stronger feature of parent–child relationships (Collins & Russell, 1991). From parents' viewpoint, the need for respect from a maturing individual becomes an important factor in the relationship.

Collins et al. (1995) provide an account of some of the normative changes in children during middle childhood. They note a growth in cognitive competence, with increased capacity for solving problems and resourcefulness, and conclude that these changes necessitate adjustments in parenting and the relationship. Part of the change is that parent–child relationships during middle childhood are less oriented to disciplinary situations than in earlier years. Collins et al. (1995) and Ambert (1997) note the expanding social worlds and networks of children during middle childhood. Relationships with peers increase in importance, with a consequent change in the significance of relationships with parents. Also at this age Ambert (1997) mentions the increased significance that children's exposure to television has for parent–child relationships.

It can be seen that child development from early childhood through middle childhood engenders associated changes in parent–child relationships, with an increased role for reciprocity, greater importance of perspective taking from both parent and child, and a reduced focus on discipline, with greater emphasis on persuasion and negotiation. Overall, the parent–child relationship is increasingly part of an expanding network of relationships for the child.

Parent characteristics: Children's relationships with mothers and fathers

A substantial empirical (see Collins & Russell, 1991; Leaper, Anderson, & Sanders, 1998; Parke, 1995) and theoretical (e.g., Chodorow, 1978; Washburn, 1994) literature is now available about differences between mother–child and father–child relationships. The degree to which these relationships differ is under dispute, and recognition needs to be given to similarities as much as to differences. Similarities between mothers and fathers, or at least the absence of differences, is a more usual finding than differences. For example, Russell and Saebel (1997) examined 116 studies of parent–child relationships that included both sexes of parents and children published in four major developmental journals over a 4-year period and found that only 16 studies reported significant differences between mother–child and father–child relationships. When such differences were found they tended to be for measures dealing with closeness/cohesion and affect (greater in relationships with mothers) (Leaper et al., 1998; Russell & Saebel, 1997). In addition, differences have been noted in terms of (a) more frequent interactions with fathers than with mothers, and (b) interactions with mothers being more around caregiving and with fathers more around play and recreation, especially with sons (Collins & Russell, 1991).

It can be seen that the extent and significance of differences in children's relationships with mothers and fathers remains in dispute. There is the further possibility that relationships are differentiated by both sex of child and sex of parent. This suggests that the four dyads of mother–son, mother–daughter, father–son, and father–daughter could involve relationships that are somewhat distinct. Despite frequent claims about the distinctness of these four relationships, however, the evidence in support of the proposition is limited (Russell & Saebel, 1997). Nevertheless, it remains an intriguing possibility worthy of further consideration.

Parent characteristics: Personality and relationships with children

It might be expected that parent–child relationships would vary according to the personality of parents and of children. This proposition has been tested to some degree in terms of parents' personality. For example, Russell (1997) examined links between parent personality and mothers' and fathers' observed warmth and affection directed to their early school-aged children during a home observation. Personality was assessed using a self-report questionnaire containing 50 items pertaining to positive personality traits, for example, appreciative, loves children, patient, and confident. Positive personality was significantly related to observed warmth and affection (positive association) only for dyads containing mothers and sons. For mother–daughter, father–son, and father–daughter dyads this correlation was negative and not significant. These results suggest that parents' positive personality characteristics were expressed in relationships with their children only for mothers with sons. This result is partially consistent with those of Belsky, Crnic, and Woodworth (1995) who found that mothering was predicted more strongly and consistently by personality than was fathering with first-born sons over the first 2 years.

Russell's (1997) and Belsky et al.'s (1995) results need to be interpreted in the context of multiple determinants of parent–child relationships. For mothers, it appears that their personality could be a factor in relationships with their children, but not so for fathers. The latter means that factors other than personality could be important for father–child relationships. In Russell (1997), for example, evidence was obtained that fathers were more likely to be warm and affectionate when their children displayed positive characteristics. This suggests that at least one of the factors affecting father–child relationships is the degree to which the child displays positive qualities such as involvement and warmth. The other side of this situation is that fathers might be especially reactive to disruptive or difficult behavior from their child.

Kochanska, Clark, and Goldman's (1997) results are also relevant here. They examined mothers with children from toddler to preschool age and found that mothers high on negative emotionality (e.g., depression, anxiety, and neuroticism) and disagreeableness (e.g., angry, aggressive/hostile) displayed more negative affect with their children and were more power-assertive and less nurturant. These results point to some important ways that mothers' personality is likely to impact on relationship with their children. In this case, the evidence suggests that negative aspects of personality are associated with mothers forming more vertical relationships with their children, with less responsiveness and warmth.

It appears, therefore, that recent evidence is pointing to a role for parents' personality in relationships with their children, but mainly for mothers. An implication is that influences on father–child relationships are likely to arise from factors other than their personality.

Parent–Child Relationships in Context: Neighborhood, Social, Ethnic and Cultural Factors

Families are part of larger social groups that can be described in social, ethnic, or cultural terms. These larger groups provide a context for families that in turn influences parent–child relationships (Bronfenbrenner, 1979, 1986; Hinde, 1997; Parke & Kellam, 1994; Tudge, Gray, & Hogan, 1997). Research in this area has included the impact on parent–child relationships of work (Crouter, 1994), stress, formal, and informal support mechanisms (Parke & Buriel, 1998), and the marital relationship (Dunn et al., 1999). From the child's perspective, their school attendance brings experiences and relationships with others (especially peers) that should have an impact on parent–child relationships. Overall, therefore, it is apparent that parent–child relationships need to be understood as connected with other relationships and influences both inside and outside of the family. For present purposes, only a selective treatment can be provided of the wider context, and it will be based on a brief mention of the neighborhood and ethnic/cultural differences.

Neighborhoods

An important recent emphasis in the literature on parenting, child development, and parent–child relationships has been on neighborhood characteristics (e.g., Parke & Buriel, 1998; Sampson, Morenoff, & Earls, 1999). Sampson et al. (1999) examined "neighborhood effects" in terms of the social mechanisms that might mediate neighborhood structural effects on the lives of children. This research emphasized the network of relationships within neighborhoods and how these impact on children's relationships and development. It was apparent that characteristics of the neighborhood (in terms of links with other parents) are an influence on parent–child relationships.

Parke and Buriel (1998) included neighborhoods as part of a discussion of ecological determinants of family socialization strategies. It is possible to extend ideas of socialization strategies to incorporate elements of parent–child relationships. For example, Parke and Buriel refer to a study by O'Neil and Parke (1997) where it was "found that when mothers and fathers perceived their neighborhoods as dangerous and low in social control, they placed more restrictions on their fourth-grade children's activities" (Parke & Buriel, 1998, p. 493). It could be inferred from this result that when families live in neighborhoods perceived as dangerous, parent–child relationships might focus more on issues about where children spend their time, with whom they spend their time, and matters relating to self-protection.

Ethnic and cultural influences on parent–child relationships

In recent years, there has been increasing interest in ethnic and cultural differences in parent–child relationships. This has arisen partly from an increase in international research in different cultures and ethnic groups (Hart, Nelson, Robinson, Olsen, & McNeilly-

Choque, 1998; Ingoldsby & Smith, 1995; Lancy, 1996), but partly from greater attention to migrant groups in countries such as the United States (Parke & Buriel, 1998). It is clear that there is a need to move beyond a white middle-class view of parent–child relationships and to incorporate either ecological or systems perspectives in attempts to understand differences in parent–child relationships. In addition, there is a need to recognize that there are cultural differences even among so-called Euro-American cultures.

Parke and Buriel (1998) use "ethnicity" to refer to an "individual's membership in a group sharing a common ancestral heritage based on nationality, language, and culture" (p. 496), with "culture" referring to "shared values, behaviors, and beliefs of a people that are transmitted from one generation to the next" (p. 496). Research on different ethnic and cultural groups has revealed profound differences in parent–child relationships. These differences show that it is critical to set parent–child relationships in the context of cultural values, beliefs, and practices. Further, this research emphasizes the diversity in parent–child relationships.

Parke and Buriel (1998) discuss a number of ethnic groups, including American Indians, Latinos, African Americans, and Asian Americans. Each group displays unique features that serve to reinforce views about the importance of cultural factors in parent–child relationships. For example, the role of extended kin systems in African-American families has a clear impact on relationships within families, the roles of parents and extended kin, and the relationships that children have with parents and related adults. Parke and Buriel (1998) note that in multigenerational households, mothers are primary caregivers, followed by grandmothers and fathers. Further, grandmothers tend to increase the moral-religious emphasis in the family. It is apparent, therefore, that parent–child relationships in African-American families where grandmothers are coresident are influenced by the role of grandmothers. This suggests that both the content (such as issues that are the focus of discussion and negotiation) and style of children's relationships with their mothers and fathers will be affected by the presence and role of the grandmother.

An important finding from recent research on African-American families has been that ostensibly similar relationship qualities could have different meaning and significance from what has been found in white middle-class families. Some of this can be illustrated around the role of authoritarian relationships and practices. Kelley, Power, and Wimbush (1992) described the disciplinary style of African-American parents as more parent-centered (with an emphasis on parental authority, and obedience) than child-centered. However, the interpretation of this finding has to take into account not only the context of many African-American families, but cultural factors as well. With respect to the context, Kelley et al. (1992) noted that obedience could be adaptive in dangerous neighborhoods and serve as a means of highlighting the need to following rules in a society where family members are part of a disadvantaged group with low power.

It can be seen that African-American parent–child relationships might be characterized as relatively vertical. However, these vertical qualities should be interpreted differently from their occurrence in white middle-class families. For example, in African-American families, harsh discipline has been found to covary with warmth and a nurturing relationship more than in white families (Deater-Deckard & Dodge, 1997a, b). Further, as Parke and Buriel (1998) note, although African-American parents may use physical discipline, this is rarely coupled with withdrawal of love from children. These findings point to vertical relationships in which the parent-centered components are combined with positive aspects of relationships with children, rather than rejection that is often assumed to be present if white parents are harsh and parent-centered. This conclusion is supported by evidence that harshness of discipline is related to externalizing problems in European-American children, but not in African-American children (Deater-Deckard & Dodge, 1997a, b; Deater-Deckard, Dodge, Bates, & Pettit, 1996). Potentially parallel findings to those of Deater-Deckard and colleagues on links between harsh discipline and externalizing behavior in African-American children have been obtained by Chao (1994) on immigrant Chinese families.

It can be seen that recent research on African American and immigrant Chinese families highlight not only ethnic and cultural differences, but also show the importance of cultural factors in shaping parent–child relationships and in providing meaning to parent and child behavior in their relationships.

Conclusions

The present discussion of parent–child relationships was informed by a model that incorporates several levels of analysis (Hinde, 1997; Levinger, 1994), from psychological processes to individual behavior and characteristics, to interactions and relationships through to system and ecological factors. An understanding of parent–child relationships requires an appreciation of factors at each of these levels. Attention was directed to some problematic matters in the current literature on parent–child relationships. In particular, there remains some dispute about the core dimensions of parent–child relationships. We argued here for the value of the vertical/horizontal distinction as a basis for understanding parent–child relationships. Second, although there is increasing recognition of a perspective that emphasizes these relationships are bidirectional and co-constructed, this emphasis has still to be fully accepted in the literature. Third, it was evident that there is considerable evolution of parent–child relationships from early childhood through middle childhood. We documented some aspects of child development over this period and showed how this development is likely to have an impact on parent–child relationships. Finally, we noted a number of broader ethnic and cultural factors linked to differences in parent–child relationships. The latter discussion helped to highlight the considerable diversity in normative parent–child relationships.

References

Ambert, A-M. (1997). *Parents, children, and adolescents: Interactive relationships and development in context*. New York: The Haworth Press.

Anderson, C., Hinshaw, S. P., & Simmel, C. (1994). Mother–child interactions in ADHD and comparison boys: Relationships with overt and covert externalizing behavior. *Journal of Abnormal Child Psychology, 22,* 247–265.

Anderson, K. E., Lytton, J., & Romney, D. M. (1986). Mothers' interactions with normal and conduct-disordered boys: Who affects whom? *Developmental Psychology, 22*, 415–419.

Barkley, R. A. (1989). Hyperactive girls and boys: Stimulant drug effects on mother–child interactions. *Journal of Child Psychology and Psychiatry and Allied Disciplines, 30*, 379–390.

Baumrind, D. (1967). Child care practices anteceding three patterns of preschool behavior. *Genetic Psychology Monographs, 75*, 43–88.

Baumrind, D. (1971). Current patterns of parental authority. *Developmental Psychology Monographs, 4*, 1–103.

Bell, R. Q. (1968). A reinterpretation of the direction of effects in studies of socialization. *Psychological Review, 75*, 81–95.

Belsky, J., Crnic, K., & Woodworth, S. (1995). Personality and parenting: Exploring the mediating role of transient mood and daily hassles. *Journal of Personality, 63*, 905–929.

Berscheid, E., & Peplau, L. A. (1983). The emerging science of relationships. In H. H. Kelley, E. Berscheid, A. Christensen, J. H. Harvey, T. L. Huston, G. Levinger, E. McClintock, L. A. Peplau, & D. R. Peterson (Eds.), *Close relationships* (pp. 1–19). New York: W. H. Freeman.

Bigelow, B. J., Tesson, G., & Lewko, J. H. (1996). *Learning the rules: The anatomy of children's relationships.* New York: Guilford Press.

Bronfenbrenner, U. (1979). *The ecology of human development.* Cambridge, MA: Harvard University Press.

Bronfenbrenner, U. (1986). Ecology of the family as a context for human development: Research perspectives. *Developmental Psychology, 22*, 723–742.

Bugental, D. B., & Goodnow, J. J. (1998). Socialization processes. In N. Eisenberg (Ed.), *Handbook of child psychology: Vol. 3. Social, emotional, and personality development* (5th ed., pp. 389–462). New York: Wiley.

Canary, D. J., & Emmers-Sommer, T. M. (1997). *Sex and gender differences in personal relationships.* New York: Guilford Press.

Chao, R. K. (1994). Beyond parental control and authoritarian parenting style: Understanding Chinese parenting through the cultural notion of training. *Child Development, 65*, 1111–1119.

Chodorow, N. (1978). *The reproduction of mothering: Psychoanalysis and the sociology of gender.* Berkeley, CA: University of California Press.

Collins, W. A., Harris, M. L., & Susman, A. (1995). Parenting during middle childhood. In M. H. Bornstein (Ed.), *Handbook of parenting: Vol. 1. Children and parenting* (pp. 65–89). Mahwah, NJ: Erlbaum.

Collins, W. A., & Russell, G. (1991). Mother–child and father–child relationships in middle childhood and adolescence. *Developmental Review, 11*, 99–136.

Colpin, H., Demyttenaere, K., & Vandemeulebroecke, L. (1995). New reproductive technology and the family: The parent–child relationship following in vitro fertilization. *Journal of Child Psychology and Psychiatry and Allied Disciplines, 36*, 1429–1441.

Crouter, A. C. (1994). Processes linking families and work: Implications for behavior and development in both settings. In R. D. Parke & S. G. Kellam (Eds.), *Exploring family relationships with other social contexts* (pp. 9–28). Hillsdale, NJ: Erlbaum.

Darling, N., & Steinberg, L. (1993). Parenting style as context: An integrative model. *Psychological Bulletin, 113*, 487–496.

Deater-Deckard, K., & Dodge, K. A. (1997a). Externalizing behavior problems and discipline revisited: Nonlinear effects and variation by culture, context, and gender. *Psychological Inquiry, 8*, 161–175.

Deater-Deckard, K., & Dodge, K. A. (1997b). Spare the rod, spoil the authors: Emerging themes in research on parenting and child development. *Psychological Inquiry, 8*, 230–235.

Deater-Deckard, K., Dodge, K. A., Bates, J. E., & Pettit, G. S. (1996). Physical discipline among African American and European American mothers: Links to children's externalizing behaviors.

Developmental Psychology, 1065–1072.

DeKlyen, M., Biernbaum, M. A., Speltz, M. L., & Greenberg, M. T., (1998). Fathers and preschool behavior problems. *Developmental Psychology, 34,* 264–275.

Duck, S. (1992). *Human relationships* (2nd ed.). London: Sage.

Duck, S., Acitelli, L. K., Manke, B., & West, L. (1999). Sowing relational seeds: Contexts for relating in childhood. In R. Mills & S. Duck (Eds.), *Developmental psychology of personal relationships* (pp. 1–14). New York: Wiley.

Dunn, J., Deater-Deckard, K., Pickering, K., Golding, J., & the ALSPAC study team. (1999). Siblings, parents, and partners: Family relationships within a longitudinal community study. *Journal of Child Psychology and Psychiatry and Allied Disciplines, 40,* 1025–1037.

Gouldner, A. J. (1960). The norm of reciprocity: A preliminary statement. *American Sociological Review, 25,* 161–178.

Hart, C. H., Nelson, D. A., Robinson, C. C., Olsen, S. F., & McNeilly-Choque, M. K. (1998). Overt and relational aggression in Russian nursery-school-age children: Parenting style and marital linkages. *Developmental Psychology, 34,* 687–697.

Hartup, W. W. (1989). Social relationships and their developmental significance. *American Psychologist, 44,* 120–126.

Hartup, W. W., & Laursen, B. (1991). Relationships as developmental context. In R. Cohen & A. W. Siegel (Eds.), *Context and development* (pp. 253–279). Hillsdale, NJ: Erlbaum.

Hinde, R. A. (1979). *Towards understanding relationships.* London: Academic Press.

Hinde, R. A. (1987). *Individuals, relationships and culture: Links between ethology and the social sciences.* Cambridge, England: Cambridge University Press.

Hinde, R. A. (1997). *Relationships: A dialectical perspective.* Hove, England: Psychology Press.

Hinshaw, S. P., Zuppan, B. A., Simmel, C., Nigg, J. T., & Melnick, S. (1997). Peer status in boys with and without attention-deficit hyperactivity disorder: Predications of overt and covert antisocial behavior, isolation, and authoritative parenting beliefs. *Child Development, 68,* 880–896.

Hodges, E. V. E., Finnegan. R. A., & Perry, D. G. (1999). Skewed autonomy-relatedness in preadolescents' conceptions of their relationships with mother, father, and best friend. *Developmental Psychology, 35,* 737–748.

Ingoldsby, B. B., & Smith, S. (Eds.). (1995). *Families in multicultural perspective.* New York: Guilford Press.

Kelley, M. L., Power, T. G., & Wimbush, D. D. (1992). Determinants of disciplinary practices in low-income Black mothers. *Child Development, 63,* 573–582.

Kochanska. G. (1992). Children's interpersonal influence with mothers and peer. *Developmental Psychology, 28,* 491–499.

Kochanska. G. (1997). Mutually responsive orientation between mothers and their young children: Implications for early socialization. *Child Development, 68,* 94–112.

Kochanska, G., Clark, L. A., & Goldman, M. S. (1997). Implications of mothers' personality for their parenting and their young children's developmental outcomes. *Journal of Personality, 65,* 387–420.

Kuczynski, L. (1997, April). Power asymmetry revisited: Power in the parent–child relationship. In D. B. Bugental (Chair), *Power and negotiation in parent–child relationships.* Paper symposium conducted at the biennial meeting of the Society for Research in Child Development, Washington, DC.

Kuczynski, L., & Lollis, S. (in press). Four foundations for a dynamic model of parenting. In J. Gerris (Ed.), *Dynamics of parenting.* Hillsdale, NJ: Erlbaum.

Kuczynski, L., Marshall, S., & Schell, K. (1997). Value socialization in a bidirectional context. In J. E. Grusec & L. Kuczynski (Eds.), *Parenting and children's internationalization of values* (pp.

23–50). New York: Wiley.

Lancy, D. F. (1996). *Playing on the mother-ground: Cultural routines for children's development.* New York: Guilford Press.

Leaper, C., Anderson, K. J., & Sanders, P. (1998). Moderators of gender effects on parents' talk to their children: A meta-analysis. *Developmental Psychology, 34,* 3-27.

Levinger, G. (1994). Figure versus ground: Micro- and macroperspectives on the social psychology of personal relationships. In R. Erber & R. Gilmour (Eds.), *Theoretical frameworks for personal relationships* (pp. 1–28). Hillsdale, NJ: Erlbaum.

Lindsey, E. W., Mize, J., & Pettit, G. S. (1997). Mutuality in parent–child play: Consequences for children's peer competence. *Journal of Social and Personal Relationships, 14,* 523–538.

Lollis, S., & Kuczynski. L. (1997). Beyond one hand clapping: Seeing bidirectionality in parent–child relations. *Journal of Social and Personal Relationships, 14,* 441–461.

Maccoby, E. E. (1984). Middle childhood in the context of the family. In W. A. Collins (Ed.), *Development during middle childhood: The years from six to twelve* (pp. 184–239). Washington, DC: National Academy of Science Press.

Maccoby, E. E. (1992). The role of parents in the socialization of children: An historical overview. *Developmental Psychology, 28,* 1006–1017.

Maccoby, E. E. (1999). The uniqueness of the parent–child relationship. In W. A Collins & B. Laursen (Eds.), *Minnesota Symposia on child psychology: Vol. 30. Relationships in developmental contexts* (pp. 13–35). Mahwah, NJ: Erlbaum.

MacDonald, K. (1996). What do children want? A conceptualization of evolutionary influences on children's motivation in the peer group. *International Journal of Behavioral Development, 19,* 53–73.

Miller, N. B., Cowan, P. A., Cowan, C. P., Hetherington, E. M., & Clingempeel, W. G. (1993). Externalizing in preschoolers and early adolescents: A cross-study replication of a family model. *Developmental Psychology, 29,* 3–18.

Mills, J., & Clark, M. S. (1994). Communal and exchange relationships: Controversies and research. In R. Erber & R. Gilmour (Eds.), *Theoretical frameworks for personal relationships* (pp. 29–42). Hillsdale, NJ: Erlbaum.

Mills, R. S. L., & Grusec, J. E. (1988). Socialization from the perspective of the parent–child relationship. In S. Duck (Ed.), *Handbook of personal relationships: Theory, research, and interventions* (pp. 177–191). Chichester, England: Wiley.

Noller, P., & Fitzpatrick, M. S. (1993). *Communication in family relationships.* Englewood Cliffs, NJ: Prentice Hall.

O'Neil, R., & Parke, R. D. (1997). Objective and subjective features of children's neighborhoods: Relations to parental regulatory strategies and children's social competence. Paper presented at the biennial meeting of the Society for Research in Child Development, Washington, DC.

Paltin, D. M. (1993). *The parent's hyperactivity handbook: Helping the fidgety child.* New York: Insight Books.

Parke, R. D. (1995). Fathers and families. In M. H. Bornstein (Ed.), *Handbook of parenting: Vol. 3. Status and social conditions of parenting* (pp. 27–63). Mahwah, NJ: Erlbaum.

Parke, R. D., & Buriel, R. (1998). Socialization in the family: Ethnic and ecological perspectives. In N. Eisenberg (Ed.), *Handbook of child psychology: Vol. 3. Social, emotional, and personality development* (5th ed., pp. 463–552). New York: Wiley.

Parke, R. D., & Kellam, S. (Eds.). (1994). *Advances in family research: Vol. 4. Family relationships with other social systems.* Hillsdale, NJ: Erlbaum.

Pelham, W. E., Lang, A. R., Aketson, B., Murphy D. A., Gnangy, E. M., Griener, A. R., Vodde-Hamilton, M., & Greenslade, K. E. (1997). Effects of deviant child behavior on parental distress and alcohol consumption in laboratory interactions. *Journal of Abnormal Psychology,*

25, 413–424.

Russell. A. (1997). Individual and family factors contributing to mothers' and fathers' positive parenting. *International Journal of Behavioral Development, 21*, 111–132.

Russell. A., Pettit, G., & Mize, J. (1998). Horizontal qualities in parent–child relationships: Parallels with and possible consequences for children's peer relationships. *Developmental Review, 18*, 313–352.

Russell, A., & Russell, G. (1992). Child effects in socialization research: Some conceptual and data analysis issues. *Social Development, 1*, 163–184.

Russell, A., & Saebel, J. (1997). Mother–son, mother–daughter, father–son, and father–daughter: Are they distinct relationships? *Developmental Review, 17*, 111–147.

Sampson, R. J., Morenoff, J. D., & Earls, F. (1999). Beyond social capital: Spatial dynamics of collective efficacy for children. *American Sociological Review, 64*, 633–660.

Selman, R. L. (1980). *The growth of interpersonal understanding.* New York: Academic Press.

Smetana, J. G. (1989). Adolescents' and parents' reasoning about actual family conflict. *Child Development, 60*, 1052–1067.

Tudge, J., Gray, J. T., & Hogan, D. M. (1997). Ecological perspectives in human development: A comparison of Gibson and Bronfenbrenner. In J. Tudge. M. J. Shanahan, & J. Valsiner (Eds.), *Comparisons in human development: Understanding time and context* (pp. 72–105). Cambridge, England: Cambridge University Press.

Washburn, M. (1994). Reflections on a psychoanalytic theory of gender difference. *Journal of American Academy of Psychoanalysis, 22*, 1–28.

Youniss, J., McLellan, J. A., & Strouse, D. (1994). "We're popular, but we're not snobs": Adolescents describe their crowds. In R. Montemayor (Ed.), Advances in adolescent development (Vol. 6, pp. 101–122). Thousand Oaks, CA: Sage.

12

Sibling Relationships

Judy Dunn

The majority of individuals (around 80% in Europe and the United States) grow up with siblings, and for many, their relationships with their brothers and sisters are the longest lasting in their lives. While siblings have had a key place in folk stories, legends, history, and literature all over the world, the scientific study of the psychology and relationships of brothers and sisters is relatively recent. Clinicians and family theorists have since early in the twentieth century argued that siblings play an important role in family relationships, and influence individual adjustment. However, with the notable exception of the classic studies of siblings conducted by Koch in the 1950s and 1960s (1954, 1960), systematic research on siblings was relatively rare until the 1980s. In the last two decades, research interest in siblings has broadened and increased greatly; it has centered chiefly on studies of childhood and adolescence (Boer & Dunn, 1990; Brody, 1996; Hetherington, Reiss, & Plomin, 1994; for a useful review of research on adult siblings see Cicirelli, 1996). Studies of siblings in childhood have focused on three general domains which we consider here: first, the nature of sibling relationships and why they differ; second, their developmental influence and the illuminating perspective they provide on key developmental issues; and third, the challenge they provide to our understanding of how families influence individual development – why siblings differ notably in personality and adjustment even though they grow up within the same family.

The Nature of Sibling Relationships

Characteristics of sibling relationships

Three characteristics of sibling relationships stand out, from the findings of systematic research. The first is that sibling relationships are from infancy through adolescence notable for their emotional power and for the uninhibited expression of these emotions. One observational study reported that around 20% of interactions between siblings of the preschool and toddler age group were characterized by intense negative emotions (Dunn, Creps, & Brown, 1996) – a far higher percentage than was found for children's interactions with their parents or friends; intense positive emotions expressed in sibling interaction were also notably high. For many siblings, the relationship is one of mixed emotional color – both positive and hostile emotions are freely expressed (Dunn, 1993).

A second characteristic of siblings' relationships is their intimacy. Most children spend more time in interaction with siblings than with parents (Larson & Richards, 1994; McHale & Crouter, 1996). They know each other extremely well, and this intimacy means the relationship can be a source of support or of conflict. Teasing, for example, depends on knowing an individual well enough to be able to gauge what will upset and annoy; teasing by siblings is observed early in the second year of life, and increases rapidly over the next months, showing considerable sophistication, thus reflecting considerable understanding of the other child (Dunn, 1988). The familiarity of siblings, coupled with the emotional power of the relationship, means that the potential for siblings' influence on one another is high.

A third characteristic of the relationship is the great range of individual differences which is evident from early infancy through to adolescence, in both observational and interview studies. Some siblings show affection, interest, cooperation, and support in the great majority of their interactions; when interviewed they describe their affection and positive feelings vividly. Other siblings show hostility, irritation, and aggressive behavior, and describe their dislike very clearly. Yet other children are ambivalent about their relations with their siblings, and show both hostility and positive interest in one another (for siblings' perceptions of their relationship, see for instance, Dunn & Plomin, 1990; McGuire, Manke, Eftekhari, & Dunn, 2000). This notable range of differences raises questions for both psychologists and parents: Why should some siblings get along so well and be important sources of support and comfort for one another, while others are so hostile?

Individual differences in sibling relationships

The answer to the question of why siblings differ markedly in their relationship quality was, until relatively recently, answered in terms of birth order, sex of siblings, and the age gap between the siblings (e.g., Ernst & Angst, 1983; Sutton-Smith & Rosenberg, 1970; for a recent approach see Sulloway, 1996). These family constellation variables were thought to affect the children's relationships through effects on the children's personalities or temperaments, their intelligence, or motivation. Since the 1980s the framework has broadened, with models that incorporate, in addition to the family constellation variables, the personality characteristics of the children themselves, the quality of relationships within the family, and the social adversities or risks faced by the family (e.g., Furman & Lanthier, 1996; Stoneman & Brody, 1993).

Temperament and personality.   Links between the temperamental characteristics of both individuals in a sibling dyad and the quality of their relationship have been reported for siblings in the preschool period, middle childhood, and early adolescence (Brody, Stoneman, & Burke, 1987; Furman & Lanthier, 1996; Munn & Dunn, 1989; Stocker, Dunn, & Plomin, 1989). However, the precise findings vary across studies, the various projects are based on very different populations, and they vary in the age of siblings studied, and in the methodologies employed. Furman and Lanthier point out one general pattern, however: The personality and temperamental characteristics are more clearly related to conflict in the sibling relationship than to the positive aspects of the relationship. This may reflect the problems of measuring the positive features, such as feelings of warmth and affection, which tend to be less evident when parents are present. In contrast, conflict between siblings is all too evident in a range of settings! The match in siblings' temperaments was found to be important in relation to the frequency of conflict and affection that they show one another, both in early and middle childhood (Brody, 1996; Munn & Dunn, 1989). This finding parallels the evidence from the adult relationship literature for the significance of *similarity* in attraction between people: "like me" attracts (Hinde, 1979).

Gender and age gap   Evidence for the significance of gender and age gap for individual differences in sibling relationship quality varies with the age of the siblings under scrutiny. For young siblings, the findings are inconsistent. During middle childhood, it appears that gender may increase in importance as an influence on the sibling relationship (Dunn, Slomkowski, & Beardsall, 1994a). Boys become increasingly less likely to report warmth and intimacy in their relationships with their siblings. Among older adults, relationships with sisters appear to be particularly important; this is generally attributed to women's emotional expressiveness and their traditional role as nurturers. While findings on gender and children's sibling relationships are mixed and inconsistent, clear associations are reported between the quality of sibling relationships and other family relationships; these are considered next.

Connections with Other Family Relationships

How far and in what ways are individual differences in sibling relationships linked to the children's relationships with their parents, or to the quality of the parents' own relationships with each other? There is some inconsistency in the research findings, and much current debate about the extent of parental influence on sibling relationships. A number of general developmental points stand out from the research.

First, there is evidence that the security of young children's attachments to their parents is correlated with individual differences in the quality of later sibling relationships. Children who were secure in their attachments to their parents were reported to have more positive sibling relationships than those who were insecure in their parent–child relationships (Teti & Ablard, 1989; Volling & Belsky, 1992). There is also an impressive consensus of evidence from research focusing on a broader range of dimensions of parent–child relationships that positive parent–child relations are associated with positive, prosocial sibling relationships (for review, see Brody, 1998). In a parallel fashion, negativity, punitiveness, and overcontrol in the parent–child relationship are correlated with aggressiveness and hostility in the sibling relationship. It is important to note that these studies are correlational, and conclusions cannot be drawn about the direction of causal influence, or the family processes that might be implicated in the links. While such connections are often interpreted as reflecting *parental influence* on siblings, it could well be that children's temperamental characteristics or other individual qualities contribute to difficult relationships with both siblings and parents. It could also be that in families in which the siblings are particularly hostile and aggressive with one another, this in turn affects the relationships of the children with their parents. In commonsense terms it appears plausible that all of these processes may contribute to the interconnections between family relationships.

Second, there are also research findings that, in contrast to the links between positivity in parent–child and sibling relationships, indicate that intense supportive sibling relationships can develop in families in which the parent–child relationships are distant or uninvolved (Bank & Kahn, 1982; Boer & Dunn, 1990). Such patterns of findings, which fit with a "compensatory" model of family relationships, may be more characteristic of families at the extremes of stress and social problems than of families within the normal range.

Third, there is consistent evidence that more conflicted, hostile sibling relationships are associated with *differential* relations between parents and their various children. That is, in families in which more affection, attention, and less discipline and control are evident in a parent's relationship with one sibling than with another, the siblings are likely to get along less well than in families in which parents and siblings do not report such differential relationships (Brody, 1998; Hetherington et al., 1994; Reiss, Neiderheiser, Hetherington, & Plomin, 2000; Stocker et al., 1989; Volling & Belsky, 1992). Such patterns are particularly evident in families that are under stress (Bank, Patterson, & Reid, 1996), such as those who have recently experienced parental separation, those with steprelationships, and those with disabled or sick siblings. It is important to note, again, that the evidence for these links is correlational and inferences about the direction of causal influence are not justified. Children's interpretation of their parents' differential behavior has been seen as key: Sibling relationships are thought to be compromised particularly when children interpret their parents' differential behavior as an indication that their parents are less concerned about them, or that they are less worthy of love than their siblings (Kowal & Kramer, 1997). Children monitor with vigilance the interactions between their parents and siblings, from a surprisingly early age: During the second year of life, one observational study showed, they ignore relatively few of the exchanges between their siblings and parents (Dunn & Munn, 1985).

Differential parent–child relationships are often associated with conflict or distress between the parents: Increased levels of differential treatment have been linked with such marital problems, and in turn both contemporaneously and longitudinally with higher levels of sibling conflict (Brody, Stoneman, & McCoy, 1992; Brody, Stoneman, & McCoy, 1994; Hetherington, Henderson, & Reiss, 1999; McHale & Crouter, 1996). More generally, several research programs report that the quality of the relationship between parents was linked to that of the sibling relationship (Brody, Stoneman, McCoy, & Forehand, 1992b; Erel, Margolin, & John, 1998; MacKinnon, 1989; Stocker, Ahmed, & Stall, 1997). Both direct pathways between marital and sibling relationships, and indirect pathways (via the parent–child relationships) are implicated (Dunn, Deater-Deckard, Pickering, Beveridge, & the ALSPAC Study Team, 1999). Interestingly, these patterns of association appear to differ in stepfamilies from those in families with two biological parents. Thus Hetherington and her colleagues (1992) reported that positive relations between mothers and their "new" partners were associated with high levels of negativity in parent–child relationships in step-father families – in direct contrast to the patterns found in nonstepfamilies. In the study by Dunn and colleagues, mother–partner hostility showed no significant relation to the hostility siblings showed one another – a pattern quite different from that of nonstep families.

Finally, it should be noted that the changes in parent–child relationships that accompany the arrival of a sibling are linked to the quality of the relationship that develops between the siblings. Both relatively small-scale intensive research (Dunn & Kendrick, 1982; Stewart, 1990; Stewart, Mobley, Van Tuyl, & Salvador, 1987) and large-scale survey studies (such as those based on the National Longitudinal Survey of Youth in the United States (Baydar, Greek, & Brooks-Gunn, 1997a; Baydar, Hyle, & Brooks-Gunn, 1997b) report consistent findings – that the birth of a sibling is accompanied by a decline in positive mother–child interactions, an increase in controlling, negative interactions, and an increase in behavioral problems in the "displaced" child. These changes are accompanied by a decline in material resources for families, which may be implicated in the sequelae for the children's adjustment and relationships – an issue we return to below. The general developmental point highlighted by these findings is that *indirect* links between parent–child and sibling relationships are likely to be important as influences on individual differences in the siblings' relationships.

Developmental change and continuities in individual differences in sibling relationships

Developmental changes in sibling relationships have been documented in studies following siblings through early and middle childhood. During the preschool years, the younger siblings in a dyad play an increasingly active role in the relationship, as their powers of understanding and communicative skills develop. They begin to initiate more games, and their ability to cooperate makes them more interesting companions in play for their older siblings (Dunn et al., 1996). The welcome recent increase in studies of siblings in middle childhood and adolescence has clarified some of the developmental changes in this period, though it should be noted that with the exception of the research of Brody and his colleagues (Brody et al., 1992a, 1992b, 1994), much of the research is cross-sectional in design. It has been concerned with charting normative changes, rather than continuities in individual differences. Such research reports changes in the balance of power between siblings as they reach middle childhood: the relationship between siblings becomes more egalitarian (Buhrmester, 1992; Buhrmester & Furman, 1990; Vandell, Minnett, & Santrock, 1987). There is some disagreement about the extent to which this reflects an increase in the power that the younger sibling is able to exert, or a decrease in the dominance that *both* older and younger attempt to exert. During adolescence, there tends to be a decrease in the warmth that siblings feel and express toward each other. This parallels the patterns of change reported for parent–child relationships over this period, as adolescents become increasingly involved with peers outside the family.

To what extent do the striking individual differences in sibling relationships evident in early childhood show continuity over time? One relatively small study that followed sibling pairs for over 7 years reported evidence for considerable stability in children's behavior and feelings toward their siblings, particularly for the older siblings during the period from 5 years to 12–13 years of age (Dunn et al., 1994a). However, many sibling pairs also changed in the relative friendliness or hostility that they felt toward each other. Increases in friendliness and support were found, for example, to follow life events with negative impact that the children faced together. In contrast, in many of the families, negative changes in the sibling relationship were attributed by both siblings and their mothers to the new friendships that the children had formed outside the family, particularly after the school transition that in the UK takes place around 8 years of age. Siblings also attributed increases in coolness or distance between them to the development of different interests by the two siblings during middle childhood, and to developmental changes in the younger siblings' powers of argument.

Developmental Influence of Sibling Relationships

The emotional intensity of siblings' interactions, their familiarity and frequent interaction during childhood, and the significance of their competitiveness over parental attention and love, all combine to suggest that they may well exert developmental influence upon one another. Two particular domains of development have been studied in relation to children's experiences with their siblings: children's adjustment, and their social understanding.

Siblings and children's adjustment

There is evidence for associations between the quality of siblings' relationships and their externalizing (aggressive, oppositional, rule-breaking) and internalizing (worrying, anxious) behavior, links found both contemporaneously and over time. Patterson and his colleagues established in the 1980s in their research with both community samples and clinical samples of conduct-disordered children, employing direct observations of the children at home, that siblings reinforce each other's aggressive behavior by fighting back, teasing, and escalating the level of conflict (Patterson, 1986). As Patterson points out, children whose family relational experiences train them to select coercive behavior are doubly handicapped: not only have they learned to be coercive, they have also *not* learned the prosocial actions required for supportive relationships (Snyder & Patterson, 1995). Longitudinal research following children from the preschool period to early adolescence has demonstrated that not only externalizing behavior but also internalizing problems in middle childhood and adolescence were more common among children whose siblings had been very negative and hostile to them during the preschool years (Dunn, Slomkowski, Beardsall, & Rende, 1994b). This pattern of associations was significant even when the mothers' current mental state was controlled for. A large-scale community study with cross-sectional data on 4 and 7 year olds found that negativity between siblings contributed to adjustment problems, and negatively to levels of prosocial behavior, beyond the contribution of poor parent–child relationships (Dunn et al., 1999). A substantial body of research findings employing cross-lagged models of analyses suggest that *younger* siblings are more influenced by their older siblings' behavior and adjustment than vice versa (e.g. Hetherington et al., 1999); longitudinal analyses in the Hetherington study of adolescents indicates that the impact of the sibling's adjustment – rather than the quality of the relationship per se – is important in predicting long-term adjustment.

The issue of how far siblings' hostile relationships contribute to the development of behavior problems independently of the parent–child relationship has been addressed recently in a number of studies. Garcia and colleagues for example in a study of conduct problems in a low-income sample of 5-year-old boys found that the interaction between destructive sibling conflict and rejecting parenting predicted aggressive behavior problems across time and informants: A rise in aggression scores was evident for children who had both high levels of sibling conflict and rejecting parent–child relationships. Sibling conflict was also directly related to later delinquency (Garcia, Shaw, Winslow, & Yaggi, 2000).

These studies implicate *direct* effects of sibling interaction on behavioral adjustment outcome. However, it should be noted that while the experience of sibling aggression not only increases the risk of aggression in other social contexts, but also leaves adolescent siblings with a sense of inadequacy and incompetence (Bank et al., 1996), these associations are not likely to develop in isolation from other sources of stress, and for many of the reported findings we have to be cautious about attributing causal effects to the siblings alone. A number of lines of evidence do indicate that *indirect* effects involving siblings are implicated in later behavioral adjustment problems. Two of these sets of evidence are noted briefly next: first, differential parent–child relationships, and second the impact of the arrival of a sibling.

Many of the studies of differential parent–child relationships have focused on the siblings' adjustment as outcome, and in particular the differences in siblings' adjustment (Conger & Conger, 1994; McGuire, Dunn, & Plomin, 1995; Reiss et al., 2000; Stocker, 1993, 1995). The least "favored" sibling was found in such studies to show greater adjustment difficulties. Differential paternal treatment has also been included in several studies, and found to be also related to adjustment outcome (Brody et al., 1992; Stocker, 1993, 1995; Volling & Elins, 1998). Volling and Elins, for instance, found that preschool aged siblings showed greater internalizing and externalizing symptoms when both mothers *and* fathers disciplined them more than their younger siblings. The findings indicate that the correlates of differential treatment with such very young siblings differ in some respects from those with older children, and that future studies need to examine differential parental treatment as a developmental process across childhood. It should also be noted that most studies of differential parental treatment and adjustment do not examine whether the effect of differential experiences is significant beyond the effect of the "absolute" level of parent–child interaction.

A second line of evidence suggesting indirect effects of siblings on children's adjustment comes from the research on the arrival of a sibling. The birth of a sibling is consistently found to be linked to increased problems of adjustment in firstborn children: Disturbance in bodily functions, withdrawal, aggressiveness, dependency, and anxiety have been reported in detailed home observations (Dunn & Kendrick, 1982; Stewart et al., 1987), and in large-scale surveys (Baydar et al., 1997a). The changes in children's adjustment that follow the arrival of a sibling are correlated with parallel changes in the interactions between the "displaced" older sibling and his or her parents. There is a notable increase in critical negative behavior from mothers, an increase in demanding difficult firstborn behavior to mothers, and a decrease in positive joint activities shared by parents and firstborn (Dunn & Kendrick, 1982). Baydar and colleagues reported similar changes in family interaction patterns, and described negative effects on adjustment, achievement, and self-perception about 2.5 years after the sibling birth, and makes two further, important points. The first is that these effects are stronger among the children of economically disadvantaged children, and the second, that there is a significant decrease in the income-to-poverty ratio with the birth of a child, and the accompanying loss of maternal employment income (Baydar et al., 1997b).

Siblings as sources of support

Siblings can also be an important source of support to children faced with stressful experiences. For example, Jenkins (Jenkins, 1992; Jenkins & Smith, 1990) reported that children growing up in disharmonious homes have fewer problems if they have a good sibling relationship. It seems that both offering comfort to, and receiving comfort from, a sibling are associated with benefits for children. Note that other studies of parental separation and family reconstitution report that siblings are relatively infrequent confidants for children (Dunn, Davies, O'Connor, & Sturgess, 2001). But children faced with other negative life events report becoming more intimate and close with their siblings following the stressful event (Dunn et al., 1994a). This is a growing area for clinical research, as in the research with siblings involved as therapists for children with eating disorders (Vandereyken & Van Vrecken, 1992), and as donors for children undergoing bone-marrow transplants.

Siblings and the development of social understanding

The study of siblings has played an important role in changing our views of the nature and development of children's discovery of the mind – their understanding of others' emotions, thoughts, beliefs, and their grasp of the links between such inner states and people's behavior. In standard experimental settings, young preschool children show limited understanding of "other minds" and feelings; in contrast, in the context of the emotional drama and the familiarity of interactions with siblings, they reveal remarkable powers of manipulating others' emotions, anticipating intentions, and of understanding the significance of inner states for human action (Dunn, 1999). Their ability to tease, deceive, manage conflict by anticipating the other's intentions and perspective, share an imaginative world in joint pretend play, and engage in conversations about why people behave the way they do, with reference to mental states as causes and consequences of action – all these are seen in their daily interactions with their siblings in the second, third, and fourth years of life. All reflect a growing sophistication about inner states and social behavior. Sibling research thus has offered a new perspective on a central aspect of early sociocognitive development.

It has also alerted us to the range of individual differences in young children's abilities in these domains, which are striking, and until very recently, little studied. Research addressing the question of what experiences contribute to these striking individual differences in understanding has clearly implicated experiences with siblings.

For example, children who have engaged in frequent shared pretend play with an older sibling, and talked about mental states (knowing, remembering, thinking, believing, and so on) with a sibling are, over time, especially successful on the standard assessments of understanding emotions and mental states (Dunn, 1999; Howe, Petrakos, & Rinaldi, 1998). Children with older siblings, in some studies, perform better on such tasks than those without siblings (Perner, Ruffman, & Leekham, 1994). Other research indicates that it is interaction with familiar others (kin or friends) that is linked to individual differences in performances on understanding of inner states – rather than interaction with siblings per se (Lewis, Freeman, Kyriakidou, Maridaki-Kassotaki, & Berridge, 1996). In general these studies demonstrate associations, and do not directly test causes, so again, we should be wary of inferring the causal contribution of experiences with siblings to social understanding. The children who are good at understanding emotions and at mind-reading are likely to be particularly effective play companions: their early sophistication at reading minds and emotions may well contribute to the development of shared imaginative play with their siblings, and this in itself is likely to foster further developments in understanding others' inner states (Howe et al., 1998).

But though direction of effects is still an intractable issue to be addressed, the sibling research has established firmly the potential significance of certain social processes within the family, for the development of the marked individual differences in the core developmental domain of understanding others.

Siblings and peer relationships

The notion that the quality of sibling relationships will be associated with, and possibly influence, children's relationships with other children outside the family is one that would be supported by a number of different developmental theories: attachment theory, social learning theory, and by those who propose that an individual's characteristics will elicit similar responses from different people (e.g., Caspi & Elder, 1988). The mechanisms suggested to underlie such links differ in these various theoretical frameworks, but each would predict positive associations between sibling and peer relationships. Within a social learning framework, it would be expected that what is learned through interaction with a sibling would generalize to interactions with familiar peers outside the family.

In contrast, it can also be argued that the clear differences between sibling and peer relationships mean that simple positive associations should not be expected. Although both are intimate, dyadic relationships with other children, friendships involve a commitment of trust and support that not all siblings feel about each other, and friendships do not involve rivalry for parental love and attention, or resentment about differential treatment. Children do not choose their siblings, but they do select their friends. The evidence for positive links between individual differences in sibling and peer relations is inconsistent. With young children, studies of conflict management, and of connected communication show some associations across the two relationships (Slomkowski & Dunn, 1992), and some correlations have been reported for aggression with siblings and with peers (Vandell et al., 1987), but other research reports no links (Abramovitch, Corter, Pepler, & Stanhope, 1986). One study of slightly older children reports links in controlling and positive behavior between sibling and friend relationships (Stocker & Mantz-Simmons, unpublished), but also notes that children who were particularly cooperative with their siblings reported lower levels of companionship with their friends. Two other studies also report evidence for "compensatory" patterns – rather than evidence for consistency across the relationships (Mendelson, Aboud, & Lanthier, 1994; Stocker & Dunn, 1990). Studies of popularity with peers also report very few associations with children's sibling relationships, either as preschoolers or as 5–10 year olds (Stocker & Dunn, 1990).

The lack of consistency across the two relationships could be interpreted in various ways. "Compensatory" mechanisms could be invoked; alternatively (or in addition) it could be that the experience of conflict and competitive interactions with siblings fosters children's capacities in social understanding – and this understanding helps children to form particularly close relationships with friends. There is some evidence that frequency of sibling arguments in the preschool period are associated with later successful performance on sociocognitive tasks (Slomkowski & Dunn, 1992), but we are very far from being able to draw conclusions about the mechanisms underlying such correlational data. Internal working models, social understanding as a mediator, and temperamental characteristics have all been invoked to explain connections across relationships.

Siblings and the Nature of Family Influence

The third aspect of sibling research that has notable implications for psychology concerns the ways in which family experiences influence individual development. One of the striking findings of recent research has been the documentation of the *differences* in personality, adjustment, and psychopathology between siblings growing up in the same family (Dunn & Plomin, 1990). These differences, which have been reported in a wide range of studies, present a considerable challenge to those who study family influence. The aspects of family life that have been seen as key influences on children's development, such as mothers' and fathers' educational and occupational level, the parents' mental health and the quality of their spousal relationship, the neighborhood in which the family lives, the social adversities faced by the family, are all apparently shared by the siblings. Yet these siblings grow up to be very different from one another. Answers to this puzzle, suggested by the findings of extensive studies by behavior geneticists, include the proposal that experiences *within* the family differ markedly for siblings, and are key to their developmental differences. It is these experiences specific to each sibling that need to be studied, rather than the between-family differences that have been chiefly studied. The message is not that family influences are unimportant, but that families are experienced very differently by the children who are members of those families (Hetherington et al., 1994).

The evidence for the significance of differential parental treatment, described above, and for the vigilance with which children monitor such differences from early childhood support this new perspective on family processes. Of course, individual differences in the temperament, adjustment, and other characteristics of each sibling are likely to play a major part in eliciting different responses from other family members, as well as in contributing to differences in their responses to others both within and outside the family, and in their responses to "shared" stresses and difficulties that the family faces.

Growing Points and Gaps in Sibling Research

Recent research on siblings has opened up a series of exciting questions about both normative development, and individual differences in development. If we include siblings in studies of the growth of social understanding, of social competence, in research on family influences on adjustment, on the nature and individual differences in peer relations, we gain a powerful new perspective on these areas of development. There is growing interest in siblings in the clinical literature, as in the research on the effects of children's response to illness, disability, or injury in their siblings (Stallard, Mastroyannopoulou, Lewis, & Lenton, 1997), and of traumatic experiences on siblings (Newman, Black, & Harris-Hendriks, 1997). A lively new area of study is investigation into the relationships of step- and half-siblings, and individual differences in their development; with the marked increase in the numbers of families that do not conform to the traditional pattern of two biological parents and their biological children, this is a growth area of considerable practical significance (Hetherington et al., 1999; O'Connor, Dunn, Jenkins, Pickering, & Rasbash, 2001). Comparison of full, half, and stepsiblings provides a useful strategy for discovering the role of genetics in the development of individual differences (Deater-Deckard et al., in press).

However, although the inclusion of siblings in research strategies represents a major opportunity to learn more about not only their relationships, but also about key issues in developmental psychology more broadly considered, there are still notable gaps in the research on siblings. Most studies focus on young or middle-childhood children, though interest in research on adolescent siblings is rapidly growing (e.g., Hetherington et al., 1999), but there is little longitudinal research in adulthood, or studies that take a life-course perspective. We are left comparatively ignorant of the long-term significance of early experiences with siblings.

Studies of siblings from minority communities are notably lacking, as are cross-cultural studies, and studies of non-Western cultures more generally. These gaps are especially striking, given that ethnographic studies have shown that siblings play important roles as caregivers for children from a very early age in many cultures (Weisner, 1989; Weisner & Gallimore, 1977). Weisner's (1989) reviews make clear siblings are key figures in children's lives in many non-Western communities, and he considers these experiences play an important role in "socialization for parenthood." Anthropological research has documented that siblings are also key in adults' lives in such communities (e.g., Nuckolls, 1993). Little research in the United States, or the UK, has focused specifically on ethnic differences in sibling relations. In a national sample in the United States, the relationships between siblings in African American, Hispanic, non-Hispanic White and Asian American adults were compared. The conclusion was that the similarities across the groups in terms of contact and social support far outweighed the differences (Riedmann & White, 1996). Parallel research on childhood and adolescence is needed.

These gaps in what we know about siblings represent opportunities for studies that are likely to prove both theoretically and practically important; the study of siblings is providing a novel perspective on widely differing domains of psychology – clinical, developmental, on family processes, on the contribution of genetics to individual differences in development.

References

Abramovitch, R., Corter, C., Pepler, D. J., & Stanhope, L. (1986). Sibling and peer interaction: A final follow-up and a comparison. *Child Development, 57*, 217–229.

Bank, L., Patterson, G. R., & Reid, J. B. (1996). Negative sibling interaction as predictors of later adjustment problems in adolescent and young adult males. In G. H. Brody (Ed.), *Sibling relationships: Their causes and consequences* (pp. 197–229). Norwood, NJ: Ablex.

Bank, S., & Kahn, M. D. (1982). *The sibling bond.* New York: Basic Books.

Baydar, N., Greek, A., & Brooks-Gunn, J. (1997a). A longitudinal study of the effects of the birth of a sibling during the first 6 years of life. *Journal of Marriage and the Family, 59*, 939–956.

Baydar, N., Hyle, P., & Brooks-Gunn, J. (1997b). A longitudinal study of the effects of the birth of a sibling during preschool and early grade school years. *Journal of Marriage and the Family, 59*, 957–965.

Boer, F., & Dunn, J. (1990). *Children's sibling relationships: Developmental and clinical issues.* Hillsdale, NJ: Erlbaum.

Brody, G. H. (1996). *Sibling relationships their causes and consequences.* Norwood, NJ: Ablex.

Brody, G. H. (1998). Sibling relationship quality: Its causes and consequences. *Annual Review of Psychology, 49*, 1–24.

Brody, G., Stoneman, Z., & Burke, M. (1987). Child temperaments, maternal differential behavior, and sibling relationships. *Developmental Psychology, 23*, 354–362.

Brody, G., Stoneman, Z., & McCoy, J. (1992). Associations of maternal and paternal direct and differential behavior with sibling relationships: Contemporaneous and longitudinal analyses. *Child Development, 63*, 82–92.

Brody, G., Stoneman, Z., & McCoy, J. (1994). Forecasting sibling relationships in early adolescence from child temperaments and family processes in middle childhood. *Child Development, 65*, 771–784.

Brody, G., Stoneman, Z., McCoy, J. K., & Forehand, R. (1992). Contemporaneous and longitudinal associations of sibling conflict with family relationship assessments and family discussions about sibling problems. *Child Development, 63*, 391–400.

Buhrmester, D. (1992). The developmental course of sibling and peer relationships. In F. Boer & J. Dunn (Eds.), *Children's sibling relationships: Developmental and clinical issues* (pp. 19–40). Hillsdale, NJ: Erlbaum.

Buhrmester, D., & Furman, W. (1990). Perceptions of sibling relationships during middle childhood and adolescence. *Child Development, 61*, 1387–1398.

Caspi, A., & Elder, G. H., Jr. (1988). Emergent family patterns: The intergenerational construction of problem behaviour and relationships. In R. Hinde & J. Stevenson-Hinde (Eds.), *Relationships within families: Mutual influences* (pp. 218–240). Oxford, England: Clarendon Press.

Cicirelli, V. (1996). Sibling relationships in middle and old age. In G. Brody (Ed.), *Sibling relation-*

ships: Their causes and consequences (pp. 47–73). Norwood, NJ: Ablex.

Conger, K., & Conger, R. (1994). Differential parenting and change in sibling differences in delinquency. *Journal of Family Psychology, 8*, 287–302.

Deater-Deckard, K., Dunn, J., O'Connor, T., Davies, L., Golding, J., & The ALSPAC Study Team. (in press). Using the step-family genetic design to examine gene-environment processes in family functioning. *Marriage and Family Review: Special issue on gene-environment processes in social behaviors and relationships.*

Dunn, J. (1988). *The beginnings of social understanding* (1st ed.). Cambridge, MA: Harvard University Press.

Dunn, J. (1993). *Young children's close relationships: Beyond attachment, Vol. 4* (1st ed.). Newbury Park, CA: Sage.

Dunn, J. (1999). Making sense of the social world: Mindreading, emotion, and relationships. In P. D. Zelazo, J. W. Astington, & D. R. Olson (Eds.), *Developing theories of intention: Social understanding and self-control* (pp. 229–242). Mahwah, NJ: Erlbaum.

Dunn, J., Creps, C., & Brown, J. (1996). Children's family relationships between two and five: Developmental changes and individual differences. *Social Development, 5*, 230–250.

Dunn, J., Davies, L., O'Connor, T. G., & Sturgess, W. (2001). Family lives and friendships: The perspectives of children in step-, single-parent and nonstep families. *Journal of Family Psychology, 15*, 272–287.

Dunn, J., Deater-Deckard, K., Pickering, K., Beveridge, M., & the ALSPAC Study Team. (1999). Siblings, parents and partners: Family relationships within a longitudinal community study. *Journal of Child Psychology and Psychiatry, 40*, 1025–1037.

Dunn, J., & Kendrick, C. (1982). *Siblings: Love, envy and understanding.* Cambridge, MA: Harvard University Press.

Dunn, J., & Munn, P. (1985). Becoming a family member: Family conflict and the development of social understanding in the second year. *Child Development, 56*, 764–774.

Dunn, J., & Plomin, R. (1990). *Separate lives: Why siblings are so different* (1st ed.). New York: Basic Books.

Dunn, J., Slomkowski, C., & Beardsall, L. (1994a). Sibling relationships from the preschool period through middle childhood and early adolescence. *Developmental Psychology, 30*, 315–324.

Dunn, J., Slomkowski, C., Beardsall, L., & Rende, R. (1994b). Adjustment in middle childhood and early adolescence: Links with earlier and contemporary sibling relationships. *Journal of Child Psychology and Psychiatry and Allied Disciplines, 35*, 491–504.

Erel, O., Margolin, G., & John, R. S. (1998). Observed sibling interaction: Links with the marital and the mother–child relationship. *Developmental Psychology, 34*, 288–298.

Ernst, C., & Angst, J. (1983). *Birth order: Its influence on personality.* Berlin: Springer-Verlag.

Furman, W., & Lanthier, R. P. (1996). Personality and sibling relationships. In G. H. Brody (Ed.), *Sibling relationships: Their causes and consequences* (pp. 127–146). Norwood, NJ: Ablex.

Garcia, M. M., Shaw, D. S., Winslow, E. B., & Yaggi, K. E. (2000). Destructive sibling conflict and the development of conduct problems in young boys. *Developmental Psychology, 36*, 44–53.

Hetherington, E. M., & Clingempeel, W. G. (1992). Coping with marital transitions: A family systems approach. *Monographs of the Society for Research in Child Development, 57* (2-3, Serial No. 227).

Hetherington, E. M., Henderson, S., & Reiss, D. (1999). Adolescent siblings in stepfamilies: Family functioning and adolescent adjustment. *Monographs of the Society for Research in Child Development, 64* (4, Serial No. 259), 1–222.

Hetherington, E. M., Reiss, D., & Plomin, R. (1994). *Separate social worlds of siblings: The impact of nonshared environment on development.* Hillsdale, NJ: Erlbaum.

Hinde, R. A. (1979). *Towards understanding relationships.* London: Academic Press.

Howe, N., Petrakos, H., & Rinaldi, C. (1998). "All the sheeps are dead. He murdered them": Sibling pretense, negotiation, internal state language and relationship quality. *Child Development, 69,* 182–191.

Jenkins, J. (1992). Sibling relationships in disharmonious homes: Potential difficulties and protective effects. In F. Boer & J. Dunn (Eds.), *Children's sibling relationships: Developmental and clinical issues.* Hillsdale, NJ: Erlbaum.

Jenkins, J., & Smith, M. (1990). Factors protecting children living in disharmonious homes: Maternal reports. *Journal of the American Academy of Child and Adolescent Psychiatry, 29,* 60–69.

Koch, H. L. (1954). The relation of "primary mental abilities" in five- and six-year-olds to sex of child and characteristics of his sibling. *Child Development, 15,* 209–223.

Koch, H. L. (1960). *The relation of certain formal attributes of siblings to attitudes held toward each other and toward their parents, Vol. 25.* Chicago: University of Chicago Press.

Kowal, A., & Kramer, L. (1997). Children's understanding of parental differential treatment. *Child Development, 68,* 113–126.

Larson, R., & Richards, M. H. (1994). *Divergent realities: The emotional lives of mothers, fathers, and adolescents.* New York: Basic Books.

Lewis, C., Freeman, N. H., Kyriakidou, C., Maridaki-Kassotaki, K., & Berridge, D. M. (1996). Social influences on false belief access: Specific sibling influences or general apprenticeship? *Child Development, 67,* 2930–2947.

MacKinnon, C. (1989). An observational investigation of sibling interactions in married and divorced families. *Developmental Psychology, 25,* 36–44.

McGuire, S., Dunn, J., & Plomin, R. (1995). Maternal differential treatment of siblings and children's behavioral problems: A longitudinal study. *Development and Psychopathology, 7,* 515–528.

McGuire, S., Manke, B., Eftekhari, A., & Dunn, J. (2000). Children's perceptions of sibling conflict during middle childhood: Issues and sibling (dis)similarity. *Social Development, 9,* 173–190.

McHale, S. M., & Crouter, A. C. (1996). The family context of children's sibling relationships. In G. Brody (Ed.), *Sibling relationships: Their causes and consequences* (pp. 173–195). Norwood, NJ: Ablex.

Mendelson, M., Aboud, F., & Lanthier, R. (1994). Kindergartners' relationships with siblings, peers and friends. *Merrill Palmer Quarterly, 40,* 416–427.

Munn, P., & Dunn, J. (1989). Temperament and the developing relationship between siblings. *International Journal of Behavioral Development, 12,* 433–451.

Newman, M., Black, D., & Harris-Hendriks, J. (1997). Victims of disaster, war, violence or homicide: Psychological effects on siblings. *Child Psychology and Psychiatry Review, 2,* 140–149.

Nuckolls, C. (1993). *Siblings in South Asia.* New York: Guilford Press.

O'Connor, T., Dunn, J., Jenkins, J., Pickering, K., & Rasbash, J. (2001). Family settings and children's adjustment: Differential adjustment within and across families. *British Journal of Psychiatry, 179,* 110–115.

Patterson, G. R. (1986). The contribution of siblings to training for fighting: A microsocial analysis. In D. Olweus, J. Block, & M. Radke-Yarrow (Eds.), *Development of antisocial and prosocial behavior* (pp. 235–261). New York: Academic Press.

Perner, J., Ruffman, T., & Leekham, S. R. (1994). Theory of mind is contagious: You catch it from your sibs. *Child Development, 65,* 1228–1238.

Reiss, D., Neiderheiser, J. M., Hetherington, E. M., & Plomin, R. (2000). *The relationship code: Deciphering genetic and social patterns in adolescent development.* Cambridge, MA: Harvard University Press.

Riedmann, A., & White, L. (1996). Adult sibling relationships: Racial and ethnic comparisons. In

G. Brody (Ed.), *Sibling relationships: Their causes and consequences* (pp. 105–126). Norwood, NJ: Ablex.

Slomkowski, C. L., & Dunn, J. (1992). Arguments and relationships within the family: Differences in young children's disputes with mother and sibling. *Developmental Psychology, 28*, 919–924.

Snyder, J., & Patterson, G. (1995). Individual differences in social aggression: A test of a reinforcement model of socialization in the natural environment. *Behavior Therapy, 26*, 371–391.

Stallard, P., Mastroyannopoulou, K., Lewis, M., & Lenton, S. (1997). The siblings of children with life-threatening conditions. *Child Psychology and Psychiatry Review, 2*, 26–33.

Stewart, R. B. (1990). *The second child.* Newbury Park, CA: Sage.

Stewart, R., Mobley, L., Van Tuyl, S., & Salvador, M. (1987). The firstborn's adjustment to the birth of a sibling. *Child Development, 58*, 341–355.

Stocker, C. (1993). Siblings' adjustment in middle childhood: Links with mother–child relationships. *Journal of Applied Developmental Psychology, 14*, 485–499.

Stocker, C. (1995). Differences in mothers' and fathers' relationships with siblings: Links with behavioral problems. *Development and Psychopathology, 7*, 499–513.

Stocker, C., Ahmed, K., & Stall, M. (1997). Marital satisfaction and maternal emotional expressiveness: Links with children's sibling relationships. *Social Development, 6*, 373–385.

Stocker, C., & Dunn, J. (1990). Sibling relationships in childhood: Links with friendships and peer relationships. *British Journal of Developmental Psychology, 8*, 227–244.

Stocker, C., Dunn, J., & Plomin, R. (1989). Sibling relationships: Links with child temperament, maternal behavior, and family structure. *Child Development, 60*, 715–727.

Stocker, C., & Mantz-Simmons, L. (unpublished). *Children's friendships and peer status: Links with family relationships, temperament and social skills.* University of Denver.

Stoneman, Z., & Brody, G. (1993). Sibling relations in the family context. In Z. Stoneman & P. Berman (Eds.), *The effects of mental retardation, disability, and illness on sibling relationships: Issues and challenges* (pp. 3–30). Baltimore: Paul H. Brooks.

Sulloway, F. (1996). *Born to rebel.* London: Little, Brown.

Sutton-Smith, B., & Rosenberg, B. (1970). *The sibling.* New York: Holt, Rinehart, & Winston.

Teti, D. M., & Ablard, K. E. (1989). Security of attachment and infant-sibling relationships: A laboratory study. *Child Development, 60*, 1519–1528.

Vandell, D. L., Minnett, A. M., & Santrock, J. W. (1987). Age differences in sibling relationships during middle childhood. *Journal of Applied Developmental Psychology, 8*, 247–257.

Vandereyken, W., & Van Vrecken, E. (1992). Siblings as co-patients and co-therapists in eating disorders. In F. Boer & J. Dunn (Eds.), *Children's sibling relationships: Developmental and clinical issues* (pp. 109–123). Hillsdale, NJ: Erlbaum.

Volling, B. L., & Belsky, J. (1992). The contribution of mother–child and father–child relationships to the quality of sibling interaction: A longitudinal study. *Child Development, 63*, 1209–1222.

Volling, B. L., & Elins, J. L. (1998). Family relationships and children's emotional adjustment as correlates of maternal and paternal differential treatment: A replication with toddler and preschool siblings. *Child Development, 69*, 1640–1656.

Weisner, T. S. (1989). Comparing sibling relationships across cultures. In P. Zukow (Ed.), *Sibling interaction across cultures: Theoretical and methodological issues* (pp. 11–25). New York: Springer-Verlag.

Weisner, T. S., & Gallimore, R. (1977). My brother's keeper: Child and sibling caretaking. *Current Anthropology, 18*, 169-190.

13

Social Development in Different Family Arrangements

Dale F. Hay and Alison Nash

Objectives

The aim of the chapter is to demonstrate the importance of studies of family arrangements for theories of social development. In line with the aims of the volume, we focus on early and middle childhood, asking how family arrangements affect children's social development, that is, their abilities to relate to others, to regulate emotion, and to function competently in the social world, free of major mental health problems.

Although some investigators of family structure highlight psychological processes (e.g., Hetherington, 1998), most studies are guided by the methods and theories of demography, family sociology, and ethnography, and thus do not test developmental theory. Rather, the existing literature arises from concerns about the increased prevalence of "nontraditional" family structures. Investigators often apply a "deficit model," using the nuclear family (two biological parents and their children) as the standard with which other families are compared. This assumption is made explicit in newer studies that use statistical modeling procedures, where conventional nuclear families are set as the baseline value (e.g., Cleveland, Wiebe, Van den Oord, & Rowe, 2000).

These comparisons are challenged by the fact that nuclear families are increasingly unrepresentative. For example, the number of families headed by single mothers in the United States has increased 25% since 1990 (U.S. Census, 2000). Only about half the children in the United States live in homes that include only their two biological parents and any full siblings (Hernandez, 1997). UK demographers estimate that, by 2010, more children will live with stepparents than two biological parents (Office of National Statistics, 2000). In much of the world, the extended family is the norm. Even in the United States and Britain, single parenting and stepfamilies are not new phenomena, being quite common in the past as a result of death during childbirth (Muzi, 2000). Because contemporary families live in diverse ways, the study of family influences on social development must draw upon representative samples, and go beyond simple pair-wise comparisons against a "normal" baseline.

Studies of family arrangements have critical implications for current theories of social development, as they provide the strongest tests of claims that family influences are not as great as once thought, in comparison with genetic predispositions (Scarr, 1992), sibling contributions (Sulloway, 1996), and the role of peers (Harris, 1998). Thus we describe how studies of family arrangements address theoretical issues in five perspectives in developmental psychology that emphasize family influences: (1) *the attachment model*, which highlights the importance of formative social experiences in very early life; (2) *the parenting model*, which is a contemporary heir to the long-standing tradition of the study of individual variation in childrearing strategies and the competence of individual parents; (3) *the nuclear family model*, which emphasizes the importance of both fathers and mothers in children's lives; (4) *the family systems model*, which characterizes families as dynamic systems in which all members play important roles and there are important effects of relationships on other relationships; and (5) *the social networks model*, in which family relationships are seen in the context of wider social networks and cultural frameworks.

In the sections that follow we illustrate ways in which different types of families have been studied in each of these five perspectives. However, before highlighting key findings, it is important to introduce a note of caution. The body of evidence on family arrangements is weakened by many methodological flaws, so that few firm conclusions can be drawn (some common methodological problems are shown in Table 13.1). Most importantly, serious confounds in many research designs lead to alternative interpretations of many findings. These confounds are illustrated clearly by the literature on divorce and remarriage.

Confounds in the Study of Family Arrangements

Intergenerational continuities

An intergenerational link between parents' and children's traits (through heritable characteristics or socialization patterns in families) might account both for children's behavioral problems and marital discord, divorce, and multiple transitions. For example, parents who are angry, aggressive, or abusive could transmit such behaviors to their children, either through genes or behavioral models, and also create a family climate that makes divorce likely (e.g. Emory, Waldron, Aaron, & Kitzmann, 1999). Evidence for genetic contributions is supported by the fact that effects of divorce are stronger in biological than adoptive families (O'Connor, Caspi, De Fries, & Plomin, 2000), and by comparisons of households containing one or two parents and sibling pairs who share both or one parent (Cleveland et al., 2000).

Table 13.1 Some Common Methodological Problems in the Study of Family Arrangements

	Type of problem	Illustrative examples[a]
Sampling problems	Small, unrepresentative samples	Many studies of rare family structures, e.g., same-sex parents (Braeways et al., 1997), families who use fertility treatments (Golombok et al., 1999), and families who rear children communally (Hamilton, 2000) rely on small, volunteer samples who may not be representative of a general population
	Secular trends and cohort effects	Large cohort studies are rooted in time and place, and long-term effects found in studies begun in the 1950s (e.g., the British NCDS Sample) might not generalize to younger cohorts
	Attrition and selective participation	There is substantial attrition in the cohort studies (e.g., NCDS). Furthermore, selective participation may compromise results, e.g., in a comparison of same-sex and heterosexual couples, all lesbian couples who were contacted agreed to participate but substantially fewer fathers did. Fathers who used donor insemination were more willing to participate than normally conceiving fathers (Braeways et al., 1997)
	Problems with matching and case-control designs	Quasi-experimental case-control designs have often been used to compare family arrangements. Matching on some variables may lead to systematic unmatching on others; problems may be exacerbated when control groups are constructed long after the original observations were made (e.g., Wallerstein, Lewis, & Blakeslee, 2000)
Measurement problems	Defining and categorizing family arrangements	Families are very fluid, shifting arrangements over short time periods (Muzi, 2000; Seltzer, 2000). Definitions are problematic. The concept of "parent" in the case of fostering, adoption, fertility treatments, and same-sex relationships is not always clear, and the concept of "family" does not always equate to "household," especially with respect to extended families and contexts such as the Bahamas, where fostering arrangements and time spent in different households are familiar parts of children's lives (Dean, personal communication)
	Informant biases	Large, representative studies often use single informants, most commonly mothers (e.g., Dunn et al., 1998). A single informant's reports about children's adjustment may be biased by the informant's own mental health problems (see Boyle & Pickles, 1997; Hay et al., 1999) or continuing conflict with the spouse before and after divorce. Role relationships also affect reporting. Step-parents provide reports of children's psychological adjustment that are much more negative than those from other informants (Hetherington & Clingempeel, 1992)

[a] The studies cited are no more flawed than others in the literature, but rather provide clear illustrations of specific problems that are common to many other studies of family arrangements. It should be noted that even the best studies in this area must make "trade-offs" between large, representative samples and reliable and valid measurement. Thus, detailed qualitative and quantitative data of psychological processes in family life are more likely to be possible in smaller, selected samples, whilst large, representative cohort studies often use standardized questionnaires completed by single informants.

Conditions that predate changes in family arrangements

Pre-existing conditions may make it more likely that children have behavioral problems and that their parents will divorce. For example, marital conflict that predates divorce may be the primary cause of children's problems. Children whose parents eventually divorce are more likely to have shown problems years prior to the divorce (e.g., Amato & Booth, 1996; Cherlin et al., 1991; Shaw, Winslow, & Flanagan, 1999). Even economic disadvantage, a common consequence of family disruption (McLanahan & Teitler, 1999), may cause it as well: for example, African-American couples living in poverty more often separated whilst those with more financial resources tended to stay together (Shaw et al., 1999).

Socioeconomic status

The correlation between income and family structure is apparent. For example, in the United States in 1995, the median income for mother-headed families was $18,000, compared to $50,000 for two-parent families (McLanahan & Teitler, 1999). When income levels and family education are controlled, the effects of family structure are either negligible (e.g., Clarke-Stewart, Vandell, McCartney, Owen, & Booth, 2000) or much reduced (e.g., Amato & Keith, 1991). Furthermore, *perceived* income affects the parents' levels of stress and their manner of coping, which in turn influence parenting style (Brody, Flor, & Gibson, 1999). In general, it is important to integrate analyses of the different economic dimensions of family arrangements (e.g., DeGarmo, Forgatch, & Martinez, 1999) with assessments of parents' mental health and parenting style.

Social perceptions of family arrangements

A particular family structure is inevitably confounded with the views of that structure held by others. Families outside the "norm" may be perceived negatively and consequently receive less support than those who live in ways closer to cultural ideals. For example, 300 professionals and 300 lay observers watched videotapes of 10-year-old boys interacting with other children (Fry & Addington, 1984). The observers were randomly informed that boys were living either with divorced mothers, divorced fathers, or in "intact" homes. Boys thought to be from "intact" families were rated the *most* well-adjusted, boys from father-headed families the *least* so. Such perceptions can result in biased reports from informants such as teachers and care workers and create self-fulfilling prophecies.

It is important to measure family members' beliefs about their circumstances, as a mismatch between ideal and reality may have profound effects. For example, Pyle (2000) found that Korean and Vietnamese immigrants to the United States contrasted their own families of origin – characterized as overly strict, emotionally distant, and deficient – with the idealized American family. Beliefs that one's own family is not ideal may affect parents' feelings of efficacy, which then affects parenting style and children's competence (Brody et al., 1999). Departures from one's own ideals of family life may be painful. For example, "loss of a cherished ideal" (such as an "ideal marriage") is a life event capable of inducing depression (Brown & Harris, 1989).

Absence of guiding theory

Families cannot be randomly assigned to live in different ways. It is almost impossible to disentangle confounds and test alternative explanations in the absence of theoretical frameworks in which to evaluate the mass of correlational studies that are characterized by many methodological problems (Table 13.1). It often seems that a variety of standardized outcome measures have been chosen on an arbitrary basis, and few studies have attempted to examine the effects of family arrangements with respect to a coherent set of questions about social development. Thus, in the sections that follow, we identify conceptual issues and highlight illustrative findings that are pertinent to current theories of social development.

The Attachment Model

Of central importance to attachment theory is the early relationship between an infant and its primary caregiver, usually, though not inevitably, the mother (Bowlby, 1969). Infants are assumed to be "monotropic," needing a focused attachment with a particular "mothering figure." Family arrangements that disrupt the tie between infants and their mothers are thought to put children at risk. Thus, attachment researchers study the consequences of maternal employment and day care (e.g., NICHD, 1997) and communal experiences such as that provided in Israeli kibbutzim (Sagi, Lamb, & Gardner, 1986). Attachment theory makes no clear predictions about the consequences of father absence. For example, Bowlby (1969) argued that the natural unit was that between mother and child, with a male (though not necessarily the biological father) in a supporting role. The security of attachment with the father is less stable over time than that with the mother (Main, Kaplan, & Cassidy, 1985). Family structure is not associated with the quality of attachment relationships in early life, but *changes* in family life result in changes in attachment classifications, in both directions. If family arrangements change, some secure children become insecure, but some insecure children become secure (Thompson, Lamb, & Estes, 1982).

Long-term longitudinal studies of attachment highlight the influence of the quality of the child's relationship with the parents in later years and the changes in family arrangements that take place after infancy (e.g., Hamilton, 2000). In one follow-up study, current feelings of security and divorce predicted adolescents' psychological adjustment, but security measured in infancy did not (Lewis, Feiring, & Rosenthal, 2000). These findings show that classic attachment theory alone is not sufficient to explain social development in middle childhood and adolescence. Rather, parent–child relationships need to be studied over time.

The Parenting Model

A dominant perspective in contemporary developmental psychology is one that focuses on parenting style as a characteristic of individuals. In this perspective, which follows from the earlier tradition of studying patterns of child rearing (e.g., Sears, Maccoby, & Levin, 1957), parents differ in skills, cognitions, warmth, and mental states (e.g., Baumrind, 1989; Bugental & Johnston, 2000; Maccoby, 2000). Individual differences in "parenting" are widely believed to mediate the effects of family arrangements on children's lives, and interventions to improve parenting are of considerable interest for public policy (Cowan, Powell, & Cowan, 1998).

Theorists in this tradition argue that some family structures place parents at risk for poor parenting (see Hetherington & Stanley-Hagen, 1999a; Waite & Gallagher, 2000). The parenting model is often applied to studies of divorce and single parenthood, which were first cast in terms of questions about "father absence" (for a review see Herzog & Sudia, 1973). Current accounts emphasize variation in parenting skill within as well as across different family structures.

Never-married mothers

Never-married mothers are thought to be at particular risk for problems in parenting. Although a substantial number of children in single-parent families live with mothers who have never married, there are few studies of this family arrangement (for a review see Weinraub & Gringlas, 1995), and most focus on adolescent motherhood, which has its own unique set of issues. In the United States, 8% of all children live with never-married mothers as opposed to 14% who live with separated or divorced mothers (Hernandez, 1997).

Never-married mothers show higher levels of rejecting parenting compared to other types of families (Shaw et al., 1999) and lower supervision and control over their children than mothers in two-parent families (Thomson, McLanahan, & Braun-Curtin, 1992). The parenting style of single mothers reflects mental health problems and worries that transcend the mother–child relationship; for example, young single mothers behave in parallel ways with their infants and their boyfriends (Hart, Field, Jones, & Yando, 1999). In a study of a London birth cohort (Schmuecker, 1998), *all* single mothers in the sample had suffered from depression by the time the children were 4 years of age. The well-established links between maternal depression, parenting problems, and poor outcomes for children (e.g., Murray & Cooper, 1997) account for some of the risks attached to single parenthood (Dunn, Deater-Deckard, Pickering, & O'Connor, 1998).

Studies of never-married mothers provide important support for the parenting model, in that they clearly document sources of variation within such families. Not all single parents are unskilled. For example, studies of poor, single African-American mothers document considerable within-sample variation in parenting style and skill (e.g., Brody et al., 1999). In a sample of 193 single mothers, most provided nurturant or cognitively stimulating behavior to their children, though some women also expressed annoyance with their children and their situations (McGroder, 2000). The minority of women who were not nurturant were themselves more likely to have had a history of abuse and a longer history of welfare dependency.

The effects of single parents' parenting difficulties on children's adjustment are unclear. As toddlers, boys living with never-married mothers had higher rates of externalizing and internalizing problems than did those from other family types, but no differences emerged beyond toddlerhood (Shaw et al., 1999). Longer-term follow-up studies of representative samples of never-married mothers are badly needed.

Divorced families

A major research question within the parenting model is the extent to which parenting deteriorates in the face of life changes, economic setbacks, and psychological stress. The study of divorce is therefore of particular interest within this perspective. Decades of correlational studies have shown that divorce is associated with deleterious outcomes for children (e.g., Hanson, McLanahan, & Thomson, 1998; Wallerstein, Lewis, & Blakeslee, 2000). The earlier "father absence" studies demonstrated social, psychological, and economic disadvantages for children whose parents divorced (Herzog & Sadia, 1973). More recent studies have demonstrated that, even under conditions of stress and turmoil, competent, emotionally responsive parenting provides opportunities for sound child adjustment (Hetherington & Stanley-Hagen, 1999a; Wyman et al., 1999). It thus becomes possible to design interventions to improve parenting skills and sensitivity (Cowan et al., 1998), even when marriages have moved beyond repair.

Distressed parents may find it very hard to provide competent parenting. Authoritative parenting helps children of divorced parents as much as those who live with both biological parents (Hetherington & Clingempeel, 1992), but divorced parents are often less able to be authoritative (Hetherington & Stanley-Hagen, 1999a). Parenting difficulties are bound up with the divorced parent's own emotional problems. The parent's mental state directly impinges on the parent–child relationship (e.g., Cummings & Davies, 1994) and some studies suggest that parents' own mental health problems often mediate the effects of divorce on children (e.g., Dunn et al., 1998). The evidence is unclear, however, in that informants who are depressed may exaggerate the extent of their children's problems (see Boyle & Pickles, 1997; Hay et al., 1999).

Some investigators have tried to observe the qualitative features of family life in different types of families, which provides interesting insights into the values held by parents in different circumstances. For example, children in divorced families participate more in family decisions and have more responsibility, which predicts higher levels of maturity, self-esteem, empathy, and androgyny (Gately & Schwebel, 1992). One study showed that single mothers read more to their children but eat fewer meals with them than do married mothers; remarried mothers spent little time either reading to or eating with their children (Thomson et al., 1992). Sometimes things can be simpler in single-parent families. For example, a study of effective single parenting showed that, under some circumstances, single mothers, who do not have to engage in conflict with a spouse who might hold different opinions and values about child rearing, provide a very peaceful, consistent family climate (Morrison, 1995). In general, future research within the parenting model needs to concentrate on family activities and values as well as the skills used by parents in different arrangements.

The Nuclear Family Model

An over-emphasis on parenting as an individual difference variable may limit our understanding of the dynamics of particular parent–child relationships (see also Russell, this volume). It is not clear whether the concept of parenting can completely account for the differential contributions of fathers and mothers to children's social development. Child rearing is not necessarily a sexless enterprise. For example, Amato's (1993) review of the divorce literature indicated that the presence of a father or stepfather added explanatory power to the prediction of boys' psychological adjustment, beyond information about parenting style. Thus some theorists still emphasize the importance of a two-parent family for social development.

The nuclear family model has a long history and several contemporary versions, which owe much to earlier psychoanalytic writings. The attachment perspective draws on Bowlby's (1958) interest in object relations and the early mother–infant bond, and studies of child rearing were influenced by concepts in ego psychology such as dependency (Cairns, 1979). In contrast, the nuclear family model is heavily influenced by another strand within psychoanalysis, Freud's account of gender roles, identification, and moral development (e.g., Freud, 1938). Freud drew attention to children's relationships with both biological parents and the effects of an initial attraction to the opposite-sex parent and a final identification with the same-sex parent. Implicit in the theory was the notion that identification with the same-sex parent occurs in the context of a stable marriage between the biological mother and father. In this perspective, boys who do not live with their fathers are thought to be at risk for identity problems and atypical gender role development. Thus the central question is not simply, are children mentally healthy and well adjusted, but also, are they acting in ways that are deemed appropriate for members of their sex? Family arrangements of particular concern here are those of separated or divorced families, single-parent families, and families headed by two same-sex parents.

Freud's concern with the dynamics of the nuclear family is echoed in current views emphasizing the importance of fathers as well as mothers (e.g., Cabrera et al., 2000), showing that positive interactions with both parents enhance development (e.g., Harris, Furstenberg, & Marmer, 1998; Hart, Nelson, Robinson, Olsen, & McNeilly-Choque, 1998; Isley, O'Neil, Clatfelter, & Parke, 1999). Although much of this work concentrates on mother–child and father–child relationships within nuclear families, rather than comparisons across family structures, these studies draw attention to the unique features of each relationship, and raise questions about "father absence." The evidence suggests that positive interactions with fathers are better than negative ones, but what are the effects of positive and negative interactions with fathers, compared to no or little interaction?

Deviation from the nuclear family structure takes different forms. "Illegitimate" children may be seen to be at some degree of social disadvantage, which may affect their social development and eventual well-being. Thus there is interest in comparing the children of married couples with those whose parents are cohabiting (Seltzer, 2000). Arrangements that include biologically unrelated family members, such as stepparent families or those created through donor insemination, also deviate from the nuclear family model. Risk here is sometimes seen to go beyond issues of social adjustment and gender identity. For example, sociobiological accounts suggest that children's lives are actually endangered when they live with unrelated individuals (Daly & Wilson, 2000). Issues concerning the importance of the nuclear family structure for children's social development often become intertwined and confounded in studies that merely compare children in nuclear families against one particular alternative. Here we highlight some current findings that bear on the importance of same-sex role models, the advantages of legal marriage and the dynamics of children's relationships with genetically unrelated family members.

Parental sex and gender role development

Father absence versus father presence.   A meta-analysis of 67 studies comparing children in father-absent and father-present families indicated that girls' sex-typed behavior appeared unaffected by the absence of fathers, whereas preschool-aged boys were less stereotypical in categorizing toys (Stevenson & Black, 1988). A more direct test of Freud's (1938) claim that identification with the same-sex parent is critical for healthy psychological development is provided by comparisons of children living with same-sex as opposed to opposite-sex parents.

Same versus opposite-sex single parents.   Very few empirical studies compare children from households with same-sex and opposite-sex single parents, but those that do demonstrate that children are *not* advantaged by living with same-sex parents (Downey & Powell, 1993). Nevertheless, strong cultural beliefs that boys model themselves after and identify with their fathers and girls with their mothers, and that same-sex parents better understand the feelings and needs of their children, are reflected in the courts, which are increasingly willing to grant same-sex requests for custody. Consequently, more sons than daughters live in single-father households (Muzi, 2000).

Relationships with non-custodial fathers.   Relationships with fathers who do not have custody differ, depending on whether the parents have ever been married or cohabiting. For example, Coley (1998) found that children of divorced mothers reported higher levels of warmth from noncustodial fathers than children from never-married mothers. Although these differences disappeared when SES was controlled, the link between paternal warmth and control and children's school achievement was greater for divorced or separated fathers than for never-married fathers, especially for girls. Thus daughters who live with their fathers for part of their lives are more influenced by them, and so the study of paternal influences needs to go beyond the issue of same-sex role models.

Same-sex parents.   Studies of families with two female parents or two male parents also provide a test of the necessity of having a parent of each sex. Earlier work in this area focused on children of heterosexual couples who subsequently divorced and forged same-sex relationships (Patterson, 1992); more recent work focuses on the children born to same-sex partners, often with the help of new reproductive technologies (Patterson, 2000). More studies focus on the children of lesbian couples than on those of gay men.

The children of lesbian mothers are not usually compared to the "baseline" of heterosexual, married biological parents. When the focus was on the children of divorced women who were now in lesbian relationships, the comparison group was single heterosexual women (Golombok, Spencer, & Rutter, 1983). Now that there is increased interest in the families created by lesbian couples with the aid of donor insemination, comparison groups include heterosexual couples who similarly availed themselves of reproductive technologies (e.g., Braeways, Panjaert, Van Hall, & Golombok, 1997). These comparisons reveal no deficiencies in parenting or the quality of the parent–child relationship in families headed by lesbians (Golombok, Tasker, & Murray, 1997; Patterson, 1992).

For example, in a European study of 4 to 8 year olds, there was no difference in the quality of the interaction between biological mother and child in three different groups: lesbian couples who had used donor insemination; heterosexual couples who had used donor insemination; and heterosexual couples who had conceived their child in the ordinary way (Braeways et al., 1997). Some comparisons favored the lesbian couples. For example, the quality of parent–child interaction was significantly more positive between children and their "social mothers" in lesbian couples than between children and fathers in the other two groups. Children in all three sets of families, boys as well as girls, expressed stronger positive feelings for their biological mothers than for the mothers' partners.

Although research on same-sex parenting has been criticized for methodological limitations (Cameron, 1999; Lerner & Nagai, 2001), the existing studies on families with same-sex parents have revealed no significant effects on the quality of parent–child interaction, on children's peer relations, or on the child's own sexual identity (Golombok et al., 1997; Patterson, 2000). Children who grow up with same-sex parents have more flexible views about gender roles, are more tolerant of homosexuality and unconventional family arrangements, and are somewhat more likely to engage in sexual experimentation with members of their own sex. However, they are no more likely than members of the population as a whole to identify as lesbian or gay (Golombok, 2001; Golombok et al., 1997).

The importance of legal marriage

Recent societal changes reflecting a decline in legal marriages are of increasing interest to researchers and policy makers. For example, U.S. 2000 census data confirm that the number of unmarried partners living together has increased 72% over the past decade (mainly opposite-sex couples). Married couples with children now account for less than a quarter of all U.S. households. Historically in the United States and in many societies, the nuclear family has not been just a social but a legal arrangement, and so-called illegitimate children have been seen as disadvantaged (e.g., Collishaw, Maughan, & Pickles, 1998). Comparisons of the children of cohabiting versus married couples thus help to specify the key elements in the lives of nuclear families that benefit children. If what is important is the presence of same- and opposite-sex parents, and the complementary skills and contributions of fathers and mothers, legal status should not matter. Alternatively, marriage as a social institution may have important effects on parents' behavior and children's lives.

Little evidence addresses this issue (see Seltzer, 2000). Many studies do not distinguish between those two-parent families where the parents are married and those where the parents' relationship has not been legalized; others do not distinguish between single mothers who are or are not living with the fathers of their children. The sociological emphasis on household structure, rather than interpersonal relationships, has identified very heterogeneous groups of cohabiting couples (Seltzer, 2000). However, many of the children who are officially born to single mothers have parents who live in stable partnerships. For example, in an urban community sample of children born in South London in the late 1980s, 63% of the mothers were married, 8% were single, and 29% were cohabiting at the time of the child's birth (Hay et al., 2001). Similar proportions were found in a large British community sample, in which there were no clear differences between married and cohabiting families (Dunn et al., 1998). However, cohabiting families are more likely than married ones to experience negative life events that could facilitate negative outcomes in children (Schmuecker, 1998). Cohabiting couples are also more likely than married ones to separate (Seltzer, 2000), though it is not clear that the legal status of the prior partnership adds to the risks associated with parental separation.

The importance of genetic relatedness

Tests of a third implication of the nuclear family model – that *biological* parents are advantageous for children – are provided by studies comparing nuclear families with stepfamilies, and with families using reproductive technologies.

Stepparent families.   The strongest claim regarding the importance of genetic relatedness is provided by Daly and Wilson (2000), who present an evolutionary argument for the adaptive value of biological parents raising their children. They support this theory with evidence of increased rates of abuse for children who live with stepparents. Thus, in this view, children are actually in danger if they live with *genetically unrelated* parental figures.

Other studies indicate that the introduction of a stepparent may solve some problems associated with divorce but creates others (Deater-Deckard & Dunn, 1999; Hetherington & Stanley-Hagen, 1999b). For example, stepchildren find it difficult to balance their relationships with biological parents and stepparents; this balancing act appears to be especially difficult for girls living with fathers and stepmothers, particularly if they spend greater amounts of time with their noncustodial biological mothers (Clingempeel & Segal, 1986). In general, meta-analyses have suggested that stepparenting has stronger negative effects on girls than on boys (Amato & Keith, 1991; Hetherington & Stanley-Hagen, 1999b).

It is not always possible to disentangle the effects of genetic relatedness from the other factors associated with stepparenting. Stepparent families do not restore the conditions existing in the original family prior to divorce. For example, stepfamilies are not necessarily likely to enjoy higher income levels and social status than families headed by single parents (Deater-Deckard & Dunn, 1999). Stepfamilies may also be more likely than "intact" families to experience life events and stressful experiences. For example, one-parent families move house more frequently than original two-parent families, but stepparents move even more often (McLanahan & Teitler, 1999). Moving house can cause disruptions for children and parents, loss of support networks, adjustment to new schools for children and new jobs for parents.

It is not clear how much *additional* risk accrues when a child acquires a stepparent, which is an event that has usually been predated by exposure to marital conflict, separation of the parents, and the exigencies of life after divorce. In a large, representative New Zealand sample, 18 year olds who had grown up in stepfamilies were at elevated risk for juvenile offending, substance use, leaving school without qualifications, and early, promiscuous sexual relationships (Nicholson, Fergusson, & Horwood, 1999). However, when factors antecedent to the experience of stepparenting were taken into account, the odds ratios were no longer significant.

Families who use fertility treatments. Currently there is great interest in a group of families that might be characterized as "stepparenting from birth," that is, those with children born through donor insemination or egg donation. In these procedures, one of the parents is not the biological parent of the child, in contrast to in vitro fertilization, where both parents are genetically related to the child. Unlike stepfamilies formed through remarriage, families formed through reproductive technology provide an opportunity for examining the influences of biological and *perceived* biological relatedness without the confounding effects of previous family disruptions.

In a study of families who had attended fertility clinics in the UK, with a comparison group of adoptive families, genetic relatedness affected dimensions of the parent–child relationship (Golombok, Murray, Brinden, & Abdalla, 1999). Mothers expressed less warmth when the child was not genetically related to the father, even when the mother herself was the child's biological parent. Parents reported more cooperation in disciplining the child when there was a genetic relationship between the child and the father. Mothers who had experienced egg donation had more serious disputes with their children than did adoptive mothers; thus mother–child conflict was more intense if the father but not the mother was genetically related to the child. No effects of genetic relatedness were found on measures of the children's behavioral problems. However, some emotional problems and issues regarding identity may later emerge, given the fact that the circumstances of the child's conception were shrouded in secrecy. None of the families who had used donor insemination and only one of those who had used egg donation had told the child that one of the parents was really a stepparent.

The studies of stepparent and donor insemination families draw attention to the complexities of the different roles and relationships within families, and the changing dynamics of family life over time, issues of major concern to family systems theory.

The Family Systems Model

In family systems theory (e.g., Cox & Paley, 1997), families are seen as dynamic wholes. This perspective emphasizes the multifaceted roles played by all family members (not just parents), including children themselves. Considerable attention is given to the dynamics of conflict and alliances across different relationships in the family. Furthermore, the idea that a family is a dynamic system incorporates the notion of change, as well as structure. Thus family systems perspectives are especially applicable to the study of the changing roles in separating or divorcing families, the balancing of roles within both heterosexual and same-sex couples, and the new alliances and animosities that emerge when families are blended together upon remarriage.

Although it seems apparent that family arrangements directly affect all family members, empirical research is rarely guided by systems theory. However, some findings in the literature on divorce provide examples of how relationships influence other relationships within a changing family system. Three illustrative examples include the effects of conflict in one relationship on the quality of other relationships in the family, children's effects on parents, and the importance of sibling relationships within the family system.

Effects of the marital relationship on parent–child relationships

Although divorce may in some circumstances place parents at risk for poor parenting, it can also provide the opportunity for increased parent mental health and better parenting through the reduction of conflict between the parents. Much research has demonstrated the negative effects of marital conflict on children (e.g., Fincham, 1998). Even the earliest relationships between parents and their infants are affected by marital conflict; taking individual differences in parents' psychological adjustment into account, both mothers and fathers interact more positively with very young infants when they are in close, confiding marriages (Cox, Owen, Lewis, & Henderson, 1989). Strong evidence for a *causal link* between conflict and parenting was provided by Kitzmann (2000), who manipulated spousal conflict experimentally, and then examined its effects on the couples' 6- to 8-year-old sons. After quarreling with their partners, fathers were less supportive of their sons, and the couples were less democratic in their parenting.

The long-term negative effects of divorce on children are primarily due to the nature of the couple's relationship prior to and following the divorce, rather than to parental absence and the change in family structure. High amounts of conflict prior to divorce mediate the link between divorce and negative child outcomes (e.g., Amato & Booth, 1996; Shaw et al., 1999). To the extent that divorce improves the custodial parent's mental state and frees children from an atmosphere of conflict, there are positive opportunities as well as risks in divorced families (see Morrison, 1995).

Children's *perceptions* of conflict between their parents may be more important than the actual extent of conflict that occurs (e.g., Harold & Conger, 1997). Furthermore, the effects of marital conflict on children's mental health are not always direct, but rather mediated by the parent–child relations; whether marital conflict has direct or indirect effects depends on whether the child in question is a girl or a boy (Paley, Conger, & Harold, 2000). Thus an understanding of gender differences in response to family change may be clarified by analyses of the family system as a whole.

Children's effects on the marital relationship

The literature on marital conflict shows that a couple's relationship affects their children's development; but children also influence parents. In divorced families, a cycle of influence could be observed in which problematic childrearing behaviors were followed by negative behaviors in children which, in turn, were followed by decreases in parents' psychological adjustment (Hetherington, Cox, & Cox, 1982). The fact that children's behavioral problems predate divorce (e.g., Amato & Booth, 1996) suggests that problems in children place additional strain on the relationship between the two parents, thus increasing the risk of divorce. Furthermore, vulnerable children may place extra strains on their parents; children who are high in impulsivity are especially likely to develop problems in response to divorce (Lengua, Wolchick, Sandler, & West, 2000).

The importance of siblings

Family systems often include more than one child. Family arrangements following upon divorce and stepparenting may have different effects on older and younger siblings in a family (e.g., Dunn et al., 1998). Patterns of conflict in the parent–child relationship may be mirrored in sibling interaction (Hay, Vespo, & Zahn-Waxler, 1998). Furthermore, the quality of relationships with siblings may either ameliorate or exacerbate the effects of parental conflict and divorce. For example, it has been observed that same-sex pairs of siblings become especially close after divorce (Kier & Lewis, 1999). It also seems likely that discordant sibling relationships, or alliances made by parents with one or another child, might add to the levels of family distress that accompany divorce and remarriage. Relationships between unrelated siblings may also contribute to problems in stepfamilies (Dunn et al., 1998).

The Social Networks Model

Finally, some developmental theorists see family relationships, including those between parents and children, in the context of the greater social network in which the family resides (e.g., Dunn, 1993; Lewis, 1982; Rheingold & Eckerman, 1975). Peers, teachers, and other adults affect children's lives, and may serve to buffer children against the deleterious effects of family conflict, separation, and divorce. The phenomenon of "social support" has usually been studied as an individualistic variable, presumed to affect an individual's parenting skills. In contrast, the social networks model holds that it is necessary to study children's various relationships directly, so that the social and cultural framework surrounding family life may be understood. Cultural and subcultural arrangements such as child rearing in the context of extended families, fostering, and communal child rearing deserve study. Furthermore, parents sometimes function as "gatekeepers" of their children's networks, and the boundary with the outside world is more permeable in some types of families than others.

Multiple influences on children's lives

Relationships with individuals other than primary caregivers affect children's development (see Nash & Hay, 1993). Positive relationships with grandmothers, siblings, other relatives, friends, and other adults have been found to buffer the effects of family turmoil (Florsheim, Tolan, & Gorman-Smith, 1998; Gadsden, 1999; Hunter, Pearson, Ialongo, & Killam, 1999; Werner, 1995; Wyman et al., 1999). However, the availability of resilience-promoting social networks for single mothers and their children is often overlooked (Brody et al., 1999), and the impact of single parents' economic distress may be reduced with access to high quality school and community support programs (Guttman & Eccles, 1999). Support from friends and extended family members, including nonpaternal men (Coley, 1998), and families' community involvement are positively associated with children's functioning (Wyman et al., 1999).

Different types of families have different types of networks

The social support available to families and the type of networks they have vary across family structures. For example, the children of divorced women who entered into lesbian partnerships had more frequent and more positive contact with their noncustodial, biological fathers than did a comparison group of children whose divorced mothers remained heterosexual (Patterson, 1992).

Single parents may draw heavily on relationships with other extended family members and friends (Amato, 1995; Barbarin, 1999; Gadsden, 1999; McLanahan & Teitler, 1999). However, Hetherington (1998) suggested that support and involvement from extended family members, especially the lost parent's family, is greater following death of a parent than divorce. On the other hand, grandparents, and especially grandfathers, forge closer ties to grandchildren whose mothers are divorced and bringing up their children on their own (Clingempeel, Colyar, Brand, & Hetherington, 1992). Grandparents are less willing to "interfere" in the child rearing of married daughters, a judgment in line with research findings. Family relationships and social networks often promote positive outcomes for the children of single mothers (Brody et al., 1999; Wyman et al., 1999), but the close involvement of grandparents in married families can lead to stress and conflict, as in the case of Muslim mothers living in extended families in Britain (Sonuga-Barke, Mistry, & Qureshi, 1998).

Communal rearing

In some cultural and ideological contexts, children are reared communally. The greater tolerance of unconventional behavior and flexibility of views about gender roles shown by the children of same-sex parents (Golombok et al., 1997) also characterizes children who have been raised in communal arrangements, either in households shared for economic reasons or ideologically based communes (Weisner & Wilson-Mitchell, 1990). The nuclear family model would imply that the presence of multiple caregivers might disrupt identification with one's same-sex parent and therefore might produce confused sexual identities. This does not appear to have occurred in the sample of children born in varying circumstances in the early 1970s (the Family Lifestyles Project, Weisner & Wilson-Mitchell, 1990).

The study of communally reared children also poses critical questions for the attachment model. Issues about attachment relationships loom large in many other studies of children reared communally along a gradient that includes paid childcare (e.g., NICHD, 1997) and institutional upbringing (Hodges & Tizard, 1989). Such studies draw attention to the effects of quality of care in communal arrangements and also raise the methodological issue of the appropriateness of conventional assessments in different types of families. Additionally, they question a central tenet of attachment theory, that is, the formative influence of the early primary attachment relationship. A recent follow-up of the Family Lifestyles Project indicated that attachment security was associated with economic and social factors and later life events. Furthermore, there were no significant effects of family type on the distribution of secure and insecure attachments (though that might be due to lack of statistical power). Rather, later experiences seemed more important than early ones and the negative impact of divorce on security of attachment was no different in conventional and unconventional families (Hamilton, 2000).

The studies of communal rearing extend Bowlby's (1969) emphasis on the importance of *monotropic* attachments to primary caregivers (see Nash, 1988). Israeli kibbutz-reared children have qualitatively distinct attachments to mothers, fathers, and familiar caregivers, each relationship predicting different dimensions of the child's later functioning (Oppenhein, Sagi, & Lamb, 1988). Decades of research on kibbutz children yield very little evidence for ill effects, save a cautionary note regarding children who spend nights as well as days away from their biological parents (Aviezer, van Ijzendoorn, Sagi, & Schuengel, 1994).

Extended families

The nuclear family in the Western world is a phenomenon that is rooted in place and time. In other places and at other times, extended families are the norm. For example, in the Sudan, the nuclear family is a relatively new invention, associated with urbanization, social isolation, and disruption of important extended family ties. Children in the Sudan who lived in nuclear families had *more* psychological problems than those who lived in traditional extended families (El Hassan El Awad, & Sonuga-Barke, 1992). Grandmother involvement was the strongest predictor of normal social and emotional adjustment in the children. Similarly, schoolchildren in Korea who lived in extended families fared better than those who lived in nuclear families (Hwang & St. James-Roberts, 1998).

The comparison of nuclear and extended family structures thus needs to be undertaken with reference to the values and ideals of different cultures. For example, the importance of grandmothers for children growing up in the Sudan (El Hassan Al Awad & Sonuga-Barke, 1992) may partly derive from the twofold role of the grandmother (*haboba*) in that culture. She provides social and practical support to inexperienced mothers and transmits cultural values to the new generation. The Sudanese nuclear families were shorn of much needed practical support and a culturally valued childrearing mechanism. Thus, in general, the social networks perspective does not just identify complex structures and webs of relationships, but also the values and cultural ideals that underpin child rearing in different communities.

Conclusions

Current research on family arrangements is fraught with conceptual and methodological problems (Table 13.1), but has nonetheless advanced considerably since the early days of studies of "father absence." Most differences between family types are accounted for by a host of mediating and moderating variables (see Baron & Kenny, 1986), including economic, social, and psychological factors (Clarke-Stewart et al., 2000; Dunn et al., 1998; Nicholson et al., 1999). The wide adoption of multivariate modeling procedures and a concomitant tendency to report effect sizes, not just significant group differences, has uncovered important mechanisms and demonstrated the rather modest contribution of family structure variables to children's social development.

We concur with other reviewers' recommendations to concentrate attention on underlying processes responsible for variation within as well as across different family arrangements (e.g., Hetherington & Stanley-Hagan, 1999a). Such process-orientated research has important implications for public policy and clinical interventions. At the same time, we have argued that the research on family arrangements is of great importance for "mainstream" theories of social development. The topic poses important challenges for each perspective on social development, but also highlights prospects for synthesis across different theories.

For example, the study of divorce shows that attachment relationships do not always remain as they were in infancy, but rather change, for better or worse, in the face of changing family arrangements. Furthermore, studies of children reared communally draw attention to the qualitatively different consequences for social development that derive from different attachment relationships. These data extend attachment theory beyond Bowlby's original speculations (see also Waters & Cummings, 2000). At the same time, the emphasis on cognitive representations and emotional regulation that derives from attachment theory provides a theoretical language in which some consequences of family disruption can be analyzed.

The studies of different family arrangements provide considerable support for the parenting model, as they demonstrate the importance of parenting style rather than family structure for many aspects of social development (Hetherington & Stanley-Hagan, 1999a). At the same time the qualitatively unique features of different family arrangements, and the clear evidence for the importance of social, economic, and ideological pressures on parents' own feelings of competence and self-esteem, extend the perspective beyond classic typologies and standardized assessments. Most critically, studies of different family arrangements have challenged the notion of parenting as a gender-neutral activity, and drawn attention to the differential contributions made by fathers and mothers, both when living together and after marriages have been dissolved.

Although it is never safe to accept null hypotheses, particularly when the power to reject the alternative hypothesis is far too low, the studies of children living in nontraditional arrangements do not show dramatic changes in gender development or psychological adjustment. The effects so far identified seem to be rather subtle ones. At the same time, research on the children in stepfamilies and those born with the aid of reproductive technologies draw attention to the importance of genetic relatedness, or at least attributions made on the basis of genetic relatedness. The meager findings with respect to cohabiting families remind us that children may be affected by marriage as a social institution as well as by their parents' overt behavior. Thus studies of family arrangements have both revived and extended the classic nuclear family model, in some cases refuting its strong claims, but, most importantly, drawing attention to the importance of parent–child relationships, not just the individual characteristics of particular parents (see also Russell, this volume; Parke this volume).

Studies of changing families, in terms of divorce and remarriage, offer some of the strongest empirical support that exists for the abstract principles outlined by family systems theorists. Family alliances and coalitions, and the effects of relationships on other relationships, are thrown into sharp relief in the context of divorce and remarriage. Studies of extended families and those that adopt communal rearing are also likely to provide data that challenge and extend current versions of family systems theory. Most importantly, family systems theory reminds us that families do change, and children do exert influence on other members of their families.

Finally, the study of different family arrangements in the context of wider social networks lends much-needed empirical support to this broader view of influences on social development. The social networks perspective has often been offered as a critical framework, providing a theoretical alternative to attachment theory (Dunn, 1993; Lewis, 1982; Nash & Hay, 1993; Rheingold & Eckerman, 1975). As an organizing framework for the analysis of children's social development in the context of different family arrangements, with access to different networks and cultural institutions, these critiques take more solid form as a developmental theory in its own right.

The study of family arrangements encourages constructive synthesis across these various theoretical perspectives. The findings call for a unified theory, which would emphasize emotion and representation; variation across individual families; unique properties of particular relationships, including those with siblings (Sulloway, 1995) and peers (Harris, 1998) as well as with parents; relationships amongst those relationships; and attention to the social and cultural context in which families reside. In other words, we require a general theory of social development, the like of which has not been seen since the rise of social learning theory in the mid-twentieth century, when child rearing was assumed to be a topic of fundamental importance for developmental psychology as a whole. The behaviorist assumptions of classic social learning theory are no longer adequate to explain social development, but a full understanding of the ways in which families affect children's development will certainly require a synthesis of existing mini-theories.

We hope that the next wave of research on children and their families will focus on mutual activities, beliefs, traditions, and individual ways of dealing with the inevitable dilemmas of family life in all sorts and conditions of families. We hope to see more emphasis on the web of important relationships that surround children and their families. Newer statistical procedures such as hierarchical linear modeling allow us to study family influences at different levels of analysis. Thus the theoretical synthesis proposed here is testable. It is surely time to move beyond the static and methodologically inadequate comparisons of different family structures that dominated research on this topic in the late twentieth century.

References

Amato, P. R. (1993). Children's adjustment to divorce: Theories, hypotheses, and empirical support. *Journal of Marriage and the Family, 55,* 23–54.

Amato, P. R. (1995). Single-parent households as settings for children's development, well-being, and attainment: A social network/resources perspective. *Sociological Studies of Children, 7,* 19–47.

Amato, P. R., & Booth, A. (1996). A prospective study of divorce and parent–child relationships. *Journal of Marriage and the Family, 58,* 356–365.

Amato, P. R., & Keith, B. (1991). Parental divorce and the well-being of children: A meta-analysis. *Psychological Bulletin, 110,* 26–46.

Aviezer, O., Van Ijzendoorn, M. H., Sagi, A., & Schuengel, C. (1994). "Children of the dream" revisited: 70 years of collective early child care in Israeli kibbutzim. *Psychological Bulletin, 116,* 99–116.

Barbarin, O. A. (1999). Social risks and psychological adjustment: A comparison of African American and South African children. *Child Development, 70,* 1348–1359.

Baron, R. E., & Kenny, D. A. (1986). The moderator–mediator variable distinction in social psychological research: Conceptual, strategic, and statistical considerations. *Journal of Personality and Social Psychology, 51,* 1173–1182.

Baumrind, D. (1989). Rearing competent children. In W. Damon (Ed.), *Child development today and tomorrow* (pp. 349–378). San Francisco: Jossey-Bass.

Bowlby, J. (1958). The nature of the child's tie to his mother. *International Journal of Psychoanalysis, 39,* 350–373.

Bowlby, J. (1969). *Attachment.* New York: Basic Books.

Boyle, M.H., & Pickles, A. (1997). Maternal depressive symptoms and ratings of emotional disorder symptoms in children and adolescents. *Journal of Child Psychology and Psychiatry, 38,* 981–992.

Braeways, A., Ponjaert, I., Van Hall, E. V., & Golombok, S. (1997). Donor insemination: Child development and family functioning in lesbian mother families. *Human Reproduction, 12,* 1349–1359.

Brody, G. H., Flor, D. L., & Gibson, N. M. (1999). Linking maternal efficacy beliefs, developmental goals, parenting practices, and child competence in rural single-parent African American families. *Child Development, 70,* 1197–1208.

Brown, G. W., & Harris, T. O. (1989). *Life events and illness.* New York: Guilford Press.

Bugental, D. B., & Johnston, C. (2000). Parental and child cognitions in the context of the family. *Annual Review of Psychology, 51,* 315–344.

Cabrera, N. J, Tamis-LeMonda, C. S., Bradley, R. H., Hofferth, S., & Lamb, M. E. (2000). Fatherhood in the twenty-first century. *Child-Development, 71,* 127–136.

Cairns, R. (1979). *Social development.* San Francisco: Freeman.

Cameron, P. (1999). Homosexual parents: Testing common sense. *Psychological Reports, 85,* 282–322.

Cherlin, A. J., Furstenberg, F. F., Chase-Landale, P. L., Kiernan, K., Robbins, P., Morrison, D., & Teitler, J. (1991). Longitudinal studies of effects of divorce on children in Great Britain and the United States. *Science, 252,* 1386–1389.

Clarke-Stewart, K. A., Vandell, D. L., McCartney, K., Owen, M. T., & Booth, C. (2000). Effects of parental separation and divorce on very young children. *Journal of Family Psychology, 14,* 304–326.

Cleveland, H. H., Wiebe, R. P., van den Oord, E. J. C. G., & Rowe, D. C. (2000). Behavior problems among children from different family structures: The influence of genetic self-selection. *Child Development, 71,* 733–751.

Clingempeel, W. G., Colyar, J. J., Brand, E., & Hetherington, E. M. (1992). Children's relationships with maternal grandparents: A longitudinal study of family structure and pubertal status effects. *Child Development, 63,* 1404–1422.

Clingempeel, W. G., & Segal, S. (1986). Stepparent–stepchild relationships and the psychological adjustment of children in stepmother and stepfather families. *Child Development, 57,* 474–484.

Coley, R. L. (1998). Children's socialization experiences and functioning in single-mother households: The importance of fathers and other men. *Child Development, 69,* 219–230.

Collishaw, S., Maughan, B., & Pickles, A. (1998) Infant adoption: Psychosocial outcomes in adulthood. *Social Psychiatry and Psychiatric Epidemiology, 33,* 57–65.

Cowan, P. A., Powell, D., & Cowan, C. P. (1998). Parenting interventions: A family systems perspective. In W. Damon (Ed.), *Handbook of child psychology, Vol. 4* (pp. 3–72) New York: Wiley.

Cox, M. J., Owen, M. T., Lewis, J. M., & Henderson, V. K. (1989). Marriage, adult adjustment, and early parenting. *Child Development, 60,* 1015–1024.

Cox, M. J., & Paley, B. (1997). Families as systems. *Annual Review of Psychology, 48,* 243–267.

Cummings, E. M., & Davies, P. (1994). Maternal depression. *Journal of Child Psychology and Psychiatry.*

Daly, M., & Wilson, M. (2000). Not quite right. *American Psychologist, 55,* 679–680.

Deater-Deckard, K., & Dunn, J. (1999). Multiple risks and adjustment in young children growing up in different family settings: A British community study of stepparent, single mother, and nondivorced families. In E. M. Hetherington (Ed.), *Coping with divorce, single parenting, and remarriage: A risk and resiliency perspective.* (pp. 47–64). Mahwah, NJ: Erlbaum.

DeGarmo, D. S., Forgatch, M. S., & Martinez, C. R. Jr. (1999) Parenting of divorced mothers as a link between social status and boys' academic outcomes: Unpacking the effects of socioecomic status. *Child Development, 70,* 1231–1245.

Downey, D. B., & Powell, B. (1993). Do children in single-parent households fare better living with the same-sex parents? *Journal of Marriage and the Family, 55,* 55–71.

Dunn, J. (1993). *Young children's close relationships: Beyond attachment.* London: Sage.

Dunn, J., Deater-Deckard, K., Pickering, K., & O'Connor, T. G. (1998). Children's adjustment and prosocial behavior in step-, single-parent, and non-stepfamily settings: Findings from a community study. *Journal of Child Psychology and Psychiatry, 39,* 1083–1095.

El Hassan Al Awad, A. M., & Sonuga-Barke, E. J. S. (1992). Childhood problems in a Sudanese City: A comparison of extended and nuclear families. *Child Development, 63,* 906–914.

Emory, R. E., Waldron, M. C., Aaron, J., & Kitzmann, K. M. (1999). Delinquent behavior, future divorce or nonmarital childbearing, and externalizing behavior among offspring: A 14-year prospective study. *Journal of Family Psychology, 13,*

Fincham, F. (1998). Child development and marital relations. *Child Development, 69,* 543–574.

Florsheim, P., Tolan, P., & Gorman-Smith, D. (1998). Family relationships, parenting practices, the availability of male family members, and the behavior of inner-city boys in single-mother and two-parent families. *Child Development, 69,* 1437–1447.

Freud, S. (1938). (J. Strachey, Tr.). *An outline of psychoanalysis.* London: Hogarth.

Fry, P. S., & Addington, J. (1984). Professionals' negative expectations of boys from father-headed single-parent families: Implications for the training of child-care professionals. *British Journal of Developmental Psychology, 2,* 337–346.

Gadsden, V. L. (1999). Black families in intergenerational and cultural perspective. In M. E. Lamb (Ed.), *Parenting and child development in "nontraditional" families* (pp. 221–246). Mahwah, NJ: Erlbaum.

Gately, D., & Schwebel, A. I. (1992). Favorable outcomes in children after parental divorce. *Journal of Divorce and Remarriage, 18,* 57–78.

Golombok, S. (2001). Paper presented to the School of Psychology, Cardiff University.

Golombok, S., Murray, C., Brinsden, P., & Abdalla, H. (1999). Social vs. biological parenting: Family functioning and the socioemotional development of children conceived by egg or sperm donation. *Journal of Child Psychology and Psychiatry. 40,* 519–527.

Golombok, S., Spencer, A., & Rutter, M. (1983). Children in lesbian and single-parent households: Psychosexual and psychiatric appraisal. *Journal of Child Psychology and Psychiatry, 24,* 551–572.

Golombok, S., Tasker, F., & Murray, C. (1997). Children raised in fatherless families from infancy: Family relationships and the socioemotional development of children of lesbian and single heterosexual mothers. *Journal of Child Psychology and Psychiatry, 28,* 783–791.

Gutman, L. M., & Eccles, J. S. (1999). Financial strain, parenting behaviors, and adolescents' achievement: Testing model equivalence between African American and European American single- and two-parent families. *Child Development, 70,* 1464–1476.

Hamilton, C. E. (2000). Continuity and discontinuity in attachment from infancy through adolescence. *Child Development, 71,* 690–694.

Hanson, T. L., McLanahan, S. S., & Thomson, E. (1998). *Social Science Research, 27,* 329–349.

Harold, G. T., & Conger, R. (1997). Marital conflict and adolescent distress: The role of adolescent awareness. *Child Development, 68,* 333–350.

Harris, J. R. (1998). *The nurture assumption.* New York: Touchstone.

Harris, K. M., Furstenberg, F. F., & Marmer, J. K. (1998). Paternal involvement with adolescents in intact families: The influence of fathers over the life course, *Demography, 35,* 201–216.

Hart, S., Field, T., Jones, N., & Yando, R. (1999). Intrusive and withdrawn behavior of mothers with their infants and boyfriends. *Journal of Child Psychology and Psychiatry, 40,* 239–245.

Hart, C. H., Nelson, D. A., Robinson, C. C., Olsen, S. F., & McNeilly-Choque, M. K. (1998). Overt and relational aggression in Russian nursery-school-age children: Parenting style and marital linkages. *Developmental Psychology, 34,* 687–697.

Hay, D. F., Pawlby, S., Sharp, D., Asten, P., Mills, A., & Kumar, R. (2001). Intellectual problems in 11-year-old children whose mothers had postnatal depression. *Journal of Child Psychology and Psychiatry, 42,* 871–889.

Hay, D. F., Pawlby, S., Sharp, D., Schmuecker, G., Mills, A., Allen, H., & Kumar, R. (1999) Parents' judgements about young children's problems: Why mothers and fathers might disagree yet still predict later outcomes. *Journal of Child Psychology and Psychiatry, 40,* 1249–1258.

Hay, D. F., Vespo, J. E., & Zahn-Waxler, C. (1998) Young children's quarrels with their siblings and mothers: Links with maternal depression and bipolar illness. *British Journal of Developmental Psychology, 16,* 519–538.

Hernandez, D. J. (1997). Child development and the social demography of childhood. *Child Development, 68,* 149–169.

Herzog, E., & Sudia, C. E. (1973). Children in fatherless families. In B. M. Caldwell & H. N. Riccuiti (Eds.), *Review of child development research. Vol. 3. Child development and social policy.*

Chicago: University of Chicago Press.

Hetherington, E. M. (1998). What matters? What does not? Five perspectives on the association between marital transitions and children's adjustment. *American Psychologist, 167–184.*

Hetherington, E. M., & Clingempeel. W. G. (1992). Coping with marital transitions. *Monographs of the Society for Research in Child Development, 57, Serial No. 227.*

Hetherington, E. M., Cox, M., & Cox, R. (1982). Effects of divorce on parents and children. In M. Lamb (Ed.), *Nontraditional families: Parenting and child development* (pp. 233–288). Hillsdale, NJ: Erlbaum.

Hetherington, E. M., & Stanley-Hagan, M. M. (1999a). The adjustment of children with divorced parents: A risk and resiliency perspective. *Journal of Child Psychology and Psychiatry, 40,* 129–140.

Hetherington, E. M., & Stanley-Hagan, M. M. (1999b). Stepfamilies. In M. E. Lamb (Ed.), *Parenting and child development in "nontraditional" families* (pp. 137–159). Mahwah, NJ: Erlbaum.

Hodges, J., & Tizard, B. (1989). Social and family relationships of ex-institutional adolescents. *Journal of Child Psychology and Psychiatry, 30,* 77–97.

Hunter, A. G., Pearson, J. L., Ialongo, N. S., & Kellam, S. G. (1998). Parenting alone to multiple caregivers: Child care and parenting arrangements in Black and White urban families. *Family Relations, 47,* 343–353.

Hwang, H. J., & St. James-Roberts, I. (1998). Emotional and behavioral problems in primary school children from nuclear and extended families in Korea. *Journal of Child Psychology and Psychiatry, 39,* 973–979.

Isley, S. L., O'Neil, R., Clatfelter, D., & Parke, R. (1999). Parent and child expressed affect and children's social competence: Modeling direct and indirect pathways. *Developmental Psychology, 35,* 547–560.

Kier, C., & Lewis, C. (1999) Preschool sibling interaction in separated and married families: Are same-sex pairs or older sisters more sociable? *Journal of Child Psychology and Psychiatry, 58,* 191–201.

Kitzmann, K. M. (2000). Effects of marital conflict on subsequent triadic family interactions and parenting. *Developmental Psychology, 36,* 3–13.

Lengua, L. J., Wolchik, S. A., Sandler, I. N., & West, S. G. (2000). The addictive and interactive effects of parenting and temperament in predicting problems of children of divorce. *Journal of Clinical Child Psychology, 29,* 232–244.

Lerner, R., & Nagai, A. (2001). *No basis: What the studies don't tell us about same-sex parenting.* Washington, DC: Ethics and Public Policy Center.

Lewis, M. (1982). The social network systems model: toward a theory of social development. In T. Field (Ed.), *Review of human development, vol. 1* (pp. 180–209). New York: Wiley.

Lewis, M., Feiring, C., & Rosenthal, S. (2000). Attachment over time. *Child Development, 71,* 707–720.

Maccoby, E. E. (2000) Parenting and its effects on children: On reading and misreading behavior genetics. *Annual Review of Psychology, 51,* 1–27.

Main, M., Kaplan, A., & Cassidy, J. (1985) Security in infancy, childhood and adulthood: A move to the level of representation. In I. Bretherton & E. Waters (Eds.), *Growing points in attachment theory and research. Monographs of the Society for Research in Child Development, 50(1–2), Serial No. 209,* 66–104.

McGroder, S. M. (2000). Parenting among low-income African American single mothers with pre-school-age children: Patterns, predictors, and developmental correlates. *Child Development, 71,* 752–771.

McLanahan, S., & Teitler, J. (1999). The consequences of father absence. In M. E. Lamb (Ed.), *Parenting and child development in "nontraditional families."* (pp. 83–102).

Morrison, N. C. (1995). Successful single-parent families. *Journal of Divorce and Remarriage, 22,* 205–219.

Murray, L., & Cooper, P. (1997). *Postpartum depression and child development.* New York: Guilford Press.

Muzi, M. J. (2000). *The experience of parenting.* Upper Saddle River, NJ: Prentice Hall.

Nash, A. (1988). Ontogeny, phylogeny, and relationships. In S. Duck (Ed.), *Handbook of personal relationships* (pp. 121–141). Chichester, England: Wiley.

Nash, A., & Hay, D. F. (1993) Relationships in infancy as precursors and causes of later relationships and psychopathology. In D. F. Hay & A. Angold (Eds.), *Precursors and causes in development and psychopathology* (pp. 199–232). Chichester, England: Wiley,.

NICHD Early Child Care Research Network (1997). The effects of infant child care on infant–mother attachment security: Results of the NICHD Study of Early Child Care. *Child Development, 68,* 860–879.

Nicholson, J. M., Fergusson, D. M., & Horwood, L. (1999). Effects on later adjustment of living in a stepfamily during childhood and adolescence. *Journal of Child Psychology and Psychiatry, 40,* 405–416.

O'Connor, T. G., Caspi, A., De Fries, J. C., & Plomin, R. (2000). Are associations between parental divorce and children's adjustment genetically mediated? An adoption study. *Developmental Psychology, 36,* 429–437.

Office of National Statistics (2000). *Social Trends Pocketbook 2000 edition.* Newport, South Wales: Government Statistical Service.

Oppenhein, D., Sagi, A., & Lamb, M. E. (1988). Infant–adult attachments on the kibbutz and their relation to socioemotional development 4 years later. *Developmental Psychology, 24,* 427–433.

Paley, B., Conger, R. D., & Harold, G. T. (2000). Parents' affect, adolescent cognitive representations, and adolescent social development. *Journal of Marriage and the Family, 62,* 761–776.

Patterson, C. J. (1992) Children of lesbian and gay parents. *Child Development, 63,* 1025–1042.

Patterson, C. J. (2000). Family relationships of lesbians and gay men. *Journal of Marriage and the Family, 62,* 271–288.

Pyle, K. (2000). "The normal American family" as an interpretative structure of family life among grown children of Korean and Vietnamese immigrants. *Journal of Marriage and the Family, 62,* 240–255.

Rheingold, H. L., & Eckerman, C. O. (1975) Some proposals for unifying the study of social development. In M. Lewis & L. A. Rosenblum (Eds.), *Friendship and peer relations* (pp. 293–298). New York: Wiley.

Sagi, A., Lamb, M., & Gardner, W. (1986). Relations between strange situation behavior and stranger sociability among infants on Israeli kibbutzim. *Infant Behavior and Development, 9,* 271–282.

Scarr, S. (1992). Developmental theories for the 1990s: Development and individual differences. *Child Development, 63,* 1–19.

Schmuecker, G. A. (1998) Family influences on mothers' and their children's affect. Unpublished Ph.D. thesis, University of London.

Sears, R., Maccoby, E. E., & Levin, H. (1957). *Patterns of child rearing.* Evanston, IL: Row, Peterson.

Seltzer, J. A. (2000). Families formed outside of marriage. *Journal of Marriage and the Family, 62,* 1247–1268.

Shaw, D. S., Winslow, E. B., & Flanagan, C. (1999). A prospective study of the effects of marital status and family relations on young children's adjustment among African American and European American families. *Child Development, 70,* 742–755.

Sonuga-Barke, E. J. S., Mistry, M., & Qureshi, S. (1998). The mental health of Muslim mothers in extended families living in Britain: The impact of intergenerational disagreement on anxiety and depression. *British Journal of Clinical Psychology, 37,* 399–408.

Stevenson, M. R., & Black, K. N. (1988). Paternal absence and sex-role development: A meta-analysis. *Child Development, 59,* 793–814.

Sulloway, F. (1996). *Born to rebel: Birth order, family dynamics and creative lives.* New York: Pantheon.

Thomson, E., McLanahan, S., & Braun-Curtin, R. (1992). Family structure, gender, and parental socialization. *Journal of Marriage and the Family, 54,* 25–37.

Thompson, R. A., Lamb, M. E, & Estes, D. (1982). Stability of infant–mother attachment and its relationship to changing life circumstances in an unselected middle-class sample. *Child Development, 53,* 144–148.

Waite, L. J., & Gallagher, M. (2000). *The case for marriage.* New York: Doubleday.

Wallerstein, J. A., Lewis, J. M., & Blakeslee, S. (2000). *The unexpected legacy of divorce: A 25-year landmark study.* New York: Hyperion.

Waters. E., & Cummings, M. E. (2000). A secure base from which to explore close relationships. *Child Development, 71,* 164–172.

Weinraub, M., & Gringlas (1995). Single parenthood. In M. Bornstein (Ed.), *Handbook of parenting, Vol. 3: Status and social conditions of parenting* (pp. 65–87). Hillsdale, NJ: Erlbaum.

Weinraub, M., & Wolf, B. M. (1983). Effects of stress and social supports on mother–child interactions in single- and two-parent families. *Child Development, 54,* 1297–1311.

Weisner, T. S., & Wilson-Mitchell, J. E. (1990) Nonconventional family life-styles and sex-typing in six-year-olds. *Child Development, 61,* 1915–1933.

Werner, E. E. (1995). Resilience in development. *Current Directions in Psychological Science, 4,* 81–85.

Wyman, P. A., Cowen, E. L, Work, W. C., Hoyt-Meyers, L., Magnus, K. B., & Fagen, D. B. (1999). Caregiving and developmental factors differentiating young at-risk urban children showing resilient versus stress-affected outcomes: A replication and extension. *Child Development, 70,* 645–659.

Part V

The Peer Group

Studies over the past several decades have emphasized the importance of competent peer group functioning and healthy interpersonal relationships for current and later life success. Alternatively, childhood difficulties with peers have been concurrently and longitudinally related to a host of psychosocial challenges (e.g., Chapter 20; and Rubin, Bukowski, & Parker, 1998).

Peer acceptance and rejection is an integral aspect of group functioning in childhood. Research in this area has a rich tradition of empirical inquiry that has illuminated many interpersonal processes that lend themselves to adaptive or maladaptive peer group functioning. Shelley Hymel, Tracy Vaillancourt, Patricia McDougall, and Peter Renshaw conduct a comprehensive historical and methodological overview of sociometry, and consider a number of sociometric approaches as well as their psychometric adequacy. They go further by synthesizing recent research in ways that provide a clear picture of social cognitive, behavioral, and academic strengths and deficits that often accompany acceptance or rejection by peers. This information is invaluable to students, researchers, clinicians, and practitioners who are concerned with understanding how children adjust to peer group dynamics.

Although competent peer group functioning is important for successful life adjustment, close interpersonal relationships with family members, friends, and even enemies can help children develop self-awareness in ways that can round out social development for good or for ill. In this context, Willard Hartup and Maurissa Abaecassis overview research that helps us understand how and why, for example, friends come together on the basis of attraction and enemies maintain their relations on the basis of mutual antipathy. They point out how friendship expectations change across early and middle childhood development, why enmities between individuals form, and what mechanisms draw children together and pull them apart. Other intriguing questions are addressed. Is there any evidence that opposites attract? How do children sort themselves out into friendship dyads? What patterns of interaction are characteristic of friends and enemies? How are boys and girls friendships and antipathies similar or different? What are the developmental implications of having friends and enemies? Hartup and Abaecassis treat readers to an enlightening discussion of these and other issues.

Susan Denham, Maria von Salisch, Tjeert Olthof, Anita Kochanoff, and Sarah Caverly focus on emotional processes that underlie peer group behavior. They provide a comprehensive overview of the research that explicates interdependencies between emotional and social competence. Broadly speaking, more positive and less negative affect is associated with more friendly interactions with and acceptance by peers. Denham and colleagues go beyond this general conclusion and explicate the processes that feed into emotional expression in terms of how children understand, experience, and regulate emotion in ways that change across the early and middle childhood years. For example, as children mature, many learn to adopt an "emotional front" to save face and survive potential peer hostilities. Of additional interest are insights that Denham and colleagues provide for how parents can socialize emotional competence through emotion talk, empathy, and nonpunitive regulation strategies. They conclude with suggestions for future research that include a greater emphasis on cross-cultural comparisons and measurement enhancements.

What about children who withdraw from peer group interaction? Ken Rubin, Kim Burgess, and Robert Coplan overview a systematic line of theory and research that helps us not only better define social withdrawal, but also understand how various forms of solitude carry with them different psychological meanings. Withdrawal is conceptualized and empirically validated as an umbrella construct for reticence, solitary-passive, and solitary-active forms of solitude, each of which plays out differently in peer group interactions across early and middle childhood. Biological factors and socialization influences that may play a role in children isolating themselves from peers are considered in depth. For example, children who are prone to solitude may be so, due to physiological mechanisms that are reflected in EEG asymmetries, vagal tone, and cortisol readings (see also Fox, Henderson, Rubin, Calkins, & Schmidt, 2001). Insecure attachment relationships, intrusive and overprotective parenting may serve to maintain and further exacerbate these predispositions in ways that lead to maladaptive withdrawal from peers. How all this plays out in peer relations, friendships, and psychological adjustment in the short and long terms is carefully considered. The emerging picture for how withdrawn children fare is not good, and underscores the need for a greater emphasis on helping children who suffer from this difficulty. Rubin and colleagues conclude by outlining some promising approaches for intervention and future directions for research in this area.

References

Fox, N. A., Henderson, H. A., Rubin, K. H., Calkins, S. D. & Schmidt, L. A. (2001). Continuity and discontinuity of behavioral inhibition and exuberance: Psychobiological and behavioral influences across the first four years of life. *Child Development, 72*, 1–21.

Rubin, K. H., Bukowski, W., & Parker, J. G. (1998). Peer interactions, relationships, and groups. In N. Eisenberg (Ed.), *Handbook of child psychology: Vol. 3: Social, emotional, and personality development* (pp. 619–700). New York: Wiley.

14

Peer Acceptance and Rejection in Childhood

Shelley Hymel, Tracy Vaillancourt, Patricia McDougall, and Peter D. Renshaw

Human beings are social animals. We live in a complex social world in which we juggle a variety of social roles and operate in a number of different groups simultaneously. We have evolved a multifaceted system of social, political, and economic interdependence that demands both competitive and cooperative skills and respect for group differences. How do we develop the competencies necessary for success within social groups? What are the consequences if we fail to function effectively within the group? This chapter considers one aspect of group functioning in childhood: peer acceptance and rejection.

Social and developmental psychologists have increasingly acknowledged the critical role of peer relations for life success (e.g., Baumeister & Leary, 1995; Goleman, 1995; Harris, 1998; McDougall, Hymel, Vaillancourt, & Mercer, 2001), echoing arguments put forward years ago by Viennese psychiatrist, Jacob L. Moreno, in his classic 1934 work, *Who Shall Survive?*. Moreno argued that human behavior must be understood in terms of the social contexts and groups in which individuals function. His emphasis on group functioning was a departure from the zeitgeist of the 1930s (Bukowski & Cillessen, 1998), when human behavior was primarily understood in terms of internal mechanisms (e.g., psychoanalysis), and the "social environment" was defined in terms of external rewards and punishments (e.g., behaviorism). However, Renshaw (1981) points out that Moreno's work was part of a larger effort to understand children's social development, including studies of children's play (e.g., Parten, 1934) and friendships (e.g., Koch, 1933).

Moreno's work has contributed in critical ways to our understanding of childhood interpersonal development, and especially to *how* we study group functioning (see Bukowski & Cillessen, 1998; Cillessen & Bukowski, 2000a, Renshaw, 1981), with the establishment of a broad measurement approach called *sociometry*. Sociometric measures offer a unique window into how individuals are received within their social world, and the degree to which they are effectively integrated within a group. The history of sociometry and its methodological issues are the focus of the first part of this chapter. We consider a range of sociometric approaches, focusing on issues of administration, measurement, and psychometric adequacy. Next, we move from measurement to meaning, as we examine the correlates of peer acceptance and rejection. Finally, we move from meaning to mechanisms, considering the processes through which peer rejection is causally implicated in long-term adjustment outcomes. Throughout the chapter, we identify future research directions.

Sociometric Measures

Sociometry involves the measurement of interpersonal attraction among members of a specified group, providing a means of quantifying information about individuals within groups. Although peers can (and have) been used as sources of information on behavior and personality (Landau & Milich, 1990; Terry, 2000), sociometric indices of attraction are distinct from peer assessments of behavior (Asher & Hymel, 1981; Gronlund, 1959). This chapter focuses on indices of attraction rather than behavior.

The use of *peers as informants* in sociometric assessments is advantageous for several reasons (Asher & Hymel, 1981; Hymel & Rubin, 1985). First, peers provide an "insider" perspective, based on the perceptions of those who ultimately determine one's status. As such, peer evaluations have clear face validity, relative to more "outside" and potentially limited adult perspectives about what constitutes appropriate peer relations. For instance, with regard to the predictive utility of peer evaluations, Cowan, Pederson, Babigian, Izzo, and Trost (1973) found that peer sociometric evaluations predicted later mental health status better than did adult evaluations. A second advantage is that peer evaluations are based on varied experiences with a child, and can reflect low frequency but potentially significant events that contribute to social status and influence within the group. Moreover, peer evaluations are derived from multiple observers, who have different experiences and information about an individual child.

Moreno (1934) hypothesized three basic dimensions of interpersonal experience – attraction, repulsion, and indifference (see Cillessen & Bukowski, 2000b). These three responses could be used to reflect two different perspectives – how others view individuals in the group and how individuals view others in the group. Despite the complexity of Moreno's model, subsequent research has focused almost exclusively on how *individuals are perceived by group members*. Two different outcomes have been emphasized, one assessing the status of individuals within the group, and the other mapping group social structures (e.g., network analysis). The former, emphasizing the *individual* as the unit of analysis, has been far more prominent than the latter, emphasizing the *group* as the unit of analysis (see Bukowski & Cillessen, 1998), and constitutes the focus of this chapter.

Over the years, sociometric studies have emphasized only two of the dimensions proposed by Moreno (1934): attraction and repulsion. Positive peer evaluations assess *acceptance*, while negative peer evaluations assess *rejection* within the group. Four types of sociometric evaluations have been used. With *nomination* methods, participants select group members according to specified sociometric criteria (e.g., "Who do you like to play with?"). Alternatively, participants are asked to *rank order* or to *rate* others according to specified criteria (e.g., "How much do you like to play with _____?"). Finally, *paired comparison* methods require that participants evaluate all possible pairs of peers (e.g., "Which person would you rather play with?"). Across methods, peer evaluations are combined in particular ways to yield summary indices of acceptance, rejection, and/or overall status. Ranking and paired comparison methods are seldom used, owing primarily to the excessive administration time required, despite the advantage of ensuring equal consideration of all group members and providing more reliable sociometric indices, based on a larger number of data points (see Cohen & Van Tassel, 1978; Vaughn & Waters, 1981). Instead, researchers have typically relied on nomination or rating scale procedures, with considerable debate regarding the relative advantages of each (e.g., Hymel, 1983; Hymel & Rubin, 1985; Landau & Milich, 1990; Rubin et al., 1998; Terry & Coie, 1991).

Nomination measures

Historically and currently, peer acceptance and rejection have been measured most often using a nomination methodology. Classmates are asked to identify peers in terms of specified positive or negative criteria. The number or proportion of positive nominations received provides an index of attraction or acceptance, whereas the number or proportion of negative nominations received provides an index of repulsion or rejection within the group. Self-nominations are typically not permitted or not counted.

Although there are many ways to phrase nomination questions (see Terry, 2000), the most common forms include *direct preference* questions (e.g., "Name three classmates you like most/least") and *task-specific* or *indirect preference* questions (e.g., "Name three classmates you like/don't like to play with/sit next to"). Moreno (1934) strongly advocated for the use of concrete, task-specific sociometric criteria rather than abstract and multidimensional criteria such as "friendship" or "liking" that reflect different things for different people, thus resulting in summary measures that are not truly meaningful.

Nomination measures also differ in how responses are indicated by participants. Asking children to spontaneously name classmates has long been considered problematic in terms of its demands on children's memory. Thus, children are usually given a list of all group members and asked to circle or check off each nominee. With younger, preliterate children, researchers have used picture nomination procedures developed by McCandless and Marshall (1957), using photographs instead of names.

Efforts to refine nomination measures have dominated this literature, with debates regarding just what is being assessed and how to categorize individuals in terms of status. One long-standing debate concerns the use of *limited versus unlimited nominations*. Should the number of nominations be restricted or can children nominate as many people as they wish? Studies in the 1950s and 60s demonstrated little difference between limited versus unlimited nomination scores (see Terry, 2000), and argued for limited nominations (usually three to five), based on observations that children typically nominate only a few individuals, and because data collection and analysis is easier. However, Terry demonstrated that unlimited nomination data yields sociometric scores with superior distributional properties (e.g., less skewed, wider range of scores). Thus, limited nominations take less time, but unlimited nominations are more psychometrically sound.

A second debate concerns the use of *weighted versus unweighted scoring* procedures. With weighted scoring, more weight is given to first nominations than subsequent nominations (e.g., Dunnington, 1957; Hartup, Glazer, & Charlesworth, 1967; Vaughn & Waters, 1981), based on the assumption that first nominations indicate a better friend or a more extreme enemy. Such an assumption may be unwarranted, since differential weighting is not indicated in instructions and is undermined by the practice of providing lists of group members. Given high correlations between weighted and unweighted scores, most subsequent studies have relied on less time-consuming, unweighted scores (e.g., Coie, Dodge & Coppotelli, 1982; Terry & Coie, 1991).

Another debate involves the use of *absolute versus probabilistic criteria* for determining status classifications. Moreno (1934) distinguished "isolates" from "stars" on the basis of whether or not the individual received positive nominations from three or more group members (see also Gronlund, 1959). Bronfenbrenner (1943, 1944) argued for relative rather than absolute criteria to account for variations in group size, using statistical, probabilistic criteria (e.g., a "star" is accepted by peers at a rate greater than chance). Although support for the probability approach continues (e.g., Newcomb & Bukowski, 1983), few studies utilize statistical probabilities. Proportion scores or standardization procedures are typically used to account for variations in group size.

Perhaps the most important debate concerns the *dimensionality of acceptance and rejection*. Initially, acceptance and rejection scores were thought to be unidimensional – low scores on one meant high scores on the other. However, studies in the 1960s and 70s demonstrated that acceptance and rejection scores were only modestly negatively related (Moore & Updegraff, 1964; Roff, Sells, & Golden, 1972) or unrelated (Hartup et al., 1967), and were differentially correlated with behavior (e.g., Gronlund & Anderson, 1957; Hartup et al., 1967). These data were used to support arguments that acceptance and rejection scores tap different aspects of attraction.

Over the years, the assumption that acceptance and rejection represent two distinct dimensions led to different approaches to assessing status. Despite arguments for a more complex, two-dimensional system (e.g., Bronfenbrenner, 1944), many early studies emphasized only the positive dimension of acceptance (e.g., Dunnington, 1957; Northway, 1940; Thompson & Powell, 1951). These were criticized (e.g., Lemann & Solomon, 1952) for not distinguishing between "rejected" individuals (not accepted and openly rejected) and "neglected" children (not accepted but not openly rejected). Others proposed single indices of status based on combinations of acceptance and rejection scores (e.g., acceptance minus rejection, Hartup et al., 1967). They were criticized for not identifying children who were less visible, or for whom the peer group was "indifferent" in Moreno's terms, although efforts to include the dimension of "indifference" (Lemann & Solomon, 1952), or "notice" (Dunnington, 1957) were limited. It was Gronlund (1959) who provided the conceptual basis for currently used status classification schemes that considered acceptance and rejection as separate dimensions. His system distinguished four groups using absolute criteria: "stars" (many positive but few or no negative nominations); "rejected" children (few or no positive but many negative nominations); "neglected" children (few or no positive or negative nominations); and "controversial" children (many positive and many negative nominations).

Two decades later, Peery (1979) developed a sociometric taxonomy that considered acceptance and rejection as well as social visibility. Peery used acceptance and rejection scores to create two orthogonal dimensions – "social impact" (acceptance plus rejection) and "social preference" (acceptance minus rejection) – reminiscent of the earlier notions of "notice" and "status" (e.g., Dunnington, 1957; Hartup et al., 1967). These dimensions were used to distinguish four groups: popular (above the mean on both impact and preference); isolated (below the mean on both impact and preference); rejected (above the mean on impact, below the mean on preference); or amiable (above the mean on preference, below the mean on impact). Although the system was not used extensively, Peery provided a clearly specified, two-dimensional model for sociometric classification that reflected all three interpersonal experiences initially proposed by Moreno (attraction, repulsion, indifference).

Subsequent classification schemes (e.g., Coie et al., 1982; Newcomb & Bukowski, 1983) followed Peery (1979), by utilizing *social preference* (i.e., relative degree of liking by peers) and *social impact* scores (i.e., visibility within the peer group), as well as acceptance and rejection, with two notable improvements (Cillessen & Bukowski, 2000b). The newer schemes allowed for greater differentiation across individuals and for more extreme group classifications, using well-defined cut-offs based on either standard scores (Coie et al., 1982) or binomial probabilities (Newcomb & Bukowski, 1983). For example, Coie et al. defined rejected children as those receiving standardized social preference scores that were one standard deviation below the mean, standardized rejection scores above the mean, and standardized acceptance scores below the mean. Newcomb and Bukowski defined rejected children as those whose rejection scores were greater than would be expected by chance and whose acceptance scores were at or below the mean of the group. Despite these differences, most children (88%) are similarly classified across the two schemes (Terry & Coie, 1991), with approximately 12–13% of elementary children classified as popular among their peers, about 12–13% classified as rejected, 6–7% classified as neglected, and another 6–7% classified as controversial in status. The remaining 58–60% of students are categorized as average in status or unclassifiable.

Recently, Maassen and colleagues (1997, 2000) have revisited the issue of unidimensionality of acceptance/rejection. They argue that the low correlations observed between acceptance and rejection are in part attributable to artifacts of measurement, including the highly skewed nature of acceptance and rejection scores that reduces the magnitude of the intercorrelation that can be obtained. Maassen et al. further argue that liking or attraction is *unidimensional at the individual level*. How one feels about another person reflects a single continuum of liking–disliking, attraction–repulsion or sympathy–antipathy. Nomination measures artificially trichotomize this single dimension by omitting the middle range. At the group level, the relation between acceptance and rejection scores depends on the nature of the group. When groups contain individuals for whom peer attraction is mixed (controversial) or not intense (neglected), a second dimension of visibility or impact influences the relation between acceptance and rejection. Furthermore, at the group level, Bukowski, Sippola, Hoza, and Newcomb (2000) have recently demonstrated that the relationship between acceptance and rejection is actually linear and negative, as well as curvilinear. Thus, at high levels of acceptance, virtually all children are low in rejection, but at low levels of acceptance, one finds a wider range of rejection scores. Similarly, although highly rejected individuals are typically low in acceptance, low rejected children are not necessarily high in acceptance.

Rating measures

With *rating-scale* measures, children are asked to rate their level of preference for each group member on a Likert-type scale (e.g., "How much do you like to play with ___?"). With elementary children, a 5-point numeric scale is typically used (e.g., Ladd, 1983), although 7-point scales have been employed (Maassen et al., 1997). Following McCandless and Marshall (1957), Asher, Singleton, Tinsley, and Hymel (1979) creatively adapted the rating procedure for use with younger (preschool) children by having children assign peer photographs to one of three boxes, distinguished with a happy, neutral, or sad face, in response to sociometric questions. The average rating received from peers provides an index of overall liking versus disliking, or popularity versus unpopularity within the group, with higher scores reflecting greater peer acceptance, liking or popularity, and lower scores reflecting greater rejection, disliking or unpopularity within the group.

Proponents of the rating approach (e.g., Asher et al., 1979; Asher & Hymel, 1981, Maassen et al., 1997; Thompson & Powell, 1951) point to the advantage of tapping perceptions of all group members, thereby providing more refined, ordinal measurement information, and yielding more reliable and stable summary scores, relative to nomination measures. The primary disadvantage (Terry & Coie, 1991) is that rating scales are unidimensional and cannot distinguish neglected and rejected children (as identified in nomination schemes). When distinct "status" groups are needed (e.g., French, 1990; Ladd, 1983), cut-off points are used to divide this single continuum into three groups of children – popular, average, and rejected – on the basis of the average or standardized ratings received (e.g., cut-offs of ± one standard deviation, Terry & Coie, 1991). Neglected children, as identified by nomination-based schemes, are not distinguished, and have been shown to receive average peer ratings that span the entire scale (Hymel & Rubin, 1985; Maassen et al., 1977, 2000). Given evidence that "neglected" children can be liked or disliked on a rating scale measure, as well as observations that neglected children are often viewed by peers as likeable (Newcomb, Bukowski, & Pattee, 1993), one might question whether sociometric neglect, as defined by nomination measures actually reflects a meaningful or consistent sociometric category. The issue of interpersonal indifference, at both the individual and group level, therefore remains a contentious one.

Are rating and nomination measures tapping the same social constructs? Bukowski et al. (2000) have shown that rating scale indices of liking/disliking are more highly related to nomination-based *social preference* scores than to *acceptance* scores. However, the number of highest ratings received from peers is comparable to nomination-based indices of acceptance, and the number of lowest ratings received is consistent with nomination-based indices of rejection at both the group (Bukowski et al., 2000) and individual levels (Maassen et al., 1997). Thus, average sociometric ratings tap the construct of social preference, although both rating scale and nomination data can be used to tap the constructs of acceptance and rejection (assessed by number or proportion of highest/lowest ratings and positive/negative nominations).

Terry and Coie (1991) compared nomination and rating-scale sociometric *status classifications* of elementary children, noting that the two sociometric approaches identified similar numbers of students as rejected and popular, with a larger average status group in the rating system. The correspondence between these classifications was only fair to moderate for popular and rejected children in grades 4–5, with lower estimates observed for younger, grade 3 students. Nevertheless, several studies indicate that children who are categorized as rejected on nomination-based classification schemes are also those rated as highly disliked on rating-scale sociometric measures (e.g., Hymel & Rubin, 1985; Rubin, Chen, & Hymel, 1993; Rubin, Hymel, Le Mare, & Rowden, 1989).

Until recently, neglected and controversial status categories could only be distinguished using nomination measures. However, Maassen and colleagues (2000) have developed a new procedure called "SSrat" for classifying students into the five traditional status groups (popular, average, rejected, neglected, controversial) using 7-point sociometric ratings. Specifically, peers are rated on a scale from –3 (extremely disliked) to +3 (extremely liked), with the midpoint of the scale (0) reflecting neutral judgments. For classification purposes, ratings of +1 to +3 are used to create acceptance (like most) scores and ratings of –1 to –3 are used to create rejection (like least) scores, with 0 ratings indicating peers who are "not nominated". These simplified rating data are then transformed using a probability approach to classify students into the five traditional status categories. Maassen et al. found that SSrat status classifications were more stable over a 1-year interval than classifications based on either the Coie et al. (1982) or the Newcomb and Bukowski (1983) systems.

In terms of prevalence rates, the traditional, unidimensional rating scale identifies about 13–14% of elementary children as popular and about 16% as rejected, with the remaining 70% of students classified as average in status (Terry & Coie, 1991, using mean ± one standard deviation criteria for these categories). With the more recent, 5-category rating-scale system, Maassen et al. (2000) identified about 10–15% of children as popular, 13–17% as rejected, 0–1% as controversial, 1–5% as neglected, and 67–70% as average in two samples of elementary children. Relative to nomination-based classifications, Maassen et al.'s system identifies proportionately more popular and rejected children and fewer neglected and controversial children, although these numbers vary depending on the cut-off criteria employed.

Debates regarding the relative utility of nomination versus rating scale approaches have dominated the sociometric literature for decades (e.g., Asher & Hymel, 1981; Hymel & Rubin, 1985; Landau & Milich, 1990; Rubin et al., 1998; Terry & Coie, 1991; Maassen et al., 2000). Although these debates have been largely methodological, issues regarding how individuals experience their relationships with others remain. Indeed, it is still not entirely clear whether interpersonal experience reflects a single continuum of liking–disliking, sympathy–antipathy (Maassen et al., 1997, 2000), or a more complex triangular model of attraction, repulsion, and indifference (Moreno, 1934). Future theoretical as well as empirical and methodological studies will likely continue to address these fundamental issues.

Psychometric adequacy

Evaluations of the psychometric adequacy of sociometric measures has been surprisingly limited within this literature, owing in part to difficulties separating issues of measurement from characteristics of the phenomenon being measured. As Terry (2000) points out, the classic criteria used to assess psychometric adequacy – reliability and validity – are problematic in evaluating measures of acceptance and rejection. Sociometric studies have focused primarily on test–retest reliability, assessing the short-term as well as long-term stability of peer assessments of status based, albeit implicitly, on the assumption that group status is a rather stable, trait-like characteristic. If groups are dynamic and changing, however, such measures reflect the stability of the group rather than the reliability of the measurement. Nevertheless, some demonstration of stability is necessary if the sociometric construct is to be useful in prediction (see Terry, 2000). The assessment of reliability in terms of internal consistency is also problematic, since sociometric judgments across members of a group are not expected to be consistent, especially in the case of some status groups (e.g., controversial students).

Despite these concerns, acceptance and rejection scores (at the group level) have been shown to be fairly stable over time for elementary school age children. Over 6 months, Asher and Dodge (1986) reported test–retest correlations of .55 for acceptance and .65 for rejection scores, for both nomination and rating measures. Over 2 years, Terry and Coie (1991) reported test–retest correlations of .45 for acceptance, .32 for rejection, .46 for social preference and .29 for social impact scores, and .46 for average ratings. Over a 3-year period (grades 3–6), Roff et al. (1972) reported test–retest correlations of .42 for acceptance, .34 for rejection, and .45 for social preference scores, and Hymel, Rubin, Rowden, and Le Mare (1990) reported correlations of .56 for peer ratings from age 8 to 11 (grades 2–5). Among preschool children, sociometric indices have been shown to be somewhat less reliable over even shorter time periods, with higher test–retest correlations reported for rating than nomination measures (see Hymel, 1983; Wu, Hart, Draper, & Olsen, 2001). For example, over an 8-week period, Wu et al. reported test–retest correlations of .47 for acceptance, .44 for rejection, and .64 for rating-scale scores among preschoolers (3–6 years).

With regard to sociometric *categories*, Cillessen, Bukowski, and Haselager (2000) reviewed 12 studies examining stability over periods of 1 month to 4 years, in children ranging from preschool to grade 12. Not surprisingly, the stability of status classifications was found to decrease as test–retest intervals increased. Moderate stability was evident over 1–3 months, among middle to late elementary age children (grades 4–6). Sociometric classifications were less stable over intervals of 4 months to 4 years. For example, Coie and Dodge (1983) reported that 41% of elementary students maintained their status over 1 year, but only 23% maintained their status classification over 4 years. The stability of status classifications also varies across status groups, with average, popular, and rejected status categories showing greater stability than controversial and neglected children (Cillessen et al., 2000).

Another consideration is the degree to which peer evaluations are consistent with assessments by others, providing information on inter-rater reliability and/or concurrent validity. Studies of preschool and elementary children have consistently demonstrated moderate correspondence between peer and teacher sociometric evaluations, with coefficients ranging from .20 to .70 across studies (see Landau & Milich, 1990; Wu et al., 2001 for reviews). Thus, peer and teacher sociometric evaluations tap both similar and unique aspects of interpersonal experience (Wu et al., 2001), with some but not complete overlap between teacher and peer perceptions of popularity and status. The meaning of these modest relationships must be considered carefully, however, given arguments that peers provide a more face-valid, "insider" perspective on group social functioning.

Inter-rater agreement has also been considered by examining the consistency of socio-metric assessments derived from same-sex versus opposite-sex peers within the same group. Same- and opposite-sex sociometric evaluations have been found to be very highly correlated for "like most" and "like least" nominations, social preference, and social impact scores, as well as average peer ratings (Asher & Hymel, 1981; Terry & Coie, 1991). Moreover, Terry and Coie found excellent agreement across the two voting populations for each of the five status groups (i.e., rejected, neglected, popular, controversial, and average students). Although there is some evidence that children tend to nominate and/or rate same-sex peers more favorably (e.g., Asher & Dodge, 1986; Hartup, 1983), the strong correspondence between same- and opposite-sex evaluations suggests that elementary school boys and girls hold quite similar perceptions of their peers. Thus, there may be no advantage to the more time-consuming practice of including both same-sex and opposite-sex sociometric evaluations at the elementary level.

Peer group context

To date, researchers have usually evaluated sociometric status within the classroom and school context, since classrooms represent a primary socialization group during childhood that can be conveniently accessed. However, the classroom and school context provides a narrow view of childhood social relations, and reflects neither the breadth nor the dynamic nature of children's peer interactions (e.g., Internet contacts, neighborhood, extracurricular groups, etc.) nor the potential compensatory role of relationships with adults, siblings (e.g., East & Rook, 1992) or high-quality friendships (Parker & Asher, 1993). Consideration of a more diverse range of social groups becomes increasingly important with age, as reference groups expand rapidly beyond the school context during adolescence (e.g., Brown, 1990). This seems an important consideration in future sociometric research.

Within the classroom context, however, it is critical that sociometric evaluations be based on an adequate sampling of peer group members, that is, on an adequate "participation rate." Crick and Ladd (1989) used computer simulations to demonstrate that the accuracy of sociometric measures becomes compromised as the proportion of peer group members who provide ratings declines. Their findings suggest that sociometric evaluations should be based on data obtained from at least 75% of the group members to preserve a reasonable degree of accuracy. It is also important to recognize that participation rates are typically nonrandom, and are often tied to issues of informed consent. Comparisons of students who did and did not receive parent consent for participation in sociometric studies have shown that nonparticipants are often viewed more negatively by teachers and peers in terms of social behavior, academic performance, and/or popularity (see Iverson & Cook, 1994; Noll, Zeller, Vannatta, Bukowski, & Davies, 1997). Thus, high rates of participation are required to increase the accuracy and minimize potential biases in sociometric evaluations (see Iverson & Cook, 1994, for effective strategies).

Ethical considerations

Some educators, parents, researchers, and ethics review committees question the use of sociometric measures, concerned that asking children to negatively evaluate peers will implicitly or explicitly sanction saying harmful things about others or contribute to poor treatment within the group (Asher & Hymel, 1986; Foster & Ritchey, 1979; Landau & Milich, 1990). Several studies have demonstrated that completion of sociometric assessments does not increase negative interactions with less accepted peers, and does not contribute to social withdrawal or to feelings of loneliness and unhappiness following testing. Indeed, most students report positive reactions to sociometric tasks (see Iverson, Barton, & Iverson, 1997 for a review).

Although encouraging, these results do not eliminate concerns regarding potential risk, as administration procedures vary widely across researchers. Several practices have been recommended to minimize potential negative effects (Asher & Hymel, 1986; Bell-Dolan & Wessler, 1994; Landau & Milich, 1990), including explicit emphasis on confidentiality in instructions, optimal scheduling (i.e., not prior to unstructured [recess] periods, embedded within other structured, distracter activities), and planned debriefing and follow-ups with participants. Others have reduced negative effects by using unlimited nominations, allowing children to identify friends outside the classroom if they had no friends in class, carefully wording negative criteria (e.g., "least preferred" or "rather not play with" rather than "disliked"), and/or avoiding negative nominations altogether. Rating scales, allowing children to evaluate peers along a continuum, are often seen as more ethically defensible, as they do not *require* children to identify peers according to negative criteria, although negative ratings are possible. Accordingly, Asher and Dodge (1986) developed procedures for combining positive nomination and rating-scale data to identify rejected and neglected children, using low ratings in lieu of negative nominations. Until recently (Maassen et al., 2000, SSrat system), this was the only alternative to negative nominations that identified both neglected and rejected children (Terry & Coie, 1991).

A second ethical consideration is whether or not to include "nonparticipants," for whom parental consent or self assent has not been received, on sociometric lists. Some interpret negative consent as complete noninvolvement, both as an evaluator and as a person who is evaluated. For others, negative consent is interpreted as not allowing the child to complete the sociometric questionnaire, with the names of "nonparticipants" retained as potential peers to be rated or nominated. As Bell-Dolan and Wessler (1994) suggest, being evaluated by peers may be as much of a concern as evaluating peers. Researchers must continue to seriously consider the ethical issues involved in sociometric research and be vigilant regarding the appropriateness of their procedures.

Concurrent Correlates

Numerous studies have examined the correlates of acceptance and rejection (see Asher & Coie, 1990; Cillessen & Bellmore, this volume; Newcomb et al., 1993; Rubin, Bukowski,

& Parker., 1998) in order to determine what it *means* to be popular, rejected, controversial, or neglected within the peer group. In a large-scale meta-analysis, Newcomb et al. (1993) identified four major areas that distinguish accepted and rejected children: aggression, withdrawal, sociability, and cognitive skills. Accepted children exhibit more sociable and less withdrawn and aggressive behavior, as well as greater cognitive competence than rejected children. The primary focus in the literature, however, has been on the correlates of peer rejection.

Rejected status is associated with a number of deficits (see McDougall et al., 2001; Rubin et al., 1998), including social-cognitive skills (poor sociability, limited perspective-taking, poor communication skills), and academic performance (low achievement, poor school adjustment). Researchers have also linked peer rejection to lower socioeconomic status (e.g., Pettit, Clawson, Dodge, & Bates, 1996) and physical unattractiveness (e.g., Coie et al., 1982). However, the two most consistent correlates of peer rejection are aggressive and withdrawn behavior. These have been viewed as two distinct pathways leading to peer rejection (Rubin, LeMare, & Lollis, 1990) and have been used to distinguish subgroups of rejected children (see Boivin, Hymel, & Bukowski, 1995). About 40–50% of rejected children are behaviorally aggressive, and about 10–20% are behaviorally withdrawn (Rubin et al., 1998).

Links between peer rejection and aggressive as well as withdrawn behavior are robust, but do appear to be influenced by the behavioral norms of the peer group in which they are studied. For instance, the link between social withdrawal and peer rejection is not evident during the preschool years (Rubin, 1982), when withdrawn behavior is neither salient nor unusual. However, withdrawal is linked to peer rejection during the elementary years (e.g., Hymel & Rubin, 1985; Rubin, Hymel, & Mills, 1989), as withdrawal becomes increasingly nonnormative with age (Younger, Gentile, & Burgess, 1993; see Rubin et al., 1998). Further, although associations between rejection and aggression are common, there is evidence that some aggressive children enjoy elevated peer acceptance in some settings (e.g., Dodge, Coie, Pettit, & Price, 1990; Vaillancourt, 2001). Also, links between aggression and peer rejection are *less* likely in classrooms where aggression is normative and *more* likely in classrooms where aggression is rare (Boivin, Dodge, & Coie, 1995; Stormshak et al., 1999; Wright, Giamarino, & Parad, 1986). These findings underscore the need to consider mitigating factors like age and peer group context before concluding that all rejected children are aggressive or withdrawn. The relationship between social behavior and rejected status is more complicated than is often assumed.

Just as peer rejection is consistently associated with a plethora of unappealing characteristics, peer acceptance (sociometric popularity) is typically associated with desirable qualities (see Newcomb et al., 1993; Rubin et al., 1998). Accepted children are more sociable, helpful, and cooperative than less accepted children, and display better leadership, perspective-taking, and problem-solving skills. Also, highly accepted individuals are perceived by peers to possess greater assets and competencies including being athletic, attractive, rich, stylish, etc. (Vaillancourt, 2001).

Far less is known about the correlates of controversial and neglected status, owing primarily to the fact that these categories are rather rare and unstable, requiring large samples to identify them in adequate numbers (see Rubin et al., 1998). The available evidence indicates that controversial children represent a behavioral mélange of popular and rejected children in that they are described as both highly sociable and highly aggressive. In fact, controversial children have been found to be *more* aggressive than rejected children (e.g., Cairns, Cairns, Neckerman, Gest, & Gariepy, 1988; Coie & Dodge, 1988), and to be perceived as *more* popular (dominant, visible) than popular children (e.g., Parkhurst & Hopmeyer, 1998). Neglected children appear to be less sociable, less aggressive, less disruptive, and less interactive than their average status peers (e.g., see Newcomb et al., 1993; Rubin et al.,1998). Although neglected status has been associated with withdrawn behavior in some (e.g., Coie & Kupersmidt, 1983; Coie & Dodge, 1988; Dodge et al., 1982), but not all studies (e.g., Coie et al., 1982; Rubin et al., 1993), social withdrawal is generally viewed as a characteristic of peer rejection, rather than neglect.

In summary, researchers have delineated the behavioral profiles of rejected and accepted children, describing what it typically means to be part of these two sociometric groups. More recent (and future) research is beginning to uncover a more complex picture in which the links between peer rejection and various characteristics differ as a function of age and group norms or priorities. The characteristics of controversial and neglected children are less clear, and this remains an important question for future research. Our knowledge of the correlates of status lends strong support to the *concurrent validity* of sociometric measures (at least for indices of acceptance and rejection), but tells us little about the processes through which children come to achieve their status and the mechanisms through which status contributes to later adjustment. The *predictive utility* of sociometric indices is considered next.

Mechanisms and Processes: Long-Term Outcomes

Although the present volume focuses on childhood, it is important to understand the implications of early peer experiences for later adjustment, extending into adolescence and adulthood. Research on the long-term correlates of social status has demonstrated predictive links between early peer rejection and three major adjustment outcomes (see McDougall et al., 2001): academic difficulties, internalizing problems (loneliness, low self-esteem, depression), and externalizing problems (aggression, acting-out behavior, criminality). Questions remain, however, regarding whether status is a cause or simply a consequence of adjustment and behavior.

Research on the consequences of one's status within the peer group has focused largely on rejected children and has commonly followed a theoretical sequence first articulated by Parker and Asher (1987). In this causal sequence, children who demonstrate deviant or negative social behavior (e.g., aggression and/or withdrawal) are predisposed to experience difficult peer relationships (rejection). Rejection, in turn, deprives them of the positive peer socialization experiences that help build adaptive social skills, and places them at risk for negative peer experiences including victimization and involvement with deviant peers (e.g., gangs) (see also Parker, Rubin, Price, & DeRosier, 1995). What evidence is there to support this causal sequence? Longitudinal research reveals strong support for the idea that the combination of negative or deviant social behavior *and* peer rejection can lead to quite damaging outcomes, although this pattern seems to vary somewhat depending on the outcome explored.

Academic outcomes

Early peer rejection has been linked to subsequent school difficulties, including grade retention, absenteeism, truancy, and school dropout (see Hymel, Comfort, Schonert-Reichl, & McDougall, 1996; McDougall et al., 2001). The causal nature of these long-term links is not always clear. For example, although peer rejection in childhood predicts early school leaving, there is no evidence that students are rejected at the time they drop out. Here, it appears that social behavior works in concert with peer rejection in contributing to academic difficulties. Specifically, students who are both aggressive and rejected seem to be at greatest risk for early school leaving (e.g., Cairns, Cairns, & Neckerman, 1989, Kupersmidt & Coie, 1990). Hymel et al. (1996) propose that these aggressive-rejected students are more likely to affiliate with what many would characterize as the "wrong" peer group, who place less value on academic pursuits and who themselves may be at risk for drop out. Thus, aggressive students who are rejected are effectively deprived of the positive socialization experiences that cultivate both the skills and the desire to remain in school, and gradually disengage from the school milieu, eventually dropping out. Future research is needed to verify the role of deviant socialization as a mechanism in the causal sequence for school dropout.

Externalizing problems

The role of peer rejection in the prediction of externalizing problems has been somewhat confusing (see McDougall et al., 2001). Although studies have shown that being poorly accepted in childhood contributes directly to later delinquency and criminality (e.g., Parker & Asher, 1987; Kupersmidt, Burchinal, & Patterson, 1995), other research suggests that it is aggressive behavior (rather than rejection) that predicts subsequent aggression and anti-social behavior (e.g., Kupersmidt et al., 1995; Kupersmidt & Coie, 1990). Still others indicate that it is the combination of aggression and rejection that most strongly predicts later externalizing difficulties like conduct problems (e.g., Bierman & Wargo, 1995), at least for boys (e.g., Coie, Terry, Lenox, Lochman, & Hyman, 1995). Within the context of our causal sequence, there is some converging evidence for the path linking aggressive behavior and difficult peer relationships to long-term externalizing problems, although peer rejection appears to play an indirect role. In particular, Patterson, Capaldi, and Bank (1991) argue that when individuals are rejected by their peers, they are more likely to become affiliated with deviant peer groups, which increases their risk of externalizing problems (e.g., delinquency, acting out). As in the case of academic outcomes, then, the negative impact of peer rejection depends in part on whether the rejected child is exposed to deviant socialization experiences. Preliminary findings support this contention (e.g., French, Conrad, & Turner, 1995), although further research is needed before definitive conclusions can be reached.

Internalizing problems

There is no shortage of research indicating that both withdrawn behavior and peer rejection are important predictors of subsequent internalizing problems (see McDougall et al., 2001), including loneliness (Renshaw & Brown, 1993) and depression (Boivin et al., 1995, 1997). The links between withdrawal, rejection, and later internalizing difficulties, however, are complex, mediated in part by negative peer experiences as well as how the individual feels about his/her social situation. Specifically, Boivin et al. documented that the pathway from withdrawn behavior and rejected status to subsequent depression was strongest when children were not only rejected but also victimized by their peers. Moreover, the impact of negative peer experiences on depression held true only for those children who felt lonely and dissatisfied with their social circumstances. Alongside socialization experiences, then, children's view of their own social circumstances might help to explain the mechanisms by which social behavior and peer rejection contributes to internalizing problems (see also Valas & Sletta, 1996). The potential significance of self-perceptions brings us back to Moreno's initial proposal that it is important to consider both the perspective of the individual as well as the perspective of the group. As Parker et al. (1995) point out, a more complete examination of mechanisms and processes involving peer acceptance/rejection requires that we track the connections between the environment (i.e., poor peer relationships) and characteristics of the child (e.g., negative social cognitions, maladaptive behavior) across time.

Conclusions

Research on childhood peer acceptance and rejection has a long and rich history, dating back to the early writings of Moreno in 1934. The primary focus, however, has been on peer-group perceptions of the child, operationalized in terms of summary sociometric scores or status categories quantifying the degree to which children are accepted or rejected within the peer group. Although much of this literature has focused on methodological issues, these studies have contributed importantly to our understanding of social development and the degree to which peer socialization and preference contributes to adjustment, both concurrently and in later life.

Over the years, progress in this area has been and will continue to be linked to the development of new statistical and analytical approaches that extend the range of possible empirical inquiries (see Rubin et al., 1998 for a discussion). In addition, however, future research will continue to echo theoretical arguments made by Moreno over 60 years ago. Like Bukowski and Cillessen (1998; Cillessen & Bukowski, 2000), we acknowledge that much of the research on acceptance and rejection has been and will continue to be inspired, directly or indirectly, by Moreno's early formulations about the nature of individuals and groups. Two important future directions are highlighted in this regard. First, our primary emphasis to date has been on how the group perceives the individual, using peer-derived indices of acceptance and rejection. As Johnson and colleagues (1991, 1994) point out, neither nomination nor rating approaches are adequate in that they fail to consider the more complex structure of the peer group in which rejected children may occupy very different levels of integration and influence within the social network. We have only begun to explore the complexities of the larger social network, although the measurement tools for such an exploration now exist (e.g., see Cairns, Xie, & Leung, 1998; Kindermann, 1998). Second, despite Moreno's (1934) suggestions for multiple perspectives on group functioning, much of our research to date has considered the perceptions of the group, rather than perceptions of the individual. However, recent recognition of the importance of the child's perspective on his/her own group functioning and social status (see McDougall et al., 2001), as well as recent advances in theory and measurement of self-perceptions (see Cillessen & Bellmore, 1999; Hymel, LeMare, Ditner & Woody, 1999; Kupersmidt, Buchele, Voegler, & Sedikides, 1996) now set the stage for a new focus in future research within this area.

References

Asher, S. R., & Coie, J. D. (1990). *Peer rejection in childhood*. New York: Cambridge University Press.

Asher, S. R., & Dodge, K. H. (1986). Identifying children who are rejected by their peers. *Developmental Psychology, 22,* 444–449.

Asher, S. R., & Hymel, S. (1981). Children's social competence in peer relations: Sociometric and behavioral assessments. In J. D. Wine & M. D. Smye (Eds.), *Social competence* (pp. 125–157). New York: Guilford Press.

Asher, S. R., & Hymel. S. (1986). Coaching in social skills for children who lack friends in school. *Social Work in Education, 8,* 205–218.

Asher, S. R., Singleton, L. C., Tinsley, B. R., & Hymel, S. (1979). A reliable sociometric measure for preschool children. *Developmental Psychology, 15,* 443–444.

Baumeister, R. F., & Leary, M.R. (1995). The need to belong: Desire for interpersonal attachments as a fundamental human motivation. *Psychological Bulletin, 117,* 497–529.

Bell-Dolan, D. J., & Wessler, A. E. (1994). Ethical administration of sociometric measures: Procedures in use and suggestions for improvement. *Professional Psychology: Research and Practice, 25,* 23–32.

Bierman, K. L., & Wargo, J.B. (1995). Predicting the longitudinal course associated with aggressive-rejected, aggressive (non-rejected), and rejected (non-aggressive) status. *Development and Psychopathology, 7,* 669–682.

Boivin, M., Dodge, K. A., & Coie, J. D. (1995). Individual-group behavioral similarity and peer status in experimental play groups of boys: The social misfit revisited. *Journal of Personality and Social Psychology, 69,* 269–279.

Boivin, M., & Hymel, S. (1997). Peer experiences and self-perceptions: A sequential model. *Developmental Psychology, 33,* 135–145.

Boivin, M., Hymel, S., & Bukowski, W. M. (1995). The roles of social withdrawal, peer rejection, and victimization by peers in predicting loneliness and depressed mood in childhood. *Development and Psychopathology, 7,* 765–785.

Bronfenbrenner, U. (1943). A constant frame of reference for sociometric research, Part I: Theory and technique. *Sociometry, 6,* 363–397.

Bronfenbrenner, U. (1944). A constant frame of reference for sociometric research, Part II: Experiment and inference. *Sociometry, 4*, 40–75.

Brown, B. B. (1990). Peer groups and peer cultures. In S. S. Feldman & G. R. Elliott (Eds.), *At the threshold: The developing adolescent* (pp. 171–196). Cambridge, MA: Harvard University Press.

Bukowski, W. M., & Cillessen, A. H. N., (1998). Sociometry then and now: Building on six decades of measuring children's experiences with the peer group. *New Directions for Child Development, 80*, San Francisco: Jossey-Bass.

Bukowski, W. M., Sippola, L, Hoza, B., & Newcomb, A. F. (2000). Pages from a sociometric notebook: An analysis of nomination and rating scale measures of acceptance, rejection and social preference. In A. H. N. Cillessen & W. M. Bukowski, (Eds.), Recent advances in the measurement of acceptance and rejection in the peer system (pp. 11–26), *New Directions for Child and Adolescent Development, 88*. San Francisco: Jossey-Bass.

Cairns, R. B., Cairns, B. D., & Neckerman, H. J. (1989). Early school dropout: Configurations and determinants. *Child Development, 60*, 1437–1452.

Cairns, R. B., Cairns, B. D., Neckerman, H. J., Gest, S. D., & Gariepy, J. (1988). Social networks and aggressive behavior: Peer support or peer rejection? *Developmental Psychology, 24*, 815–823.

Cairns, R., Xie, H., & Leung, M-C. (1998). The popularity of friendship and the neglect of social networks: Toward a new balance. In W. M. Bukowski & A. H. N. Cillessen (Eds.), Sociometry then and now: Building on six decades of measuring children's experiences with the peer group (pp. 25–54), *New Directions for Child Development, 80*. San Francisco: Jossey-Bass.

Cillessen, A. H. N., & Bellmore, A. (1999). Accuracy of social self-perceptions and peer competence in middle childhood. *Merrill Palmer Quarterly, 45*, 650–676.

Cillessen, A. H. N., & Bukowski, W. M. (Eds.) (2000a). Recent advances in the measurement of acceptance and rejection in the peer system. *New Directions for Child and Adolescent Development, 88*. San Francisco: Jossey-Bass.

Cillessen, A. H. N., & Bukowski, W. M. (2000b). Conceptualizing and measuring peer acceptance and rejection. In A. H. N. Cillessen & W. M. Bukowski (Eds.), Recent advances in the measurement of acceptance and rejection in the peer system (pp. 3–10), *New Directions for Child and Adolescent Development, 88*, San Francisco: Jossey-Bass.

Cillessen, A. H. N., Bukowski, W. M., & Haselager, G. T. (2000). Stability of dimensions and types of sociometric status. In A. H. N. Cillessen & W. M. Bukowski (Eds.), Recent advances in the measurement of acceptance and rejection in the peer system (pp. 75–93), *New Directions for Child and Adolescent Development, 88*. San Francisco: Jossey-Bass.

Cohen, A. S., & Van Tassel, E. (1978). A comparison of partial and complete paired comparisons in sociometric measurement of preschool groups. *Applied Psychological Measurement, 2*, 31–40.

Coie, J. D., & Dodge, K. A. (1983). Continuities and changes in children's social status: A five-year longitudinal study. *Merrill-Palmer Quarterly, 29*, 261–282.

Coie, J. D., & Dodge, K. A. (1988). Multiple sources of data on social behavior and social status. *Child Development, 59*, 815–829.

Coie, J. D., Dodge, K.A., & Coppotelli, H. (1982). Dimensions and types of social status: A cross-age perspective. *Developmental Psychology, 18*, 557–570.

Coie, J. D., & Kupersmidt, J. B. (1983). An analysis of emerging social status in boy's groups. *Child Development, 54*, 1400–1461.

Coie, J., Terry, R., Lenox, K., Lochman, J., & Hyman, C. (1995). Childhood peer rejection and aggression as predictors of stable patterns of adolescent disorder. *Development and Psychopathology, 7*, 697–713.

Cowan, E., Pederson, A., Babigian, H., Izzo, L., & Trost, M. (1973). Long-term follow-up of early detected vulnerable children. *Journal of Consulting and Clinical Psychology, 41*, 438–446.

Crick, N. R., & Ladd, G. W. (1989). Nominator attrition: Does it affect the accuracy of children's sociometric classifications? *Merrill-Palmer Quarterly, 35,* 197–207.

Dodge, K. A., Coie, J. D., & Brakke, N. P. (1982). Behavior patterns in socially rejected and neglected preadolescents: The role of social approach and aggression. *Journal of Abnormal Psychology, 10,* 389–410.

Dodge, K. A., Coie, J. D., Pettit, G. S., & Price, J. M. (1990). Peer status and aggression in boys' groups: Development and contextual analyses. *Child Development, 61,* 1289–1309.

Dunnington, M. J. (1957). Investigations of areas of disagreement in sociometric measurement of preschool children. *Child Development, 28,* 93–102.

East, P. L., & Rook, K. S. (1992). Compensatory patterns of support among children's peer relationships: A test using school friends, nonschool friends and siblings. *Developmental Psychology, 28,* 163–172.

Foster, S. L., & Ritchey, W. (1979). Issues in the assessment of social competence in children. *Journal of Applied Behavior Analysis, 12,* 625–638.

French, D. C. (1990). Heterogeneity of peer-rejected girls. *Child Development, 61,* 2028–2031.

French, D. C., Conrad, J., & Turner, T. M. (1995). Adjustment of antisocial and nonantisocial rejected adolescents. *Development and Psychopathology, 7,* 857–874.

Goleman, D. (1995). *Emotional intelligence.* New York: Bantam Books.

Gronlund, N. E. (1959). *Sociometry in the classroom.* New York: Harper.

Gronlund, N. E., & Anderson, L. (1957). Personality characteristics of socially accepted, socially neglected, and socially rejected junior high school pupils. *Educational Administration and Supervision, 43,* 329–338.

Harris, J. R. (1998). *The nurture assumption.* New York: Free Press.

Hartup, W. W. (1983). Peer relations. In E. M. Hetherington (Ed.), *Handbook of child psychology, Vol. 4: Socialization, personality and social development* (pp. 103–198). New York: Wiley.

Hartup, W. W., Glazer, J. A., & Charlesworth, R. (1967). Peer reinforcement and sociometric status. *Child Development, 38,* 1017–1024.

Hymel, S. (1983). Preschool children's peer relations: Issues in sociometric assessment. *Merrill Palmer Quarterly, 29,* 237–260.

Hymel, S., Comfort, C., Schonert-Reichl, K., & McDougall, P. (1996). Academic failure and school dropout: The influence of peers. In K. Wentzel & J. Juvonen (Eds.), *Social motivation: Understanding children's school adjustment* (pp. 313–345). New York: Cambridge University Press.

Hymel, S., LeMare, L., Ditner, E., & Woody, E. (1999). Assessing self-concept in children: Variations across self-concept domains. *Merrill Palmer Quarterly, 45,* 602–623.

Hymel, S., & Rubin, K. H. (1985). Children with peer relationship and social skills problems: Conceptual, methodological and developmental issues. In G. J. Whitehurst (Ed.), *Annals of Child Development, Vol. 2* (pp. 251–297). Greenwich, CT: JAI Press.

Hymel, S., Rubin, K. H., Rowden, L., & Le Mare, L. (1990). Children's peer relationships: Longitudinal predications of internalizing and externalizing problems from middle to late childhood. *Child Development, 61,* 2004–2021.

Iverson, A. M., Barton, E. A., & Iverson, G. L. (1997). Analysis of risk to children participating in a sociometric task. *Developmental Psychology, 33,* 104–112.

Iverson, A. M., & Cook, G. L. (1994). Guardian consent for children's participation in sociometric research. *Psychology in the Schools, 31,* 108–112.

Johnson, J. C., Poteat, G. M., & Ironsmith, M. (1991). Structural vs. marginal effects: A note on the importance of structure in determining sociometric status. *Journal of Social Behavior and Personality, 6,* 489–508.

Johnson, J. C., Ironsmith, M., & Poteat, G. M. (1994). Assessing children's sociometric status: Issues and the application of social network analysis. *Journal of Group Psychotherapy, Psychodrama, and Sociometry, 47,* 36–48.

Kindermann, T. (1998). Children's development within peer groups: Using composite social maps to identify peer networks and to study their influences. In W. M. Bukowski & A. H. N. Cillessen (Eds.), Sociometry then and now: Building on six decades of measuring children's experiences with the peer group_(pp. 25–54), *New Directions for Child Development, 80.* San Francisco: Jossey-Bass.

Koch, H. L. (1933). Popularity in preschool children. *Child Development, 4,* 164–175.

Kupersmidt, J. B., Burchinal, M., & Patterson, C. J. (1995). Developmental patterns of childhood peer relation as predictors of externalizing behavior problems. *Development and Psychopathology, 7,* 825–843.

Kupersmidt, J. B., & Coie, J. D. (1990). Preadolescent peer status, aggression and school adjustment as predictors of externalizing problems in adolescence. *Child Development, 61,* 1350–1362.

Kupersmidt, J. B., Buchele K. S., Voegler, M. E., & Sedikides, C. (1996). Social self-discrepancy: A theory relating peer relations problems and school maladjustment. In J. Juvonen & K. R. Wentzel (Eds.), *Social motivation: Understanding children's school maladjustment* (pp. 66–97). New York: Cambridge University Press.

Ladd, G. W. (1983). Social networks of popular, average and rejected children in school settings. *Merrill Palmer Quarterly, 29,* 283–308.

Ladd, G. W. (1990). Having friends, keeping friends, making friends, and being liked by peers in the classroom: Predictors of children's early school adjustment? *Child Development, 61,* 312–331.

Landau, S., & Milich, R. (1990). Assessment of children's social status and peer relations. In A. M. LaGreca (Ed.), *Through the eyes of the child: Obtaining self-reports from children and adolescents* (pp. 259–291). Boston: Allyn & Bacon.

Lemann, T. B., & Solomon, R. L. (1952). Group characteristics as revealed in sociometric patterns and personality ratings. *Sociometry, 15,* 7–90.

Maassen, G. H., van der Linden, J. L., & Akkermans, W. (1997). Nominations, ratings and dimensions of sociometric status. *International Journal of Behavioral Development, 21,* 179–199.

Maassen, G. H., van der Linden, J. L., Goossens, F. A., & Bokhorst, J. (2000). A ratings-based approach to two-dimensional sociometric status determination. In A. H. N. Cillessen & W. M. Bukowski (Eds.), Recent advances in the study and measurement of acceptance and rejection in the peer system (pp. 55–73), *New Directions for Child and Adolescent Development, 88,* San Francisco: Jossey-Bass.

McCandless, B. R., & Marshall, H. R. (1957). A picture sociometric technique for preschool children and its relation to teacher judgements of friendship. *Child Development, 28,* 139–147.

McDougall, P., Hymel, S., Vaillancourt, T., & Mercer, L. (2001). The consequences of childhood peer rejection. In M. Leary (Ed.), *Interpersonal rejection.* London: Oxford University Press.

Moore, S. G., & Udpegraff, R. (1964). Sociometric status of preschool children related to age, sex, nurturance-giving, and dependency. *Child Development, 35,* 519–524.

Moreno, J. L. (1934). *Who shall survive? A new approach to the problem of human interrelations.* Washington, DC: Nervous and Mental Disease Publishing Co.

Moreno, J. L. (1951). *Sociometry, experimental method and the science of society.* Beacon, NY: Beacon House.

Newcomb, A. F., & Bukowski, W. M. (1983). Social impact and social preference as determinants of children's peer group status. *Developmental Psychology, 19,* 856–867.

Newcomb, A. F., Bukowski, W. M., & Pattee, L. (1993). Children's peer relations: A meta-analytic review of popular, rejected, neglected, controversial, and average sociometric status. *Psychological Bulletin, 111,* 99–128.

Noll, R. B., Zeller, M. H., Vannatta, K., Bukowski, W. M., & Davies, W. H. (1997). Potential bias in classroom research: Comparison of children with permission and those who do not receive permission to participate. *Journal of Clinical Child Psychology, 26,* 36–42.

Northway, M. L. (1940). Appraisal of the social development of children at a summer camp. *University of Toronto Studies, Psychology Series, 5,* 62.

Parker, J. G., & Asher, S. R. (1987). Peer relations and later personal adjustment: Are low-accepted children at risk? *Psychological Bulletin, 102,* 357–389.

Parker, J. G., & Asher, S. R. (1993). Friendship and friendship quality in middle childhood: Links with peer group acceptance and feelings of loneliness and social dissatisfaction. *Developmental Psychology, 29,* 357–389.

Parker, J. G., Rubin, K. H., Price, J., & DeRosier, M. E. (1995). Peer relationships, child development and adjustment: A developmental psychopathology perspective. In D. Cicchetti & D. Cohen (Eds.), *Developmental psychopathology, Vol. 2: Risk, disorder and adaptation* (pp. 96–161). New York: Wiley.

Parkhurst, J. T., & Hopmeyer, A. (1998). Sociometric popularity and peer-perceived popularity: Two distinct dimensions of peer status. *Journal of Early Adolescence, 18,* 125–144.

Parten, M. (1932). Social participation among preschool children. *Journal of Abnormal and Social Psychology, 27,* 243–269.

Patterson, G. R., Capaldi, D., & Bank, L. (1991). An early starter model for predicting delinquency. In D. J. Pepler & K. H. Rubin (Eds.), *The development and treatment of childhood aggression* (pp. 139–168). Hillsdale, NJ: Erlbaum.

Peery, J. (1979). Popular, amiable, isolated, rejected: A reconceptualization of sociometric status in preschool children. *Child Development, 50,* 1231–1234.

Pettit, G. S., Clawson, M. A., Dodge, K. A., & Bates, J. E. (1996). Stability and change in peer-rejected status: The role of child behavior, parenting, and family ecology. *Merrill-Palmer Quarterly, 42,* 267–294.

Renshaw, P. D. (1981). The roots of peer interaction research: An historical analysis of the 1930s. In S. R. Asher & J. M. Gottman (Eds.) *The development of children's friendships* (pp. 1–25). New York: Cambridge University Press.

Renshaw, P. D., & Brown, P. J. (1993). Loneliness in middle childhood: Concurrent and longitudinal predictors. *Child Development, 64,* 1271–1284.

Roff, M., Sells, S. B., & Golden, M. M. (1972). *Social adjustment and personality development in children.* Minneapolis, MN: University of Minnesota Press.

Rubin, K. H. (1982). Social and social-cognitive developmental characteristics of young isolate, normal and sociable children. In K. H. Rubin & H. S. Ross (Eds.), *Peer relationships and social skills in childhood* (pp. 353–374). New York: Springer-Verlag.

Rubin, K. H., Bukowski, W., & Parker, J. G. (1998). Peer interactions, relationships and groups. In W. Damon (Series Ed.) & N. Eisenberg (Vol. Ed.), *Handbook of child psychology: Vol. 3, Social emotional and personality development* (5th ed., pp. 619–700). New York: Wiley.

Rubin, K. H., Chen, X., & Hymel, S. (1993). Socioemotional characteristics of withdrawn and aggressive children. *Merrill-Palmer Quarterly, 39,* 518–534.

Rubin, K. H., Hymel, S., LeMare, L., & Rowden, L. (1989). Children experiencing social difficulties: Sociometric neglect reconsidered. *Canadian Journal of Behavioral Science, 21,* 94–111.

Rubin, K. H., Hymel, S., & Mills, R. (1989). Sociability and social withdrawal in childhood: Stability and outcomes. *Journal of Personality, 57,* 238–255.

Rubin, K. H., LeMare, L., & Lollis, S. (1990). Social withdrawal in childhood: Developmental pathways to peer rejection. In S. R. Asher & J. D. Coie (Eds.), *Peer rejection in childhood* (pp. 217–249). New York: Cambridge University Press.

Stormshak, E. A., Bierman, K. L., Bruschi, C., Dodge, K., Coie, J. D., & The Conduct Problems Prevention Research Group (1999). The relation between behavioral problems and peer preference in different classroom contexts. *Child Development, 70,* 169–182.

Terry, R. (2000). Recent advances in measurement theory and the use of sociometric techniques. In A. H. N. Cillessen & W. M. Bukowski (Eds.), Recent advances in the measurement of acceptance and rejection in the peer system, *New Directions for Child and Adolescent Development, 88* San Francisco: Jossey-Bass.

Terry, R., & Coie, J. D. (1991). A comparison of methods for defining sociometric status among children. *Developmental Psychology, 27,* 867–880.

Thompson, G. G., & Powell, M. (1951). An investigation of the rating-scale approach to the measurement of social status. *Educational and Psychological Measurement, 11,* 440-445.

Vaillancourt, T. (2001). Competing for hegemony during adolescence: A link between aggression and social status. Unpublished doctoral dissertation, University of British Columbia, Vancouver, British Columbia, Canada.

Valas, H., & Sletta, O., (1996). Social behavior, peer relations, loneliness and self-perceptions in middle school children: A mediational model. Paper presented at the XIVth biennial meeting of the International Society for the Study of Behavioral Development, Quebec City, Canada.

Vaughn, B. E., & Waters, E. (1981). Attention structure, sociometric status, and dominance: Interrelations, behavioral correlates, and relationships to social competence. *Developmental Psychology, 17,* 275–288.

Wright, J. C., Giammarino, M., & Parad, H. W. (1986). Social status in small groups: Individual-group similarity and the social "misfits". *Journal of Personality and Social Psychology, 50,* 523–536.

Wu. X., Hart, C. H., Draper, T. W., & Olsen, J. A. (2001). Peer and teacher sociometrics for preschool children: Cross-informant concordance, temporal stability, and reliability. *Merrill Palmer Quarterly, 47,* 416–443.

Younger, A. J., Gentile, C., & Burgess, K. (1993). Children's perceptions of social withdrawal: Changes across age. In K. Rubin & J. B. Asendorpf (Eds.), *Social withdrawal, inhibition and shyness in childhood* (pp. 215–235). Hillsdale, NJ: Erlbaum.

15

Friends and Enemies

Willard W. Hartup and Maurissa Abecassis

Relationships are the contexts in which our social selves originate. Social referencing, emotional regulation, and language emerge in relationships with family members, friends, and even enemies. Within these contexts, self-awareness emerges along with a variety of attitudes and skills that carry over into other relationships.

Close relationships are usually portrayed by social scientists with an emphasis on harmony, on the one hand, and disharmony, on the other. At one and the same time, however, relationships can be dark as well as bright, constricting as well as actualizing, and constitute both developmental risk and developmental protection. Most relationships have dark sides, and developmental impact is determined by the manner in which these darker elements are intertwined with brighter ones. Other relationships are characterized almost exclusively in terms of hatred, fear, anxiety, aversion, and nonsupportiveness. Although empirical studies are rare, recent work shows that these "negative" relationships are also developmentally significant – by middle childhood if not before.

Friends and enemies, examined together, provide an opportunity to better understand the crosscurrents existing in children's social networks. On the one hand, friends come together and maintain their relationships on the basis of attraction (liking). Attraction stems from common ground and the expectation that cost–benefit ratios across social exchanges will be generally favorable. On the other hand, enemies maintain their relations with one another on the basis of antipathy (disliking). Enmities may derive from bullying and aggression, contractual violations, and expectations that cost–benefit ratios in the social exchange will be unfavorable. Relatively little is known, however, about similarities and differences between enemies as contrasted with friends, distinctive modes of interaction, and the adaptational significance of mutual antipathies as contrasted with mutual attractions. Nevertheless, these two types of relationships are brought together in this chapter based on the argument that, within children's social networks, darker relationships co-exist with brighter ones and developmental outcomes derive from both.

We believe that the state of knowledge in these fields can be most clearly described by comparing these relationships with respect to the following issues: (a) children's expectations about friends and enemies and the social provisions they associate with them; (b) relationship formation; (c) the incidence of friends and enemies in children's experience at various ages; (d) similarities (homophilies) between friends and between enemies; (e) distinctive patterns of social interaction associated with these relationships; (f) correlates and consequences of having friends and having enemies, respectively; (g) characteristics of children's friends and enemies and their developmental implications; and (h) socioemotional qualities among friendships and among enmities, along with their developmental significance. One note: The terms "enemies" and "mutual antipathies" are used interchangeably in this chapter even though we recognize that the latter construct is more inclusive than the former. Future studies may well demonstrate that these terms should be used more precisely.

Relationship Expectations

Friends

The friendship expectations of younger and older children are both similar and different. The most striking similarities involve the centrality of *reciprocity* and *mutuality* in the meaning structure. Friends are not described by children as abiding by equivalence norms, in the sense that resource exchanges must be exactly equal or that one individual's behavior must match the other's. Nevertheless, interviews with children show that giving and taking in a broad sense ("symmetrical reciprocity") are emphasized in friendship expectations at all ages (Hartup & Stevens, 1997; Youniss, 1980). Even so, preschool-aged children describe their friends in terms of concrete reciprocities ("We play "); primary-school children describe their friends in terms of loyalty, trustworthiness, and time spent together; and preadolescents emphasize sympathy, self-disclosure, and other aspects of social intimacy (Bigelow, 1977). The cognitive representations of friendships thus undergo extensive change during childhood even though the underlying meaning structure remains the same. Stated another way, continuity marks the friendship "deep structure" but discontinuity its "surface structure" (Chomsky, 1965).

Some of the age changes in friendship expectations reflect increases in the number of psychological constructs children use to describe their friends, their greater complexity, and a re-organization of information and ideas; that is, these changes reflect general changes in cognitive development (Livesley & Bromley, 1973). Changes in friendship expectations may also reflect changes in the developmental tasks that confront children as they grow older. Young children expect their friends to behave in ways that are consistent with their own struggles in mastering new social skills, especially cooperation and conflict management. Older children's concerns, however, shift to intimacy, identity, sensitivity to the needs of others, and what it takes to keep relationships going (Hartup & Stevens, 1997). Both these continuities and discontinuities demonstrate how friendships support the development of social understanding and social skill from early childhood into adolescence.

Children's friendship expectations are different from their expectations about other relationships. Preschool children, for example, recognize the existence of differences in social power between themselves and their parents but not between themselves and their friends; they also expect friends to be less likely to give them help than parents. At the same time, young children expect conflict to occur more frequently with siblings than with either parents or friends (Gleason, 1998). Older children make similar differentiations: Friendships are understood by school-aged children to provide companionship and intimacy more frequently than parent–child relationships, but compliance and control less frequently. Nurturance, in general, is understood by older children to be provided by both friends and parents; overt affection, however, less frequently by friends. Power sharing continues to be seen by school-aged children as a hallmark of relations between friends – not relationships between children and adults (Furman & Buhrmester, 1985). Differentiation between friendships and other close relationships is thus established in early childhood and remains relatively constant thereafter. Elaborations in the way children think about these relationships occur as children grow older, but relationship schemas emerge early and their deep structures are relatively stable across time (Gleason, 1998).

Enemies

Enemies are individuals who mutually dislike one another and perceive one another as threats to desired goals (Abecassis, 1998). Sometimes, a child regards another child as an enemy when this attitude is not reciprocated. Nothing, however, is known about children's use of the word "enemy" – for example, when it enters the working vocabulary and what meanings are attached to it. Although children use the word "friend" by the fourth year, anecdotal evidence suggests that the word "enemy" is not used as soon. Investigators who are experienced in sociometric testing know that young children understand what it means to "not like" somebody; disliking someone, however, is a necessary, but not sufficient criterion for identifying that person as an enemy.

The reasons given by young children for not liking someone are similar to those given by older ones, the main reason being aggressiveness (Hayes, Gershman, & Bolin, 1980; Moore, 1967). Engaging in rule violations and other aberrant behavior are also mentioned, again by both preschool children and preadolescents (preadolescent boys only since girls at that age have not been studied). Older boys also dislike classmates who are insincere and not helpful (Hayes, Gershman, & Halteman, 1996). Such conditions suggest that enmity may be based on aggression or inappropriate behavior directed from one child to another but this extrapolation needs to be made cautiously. Enmities, especially mutual ones, may have intense affects associated with them (e.g., hatred) and complex expectations (that one's enemy is a threat to obtaining one's goals). Beyond these observations, child development research tells us nothing about the social expectations associated with either mutual enmities or mutual antipathies among preschool- or school-aged children.

Becoming Friends and Becoming Enemies

Friends

Friendship formation begins with "propinquity," that is, the condition that children cannot become friends if they never meet. Consequently, the social forces that bring two children together in the same place at the same time need to be taken into account in any workable theory of friendship formation: for example, what draws children and their families to the same neighborhoods, the same schools, and the same playgrounds.

Although relatively little is known about first encounters, the available evidence indicates that these initial meetings are largely devoted to establishing common ground (or its absence). Social interaction is mostly driven by the activities or tasks at hand; the social exchange is thus task constrained. Emotionally speaking, relationships are superficial in these early stages. As children begin to "hit it off," a shift occurs from an ego-centered to a relationship-centered orientation. Those who get along best show connected communication, successful conflict management, attention to similarities between themselves, and self-disclosure (Gottman, 1983). Relationships, however, are not very stable in this "build-up" stage: Should children not maintain common interests, they must exchange relevant information again, much as they did during their first encounters. Over the long term, friendships are maintained largely through continued validation of common interests and by commitment to the relationship that older children believe friends are obliged to have. Not much is known, however, about commitment and its role in children's social relations.

Children terminate their friendships for many reasons although disagreements, fights, and commitment violations are less salient than one might expect. Friendships are known to be less stable when the "friendship talk" of the individual children is negative and nonsupportive (Berndt & Perry, 1986). On many occasions children simply drift apart (and sometimes regret it) but cannot explain exactly why. Observations in one first-grade classroom demonstrated that friendships ceased mainly because children stopped interacting; neither emotional outbursts nor arguments foreshadowed these endings, nor did the children make much fuss (Rizzo, 1989).

Enemies

The events that establish mutual antipathies among children are unclear. Survey studies among adults (Wiseman & Duck, 1995) suggest that enmities are unanticipated and often come as a surprise. Sometimes, an aura occurs (bad "vibes," slights, sneers) but some kind of hostile action, viewed as malicious, is the inciting incident that most frequently establishes two individuals as enemies. Enmities carry relatively few social expectations because role responsibilities do not exist in the same sense as in friendship relations. Control issues (including threats to one's rights and privileges) are associated with relationship animosities among many adults.

Some theorizing suggests that the prehistories of enemy relationships are quite varied:

Some involve falling away from a friendship (see above), some involve dispositional or personality clashes, some are based in encounters between bullies and victims, and some stem from scapegoating (Abecassis, 1998). Although no one knows the extent to which these prehistories are involved in generating enmities between children, each undoubtedly is relevant.

Incidence

Friends

Social preferences can be identified among toddlers (Howes, 1983), but these relationships do not carry the same nuances evinced among older children. By 4 years of age, about three quarters of children are involved in mutual friendships as indicated by time spent together, cooperation and reciprocities in social interaction, and various affective markers (Hinde, Titmus, Easton, & Tamplin, 1985; Howes, 1983). Observations, teachers' reports, and maternal interviews – singly or in combination – have been used to arrive at these estimates. Friendship frequencies rise only slightly through middle childhood (to about 85%). Children who have friends at one age are likely to have them at other ages (Elicker, Englund, & Sroufe, 1992) thus illustrating an important continuity in childhood social relations.

Friendship networks are relatively small among preschool children, averaging 1.7 for boys and 0.9 for girls (Hartup, Laursen, Stewart, & Eastenson, 1988) increasing to 3.0–5.0 during middle childhood, depending on whether one includes unreciprocated choices as well as reciprocated ones (Hallinan, 1980). Time spent with friends increases through the school years, too, rising to its peak (29% of time awake) in adolescence.

The vast majority of children's friendships are gender concordant. Opposite-sex friendships occur in relatively small numbers, even among preschoolers. The proportion of boys and girls who have friends does not differ – among either younger or older children – although friendship networks are likely to be somewhat smaller among girls than among boys (Eder & Hallinan, 1978).

Enemies

More children have friends than enemies. Observational studies have failed to establish that preschool-aged children fight or quarrel disproportionately with certain classmates. To the contrary, aggressive young children tend to "spread it around" rather than quarrel or fight consistently with the same partners (Dawe, 1934; Ross & Conant, 1992). Mutual antipathies, identified by asking children to name other children "whom you dislike more than anyone else," are also rare among young children. In one investigation (Hayes et al., 1980), 59 of the 78 children who were interviewed identified children that they disliked, but mutual antipathies were revealed in only two instances, suggesting either that these nominations are not reliable or that these relationships are very uncommon among young children.

This situation changes during middle childhood. Same-sex mutual antipathies were studied among 8-year-old school children by Hembree and Vandell (2000), with the results revealing that 65% were involved in at least one (half of these in more than one). Mutual antipathies were identified by comparing children's nominations lists of three same-sex classmates whom "you would not like to play with." Although significant concordance was observed between sociometric status and the prevalence of these antipathies, involvement in these relationships occurred in all sociometric groups: Popular children had fewer mutual antipathies (32%) than neglected (39%), average (70%), rejected (95%), or controversial children (100%). Sex differences were not reported nor the incidence of mixed-sex antipathies.

Similar data were obtained with 10 and 14 year olds, using sociometric nominations requiring the children to list three classmates "whom you do not like at all" (Abecassis, Hartup, Haselager, Scholte, & Van Lieshout, 2001). Prevalence rates were established separately for the two sexes and separately for same- and mixed-sex mutual antipathies. In this instance, same-sex mutual antipathies were identified for 9% of the school-aged girls but 25% of the boys, and for 14% of the adolescent girls and 20% of the adolescent boys. Mixed-sex antipathies, however, were identified for 17% and 16% of the school-aged boys and girls, respectively, and for 15% and 14% of young adolescent girls and boys, respectively. Comparisons across these studies are difficult because a more conservative sociometric criterion was used with the older children and the adolescents (Abecassis et al., 2001) than was used earlier with the 8 year olds (Hembree & Vandell, 2000). Moreover, the children differed in country of residence (the Netherlands, and the United States, respectively) as well as chronological age. Since these are the only studies available, it is impossible to conclude now whether or not the incidence of mutual antipathies changes with age.

Similarities Between Friends and Between Enemies

Friends

Since common ground is necessary for the formation and maintenance of friendships from early childhood onwards (Gottman, 1983), friends can be expected to be similar to one another in many ways. The weight of the evidence supports this thesis, beginning in early childhood and extending through the school-aged years. Friends are more concordant than nonfriends in age, gender, ethnicity, and sociometric status. Behavioral concordances occur, too, although not as extensively among preschool-aged children as among their school-aged counterparts. Even so, research shows that the probability that two young children will be friends varies directly as a function of the number of behavioral attributes they share (Kupersmidt, DeRosier, & Patterson, 1995). And, among 8 year olds, initially strangers to one another, greater attraction between children occurs during play sessions when cognitive and play styles are similar than when they are different (Rubin, Lynch, Coplan, Rose-Krasnor, & Booth, 1994).

Behavioral similarity is clearly evident among school-aged friends. Comparisons between children and their friends and between children and "neutral" classmates show greater similarity between friends in prosocial behavior, antisocial behavior, shyness-dependency, depression, sociometric status, and achievement in both Western and Eastern cultures (French, Jansen, Riansari, & Setiono, 2000; Haselager, Hartup, Van Lieshout, & Riksen-Walraven, 1998; Poulin & Boivin, 2000). Concordant similarities are evinced for children who are victimized: Friends of victimized children are physically weak, have internalizing problems, and are victimized, too (Hodges, Malone, & Perry, 1997).

Friends also share biases in their perceptions of both persons and relationships: For example, when two friends rate other children's behavior, their ratings are more similar to one another than nonfriends' ratings are (Haselager et al., 1998). Friends are also more concordant than non-friends in relationship stance (being "preoccupied" or "avoidant") both with one another and with their mothers and fathers (Hodges, Finnegan, & Perry, 1999).

Similarities between friends come about for a number of reasons. Schools and neighborhoods are organized so children come together in classrooms, on playgrounds, and on street corners with others who are similar to themselves rather than dissimilar. Subsequently, children in these "homophilous pools" are exposed to similar socialization agents in schools and elsewhere. In addition, children are especially attracted to other children who resemble themselves (Kupersmidt et al., 1995; Rubin et al., 1994). Children are also more likely to *dislike* associates who are different from themselves (Rosenbaum, 1986) and to terminate relationships with children who are different rather than similar (Poulin & Boivin, 2000). No evidence exists to suggest that "opposites attract."

While the "similarity-attraction" hypothesis thus explains some of the similarity between children and their friends, no one knows exactly how children go about sorting themselves into friendship dyads. Similarities between friends do not seem to derive from carefully weighed decisions made by the children themselves but from complex assortments that some investigators have called "shopping expeditions" (Dishion, Patterson, & Greisler, 1994). Children seem to make their social choices in terms of what "feels right" and what does not. These shopping expeditions frequently occur within social networks, so that friendship similarities emerge within two interconnected selection systems: dyadic interaction and assortative dialectics.

Friendship similarities are also known to derive from mutual socialization, that is, children become more alike as a consequence of their interaction with one another over time. The relative extent to which mutual selection and mutual socialization contribute to the similarity between friends, however, depends on many conditions including characteristics of the children themselves, the nature of their interaction, and the behavioral characteristics being measured (Kandel, 1978; Poulin & Boivin, 2000; Urberg, 1999).

Enemies

Whether children involved in mutual antipathies are similar or different from one another as compared with neutral associates is not known.

Patterns of Interaction

Friends

Children spend more time with their friends than with nonfriends, suggesting to some researchers that time sharing is a valid means of identifying friendships, especially in early childhood (Hinde et al. 1985). The activities of boys and their friends differ from those of girls and their friends (this is obvious to everyone). The two sexes also differ in the behavioral provisions that children expect from these relationships: Girls anticipate greater affection, intimacy, and instrumental help from their friends than boys do (Furman & Buhrmester, 1985). Moreover, intimacy is more central in girls' talk about friends than in boys' talk, self-ratings of friendships by girls are more intimate than boys' self-ratings, and self-disclosure is more common (Sharabany, Gershoni, & Hofman, 1981). Intimacy has been studied largely, however, with constructs especially applicable to girls (e.g., empathy and self-disclosure) rather than ones applicable to boys (i.e., task mastery and camaraderie). Good reason exists, therefore, to refine the measurement of intimacy before drawing final conclusions about sex differences in children's friendships.

Social exchanges differ between friends and nonfriends beginning in early childhood. Children identified as friends are more cooperative than nonfriends, and reciprocities are more evident in their interaction (Howes, 1983). Behaviors differentiating friends from nonfriends among school-aged children have been examined in a large number of investigations, and have been scrutinized in both narrative reviews (e.g., Hartup, 1996) and one meta-analysis (Newcomb & Bagwell, 1995). Differences occur in four broad categories: *positive engagement* (friends talk, smile, and laugh more frequently than nonfriends); *relationship mutuality* (friends are more supportive, more mutually oriented, and emphasize equality (parity) more frequently in their exchanges than nonfriends); *task behavior* (friends talk more about the task at hand and spend more time on-task than nonfriends); and *conflict management* (although friends do not have more frequent conflicts than nonfriends, they use disengagement and negotiation proportionally more often and their conflicts are not as intense). These results demonstrate once again that reciprocity and symmetry are the behavioral hallmarks of friendship during middle childhood.

Enemies

The behavior of enemies toward one another has never been systematically described, either in early or middle childhood. In certain instances, investigators have considered two children who fight frequently with one another to be enemies (Ross & Conant, 1992) but the fact of the matter is that not many preschool-aged dyads do this. Since children do not concentrate hostile actions on specific associates, this must mean one of two things: either enemies do not exist among young children (as mentioned above) or enemies consistently use other strategies, for example, avoiding one another. Avoidance indeed seems likely to be a coping mechanism used by children who mutually consider themselves to be enemies or who dislike each other. Adults report that they minimize contact with their enemies and avoid them whenever possible (Holt, 1989). Demonstrating avoidance with young children, however, is surprisingly difficult.

Motives attributed by children to their enemies are likely to be more hostile than those attributed to friends or acquaintances. In one investigation (Ray & Cohen, 1997), school-aged children were asked to evaluate the victim's attributions in hypothetical scenarios when either a friend, an acquaintance, or an enemy committed a hurtful act under either accidental, ambiguous, or hostile circumstances. In ambiguous situations, an enemy's intentions were evaluated less positively than were the intentions of friends or acquaintances. In accidental situations, victims were believed to be more likely to retaliate when provoked by enemies than by either friends or acquaintances. Finally, self-reported liking for enemies (as provocateurs) was low regardless of motivational condition; in contrast, liking for friends and acquaintances (relatively high prior to the provocation) decreased. School-aged children thus display attribution biases suggesting that they assume "the worst" of their enemies.

Persuasion studies suggest that enemies, in general, are seen as power-assertive, threatening, and uncooperative: 6 and 7 year olds were asked how they would make requests of a friend or an enemy, respectively (Bernicot & Mahrokhian, 1989). Results showed that children were more direct and more imperative in persuading friends (e.g., "give me the toy") than enemies ("gee, that toy looks like it would be fun to play with"). Apparently, children believe that one approaches enemies cautiously when attempting to exert social influence – the same caution they display in attempting to persuade parents and other persons possessing greater power and authority than they do (Cowan, Drinkard, & MacGavin, 1984). While scattered, these findings nevertheless indicate that the "enemy construct" is behaviorally salient by middle childhood.

Having Friends and Having Enemies: Developmental Implications

Friends

Children differ from one another according to whether or not they have mutual friends. Such differences are significant because friendships may be contexts that enhance social competence (Sullivan, 1953); concomitantly, social competence may enhance the likelihood that a child has friends. Indeed, correlational studies suggest such a linkage. Among preschool-aged children, individuals with emotional difficulties are friendless more frequently than better-adapted children, and are less likely to maintain the friendships they have (Howes, 1983). Children with reciprocated friendships enter groups more easily, engage in more cooperative play, are more sociable, more prosocial, and are less aggressive and have fewer conflicts with other children than those who do not have friends (Howes, 1989; Sebanc, 1999). Moreover, these conditions hold true for both Caucasian and African American children in the United States (Vaughn, Azria, Krzysik, Caya, Newell, & Cielinski, 2000). Among young children who have friends, a significant advantage also accrues in having several friendships as opposed to one (Vaughn et al., 2000).

Cross-sectional studies also show that, among school-aged children, those who have friends are more socially competent than those who do not: They are more sociable, coop-erative, altruistic, self-confident, and less lonely (Newcomb & Bagwell, 1995). Children who lack friends are more likely to endorse revenge as an appropriate goal in social rela-tions than those who have friends (Rose & Asher, 1999a) as well as goals involving distanc-ing oneself from other children (Rose & Asher, 1999b). Finally, among children who are at risk of being victimized (owing to both internalizing and externalizing problems), the occurrence of abuse varies negatively with the number of friends the children have: Nu-merous friends appear to offer physical protection to victimized children, are feared by the child's bullies, and are sources of advice concerning how to handle conflicts and threats (Hodges et al., 1997).

Although research is consistent in showing that children who have friends evince better social adaptation than those who do not (and that having more friends is better than having few), the meaning of these results is not clear. First, the results can be over-inter-preted: Having friends may not be as closely linked to social adaptation as certain other measures (e.g., social rejection). In one investigation involving 8 year olds (Gest, Graham-Bermann, & Hartup, 2001), the number of mutual friends was correlated only with lead-ership, humor, and not being teased whereas peer rejection was correlated with a wide range of different behaviors (e.g., peer rejection was negatively related to cooperation and prosocial behavior and positively to aggression and antisocial behavior). In one other in-stance (Schwarz, Hess, & Atkins, 1999), the number of the child's friends did not contrib-ute unique variance to any peer-rated behavior except shyness. Second, other close relationships (e.g., family relationships) may moderate the relation between having mutual friendships and psychological well-being. Among older children, for example, having friends is more strongly related to social adjustment among children from noncohesive and nonadaptable families than among children from better family environments. At the same time, family environments are more strongly linked to adjustment among children who do not have mutual friends than among those who do (Gauze, Bukowski, Aquan-Assee, & Sippola, 1996). The outcomes of *either* relationship, then, are moderated by the other. Clearly, univariate studies do not reveal the complex developmental implications of having mutual friends.

Longitudinal studies assist in sorting out these issues. Such studies of preschool-aged children, however, are rare: One investigation shows that social competence is a better predictor of friendship status across time than the reverse (Vaughn et al., 2000) which assists with causal questions. Certain other studies show that the transition to kindergarten is made more easily among children who have friends and keep them (Ladd, 1990). Longer term derivatives of preschool friendships have not been studied, however.

Among older children, having friends increases self-esteem and decreases psychosocial difficulties during changes from lower to middle to high school (Simmons, Burgeson, & Reef, 1988). The relation between behavior problems and increases over time in victimiza-tion is attenuated among children who have friends (Hodges, Finnegan, & Perry, 1999). The relation between having friends and later outcomes, however, is complex. For exam-ple, having friends in middle childhood predicts adult feelings of self-worth in early adult-hood, family attitudes, and the absence of depression but not sociability, school performance, educational aspirations, and job performance, which are better predicted by sociometric status (Bagwell, Newcomb, & Bukowski, 1998). Once again, having a mutual friend predicts some outcomes but not others. Finally, moderator effects occur in social development: Adjustment outcomes when one gains or loses a friend (either one) are greater among children from nonadaptable families than more adaptable ones (Gauze et al., 1996).

One other consequence of having friends in childhood is success is romantic relationships. First, having same-sex friends during middle childhood forecasts having romantic relationships in early adolescence (Neeman, Hubbard, & Masten, 1995). Second, having friends enhances success in adolescent romantic relationships (Sroufe, Egeland, & Carlson, 1999) as well as successful functioning in romantic relationships in early adulthood (Collins, Hennighausen, & Ruh, 1999). Other-sex friendships are related to romantic affiliations as well, but not until adolescence (Feiring, 1999). The weight of the evidence thus supports Sullivan's (1953) notions concerning the importance of same-sex friendships during "the juvenile era" in generating the intimacy required subsequently for success in opposite-sex relationships.

Enemies

Relatively little attention has been given to the developmental significance of having enemies. Since the central dynamic in these relationships is reciprocal rejection (Hembree & Vandell, 2000), the children involved could be affected by the conflict and aggression associated with being disliked. Alternatively, one can argue that a mutual antipathy is an especially intense and personalized rejection and, as such, increases developmental risk over and beyond the risk that derives from general peer rejection. No one knows whether these conditions represent the phenomenology of mutual antipathies but the possibility makes the linkage between having enemies and social development worth studying.

Neither cross-sectional nor longitudinal studies addressing these questions have been conducted with preschool-aged children. Cross-sectional studies with school-aged children, however, have been carried out separately with 8 and 10 year olds. Hembree and Vandell (2000) examined the relation between involvement in same-sex mutual antipathies (mutual nomination as "someone I don't want to play with") and four composite measures: *social-emotional adjustment*, including prosocial and antisocial behavior rated separately by parents and teachers; *academic adjustment*, including grades, test scores, and work habits; and self-ratings of *perceived competence*. Teacher-rated social adjustment and the measure of academic adjustment were both negatively related to involvement in same-sex antipathies with parent education, single-parent status, *and* peer rejection factored out.

Using assessments of several thousand Dutch 10 year olds, Abecassis et al.,(2001) studied the relation between involvement in mutual antipathies and a wide variety of social and adaptational behaviors. Same-sex and mixed-sex antipathies (defined as children who mutually nominate one another as "someone not liked at all") were both linked to social competence using composite measures based on peer and self-ratings. Sociometric assessment (i.e., peer rejection) was included as a covariate in the analyses in order to determine whether unique adaptational variance was associated with antipathy involvement. Results showed that same-sex antipathies were positively associated with antisocial behavior, especially fighting and bullying, social ineffectiveness, and being victimized; prosocial behavior was not related to involvement in these antipathies. These data are consistent with earlier findings that both bullies and victims have more enemies than nonbullies or nonvictimized children, respectively (Hodges et al., 1999), but apply to children more widely than to bully–victim dyads.

Mixed-sex antipathies were associated with more dysfunctional behavior in girls than in boys: Girls with mixed-sex antipathies were less antisocial than girls without, but more socially ineffective, less prosocial, more victimized, had fewer friends, and more frequently reported depressive symptoms and somatic complaints. In contrast, boys with mixed-sex antipathies were more antisocial than boys who were not involved in these relationships (including fighting, bullying, and being disruptive), but were also more prosocial, socially effective, less frequently victimized, and suffered no negative consequences in terms of depression or somatic complaints. Taken together, the results show that mutual antipathies are associated with a wide range of socially maladaptive behaviors for school-aged children, carrying predictive variance not shared entirely with peer rejection.

One longitudinal study shows that involvement in same-sex antipathies among 10-year-old boys predicts social behavior when they have become adolescents. Abecassis (1999) found, among boys only, that a group of intercorrelated social behaviors measuring social reservedness and social withdrawal (e.g., noninvolvement in addictive behaviors, nonparticipation in delinquency, fewer somatic complaints, lack of support from parents, and parental unwillingness to respect the adolescent's autonomy) were forecast by earlier involvement in same-sex antipathies. Baseline controls were included in the analyses, so that the results suggest that involvement in same-sex antipathies as children translates into behavior in adolescence that *differs* from the concurrent correlates at either age. Actually, since a *combination* of antipathies involvement and depression among the boys during childhood predicted the social reservedness pattern, developmental trajectories need to be studied more closely. The results demonstrate, however, that involvement in inimical relationships in middle childhood may have long-term significance.

Characteristics of Friends and Enemies: Developmental Implications

Social interaction between friends or between enemies reflects characteristics of both children; each is being socialized simultaneously within these relationships. Consequently, the variance deriving from the characteristics of children's friends or enemies is conflated with characteristics of the children themselves. Only longitudinal studies convincingly demonstrate the extent to which developmental outcome depends on who a child's friends or enemies are.

Friends

Friendships ought to enhance social competence when a child's friend is socially competent but not when friends are incompetent. Friendships may actually contribute deleteriously to developmental outcome when the child's friend is antisocial, not well socialized, or socially rejected. According to these arguments, the social advantage for the individual child does not reside merely in having friends but in having socially competent, well-adjusted friends.

Several kinds of evidence support these notions: (a) Among 12 year olds, social adjustment improves across a one-year school transition when friends are well adjusted but not otherwise (Berndt, Hawkins, & Jiao, 1999). (b) School-aged children whose friends have conventional social orientations and good social skills become even more likely to endorse normative values as time passes (Kandel & Andrews, 1987). (c) Among children experiencing the stress of marital transitions (e.g., divorce or remarriage of their parents), having socially well-adjusted friends who have few behavior problems promotes resilience whereas having immature friends or friends with behavior problems does not (Hetherington, 1999). (d) "Desisting" delinquency is forecast among children at risk for antisocial behavior more strongly by turning away from antisocial friends to more socially skilled friends than by any other variable (Mulvey & Aber, 1988). (e) Increases in victimization among children at risk are inversely related to the number of externalizing problems evinced by their friends, suggesting that children with externalizing difficulties may retaliate in defense of their friends, thereby protecting them from escalating victimization (Hodges & Perry, 1999). Taken together, these results suggest that friendships with socially well-adjusted children promote better developmental outcomes than friendships with poorly adjusted children. Complicating the situation, however, are social comparison processes occurring between children and their friends: Children's evaluations of their own academic achievement, for example, are more accurate when their friends are low rather than high achievers (Guay, Boivin, & Hodges, 1999). Such results suggest that social comparisons with friends have more positive outcomes when they reflect positively on the child rather than negatively (Tesser, Campbell, & Smith, 1984).

On the other side of the coin, association with antisocial friends increases a child's antisocial behavior, especially among children already identified as aggressive and rejected (Dishion, 1990; Kupersmidt, Burchinal, & Patterson, 1995; Tremblay, Masse, Vitaro, & Dobkin, 1995). One reason is that antisocial friends oftentimes are not socially skilled, and thus lack the capacity to instigate socially competent behavior in their companions. Second, the interaction between aggressive children and their friends is more contentious and conflict-ridden than interaction between matched controls (Dishion, Andrews, & Crosby, 1995). Still other studies show that overtly aggressive children are not notably intimate with one another and are not as exclusive in their relationship attitudes as their nonaggressive counterparts (Grotpeter & Crick, 1996).

Taken together, then, the friendships of some children are mixed blessings: On the one hand, these friends support good developmental outcomes through social support and the increased sense of well-being that accompanies experience in close relationships. On the other hand, aggressive friends are risk factors since the children are not well socialized and instigate aggressive behavior in one another. Whether other socially incompetent children (e.g., extremely shy children) socialize one another toward increased maladaptation is not known. Actually, shy friends may assist one another in alleviating the loneliness that accompanies and exacerbates the risk associated with shyness (Asher, Parkhurst, Hymel & Williams, 1990).

Enemies

The developmental implications of the characteristics of children's enemies are largely unknown. In a cross-sectional study of victimization among 10 to 14 year olds (Card, Isaacs, & Hodges, 2000), the investigators identified children with same-sex mutual antipathies (least like to work or play with) and correlated the children's victimization scores with four theoretically relevant characteristics of their enemies: aggression, physical strength, victimization, and internalizing behaviors. Results show that the first three variables significantly and uniquely predicted victimization. Although not longitudinal in design, these results suggest that making enemies with aggressive, strong, and nonvictimized children may be a risk factor in victimization, supplementing the risk these children experience by virtue of having friends who are themselves physically weak and nonaggressive. Whether children consciously select friends who are different from their enemies (or the reverse) is an interesting inference that can be drawn from the results. Regardless of the limitations on these results, there is a suggestion that the developmental significance of having enemies may lie in who one's enemies are, not merely in whether one has an enemy.

Relationship Quality: Developmental Implications

Friends

Friendships vary in their social and emotional qualities: Some children have supportive and intimate relationships with their friends, some nonsupportive and contentious ones. Differences among the friendships of young children can be measured either with behavioral observations or reports based on the observations of teachers or mothers. The *Dyadic Relationships Q-set* (Park & Waters, 1989) uses detailed behavioral observations and encompasses a two-factor structure including positive and coordinated interactions, respectively. Teacher ratings have been used to differentiate the friendships of young children according to a somewhat more elaborated structure consisting of supportiveness, exclusivity, conflict, and asymmetry (Sebanc, 1999).

Using these measures, several investigators have reported that the quality of relationships between mothers and children is related to the quality of friendships among preschool-aged children. Secure mother–infant relationships in both members of 4-year-old friendship pairs are associated with more harmonious, less controlling, and greater responsivity between the children than when one child has a history of insecure attachment (Park & Waters, 1989) and are more positive and coordinated one year later (Kerns, 1994). Children with secure attachment histories are also less likely to have negative and asymmetrical friendships during the preschool years than children with insecure attachments (Youngblade & Belsky, 1992) and to be sadder when their friends move away (Park, 1992). Mechanisms responsible for these associations have not been clearly identified but it is clear that certain continuities exist between the mother–child attachment system and friendship quality. Moreover, these extend into middle childhood (Elicker et al., 1992; Sroufe et al., 1999). Other correlates of friendship quality have not been explored extensively among preschool-aged children, although supportive relationships have been linked to prosocial behavior displayed by the children, relationship exclusivity linked to relational aggression, and relationship conflict linked to overt aggression (Sebanc, 1999).

Among older children, friendship qualities have been assessed with instruments that differentiate between "positive" and "negative" relationships (Furman, 1996) although more finely grained assessments are also available (Parker & Asher, 1993). Correlational studies show that: (a) friendship success is positively related to sociability and negatively related to emotionality (Stocker & Dunn, 1990); (b) supportiveness in friendship relations among school-aged children is positively related to popularity and good social reputations (Cauce, 1986), self-esteem (McGuire & Weisz, 1982), social involvement and achievement (Berndt, 1996) and good psychosocial adjustment (Kurdek & Sinclair, 1988; Gauze et al., 1996); and (c) good-quality friendships are negatively related to children's endorsement of revenge, avoidance, and blaming as social goals and strategies in relating to other children (Rose & Asher, 1999a, b). The weight of the evidence thus suggests that supportiveness and harmony in friendship relations are linked to good social adaptation.

Longitudinal studies support the hypothesis that friendship quality affects developmental outcome but also demonstrate that these linkages are complex. In making the transition into kindergarten, for example, children who enter with supportive friendships, as contrasted with nonsupportive ones, are happier at school, perceive classmates as more supportive, and show increasingly positive attitudes toward school over the course of the year; school adjustment difficulties occur less frequently, especially among boys (Ladd, Kochenderfer, & Coleman, 1996). The transition from elementary school to secondary school is also affected by friendship quality: Supportiveness of the child's friends, assessed shortly after school entrance, predicts increasing sociability, positive attitudes about classmates, and popularity over the next year, especially in stable relationships (Berndt et al., 1999).

Oftentimes, however, the developmental effects of friendship quality depend on other conditions and characteristics. For example, friendships that children regard as providing them with companionship, support, security, and closeness compensate for vulnerabilities and stresses that derive from poor family environments (Gauze et al., 1996; Sesma, 2001) but provide fewer benefits when family environments are good. Concomitantly, an adaptive or cohesive family environment helps children with poor quality friendships more than those with good quality relationships (Gauze et al., 1996).

Child characteristics moderate the effects of friendship quality, too: (a) Among aggressive, but not nonaggressive children, increases over time in delinquency are greater for those who have low quality friendships than better quality ones (Poulin, Dishion, & Haas, 1999); and (b) the relation between internalizing behaviors and increases over time in victimization is attenuated when children have a "protective" friendship (Hodges, Boivin, Vitaro, & Bukowski, 1999). Taken together, then, the evidence suggests that good developmental outcomes are most likely when a child has friends, those friends are socially skilled, and these friendships are supportive and intimate. Friendships between children who are aggressive or not well socialized are mixed blessings, as are friendships which are negative and contentious. Moderator effects, however, are common.

Enemies

No one has yet studied qualitative features of mutual antipathies as related to developmental outcome. Certainly, all enmities are not alike either in affective intensity or modes of social interaction.

Conclusion

Several generalizations can be made about friends and enemies in child development: First, both of these relationships account for unique variance in long-term as well as concurrent adaptation. Too little is known, however, about the developmental dynamics of mutual antipathies to be able to determine whether "being friends" and "being enemies" are relationship opposites or relationship orthogonalities in children's experience.

Second, these relationships may not be as important developmentally speaking as whether children are generally accepted or rejected. Comparative studies suggest that being disliked by other children, especially one's same-sex peers, accounts for greater amounts of unique variance than having friends or occupying a central position in the social network. Peer rejection also identifies children at risk across a wider range of social behaviors than friendlessness does. Although the developmental consequences of having good friends encompass self-esteem, success in romantic relationships, and good relationship attitudes, friendships may still have more restricted consequences than peer acceptance/rejection.

Third, children's enemies should not be ignored in developmental research. Effect sizes in the existing data are small and only one longitudinal study suggests that these relationships have long-term consequences, but these relationships may be more important in child development than previously suspected. Mutual antipathies may not predict developmental outcomes as powerfully as being generally disliked and one can guess that these antipathies are more critical to the development of certain behaviors (e.g., antisocial dispositions, victimization) than others. But we do not know these things. One must also consider the possibility that childhood antipathies are more important in the social development of some individuals than others.

Fourth, we know relatively little about the processes (mechanisms) through which friends and enemies influence the development of the individual child. Laboratory studies demonstrate that friends talk more with each other than nonfriends, are more mutually oriented, and manage conflicts more constructively. One can assume that these behaviors are evinced in everyday circumstances when observers are not present. Friends may be better socializers than nonfriends (for example, in the induction of scientific reasoning on difficult tasks through the use of constructive conflicts (Azmitia & Montgomery, 1993)). Few investigators, however, have identified developmental mechanisms like these. We know as little about the processes by which friends and enemies influence the individual child as we do about the processes through which peer rejection brings about its effects (Rubin, Bukowski, & Parker, 1998).

Process-oriented studies of several kinds ought to be conducted: Macro-analytic studies are needed to show the manner in which relationships with friends and enemies combine over time with temperament and early experience, family relationships, the social context, and emerging social competence in the child. Good beginnings can be made by showing how relationships affect coping and children's encounters with stress. Close examination of naturally occurring stressors such as being victimized or being a child of divorce can greatly enhance our understanding of both friendship and inimical processes.

Micro-analytic investigations are also needed. Models need to be constructed for utilizing information about behavioral mechanisms to predict long-term developmental outcomes. One of the most successful attempts to build a developmental model at both microscopic and macroscopic levels has been "the performance model" of antisocial development developed by Gerald R. Patterson and his colleagues (cf., Patterson, Reid, & Dishion, 1992). Friendship experience is woven into that model and empirical studies have verified some of the processes that may be involved (Dishion et al., 1995). Other models in other domains of social development now need to reflect the same attention to friends and enemies and the mechanisms through which these relationships have (or do not have) developmental effects.

Our review shows that, while much is known about friends and a little is known about enemies, much is not known about these relationships. Investigators need to examine them more closely, tying distinctive modes of interaction to both developmental antecedents and developmental consequences. Attention must also be given to the manner in which different children utilize these relationships to arrive at different adaptations in childhood and beyond.

References

Abecassis, M. (1998). The Hatfields and the McCoys: Understanding the development of enemy relationships. Unpublished manuscript, University of Minnesota.

Abecassis, M. (1999). I dislike you and you dislike me: Prevalence and developmental significance of mutual antipathies among preadolescents and adolescents. Unpublished doctoral dissertation, University of Minnesota.

Abecassis, M., Hartup, W. W., Haselager, G. J. T., Sholte, R., & Van Lieshout, C. F. M. (2001). Mutual antipathies and their significance in middle childhood and adolescence. Unpublished manuscript, University of Minnesota.

Asher, S. R., Parkhurst, J. T., Hymel, S., & Williams, G. A. (1990). Peer rejection and loneliness in childhood. In S. R. Asher & J. D. Coie (Eds.), *Peer rejection in childhood* (pp. 253–273). New York: Cambridge University Press.

Azmitia, M., & Montgomery, R. (1993). Friendship, transactive dialogues, and the development of scientific reasoning. *Social Development, 2*, 202–221.

Bagwell, C. L., Newcomb, A. F., & Bukowski, W. M. (1998). Preadolescent friendship and peer rejection as predictors of adult adjustment. *Child Development, 69*, 140–153.

Berndt, T. J. (1996). Exploring the effects of friendship quality on social development. In W. M. Bukowski, A. F. Newcomb, & W. W. Hartup (Eds.), *The company they keep: Friendship in childhood and adolescence* (pp. 346–365). Cambridge, England: Cambridge University Press.

Berndt, T. J., Hawkins, J. A., & Jiao, Z. (1999). Influences of friends and friendships on adjustment to junior high school. *Merrill-Palmer Quarterly, 45*, 13–41.

Berndt, T. J., & Perry, T. B. (1986). Children's perceptions of friendship as supportive relationships. *Developmental Psychology, 22,* 640–648.

Bernicot, J., & Mahrokhian, A. (1989). Asking and insisting after a refusal: How do 6- to 7-year olds proceed? *International Journal of Psychology, 24,* 409–428.

Bigelow, B. J. (1977). Children's friendship expectations: A cognitive developmental study. *Child Development, 48,* 246–253.

Card, N. A., Isaacs, J., & Hodges, E. V. E. (2000, August). *The hazards of developing enemies: Relations with peer victimization.* Paper presented at the meetings of the American Psychological Association, Washington, DC.

Cauce, A. M. (1986). Social networks and social competence: Exploring the effects of early adolescent friendships. *American Journal of Community Psychology, 14,* 607–628.

Chomsky, N. (1965). *Aspects of a theory of syntax.* Cambridge, MA: MIT Press.

Collins, W. A., Hennighausen, K., & Ruh, J. (1999, April). *Peer competence in middle childhood and behavior in romantic relationships in adolescence and young adulthood.* Paper presented at the biennial meetings of the Society for Research in Child Development, Albuquerque, NM.

Cowan, G., Drinkard, J., & MacGavin, L. (1984). The effect of target, age, and gender on use of power strategies. *Journal of Personality and Social Psychology, 47,* 1391–1398.

Dawe, H. C. (1934). An analysis of two hundred quarrels of preschool children. *Child Development, 5,* 139–157.

Dishion, T. J. (1990). The peer context of troublesome child and adolescent behavior. In P. Leone (Ed.), *Understanding troubled and troublesome youth* (pp. 128–153). Newbury Park, CA: Sage.

Dishion, T. J., Andrews, D. W., & Crosby, L. (1995). Anti-social boys and their friends in early adolescence: Relationship characteristics, quality, and interactional processes. *Child Development, 66,* 139–151.

Dishion, T. J., Patterson, G. R., & Greisler, P. C. (1994). Peer adaptations in the development of antisocial behavior: A confluence model. In L. R. Huesmann (Ed.), *Current perspectives on aggressive behavior* (pp. 61–95). New York: Plenum.

Eder, D., & Hallinan, M. T. (1978). Sex differences in children's friendships. *American Sociological Review, 43,* 237–250.

Elicker, J., Englund, M., & Sroufe, L. A. (1992). Predicting peer competence and peer relationships in middle childhood from early parent–child relationships. In R. Parke & G. W. Ladd (Eds.), *Family–peer relationships: Modes of linkage* (pp. 77–106). Hillsdale, NJ: Erlbaum.

Feiring, C. (1999). Other-sex friendship networks and the development of romantic relationships in adolescence. *Journal of Youth and Adolescence, 28,* 495-512.

French, D. C., Jansen, E. A., Riansari, M., & Setiono, K. (2000). Similarities between Indonesian friends and nonfriends during middle childhood. Unpublished manuscript, Illinois Wesleyan University.

Furman, W. (1996). The measurement of friendship perceptions: Conceptual and methodological issues. In W. M. Bukowski, A. F. Newcomb, & W. W. Hartup (Eds.), *The company they keep: Friendship in childhood and adolescence* (pp. 41–65). Cambridge, England: Cambridge University Press.

Furman, W., & Buhrmester, D. (1985). Children's perceptions of the personal relationships in their social networks. *Developmental Psychology, 21,* 1016–1022.

Gauze C., Bukowski, W. M., Aquan-Assee, J., & Sippola, L. K. (1996). Interactions between family environment and friendship and associations with self-perceived well-being during early adolescence. *Child Development, 67,* 2201–2216.

Gest, S. D., Graham-Bermann, & Hartup, W. W. (2001). Peer experience: Common and unique features of number of friendships, social network centrality, and sociometric status. *Social Development, 10,* 23-40.

Gleason, T. R. (1998). Social provisions of real and imaginary relationships in early childhood. Unpublished Ph.D. dissertation, University of Minnesota.

Gottman, J. M. (1983). How children become friends. *Monographs of the Society for Research in Child Development, 48* (3, Serial No. 201).

Grotpeter, J. E., & Crick, N. R. (1996). Relational aggression, overt aggression, and friendship. *Child Development, 67*, 2328–2338.

Guay, F., Boivin, M., & Hodges, E. V. E. (1999). Social comparison processes and academic achievement: The dependence of the development of self-evaluations on friends' performance. *Journal of Educational Psychology, 91*, 564-568

Hallinan, M. T. (1980). Patterns of cliquing among youth. In H. C. Foot, A. J. Chapman, & J. R. Smith (Eds.), *Friendship and peer relations in children* (pp. 321–342). New York: Wiley.

Hartup, W. W. (1996). The company they keep: Friendships and their developmental significance. *Child Development, 67*, 1–13.

Hartup, W. W., Laursen, B., Stewart, M. I., & Eastenson, A. (1988). Conflict and the friendship relations of young children. *Child Development, 59*, 1590–1600.

Hartup, W. W., & Stevens, N. (1997). Friendships and adaptation in the life course. *Psychological Bulletin, 121*, 355–370.

Haselager, G. J. T., Hartup, W. W., Van Lieshout, C. F. M., & Riksen-Walraven, M. (1998). Similarities between friends and nonfriends in middle childhood. *Child Development, 69*, 1198–1208.

Hayes, D., Gershman, E., & Bolin, L. (1980). Friends and enemies: Cognitive bases for preschool children's unilateral and reciprocal relationships. *Child Development, 51*, 1276–1279.

Hayes, D., Gershman, E., & Halteman, W. (1996). Enmity in males at four developmental levels: Cognitive bases for disliking. *Journal of Genetic Psychology, 157*, 153–160.

Hembree, S. E., & Vandell, D. L. (2000). Reciprocity in rejection: The role of mutual antipathy and children's adjustment. Unpublished manuscript, University of Wisconsin.

Hetherington, E. M. (1999). Social capital and the development of youth from nondivorced, divorced, and remarried families. In W. A. Collins & B. Laursen (Eds.), *Minnesota symposia on child psychology* (Vol. 30, pp. 177–209). Mahwah, NJ: Erlbaum.

Hinde, R. A., Titmus, G., Easton, D., & Tamplin, A. (1985). Incidence of "friendship" and behavior with strong associates versus nonassociates in preschoolers. *Child Development, 56*, 234–245.

Hodges, E. V. E., Bovin, M., Vitaro, F., & Bukowski, W. M. (1999). The power of friendship: Protection against an escalating cycle of peer victimization. *Developmental Psychology, 35*, 94–101.

Hodges, E. V. E., Finnegan, R. A., & Perry, D. G. (1999). Skewed autonomy-relatedness in preadolescents' conceptions of their relationships with mother, father, and best friend. *Developmental Psychology, 35*, 737–748.

Hodges, E. V. E., Malone, M. J., & Perry, D. G. (1997). Individual risk and social risk as interacting determinants of victimization in the peer group. *Developmental Psychology, 33*, 1032–1039.

Hodges, E. V. E., & Perry, D. G. (1999). Personal and interpersonal antecedents and consequences of victimization by peers. *Journal of Personality and Social Psychology, 76*, 677–685.

Holt, R. (1989). College students' definitions and images of enemies. *Journal of Social Issues, 45*, 33–50.

Howes, C. (1983). Patterns of friendship. *Child Development, 54*, 1041–1053.

Howes, C. (1989). Peer interaction of young children. *Monographs of the Society for Research in Child Development, 53* (Serial No. 217).

Kandel, D. B. (1978). Similarity in real-life adolescent pairs. *Journal of Personality and Social Psychology, 36*, 306–312.

Kandel, D. B., & Andrews, K. (1987). Processes of adolescent socialization by parents and peers.

International Journal of the Addictions, 22, 319–342.

Kerns, K. A. (1994). A longitudinal examination of links between mother–child attachment and children's friendships in early childhood. *Journal of Social and Personal Relationships, 11,* 379–381.

Kupersmidt, J. B., Burchinal, M., & Patterson, C. J. (1995). Developmental patterns of childhood peer relations as predictors of externalizing behavior problems. *Development and Psychopathology, 7,* 649–668.

Kupersmidt, J. B., DeRosier, M. E., & Patterson, C. P. (1995). Similarity as the basis for children's friendships: The roles of sociometric status, aggressive and withdrawn behavior, academic achievement, and demographic characteristics. *Journal of Social and Personal Relationships, 12,* 439–452.

Kurdek, L. A., & Sinclair, R. J. (1988). Adjustment of young adolescents in two-parent nuclear, stepfather, and mother-custody families. *Journal of Consulting and Clinical Psychology, 56,* 91–96.

Ladd, G. W. (1990). Having friends, keeping friends, making friends, and being liked by peers in the classroom: Predictors of children's early school adjustment? *Child Development, 61,* 1081–1100.

Ladd, G. W., Kochenderfer, B. J., & Coleman, C. C. (1996). Friendship quality as a predictor of young children's early school adjustment. *Child Development, 67,* 1103–1118.

Livesley, W. J., & Bromley, B. D. (1973). *Person perception in childhood and adolescence.* London: Wiley.

McGuire, K. D., & Weisz, J. R. (1982). Social cognition and behavior correlates of preadolescent chumship. *Child Development, 53,* 1478–1484.

Moore, S. G. (1967). Correlates of peer acceptance in nursery school children. In W. W. Hartup & N. L. Smothergill (Eds.), *The young child* (pp. 229–247). Washington, DC: National Association for the Education of Young Children.

Mulvey, E. P., & Aber, M. S. (1988). Growing out of delinquency: Development and desistance. In R. Jenkins & W. Brown (Eds.), *The abandonment of delinquent behavior: Promoting the turnaround.* New York: Prager.

Neeman, J., Hubbard, J., & Masten, A. (1995). The changing importance of romantic relationship involvement to competence from late childhood to late adolescence. *Development and Psychopathology, 7,* 727–750.

Newcomb, A. F., & Bagwell, C. (1995). Children's friendship relations: A meta-analytic review. *Psychological Bulletin, 117,* 306–347.

Park, K. A. (1992). Preschoolers' reactions to loss of a best friend: Developmental trends and individual differences. *Child Study Journal, 22,* 233–252.

Park, K. A., & Waters, E. (1989). Security of attachment and preschool friendships. *Child Development, 60,*1076–1081.

Parker, J. G., & Asher, S. R. (1993). Friendship and friendship quality in middle childhood: Links with peer group acceptance and feelings of loneliness and social dissatisfaction. *Developmental Psychology, 29,* 611–621.

Patterson, G. R., Reid, J. B., & Dishion, T. J. (1992). *Antisocial boys.* Eugene, OR: Castalia.

Poulin, F., & Boivin, M. (2000). The role of proactive and reactive aggression in the formation and development of boys' friendships. *Developmental Psychology, 36,* 233–240.

Poulin, F., Dishion, T. J., & Haas, E. (1999). The peer influence paradox: Friendship quality and deviancy training within male adolescent friendships. *Merrill-Palmer Quarterly, 45,* 42–61.

Ray, G., & Cohen, R. (1997). Children's evaluations of provocation between peers. *Aggressive Behavior, 23,* 417–431.

Rizzo, T. A. (1989). *Friendship development among children in school.* Norwood, NJ: Ablex.

Rose, A. J., & Asher, S. R. (1999a). Children's goals and strategies in response to conflicts within a friendship. *Developmental Psychology, 35,* 69–79.

Rose, A. J., & Asher, S. R. (1999b, April). *Seeking and giving support within a friendship.* Paper presented at the biennial meetings of the Society for Research in Child Development, Albuquerque, NM.

Rosenbaum, M. E. (1986). The repulsion hypothesis: On the nondevelopment of relationships. *Journal of Personality and Social Psychology, 51,* 1156–1166.

Ross, H., & Conant, C. (1992). The social structure of early conflicts: Interaction, relationships, and alliances. In C. U. Shantz & W. W. Hartup (Eds.), *Conflict in child and adolescent development* (pp. 153–185). Cambridge, England: Cambridge University Press.

Rubin, K. H., Bukowski, W. M., & Parker, J. G. (1998). Peer interaction, relationships, groups. In W. Damon & N. Eisenberg (Eds.), *Handbook of child psychology* (Vol. 3, pp. 619–700). New York: Wiley.

Rubin, K. H., Lynch, D., Coplan, R., Rose-Krasnor, L., & Booth, C. L. (1994). "Birds of a feather…": Behavioral concordances and preferential personal attraction in children. *Child Development, 65,* 1778–1785.

Schwarz, R. L., Hess, L. E., & Atkins, M. S. (1999, April). *Friendships, peer status, and Social networks: Relative contributions to children's adjustment.* Paper presented at the biennial meetings of the Society for Research in Child Development, Albuquerque, NM.

Sebanc, A. M. (1999). Friendship experiences among preschool children: Links with prosocial behavior and aggression. Unpublished doctoral dissertation, University of Minnesota.

Sesma, A. (2001). The conditional significance of friendship intimacy for well-being in childhood and adolescence: Adversity and parent-child outcomes as moderators. Unpublished doctoral dissertation, University of Minnesota.

Sharabany, R., Gershoni, R., & Hofman, J. E. (1981). Girlfriend, boyfriend: Age and sex differences in intimate friendship. *Developmental Psychology, 17,* 800–808.

Simmons, R. G., Burgeson, R., & Reef, M. J. (1988). Cumulative change at entry to adolescence. In M. Gunnar & W. A. Collins (Eds.), *Minnesota symposia on child psychology* (Vol. 21, pp. 123–150). Hillsdale, NJ: Erlbaum.

Sroufe, L. A., Egeland, B., & Carlson, E. A. (1999). One social world: The integrated development of parent–child and peer relationships. In W. A. Collins & B. Laursen (Eds.), *Minnesota symposia on child psychology* (Vol. 30, pp. 241–261). Mahwah, NJ: Erlbaum.

Stocker, C., & Dunn, J. (1990). Sibling relationships in childhood: Links with friendships and peer relationships. *British Journal of Developmental Psychology, 8,* 227–244.

Sullivan, H. S. (1953). *The interpersonal theory of psychiatry.* New York: Norton.

Tesser, A., Campbell, J., & Smith, M. (1984). Friendship choice and performance: Self-evaluation maintenance in children. *Journal of Personality and Social Psychology, 46,* 561–574.

Tremblay, R. E., Masse, L. C., Vitaro, F., & Dobkin, P. L. (1995). The impact of friends' deviant behavior on early onset of delinquency: Longitudinal data from 6 to 13 years of age. *Development and Psychopathology, 7,* 649–667.

Urberg, K. A. (1999). Introduction to invitational issue: Some thoughts about studying the influence of peers on children and adolescents. *Merrill-Palmer Quarterly, 45,* 1–12.

Vaughn, B. E., Azria, M. R., Krzysik, L., Caya, L. R., Newell, W., & Cielinski, K. L. (2000). Friendship and social competence in a sample of preschool children attending Head Start. *Developmental Psychology, 36,* 326–338.

Wiseman, J., & Duck, S. (1995). Having enemies and managing enemies: A very challenging relationship. In S. Duck & J. Wood (Eds.), *Understanding relationship processes, Vol. 5: Confronting relationship challenges* (pp. 43–72). Thousand Oaks, CA: Sage.

Youngblade, L. M., & Belsky, J. (1992). Parent-child antecedents of five-year-olds' close friendships: A longitudinal analysis. *Developmental Psychology, 28*, 107–121.

Youniss, J. (1980). *Parents and peers in social development: A Sullivan–Piaget perspective.* Chicago: University of Chicago Press.

16

Emotional and Social Development in Childhood

Susanne Denham, Maria von Salisch, Tjeert Olthof, Anita Kochanoff, and Sarah Caverly

Gary and Ron are practicing soccer moves on the playground. They have all their equipment – goal, shinpads, regulation ball – and they're having fun together. Ron shows Gary how to head the ball into the goal, both shouting, "Hurray!" But then things get complicated, changing fast, as interaction often does. Ron, thinking twice about sharing his best technique, kicks the ball ferociously away from Gary on the next play. Then Huynh, who had been watching from the sidelines, shyly asks Gary if he can join them. Simultaneously, Gary trips over a swiftly kicked ball, and slumps to the ground. And just then, Jack, the class bully, approaches, laughing at Gary's discomfort and demanding they leave so that he and his buddies can use the field. Somehow, Gary deals with all of this. He hands the ball to Huynh, extends a hand to Ron, and calmly tells Jack, "It's our turn now." When the teacher calls them inside, everybody except Jack is satisfied with recess.

What do emotions have to do with social development? Our example abounds with instances where emotions help determine the flow and outcome of interaction. First, behaviors of others in one's social group often constitute antecedent conditions for a child's emotions. When Ron became angry, it was because his goal of being "the best" was threatened. Huynh approached diffidently because he often had been "left out" from play. Second, when the child exhibits emotion within a dyad or group, this emotional expressiveness also is important information for these others. When Gary experienced delight at making a goal, he probably wanted to keep playing; others, like Huynh, want to join him. Jack is cranky, irritable, and easily provoked; he often strikes out at those he perceives to be "in his way." His classmates, observing his emotional behaviors, wisely seek to leave the scene. Third, one child's expressions of emotion may form antecedent conditions for others' experience and expression of emotions. Playmates exiting from Jack's wrath may themselves feel some combination of discomfort at his uncontrolled display, fear at his targeted nastiness, answering anger, and even spiteful delight when he *doesn't* get his way.

In concert with these views, theorists highlight the interdependency of emotional and social competence (Denham, 1998; Saarni, 1999). The interpersonal function of emotion is central to its expression and experience, its very meaning. Conversely, social interactions and relationships are guided, even defined, by emotional transactions (Halberstadt, Denham, & Dunsmore, 2001). Emotional and social competence are intimately intertwined, and, we argue, become even more so with development. Unfortunately, however, the peer literature still lags in integrating explicit elements of emotional competence into its models (Ladd, 1999; but cf. Hubbard & Coie, 1994; Lemerise & Arsenio, 2000).

Given these considerations, our *first goal* is to outline how social developmental tasks differ across childhood. The defining social issues of each age help clarify the role of emotion within each period. Our *second goal* is to describe aspects of emotional competence important to social interaction and relationship building with parents, peers, and friends (Denham, 1998; Halberstadt et al., 2001). The social tasks and emotional competencies of each period of childhood are situated within ascendant social relationships. Our *third goal* is to detail and evaluate existing research on the contribution of emotional competence to social competence, using the framework of aspects of emotional competence changing across developmental epochs and differing within relationships. We will identify gaps in theory, methodology, and evidence, to suggest future directions.

Developmental Tasks of Social Competence

The nature of adaptive social functioning changes with development; what is useful for coordinating preschoolers' interactions may be less helpful later. These changes in children's social competence and relationships are accompanied by parallel reorganizations of ways to deal with emotional issues.

Preschoolers' social tasks include managing emotional arousal within interaction and beginning to meet social expectations of persons other than their parents (Gottman & Mettetal, 1986). Coordination of play is the preschool child's overriding goal. Serving this goal are social processes of common-ground activity, conflict management, creation of a "me too" climate, shared fantasy, and achievement of good will and harmony. The processes inherent in succeeding at these social tasks call for skills of emotional competence – arguments must be resolved so that play can continue; enjoying one another's company greases the cogs of sustained interaction. Emotion regulation is key; young children must learn to avoid the disorganization of a tantrum, to think reflectively about a distressing situation.

The goals, social processes, and emotional tasks central to social competence then change radically, as gradeschoolers become aware of a wider social network than the dyad. Peer norms for social acceptance are complex and finely tuned, with inclusion by one's peers and avoiding rejection or embarrassment paramount (Gottman & Mettetal, 1986). Instead of reining in vivid emotions, gradeschoolers want to avoid embarrassment, rejecting sentiment in favor of logic. Hence, socially competent responses to many salient social situations, such as group entry and provocation, are to be guarded, cool, and unflappable.

Social processes of gossip, social support, relationship talk, self-disclosure, and informa-tion exchange serve this goal. Conversation assumes particular importance, perhaps carry-ing the weight of earlier, more overt, emotionality. Managing how and when to show emotion becomes crucial, as does knowing with whom to share emotion-laden experiences and ideas.

Elements of Emotional Competence

Next, we elaborate a model of emotional competence, showing its complex relation with social competence. We focus on three basic components crucial for success in these social developmental tasks: experiencing, expressing, and understanding emotion. Each compo-nent of emotional competence follows a partially independent developmental trajectory, which we now describe.

Experience of emotions

We refer to "experience of emotions" as not only the awareness and recognition of one's own emotions, but also as the effective regulation of one's emotional expression in the context of an ongoing social interaction (Halberstadt et al., 2001). In Figure 16.1, we depict the process of emotional experience (Denham, 1998). First, there is arousal. Some-thing happens – an environmental event (as when Gary fell down on the soccer field), one's actions (as when Ron made a goal), the actions of others (as when Jack came up to boss them), or even memories (as when Ron ruminated over giving up his "soccer se-crets").

Sometimes this arousal is automatic – when Gary fell down, he didn't need contempla-tion to experience his pain and dismay. Emotion ensued automatically, along with its attendant behavior – holding his knee, trying unsuccessfully not to cry (leftmost column, Figure 16.1). Sometimes emotional arousal needs to be understood, not just reacted to, because children create an increasingly complicated network of desires and outcomes they want to attain – their goals. Huynh needed to represent the notable change, what hap-pened to him as he walked up to Gary. How do the "butterflies" in his stomach impact his goal of joining play, if at all? What does this arousal mean? Does he acknowledge it as apprehension? Before any specific emotional reaction was felt by Huynh, or noticed by Gary, Huynh attended to the event, comprehended it, and interpreted it (middle column, Figure 16.1).

Interpretations of events' relations to ongoing goals lead not only to felt emotions, but also to actions associated with each specific emotion, and new changes in arousal (rightmost column, Figure 16.1). Does Huynh try to "deal with" his jitters so that he can present himself as a worthy teammate, maybe taking a deep breath and making an effort to walk steadily? Do these attempts at regulation work, so that he really is calmer, and his chances with Gary are better? Ability to access and manage emotions, and to communicate (or *not* communicate) them to others, is important to relationships' success.

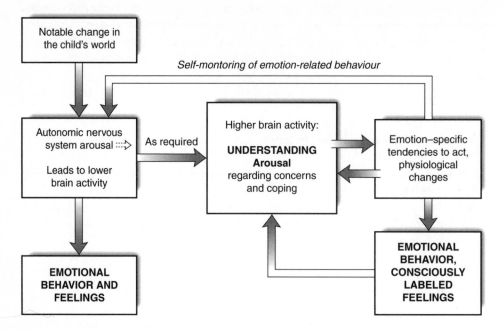

Figure 16.1 Emotional experience

To be emotionally competent, one must first recognize an emotion is being experienced. The valence of the emotion is registered at this level of skill. This low-level awareness is necessary for higher level abilities of understanding – What emotional signal am I sending to others? How do my emotional signals affect them? Identifying one's emotions accurately is also important intrapersonally. If Ron is not able to recognize his annoyance, that it stems from wanting to be "the best," he is in danger of experiencing a cascade of feelings and behaviors related to misplaced anger – which, once enacted, are resistant to reorganization.

One also must comprehend one's emotional experience within the constraints of the emotion scripts that are active, and the ongoing social context. Knowledge of feeling rules may guide children in selecting aspects of their emotional experiences upon which to focus. The glee that Gary experiences at getting a goal is more complicated than it appears. He may experience a conglomeration of delight, mild "macho" contempt, and fear when he almost didn't make it; the feeling rule, "when you win, you feel happy," may help him discern the emotional tone of his experience, or decide which aspects to communicate to others. Further, understanding that inner and outer emotional states may differ ("I know I'm scared of Jack, but I am going to put on a calm face"), also is important.

Next, the management or regulation of emotional experience is necessary when the presence or absence of emotional expression and experience interfere with a person's goals – when emotions are distressing, positive but possibly overwhelming, or needing amplification for intra- or interpersonally strategic reasons. By preschool age, such emotion regulation becomes both necessary, due to the increasing complexity of children's emotionality

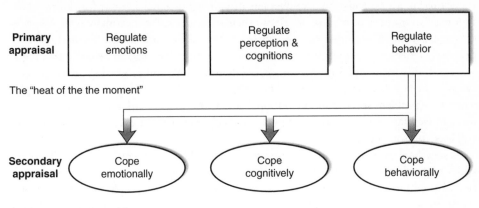

Figure 16.2 Model of emotion regulation

and the demands of their social world, and possible, because of their increased comprehension and control of their emotionality. The child chooses responses that serve the goal of modulating emotional experience (Denham, 1998). "Doing something" about the experience of emotion need not be overt and active; regulatory responses may be emotional, cognitive, or behavioral (Figure 16.2). The experience of emotion may need to be diminished or modulated, or even transformed; a child feeling anxious at preschool may smile to convince herself and others that she is happy.

Perceptual and cognitive coping steps are also possible. Refocusing attention is a useful perceptual means of regulating emotional experience – Huynh may focus on the soccer ball rather than the boys whose social status makes him uncomfortable. Problem-solving reasoning can be particularly useful. The child may relinquish a goal, choose a substitute goal, or conceive new attributions that bring comfort. A boy who is sad about not going swimming may say, "I didn't want to go anyway." Children also *do* things to cope with the experience of emotion – enacting a solution to the emotional situation, looking for support from adults, lashing out, or crying.

To succeed at emotion regulation, then, several abilities are key. One must experience clear rather than diffuse feelings, to know what to regulate! Managing false self-signals is also crucial – sometimes we may experience self-signals that aren't actually emotional, but could be mistaken for feelings (e.g., Huynh had a sudden "tummy rumble" as he approached Gary, but ignored it as not pertinent). One must also know what to feel and what not to, to attain one's goals. Children learn to retain or enhance relevant and helpful emotions, to attenuate relevant but not helpful ones, and to dampen those that are irrelevant; these regulatory behaviors help them to maintain genuine and satisfying relationships.

Experiencing and regulating emotion during the preschool period.   Little research has focused specifically on how preschoolers experience emotion. More has been done with respect to emotion regulation. Preschoolers often need external support for skillful emotion regulation; caregivers' support allows their strategies to be maximally effective. Parents assist them in cognitive coping strategies they will eventually use themselves (e.g., purposely redeploying attention). Adults also use emotion language to help children regulate emotion – by identifying and construing their feelings, and processing causal associations between events and emotions. They also demonstrate behavioral coping strategies when they problem solve around emotional situations, or structure their child's environment to facilitate regulation (e.g., a father avoids arranging a play date with someone who will leave his son cranky).

As preschoolers become more autonomous and capable of cooperation, they collaborate with caregivers' regulation efforts. They also make independent attempts, such as orientation of attention toward or away from a stimulus, self-distraction via physical self-comforting or self-stimulation, approaching or retreating from a situation, or symbolic manipulations of a situation through play (Grolnick, Bridges, & Connell, 1996). Next, young children slowly see connections between their emotion regulation efforts and changes in their feelings. Their awareness of the need for, and use of, coping strategies increases. Finally, they begin to appreciate the success or failure of their emotion regulation, and become more flexible in choosing optimal ways of coping in specific contexts. Behavioral disorganization resulting from strong emotion decreases dramatically.

Experiencing and regulating emotion during middle childhood.   Age changes in emotion regulation occur due to the socialization messages of others, as well as cognitive abilities to appraise the controllability of emotional experience, shift one's thoughts intentionally, reframe situations, and examine different aspects of the situation so that new solutions are possible (Denham, 1998; Saarni, 1999; Salisch, 2000a). Thus, gradeschoolers use and refine the same coping strategies as preschoolers – in different frequencies (Saarni, 1997). They increasingly use cognitive and problem-solving behavioral coping strategies to regulate emotion, and rely less on support seeking. Finally, they endorse distancing when stressors are not controllable. They are aware of the multiple strategies at their command, and that some strategies are most adaptive in specific situations.

Expression of emotions

Another key element of emotional competence is expressiveness. Emotions must be expressed in keeping with the child's goals, and in accordance with the social context. Thus, emotional competence includes *expressing emotions* in a way that is advantageous to moment-to-moment interaction and relationships over time. First, emotionally competent individuals are aware that an affective message should be sent in a given context (Barrett, 1995). Perhaps Ron ruminates that Gary is becoming a better soccer player because Ron showed him new moves. Gary inadvertently pokes him on the way to the pencil sharpener; because of his emotionally toned rumination, Ron may feel like sending a high intensity message – "come closer at your own risk!" But what affective message *should* be sent, for interaction to proceed smoothly? Second, children learn which expressions of emotion facilitate their goals in a given social context. Third, after determining the affective message appropriate in the current context, children must also send it convincingly. The method, intensity, and timing of sending an affective message are crucial to its meaning and eventual success or failure. Showing brief annoyance over a friend winning a game conveys a very different message than remaining angry for days. Fourth, affective messages must be sent within the constraints of display rules. Finally, the unique characteristics of interaction partners and of their interpersonal interchange must be considered (Halberstadt et al., 2001). Some situations, like a raucous game of street hockey, and some people, like Great Aunt Martha, "pull for" particular modes of expressiveness.

Accordingly, it is important to express clear, nonredundant emotional messages. Often it is most productive for a child to show what she feels, such as anxiety when lost in a store. Nonetheless, real affective messages often need to be managed – what affective message is relevant and helpful? There are also times when real affective messages are not appropriate – some are relevant to the situation but not the context, and some irrelevant ones need to be masked. The quite relevant emotions of disappointment and rage at being barred from playing Scrabble with the adults make sense, but are inappropriate in front of company. Anxiety when meeting a new friend is probably irrelevant to the goal of fun, and should be suppressed.

Expressiveness during the preschool period.   Preschoolers' emotional lives become quite complex. They are aware of the need to send an affective message, and can express vividly all the "basic" emotions. They also begin to show "social" emotions that require a sense of self and of others, including empathy, shame, guilt, and contempt (Barrett, 1995; Denham, 1998). Preschoolers also begin to show blended emotions. After his best friend leaves angrily – "You broke my truck – I won't be your friend anymore" – Antonio expresses a multifaceted mixture of sadness, guilt, and anger.

Young children's propensity to show emotions also tends to become stable across time, and across some situations. Preschoolers also have a rudimentary awareness that there are important contextual differences about what to send or not send (Zeman, Penza, Shipman, & Young, 1997). They begin to use, but not completely understand, display rules and "dissembling" emotions (Cole, 1986). Perhaps, despite feeling sad and guilty, Antonio may show his friend only his righteous anger. To look sad or act guilty would only make things worse.

Expressiveness during middle childhood.   With time and experience, older children learn that goals are not always met by showing their most intense feelings. They often do not express emotions as directly and vividly as they did earlier, with emotional expression depending on the person with whom, and the situation in which, they are interacting. For example, they regulate anger due to the negative consequences they expect (Zeman & Shipman, 1996). Along with the "cool rule" that mandates their more muted emotions within most settings, older children's emotional messages can be more complex, with the use of more blended signals and better-differentiated expressions of the social emotions. Their new ability to express (and experience) guilt, pride, and shame is buttressed by attributions of responsibility and normative standards (Harris, 1989; Olthof, Ferguson, & Luiten, 1989). Although empirical evidence is sparse, social emotions undoubtedly influence the nature of interactions and relationships.

Understanding emotions

Understanding emotion lies at the heart of emotional competence, with both experiencing and expressing emotions contributing to understanding, and understanding contributing to both other aspects. An initial appraisal that another individual is sending affective information is necessary – missing such information definitely puts one at a disadvantage (e.g., if Gary misses the muted expressions of annoyance on Ron's face, he may gloat about learning to head the soccer ball, to the dismay of both). Once perceived, the other's affective message must be interpreted accurately. Then this information must be understood within the constraints of display rules and applied within the "ongoing flow" of the context. The key here is receiving as clearly and nonredundantly as possible, the emotional messages of others.

Realizing that inner and outer emotional states may differ, that different individuals have differing emotional "styles," is also important. It is tricky to manage true *or* false emotional signals from others. One must be able to ignore false affective messages if ignoring benefits one's goals, or to accept them as real if that is advantageous. Ron may notice Gary's attempts to mask his pain and accept them, to allow Gary to save face. One must also: (1) pick up real, relevant, helpful messages; (2) ignore real but irrelevant messages; and (3) somehow deal with real and relevant but not helpful messages. When Ron notices Gary's real but not helpful message of annoyance, he has to decide whether to ignore this expressiveness as a momentary "blip."

Understanding emotions during the preschool period.   Preschoolers can name and recognize expressions for most basic emotions, and identify common emotion-eliciting situations (Denham, 1998). They can talk about emotions' causes and consequences, especially when ecologically valid measures are used. Young children also are acquiring the beginnings of even more sophisticated knowledge of emotion. They are becoming aware of equivocal emotions (some people love oatmeal, others would be angry to be served it) and using personalized information about emotional reactions (Gnepp, 1989). They are just beginning to understand emotion regulation, display rules, simultaneity, and ambivalence; often they can grasp these concepts if assistive methods are utilized (Josephs, 1994; Kestenbaum & Gelman, 1995). However, there are limits to preschooler's understanding of emotions; despite emerging abilities, they often remain wedded to an emotion's outward expression *or* its eliciting situation, which of necessity hampers their accuracy (Hoffner & Badzinski, 1989).

Understanding emotions during middle childhood.   Intricate understanding of emotions blossoms during this period. Gradeschoolers show marked improvement in understanding that different events elicit different emotions in different people, and that enduring patterns of personality affect individuals' emotional reactions (Gnepp & Chilamkurti, 1988). They better understand finer nuances of emotions in self and others, including (1) display rules, serving both prosocial and self-protective functions (Gnepp & Hess, 1986); (2) multiple emotions (Harris, 1989; Olthof, Meerum Terwogt, Van Eck, & Koops, 1987); (3) the time course of emotions and sophisticated means to regulate them (Meerum Terwogt

& Olthof, 1989); and (4) social emotions (Nunner-Winkler & Sodian, 1988). Taken together, these new understandings bode well for emotional competence as children mature, affecting their reactions to others' emotions, and their understanding of how others perceive emotions in themselves.

Relationship-Specific Interconnectedness of Emotional and Social Competence

The utility of such emotional competence, its relation to socially competent outcomes, often depends on the specific relationship in which it is embedded. In the following, we consider the unique links between social and emotional competence in three relationships differing along the dimensions of symmetry and closeness, that is, "ordinary" peers (symmetrical and not close), friends (symmetrical and close), and parents (asymmetrical and close). When considering relationships influential in the development of emotional competence, many minds first turn to parents, as we do now.

Emotional development in parent–child relationships

Children's relationships with their parents are close dyadic relationships. In contrast to peer relationships and friendships, however, these relationships are asymmetrical and complementary (Youniss, 1980); for example, most children rarely give advice on their parents' emotional problems. The complementary nature of the parent–child relationship has implications for children's emotional competence in four respects. First, from birth, parents are primary attachment figures in times of pain, anxiety, or distress. As children develop, the importance of this support gradually diminishes, but parents still play a major role in times of need. A secure attachment to mother tends to promote preschoolers' understanding of basic emotions (Laible & Thompson, 1998; Suess, Grossmann, & Sroufe, 1992) and mixed emotions (Steele, Steele, Croft, & Fonagy, 1999). Children with an insecure attachment to their mother are more likely to express hostility during the preschool years (DeMulder, Denham, Schmidt, & Mitchell, 2000).

Second, parents are experienced adults. Their children are likely to model their emotional behavior, to be exquisitely attentive to parental reactions to their emotions, and learn much from their emotion language (Denham, 1998; Eisenberg, Cumberland, & Spinrad, 1998; Halberstadt, 1991). These aspects of socialization contribute to strengths and weaknesses in all elements of children's emotional competence.

Parents also have a more advanced knowledge of emotions and of strategies for regulating them than children. Because of their life experience and sophisticated knowledge, parents can teach children about appraisals of emotional events, verbal labels for emotional experiences, and antecedents and consequences of expressive displays (Dunn, Brown, Slomkowski, Tesla, & Youngblade, 1991). Such teaching promotes children's later emotional understanding (Brown & Dunn, 1996; Denham, Zoller, & Couchoud, 1994), as well as their moral sensitivity (Dunn, Brown, & Maguire, 1995). Type of emotion talk also may be important –

empathy-related statements, explanations about causes and consequences of emotions, and descriptions of parents' own emotions appear especially compelling for children (Garner, Jones, Gaddy, & Rennie, 1997; Kochanoff, Denham, & Caswell, 1998).

When parents' admonitions about emotions are misleading or idiosyncratic, children may develop distorted emotion understanding. The anger-intensifying tendency to attribute hostile intentions to another, even when none are present, is a particular problem (Weiss, Dodge, Bates, & Pettit, 1992). Although there are no studies on "feeling talk" in middle childhood, we can assume that parents also speak to school-age children about emotion-relevant issues, such as complex emotions, mixed feelings, masked emotions, and regulatory strategies (Harris, 1989; see also Gottman, Katz, & Hooven, 1996).

Third, parents introduce their children to cultural rules about experiencing, expressing, and regulating emotions, such as expressing politeness toward the elderly (Hochschild, 1983; Joshi & MacLean, 1994; Saarni, 1999; Weber, 1996). In addition, parents usually have subcultural, familial, or personal goals and values for appraising emotional events, as well as ways of feeling and displaying emotions in certain situations (e.g., Zahn-Waxler, Friedman, Cole, Mizuta, & Hiruma, 1996). Baltimore working-class mothers' childrearing values motivate them to teach their toddlers "toughness," to prepare them for the challenges of their inner-city neighborhood (Miller & Sperry, 1987).

Fourth there are possible negative contributions of parents to children's emotional competence. Because parents are adults, their understanding of their children's emotional appraisals may be limited. Parents may also vary in how much they value children's emotional lives; for example, a ghost that frightens their child may not impress them. Childrearing values also may stand in the way of parents' ability to empathize with their children's emotions. Further, even well-meaning, empathic parents cannot know all of today's peer norms about appraisal, experience, and display of emotions.

Parents may differ in their willingness and ability to share children's joy and exuberance (Downey & Coyne, 1990; Halberstadt, 1986). Some parents also have difficulties with negative emotion – depressed parents tend to instill higher levels of unjustified guilt in their children (Zahn-Waxler, Kochanska, Krupnick, & McKnew, 1990). Angrier mothers tend to have less empathic, more defiant children (Denham, 1998). Witnessing interadult anger causes distress and sometimes anger in children (El Sheikh & Reiter, 1996), alleviated only when the adults resolve their disagreement and show positive emotions (Shifflett-Simpson & Cummings, 1996).

Despite possible negative trajectories, parents of gradeschoolers continue to be important supports for their children's growing emotional competence. Most school-age boys still share their fears with their parents (Rimé, Dozier, Vandenplas, & Declercq 1996). A majority of elementary school children endorsed the genuine expression of anxiety, sadness, and pain in hypothetical vignettes in which their parents watched their emotional reactions (Saarni, 1988, 1989; Zeman & Shipman, 1996). But, gradeschoolers also expected that their expressions of anger about third parties would displease their parents. These findings may depend on the gender of child and parent; when disclosing their sadness, elementary school boys expected fathers to react more negatively than mothers (Zeman & Garber, 1996).

Experience and regulating of emotion and parent–child relationships.   No research that we know directly addresses parent–child *experience* of emotion and its association with social competence. As noted, however, parents do use emotion language to support their young children's emotion regulation efforts. Preschoolers with access to more sophisticated maternal language about emotion coped more productively with their own emotions expressed in their preschool classroom (Denham, Cook, & Zoller, 1992). Teachers and peers alike viewed these more affectively balanced children as more socially competent (Denham, McKinley, Couchoud, & Holt, 1990). In contrast, with depressed mothers who did not talk productively about emotion, the opposite pattern of findings obtained (Zahn-Waxler, Ridgeway, Denham, Usher, & Cole, 1993).

Parents' means of coping with their children's negative emotions also has received some attention. Concern over the child's need for emotion regulation, if not punitive, fosters the child's awareness of, and attention to, his or her own emotions (Denham, 1997; Roberts & Strayer, 1987). In contrast, overly strict sanctions about emotional expressiveness may motivate children to hide, not regulate, their easily aroused negativity. In turn, children's coping is associated with their social functioning, and with sociometric status, even with the contribution of child temperament partialled (Eisenberg & Fabes, 1994; Eisenberg, Fabes, & Murphy, 1996; Eisenberg et al., 1999).

Expression of emotion.   Fruitful investigation of the contribution of parental emotion to children's social competence, as mediated by children's emotion expressed during interaction with parents, has begun. Isley, O'Neil, Clatfelter, and Parke (1999) have found that parents' positive affect during game playing was related to their children's social competence, as mediated by the children's positive affect while interacting with their parents (see also Denham & Grout, 1993; Jones & Eisenberg, 1997). Parental negative affect had only a direct, negative contribution to children's social competence (Isley et al., 1999). Angry interchanges with mothers and fathers unfortunately can help children become easily aroused during interaction, and/or learn a confrontational style, that carry over to peer aggression and avoidance (Carson & Parke, 1996; Denham & Grout, 1993). Parental affect is especially related to social competence for father–son shared negativity and maternal positive emotion. Taken together, these investigations suggest an important alignment of parents' expressiveness with children's emotional and social competence.

Understanding of emotion.   Parents', especially mothers', contributions to their preschool-aged children's understanding of emotion have been investigated with some interesting results. Denham, Zoller, and Couchoud (1994) found that when mothers explained emotions, showed predominantly positive emotion, and were positively rather than negatively responsive to the children's emotions, children evidenced greater emotion understanding (see also Dunn, Brown, & Beardsall, 1991). Presumably, children who experience mothers' positive meta-emotion philosophy (Gottman et al., 1996) are more willing to explore, and have greater access to, the world of emotions, which in turn enhances their social interactions and relationships (Dunn & Cutting, 1998; Dunn & Herrera, 1997).

Emotional development in interaction with peers

The peer group is expected to have a pervasive influence on children's emotional develop-ment for two reasons. First, because of their similarity, peers are in a better position to understand the emotional life of age-mates than parents or children of other age groups (Dunn & Hughes, 1998). Age-mates argue at about the same sociocognitive and moral level, face the same transitions and (normative) life events, and share the same role vis-à-vis school and teachers (Salisch, 2000c). Second, being with a group of like-minded peers may intensify children's emotional experiences, such as glee over a teacher's faux pas or panic over crawling insects. Children create group cultures with their own norms and values (Corsaro & Eder, 1990), including the shared appraisal of emotion-eliciting events, and explicit and implicit rules about the expression and the regulation of emotions.

Experiencing and regulating emotion and peer relations.   From preschool through the pri-mary grades, children who improve, or are consistently average or high in emotion regula-tion, show higher social competence than those whose regulation ability is consistently low or declining. Experience of emotions and their regulation also interact in contributing to social competence. Especially for highly negative children, attentional and behavior regu-lation are related to social functioning and sociometric status (Eisenberg, Fabes, Shepard, Murphy, et al., 1997; Eisenberg, Fabes, Guthrie, Murphy et al., 1996; Eisenberg, Guthrie, Fabes, Reiser, et al., 1997). Further, high attentional regulation and *low* emotional inten-sity, as well as their interaction, predict sympathy concurrently and over time (Eisenberg, Fabes, Murphy, Maszk, et al., 1995).

Gradeschoolers learn to adopt an "emotional front" (Saarni, 1988, 1989). "Letting it all hang out" is uniformly selected as the worst reaction to negative emotional experiences with peers (Saarni, 1997). Gradeschoolers apply differing strategies to achieve their "fronts"; they report cognitively distancing themselves from anger-provoking situations, redirecting attention to alleviate distress, avoiding confrontations altogether, or problem solving calmly (Murphy & Eisenberg, 1996; Stegge & Meerum Terwogt, 1998; Salisch, 2000a). Although these "fronts" make children's expressions less genuine, they also have positive aspects, including saving face and "surviving" in a possibly hostile environment.

Expressiveness and peer relations.   Preschoolers' expression of specific emotions also relates to their peer status and to teachers' evaluations of their friendliness and aggression. *Positive* affect is important in the initiation and regulation of social exchanges, and for communi-cation during socially directed acts; sharing positive affect may facilitate the formation of friendships. Happier, less angry preschoolers react more prosocially to peers' emotions, are better liked by peers, and are rated as friendlier and more cooperative by teachers (Denham et al., 1990). Conversely, preschoolers, who show larger proportions of negative affect, are often seen as troublesome and difficult (Denham et al., 1990). Sadness is related to teacher-rated withdrawal (Denham & Burger, 1989).

The relation of emotional expressiveness to social competence is often context-depend-ent. Arsenio, Cooperman, and Lover (2000) have examined preschoolers' emotions within and outside periods of conflict, to investigate these emotions' relations to aggression and social competence. Children's nonconflict anger (and less nonconflict happiness), and happiness during conflict were positively related to initiation of aggression and negatively related to sociometric status. Anger during conflict appears normative – after all, it is a conflict. A generally irascible demeanor, or glee at another's discomfort, however, is incongruent with social competence.

Little work has described observed expressiveness and social competence in older children. It becomes more difficult to code emotion because of the "cool rule!" There are clear indications, however, that rejected and accepted children's emotional profiles differ (Underwood, Hurley, Johanson, & Mosley, 1999). To avoid peer rejection, gradeschoolers are challenged to reduce expressions of anger, triumph over others' failures, and envy, in favor of polite negotiation (Krappmann & Oswald, 1995; Tassi & Schneider, 1997). Children also say they would express only extreme or visible anxiety and hurt to peers (Saarni, 1989), and expect harsher reactions when expressing sadness or pain in front of peers rather than parents (Zeman & Garber, 1996). Some expectations are gender dependent. Boys say they are unlikely to share fears, but girls report not displaying anger (Underwood, Coie, & Herbsman, 1992). Finally, although some studies support that children prefer to befriend peers who are "fun" (Parker & Seal, 1996), there is little research on rules about expressing positive emotions.

Understanding emotions and peer relations. Children who strategically apply emotion knowledge more often succeed in peer interactions. Preschoolers' understanding of emotion is related to their positive peer status, to teachers' views of their social competence, and to their prosocial reactions to the emotions of peers and adults (Denham, 1986; Denham et al., 1990). Barth and Bastiani (1997) have uncovered a more subtle relation: Preschoolers' mistaken perceptions of peers as angry – a recognition bias similar to the hostile attribution bias of later years – are associated with negative social behavior.

Other discrete types of positive social behavior also are related to preschoolers' emotion knowledge. For example, preschoolers' emotion knowledge is related to use of reasoned argument, and caregiving, with siblings (Dunn, Slomkowski, Donelan, & Herrera, 1995; Garner, Jones, & Miner, 1994). Older children's understanding of prosocial display rules is related to: (1) prosocial behavior; (2) prosocial responses to hypothetical conflicts; and (3) teacher- and peer-rated social competence (Garner, 1996; Jones, Abbey, & Cumberland, 1998).

Emotional development within friendships

Because friendships now attain a new quality of intimacy, friends' emotions are experienced "close up" (Krappmann, 1996). Observing another's emotions in a symmetrically reciprocal relationship, where the child takes more responsibility for successful interaction, may be accompanied by attention that facilitates learning. A friend's conformance to display rules, display of complex emotions, and demonstration of ambivalence may be especially instructive. Thus, sharing emotions with friends may contribute to children's emotional competence, but these theoretical speculations badly need empirical support.

Caution is warranted, however, against assuming only beneficial aspects of friendships;

all friends and friendships are not equal (Hartup, 1999). Reciprocal negative, as well as positive, effects can operate (Salisch, 2000b). Several issues to consider are: (1) Is the friend socially competent? (2) Is the friendship amicable? intimate? conflictual? (3) Child characteristics, including temperament and family processes.

Experiencing and regulating emotion within friendship.   Friends may assist each other to manage their experience of emotion, for example, by reframing the break-up of another friendship ("he's not worth crying over"), or by giving explicit advice on emotion regulation ("don't think about it any more"; Gottman & Mettetal, 1986). Preadolescent friends also use distraction to keep their friends from ruminating over negative attributions that accentuate emotions like shame, guilt, or depression (Denton & Zarbatany, 1996). Not all is amiable, however. Gradeschoolers who endorsed revenge goals and hostile strategies in conflict scenarios quarreled more in their best friendships and had fewer reciprocal best friends (Rose & Asher, 1999a). In conflicts during a computer game, competitive friends expressed anger, contempt, and disgust, and self-reported more intense experiences of shame and guilt (Salisch, 1999).

Expressiveness within friendship.   Preschoolers display positive affective reciprocity more frequently, and are more expressive overall, with friends than with siblings (Brachfeld-Child & Schiavo, 1990; Volling, Youngblade, & Belsky, 1997). Although preschoolers' experience similar intensity of anger with liked and disliked peers, their behavioral responses, especially boys', are more controlled to liked peers (Fabes, Eisenberg, Smith, & Murphy, 1996). Children also are more sympathetic to the hypothetical plight of a friend than a nonfriend, and more readily propose an intervention (Costin & Jones, 1992). Because the tasks of middle childhood friendship include caring, concern, help, conflict management, forgiving, and affection, friends are children's "best bets" for sharing emotional experience, especially feelings of vulnerability, and helping each other acquire emotional competencies (Rose & Asher, 1999b; Saarni, 1988, 1989).

Understanding emotions and friendship.   Preschoolers' understanding of the causes and consequences of emotions already is differentiated by relationship (Dunn & Hughes, 1998). Understanding of emotions and others' minds is related to 4 year olds' positive interaction with friends – both child and friends' emotion knowledge contribute to cooperative shared pretend, low frequency of conflict, and successful communication (Dunn & Cutting, 1999). Child–friend conversation about emotion also is related to cooperative interaction (Brown, Donelan-McCall, & Dunn, 1996). Finally, positive play within friendships predicts understanding of mixed emotions at the end of the preschool period (Maguire & Dunn, 1997), suggestive of a bidirectional relation.

The shifting developmental tasks served by conversations between friends (Gottman & Mettetal, 1986) point to middle childhood as a time when friends may use emotion talk in various ways, specifically about the aspects of emotion understanding undergoing rapid development at this age – display rules, ambivalence, and complex emotions like guilt. First, friends' ubiquitous gossip allows them to mention potential insecurities without naming them, similar to earlier fantasy play (e.g., "I hate it when he 'blows up', don't you?"). Second, close friendships challenge preadolescents to be helpful to the friend in need, to not respond in an ignoring or hostile way (Rose & Asher, 1999b). Friends' approval, sympathy, and affection could easily include emotion language. Emotion-colored accounts are compared, contrasted, and validated as friends help each other to sort out their shared and idiosyncratic feelings (Sullivan, 1953). Third, conflict processes also rear their not-necessarily-ugly head, with conversations replete with emotion talk about regulating anger, sadness, envy, jealousy, shame, guilt, and hurt feelings. Fourth, friends react to each other's emotions during their conversations. Reactions that comfort ("Don't worry about the test") and exhort ("Stop crying – everybody's looking!") may be pivotal in assisting the friend learn about emotions and feel generally positive, while conforming to group norms. Research on emotion-related aspects of elementary school-aged friends' conversation and behaviors, especially their relations to other aspects of their emotional competence, is sorely needed.

Where Do We Go From Here?

It should be obvious that much exciting work has been done, to show the ways in which emotional competence is an integral part of social competence. There also are many readily discernible ways to expand upon this work, primary among them to follow children's lives across time – what is the predictive power of emotional (in)competence? What happens to Gary, Ron, Huynh, and Jack? Only longitudinal study can spell out the significance of emotional development for children's long-term adaptation and settle issues about the direction of causality. Thus, although our evaluations may be somewhat biased, it seems clear that we must:

- Flesh out the dual roles of each relationship partner – parent, peer, and friend. That is, it is probably apparent to the reader that our exposition of parents' influence centered on socializing emotional competence, whereas discussion of peers and friends focused on the role of the child's emotional competence within such relationships. We need to know: (1) how children's emotional competence in interaction with parents is related to successful parent–child relationships; and (2) how peers and friends act as socializers of other children's emotional competence. *What does Huynh learn about expressing emotions from Gary, or from Jack? Conversely, how does Gary's shrewdness about emotions play out in the transformations of his relationship with his father, as he nears adolescence?*
- Make more headway in the investigation of children's "live" experience of emotions, especially during preschool (e.g., Olthof & Engelberts-Vaske, 1997). *Was Jack really feeling so dominant in his bullying, or was that a "front"? What emotions does he experience and display in high school, and how do they affect his relationships?*
- Plumb the relation between use of display rules and social competence, despite the efforts of Zeman and Shipman (e.g., 1996); in fact, the union of investigation of social and emotional competence still lags, in our view. *What if Huynh hadn't managed to conceal his fear? What sort of peer relations and friendships would he have years later?*
- Investigate more thoroughly the emotional world of gradeschoolers, especially in comparison to more easily accessible preschoolers; more work on emotional/social compe-

tence links in middle childhood friendships is sorely needed. *Did Ron and Gary continue to use their emotional competence skills to the utmost with each other? Are they still friends in high school?*

● Examine these phenomena with minority and low SES children (with the exception of Garner's work, which often suggests that low SES, minority children's emotional competence milestones, and their socialization, often are similar to more affluent children's). *If the boys had been playing stickball in an inner-city neighborhood, would they need the same or different emotional competence skills? And what would their trajectory be?*

● Uncover possible gender effects, going beyond main effects (which seem to be sparse); the ways in which emotional competence contributes to social competence may differ for boys and girls (but see Eisenberg, Fabes, et al., 1997). *What if the four children playing soccer had been girls?*

● Consider that emotional competence is not always beneficial for establishing and maintaining harmonious relationships. For example, even though a well-developed empathic sense might keep aggressors from attacking their victims, they might use it to enhance the maliciousness of their attacks (Sutton, Smith, & Swettenham, 1999). Similarly, developmental change in competence concerning envy, jealousy, and anger may influence social development negatively. *Did Jack's perceptive reading of peers' weaknesses allow him to become an ever more powerful thug?*

These specific needs must be addressed in future research. Steps toward rapprochement of peer and emotions subdisciplines are hopeful signs. For example, Lemerise and Arsenio's (2000) inclusion of emotions with their model of social information processing should spawn much fruitful work.

There also are more overarching areas needing attention. One problem area is cultural. Most of the studies reviewed so far come from the Western industrialized countries. This limits the generalizability of their results. *What if the four soccer players had been Nigerian? Or Chinese? How would "emotional competence" be different for the children?*

A further limitation is measurement related. Many studies of gradeschoolers use self-report measures, especially in research on emotional competence with peers and friends. Self-reports are subject to biases, and may be influenced by gender-role concepts or cultural styles of self-presentation. Many investigations on emotional development in gradeschoolers' relationships use hypothetical vignettes, sometimes of questionable ecological validity. New, more ingenious, methods of self-report also can be devised. To measure experiencing and regulating, children could review videotapes of themselves, pressing a button when they were feeling (and showing or not showing) an emotion. They could describe their feelings and causes, as well as means of regulation. To measure expressiveness, children could view a videotape of social interaction, and press a button when an affective message needed to be sent. They could be asked, as well, what message *should* be sent? Emotional reactions to others can be measured within "created" situations in the laboratory or within real social settings, for example, helping an older confederate, consoling an adult, and discussing the experience during a post-event interview (Denham, 1986; Saarni, 1992). To measure understanding, a child could press a button when there is an affective message on videotape, and identify it.

Observational research covering a broad range of age groups and emotion-eliciting situations is especially needed for the joint study of peer influences and emotional development (e.g. Denham et al., 2001; Underwood et al., 1999). For example, observed facial expressions of anger do not become less frequent across middle childhood, nor is a subtler variant substituted for the full anger expression, as might be expected (Salisch, 1997; cf. nonobservational studies, Zeman & Garber, 1996; Underwood et al., 1992).

We also must integrate inter- and intrapersonal aspects of emotional competence in our investigations, rather than centering on one or another, because bidirectionality can be assumed between them. For example, intrapersonal representations, such as lack of emotion understanding or a hostile attribution bias, may influence the expression of anger and hostility in interpersonal contexts, ultimately leading to peer rejection. Conversely, interpersonal practices, such as ample emotion talk in the family, are likely to promote children's intrapersonal understanding of emotions. A transactional model that depicts the reciprocal influences between intra- and interpersonal features of emotional competence, both concurrently and longitudinally, is necessary.

Finally, we realize that at the interpersonal level, it is somewhat artificial to tease apart the differential influences of parents, peers, and friends because most children take part in each of these kinds of relationships. In addition, some influences may not be specific to one type of relationship. Nevertheless, differentiating between the emotion components of experience, expression, understanding, and regulation strategies, and tracing the influences of different interpersonal relationships on the development of the emotion components, seems to be a worthwhile undertaking for the future, considering how important emotions and relationships are to the participants.

References

Arsenio, W. F., Cooperman, G., & Lover, A. (2000). Affective predictors of preschoolers' aggression and peer acceptance: Direct and indirect effects. *Developmental Psychology, 36*, 438–448.

Barrett, K. C. (1995). A functionalist approach to shame and guilt. In J. Tangney & K. Fischer (Eds.), *Self-conscious emotions: The psychology of shame, guilt, embarrassment, and pride* (pp. 25–63). New York: Guilford Press.

Barth, J. M., & Bastiani, A. (1997). A longitudinal study of emotion recognition and preschool children's social behavior. *Merrill-Palmer Quarterly, 43*, 107–128.

Brachfeld-Child, S., & Schiavo, R. S. (1990). Interactions of preschool and kindergarten friends and acquaintances. *Journal of Genetic Psychology, 151*, 45–58.

Brown, J. R., Donelan-McCall, N., & Dunn, J. (1996). Why talk about mental states? The significance of children's conversations with friends, siblings, and mothers. *Child Development, 67*, 836–849.

Brown, J. R., & Dunn, J. (1996). Continuities in emotion understanding from three to six years. *Child Development, 67*, 789–802.

Carson, J. L., & Parke, R. D. (1996). Reciprocal negative affect in parent–child interactions and children's peer competency. *Child Development, 67*, 2217–2226.

Cole, P. M. (1986). Children's spontaneous control of facial expression. *Child Development, 57*, 1309–1321.

Corsaro, W., & Eder, D. (1990). Children's peer culture. *Annual Review of Sociology, 16*, 197–220.

Costin, S. E., & Jones, D. C. (1992). Friendship as a facilitator of emotional responsiveness and prosocial interventions among young children. *Developmental Psychology, 28*, 941–947.

DeMulder, K. E., Denham, S. A., Schmidt, M., & Mitchell, J. (2000). Q-sort assessment of attachment security during the preschool years: Links from home to school. *Developmental Psychology, 36*, 274–282.

Denham, S. A. (1986). Social cognition, social behavior, and emotion in preschoolers: Contextual validation. *Child Development, 57*, 194–201.

Denham, S. A. (1997). "When I have a bad dream, Mommy holds me." Preschoolers' consequential thinking about emotions and social competence. *International Journal of Behavioral Development, 20,* 301–319.

Denham, S. A. (1998). *Emotional development in young children.* New York: Guilford Press.

Denham, S. A., & Burger, C. (1991). Observational validation of teacher-rating scales. *Child Study Journal, 21*, 185–202.

Denham, S. A., Cook, M. C., & Zoller, D. (1992). "Baby looks very sad": Discussions about emotions between mother and preschooler. *British Journal of Developmental Psychology, 10*, 301–315.

Denham, S. A., & Grout, L. (1993). Socialization of emotion: Pathway to preschoolers' emotional and social competence. *Journal of Nonverbal Behavior, 17*, 205–227.

Denham, S. A., Mason, T., Caverly, S., Schmidt, M., Hackney, R., Caswell, R., & DeMulder, E. (2001). Preschoolers at play: Co-socializers of emotional and social competence. *International Journal of Behavioral Development, 25*, 290–301.

Denham, S. A., McKinley, M., Couchoud, E. A., & Holt, R. (1990). Emotional and behavioral predictors of peer status in young preschoolers. *Child Development, 61*, 1145–1152.

Denham, S. A., Zoller, D. & Couchoud, E. A. (1994). Socialization of preschoolers' emotion understanding. *Developmental Psychology, 30*, 928–936.

Denton, K., & Zarbatany, L. (1996). Age differences in support processes in conversations between friends. *Child Development, 67*, 1360–1373.

Downey, G., & Coyne, J. (1990). Children of depressed parents: An integrative review. *Psychological Bulletin, 108*, 50–76.

Dunn, J., Brown, J., & Beardsall, L. (1991). Family talk about emotions, and children's later understanding of others' emotions. *Developmental Psychology, 27*, 448–455.

Dunn, J., Brown, J. B., & Maguire, M. (1995). The development of children's moral sensibility: Individual differences and emotion understanding. *Developmental Psychology, 31*, 649–659.

Dunn, J., Brown, J. R., Slomkowski, C., Tesla, C., & Youngblade, L. (1991). Young children's understanding of other people's feelings and beliefs: Individual differences and their antecedents. *Child Development, 62*, 1352–1366.

Dunn, J., & Cutting, A. L. (1999). Understanding others and individual differences in friendship interactions in young children. *Social Development, 8*, 201–219.

Dunn, J., & Herrera, C. (1997). Conflict resolution with friends, siblings, and mothers: A developmental perspective. *Aggressive Behavior, 23*, 343–357.

Dunn, J., & Hughes, C. (1998). Young children's understanding of emotions within close relationships. *Cognition and Emotion, 12*, 171–190.

Dunn, J., Slomkowski, C., Donelan, N., & Herrera, C. (1995). Conflict, understanding, and relationships: Developments and differences in the preschool years. *Early Education and Development, 6*, 303–316.

Eisenberg, N., Cumberland, A, & Spinrad, T. L. (1998). Parental socialization of emotion. *Psychological Inquiry, 9*, 241–273.

Eisenberg, N., & Fabes, R. A. (1994). Mothers' reactions to children's negative emotions: Relations to children's temperament and anger behavior. *Merrill-Palmer Quarterly, 40*, 138–156.

Eisenberg, N., Fabes, R. A., Guthrie, I. K., Murphy, B., C., et al. (1996). The relations of regulation and emotionality to problem behavior in elementary school children. *Development and Psycho-*

pathology, 8, 141–162.

Eisenberg, N., Fabes, R. A., & Murphy, B. C. (1996). Parents' reactions to children's negative emotions: Relations to children's social competence and comforting behavior. *Child Development, 67*, 2227–2247.

Eisenberg, N., Fabes, R. A., Murphy, B. C, Maszk, P., et al. (1995). The role of emotionality and regulation in children's social functioning: A longitudinal study. *Child Development, 66*, 1360–1384.

Eisenberg, N., Fabes, R. A., Shepard, S. A., Guthrie, I., Murphy, B. C., & Reiser, M. (1999). Parental reactions to children's negative emotions: Longitudinal relations to quality of children's social functioning. *Child Development, 70*, 513–534.

Eisenberg, N., Fabes, R. A., Shepard, S. A., Murphy, B. C., Guthrie, I., Jones, S., Friedman, J., Poulin, R., & Maszk, P. (1997). Contemporaneous and longitudinal prediction of children's social functioning from regulation and emotionality. *Child Development, 68*, 642–664.

Eisenberg, N., Guthrie, I. K., Fabes, R. A., Reiser, M., Murphy, B. C., Holgren, R., Maszk, P., & Losoya, S. (1997). The relations of regulation and emotionality to resiliency and competent social functioning in elementary school children. *Child Development, 68*, 295–311.

El-Sheikh, M., & Reiter, S. (1996). Children's responding to live interadult conflict: The role of form of anger expression. *Journal of Abnormal Child Psychology, 24*, 401–415.

Fabes, R. A., Eisenberg, N., Smith, M. C., & Murphy, B. C. (1996). Getting angry at peers: Associations with like of the provocateur. *Child Development, 67*, 942–956.

Garner, P. W. (1996). The relations of emotional role taking, affect/moral attributions, and emotional display rule knowledge to low-income school-age children's social competence. *Journal of Applied Developmental Psychology, 17*, 19–36.

Garner, P. W., Jones, D. C., Gaddy, G., & Rennie, K. (1997). Low income mothers' conversations about emotions and their children's emotional competence. *Social Development*.

Garner, P. W., Jones, D. C., & Miner, J. L. (1994). Social competence among low-income preschoolers" Emotion socialization practices and social cognitive correlates. *Child Development, 65*, 622–637.

Gnepp, J. (1989). Personalized inferences of emotions and appraisals: Component processes and correlates. *Developmental Psychology, 25*, 277–288.

Gnepp, J., & Chilamkurti, C. (1988). Children's use of personality attributions to predict other people's emotional and behavioral reactions. *Child Development, 59*, 743–754.

Gnepp, J., & Hess, D. L. R. (1986). Children's understanding of verbal and facial display rules. *Developmental Psychology, 22*, 103–108.

Gottman, J. M., Katz, L. F., & Hooven, C. (1996). *Meta-emotion: How families communicate emotionally, links to child peer relations, and other developmental outcomes*. Mahwah, NJ: Erlbaum.

Gottman, J. M., & Mettetal, G. (1986). Speculations about social and affective development of friendship and acquaintanceship through adolescence. In J. M. Gottman & J. Parker (Eds.), *Conversations of friends: Speculations on affective development* (pp. 192–237). New York: Cambridge University Press.

Grolnick, W. S., Bridges, L. J., & Connell, J. P. (1996). Emotion regulation in two-year-olds: Strategies and emotional expression in four contexts. *Child Development, 67*, 928–941.

Halberstadt, A. G. (1986). Family socialization of emotional expression and nonverbal communication styles and skills. *Journal of Personality and Social Psychology, 51*, 827–836.

Halberstadt, A. G. (1991). Socialization of expressiveness: Family influences in particular and a model in general. In R. S. Feldman & S. Rimé (Eds.), *Fundamentals of emotional expressiveness* (pp. 106–162). Cambridge, England: Cambridge University Press.

Halberstadt, A., Dunsmore, J., & Denham, S. A. (2001). Spinning the pinwheel, together: More thoughts on affective social competence. *Social Development, 10*, 130–136.

Harris, P. L. (1989). *Children and emotion: The development of psychological understanding.* Cambridge, MA: Blackwell.

Hartup, W. W. (1999). Constraints on peer socialization: Let me count the ways. *Merrill-Palmer Quarterly, 45,* 172–183.

Hochschild, A. R. (1983). *The managed heart: Commercialization of human feelings.* Berkeley, CA: University of California Press.

Hoffner, C., & Badzinski, D. M. (1989). Children's integration of facial and situational cues to emotion. *Child Development, 60,* 415–422.

Hubbard, J. A., & Coie, J. D. (1994). Emotional correlates of social competence in children's peer relationships. *Merrill-Palmer Quarterly, 40,* 1–20.

Isley, S. L., O'Neil, R., Clatfelter, D., & Parke, R. D. (1999). Parent and child expressed affect and children's social competence: Modeling direct and indirect pathways. *Developmental Psychology, 35,* 547–560.

Jones, D. C., Abbey, B., & Cumberland, A. (1998). The development of display rule knowledge: Linkages with family expressiveness and social competence. *Child Development, 69,* 1209–1222.

Jones, S. M., & Eisenberg, N. (1997, April). Parent socialization and children's social competence: The mediating role of children's affective displays. Presented at the biennial meeting of the Society for Research in Child Development, Washington, DC.

Josephs, I. E. (1994). Display rule behavior and understanding in preschool children. *Journal of Nonverbal Behavior, 18,* 310–326.

Joshi, M. S., & MacLean, M. (1994). Indian and English children's understanding of the distinction between real and apparent emotion. *Child Development, 65,* 1372–1384.

Kestenbaum, R., & Gelman, R. (1995). Preschool children's identification and understanding of mixed emotions. *Cognitive Development, 10,* 443–458.

Kochanoff, A., Denham, S. A., & Caswell, C. (1998, March). The effects of parental emotion language function and self/other referencing on preschoolers' social competence. Poster presented at the Conference on Human Development, Mobile, AL.

Krappmann, L. (1996). The development of diverse relationships in the social world of childhood. In A. E. Auhagen & M. von Salisch (Eds.), *The diversity of human relationships* (pp. 52–78). New York: Cambridge University Press.

Krappmann, L., & Oswald, H. (1995). *Alltag der Schulkinder. Beobachtungen und Analysen von Interaktionen und Sozialbeziehungen.* Weinheim, Germany: Juventa.

Ladd, G. (1999). Peer relationships and social competence during early and middle childhood. *Annual Review of Psychology, 50,* 333–359.

Laible, D., & Thompson, R.A. (1998). Attachment and emotional understanding in preschool children. *Developmental Psychology, 34,* 1038–1045.

Lemerise, E., & Arsenio, W. F. (2000). An integrated model of emotion processes and cognition in social information processing. *Child Development, 71,* 107–118.

Maguire, M. C., & Dunn, J. (1997). Friendships in early childhood, and social understanding. International *Journal of Behavioral Development, 21,* 669–686.

Meerum Terwogt, M., & Olthof, T. (1989). Awareness and self-regulation of emotion in young children. In C. Saarni & P. Harris (Eds.), *Children's understanding of emotion* (pp. 209–237). New York: Cambridge University Press.

Miller, P., & Sperry, L. (1987). The socialization of anger and aggression. *Merrill-Palmer Quarterly, 33,* 1–31.

Murphy, B., & Eisenberg, N. (1996). Provoked by a peer: Children's anger related responses and their relation to social functioning. *Merrill-Palmer Quarterly, 42,* 103–124.

Nunner-Winkler, G., & Sodian, B. (1988). Children's understanding of moral emotions. *Child*

Development, 59, 1323–1338.

Olthof, T., & Engelberts-Vaske, A. (1997). Kindergarten-aged children's reactions to an emotionally charged naturalistic event: Relations between cognitions, self-reported emotions and emotional behavior. *Journal of Child Psychology and Psychiatry, 38*, 449–456.

Olthof, T., Ferguson, T. J., & Luiten, A. (1989). Personal responsibility antecedents of anger and blame reactions in children. *Child Development, 60*, 1328–1336.

Olthof, T., Meerum Terwogt, M., Van Eck, O. V., & Koops, W. (1987). Children's knowledge of the integration of successive emotions. *Perceptual and Motor Skills, 65*, 407–414.

Parker, J. G., & Seal, J. (1996). Forming, losing, renewing and replacing friendships: Applying temporal parameters to the assessment of children's friendship experiences. *Child Development, 67*, 2248–2268.

Rimé, B., Dozier, S., Vandenplas, C. & Declercq, M. (1996). Social sharing of emotion in children. In N. Frijda (Ed.), *Proceedings of the 9th Conference of the International Society for Research on Emotions, Toronto, Canada* (pp. 161–163). Storrs, CT: ISRE.

Roberts, W. R., & Strayer, J. (1987). Parents' responses to the emotional distress of their children: Relations with children's competence. *Developmental Psychology, 23*, 415–422.

Rose, A., & Asher, S. (1999a). Children's goals and strategies in response to conflicts within a friendship. *Developmental Psychology, 35*, 69–79.

Rose, A., & Asher, S. (1999b). Seeking and giving social support within a friendship. Paper presented at the Society for Research in Child Development, Albuquerque, NM.

Saarni, C. (1988). Children's understanding of the interpersonal consequences of dissemblance of nonverbal emotional-expressive behavior. *Journal of Nonverbal Behavior, 12*, 275–294.

Saarni, C. (1989). Children's understanding of the strategic control of emotional expression in social transactions. In C. Saarni & P. Harris (Eds.), *Children's understanding of emotions* (pp. 181–208). Cambridge England: Cambridge University Press.

Saarni, C. (1992). Children's emotional-expressive behaviors as regulators of others' happy and sad emotional states. *New Directions for Child Development, 55*, 91–106.

Saarni, C. (1997). Coping with aversive feelings. *Motivation and Emotion, 21*, 45–63.

Saarni, C. (1999). *The development of emotional competence.* New York: Guilford Press.

Salisch, M. von (1997). Zur Entwicklung der Ärgerregulierung in der mittleren Kindheit (DFG Endbericht).

Salisch; M. von (1999). Kooperation und Konkurrenz unter gleichrangigen Partnern. In L. Krappmann, H.-P. Kuhn, & H. Uhlendorff (Eds.), *Sozialisation zur Mitbürgerlichkeit.* Opladen, Germany: Leske & Budrich.

Salisch, M. von (2000a). *Wenn Kinder sich ärgern. Emotionsregulierung in der Entwicklung.* Göttingen, Germany: Hogrefe Verlag.

Salisch, M. von (2000b). The emotional side of sharing, social support, and conflict negotiation between siblings and between friends. In R. Mills & S. Duck (Eds.), *Developmental psychology of personal relationships* (pp. 49–70). Chichester, England: Wiley.

Salisch, M. von (2000c). Zum Einfluß von Gleichaltrigen (Peers) und Freunden auf die Persönlichkeitsentwicklung. In M. Amelang (Ed.), *Enzyklopädie der Psychologie, Differentielle Psychologie, Band 4: Determinanten individueller Differenzen* (pp. 345–405). Göttingen, Germany: Hogrefe Verlag.

Shifflett-Simpson, K., & Cummings, E. M. (1996). Mixed message resolution and children's responses to interadult conflict. *Child Development, 67*, 437–448.

Steele, H., Steele, M., Croft, C., & Fonagy, P. (1999). Infant–mother attachment at one year predicts children's understanding of mixed emotions at six years. *Social Development, 7*, 161–178.

Stegge, H., & Meerum Terwogt, M. (1998). Perspectives on the strategic control of emotions: A developmental account. In A. Fischer & N. Frijda (Eds.), *Proceedings of the 10th Meeting of the*

International Society for Research on Emotions, Würzburg, 1998 (pp. 45–47). Amsterdam: ISRE Publications.

Suess, G. J., Grossmann, K. E., & Sroufe, L. A. (1992). Effects of infant attachment to mother on quality of adaptation in preschool. From dyadic to individual organization of self. *International Journal of Behavioral Development, 15*, 43–65.

Sullivan, H. S. (1953). *The interpersonal theory of psychiatry*. New York: Norton.

Sutton, J., Smith, P. K., & Swettenham, J. (1999). Social cognition and bullying: Social inadequacy or skilled manipulation? *British Journal of Developmental Psychology, 17*, 435–450.

Tassi, F., & Schneider, B. H. (1997). Task-oriented vs. other-referenced competition: Differential implications for children's peer relations. *Journal of Applied Social Psychology, 27*, 1557–1580.

Underwood, M., Coie, J. D., & Herbsman, C. (1992). Display rules for anger and aggression in school age children. *Child Development, 63*, 366–380.

Underwood, M., Hurley, J., Johanson, C., & Mosley, C. (1999). An experimental, observational investigation of children's responses to peer provocation: Developmental and gender differences in middle childhood. *Child Development, 70*, 1428–1446.

Volling, B. L., Youngblade, L. M., & Belsky, J. (1997). Young children's social relationships with siblings and friends. *American Journal of Orthopsychiatry, 67*, 102–111.

Weber, H. (1996). Social constructivist approaches to understanding how we cope with stress. In N. Frijda (Ed.), *Proceedings of the 9th Meeting of the International Society for Research on Emotions in Toronto* (pp. 174–178). Storrs, CT: ISRE Publications.

Weiss, B., Dodge, K., Bates, J., & Pettit, G. (1992). Some consequences of early harsh discipline: Child aggression and a maladaptive information processing style. *Child Development, 63*, 1321–1335.

Youniss, J. (1980). *Parents and peers in social development*. Chicago: University of Chicago Press.

Zahn-Waxler, C., Friedman, R., Cole, P., Mizuta, I., & Hiruma, N. (1996). Japanese and United States preschool children's responses to conflict and distress. *Child Development, 67*, 2462–2477.

Zahn-Waxler, C., Kochanska, G., Krupnick, J., & Mc Knew, D. (1990). Patterns of guilt in children of depressed and well mothers. *Developmental Psychology, 26*, 51–59.

Zahn-Waxler, C., Ridgeway, D., Denham, S. A., Usher, B., & Cole, P. M. (1993). Research strategies for assessing mothers' interpretations of infants' emotions. In R. Emde, J. Osofsky, & P. Butterfield (Eds.), *The IFEEL pictures: A new instrument for interpreting emotions* (pp. 217–236). Madison, CT: International Universities Press.

Zeman, J., & Garber, J. (1996). Display rules for anger, sadness, and pain: It depends on who is watching. *Child Development, 67*, 957–973.

Zeman, J., Penza, S., Shipman, K., & Young, G. (1997). Preschoolers as functionalists: The impact of social context on emotion regulation. *Child Study Journal, 27*, 41–67.

Zeman, J., & Shipman, K. (1996). Children's expression of negative affect: Reasons and methods. *Developmental Psychology, 32*, 842–849.

17

Social Withdrawal and Shyness

Kenneth H. Rubin, Kim B. Burgess, and Robert J. Coplan

And the Lord God said "It is not good that the man should be alone."

Genesis 2:18

I live in that solitude which is painful in youth, but delicious in the years of maturity.

Albert Einstein

There are days when solitude is a heady wine that intoxicates you with freedom, others when it is a bitter tonic, and still others when it is a poison that makes you beat your head against the wall.

Colette, *Earthly Paradise*

For centuries philosophers, writers, artists, and psychologists alike have offered opinions, hypotheses, and data pertaining to the phenomenon of solitude. For many writers, solitude is viewed romantically as a phenomenon that brings safety, quiet, and escape from the "madding crowd." Solitude is viewed as a source of inspiration, as a psychological venue for quiet reflection. For others, however, solitude brings with it loneliness and suffering. In this chapter, we describe the origins, correlates, and consequences of this second vision of solitude – that which brings wariness in social company, fear of rejection, victimization, and loneliness. Thus, our focus is on the topic of *social withdrawal*.

For many years, researchers neglected the study of solitude and withdrawal from social company. In part, this neglect stemmed from assumptions that shyness (not withdrawal) was neither an accompaniment of maladaptation nor a predictor of subsequent psychological difficulty. In the past 20 years, however, a burgeoning literature has accumulated on the topic. The phenomenon has undergone definitional scrutiny, developmental examination, and theory generation.

Defining Social Withdrawal

Prior to the contemporary research and thinking of the past decade, researchers and clinical psychologists were habitually using the following terms interchangeably: *social withdrawal (passive or solitary-passive), isolation, shyness,* and *inhibition.* In an edited volume, Rubin and Asendorpf (1993) attempted to bring order to the perceived chaos endemic in the study of children's solitary behavior and solitude. In their leadoff chapter, they defined *inhibition* as the disposition to be wary and fearful when encountering *novel* (unfamiliar) situations. *Fearful shyness* refers to inhibition in response to novel social situations; in middle childhood, *self-conscious shyness* is reflected by the display of inhibition in response to social-evaluative concerns. Social isolation has little to do with the behavioral expression of wariness; rather the term reflects the experience of solitude that derives from peer rejection, as in being isolated (rejected) by the peer group. Finally, *social withdrawal* refers to *the consistent (across situations and over time) display of all forms of solitary behavior when encountering familiar and/or unfamiliar peers.* Simply put, social withdrawal is construed as isolating oneself from the peer group.

Unfortunately, the two constructs of passive withdrawal and solitary-passive withdrawal have created an understandable confusion in the literature. *Passive withdrawal* refers to the child's withdrawal *from* the peer group. Typically, this construct is drawn from rating scale data (e.g., Revised Class Play, Pupil Evaluation Inventory) and is illustrated by items such as "very shy," "feelings hurt easily," "rather play alone than with others." The passive withdrawal construct may be contrasted with *active isolation,* a term which suggests that the child is actively isolated by the peer group (e.g., "often left out," "can't get others to listen"). *Solitary-passive withdrawal* is **observed** solitary behavior that involves exploratory and constructive activity. Since we were responsible for using the term "passive" in several ways, we hereby provide a clarification and offer an apology for any possible confusion. Moreover, we fully recognize that solitary-passive withdrawal is actually not passive at all given that it consists of active exploration and construction.

Reticence is a construct embodied within social withdrawal and should not be confused with the broader construct of social withdrawal. Reticence has been operationalized as the demonstration of solitary, wary behavior. It appears to be a reflection of *shyness* in unfamiliar peer settings and social wariness among familiar peers (Coplan & Rubin, 1998; Coplan, Rubin, Fox, Calkins, & Stewart, 1994; Rubin, 1982a). Behavioral reticence stands in contrast with solitude that reflects social disinterest (e.g., solitary-passive play in *early* childhood) or social immaturity (e.g., solitary-active play in early childhood). Solitary-active play comprises sensorimotor and/or dramatic activity acted out by oneself despite being in social company (Rubin, 1982a). Social withdrawal, on the other hand, is operationalized by *all* forms of solitude across contexts of familiarity and unfamiliarity; thus, reticence and solitary-passive and -active play *together* comprise the "umbrella" construct of social withdrawal.

To this constellation of related constructs, one can now add the clinical terms *social phobia* or *social anxiety disorder.* This phenomenon is marked by a fear of saying or doing things in public that will result in humiliation and embarrassment (Beidel, Turner & Morris, 1999). This latter construct is viewed as a clinical disorder (DSM IV, 1995) and appears to share much in common with social withdrawal at the extreme.

The forms of solitude described above carry with them different psychological meanings. For instance, there may be different motivations underlying the shy or withdrawn behaviors. Children, and adults for that matter, may spend time alone because they choose to do so, even when they are amongst others (e.g., socially disinterested). In this regard they may be said to lack an approach motivation while at the same time not necessarily having the motivation to avoid others (Asendorpf, 1993). In short, when such individuals are approached by others, they do not back away and exhibit wariness and social anxiety. Instead, they welcome the approach and thereafter make the choice to continue interacting or to return to that which occupied their solitary pursuits.

Other individuals may have conflicting motivations; that is, they may be motivated to approach others whilst at the same time feel the need to avoid those in their social milieu (e.g., socially wary; Rubin & Asendorpf, 1993). For some individuals, this approach–avoidance conflict is demonstrated mainly when in the company of unfamiliar others; for others, the motivational conflict exists across time and venue, including with familiar others. Lastly, some individuals may have a high approach motive and low avoidance motive, but for one reason or another they are rejected, and thus isolated by those in their social community of peers (Rubin, LeMare, & Lollis, 1990). In short, there are various reasons for the behavioral expression of solitude or social withdrawal.

Keeping in mind the psychological meanings and definitional issues, we now elaborate and explain why social withdrawal may bring social costs and angst rather than the pleasures to which the above quotes refer.

The Developmental Significance of Solitude and Social Withdrawal

Theories pertaining to social interaction

Piaget.   Early developmental research on social withdrawal had, as its theoretical origins, the writings of Piaget and Mead about the significance of social interaction for normal development. Piaget (1932), for example, posited that peer interaction provided a unique cognitive and social-cognitive growth context for children. He focused specifically on the relevance of disagreements with age-mates and the opportunities for negotiation arising from disagreements. These naturally occurring differences of opinion were assumed to engender cognitive conflict that required both intra- and interpersonal resolution in order for positive peer exchanges and experiences to occur. The resolution of interpersonal disputes was thought to result in a better understanding of others' thoughts and emotions, the broadening of one's social repertoire with which to solve interpersonal disputes and misunderstandings, and the comprehension of cause–effect relations in social interaction.

Support for these Piagetian notions derived from research demonstrating that peer exchange, conversations, and interactions produced intrapersonal cognitive conflict and a subsequent decline in egocentric thinking (e.g., Damon & Killen, 1982). Evidence was also offered for the associations between the *inability* to perspective-take and the demonstration of *maladaptive* social behavior (e.g., Crick & Dodge, 1994). Finally, researchers found that perspective-taking skills could be improved through peer interactive experiences, particularly those experiences that involved role-play. In turn, such improvement led to increases in prosocial behavior and to decreases in aggressive behavior (e.g., Selman & Schultz, 1990).

Mead.   Like Piaget, Mead (1934) emphasized the importance of the development of perspective-taking (and the corresponding decline of egocentrism) through peer interaction. In his theory of symbolic interactionism, Mead suggested that the ability to reflect on the self developed gradually over the early years of life, primarily as a function of peer interaction experiences. Participation in rule-governed games and activities with peers was believed to help children understand and coordinate the perspectives of others in relation to the self. Thus, perspective-taking experiences led to the conceptualization of the "generalized other" or the organized perspective of the social group, which in turn led to the emergence of an organized sense of self.

Summary.   Early developmental theories and the data supportive of them (see Rubin, Bukowski, & Parker, 1998 for a review) allow the conclusion that peer interaction influences the development of social cognition and, ultimately, the expression of competent social behavior. Peer interaction also influences children's understanding of the rules and norms of their peer subcultures. It is this understanding of normative performance levels that engenders in the child an ability to evaluate her/his own competency against the perceived standards of the peer group.

   If peer interaction does lead to the development of social competencies and the understanding of the self in relation to others, it seems reasonable to think about the developmental consequences for those children who, for whatever reason, refrain from engaging in social interaction and avoid the company of their peers. It is this reasonable thought that "drives" much of the current research on social withdrawal.

Developmental Origins of Social Withdrawal

Biology and behavioral inhibition

Where might social withdrawal come from? One line of thinking is that it derives from a *biological disposition* to be emotionally primed to react to novelty with wariness and fear. Drawing from the writings of Rothbart and Derryberry (1981), it has been suggested that *temperament*, or the degree to which individuals vary with regard to reactivity, frequency, intensity, and latency of response in the expression of emotions, may play a significant role in the early demonstration of *behavioral inhibition*. Supporting this premise, Kagan and Fox (e.g., Calkins, Fox, & Marshall, 1996; Kagan, Snidman, & Arcus, 1998) have identified groups of infants who display a high degree of reactivity and who are likely to express this reactivity via singular discrete emotions. Kagan and colleagues identified infants who exhibited not only a high degree of motor reactivity, but also cried when presented with novel visual and auditory stimuli. Calkins et al. (1996) singled out infants who were both highly reactive to novelty and expressed this reactivity via a high frequency of negative affect and distress. In both instances, these infants displayed more fearfulness and behavioral inhibition as toddlers than did other children (Calkins et al., 1996).

Following from this research, it has been argued that behavioral inhibition emanates from a physiological "hard wiring" that evokes caution, wariness, and timidity in unfamiliar social and nonsocial situations (Kagan, 1997). Inhibited infants and toddlers differ from their uninhibited counterparts in ways that imply variability in the threshold of excitability of the amygdala and its projections to the cortex, hypothalamus, sympathetic nervous system, corpus striatum, and central gray (Calkins et al., 1996). Stable patterns of right frontal EEG asymmetries in infancy predict temperamental fearfulness and behavioral inhibition in early childhood. Fox and colleagues (Fox & Calkins, 1993) recorded brain electrical activity of children at ages 9, 14, and 24 months and found that infants who displayed a pattern of stable right frontal EEG asymmetry across this 15-month period were more fearful, anxious, compliant, and behaviorally inhibited as toddlers than were other infants. The findings suggest that unique patterns of anterior brain electrical activity may be involved in the expression of fear and anxiety (Schmidt, 1999) and may reflect a particular underlying temperamental type. Indeed, a profile of asymmetric resting right frontal EEG activity has consistently been associated with social fear, withdrawal, and anxiety in both adults and young children; on the other hand, left frontal EEG activity has been associated with sociability and approach (Schmidt & Schulkin, 1999).

Another physiological entity that distinguishes wary from nonwary infants/toddlers is vagal tone, an index of the functional status or efficiency of the nervous system (Porges & Byrne, 1992), marking both general reactivity and the ability to regulate one's level of arousal. Reliable associations have been found between vagal tone and inhibition in infants and toddlers (Andersson, Bohlin, & Hagekull, 1999; Garcia Coll, Kagan, & Reznick, 1984): children with lower vagal tone (consistently high heart rate due to less parasympathetic influence) tend to be more behaviorally inhibited.

Lastly, the hypothalamic–pituitary–adrenocortical (HPA) axis is affected largely by stressful or aversive situations that involve novelty, uncertainty, and/or negative emotions (Levine, 1993); and behaviorally inhibited infants evidence significant increases in cortisol as a function of exposure to stressful social situations (Spangler & Schieche, 1998). Moreover, socially wary, fearful children have shown elevated home baseline cortisol readings relative to nonwary children, suggesting that they are continually "primed" to react with wariness to novel or unsettling social situations (Schmidt, Fox, & Schulkin, in press).

Stability of behavioral inhibition. Those who have argued for a biological cause of behavioral inhibition point not only to the physiological concomitants and predictors of the phenomenon, but also to the reasonably consistent finding that wary, fearful behavior is stable. Kagan and colleagues have suggested that *extremely* inhibited toddlers may be characterized as inhibited with adults and peers in later childhood (Kagan, 1989; Kagan, Reznick, & Snidman, 1987, 1989; Reznick et al., 1986); and have shown that toddlers identified as extremely inhibited are likely to be similarly identified five years later (Kagan et al., 1988). Others have shown that behavioral inhibition, from early through late childhood and adolescence is stable, but only moderately so (Broberg, 1993; Hart, Hofman, Edelstein, & Keller, 1997; Rubin, Burgess, & Hastings, in press; Rubin, Nelson, Hastings, & Asendorpf, 1999; Sanson, Pedlow, Cann, Prior, & Oberklaid, 1996).

Given the modest stability of behavioral inhibition, it seems reasonable to argue that it is hardly immutable. Therefore, the interplay of endogenous, socialization, and early relationship factors might be responsible for the development, maintenance, and dissolution of inhibition and its putatively negative consequences.

Attachment relationships and behavioral inhibition

According to attachment theorists, children develop an internalized model of the self in relation to others from the quality of their early parenting experiences (Bowlby, 1973). In the case of a secure parent–child relationship, the internal working model allows the child to feel confident and self-assured when introduced to novel settings. This sense of "felt security" fosters the child's active exploration of the social environment (Sroufe, 1983). *Exploration* of the social milieu allows the child to answer such *other-directed* questions as "What are the properties of this other person?", "What is she/he like?", "What can and does she/he do?" (Rubin, Fein, & Vandenberg, 1983). Once these exploratory questions are answered, the child can address self-directed questions such as "What can I do with this person?" Thus, *felt security* is viewed as a central construct in socioemotional development: it enhances social exploration, which results in interactive peer play. Peer play, in turn, plays a significant role in the development of social competence (Rubin & Rose-Krasnor, 1992).

Not all children are fortunate enough to develop internal working models of security. Approximately one third of all children develops insecure internal working models of social relationships and come to view the world as unpredictable, comfortless, and unresponsive (Sroufe, 1983). That subgroup of insecurely attached young children who refrain from exploring their social environments have typically been classified as *anxious-resistant* or "C" babies. In novel settings these infants maintain close proximity to the attachment figure; and when the attachment figure (usually the mother) leaves the paradigmatic "Strange Situation" for a short period of time, "C" babies become disturbingly unsettled. Upon reunion with the attachment figure, these infants show ambivalence – angry, resistant behaviors interspersed with proximity, contact-seeking behaviors (e.g., Greenspan & Lieberman, 1988).

Direct evidence for a predictive relation between infant temperament and insecure "C" attachment status derives from several sources. Infants who are dispositionally reactive to mildly stressful, novel social events are more likely to be classified as insecurely attached "C" (anxious-resistant) babies than their less reactive counterparts (Calkins & Fox, 1992). Spangler and Schieche (1998) reported that of 16 "C" babies they identified, 15 were rated by mothers as behaviorally inhibited.

Although support exists for a direct relation between temperament and insecure attachment, recent research indicates that this association is rather complex. It appears that when behaviorally inhibited toddlers are faced with novelty or social unfamiliarity, they become emotionally dysregulated: it is this dysregulation that seems to lead toddlers to retreat from unfamiliar adults and peers. That these youngsters become unsettled is supported by findings that confrontation with unfamiliarity brings with it increases in hypothalamic–pituitary–adrenocortical (HPA) activity (Spangler & Schieche, 1998). Interestingly, this relation

between confrontation with unfamiliarity and increases in HPA activation has been re-
ported for insecurely attached children in the Strange Situation (e.g., Gunnar, Mangelsdorf,
Larson, & Hertsgaard, 1989; Nachmias, Gunnar, Mangelsdorf, Parritz, & Buss, 1996).
More to the point, this increased HPA activity is experienced by "C" babies (Spangler &
Schieche, 1998).

Taken together, both insecure "C" attachment status and behavioral inhibition might
predict the subsequent display of socially reticent and withdrawn behaviors among peers.
Empirical support for such conjecture derives from findings that anxious-resistant ("C")
infants are more whiny, easily frustrated, and socially inhibited at age 2 than their secure
("B") counterparts (Calkins & Fox, 1992); and they also tend to be rated by their teachers
as more dependent, helpless, tense, and fearful (Pastor, 1981). Finally, "C" babies lack
confidence and assertiveness at age 4 years (Erickson, Sroufe, & Egeland, 1985); then, at
age 7 years they are observed to be socially withdrawn (Renken, Egeland, Marvinney,
Sroufe, & Mangelsdorf, 1989).

It might appear that the putative consequences of disposition-based behavioral inhibition and insecure-ambivalent attachment status are identical. Indeed, some have argued
that the behavior displayed by "C" babies in the Strange Situation is little more than the
expression of inhibited temperament (Kagan, 1998). However, Spangler and Schieche
(1998) found that the relation between behavioral inhibition and the increased production
of cortisol after being observed in the Strange Situation was significant, but only for infants
who had an insecure attachment relationship with their mother; for children with a secure
attachment relationship, there appeared to be a buffering effect on felt or experienced
stress for behaviorally inhibited babies. These data suggest that the instability of behavioral
inhibition from one year to the next may well be a function of the quality of the parent–
child relationship.

Parenting and behavioral inhibition

Thus far, we have described factors that may be responsible for the development of behavioral
inhibition, and ultimately the demonstration of social withdrawal in childhood – factors
such as the child's dispositional characteristics, the quality of the parent–child attachment
relationship, and the interaction between dispositional and social relationship factors. Note,
however, that an insecure attachment relationship is itself predicted by maternal behavior.
For example, mothers of insecurely attached "C" babies are more controlling and
overinvolved than are mothers of securely attached babies (Erickson et al., 1985). It is this
particular parenting style that is significant in the lives of behaviorally inhibited infants
and toddlers.

Maternal overcontrol and oversolicitousness. The developmental course of behavioral inhibition is better understood by referring to the quality of parenting associated with it. Given
that inhibited children may fail to adequately explore the social and nonsocial environment, it has been suggested that their parents may arrive at the belief that the best (if not
only) way to help their children understand their "worlds" is to either manipulate their
child's behaviors in a power assertive, highly directive fashion (e.g., telling the child how to

act or what to do) or to intervene and take over for the child the management of his/her interpersonal or impersonal dilemmas (see Burgess, Rubin, Cheah, & Nelson, 2001, for a review). The upside is that the child's difficulties will be solved. The downside is that for socially fearful children, the experience of such parental overcontrol is likely to maintain or exacerbate, rather than ameliorate, their difficulties. Parental overdirection will not allow the child to solve impersonal or interpersonal problems on her/his own. In controlling what their children are exposed to and how such situations are handled, these parents may prevent their children from engaging in necessary, self-initiated coping techniques. Lacking practice in behavioral self-regulation, children who are poor physiological regulators may not learn to overcome their dispositional vulnerabilities. Further, such parenting experiences may prevent the development of a belief system of self-efficacy, and likely will perpetuate feelings of insecurity within and outside the family.

Given the above scenario, is there evidence that intrusively controlling parenting is an accompaniment and/or response to behavioral inhibition? Recent studies have demonstrated that parental influence and control does appear to maintain and exacerbate children's inhibition and social withdrawal. For example, Rubin, Hastings, Stewart, Henderson, and Chen (1997) found that mothers of inhibited toddlers were "oversolicitous"; that is, they were observed to be highly affectionate and shielding of their toddlers when it was neither appropriate nor sensitive to do so. In a recent follow-up of these children, Rubin, Burgess, and Hastings (in press) found that behavioral inhibition at 2 years did predict socially reticent behavior during the preschool years; however, maternal overcontrol was a significant predictor as well. For toddlers whose mothers were highly intrusive, inhibited behavior among peers predicted subsequent reticent behaviors; but for toddlers whose mothers were *not* intrusively controlling, the relation between toddler inhibition and preschool reticence was nonsignificant.

Henderson and Rubin (1997) explored whether emotion regulation, as measured physiologically, interacted with parental behavior to predict preschoolers' socially reticent behavior among preschool peers. These researchers began with the premise that vagal tone, a marker of the tonic level of functioning of the parasympathetic nervous system (Porges & Byrne, 1992), should be associated with the display of social behavior in the peer group. For preschoolers who exhibited low resting vagal tone, observations and maternal reports of highly intrusive and critical behavior with the child were associated with observed child reticent, wary and anxious behaviors among peers; but for preschoolers with high resting vagal tone, such maternal intrusiveness and criticism were not associated with behavioral reticence.

Examining parents' behaviors toward anxious-withdrawn children (ages 2.5 to 6 years), LaFreniere and Dumas (1992) found that mothers were poor reciprocators of their own child's displays of positive behavior and positive affect. In addition, these mothers responded aversively to their child's negative behavior and negative affect. Such noncontingent responding to their children's positive behavior accompanied by punishment of negative behavior could hinder a child's development of self-worth and felt security.

Finally, in a recent examination of reported (rather than observed) parenting styles, Rubin and colleagues found that for both mothers and fathers, perceptions of their toddlers as shy and inhibited at age 2 years were (a) stable to age 4 years, and (b) predicted a lack of parental encouragement of independence at age 4 years (Rubin, Nelson, Hastings,

& Asendorpf, 1999). Parents' expressed lack of encouragement of independence, although stable from 2 to 4 years, failed to predict child shyness at age 4 years. These findings suggest that parents are responsive to child characteristics; and from the longitudinal data described above (Rubin et al., in press), it appears that those inhibited toddlers whose mothers are intrusively controlling and likely to discourage independence would be more likely to continue on a developmental trajectory of social withdrawal than those whose mothers were not inclined toward intrusiveness and overcontrol.

From inhibition to reticence and withdrawal

Investigators have consistently demonstrated that inhibited toddlers are likely to remain inhibited in the early and middle years of childhood (e.g., Broberg, Lamb, & Hwang, 1990; Reznick, Kagan, Snidman, Gersten, Baak, & Rosenberg, 1986). Notably, Kochanska and Radke-Yarrow (1992) reported that social but not nonsocial toddler inhibition predicted shy, inhibited behavior at age 5 years when children played with an unfamiliar peer. Rubin et al. (in press) found that toddlers' inhibited behavior either in the company of an unfamiliar adult or an unfamiliar peer predicted subsequent preschoolers' social reticence. Thus, behaviorally inhibited toddlers are at risk for becoming socially reticent as preschoolers.

Children's shy/reticent behaviors in *unfamiliar* contexts are not strongly predictive of socially withdrawn behaviors of any form in *familiar* contexts (Asendorpf, 1990; Paquette & LaFreniere, 1994). Asendorpf (1994) has argued that the relation between children's social behaviors in familiar and unfamiliar novel settings is mediated by the quality of children's peer relationships and their internalized thoughts about these relationships, a premise that has not been well studied in the literature.

Social withdrawal in early childhood

Social withdrawal and social skills.   If socially withdrawn children fail to engage in much peer interaction, do they also fail to develop those social and social-cognitive skills that purportedly emanate from such peer experiences? In early research on the construct of social withdrawal, researchers did not distinguish between its various forms. With this understood, it was found that socially withdrawn 4 and 5 year olds differed from their more sociable counterparts in the ways that they *think about* solving interpersonal dilemmas. For example, Rubin and colleagues have reported that when 5 year olds were asked what a cartoon character might do or say to obtain an attractive object from another cartoon character, withdrawn children produced fewer alternative solutions compared to their more sociable age-mates. Moreover, when informed that the strategies suggested would be unsuccessful, withdrawn youngsters displayed more rigidity in generating alternative responses: they were more likely to persevere and repeat the first strategy when compared to their more sociable counterparts. A qualitative analysis of strategies indicated that, compared to more sociable age-mates, withdrawn children were more likely to suggest adult intervention to aid in the solution of hypothetical social problems (Rubin, 1982b; Rubin,

Daniels-Beirness, & Bream, 1984). Consistent with these findings, LeMare and Rubin (1987) reported that social withdrawal in early childhood is associated with deficits in the ability to take the perspectives of others.

Rubin and colleagues (Rubin et al., 1984) have also found that socially withdrawn 4 and 5 year olds have relatively poor interpersonal problem-solving skills when *observed* during peer interaction. These researchers focused on children's social goals, the means by which they attempted to meet these goals, and the success rates of these strategies in relation to the sociability of the child. Their findings revealed that, compared to the more sociable children: (1) The *goals* of socially withdrawn children's requests appeared less "costly"; for example, they were more likely to attempt to request attention from a playmate rather than attempt to obtain an object or elicit active behaviors from their playmates; (2) the *strategies* used by withdrawn children were less assertive and less direct; specifically, the requests of withdrawn children were less likely to be spoken in the imperative; and (3) the *outcomes* of withdrawn preschoolers' requests were more likely to result in failure despite the fact that such overtures were less costly and less direct.

This latter finding pertaining to peer rebuff and nonattainment of social goals is true not only for socially withdrawn children (identified by using *all* forms of solitude) when they are observed with *familiar* peers, but also for reticent children when observed among *unfamiliar* peers (Nelson, 2000). Importantly, this connection between peer rebuff and social withdrawal or reticence alone may be taken as an in vivo assessment of peer rejection. Note that sociometric measures of peer group rejection do not assess the personal experience of felt rejection.

The early experience of social failure as one goes about one's life in the "real world" may well give already fearful and insecure children good reason to further withdraw from their peer milieu. For example, as a result of frequent interpersonal rejection by peers, withdrawn children may begin to attribute their social failures to internal causes: they may come to believe that there is something wrong with themselves rather than attributing their social failures to other people or situations. Supporting these notions, Rubin and Krasnor (1986) found that extremely withdrawn children tended to blame social failure on personal, dispositional characteristics rather than on external events or circumstances. The combination of peer rejection and internal (dispositional) attributions for peer noncompliance could be construed as creating a feedback loop whereby an initially fearful, withdrawn child begins to believe that his/her social failures are personality based, and then these beliefs are reinforced by increasing failure of social initiatives or interactions (Rubin & Stewart, 1996). Ultimately, the consequence of such cognitions may be further withdrawal from the social environment.

Social withdrawal during mid-to-late childhood

In almost all research on social withdrawal in middle childhood, a distinction is not made between reticence and solitary-passive behavior. The rationale for not doing so is drawn from the writings (and findings) of Asendorpf (e.g., 1993) who suggested that the varying types of solitude become "blended" by mid-childhood. Moreover, by middle childhood all types of social withdrawal become highly salient to the peer group (Younger, Gentile, &

Burgess, 1993). As such, the literature reviewed below is drawn from research on the "umbrella" construct of social withdrawal and not its subtypes.

Self-perceptions and internalizing problems. Previously, we have argued that the constellation of social withdrawal, social inadequacy, and peer rejection sows the seeds for internalizing problems such as low self-esteem, anxiety, depression, and loneliness (Rubin, 1993; Rubin et al., 1995; Rubin & Burgess, 2001). In fact, investigators have found that beginning in middle childhood, socially withdrawn children have negative self-perceptions of their social competence and interpersonal relationships (e.g., Hymel, Bowker, & Woody, 1993; Rubin, Hymel, & Mills, 1989). In addition to negative self-perceptions, socially withdrawn children actually do experience feelings of anxiety, loneliness, and depressed mood by mid-to-late childhood (e.g., Bell-Dolan, Reaven, & Peterson, 1993; Burgess & Younger, under review; Rubin et al., 1989). Considering the unpleasant nature of their psychological state, it would be useful to explore whether aspects of their peer relationships can exacerbate or ameliorate these negative experiences.

Peer relationships. The kinds of relationships that shy/withdrawn children have with peers may have an important bearing on their psychological adjustment and social-behavioral outcomes (Boivin & Hymel, 1997; Burgess, Ladd, Kochenderfer, Lambert, & Birch, 1999; Ladd & Burgess, 1999). Given the theoretical and practical significance of peer interaction for development, *and* the lack of social participation by shy/withdrawn children, one wonders about the nature of their peer relationships. Whereas much knowledge has been gained about socially withdrawn children's adjustment with respect to social and social-cognitive skills, surprisingly little is known about these children's *relationships* with peers during childhood. Yet, withdrawn children's social and psychological adjustment may partly stem from the quality of their experiences in peer relationships.

In the peer relationship literature, the prominent foci of investigators have been *friendship, peer acceptance/ rejection,* and *bully–victim relationships* (see Rubin, Bukowski, & Parker, 1998 for an extensive review). Although these three forms of peer relationships bear an empirical connection to each other, they have unique conceptual and operational definitions and represent distinct social experiences for children (Ladd, Kochenderfer, & Coleman, 1997; Vandell & Hembree, 1994). An argument could be made, however, that the construct of peer acceptance/ rejection does not necessarily imply that a "relationship" exists in the same way that friendship and victimization involve dyadic, mutual or reciprocated behaviors, affect, and social processes. The peer acceptance or rejection of withdrawn children is nevertheless considered here because it has typically been considered within the peer relationship domain.

Peer acceptance/rejection and social withdrawal. Peer acceptance or rejection refers to evidence of consensual liking or disliking, respectively, by group members for individuals in the peer group (see Asher & Coie, 1990). Consequently, if the peer group rejects a withdrawn child, it could be seen as a unilateral situation (i.e., not a reciprocal event), one in which there is not necessarily a response or effect. There may be negative effects, though, particularly for certain types of withdrawn children as opposed to others; for instance, shy or reticent children whose fear or self-consciousness drives the social decisions they make.

Based on traditional sociometric assessments, which have been utilized in numerous studies, it appears that findings pertaining to the relation between social withdrawal and peer rejection in *early* childhood are equivocal. When preschoolers' solitude was observed in the classroom, Rubin (1982a) found that reticent behavior was not associated with sociometric ratings of acceptance, but solitary-sensorimotor and solitary-dramatic behaviors were negatively associated with sociometric acceptance. In contrast, Hart et al. (2000) reported that preschoolers' reticent behavior assessed via teacher ratings was associated with sociometric peer rejection; but teacher-rated solitary-passive behavior was not. Ladd and Burgess (1999) found that teacher-rated passive withdrawal was not associated with peer rejection from kindergarten to second grade.

Evidence from *observational* studies of small peer-group interaction (Stewart & Rubin, 1995; Rubin & Borwick, 1984; Rubin & Krasnor, 1986) has shown that young withdrawn children's peers are less likely to comply with their requests or reciprocate social initiations than is the case for non-withdrawn children. Thus, peer rejection (observed noncompliance and rebuff) may actually occur in large groups and yet not be captured with general ratings of peer likeability or acceptance. Taken together, it seems that the relation between different forms of solitude and sociometric rejection may vary depending upon whether the data were derived from observed or rated behavior, who assessed the behavior (observers vs. teachers), where the behavior was observed (familiar vs. unfamiliar settings), and whether the sociometric measure was a rating or nomination scale.

With increasing age, the equivocal findings reported above become relatively congruent. Observed and peer-assessed withdrawal becomes strongly associated with sociometric measures of peer rejection or unpopularity by mid-to-late childhood (Boivin, Hymel, & Bukowski, 1995; Rubin, Chen, & Hymel, 1993). These consistent findings may be attributed to the suggestion that social withdrawal becomes increasingly noticeable as children get older. Recognizing that social solitude represents behaviors outside the norm, the peer group begins to view it as deviant (Younger et al., 1993). Also, older children are better able to perceive others' "internally driven" problems, such as anxiety and hypersensitivity, which often accompany social withdrawal. Moreover, relatively poorer social skills undoubtedly contribute to the lower likeability ratings of some withdrawn children.

Friendship and social withdrawal.   Friendship refers to a voluntary, reciprocal, and mutually regulated relationship between a child and a peer. During childhood, friendships have been viewed as support systems that facilitate psychological and social development (Ladd, Kochenderfer, & Coleman, 1996). Several indices have evolved to represent aspects of this relationship, including the size of the child's friendship network (i.e., number of mutual friendships), participation in a very best friendship, and quality of the friendships (see Bukowski & Hoza, 1989; Parker & Asher, 1993). Unfortunately, a paucity of information exists with respect to shy, withdrawn children's friendships; and the data are limited for all ages and for all aspects of friendship. Much more is known about average and aggressive children's friendships from early childhood to adolescence.

Children with larger networks of mutual friends may receive higher levels of support; in turn, friendship network size may be associated with better psychological health (Ladd & Burgess, 2001). Whilst one might expect that withdrawn children would have fewer mutual friendships than average children because they seldom initiate exchanges with peers and respond to peers' initiations less often (Wanlass & Prinz, 1982), Ladd and Burgess (1999) found that they had as many mutual friends as their normative counterparts. The authors speculated that even though withdrawn children interact with peers less often than average, they may still interact occasionally and engage in parallel play; and these encounters may be enough for them to nominate and be nominated as a friend. Note that this result was obtained among young children (ages 5–8) and that these withdrawn children were considered solitary-passive (asocial, disinterested) as opposed to reticent.

Being part of one very best friendship, especially a mutual positive one, may also help children's adjustment. Ladd and Burgess (1999) found that young withdrawn children were as likely to possess a mutual very best friendship as average/normative and aggressive children. But we have yet to discover whether this type of friendship could buffer withdrawn children from psychological difficulties such as low self-esteem, loneliness, and depression.

Lastly, the quality of children's friendships, also linked with psychological and school adjustment (Ladd et al., 1996), usually refers to supportive features such as validation/caring, help/guidance, and self-disclosure or to stressful features such as conflict and betrayal of trust (Parker & Asher, 1993). Again, it remains an empirical question as to whether socially withdrawn children's friendships differ in quality from those of other children.

Victimization and social withdrawal.   Victimization has been viewed in a relationship context because it is marked by a unique and enduring pattern of interactions that occur between children and *specific* bullies or attackers (Elicker, Englund, & Sroufe, 1992; Troy & Sroufe, 1987). Being victimized by peers implies that a child is regularly exposed to abusive interactions (e.g., physical or verbal aggression), and these negative events lead to fear of classmates, and ultimately to further withdrawal from peer interaction and possibly from school-related activities.

During early childhood, socially withdrawn children do not seem to be victimized by their peers. By mid-to-late childhood, however, evidence reveals that some peers do victimize them (Boivin, Hymel, & Bukowski, 1995). Thus, similar to the findings about peer rejection, social withdrawal has not been associated with peer victimization during early childhood (Ladd & Burgess, 1999) but does seem to be related to victimization by late childhood. Perhaps with age, fearful/withdrawn children become viewed as "easy marks" to their peers; and their anxiety may render them vulnerable to peer victimization.

Consequences of social withdrawal.   Highlighting the potential long-term outcomes of social withdrawal is a recent report which showed that a composite of observed and peer assessed social withdrawal at age 7 years predicted negative self-perceived social competence, low self-worth, loneliness, and felt peer group insecurity among adolescents aged 14 years (Rubin, Chen, McDougall, Bowker, & McKinnon, 1995). These latter findings are augmented by related research findings. Renshaw and Brown (1993) found that passive withdrawal at ages 9 to 12 years predicted loneliness assessed one year later. Ollendick, Ross, Weist, and Oswald (1990) reported that 10-year-old socially withdrawn children were more likely to be perceived by peers as withdrawn and anxious, more disliked by peers, and more likely to have dropped out of school than their well-adjusted counterparts five years later. Morison and Masten (1991) indicated that children perceived by peers as withdrawn and isolated in middle childhood were more likely to think negatively of their social competencies and relationships in adolescence. Consequently, it appears that early social withdrawal, or its relation to anxiety, represents a behavioral marker for psychological and interpersonal maladaptation in childhood and adolescence.

Summary.   By the time children reach the mid-to-late childhood years, social withdrawal becomes a full-fledged risk factor. Socially withdrawn children become salient to peers, and many become rejected by them. The seeming upshot of their salience and rejection is the development of negative self-perceptions of their social relationships and skills, as well as felt loneliness. In short, their internal working models of the social world comprise negative representations. Whether the existence of friends, or even a single close friendship, buffers withdrawn children from feeling negatively about themselves and their peer relationships is not yet known.

Social Withdrawal and Gender

Only recently have researchers begun to investigate questions pertaining to sex differences in social withdrawal in its various forms. One question is whether the prevalence of withdrawal varies between boys and girls. A second question pertains to whether the concomitants and predictive outcomes of withdrawal vary between the sexes.

Sex differences in the prevalence of social withdrawal.   Gender differences in the prevalence of behavioral inhibition and shyness have not typically been reported for young children (Mullen, Snidman, & Kagan, 1993; Rowe & Plomin, 1977; Simpson & Stevenson-Hinde, 1985). In one recent longitudinal study, however, parents rated their daughters as slightly more shy than sons at 18 and 30 months, but not subsequently at 50 months (Mathiesen & Tambs, 1999). Also, girls are not more likely than boys to be nominated by their peers as shy/anxious or socially withdrawn in preschool (Lemerise, 1997), middle childhood (Pekarik, Prinz, Leibert, Weintraub, & Neale, 1976), or late childhood (Rubin, Chen, & Hymel, 1993). Yet, in early adolescence some evidence indicates that girls tend to self-report being shy more than boys (Crozier, 1995). This is consistent with Lazarus' (1982) study of 396 fifth graders in which almost twice as many girls as boys labeled themselves "shy".

Although these latter findings cast some doubt on the notion that boys and girls do not differ in terms of shyness level, some inconsistencies in the literature may be attributed to differences in the conceptualization of the constructs (i.e., shyness, inhibition, or social withdrawal), the age of the participants, the informant source, and method of assessment (i.e., self-reports, peer reports, parental ratings, or observations). It is also possible that gender differences in children's perceptions and schemas for shyness/withdrawal are related to these findings. For example, children tend to recall information about a hypothetical peer described as socially withdrawn when that peer is a girl, and the schema for withdrawal seems to be more accessible for girls than for boys (Bukowski, 1990).

Sex differences in the concomitants and outcomes of social withdrawal.   Evidence drawn from concurrent and predictive studies suggests that being shy, inhibited, or socially withdrawn has greater psychological costs for males than females. Shyness in girls is more likely to be rewarded and accepted by parents, whereas shyness in boys is more likely to be discouraged (Engfer, 1993; Stevenson-Hinde, 1989). Radke-Yarrow, Richters, and Wilson (1988) reported that mothers were less accepting of their shy sons, and more affectionate and tender with their shy daughters. Similarly, shy boys tend to have more negative interactions with parents while shy girls have more positive ones (Simpson & Stevenson-Hinde, 1985). A similar pattern of results has been found in the school environment, as teachers tend to praise boys for outspoken behaviors but praise girls for restraining spontaneous conversation in the classroom (AAUW Educational Foundation, 1995).

Further, evidence has accumulated to suggest that *shyness* and *withdrawal* are associated with more negative outcomes for boys than for girls. In early childhood, extremely shy preschool-aged boys have more behavior problems than extremely shy girls (Stevenson-Hinde & Glover, 1996). In middle childhood, socially withdrawn boys, but not girls, describe themselves as more lonely and as having poorer social skills than their average peers (Rubin, Chen, & Hymel, 1993). Morison and Masten (1991) reported that withdrawn adolescent boys had lower self-esteem than girls. Finally, Caspi, Elder, and Bem (1988) found that males who were shy in childhood married, became fathers, and established careers at a later age than their non-shy peers. In contrast, females who were shy in childhood did not marry or start families later than other women in the same cohort.

It seems reasonable to assume that the different outcomes associated with social withdrawal for boys may be partly attributable to differential societal or cultural expectations; in western societies, shyness/withdrawal appears to be less acceptable for boys than for girls (Sadker & Sadker, 1994). Results from recent work, however, hints that there may be subtle gender differences in underlying substrates of shyness/withdrawal for boys and girls. Henderson, Fox, and Rubin (in press) reported that negative reactivity at 9 months predicted displays of social wariness at age 4 years for boys, but not for girls.

Finally, some preliminary evidence suggests that shy boys and girls may actually differ *physiologically*. Dettling, Gunnar, and Donzella (1999) reported that shyness in preschool-aged boys, but not girls, was associated with increased cortisol level over the day at childcare. Clearly, future research is required to elucidate these provocative findings.

Interventions for Social Withdrawal

As the psychological and social risks associated with shyness/withdrawal have become apparent, researchers have developed and implemented ameliorative intervention programs designed to benefit children. In most cases, the goal of intervention programs has been to increase the frequency of social interaction of shy and socially withdrawn children.

Many researchers have developed interventions involving concepts derived from *social learning theory*, including symbolic modeling (O'Connor, 1972) and contingent reinforcement (Hops, Walker, & Greenwood, 1977). Consistent with this theoretical position, researchers have involved *adult* figures such as teachers, adult "consultants," and parents to prompt, praise, and reinforce social behaviors, as well as to provide direct instruction and coaching (e.g., Lindeman, Fox, & Redelheim, 1993; Storey, Smith, & Strain, 1993). Parent participation putatively improves the generalizability of intervention beyond the school setting.

Other researchers have developed interventions that make extensive use of *peers*. Most peer-mediated interventions have focused on providing peers with incentives and/or training to increase their rate of positive social interaction (Christopher, Hansen, & MacMillan, 1991). In this vein, Fantuzzo, Stovall, Schachtel, Goins, and Hal (1987) trained more sociable children to make competent social initiations to withdrawn peers as means of encouraging more positive social experiences. Sainato, Maheady, and Shook (1986) assigned withdrawn children as classroom managers for various preferred classroom activities.

Related to this approach is the concept of *peer pairing*, whereby withdrawn children are provided with opportunities to engage in joint-task activities with non-withdrawn peers (Furman, Rahe, & Hartup, 1979). The use of peer pairing may constitute a particularly effective intervention strategy for socially wary and anxious children because a sociable peer may serve as a role model, provide positive reinforcement, decrease anxiety, increase confidence, and enhance generalization (Beidel & Turner, 1998).

Perhaps the most popular intervention strategy for withdrawn children is social skills training. This type of intervention dates back over 30 years (see Conger & Keane, 1981 for a review), and involves having children learn and practice a predetermined set of identified skills that would facilitate social interaction. It has had moderate effects on increasing the social interactions of those children who have mild to moderate levels of social withdrawal (Sheridan et al., 1990; Whitehill, Hersen, & Bellack, 1980).

Although most intervention programs have demonstrated at least some success, the literature is hampered by conceptual and methodological difficulties. Conceptually, it is not enough to teach shy/withdrawn children social skills. In many cases, socially wary children *know* what they *should* do in social situations (Rubin & Krasnor, 1986), but their problem lies with "moving" thought to action; and action appears to be inhibited by withdrawn children's inability to regulate feelings of social fear or anxiety.

Methodologically, many intervention programs have involved single-subject or numerically small designs (e.g., Lindeman et al. 1993; Mastropieri & Scruggs, 1986; Sainato et al., 1986). Further, most studies do not include a control group (e.g., Lindeman et al. 1993; Sainato et al., 1986; Sheridan et al., 1990), and the few with an average control group (Hodges & McCoy, 1990; Storey et al., 1993) do not include a nontreatment control group of withdrawn children. Other problems include the sole reliance on teacher referrals to identify withdrawn children (e.g., Lindeman et al., 1993; Sheridan et al., 1990; Storey et al., 1993). Ambiguity in the definitions of social withdrawal may result in the selection of a heterogeneous treatment group that could include socially wary, socially disinterested, and actively isolated children; therefore, the results of these studies are often inconsistent among participants. Lastly, follow-up assessments are often too short term (Lindeman et al., 1993; Sainato et al., 1986), and the gains fail to generalize across settings (Hops et al., 1985; McConnell, 1987). Despite these difficulties, the interventions extant are a reasonable starting point for future ameliorative efforts.

Conclusion

The study of the developmental course of social withdrawal has garnered an enormous amount of attention in the past decade. A glance at the dates of the cited material in this review will attest to this fact. Much work has been directed toward establishing the developmental origins of social withdrawal and its related constructs, as well as examining the contemporaneous and predictive correlates of social withdrawal at different points in childhood and adolescence. With regard to the latter, relatively few longitudinal studies exist; therefore, additional data are required to examine the premise that social withdrawal represents a risk factor in childhood and adolescence.

Although we have suggested a number of etiological factors that conspire to produce a socially withdrawn profile in childhood, the supportive data derive from very few developmental laboratories. The extent to which biologically based, dispositional factors interact with parenting styles and parent–child relationships to predict the consistent display of socially withdrawn behavior in both familiar and unfamiliar peer contexts needs to be established. Further, data are required to more precisely examine the consistency of socially reticent and solitary-passive behaviors across settings.

Our knowledge about the developmental course of social withdrawal is obviously constrained by the cultures in which the phenomenon has been studied. The vast majority of the published literature is derived from studies conducted in North America and Western Europe. Interestingly, though, recent research in the East indicates that behavioral inhibition and shyness are more prevalent in China and viewed as more normative than in the West (Chen, Rubin, & Li, 1997; Chen, Rubin, Li, & Li, 1999; Chen, Hastings, Rubin, Chen, Cen, & Stewart, 1998). Like all social behaviors, then, it would behoove us to examine cultural norms, the means by which such norms are socialized, and the developmental prognoses for children who, whilst perhaps displaying normative behavior in one culture, do not conform to expected behavioral norms in their own country. Certainly such a program of research will go a long way toward helping psychologists appreciate and be sensitive to cultural similarities, differences, and local definitions of normality and abnormality.

In summary, the literature we have reviewed suggests that the quality of life for socially inhibited and withdrawn children is less than pleasant. Withdrawn children are socially deferent, anxious, lonely, rejected and insecure in the company of peers. They fail to exhibit age-appropriate interpersonal problem-solving skills and tend to believe themselves to be deficient in social skills and relationships. The home lives of inhibited and withdrawn children are no more comforting: as we have noted here, they have insecure attachment relationships with their mothers and they are recipients of overcontrolling, intrusive parenting. Taken together, these characteristics do not augur well for socially withdrawn children. As such, researchers would do well to be more active in developing ameliorative, if not preventive interventions for these children.

References

AAUW Educational Foundation (1995). *The AAUW Report: How schools shortchange girls*. New York: Marlowe.

American Psychiatric Association (1995). *Diagnostic and statistical manual of mental disorders (DSM IV)*. Washington, DC: Author.

Andersson, K., Bohlin, G., & Hagekull, B. (1999). Early temperament and stranger wariness as predictors of social inhibition in 2-year-olds. *British Journal of Developmental Psychology, 17*, 421–434.

Asendorpf, J. (1990). Beyond social withdrawal: Shyness, unsociability and peer avoidance. *Human Development, 33*, 250–259.

Asendorpf, J. (1993). Abnormal shyness in children. *Journal of Child Psychology and Psychiatry, 34*, 1069–1081.

Asendorpf, J. (1994). The malleability of behavior inhibition: A study of individual developmental functions. *Developmental Psychology, 30*, 912–919.

Asher, S. R., & Coie, J. D. (1990). *Peer rejection in childhood*. New York: Cambridge University Press.

Beidel, D. C., & Turner, S. M. (1998). *Shy children, phobic adults*. Washington, DC: American Psychological Association.

Beidel, D. C., Turner, S. M., & Morris, T. L. (1999). Psychopathology of childhood social phobia. *Journal of the American Academy of Child and Adolescent Psychiatry, 38*, 643–650.

Bell-Dolan, D., Reaven, N. M., & Peterson, L. (1993). Depression and social functioning: A multidimensional study of the linkages. *Journal of Clinical Child Psychology, 22*, 306–315.

Boivin, M., & Hymel, S. (1997). Peer experiences and social self-perceptions: A sequential model. *Developmental Psychology, 33*, 135–145.

Boivin, M., Hymel, S., & Bukowski, W. (1995). The roles of social withdrawal, peer rejection, and victimization by peers in predicting loneliness and depressed mood in childhood. *Development and Psychopathology, 7*, 765–785.

Bowlby, J. (1973). *Attachment and loss: Separation, anxiety, and anger*. New York: Basic.

Broberg, A. G. (1993). Inhibition and children's out-of-home care. In K. Rubin & J. Asendorpf (Eds.), *Social withdrawal, inhibition, and shyness in childhood*. Hillsdale, NJ: Erlbaum.

Broberg, A., Lamb, M. E., & Hwang, P. (1990). Inhibition: Its stability and correlates in sixteen- to forty-month old children. *Child Development, 61*, 1153–1163.

Bukowski, W. M. (1990). Age differences in children's memory of information about aggressive, socially withdrawn, and prosocial boys and girls. *Child Development, 61*, 1326–1334.

Bukowski, W. M., & Hoza, B. (1989). Popularity and friendship: Issues in theory, measurement, and outcome. In T. J. Berndt & G. W. Ladd (Eds.), *Peer relations in child development* (pp. 15–45). New York: Wiley.

Burgess, K. B., Ladd, G. W., Kochenderfer, B. J., Lambert, S. F., & Birch, S. H. (1999). Loneliness during early childhood: The role of interpersonal behaviors and relationships. In K. J. Rotenberg & S. Hymel (Eds.), *Loneliness in childhood and adolescence* (pp. 109–134). New York: Cambridge University Press.

Burgess, K. B., Rubin, K.H., Cheah, C., & Nelson, L. J. (2001). Behavioral inhibition, social withdrawal, and parenting. In W. R. Crozier & L. Alden (Eds.), *International handbook of social anxiety: Concepts, research, and interventions relating to the self and shyness* (pp. 137–158). Chichester, UK: Wiley.

Calkins, S. D., & Fox, N. A. (1992). The relations among infant temperament, security of attachment, and behavioral inhibition at 24 months. *Child Development, 63*, 1456–1472.

Calkins S. D., Fox, N. A., & Marshall, T. R. (1996). Behavioral and physiological antecedents of inhibition in infancy. *Child Development ,67*, 523–540.

Caspi, A., Elder, G. H., Jr., & Bem, D. J. (1988). Moving away from the world: Life-course patterns of shy children. *Developmental Psychology, 24*, 824–831.

Chen, X., Hastings, P. D., Rubin, K. H., Chen, H., Cen, G., & Stewart, S. L. (1998). Child-rearing practices and behavioral inhibition in Chinese and Canadian toddlers: A cross-cultural study. *Developmental Psychology, 34*, 677–686.

Chen, X., Rubin, K. H., & Li, D. (1997). Relation between academic achievement and social adjustment: Evidence from Chinese children. *Developmental Psychology, 33*, 518–525.

Chen, X., Rubin, K. H., & Li, D., & Li, Z. (1999). Adolescent outcomes of social functioning in Chinese Children. *International Journal of Behavioral Development, 23*, 199–223.

Christopher, J. S., Hansen, D. J., & MacMillan, V. M. (1991). Effectiveness of a peer-helper intervention to increase children's social interactions: Generalization, maintenance, and social validity. *Behavior Modification, 15*, 22–50.

Conger, J. C., & Keane, S. P. (1981). Social skills interventions in the treatment of isolated or withdrawn children. *Psychological Bulletin, 90*, 478–495.

Coplan, R. J., & Rubin, K. H. (1998). Exploring and assessing nonsocial play in the preschool: The development and validation of the Preschool Play Behavior Scale. *Social Development, 7*, 72–91.

Coplan, R. J., Rubin, K. H., Fox, N. A., Calkins, S. D., & Stewart, S. L. (1994). Being alone, playing alone, and acting alone: Distinguishing among reticence and passive and active solitude in young children. *Child Development, 65*, 129–137.

Crick, N. R., & Dodge, K. A. (1994). A review and reformulation of social information-processing mechanisms in children's social adjustment. *Psychological Bulletin, 115*, 74–101.

Crozier, W. R. (1995). Shyness and self-esteem in middle childhood. *British Journal of Educational Psychology, 65*, 85–95.

Damon, W., & Killen, M. (1982). Peer interaction and the process of change in children's moral reasoning. *Merrill-Palmer Quarterly, 28*, 347–378.

Dettling, A. C., Gunnar, M.R., & Donzella (1999). Cortisol levels of young children in full-day childcare centers: Relations with age and temperament. *Psychoneuroendocrinology, 24*, 519–536.

Elicker, J., Englund, M., & Sroufe, L. A. (1992). Predicting competence and peer relationships in childhood from early parent–child relationships. In R. D. Parke & G. W. Ladd (Eds.), *Family–peer relationships: Modes of linkage* (pp. 77–106). Hillsdale, NJ: Erlbaum.

Engfer, A. (1993). Antecedents and consequences of shyness in boys and girls: A 6-year longitudinal study. In K. H. Rubin & J. B. Asendorpf (Eds.), *Social withdrawal, inhibition, and shyness in childhood* (pp. 49–79). Hillsdale, NJ: Erlbaum.

Erikson, M. F., Sroufe, L. A., & Egeland, B. (1985). The relationship between quality of attachment and behavior problems in preschool in a high risk sample. In I. Bretherton & E. Waters (Eds.), *Growing points of attachment theory and research. Monographs of the Society for Research in Child Development, 50* (Nos. 1–2, Serial No. 209).

Fantuzzo, J. W., Stovall, A., Schachtel, D., Goins, C., & Hal (1987). The effects of peer social initiations on the social behavior of withdrawn maltreated preschool children. *Journal of Behavior Therapy and Experimental Psychiatry, 18*, 357–363.

Fox, N. A., & Calkins, S. D. (1993). Pathways to aggression and social withdrawal: Interactions among temperament, attachment, and regulation. In K. Rubin & J. Asendorpf (Eds.), *Social withdrawal, inhibition, and shyness in childhood*. Hillsdale, NJ: Erlbaum.

Furman, W., Rahe, D. F., & Hartup, W. W. (1979). Rehabilitation of socially withdrawn preschool children through mixed-age and same-age socialization. *Child Development, 50*, 915–922.

Garcia-Coll, C., Kagan, J., & Reznick, J.S. (1984). Behavioral inhibition in young children. *Child Development, 55*, 1005–1019.

Greenspan, S. I., & Lieberman, A. F. (1988). A clinical approach to attachment. In J. Belsky & T. Nezworski (Eds.), *Clinical implications of attachment* (pp. 387–424). Hillsdale, NJ: Erlbaum.

Gunnar, M., Mangelsdorf, S., Larson, M., & Herstgaard, L. (1989). Attachment, temperament, and adreno-cortical activity in infancy: A study of psychoendocrine regulation. *Developmental Psychology, 25*, 355–363.

Hart, C. H., Yang, C., Nelson, L. J., Robinson, C. C., Olsen, J. A., Nelson, D. A., Porter, C. L., Jin S., Olsen, S. F., & Wu, P. (2000). Peer acceptance in early childhood and subtypes of socially withdrawn behavior in China, Russia, and the United States. *International Journal of Behavioral Development, 24*, 73–81.

Hart, D., Hofman, V., Edelstein, W., & Keller, M. (1997). The relation of childhood personality types to adolescents' behavior and development: A longitudinal study of Icelandic children. *Developmental Psychology, 33*, 195–205.

Henderson, H. A., & Rubin, K. H. (1997, April). Internal and external correlates of self-regulation in preschool aged children. Poster presented at the Biennial Meetings of the Society for Research in Child Development, Washington, DC.

Henderson, H. A., Fox N. A., & Rubin, K. H. (in press). Temperamental contributions to social behavior: The moderating roles of frontal EEG asymmetry and gender. *Journal of the American Academy of Child and Adolescent Psychiatry.*

Hodges, J. B., & McCoy, J. F. (1990). Effects of coaching and per utilization procedures on the withdrawn behaviors of preschoolers. *Child and Family Behavior Therapy, 12*, 25–47.

Hops, H., Walker, H. M., & Greenwood, C. R. (1977). *PEERS: A program for remediating social withdrawal in the school setting: Aspect of a research and development process. Report #3.* Center at Oregon for Research in the Behavioral Education of the Handicapped. Eugene, OR: University of Oregon.

Hymel, S., Bowker, A., & Woody, E. (1993). Aggressive versus withdrawn unpopular children: Variations in peer- and self-perceptions in multiple domains. *Child Development, 64*, 879–896.

Kagan, J. (1989). Temperamental contributions to social behavior. *American Psychologist, 44*, 668–674.

Kagan, J. (1997). Temperament and the reactions to the unfamiliarity. *Child Development, 68*, 139–143.

Kagan, J. (1998). *Three seductive ideas.* Cambridge, MA: Harvard University Press.

Kagan J., Reznick, J. S., & Snidman, N. (1987). The physiology and psychology of behavioral inhibition in children. *Child Development, 58*, 1459–1473.

Kagan J., Reznick, J. S., & Snidman, N. (1988). Biological basis of childhood shyness. *Science, 240*, 167–171.

Kagan, J., Snidman, N., & Arcus, D. (1998). Childhood derivatives of high and low reactivity in infancy. *Child Development, 69*, 1483–1493.

Kochanska, G., & Radke-Yarrow, M. (1992). Early childhood inhibition and the dynamics of the child's interaction with an unfamiliar peer at age five. *Child Development, 63*, 325–335.

Ladd, G. W. & Burgess, K. B. (1999). Charting the relationship trajectories of aggressive, withdrawn, and aggressive/withdrawn children during early grade school. *Child Development, 70*, 910–929.

Ladd, G. W., & Burgess, K. B. (2001). Do relational risks and protective factors moderate the linkages between childhood aggression and early psychological and school adjustment? *Child Development, 72*, 1579–1601.

Ladd, G. W., Kochenderfer, B. J., & Coleman, C. C. (1996). Friendship quality as a predictor of young children's early school adjustment. *Child Development, 67*, 1103–1118.

Ladd, G. W., Kochenderfer, B. J., & Coleman, C. C. (1997). Classroom peer acceptance, friendship, and victimization: Distinct relational systems that contribute uniquely to children's school adjustment? *Child Development, 68*, 1181–1197.

LaFreniere, P. J., & Dumas, J. E. (1992). A transactional analysis of early childhood anxiety and social withdrawal. *Development and Psychopathology, 4*, 385–402.

Lazarus, P. J. (1982). Incidence of shyness in elementary-school age children. *Psychological Reports, 51*, 904–906.

LeMare, L., & Rubin, K. H. (1987). Perspective-taking and peer interactions: Structural and developmental analyses. *Child Development, 58*, 306–315.

Lemerise, E. A. (1997). Patterns of peer acceptance, social status, and social reputation in mixed-age preschool and primary classrooms. *Merrill-Palmer Quarterly, 43*, 199–218.

Levine, S. (1993). The influence of social factors on the response to stress. *Psychotherapy and Psychosomatics, 60*, 33–38.

Lindeman, D. P., Fox, J. J., & Redelheim, P. S. (1993). Increasing and maintaining withdrawn preschoolers' peer interactions: Effects of double prompting and booster session procedures. *Behavior Disorders, 11*, 54–66.

Mastropieri, M. A., & Scruggs, T. E. (1986). Early intervention for socially withdrawn children. *Journal of Special Education, 19*, 429–441.

Mathiesen, K. S., & Tambs, K. (1999). The EAS temperament questionnaire: Factor structure, age trends, reliability, and stability in a Norwegian sample. *Journal of Child Psychology and Psychiatry and Allied Disciplines, 40*, 431–439.

McConnell, S. R. (1987). Entrapment effects and the generalization and maintenance of social skills training for elementary school students with behavioral disorders. *Behavioral Disorders, 12*, 252–263.

Mead, G. H. (1934). *Mind, self, and society.* Chicago: University of Chicago Press.

Morison, P., & Masten, A. (1991). Peer reputation in middle childhood as a predictor of adaptation in adolescence: A seven-year follow-up. *Child Development, 62*, 991–1007.

Mullen, M., Snidman, N., & Kagan, J. (1993). Free-play behavior in inhibited and uninhibited children. *Infant Behavior and Development, 16*, 383–389.

Nachmias, M., Gunnar, M., Mangelsdorf, S., Parritz, R. H., & Buss, K. (1996). Behavioral inhibition and stress reactivity: the moderating role of attachment security. *Child Development, 67*, 508–522.

Nelson, L. J. (2000). Social and nonsocial behaviors, and peer acceptance: A longitudinal model of the development of self-perceptions in children ages 4 to 7 years. Unpublished doctoral dissertation, University of Maryland, USA.

O'Connor, R. D. (1972). The relative efficacy of modeling, shaping, and combined procedures. *Journal of Abnormal Psychology, 79*, 327–334.

Ollendick, T. H., Ross, W. G., Weist, M. D., & Oswald, D. P. (1990). The predictive validity of teacher nominations: A five-year followup of at-risk youth. *Journal of Abnormal Child Psychology, 18*, 699–713.

Paquette, D., & LaFreniere, P. J. (1994). Are anxious-withdrawn children inhibited in a new social context? *Canadian Journal of Behavioral Science, 26*, 534–550.

Parker, J. G., & Asher, S. R. (1993). Friendship and friendship quality in middle childhood: Links with peer group acceptance and feelings of loneliness and social dissatisfaction. *Developmental Psychology, 29*, 611–621.

Pastor, D. (1981). The quality of mother–infant attachment and its relationship to toddler's initial sociability with peers. *Developmental Psychology, 17*, 326–335.

Pekarik, E., Prinz, R., Leibert, C., Weintraub, S., & Neale, J. (1976). The Pupil Evaluation Inventory: A sociometric technique for assessing children's social behavior. *Journal of Abnormal Child Psychology, 4*, 83–97.

Piaget, J. (1932). *The moral judgment of the child*. Glencoe, IL: Free Press.

Porges, S. W., & Byrne, E. A. (1992). Research methods for measurement of heart rate and respiration. *Biological Psychology, 34*, 93–130.

Radke-Yarrow, M., Richters, J., & Wilson, W. E. (1988). Child development in a network of relationships. In R. A. Hinde & J. Stevenson-Hinde (Eds.), *Relationships within families: Mutual influences* (pp. 48–67). Oxford, England: Clarendon Press.

Renken, B., Egeland, B., Marvinney, D., Sroufe, L.A., & Mangelsdorf, S. (1989). Early childhood antecedents of aggression and passive withdrawal in early elementary school. *Journal of Personality, 57*, 257–281.

Renshaw, P. D., & Brown, P. J. (1993). Loneliness in middle childhood: Concurrent and longitudinal predictors. *Child Development, 64*, 1271–1284.

Reznick, J. S., Kagan, J., Snidman, N., Gersten, M., Baak, K., & Rosenberg, A. (1986). Inhibited and uninhibited children: A follow-up study. *Child Development, 57*, 660–680.

Rothbart, M. K., & Derryberry, D. (1981). Development of individual differences in temperament. In M. E. Lamb & A. L. Brown (Eds.), *Advances in developmental psychology* (Vol. 1). Hillsdale, NJ: Erlbaum.

Rowe, D. C., & Plomin, R. (1977). Temperament in early childhood. *Journal of Personality Assessment, 41*, 150–156.

Rubin, K. H. (1982a). Non-social play in preschoolers: Necessary evil? *Child Development, 53*, 651–657.

Rubin, K. H. (1982b). Social and cognitive developmental characteristics of young isolate, normal, and sociable children. In K. H. Rubin & H. S. Ross (Eds.), *Peer relationships and social skills in childhood*. New York: Springer-Verlag.

Rubin, K. H. (1993). The Waterloo Longitudinal Project: Correlates and consequences of social withdrawal from childhood to adolescence. In K. H. Rubin & J. B. Asendorpf (Eds.), *Social withdrawal, inhibition, and shyness in childhood* (pp. 291–314). Hillsdale, NJ: Erlbaum.

Rubin, K. H., & Asendorpf, J. B. (1993). *Social withdrawal, inhibition, and shyness in childhood*. Hillsdale, NJ: Erlbaum.

Rubin, K. H., & Borwick, D. (1984). The communication skills of children who vary with regard to sociability. In H. Sypher & J. Applegates (Eds.), *Social cognition and communication*. Hillsdale, NJ: Erlbaum.

Rubin, K. H., Bukowski, W., & Parker, J. (1998). Peer interactions, relationships, and groups. In W. Damon (Ed.) & N. Eisenberg (Vol. Ed.), *Handbook of child psychology. Vol. 3: Social, emotional, and personality development* (5th ed., pp. 619–700). New York: Wiley.

Rubin, K. H., & Burgess, K. B. (2001). Social withdrawal and anxiety. In M. W. Vasey & M. R. Dadds (Eds.), *The developmental psychopathology of anxiety* (pp. 407–434). New York: Oxford University Press.

Rubin, K. H., Burgess, K. B., & Hastings, P. D. (in press). Stability and social-behavioral consequences of toddlers' inhibited temperament and parenting behaviors: *Child Development*.

Rubin, K. H., Chen, X., & Hymel, S. (1993). The socio-emotional characteristics of extremely aggressive and extremely withdrawn children. *Merrill-Palmer Quarterly, 39*, 518–534.

Rubin, K. H., Chen, X., McDougall, P., Bowker, A., & McKinnon, J. (1995). The Waterloo Longitudinal Project: Predicting adolescent internalizing and externalizing problems from early and mid-childhood. *Development and Psychopathology, 7*, 751–764.

Rubin, K. H., Coplan, R. J., Fox, N. A., & Calkins, S. D. (1995). Emotionality, emotion regulation, and preschoolers' social adaptation. *Development and Psychopathology, 7*, 49–62.

Rubin, K. H., Daniels-Beirness, T., & Bream, L. (1984). Social isolation and social problem solving: A longitudinal study. *Journal of Consulting and Clinical Psychology, 52*, 17–25.

Rubin, K. H., Fein, G., & Vandenberg, B. (1983). Play. In E. M. Hetherington (Ed.), *Handbook of child psychology: Vol 4. Socialization, personality, and social development*. New York: Wiley.

Rubin, K. H., Hastings, P. D., Chen, X., Stewart, S. L., & McNichol, K. (1998). Intrapersonal and maternal correlates of aggression, conflict, and externalizing problems in toddlers. *Child Development, 69*, 1614–1629.

Rubin, K. H., Hymel, S., & Mills, R. S. (1989). Sociability and social withdrawal in childhood: Stability and outcomes. *Journal of Personality, 57*, 237–255.

Rubin, K. H., & Krasnor, L. R. (1986). Social cognitive and social behavioral perspectives on problem-solving. In M. Perlmutter (Ed.), *Minnesota Symposia on Child Psychology* (Vol. 18, pp. 1–68). Hillsdale, NJ: Erlbaum.

Rubin, K. H., LeMare L. J., & Lollis, S. (1990). Social withdrawal in childhood: Developmental pathways to rejection. In S. R. Asher & J. D. Coie (Eds.), *Peer rejection in childhood* (pp. 217–249). New York: Cambridge University Press.

Rubin, K. H., Nelson, L. J., Hastings, P., & Asendorpf, J. (1999). Transaction between parents' perceptions of their children's shyness and their parenting styles. *International Journal of Behavioral Development, 23*, 937–957.

Rubin, K. H., & Rose-Krasnor, L. (1992). Interpersonal problem-solving and social competence in children. In V. B. van Hasselt & M. Hersen (Eds.), *Handbook of social development: A lifespan perspective*. New York: Plenum.

Rubin, K. H. & Stewart, S. L. (1996). Social withdrawal and inhibition in childhood. In E. Mash & R. Barkley (Eds.), *Child psychopathology* (pp. 277–307). New York: Guilford Press.

Sadker, M., & Sadker, D. (1994). *Failing at fairness: How America's schools cheat girls*. New York: Charles Scribner.

Sainato, D. M., Maheady, L., & Shook, G. L (1986). The effects of a classroom manager role on the social interaction patterns and social status of withdrawn kindergarten students. *Journal of Applied Behavior Analysis, 19*, 187–195.

Sanson, A. V., Pedlow, R., Cann, W., Prior, M., & Oberklaid, F. (1996). Shyness ratings: Stability and correlates in early childhood. *International Journal of Behavioral Development, 19*, 705–724.

Schmidt, L. A., (1999). Frontal brain electrical activity in shyness and sociability. *Psychological Science, 10*, 316–320.

Schmidt, L. A., Fox, N. A. & Schulkin, J. (in press). Behavioral and psychophysiological correlates of self-presentation in temperamentally shy children. *Developmental Psychobiology*.

Schmidt, L. A., & Schulkin, J. (Eds.) (1999). *Extreme fear, shyness, and social phobia: Origins, biological mechanisms, and clinical outcomes*. New York: Oxford University Press.

Selman, R, L., & Schultz, L. H. (1990). *Making a friend in youth: developmental theory and pair therapy*. Chicago: University of Chicago Press.

Sheridan, S. M., Kratochwill, T. R., & Elliott, S. N. (1990). Behavioral consultation with parents and teachers: Delivering treatment for socially withdrawn children at home and school. *School Psychology Review, 19*, 33–52.

Simpson, A. E., & Stevenson-Hinde, J. (1985). Temperamental characteristics of three- to four-year-old boys and girls and child-family interactions. *Journal of Child Psychology and Psychiatry, 26*, 43–53.

Spangler, G., & Schieche, M. (1998). Emotional and adrenocortical responses of infants to the Strange situation: The differential function of emotional expression. *International Journal of Behavioral Development, 22*, 681–706.

Sroufe, L. A. (1983). Infant-caregiver attachment and patterns of adaptation in preschool: The roots maladaptation and competence. In M. Perlmutter (Ed.), *Minnesota Symposium in Child Psy-*

chology, 16. Hillsdale, NJ: Erlbaum.

Stevenson-Hinde, J. (1989). Behavioral inhibition: Issues of context. In J. S. Reznick (Ed.), *Perspectives on behavioral inhibition* (pp. 125–138). Chicago: University of Chicago Press.

Stevenson-Hinde, J., & Glover, A. (1996). Shy girls and boys: A new look. *Journal of Child Psychology and Psychiatry, 37*, 181–187.

Stewart, S. L., & Rubin, K. H. (1995). The social problem-solving skills of anxious-withdrawn children. *Development and Psychopathology, 7*, 323–336.

Storey, K., Smith, D. J., & Strain, P. S. (1993). Use of classroom assistants and peer-mediated intervention to increase integration in preschool settings. *Exceptionality, 4*, 1–16.

Troy, M., & Sroufe, L. A. (1987). Victimization among preschoolers: Role of attachment relationship history. *Journal of the American Academy of Child and Adolescent Psychiatry, 26*, 166–172.

Vandell, D. L., & Hembree, S. E. (1994). Peer social status and friendship: Independent contributors to children's social and academic adjustment. *Merrill-Palmer Quarterly, 40*, 461–477.

Wanlass, R. L., & Prinz, R. J. (1982). Methodological issues in conceptualizing and treating childhood social isolation. *Psychological Bulletin, 92*, 39–55.

Whitehill, M. B., Hersen, M., & Bellack, A. S. (1980). Conversation skills training for socially isolated children. *Behaviour Research and Therapy, 18*, 217–225.

Younger, A. J., Gentile, C., & Burgess, K. B. (1993). Children's perceptions of social withdrawal: Changes across age. In K. Rubin & J. Asendorpf (Eds.), *Social withdrawal, inhibition, and shyness in childhood* (pp. 215–235). Hillsdale, NJ: Erlbaum.

Part VI

Social Skills and Social Cognition

Competence in social understanding and social skills are important for individual psychological well-being and peer group adjustment. While the term social cognition implies an understanding of the social world, literature reviewed by Charlie Lewis and Jeremy Carpendale shows that the terminology reflects a far more complicated and diversified construct than what appears at first glance. Likewise, how social skills are defined represents levels of complexity that are not readily apparent. We begin with a chapter by Antonius Cillessen and Amy Bellmore on the topic of social skills and interpersonal perception, followed by an illuminating chapter by Lewis and Carpendale that explicates two contrasting views of social cognition. Gary Ladd, Eric Buhs, and Wendy Troop then focus on interpersonal skills and relationships in school settings with implications for school-based prevention and intervention programs.

Cillessen and Bellmore approach their topic by distinguishing two traditions in the study of social skills during early and middle childhood. The first tradition focuses on "behavioral assessment" where social skills are defined and measurements are created to assess the veracity of the behavioral constructs. The second tradition stems from a "behavioral process" definition that explicates how child behaviors lend themselves to competent play with peers, emotion regulation, peer group entry, and conflict resolution. Behavioral processes of socially skilled and unskilled children in these critical social tasks are examined with the intent of linking these processes with interpersonal perception skills. The second half of the chapter accomplishes just that. Individual differences in how the social world is accurately perceived are shown to be associated with social self-perceptions of liking and disliking by peers. Research reviewed by the authors suggests that more socially skilled children tend to be more accurate in their self-perceptions of how well they are liked than socially unskilled children. Where do individual differences in perception accuracy come from? They conclude with a discussion of several mechanisms that might be at work and an overview of directions for future research in this area.

Lewis and Carpendale illustrate how vastly complex the study of social cognition is.

Two contrasting views of social cognition are explicated; one focuses on the cognitive approach to the study of children's social understanding while the other highlights the social approach. Surprisingly, the social and the cognitive traditions have never been fully integrated. The authors explain how the division created by these two approaches is problematic in current research on "theories of the mind." Recent developments in the "theory of the mind" literature are reviewed, followed by a discussion of domain specificity in mental-state understanding versus domain-general processes of reasoning and executive function. The false-belief test is critiqued and social approaches to children's understanding of mental states are introduced. Evidence is presented indicating that there is a relationship between children's social interactions and "theory of the mind" understandings. They culminate with a call for integrating the social and cognitive approaches in the study of children's social understanding. Suggestions are provided for how to do so.

On a somewhat different note, interpersonal challenges that children confront at school create difficult tasks for children as they apply their social skills to negotiate needs and establish relationships with other children and teachers. Little attention has been directed towards the many types of relationship difficulties that children work through in their quest to adapt to school environments. Given this backdrop, Ladd and colleagues expound upon a child by environment model that illustrates how child background variables, child attributes, behavioral styles, and supportive and stress-inducing interpersonal factors affect each other and children's adjustment to school. Research-based evidence for linkages among aspects of the model are carefully examined with regard to peer acceptance, friendship, peer victimization, and teacher–child relationships. Given all these factors, how might children's adjustment to school be enhanced? Of great interest to researchers, clinicians, and practitioners are descriptions of school-based interventions that can foster positive social cognitions, social skills, and peer acceptance and that have been empirically shown to reduce problematic behaviors. The authors note, however, that there are still needs for developing interventions that help children form and improve friendships, as well as cope with the effects of peer abuse at individual, rather than at school-wide levels. Future directions are provided for enhancing interventions and for conducting research that can further our understanding of processes associated with children's adjustment to school.

18

Social Skills and Interpersonal Perception in Early and Middle Childhood

Antonius H. N. Cillessen and Amy D. Bellmore

The definition of social skills is a much debated and complex issue. General definitions refer to adequacy, effectiveness, or competence in interactions with peers. Beyond these general definitions, what efforts have researchers made to conceptualize and define social skills more precisely and to observe the behavior of children who differ in social skills? The answers to these questions have been sought in two parallel research traditions. Both have made important contributions.

The first research tradition has its roots in educational psychology, has primarily a psychometric orientation, and may be called the "behavioral assessment" tradition. Researchers who follow this approach have made explicit attempts to define social skills and several converging definitions of this construct have been given. The main goals of this research have been instrument development, the identification of children with deficient social skills, and the evaluation of the effectiveness of intervention programs. Typically, teacher-rating scales have been used to assess social skills.

The second research tradition has its roots in social developmental psychology and may be called the "behavioral process" definition. Researchers in this approach often do not define the term social skills explicitly and use it interchangeably with terms such as social competence or social effectiveness. Research in this approach begins with a general indicator of social skills, such as social acceptance, popularity, or general measures of aggression and withdrawal. Next, children who differ on these dimensions are observed in critical social tasks, such as entering a new peer group, playing with peers, or handling conflict and competition. The goal of this research is to observe in detail the behaviors of socially skilled and socially unskilled children in those situations. The preferred research method is direct observation of actual behavior, although children's verbalizations of how they would respond in the task situations (presented to them as hypothetical vignettes) have been used as well. The strengths of this approach are its orientation on behavioral processes and its potential to compare between age groups.

In the first section of this chapter, we will distinguish the two traditions in the study of social skill through discussion of their postulates. We will limit our review of relevant research to studies that have followed the behavioral processes approach because these studies extend the focus from the assessment of individual behaviors to the role that these behaviors play in adaptive social functioning. We will detail the behaviors of children in critical tasks in relation to their peer acceptance (competent play with peers, peer group entry, emotion regulation, and conflict resolution). We are choosing peer acceptance as our indicator of social competence because it is a frequently used index of social competence as well as a good measure of social skillfulness because it incorporates the judgments of many individuals.

An additional line of investigation concerning children's social skills considers how behavior and acceptance by peers are related to social cognition (see Crick & Dodge, 1994). Specifically, competent play with peers, peer group entry, emotion regulation, and conflict resolution not only depend on children's behavioral skills, but also require adequate interpersonal perception skills. A process-oriented view of social skills should not only examine behavioral processes, but also the interpersonal perception processes that both depend on and influence interactive behavior. Consequently, in the second section of this chapter, we will consider children's interpersonal perception processes and their association with social skillfulness as measured by peer acceptance. Specifically, we consider children's understanding of themselves and of others in relation to their social status. We limit our discussion to individual differences in children's perceptions of their own and others' characteristics and to their estimations of how well liked they are by their peers because these basic perceptions may be particularly influential in determining their behavior with peers. We also discuss how research on this topic has contributed to understanding the process of how children arrive at their perceptions.

Assessment of Social Skills in Early and Middle Childhood

The first approach to the study of children's social skills, the behavioral assessment tradition, has proven useful in identifying the dimensions of children's problem behavior that disrupt adaptive social functioning (Gresham, 1986). Typically, the behavioral dimensions that contribute to social adjustment are assessed via teacher-, parent-, peer-, or self-ratings on multi-item behavior checklists. This approach can be described by the following three main characteristics.

First, social skillfulness is viewed as a multidimensional construct. Although researchers emphasize the significance of different social skills in their work, Caldarella and Merrell (1997) established five behavioral dimensions that occurred consistently in 19 separate instruments of children's social skills: peer relations skills, self-management skills, academic skills, compliance skills, and assertion skills. They also found that these dimensions were neither completely distinct nor independent of one another, indicating that although some skills contribute only to one dimension, other skills contributed to more than one dimension. Thus, although different dimensions have been identified, some of the behaviors of which they are comprised are relevant across situations.

Second, this approach places social skillfulness as a behavioral construct at an intermediate level of complexity, more specific than higher-level constructs such as social competence but more general than specific individual behavioral skills. This is useful because separate dimensions of social skill which represent a cluster of related behaviors can be identified and used for identification, diagnostic, and intervention purposes. However, given Gresham and Elliott's (1984) conclusion that social skillfulness is situationally specific, it would seem that this approach could be further validated by studying children's effective and ineffective social behaviors in specific social contexts.

Third, this approach views social skills relative to a child's age group or developmental stage. The main focus is not on changes in social skills across age groups, but rather on individual differences in social skills within age groups. Accordingly, although the scores are typically standardized within age groups, the main assessment instruments are used across developmental stages. For example, Caldarella and Merrell (1997) reported that most of the 19 studies in their review identified similar dimensions across age levels. This is a limitation of this approach because the dimensions that are most relevant to younger and older children likely differ. Thus, this approach could benefit from more research devoted to identifying age differences in the dimensions of behaviors that are effective in social interactions.

In summary, this assessment approach to social skills is extremely useful for diagnostic purposes. However, it is a relatively static approach and therefore less useful for the developmental study of social competence. To understand the development of social competence, a focus is needed on the developmental processes that underlie the social skills of children of differing ages in various social contexts. Therefore, in the next section, we will describe more extensively the efforts undertaken by researchers interested in these developmental processes.

Behavioral Processes of Socially Skilled and Unskilled Children

The second approach to the study of children's social skills involves identifying how children who differ in social skill respond when they encounter potentially problematical social tasks. This approach has been valuable because researchers have identified numerous behavioral correlates of social skillfulness (i.e., peer acceptance) for various critical social tasks. In this section we will consider four tasks that have been particularly useful in identifying differences between socially skilled and unskilled children. Specifically, we will consider social status differences in how children play with their peers, enter the ongoing activities of groups of their peers, regulate their emotions, and generate strategies to resolve conflicts. Each of these tasks is relevant to the social lives of preschool and elementary school children and requires them to adapt their behavior to allow for continued interaction with their peers. Further, the study of these tasks has utilized observational methods (both experimental and naturalistic), and is therefore particularly valuable because it informs us of what children actually do in their social worlds.

We review differences in children's behavior in each situation separately, because researchers have not examined the connections in children's behavior across these situations. Thus, we are able to determine the critical components of socially skilled behavior within each task setting. However, by focusing on single behaviors in specific contexts, we are not able to recognize how children organize and integrate their skills to produce global adaptive social functioning across multiple social settings. Although we present research relating children's behavior to their social skillfulness in each task separately, we recognize the need to consider the cross-contextual connections in future research.

Competent play with peers

Individual differences in play behavior and play competency have been assessed in early childhood because play is the context in which young children most frequently interact with their peers. Because play is a salient context for preschool age children, it is believed that it should both reflect and promote social competence (Creasey, Jarvis, & Berk, 1998). In this section, we examine preschool children's play behavior in relation to their social adjustment in the peer group.

Play behavior is most frequently observed in naturalistic settings such as preschool classrooms or childcare settings during periods where children may freely choose both their playmates and activities (e.g., Howes & Matheson, 1992). Within this context, researchers have attended to different aspects of play. For example, Howes (1988) assessed the complexity of social play forms (e.g., complementary and reciprocal play) and suggested that children's play forms follow a developmental sequence. Ladd, Price, and Hart (1988) attended to differences in the behavioral styles of preschool children's play (e.g., solitary play) as well as structural characteristics (e.g., the average size of the group in which play occurs).

Investigators have established that these various measures of play behavior are related to both concurrent and later indicators of a child's functioning with peers. Howes and Matheson (1992) reported that preschool-age children who engaged in more complex peer play at earlier developmental periods were rated by teachers as having less difficulty with their peers. Doyle and Connolly (1989) found that social acceptance, as measured by peer nominations, was positively associated with the frequency of engaging in social pretend play. Moreover, Ladd et al. (1988) reported that some styles of play predicted changes in peer acceptance over the course of one school year. They found that the cooperative play of preschoolers in the fall of the school year predicted gains in peer acceptance by spring and that arguing during play in the fall predicted lower peer acceptance by winter of the school year.

In more recent studies, cultural differences in children's play behavior have received attention. As Fantuzzo, Coolahan, Mendez, McDermott, and Sutton-Smith (1998) argued, given the presumed contextual specificity of play, relationships between competent play behaviors and peer acceptance should be considered within cultural groups. As a first step, these authors established the validity of an instrument designed to specifically assess play competencies that differentiate children who have positive peer relationships from children who have poor peer relationships within a sample of African American Head Start children.

Farver, Kim, and Lee (1995) presented evidence that play complexity may be affected by culture specific socialization practices. They found that Korean American preschool children participated in less social pretend play than their Anglo-American counterparts and suggested that this difference may be related to either the more structured classroom setting of Korean American preschools or to the collectivist orientation of Korean culture. Whatever the reason, this finding demonstrates the importance of assessing the relationship between play behaviors and peer acceptance within natural play settings for diverse groups of children as the norms for play styles may vary among different cultural groups.

Researchers have also established sex differences in the play behaviors that predict peer acceptance. For example, Hart, DeWolf, and Burts (1993) reported that lower peer preference was associated with observed solitary-passive play for preschool girls but not for boys and was linked to withdrawn/reticent behavior (onlooker and unoccupied) for preschool boys but not for girls. Additionally, Hart, DeWolf, Wozniak, and Burts' (1992) observations of preschoolers' social behaviors revealed that prosocial behavior was related to peer acceptance for girls only. In addition to sex differences in play styles, researchers have also attended to sex differences in peer interaction contact patterns. For example, Ramsey (1995) reported that older preschool children decreased their mixed-sex peer contacts over the course of one school year (i.e., fall to spring), whereas younger preschool children increase their contacts. Playground behaviors and group composition (e.g., network intensivity vs. extensivity and network homogeneity vs. diversity) have also been found to predict peer acceptance differentially for elementary-school age boys and girls (see, e.g., Ladd, 1983).

We expect children's play behaviors to be sensitive to other contextual effects (e.g., the play environment and the composition of the playgroup), and the effects of these variables on the relationship between peer group acceptance and play should be examined. Additionally, the stability of children's play behaviors from preschool to middle childhood should be studied. There is evidence that the quality of elementary school children's rough-and-tumble play is positively related to their peer-group acceptance (Pellegrini, 1988), but negatively related for preschoolers (Hart et al., 1992). However, no evidence exists showing that play behavior is stable from preschool to middle childhood. Thus, an additional avenue for future research is to establish the degree to which age moderates the relationship between specific play behaviors and peer acceptance.

Peer group entry

The ability to successfully enter into a ongoing social interaction is considered a marker of social skill because adequately initiating social contact and being accepted by the peer group is a prerequisite to developing stable social relationships. Therefore, the behaviors that result in successful peer group entry are important indicators of social competence. The research reviewed here includes studies that have examined which aspects of children's peer group entry behavior are related to their social status.

Following the protocol established by Putallaz and Gottman (1981), a target child's bid behavior is usually assessed in a laboratory with experimenter-formed groups of children who are involved in a game-like task when the target child arrives. Some experimenters comprise the "host" group of children with whom the target "guest" child is acquainted (e.g., Zarbatany, Van Brunschot, Meadows, & Pepper, 1996). Others use host children who are unacquainted with the guest (e.g., Russell & Finnie, 1990) or hosts who are confederates who follow the experimenter's instructions during the observation session (e.g., Wilson, 1999). Less frequently, target children have been observed in more naturalistic settings including the classroom (Dodge, Coie, & Brakke, 1982) and playground (Putallaz & Wasserman, 1989).

Using these methods, researchers have established the relationship between peer acceptance and group-entry behavior (see Putallaz & Wasserman, 1990, for a review). Specifically, unpopular children are more likely to call attention to themselves, attempt to control the interaction, and take longer to enter the peer group than higher status children (e.g., Dodge, Schlundt, Schocken, & Delugach, 1983; Putallaz & Gottman, 1981). These disruptive and self-centered behaviors are ineffective strategies because the children who use them are less likely to be accepted by the host children (Borja-Alvarez, Zarbatany, & Pepper, 1991; Putallaz & Gottman, 1981). Conversely, popular children successfully become a part of the group by sharing in the group's interest and offering relevant statements to the ongoing interaction (e.g., Dodge et al., 1983; Putallaz & Wasserman, 1989).

Investigators also have considered other factors that may influence children's group-entry behaviors and their resulting success. Gelb and Jacobson (1988) examined social-contextual factors and found that unpopular children are less likely to behave aversively in noncompetitive peer group entry situations than in competitive peer group entry situations. Rabiner and Coie (1989) examined intrapersonal factors and found that when rejected children have positive expectations about an upcoming play session with unfamiliar peers, they are more likely to be preferred by these unfamiliar peers during a peer group entry situation than when their initial expectations are neutral.

In addition, researchers have examined the effects of the interactions between the sex composition of the principal group and the sex of the guest child on the success of the guest child's entry behavior. Putallaz and Gottman (1981) failed to find sex differences in their laboratory study of peer group entry behavior, but naturalistic observations on the playground showed that girls were less effective and rejected more often than boys during entry bids with peers (Putallaz & Wasserman, 1989). When only same-sex interactions were considered, however, girls were more effective and more likely to be accepted than boys. This may result from the fact that girls are more likely to include newcomers than boys when they are the hosts in the peer entry paradigm (Zarbatany et al., 1996).

The findings reported above are based on elementary school children's social interactions. Hazen and Black (1989) reported similar findings for preschool children. Putallaz and Wasserman (1989) found that the group entry skills of first-, third-, and fifth-grade children differed. Specifically, older children were more likely to remain with the peers they initially approached, whereas younger children were more likely to engage in entry bids with various groups of peers. An important goal for future research is to further these age differences.

An additional goal for research is to consider the effects of additional social contextual variables on children's peer group entry behavior. For example, previous research suggests that group size (see Putallaz & Wasserman, 1989), sociometric status composition (see Gelb & Jacobson, 1988), and its psychological state (see Zarbatany & Pepper, 1996) all may affect the guest's behavior and entry success. These studies further highlight the interactional nature of the relationship between the target child and the hosts, further suggesting that children's social skills need to be considered in the social context.

Emotion regulation

Because effective social functioning with peers requires attending and adapting to the demands of specific social situations, children's ability to modulate emotions is expected to be an important aspect of their social competence. To assess this relationship between social skill and emotion regulation, researchers recently have designed observational studies that focus on children's responses to emotionally arousing situations, using sociometric status as an indicator of their social competence.

Observational studies of emotion regulation have been conducted in both naturalistic and experimental settings. Naturalistic observations usually take place in classroom or playground settings. For example, Denham, McKinley, Couchoud, and Holt (1990) attended to the emotional expression of target children in their preschool classrooms. Fabes and Eisenberg (1992) observed children on the playground, limiting their observations to children's behavioral responses to provocation during free play.

Observation of children's responses to provocation is considered a good paradigm to assess emotion *regulation*, because it allows us to compare children's actual feelings in addition to the behavioral and facial indices of emotion that they display (Hubbard & Coie, 1994). Various experimental paradigms have been designed that provoke children into a specific emotion, followed by recordings of children's recovery from that emotion. For example, Saarni (1984) provoked disappointment in children, whereas Underwood, Hurley, Johanson, and Mosley (1999) provoked anger in target children through the use of a confederate child actor. Once the target child was provoked, his or her facial expressions, gestures, and verbal responses were then recorded.

Naturalistic observations of preschool children have revealed a concurrent relationship between emotion regulation and peer-group acceptance. The expression of positive affect has been found to be related positively to liking by peers (Denham et al., 1990; Walter & LaFreniere, 2000), whereas the expression of anger is negatively related to peer-rated likability (Denham et al., 1990). Similarly, Fabes and Eisenberg (1992), studying preschool children's responses to real anger conflicts, found that children who were accepted peers dealt with anger provocations in direct and nonaggressive ways.

Underwood et al. (1999) demonstrated developmental differences in response to anger provocation in middle childhood through the use of an experimental, observational paradigm. They reported that outward expressions of anger decreased with age in a sample of 8-, 10-, and 12-year-old children. This observational study is unique in that the majority of studies of the relationship between emotion regulation and peer status with elementary school children have relied on hypothetical vignettes or self-report measures. Given the finding of Underwood et al. (1999), further insight into the relationship between emotion regulation and peer competence at different developmental stages, in particular through observational methods, is an important goal for future research.

An additional goal for future work is the assessment of sex differences in emotion regulation. To date, the findings from observational studies indicate that girls are less likely than boys to express angry feelings (e.g., Fabes & Eisenberg, 1992; Underwood et al., 1999). Further evidence exists that sex differences in emotion regulation interact with sociometric status. For example, Walter and LaFreniere (2000) found that girls' anger was negatively related to peer rejection whereas boys' anger was positively related to peer rejection. More research is needed to identify similar differentiations by sex and sociometric status for positive emotions.

The studies reviewed here highlight the utility of the observational paradigm for understanding the relationship between emotion regulation and peer acceptance. Investigators should continue to modify these methods to assess which situational and interpersonal variables moderate the status-emotion regulation link. Explicit attention should be given to identifying specific interpersonal factors (such as liking of the provocateur, see Fabes, Eisenberg, Smith, & Murphy, 1996) in addition to intrapersonal factors that may affect children's emotion regulation skills.

Conflict resolution

Shantz (1987) defines conflict as a dyadic social exchange characterized by mutual opposition between two parties. Because adequate management of conflict is necessary for the maintenance of children's interpersonal relationships, researchers have identified children's conflict resolution strategies as an important social skill. This research is corroborated empirically by research showing that preschool and elementary school children's conflict resolution strategies are related to their peer acceptance.

Because conflict responses are situation specific (Putallaz & Sheppard, 1992), the relation between peer acceptance and conflict resolution strategies needs to be examined in various settings. Children's behavioral strategies (e.g., seeking an adult's help or using physical aggression) and verbal strategies (e.g., discussing the situation or using verbal aggression) in peer conflict situations have been investigated by observing children's naturally occurring interactions in field settings such as classroom free play (e.g., Hartup, Laursen, Stewart, & Eastenson, 1988). They have also been examined in controlled laboratory settings where the composition of dyads and the activities are manipulated by the experimenter (e.g., Hartup, French, Laursen, Johnston, & Ogawa, 1993). Observations of young children's naturally occurring conflicts in free play have revealed that being disliked by peers is positively correlated with more frequent participation in conflict episodes (D. Shantz, 1986) and verbal strategies are used far more frequently than physical force within conflict episodes (Eisenberg & Garvey, 1981). However, research in which observations of children's behavior in conflict situations is related to their peer acceptance is lacking.

The most widely used method to investigate the relation between peer acceptance and conflict resolution is to examine children's responses to hypothetical conflict situations. Typically, children are presented with a realistic hypothetical situation that involves a conflict with a peer and are asked to indicate how they themselves would respond in that situation. Because every participating child is exposed to the same social scenarios, this method allows researchers to make controlled comparisons between children. Rose and Asher (1999) used this method to assess the strategies that fourth- and fifth-grade children use in response to conflict with a friend. They found that children's use of hostile strategies (e.g., physical or verbal aggression) was negatively correlated with peer acceptance. Chung and Asher (1996) assessed fourth- through sixth-grade children's strategies in conflict situations with a same-sex classmate and reported that selection of prosocial strategies (e.g., accommodation of the needs of both parties) was positively correlated with peer acceptance. They also found that sex moderated the relationship between peer acceptance and conflict strategies. Specifically, the selection of hostile strategies was negatively correlated with peer acceptance for girls, whereas the selection of adult-seeking strategies (e.g., request help from an adult) was negatively correlated with peer acceptance for boys.

These sex differences in the relation between peer conflict responses to conflict and social status correspond with the different social orientations expected of boys and girls. In response to both actual and hypothetical conflict situations (Chung & Asher, 1996; Hartup et al., 1993; Miller, Danaher, & Forbes, 1986; Murphy & Eisenberg, 1996; Rose & Asher, 1999), girls are more likely to select relationship-oriented strategies, while boys are more likely to select assertive, self-centered strategies. These sex differences are further qualified depending on the sex of the interaction partner. Miller et al.'s observational study of children's actual conflict behavior revealed that boys used assertive strategies when interacting with boys and girls, whereas girls were more likely to use prosocial strategies with girls than with boys. These differences have not been corroborated by hypothetical vignette studies as these typically have focused on children's interactions with same-sex peers.

Although clear sex differences have emerged, there is little information regarding developmental differences in children's conflict resolution strategies. Most studies of children's strategies have used elementary-school age children, and within these studies, age differences typically have not been examined. Finally, in addition to individual characteristics such as age, sex, and ethnicity, various social-contextual factors are expected to influence children's responses to conflict (see Hartup & Laursen, 1993). Future research should examine how contextual variables such as relationship characteristics (e.g., friend vs. nonfriend), characteristics of the setting (e.g., space, resources, and activities), and conflict type (e.g., object acquisition, peer provocation, and rights infraction) influence children's behavioral and social-cognitive responses to conflict.

Conclusion

Taken together, these results indicate that children's behavior in various critical social tasks is related to their peer acceptance and that these social tasks are diagnostic to assess socially skillful behavior. In spite of these results, the critical social task approach has not provided much information about developmental changes in the relationship between children's behavior and acceptance. While age differences can be identified indirectly by comparing the findings of studies assessing different age groups for each task, no direct comparisons of developmental differences in relation to sociometric status exist for any task reviewed here. Additionally, researchers have not consistently attended to sex differences for every task. For example, while clear differences between the conflict resolution strategies of boys and girls have been identified, differences in boys' and girls' play styles have not received much attention. Given the findings from research on peer group entry showing that sex differences of the actor interacted with the sex of his or her peers, more research is needed on the situational specificity of skillful behaviors. In particular, researchers should conduct more detailed analyses of individual characteristics of both the actor and their dyadic or group partners in particular situations. Finally, researchers should attend to how children form the strategies that guide their behavior in these specific social situations. Because appropriate behavior may be dependent on accurate perception of the actions and intentions of the participants in a given social situation, the second section of this chapter considers this ability in relation to social acceptance.

Interpersonal Perception

Interpersonal perception refers to one's understanding of self and of others that results from social interactions. As indicated in the introduction to this chapter, children's understanding of self and others in relationships is expected to both reflect and influence their social behavior in the domains of peer play, peer group entry, emotion regulation, and conflict. Therefore, in this section, we consider children's interpersonal perception skills in detail and examine, both conceptually and empirically, how they are related to social competence as measured by peer acceptance.

Basic questions of interpersonal perception research

Most early research on the development of interpersonal perception was directed towards establishing its normative development. For example, researchers addressed the types of perceptions children form of themselves and others (see Dubin & Dubin, 1965, for a review). More recent research has focused on establishing individual differences in children's interpersonal perceptions and the factors that are related to these differences (see Berndt & Burgy, 1996, for a review). In this more recent research trend, researchers have examined children's perceptions of their own and others' general characteristics and competencies in the social, behavioral, cognitive, and physical domains, including their general peer sociability and liking by peers. In addition, researchers have examined children's assessments of how well liked they are by specific peers. A major question guiding recent research on children's interpersonal perceptions addressed the degree to which children's general and dyad-specific interpersonal perceptions are accurate.

In research on the accuracy of children's interpersonal perceptions, an important distinction is maintained between accuracy of perceptions of competencies and accuracy of perceptions of liking because they do not necessarily reflect the same underlying ability, nor have they been assessed in the same manner. For example, perception accuracy of characteristics and competencies is usually measured by comparing one child's ratings of the self on some characteristic (e.g., disruptive behavior in school) with another person's ratings of the same behavior (e.g., teacher ratings of disruptive behavior). In some instances, a child's self-perceptions are compared to the perceptions of a social group (e.g., all peers in her grade). Accuracy of liking perceptions, however, is usually assessed by comparing the sociometric nominations or ratings a target child expects to receive from others with others' actual nominations or ratings of the target child. This has been done at both the dyadic and group levels.

Development of interpersonal perception accuracy

Research on the development of interpersonal perception accuracy has been guided by the assumption that children's social perception skills develop in accordance with general cognitive abilities (cf. social perspective taking, see Piaget, 1983). For example, based on Piaget's conclusion that young children's egocentric thinking prevents them from being accurate perceivers of others, most studies of perception accuracy have excluded children under age 6. Consistent with Piaget's theory, interpersonal perception accuracy has been demonstrated in children age 6 and older (e.g., Malloy, Yarlas, Montvilo, & Sugarman, 1996). Additionally, perception accuracy increases throughout middle childhood and into early adolescence, although the amount of improvement tends to be small across various domains (Ausubel, Schiff, & Gasser, 1952; DeJung & Gardner, 1962; Krantz & Burton, 1986; Malloy et al., 1996; Phillips, 1963).

Although perception accuracy does increase minimally with age throughout middle childhood, the notion that interpersonal perceptions will not be accurate until middle childhood has not been supported empirically. Smith and Delfosse (1980) found that preschool age children are able to correctly identify who their own friends are as well as who their classmates' friends are. Thus, the specific cognitive skills that underlie this ability might be established as early as 4 years of age.

Interpersonal perception accuracy as an indicator of social skill

The notion that interpersonal perception is related to social skillfulness has been propelled by demonstrations of individual differences in accuracy. The majority of studies that have addressed this topic have used sociometric status as an indicator of social competence. Rose-Krasnor (1997) argued that this is not only the most widely used, but also the best measure of social skill. Consequently, for all studies reviewed here, peer acceptance as measured by sociometric techniques will be used as the measure of social skill.

Perception of traits and competencies.   Studies investigating individual differences in perception accuracy for characteristics of self (e.g., the domains outlined by Harter, 1982) have been conducted almost exclusively with elementary-school age children. These studies have consistently revealed that low status children are the least able to assess themselves or others accurately on various traits compared to evaluations by others, while high status children's perceptions are more congruent with others' perceptions.

In one study, Kurdek and Krile (1982) assessed the social self-perceptions of children in grades 3–8 and found that children who were seen as the most socially competent also reported the highest perceived social self-competence. This finding indicates that popular children do have some awareness of their social acceptance. In another study, Patterson, Kupersmidt, and Griesler (1990) tested the relationship between accuracy of self-perceptions and social status more explicitly. They classified children in grades 3 and 4 into sociometric status categories and compared these children's self-perceptions in the social, academic, and behavioral domains with independent assessments by others. They reported that rejected children overestimated their social acceptance, popular and average children underestimated their peer acceptance, and neglected children underestimated their behavioral competence. Cillessen and Bellmore (1999) also examined the social self-perceptions of fourth graders who were classified into sociometric status groups. They compared self- and teacher perceptions in four domains (disruptive conduct, anxiety/withdrawal, peer sociability, and school adjustment), and found that rejected children's self-ratings showed the smallest amount of agreement with their teachers' ratings in the areas of conduct, peer sociability, and school adjustment.

Overall, the self-perceptions of rejected children have received more attention than those of other children. Boivin and Bégin (1989) reported that two clusters of rejected children could be identified based on their self-perceptions: one group who reported lower competence in various domains than other children, and one group who reported higher ratings in some domains than other children. These differential patterns of self-perceptions complement other evidence for subgroups of rejected children, typically labeled aggressive-rejected and withdrawn-rejected (see Boivin, Hymel, & Bukowski, 1995, for a review). Together, the behavioral and social-perceptual differences suggest that different negative outcomes may be expected for each group (externalizing vs. internalizing problems), and that these differences may be related to the accuracy of children's self-perceptions.

To test this idea, Patterson et al. (1990) used peer nominations to assign third- and fourth-grade children to one of three groups: rejected only, rejected-aggressive, and aggressive only. When they compared children's self-reports of their competencies to more objective assessments they found that relative to peer reports, rejected-aggressive children but not rejected children overestimated their peer acceptance compared to average children. Rejected-aggressive children also overestimated their behavioral competence compared to rejected and average children, even though they rated themselves lower than the other two groups did on this attribute.

Hymel, Bowker, and Woody (1993) also investigated the perception accuracy of subgroups of rejected children. They classified fourth and fifth graders into one of four groups: aggressive unpopular, withdrawn unpopular, aggressive-withdrawn unpopular, and average. They assessed accuracy by comparing discrepancies between children's self-ratings and their peers' ratings of their competencies in four domains: academic, athletic, peer relations, and appearance. The authors reported that average and withdrawn-unpopular children were the most accurate perceivers while children in both aggressive subgroups were more likely to overestimate their competencies in all four domains.

Although the sex of the perceiver child is gaining increasing attention in childhood social perception research, few researchers have included perceiver sex as a variable. The few studies that have considered perceiver sex indicate that the self- and other-perceptions of competencies are somewhat more concordant for girls than for boys (Bellmore, 2000; Cillessen & Bellmore, 1999; Kurdek & Krile, 1982). Clearly, however, there is a need to include perceiver sex as a variable in future studies.

Perception of liking and disliking.   Investigation of individual differences in accuracy of perceived liking and disliking has been limited to samples of elementary school children. Most studies of liking perceptions have focused on whether or not children are able to accurately identify who likes or dislikes them. An exception is the study by Krantz and Burton (1982), who tested the ability of kindergarten through third-grade children to identify their classmates' peer preferences. They found that popularity was positively correlated with greater accuracy in identifying the specific friendship preferences of their friends.

Cillessen and Ferguson (1995) compared the accuracy of perceptions of liking and disliking for kindergarten and first-grade boys who were classified into sociometric status groups. They created accuracy scores at two levels: the dyadic level (the extent to which each boy knew which specific other classmates liked him) and at the group level (the extent to which each boy knew how well liked he was by the group as a whole). They found that rejected boys were the least accurate perceivers of liking perceptions at the dyadic level and least accurate in both liking and disliking perceptions at the group level.

MacDonald and Cohen (1995) examined dyadic accuracy scores of liking and disliking for first through sixth graders. They reported that rejected children were least accurate in their judgments of who liked them and popular children were the least accurate in their judgments of who disliked them. Cillessen and Bellmore (1999) tested the accuracy of fourth-grade children's perceptions of liking and disliking by their peers using a similar method. They also formed dyadic accuracy scores by comparing liking and disliking nominations received and expected, but did not find any status differences for perceptions of liking or disliking with this sample.

Zakriski and Coie (1996) compared the accuracy of perceived liking and disliking by peers using a sample of fourth-grade children who were classified as aggressive-rejected, nonaggressive-rejected, or average. They found that aggressive-rejected children underestimated their social rejection more than nonaggressive-rejected did. Interestingly, they also reported that this inaccuracy did not generalize to perceptions of others but was limited to perceptions of self and therefore may serve a self-protective function. This study is also important because it is the only study to find an effect of ethnicity in the study of children's social self-perceptions. They authors found that African American children were less accurate than white children, but attributed this effect to methodological aspects of their study. The authors concluded that rejected-aggressive children were the least accurate social perceivers, and that no differences in perception accuracy were associated with ethnicity.

Few researchers have examined perceiver sex differences in accuracy of perceived liking and disliking by peers and those that have reported different results. Cillessen and Bellmore (1999) found that girls were more accurate than boys for perceptions of liking only, whereas MacDonald and Cohen (1995) found no sex differences in perception accuracy. One important difference between these two studies is that Cillessen and Bellmore allowed cross-sex nominations in their sociometric procedure, whereas MacDonald and Cohen allowed only same-sex nominations. Sex differences could not be examined in other studies because only boys served as participants (Cillessen & Ferguson, 1995; Zakriski & Coie, 1996).

Origins of interpersonal perception skill

Given the individual differences in perception accuracy discussed above, the question of how children arrive at their perceptions of self and others needs to be addressed. Two processes have been offered to explain the link between children's social cognitions and their interactions with others. The first process describes how perceptions are formed and is congruent with the ideas of symbolic interactionists (e.g., Cooley, 1902) who claim that others' perceptions are internalized to form self-perceptions. Indeed, Cole (1991) found that teacher and peer perceptions influenced the self-perceptions of fourth graders over the course of a school year. Felson (1989) found a similar effect of parents' perceptions on children's self-perceptions. Although these findings provide evidence that other's perceptions do affect self-perceptions, how this occurs has not yet been established.

According to symbolic interactionists, the accuracy of children's perceptions depends on the extent to which they have had social interactions with others. Theorists agree that relations with others afford children the opportunity to acquire the skills they need to successfully interact with others (e.g., Hartup, 1992). Thus, rejected children who are excluded from peer interaction may be inaccurate social perceivers because they lack the opportunities to practice this important social skill.

The second process that describes the relationship between social perceptions and social interactions considers the social cognitions of the child as the antecedent to social interactions. Accordingly, inaccurate self-perceptions are presumed to have negative consequences for social behavior and peer acceptance. This notion mirrors Dodge's (1986) model of the link between social information processing and social adjustment: perception deficits cause problematic social interactions. Research on social cognition and peer relations has demonstrated that children's self-perceptions may determine their peer relations (Crick & Dodge, 1994).

The processes explaining the link between interpersonal perceptions and social relationships that are specified by the symbolic interactionist and social-cognitive perspectives should not be considered mutually exclusive. The accuracy of children's interpersonal perceptions likely depends on the frequency and/or quality of their peer interactions and, in turn, the accuracy of children's interpersonal perceptions is likely to affect the quality and/or frequency of their social interactions. An important goal for future research is to explore the directionality of the link between children's perceptions and their peer relationships. Longitudinal studies will help to establish the point at which status differences in perception accuracy emerge and whether they decrease with age and maturing social-cognitive abilities.

Future directions in interpersonal perception research

Current debate exists about whether normative development or individual differences in interpersonal perception accuracy should be emphasized. Researchers should continue to devote attention to each aspect and its related theoretical perspectives, methods, and findings. The findings presented here indicate the necessity of continued study of individual differences in accuracy, because although differences have emerged, many questions remain. For example, all existing studies have examined perceiver differences, however, social perception is dependent on qualities of the target as well as the perceiver (Kenny, 1994). Thus, researchers need to consider characteristics of the perceiver, target, and their relationship in future research.

This interaction between perceiver and target is especially relevant for social interactions that occur between children from different groups (e.g., culture, sex, sociometric status). For example, interpersonal perception accuracy for children who come from different cultures should be examined because they participate in different types of social interactions that may affect perceptions. It might be expected that more inaccurate social perceptions would occur for interactions between children from different cultures than between children from the same culture. Thus, children's interpersonal perception accuracy for children from the same group and children from a different group should be investigated. This requires research in peer groups that are culturally heterogeneous in nature.

In addition to examining cultural differences, sex differences also require further attention. Although some sex differences have been reported, they tend to be small and inconsistent. Also, in addition to establishing whether boys or girls have different perception abilities, their perceptions of same-sex peers and other-sex peers should be studied. Children's perceptions of the opposite sex are particularly intriguing because of the sex-segregated social context of middle childhood. Accordingly, children might be more accurate about their same-sex peers' perceptions than about the perceptions of other-sex peers.

There is also a need to extend interpersonal perception research to younger age groups. The bias towards studying elementary-school age children derives from the assumption that very young children have limited cognitive abilities that prevent accurate social perception. However, this assumption has hardly been tested empirically and the limited available evidence suggests, contrary to the expectations, that perception accuracy may exist in children as young as 4 years of age. However, more research is needed to determine when in early childhood this ability emerges, how it is related to other social-cognitive skills (e.g., perspective taking), and to what domains it extends (e.g., perceptions of friendships vs. perceptions of traits and behaviors).

Finally, consideration should be given to the use of the term "accuracy" in research on children's interpersonal perceptions. Use of this term is only valid when children's self-perceptions are compared with an objective standard. The term "accuracy" is not appropriate in studies where children's self-perceptions of their competencies are compared to perceptions by others such as teachers, peers, and parents, because these are not necessarily unbiased judges of children's behavior. In those cases, it is more appropriate to use the term self-other agreement instead (Kenny, 1994). The term "accuracy" is appropriate in studies where children's self-perceptions of liking are compared to peers' actual liking judgments. Thus, consideration to variations in the assessment task may improve the consistency between findings from various studies.

Conclusion

In this chapter, we have examined two important domains of children's social skillfulness: evidence for behavioral processes related to social skills in various critical social situations, and evidence for the accuracy of children's interpersonal perceptions in interactions with others. As indicated by Rose-Krasnor (1997), the definition of social competence remains a complicated issue, but what is clear in her review is that social competence or social skill can and should not be conceptualized in terms of a single domain or a limited number of behaviors. We believe therefore that the examination of both interpersonal behaviors and interpersonal perceptions in concert may contribute to our understanding of children's social competence.

Throughout our review, we have used peer acceptance or sociometric status as an index of children's social competence. While peer acceptance provides a useful working definition of social competence, allowing us to include and examine a wide variety of research studies, there are limitations to this approach. As indicated by Rose-Krasnor, sociometric status is a group-based construct, that does not necessarily always adequately reflect a child's social skill. For example, popularity with peers may be a questionable index of social competence in deviant peer groups, whereas in other circumstances the ability to form individual friendship relations may provide a better indicator of social skill than group acceptance. The current status of the literature on interpersonal behaviors and interpersonal perception, however, does not allow us to make these finer distinctions. Thus, an important goal for future research is to examine children's social-behavioral and social-cognitive skills more precisely at each of the individual, dyadic, and group levels of peer interaction.

Finally, our review indicates that more research is needed that examines the effects of development, gender, and ethnicity on children's behavioral and perception skills. In the behavioral domain, various age groups have been examined, but few studies exist that include direct comparisons of age groups. The same is true for studies on children's interpersonal perceptions. In both domains, the roles of gender and ethnicity need to be examined further, and the examination of these effects need to become part of a more complex conceptualization of interpersonal processes than currently exists. Behaviors and perceptions in groups can be considered from a perspective known as the social relations model (Kenny, 1994). This perspective distinguishes effects due to children as actors towards or perceivers of others, children as recipients or targets of behaviors and perceptions by others, and the unique effects due to specific dyadic relationships than cannot be explained by actor or partner effects.

Moreover, this approach can take into account individual differences variables such as gender and ethnicity. That is, the actor, partner, and relationship effects can be qualified further depending on whether boys and girls interact with same-sex or other-sex peers, and whether nonminority or minority children perceive or interact with peers of their own or other ethnicity. This methodological approach will provide a useful tool for estimating children's social interaction and interpersonal perception skills in the increasingly diverse peer system.

References

Ausubel, D. P., Schiff, H. M., & Gasser, E. B. (1952). A preliminary study of developmental trends in sociempathy: Accuracy of perception of own and others' sociometric status. *Child Development, 23,* 111–128.

Bellmore, A. D. (2000). Social perception accuracy for same-sex and other-sex peers: Links with social experiences and social competence. Unpublished Master's thesis, University of Connecticut, Storrs.

Borja-Alvarez, T., Zarbatany, L., & Pepper, S. (1991). Contributions of male and female guests and hosts to peer group entry. *Child Development, 62,* 1079–1090.

Berndt, T. J., & Burgy, L. (1996). The social self-concept. In B. A. Bracken (Ed.), *Handbook of self-concept: Developmental, social, and clinical considerations* (pp. 171–209). New York: Wiley.

Boivin, M., & Bégin, G. (1989). Peer status and self-perception among early elementary school children: The case of the rejected children. *Child Development, 60,* 591–596.

Boivin, M., Hymel, S., & Bukowski, W. M. (1995). The roles of social withdrawal, peer rejection, and victimization by peers in predicting loneliness and depressed mood in children. *Development and Psychopathology, 7,* 765–785.

Caldarella, P., & Merrell, K. W. (1997). Common dimensions of social skills of children and adolescents: A taxonomy of positive behaviors. *School Psychology Review, 20,* 264–278.

Chung, T., & Asher, S. R. (1996). Children's goals and strategies in peer conflict situations. *Merrill-Palmer Quarterly, 42,* 125–147.

Cillessen, A. H. N., & Bellmore, A. D. (1999). Accuracy of social self-perceptions and peer competence in middle childhood. *Merrill-Palmer Quarterly, 45,* 650–676.

Cillessen, A. H. N., & Ferguson, T. J. (1995, March). Accuracy of children's interpersonal perceptions in early elementary school: Correlates and consequences. Paper presented at the biennial meeting of the Society for Research in Child Development, Indianapolis, IN.

Cole, D. A. (1991). Change in self-perceived competence as a function of peer and teacher evaluation. *Developmental Psychology, 27,* 682–688.

Cooley, C. H. (1902). *Human nature and the social order* (Rev. ed.). New York: Scribner.

Creasey, G. L., Jarvis, P. A., & Berk, L. E. (1998). Play and social competence. In O. N. Saracho & B. Spodek (Eds.), *Multiple perspectives on play in early childhood education* (pp. 116–143). Albany, NY: State University of New York Press.

Crick, N. R., & Dodge, K. A. (1994). A review and reformulation of social information processing in children's social adjustment. *Psychological Bulletin, 115,* 74–101.

DeJung, J. E., & Gardner, E. F. (1962). The accuracy of self-role perception: A developmental study. *Journal of Experimental Education, 31,* 27–41.

Denham, S. A., McKinley, M., Couchoud, E. A., & Holt, R. (1990). Emotional and behavioral predictors of preschool peer ratings. *Child Development, 61,* 1145–1152.

Dodge, K. A. (1986). A social-information processing model of social competence in children. In M. Perlmutter (Ed.), *The Minnesota Symposia on Child Psychology: Vol. 18. Cognitive perspectives in children's social and behavioral development* (pp. 77–125). Hillsdale, NJ: Erlbaum.

Dodge, K. A., Coie, J. D., & Brakke, N. P. (1982). Behavior patterns of socially rejected and neglected preadolescents: The roles of social approach and aggression. *Journal of Abnormal Child Psychology, 10,* 389–409.

Dodge, K. A., Schlundt, D. C., Schocken, I., & Delugach, J. D. (1983). Social competence in children's sociometric status: The role of peer group strategies. *Merrill-Palmer Quarterly, 29,* 309–336.

Doyle, A., & Connolly, J. (1989). Negotiation and enactment in social pretend play: Relations to social acceptance and social cognition. *Early Childhood Research Quarterly, 4,* 289–302.

Dubin, R., & Dubin, E. R. (1965). Children's social perceptions: A review of research. *Child Development, 36,* 809–838.

Eisenberg, A. R., & Garvey, C. (1981). Children's use of verbal strategies in resolving conflicts. *Discourse Processes, 4,* 149–170.

Fabes, R. A., & Eisenberg, N. (1992). Young children's coping with interpersonal anger. *Child Development, 63,* 116–128.

Fabes, R. A., Eisenberg, N., Smith, M. C., & Murphy, B. C. (1996). Getting angry at peers: Associations with liking of the provocateur. *Child Development, 67,* 942–956.

Fantuzzo, J., Coolahan, K., Mendez, J., McDermott, P., & Sutton-Smith, B. (1998). Contextually-relevant validation of peer play constructs with African American Head Start children: Penn Interactive Peer Play Scale. *Early Childhood Research Quarterly, 13,* 411–431.

Farver, J., Kim, Y. K., & Lee, Y. (1995). Cultural differences in Korean- and Anglo-American preschoolers' social interaction and play behaviors. *Child Development, 66,* 1088–1099.

Felson, R. B. (1989). Parents and the reflected appraisal process: A longitudinal analysis. *Journal of Personality and Social Psychology, 56,* 965–971.

Gelb, R., & Jacobson, J. L. (1988). Popular and unpopular children's interactions during cooperative and competitive peer group activities. *Journal of Abnormal Child Psychology, 16,* 247–261.

Gresham, F. M. (1986). Conceptual and definitional issues in the assessment of children's social skills: Implications for classification and training. *Journal of Clinical Child Psychology, 15,* 3–15.

Gresham, F. M., & Elliott, S. N. (1984). Assessment and classification of children's social skills: A review of methods and issues. *School Psychology Review, 13,* 292–301.

Hart, C. H., DeWolf, M., & Burts, D. C. (1993). Parental disciplinary strategies and preschoolers' play behavior in playground settings. In C. H. Hart (Ed.), *Children on playgrounds: Research perspectives and applications* (pp. 271–313). Albany, NY: State University of New York Press.

Hart, C. H., DeWolf, M., Wozniak, P., & Burts, D. C. (1992). Maternal and paternal disciplinary styles: Relations with preschoolers' playground behavioral orientations and peer status. *Child Development, 63,* 879–892.

Harter, S. (1982). The perceived self-competence scale for children. *Child Development, 53,* 87–97.

Hartup, W. W. (1992). Peer relations in early and middle childhood. In V. B. Van Hasselt & M. Hersen (Eds.), *Handbook of social development: A lifespan perspective* (pp. 257–281). New York: Plenum.

Hartup, W. W., French, D. C., Laursen, B., Johnston, M. K., & Ogawa, J. R. (1993). Conflict and friendship relations in middle childhood: Behavior in a closed-field situation. *Child Development, 64,* 445–454.

Hartup. W. W., & Laursen, B. (1993). Conflict and context in peer relations. In C. H. Hart (Ed.), *Children on playgrounds: Research perspectives and applications* (pp. 44–84). Albany, NY: State University of New York Press.

Hartup, W. W., Laursen, B., Stewart, M. I., & Eastenson, A. (1988). Conflict and the friendship relations of young children. *Child Development, 59,* 1590–1600.

Hazen, N. L., & Black, B. (1989). Preschool peer communication skills: The role of social status and interaction context. *Child Development, 60,* 867–876.

Howes, C. (1988). Peer interaction of young children. *Monographs of the Society for Research in Child Development, 53* (1, Serial No. 217).

Howes, C., & Matheson, C. C. (1992). Sequences in the development of competent play with peers: Social and social pretend play. *Developmental Psychology, 28,* 961–974.

Hubbard, J. A., & Coie, J. D. (1994). Emotional correlates of social competence in children's peer relationships. *Merrill-Palmer Quarterly, 40,* 1–20.

Hymel, S., Bowker, A., & Woody, E. (1993). Aggressive versus withdrawn unpopular children: Variations in peer and self-perceptions in multiple domains. *Child Development, 64*, 879–896.

Kenny, D. A. (1994). *Interpersonal perception: A social relations analysis.* New York: Guilford Press.

Krantz, M., & Burton, C. (1986). The development of the social cognition of social status. *Journal of Genetic Psychology, 147*, 89–95.

Kurdek, L. A., & Krile, D. (1982). A developmental analysis of the relation between peer acceptance and both interpersonal understanding and perceived social self-competence. *Child Development, 53*, 1485–1491.

Ladd, G. W. (1983). Social networks of popular, average, and rejected children in school settings. *Merrill-Palmer Quarterly, 29*, 283–307.

Ladd, G. W., Price, J. M., & Hart, C. H. (1988). Predicting preschoolers' peer status from their playground behaviors. *Child Development, 59*, 986–992.

MacDonald, C. D., & Cohen, R. (1995). Children's awareness of which peers like them and which peers dislike them. *Social Development, 4*, 182–193.

Malloy, T. E., Yarlas, A. S., Montvilo, R. K., & Sugarman, D. B. (1996). Agreement and accuracy in children's interpersonal perceptions: A social relations analysis. *Journal of Personality and Social Psychology, 71*, 692–702.

Miller, P. M., Danaher, D. L., & Forbes, D. (1986). Sex-related strategies for coping with interpersonal conflict in children aged five and seven. *Developmental Psychology, 22*, 534–548.

Murphy, B. C., & Eisenberg, N. (1996). Provoked by a peer: Children's anger-related responses and their relations to social functioning. *Merrill-Palmer Quarterly, 42*, 103–124.

Patterson, C. J., Kupersmidt, J. B., & Griesler, P. C. (1990). Children's perceptions of self and relationships with others as a function of sociometric status. *Child Development, 61*, 1335–1349.

Pellegrini, A. D. (1988). Elementary school children's rough-and-tumble play and social competence. *Developmental Psychology, 24*, 802–806.

Phillips, B. N. (1963). Age changes in accuracy of self-perceptions. *Child Development, 34*, 1041–1046.

Piaget, J. (1983). Piaget's theory. In P. H. Mussen (Series Ed.) & W. Kessen (Vol. Ed.), *Handbook of child psychology: Vol. 1. History, theory and methods* (4th ed., pp. 103–128). New York: Wiley.

Putallaz, M., & Gottman, J. M. (1981). An interactional model of children's entry into peer groups. *Child Development, 52*, 986–994.

Putallaz, M., & Sheppard, B. H. (1992). Conflict management and social competence. In C. U. Shantz & W. W. Hartup (Eds.), *Conflict in child and adolescent development* (pp. 330–355). New York: Cambridge University Press.

Putallaz, M., & Wasserman, A. (1989). Children's naturalistic entry behavior and sociometric status: A developmental perspective. *Developmental Psychology, 25*, 297–305.

Putallaz, M., & Wasserman, A. (1990). Children's entry behavior. In S. R. Asher & J. D. Coie (Eds.), *Peer rejection in childhood* (pp. 60–89). New York: Cambridge University Press.

Rabiner, D., & Coie, J. D. (1989). Effect of expectancy inductions on rejected children's acceptance by unfamiliar peers. *Developmental Psychology, 23*, 450–457.

Ramsey, P. G. (1995). Changing social dynamics in early childhood classrooms. *Child Development, 66*, 764–773.

Rose, A. J., & Asher, S. R. (1999). Children's goals and strategies in response to conflicts within a friendship. *Developmental Psychology, 35*, 69–79.

Rose-Krasnor, L. (1997). The nature of social competence: A theoretical review. *Social Development, 6*, 111–135.

Russell, A., & Finnie, V. (1990). Preschool children's social status and maternal instructions to assist group entry. *Developmental Psychology, 26*, 603–611.

Saarni, C. (1984). An observational study of children's attempts to monitor their expressive behavior. *Child Development, 55*, 1504–1513.

Shantz, C. U. (1987). Conflicts between children. *Child Development, 58*, 283–305.

Shantz, D. W. (1986). Conflict, aggression, and peer status: An observational study. *Child Development, 57*, 1322–1332.

Smith, P. K., & Delfosse, P. (1980). Accuracy of reporting own and others' companions in young children. *British Journal of Social and Clinical Psychology, 19*, 337–338.

Underwood, M. K., Hurley, J., Johanson, C. A., & Mosley, J. E. (1999). An experimental, observational investigation of children's responses to peer provocation: Developmental and gender differences in middle childhood. *Child Development, 70*, 1428–1446.

Walter, J. L., & LaFreniere, P. J. (2000). A naturalistic study of affective expression, social competence, and sociometric status in preschoolers. *Early Education and Development, 11*, 109–122.

Wilson, B. J. (1999). Entry behavior and emotion regulation abilities of developmentally delayed boys. *Developmental Psychology, 35*, 214–222.

Zakriski, A. L., & Coie, J. D. (1996). A comparison of aggressive-rejected and nonaggressive-rejected children's interpretations of self-directed and other-directed rejection. *Child Development, 67*, 1048–1070.

Zarbatany, L., & Pepper, S. (1996). The role of the group in peer group entry. *Social Development, 5*, 251–260.

Zarbatany, L., Van Brunschot, M., Meadows, K., & Pepper, S. (1996). Effects of friendship and gender on peer group entry. *Child Development, 67*, 2287–2300.

19

Social Cognition

Charlie Lewis and Jeremy Carpendale

Introduction

The term "social cognition" is deceptively simple. On the surface it refers to an understanding of the social world. Yet it hides a continuing debate between cognitive models of social behavior and development, and claims about the social origins of cognition. In this chapter we explicate and suggest an integration of these two approaches to development. A complete review of the complexities of this literature would be impossible within the framework of this chapter and there are many valiant attempts at such a summary of the history (e.g., Valsiner, 1998) and current research elsewhere (e.g., Bennett, 1992; Hala, 1997). Rather, we review the recent literature on children's understanding of the mind; for the past 20 years this has been the crucible for a lively and often heated debate on the nature of social-cognitive development and its role in children's developing competence in interacting with others.

We begin by tracing the cognitive and social approaches to the study of children's social understanding. Piaget's is usually assumed to be a prime example of a cognitive or individualistic approach to development and he is criticized for neglecting social factors in development, whereas Vygotskian theory is taken as a source of the social approach. However, in Piaget's (1977/1995) "sociological studies" he claimed that social interaction is essential in the development of knowledge. He argued that individualism ignores the role of social life in development and collectivism provides no way to distinguish between collective beliefs that are or are not based on reason. As an alternative, Piaget argued for relationism, focusing on the relations between individuals as the basis of cognition. As Chapman (1991) pointed out, Piaget is now known for his later interest in subject–object interaction, yet his early work concerned the idea that interpersonal interaction is the source of intrapersonal reflection. His first two books were, ironically, criticized by Vygostsky (1934/1986) for neglecting the child's interaction with objects. Vygotsky's ideas about the role of social interaction obviously preserved this relational approach and yet are often depicted in textbooks as the antithesis to Piaget's theory. We join other commentators in suggesting that they actually have much more in common than is often argued (L. Smith, 1996).

This apparent contrast between social and individual approaches to development filtered into the literature on social cognition. Such a division has become problematic in the current research on children's social understanding referred to under the banner "theories of mind." It is our contention that most approaches are individualistic in nature and minimize the social, even though many reject Piaget's theory (Perner, 1991). The alternative perspective rejects the cognitive approach to social cognition (e.g. Forrester, 1992) and is often seen as an enculturation approach in which children simply adopt cultural views about the mind.

The chapter is divided into five sections. The first briefly describes developments in the "theory-of-mind" literature over the past few years (for more extensive reviews see Lewis & Mitchell, 1994; Mitchell & Riggs, 2000; Zelazo, Astington, & Olson, 1999). The second section suggests that a crucial issue in the current literature concerns domain specificity in mental state understanding versus domain general processes of reasoning and executive function. Section 3 reviews critiques of the false-belief test and introduces social approaches to children's understanding of mental states. Section 4 explores recent theory and evidence suggesting a close relationship between "theory-of-mind" understanding and the child's interactions in her/his social world. As a result, the fifth part suggests that only a theoretical perspective based upon relationism can reveal the complete story of development.

Children's Understanding of Mind

The centrality of false belief

The focus of studies on the development of social cognitive skills has changed dramatically over the past 20 years. While some continuity is clear, Flavell and Miller (1998) suggest that there have been three shifts in interest. In the 1970s researchers explored the question of how and when children overcome an inherent egocentrism (see e.g., Shantz, 1983). This literature was replaced first by a short wave of research into the executive processes involved in monitoring and regulating one's activities, under the heading metacognition, and subsequently by the most recent phase of studies into the child's "theory of mind," which now dominates this area: "Indeed, it could be argued that it almost dominates the whole field of cognitive development" (Flavell, 1999, p. 23).

In most of the reviews a reader might gain the impression that the field was miraculously created either in 1978 upon the publication of Premack and Woodruff's target article concerning the question of whether chimpanzees had what the authors referred to as a "theory of mind," or a few years later with the publication of Wimmer and Perner's (1983) report of a false-belief task, based on suggestions from three philosophers commenting on Premack and Woodruff's article. Although these are not clear starting dates, it is agreed that the false-belief test has been central both as a critical test of developments which occur in the preschool period and as a point of comparison for other developments.

There are two main versions of the false-belief test. In the *Unexpected Transfer* test, a character (e.g., Maxi) leaves an object, like a chocolate bar, in one location and while he is away it is moved to a new location. Since the protagonist did not see the change in location of his chocolate we expect him to act on his now outdated, and in fact false, belief and look in the old location for his chocolate. In the *Deceptive Box* test the child becomes the protagonist. She is shown a familiar looking (e.g., confectionery) box and asked what is inside. Having guessed that appropriate items would be inside (e.g., chocolates) and been shown than something else was present (e.g., pencils) the child is asked to recall what she had said/ thought was inside and/or what someone else would think.

The counterintuitive, yet robust, finding is that young 3 year olds regularly fail these standard tests by claiming that Maxi would look in the new location for his chocolate, or that they and others would know the unexpected contents of the candy box. Four year olds generally realize that people have and act on false beliefs. Hundreds of research papers have used these procedures and a meta-analysis of over 50 of these shows that the 3–4-year shift is reliable (Wellman, Cross, & Watson, in press). In addition, children with autism tend to fail false-belief tasks until they reach a verbal age somewhat older than 5 years and/or a chronological age in the secondary school years (Baron-Cohen, Leslie, & Frith, 1985; Happé, 1995). However, there are deep divisions about why such a shift occurs.

Theoretical controversies

Since the Premack/Woodruff and Wimmer/Perner papers a deluge of research and theory has followed on the child's understanding of mind, not only within developmental psychology but also across other disciplines, particularly comparative psychology, philosophy, and cognitive science. One of the most interesting aspects of the development of the field is that there has always been dominant grouping of researchers and a healthy number of opposition groups. In the first volume of papers (Astington, Harris, & Olson, 1988), the majority subscribed to a belief that the development of an understanding of mind is theory like in so far as the child appears to develop a consistent set of principles about the working of the mind. These principles appear to change in the preschool years in the same way as a theory changes in science, through a conceptual shift at about the age of 4 when the false-belief test is passed.

The official opposition, led by Leslie (1987), contrasted the idea of theory change with a claim that an understanding of mind must be innately specified in a discrete mental module. The debate between Leslie and the majority greatly influenced the field over the late 1980s and 1990s. Leslie's work focused upon symbolic play, which he depicted as a precursor to a theory of mind: "The emergence of pretence is not seen as a development in the understanding of events and objects as such, but rather as the beginnings of a capacity to understand cognition itself. It is an early symptom of the human mind's ability to characterize and manipulate its own attitudes towards information" (Leslie, 1987, p. 416). Leslie's focus upon pretence was important for three reasons and each stems from the fact that it emerges so early in the child's development. First, it heralded a shift occurring elsewhere in developmental psychology toward a closer link between developmental theory and cognitive science, somewhat at the expense of social processes. By focusing attention on a spontaneously emerging ability Leslie's theoretical analysis homes in on how the cognitive system computes relations between contrastive truth conditions – real versus imagined use of an object; true versus false beliefs etc. The debate on the mechanics of pretence narrowed most researchers' attention on children's understanding of the mind to the cognitive processes involved.

Secondly, the interest in the specific relationship between an understanding of mind and pretence led Harris (e.g., 1991) and others to suggest that both capacities reflect an ability to be flexible in one's imagination. He claimed that just as 18 month olds can use one object (e.g., a block of wood) as something else (e.g., as a "cup" to pretend to drink from), so too can the 4 year old come to imagine another's beliefs. Known as simulation theory, this approach attempted to avoid elaborate explanations for our understanding of mental states. All that is required is the ability to put yourself into the shoes of the protagonist and reason by analogy: children "need only imagine another person – or their past self – aiming or failing to aim their mental arrows of seeing, expecting, knowing, liking and wanting at specific targets within a set of possible targets" (Harris, 1991, p. 292). A great deal of theoretical debate between simulation theory and the main group who coined the term theory of mind culminated in the early 1990s in a series of conferences in which most authors came to the conclusion that an understanding of the mind is likely to involve both theory-like understanding and the imagination (Carruthers & Smith, 1996; Davies & Stone, 1995).

Thirdly, Leslie's theoretical analysis of play reflected a move to explain "the human mind's ability to characterize and manipulate its own attitudes towards information." His claim of an innate propensity to understand mental states or "theory of mind mechanism" (ToMM) suggests that an ability to understand mental states emerges early but is constrained by a gradually developing information-processing device, labeled the Selection Processor (Leslie, 1994). Thus the developmental issues, according to this approach, concern information-processing capacity rather than the construction of an understanding of the mind as a separate entity. This approach, often referred to as the Innate Module account, contrasts with the view that the child constructs theory-like understanding of mental representations. This latter perspective is known as the Theory Theory, but there are a number of understandings of what the child's theory might be like and we will describe two briefly here. The first is that of Josef Perner (1991) who, in keeping with Leslie, suggests that central to understanding the child's social-cognitive skills is the ability to understand that mental states serve a representational function. Unlike Leslie he claims that the realization that the mind is an active entity is constructed by the child and has a profound influence upon the child's understanding. This results in a theory-like shift: "One can think of the concept of 'representation' as playing a catalytic role in children's reconceptualisation of what the mind is, similar to the catalytic role that important scientific concepts play in the development of new scientific concepts" (Perner, 1991, p. 11).

The other main interpretation of the term Theory Theory derives largely from the work of Henry Wellman (e.g., 1990). He claims that children have to make ontological distinctions between the plethora of mental states which are identified in natural language – beliefs, emotion states, desires, values, intentions, etc. – and they have to construct an understanding of each into a causal explanatory framework. Wellman (1990) suggests that children develop an understanding of the mind based initially on desires and that in the third year of life this transforms into a belief–desire framework. This approach is supported by evidence from a number of areas (see Wellman & Lagattuta, 2000, for a review) including language development, which shows that desire terms like "want" emerge before belief terms like "think" and that they gradually become used in a way which suggests an understanding of false beliefs (e.g., Bartsch & Wellman, 1995).

A theoretical impasse?

A major reason why the child's understanding of mind has received so much attention centers around the elegance of the three mainstream theories which have been put forward. Each of the perspectives – the Simulation, "Theory", and Innate Module – provides us with an interesting process model of the development of social-cognitive skills and the debate between each has been both stimulating and insightful. However, this has had the effect of narrowing the focus two ways. First, there is the presumption that these are "the only games in town" as one of the players in the field has arrogantly put it. The main debate has often been very inward looking as a result. Secondly, the nature of exchange between the various camps has resulted in two types of conclusion. As stated above the simulation–theory debate has led to something of a coalescence between the two. The theory–innate module debate has been more divisive, in that they are mutually exclusive, to the extent that there appears to be so little common ground between them that each interprets the same data in radically different ways, each effectively denying the claims of the other. So, for example, German and Leslie (2000) have recently claimed (not for the first time) that the theory approach has not shown how a single mental state concept is constructed by children, how the proposed sequences of theoretical constructs might take place, or the nature of the critical evidence which might effect a paradigm shift in the child's theoretical stance. Critics of the innate module approach have stressed that it does not appear not to explain the shift which occurs at around age 4 (Frye, 2000; Wellman et al., in press) and that the evidence from evolution does not support the idea of the emergence of a specifically human ability to understand mental states (Moore, 1996; Tomasello, 1999). More recently, the debate has turned in a different direction.

Current Cognitive Positions

Over the past decade the cognitive debate concerning children's understanding of mind has shifted away from an exclusive analysis of the nature and origins of mental-state understanding to a fierce debate over the relation between this domain-specific skill and other more domain-general abilities. Although there are many variations within each position (e.g., Mitchell & Riggs, 2000), two main perspectives have emerged in opposition to the theory-of-mind perspective advocated by Perner. The first we call the reasoning position, while the second concerns the development of executive control.

Reasoning and mental-state understanding

In the mid-1990s the false-belief task came under a great deal of critical scrutiny from a number of groups who argued that children find this test difficult because it requires the comparison of a set of contrasting hypothetical premises. For example, Frye, Zelazo, and Palfai (1995) found that success on a false-belief task correlated with an ability to perform a card-sort task in which children were required to switch from one rule to another, incompatible rule. In one experiment the children had to sort a group of blue and red pictures, some of which were boats and the rest were flowers. When told that they were now going to play the "shape game," 3 year olds continued to sort by color even when explicitly told to "Put the flowers here; put the boats here." According to the cognitive complexity and control (CCC) theory 3 year olds cannot deliberately contrast two contradictory rules. This skill emerges with the development of other skills, notably working memory, which permit successively higher levels of understanding of conscious control (Zelazo, 2000).

At the same time Riggs, Peterson, Robinson, and Mitchell (1998) explored the relation between false-belief understanding and reasoning in comparable tasks which do not involve mental states. For example, they gave children a variant on the unexpected transfer test in which John's coveted chocolate is used by his mother to make a cake. Children's performance was almost identical on a false-belief question ("Where will John look for the chocolate?") and a question which asks children to make a hypothetical or counterfactual contrast ("If Mummy had not baked the cake, where would the chocolate be?"). This latter question relies upon children's ability to reason from false premises, but ones that are not contingent upon an understanding of the protagonist's mental states.

The work on reasoning has led to a heated chicken and egg discussion (see chapters 5, 6, & 18 in Mitchell & Riggs, 2000), in which each logical position (that an understanding of counterfactuals causes a representational theory of mind, that the representations come first, or that they both depend on some other influence like processing capacity) has been suggested and debated.

Executive control

Research inspired by studies of the relationship between cognitive performance and neurological functioning gave rise to the claim that false-belief tasks require the inhibition of the prepotent response to say where the chocolate is or what is inside the deceptive box. Early evidence came from work with autistic children in which it was found that success on a battery of false-belief tasks correlated with the ability to switch rules on a card-sort task and carry out a planned sequence of actions on the Tower of Hanoi, in which the child has to move a set of disks from one pole to two others to match an array presented by the experimenter (Ozonoff, Pennington, & Rogers, 1991). At the same time Russell developed a procedure in which children had to deceive an experimenter into selecting the empty box in successive trials where a reward was placed in one of two boxes. Known as the windows task it was found that if the child could see into the boxes, 3 year olds and older children with autism persisted in telling the experimenter to open the baited box on up to 20 successive trials even though they were "punished" on each trial by not getting the reward (Russell, Mauthner, Sharpe, & Tidswell, 1991).

Two developments are noteworthy. First, the association between false-belief understanding and executive control has led to a close analysis of the nature of the latter. It has been shown that there are at least three skills involved – inhibitory control, attentional flexibility, and working memory (following Welsh, Pennington, & Grossier, 1991). Claire Hughes (1998) has provided evidence suggesting that different executive skills relate to particular aspects of social understanding. In particular, the ability to deceive appears to be related to the ability to inhibit a prepotent response.

Secondly, the literature has led to a reconsideration of theory in the area, particularly in light of Jim Russell's (1996) book *Agency*. One problem with research showing a relation between two functions like executive skills and false belief is that a causal relationship is not implied. Some, like Ozonoff et al. (1991), assumed that both are controlled by the development of the same area of the prefrontal cortex, but such accounts pinpoint possible functional relatedness, not necessarily a causal link between them. Russell claims that executive functions are important in theory-of-mind development, but he is careful to draw together many of the ideas in the theories discussed in section 2. He attempts to provide an a priori case for the coexistence of a few innate skills (what he terms "minimal vitalism"), a connectionist approach to the development (at a subsymbolic level rather than a theoretical level as described by Theory Theory) and the construction of an understanding of the mind as a representational system in keeping with Perner's (1991) theory. However, unlike Perner, he argues that a grasp of false belief, like other major achievements (notably object permanence), is part of a general process by which the child constructs a sense of self-awareness and a self-world dualism as defined by Piaget.

Whither?

The research on domain-general reasoning and the development of executive control has led to a debate which echoes that between the theoretical positions discussed in section 2. On both topics there are several "camps" (see Perner, 2000; Perner & Lang, 2000). However, the safest conjecture seems to be on theoretical accounts of the development of social skills that do not naively assume that the child constructs a theory-like understanding of the mind, but which attempt to account for the parallel achievements. Russell's (1999) idea of an active agent reintroduces Piagetian theory, although only in a "homeopathic dose." Perner's (Perner & Lang, 2000) view is that the acquisition of a representational theory of mind is a precursor to other skills. However, we believe that another, complementary, approach is required.

There is More to Social Cognition than the False-Belief Test

Thus far we have focused on "mainstream" approaches. However, there has always been a diversity of opinion and we now attempt to piece together an account of the "social" approach to development. In this section we re-examine the false-belief task from this perspective, and review evidence of the many correlates of false-belief performance which put social explanations squarely on the agenda.

Re-analysis of the false-belief test

In addressing the question of whether the false-belief test should be the primary measure of mental-state understanding many researchers have found that modifying the procedure allows younger children to demonstrate a competence which appeared lacking when the standard procedures are employed (e.g., sections 4 & 5 in Lewis & Mitchell, 1994). These experiments are often perceived by theory theorists as attempts to undermine the theory-of-mind enterprise by showing that no developmental shifts take place (e.g., Perner, 2000, pp. 368–375). Indeed some researchers have attempted to show that the test is unreliable (Mayes, Klin, Tercyak, Cicchetti, & Cohen, 1996), but others find sufficient reliability (Hughes, Adlam, Happé, Jackson, Taylor, & Caspi, 2000). However, most have modified the tasks in order to identify the factors that are important in the development of the child's understanding of mind.

Three year olds can act to deceive another person (e.g., Chandler, Fritz, & Hala, 1989) even though they appear to be readily confused into deceiving someone they are supposed to help (Sodian, 1994). They perform better when they act out the protagonist's search pattern (Freeman, Lewis, & Doherty, 1991), if they are actively involved (Hala & Chandler, 1996), if their earlier mental state is made salient by a pictorial cue (Freeman & Lacohée, 1995; Mitchell & Lacohée, 1991), if they are familiar with the "narrative" of the unexpected transfer procedure (Lewis, Freeman, Hagestadt, & Douglas, 1994), or if the test question is phrased so that it refers to a specific point in time (Lewis & Osborne, 1990).

There has been much debate about the importance of these modifications of false-belief tasks. Wellman et al.'s (in press) meta-analysis has been helpful in teasing apart the factors which reliably facilitate performance. Examining 178 experiments with 591 conditions across a range of (mainly industrial) countries, they found that factors like the type of task used, or whether the target question focused on the protagonist's thoughts or actions, did not vary systematically across studies. Five factors did show significantly improved performance in preschoolers across studies: a motive for the protagonist is made explicit; the child actively participates in the procedure; the object is either not shown to the child or is destroyed (i.e., eaten) before the test question is asked; the protagonist's mental state is made salient – for example by the child being told that Maxi is gone and cannot see the object being moved; the child is shown a picture which represents the protagonist's belief or is reminded of it. None of these factors interacted with age. This suggests that none has a magic effect of revealing false-belief understanding which is hidden in standard procedures. Indeed Wellman et al. found consistent improvement across the fifth year of life, suggesting that the task does assess a skill which is mastered at about this time. Only one factor, temporal marking (following Lewis & Osborne, 1990), interacted with age, but this seemed to show greater effects in older, not younger, preschoolers.

The Wellman et al. meta-analysis seems to validate the false-belief procedure as a means of demonstrating the development of mental-state understanding at around age 4. However, the range of factors which have been shown consistently to relate to children's success suggest that performance on the test is contingent upon the nature of experimenter–child interaction, as we see in the influence of, for example, the adults' questioning of the child or casting the test as a competitive game. It thus seems fair to suggest that such variations give us insights into the *social* nature of early social cognitive development.

Social correlates of mental-state understanding

The theory-of-mind tradition has long been criticized for being too individualistic (Bruner, 1990; Raver & Leadbeater, 1993), although it has been reluctant to address this criticism. However, in the mid-1990s a quest to explore individual differences in false-belief performance put social factors squarely on the map even within the theory-of-mind camp.

In one of the early demonstrations that social interaction influences the development of social understanding, Perner, Ruffman, and Leekam (1994) reported that children with siblings passed false-belief tests up to a year before children without siblings. Subsequent research has extended and complicated the "sibling effect." For a start, in middle-class homes, the presence of older siblings, more than younger ones, has been more consistently found to predict false-belief performance (Jenkins & Astington 1996; Lewis, Freeman, Kyriakidou, Maridaki-Kassotiaki, & Berridge, 1996; Ruffman, Perner, Naito, & Parkin, 1998). However, some studies suggest that the frequency of daily interactions with older kin (Lewis et al., 1996) or the child's language level (Jenkins & Astington, 1996) were stronger predictors. More recent studies of working-class children have failed to replicate the sibling effect (Cole & Mitchell, 2000; Cutting & Dunn, 1999) and suggest a later onset of false-belief success in impoverished children (Holmes, Black, & Miller, 1996).

As well as the influence of social background and poverty on social cognitive development, culture also seems to be important. Wellman et al.'s (in press) meta-analysis shows small but statistically significant differences in age of acquisition across cultures which are mainly similar in their levels of industrialization. Vinden (1996) reported that false-belief performance in Quechuan people of Peru lagged behind Western children by at least 3 years (and possibly much longer), perhaps because their language appears not to refer directly to mental states. A more recent study shows that among the Tainae people of Papua, New Guinea, even 15 year olds were at chance when asked about another's thoughts (Vinden, 1999).

These data on siblings, social class, and cultural differences pinpoint a glaring weakness in the literature on theory of mind. It purports to provide insights into the social functioning of children, yet it rarely compares children's social interaction with their performance on false-belief tests. The "sibling effect" raises much speculation about possible influences but tells us little about how social interaction influences social-cognitive development. To address this question we need to turn to additional evidence.

"One miracle"?: From infancy to adolescence

One problem with the literature is that false-belief understanding is treated as a fulcrum around which development takes place. Chandler (e.g., 1988) has long criticized what he refers to as the "one miracle" view of development, that false-belief understanding is the major step into a "theory of mind" which is essentially equivalent to adults' understanding. This assumption has been attacked from two sides. First, there has been growing interest in obtaining a more complete view of children's social-cognitive development by studying infants' joint attention behaviors that seem to indicate some level of social understanding (e.g., Moore & Dunham, 1995).

Secondly, attention has turned to developments in children's social understanding beyond false-belief understanding. The term "interpretation" has featured centrally in discussion of developments after the preschool years. Some researchers argue that passing a false-belief test or related theory-of-mind tasks already indicates an understanding of interpretation (e.g., Perner, 1991). Others argue for a distinction between understanding that beliefs depend on having access to information (i.e., false-belief comprehension) and the more complex understanding that even with access to the same information people may interpret it differently and, thus, end up with different beliefs, an insight achieved several years after false-belief understanding (Carpendale & Chandler, 1996; Chandler & Carpendale, 1998; Chandler & Lalonde, 1996). A related insight, also achieved some years after false-belief understanding, is the understanding that people's interpretation of an ambiguous social event may be biased by their previous expectations about the people involved (Pillow, 1991). Further mentalistic insights that preschoolers still have to acquire include their understanding of the nature of thinking (Flavell, Green, & Flavell, 1995), and inference (Varouxaki, Freeman, Peters, & Lewis, 1999).

This research on older children alerts us to a need to tie the explosion of theory-of-mind research into both a longer time perspective and the wider tradition of social-cognitive studies. However, the field is only now beginning to explore some of these potential connections. Dunn (1996) and others have called for research on connections between theory of mind and other aspects of children's development such as morality and emotional understanding. Competence in social understanding may be important for a number of different aspects of development such as self-awareness (Chandler & Carpendale, 1998), drawing inferences regarding social situations and the pragmatics of interaction.

Some recent work suggests a relationship between false-belief understanding and wider social skills. For example, young children's performance on false-belief tests was found to be positively correlated with teacher ratings of social skills (Lalonde & Chandler, 1995; Watson, Nixon, Wilson, & Capage, 1999). But with preadolescents, peers' ratings were related to social understanding, not teacher ratings (Bosacki & Astington, 1999). As Watson et al. acknowledge, these studies are correlational and give rise to many possible explanations. Competence in mentalistic understanding could lead to improved social skills, or children who are involved in more social interaction may develop more competence in understanding the mental world. Alternatively, a third factor involving children's family background may facilitate development of mentalistic understanding and social skills. Even more likely perhaps, this relationship may be bidirectional. That is, involvement in more social interaction facilitates more understanding and this in turn leads to more successful interaction with peers. Such speculation, of course, requires evaluation with longitudinal and experimental research.

Recent research has attempted to use the theory of mind to examine real-world issues like bullying. Sutton, Smith, and Swettenham (1999) argue that the image of the bully as socially naive is not based on good research and they report evidence that, in fact, bullies tend to score higher on measures of social understanding. This type of research demonstrates the close connection between social understanding and morality (Chandler, Sokol, & Wainryb, 2000), but here more conceptual and empirical work is needed.

Social Interaction and Social-Cognitive Development

Recent links made between children's understanding of the mind and other social skills are symptomatic of a move toward a more consolidated theory which integrates the two. In this section we describe what we feel is an emerging, or continuing, consensus in the field. First we report the longitudinal evidence which shows that mental-state understanding at age 4 seems to be related to patterns in the child's earlier relationships. Secondly we home in on language as the main means by which children come to develop this understanding.

Longitudinal patterns

Longitudinal research suggests that factors in the child's early relationships are important predictors of earlier false-belief understanding. In the area of family relationships, not only is concurrent attachment security related to theory-of-mind performance (Fonagy, Redfern, & Charman, 1997), but similar results are found in longitudinal studies (Symons & Clark, 2000). For example, Meins (1997) found that children who were securely attached at 11 to 13 months were more likely than insecurely attached children to pass a false-belief task at 4 years, and more complex tasks at 5 years. However, a number of explanations are possible and even more complexity in research design is required to tease apart possible lines of causality. Here the work of Dunn has been seminal.

In a series of longitudinal studies, Dunn and her colleagues found that a number of factors in family interactions predict levels of performance in theory-of-mind tasks. For example, cooperative interaction between siblings at 33 months was positively related to belief understanding at 40 months (Dunn, Brown, Slomkowski, Tesla, & Youngblade, 1991). The most consistent link in Dunn's and related research is between family talk about mental states and children's social understanding (e.g., Brown, Donelan-McCall, & Dunn, 1996; Dunn, 1996). In one of the first of these studies, Dunn et al. (1991) found that children who at 33 months participated more in family talk about emotions and the causes of behavior were more competent on a test of belief understanding 7 months later. Similar results were found in another longitudinal study in which mothers' use of mental-state terms was associated with their child's later competence in understanding belief (Moore, Furrow, Chiasson, & Patriquin, 1994). Much of this initial research has focused on words that are clearly mental-state terms, but some words may be important in learning about the mind even if they are not obviously mental-state terms such as "see," "look," or "hide" (Turnbull & Carpendale, 1999). Competence in understanding belief is also associated with mothers who report asking their children to reflect on others' mental states and feelings in disciplinary situations (Ruffman, Perner, & Parkin 1999), and with mothers who treat their children as individuals with minds (Meins & Fernyhough, 1999).

Another source of evidence for the role of language comes from research showing that deaf children tend to be delayed in false-belief understanding (Peterson & Siegal, 2000). This seems to be because most of these children have hearing parents who are not fluent in sign language, and thus there is no shared language complex enough to talk about inner states. In contrast, deaf children with deaf parents who are competent users of sign language may not be delayed. Peterson and Siegal (2000) have now reviewed 11 studies that support these conclusions and point to the role of conversation in the development of false-belief understanding.

If family talk about mental states is important in the development of social understanding then we might expect that suitable training or teaching might facilitate such development, and this approach has demonstrated some success. For example, Appleton and Reddy (1996) found that discussion of situations involving false beliefs led to 3 year olds' success on post tests and to generalize this insight to other tests of belief understanding beyond the training situations.

The studies described here conflict with ones which rely on laboratory procedures in that they suggest that young children who consistently fail standard false-belief tasks may still appear to engage in a wide variety of acts such as deception that seem to reflect some mentalistic understanding (e.g., Newton, Reddy, & Bull, 2000). Such evidence contrasts with the idea of a sudden shift into an understanding of false beliefs. For example, Newton et al.'s close observations of a 2 year old suggest that deception skills emerge from pragmatic need at around the second birthday rather than as a result of a conceptual miracle. Instead, such data support the theoretical claims regarding gradual development of concepts concerning the mind (Russell, 1996; Woodfield, 1996).

Language and social understanding

Evidence of the role of family talk about the mental world in the development of social understanding has led many to the more general issue of the relationship between language and social understanding (e.g., P. K. Smith, 1996). Several researchers have reported that false-belief understanding is closely related to language ability, assessed with various measures (e.g., Cutting & Dunn, 1999; Happé, 1995; Jenkins & Astington, 1996). Further, children with autism have problems with both language and theory-of-mind tasks. There are a number of possible relations between language and social understanding more generally, and false-belief understanding specifically. Language may reveal children's understanding, but language may also be a context for the development of understanding.

Children's talk about mental states can provide a window on their social understanding. For example, Bartsch and Wellman's (1995) exploration of the CHILDES database revealed that children consistently use desire terms like "want" at a younger age than belief terms like "think." Although they use this in support of their claim for the development of a desire-based theory as a precursor to a belief–desire theory, other explanations are possible. For example, Harris (1996) suggests that it is conversation, not word use, that is an important context in which children learn about beliefs (see also Tomasello, 1999, pp. 176–178). Here language is considered a context for development. In particular, Harris argues that information is exchanged in conversation, which should be a constant demonstration that people differ in what they think, believe, and know about a topic.

Another aspect of language that may be important in learning about mental states is syntax. De Villiers and de Villiers (2000) argue that language provides a syntactical structure, known as complementation, with which to talk about mental states. For example, in "He thought it was a lion" (de Villiers & de Villiers, 2000, p. 196), the overall sentence can be true although the embedded complement ("it was a lion") can be false. In this view, a grasp of language is required for social-cognitive development because it provides a syntactical structure for thinking about false beliefs. However, there is controversy over whether this aspect of syntax provides a necessary or a sufficient condition for grasping false belief (Astington & Jenkins, 1999).

The current longitudinal evidence on language and theory of mind suggests that earlier language abilities predict later performance on false-belief tests, but not vice versa (Astington & Jenkins, 1999). Such results support the view that theory of mind depends on language, at least when the former is defined by false-belief understanding. If we consider social understanding more generally, then it may be that some initial level of social understanding is required in order to achieve joint attention and determine others' referential intent in the process of word learning. Beyond this, language may be an important context in which to learn how to talk about and reflect on inner experience.

The first two possibilities considered by Astington and Jenkins – that theory of mind depends on language, or that language depends on theory of mind – assume that these two abilities are separable. Instead, others argue that they are inextricably intertwined. Arguments from Wittgenstein suggest that thinking about the mental world is not separate from learning to talk about the mental world (Turnbull & Carpendale, 1999; submitted). Several authors have pointed out that Wittgenstein's (1968) private language argument is an argument against the view, based on simulation theory, that children learn about the mind through introspection (Chapman, 1987; Montgomery, 1997; Russell, 1996). Instead, public criteria are needed in order to learn the meaning of mental-state terms. Criteria are those public circumstances in which it is appropriate to use certain mental-state terms (Chapman, 1987). In the case of psychological terms such as "look," "want," "think," "guess," and "forget" the criteria that justify their use are actions. Children learn the use and meaning of mental-state terms through the process of the words being grafted onto earlier or more primitive behavior (Hacker, 1997; Turnbull & Carpendale, submitted). The conclusion following from this argument is that developing social understanding is fundamentally social because children must learn the meaning of mental-state terms within family talk about the mental world.

Conclusion: Integrating the Social and Cognitive Approaches

In this chapter we have explicated two contrasting views of social cognition, that have long been present within the literature but which have manifested themselves in particular ways in recent years. As we have suggested in sections 2 and 3, much of the debate on the child's understanding of mind concerns the nature of her/his "representation" of mental states. This once focused on whether they are innate, constructed in a theoretical way, or simply simulated, but in recent years has concerned, firstly, whether a representational theory of mind (Perner, 1991) is distinct from other types of counterfactual thinking and, secondly, how it relates to other higher order or executive thinking skills. In section 4 we have tried to return the social dimension to the term social cognition by showing that the child's entry into an understanding is grounded in her/his communication with others.

We conclude by suggesting that the cognitive and social approaches be integrated. Calls for such an integration have come from both within (Astington & Olson, 1995; Vinden & Astington, 2000) and outside (Raver & Leadbeater, 1993) the theory-of-mind movement. We need a theory that takes the role of social interaction seriously, yet is not a simple enculturation position, according to which children passively adopt culturally available concepts concerning the mind. We suggest that Chapman's (1991, 1999) integration of the Piagetian and Vygotskian ideas mentioned at the start of this chapter may provide a suitable framework within which to integrate the individual and social aspects of the development of social understanding.

Chapman (1991) suggested that integrating Piaget's early work on the notion that argumentation is the source of reflective thought with his later interest in subject–object interaction into a single system results in an "epistemic triangle" involving triadic interaction between the self, others, and the world. Vygotsky's ideas concerning the role of social interaction are also preserved in this approach. From this perspective, the development of children's social understanding occurs within triadic interaction involving the child's experience of the world as well as her communicative interaction with others about their, often differing, experience and beliefs. This essential role of social interaction implies that the extent and nature of the interaction children experience will influence the development of their social understanding. More interaction and talk about the mental world should facilitate the development of social understanding through learning the criteria for mental state terms. Aspects of relationships such as cooperation that influence children's understanding of others" perspectives should also facilitate development. These expectations are consistent with the research reviewed above. Vygotsky's concept of the zone of proximal development is also important in this context because it is helpful in thinking about a gradual process of development and the role of adults in supporting such development. This is a perspective that has been lacking in the field and may be helpful in making sense of the gap between naturalistic observation and experimental evidence of belief understanding.

There are several approaches within the field that are consistent with such a framework. For example, Fernyhough's (1996) Vygotskian account is not an enculturation view, but rather proposes that children develop a dialogical form of thinking through internalizing interpersonal dialogue. This form of thinking, involving the ability to consider more than one perspective, is required in situations involving false beliefs. Hobson's (1993) work also has much in common, in fact he proposes a "relatedness triangle," similar to Chapman's epistemic triangle. Hobson argues that the capacity for symbolism arises in the interpersonal activity of relating to others about their attitudes to objects. That is, symbolic thought follows developmentally from symbolic communication. This is based on the Vygotskian (1934/1986) insight that higher mental functions arise through the internalization of social interaction. Similarly, Tomasello (1999) argues against the common view of linguistic reference as a connection between the symbol and the referent. Instead, Tomasello writes about a "referential triangle" – consistent with Chapman (1991) and Hobson (1993) – and he argues that "reference is a *social* act in which one person attempts to get another person to focus her attention on something in the world" (p. 97). This species-unique capacity for reference allows children to participate in language and culture, and to take advantage of cultural learning.

The essence of the approaches discussed in this section is that they are relational in nature and assume that development occurs in social interaction. The individual characteristics and capabilities of the child as well as of the other people involved contribute to this interaction – that is, they respond to each other. Social cognition develops within the relations between the child and others, and it is central to human life.

References

Appleton, M., & Reddy, V. (1996). Teaching three year-olds to pass false-belief tests: A conversational approach. *Social Development, 5*, 275–291.

Astington, J. W., Harris, P. L., & Olson, D. (1988). *Developing theories of mind.* Cambridge, England: Cambridge University Press.

Astington, J. W., & Jenkins, J. M. (1999). A longitudinal study of the relations between language and theory-of-mind development. *Developmental Psychology, 35*, 1311–1320.

Astington, J. W., & Olson, D. R. (1995). The cognitive revolution in children's understanding of mind. *Human Development, 38*, 179–189.

Baron-Cohen, S., Leslie, A. M., & Frith, U. (1985). Does the autistic child have a "theory of mind"? *Cognition, 21*, 37–46.

Bartsch, K., & Wellman, H. W. (1995). *Children talk about the mind.* New York: Oxford University Press.

Bennett, M. (Ed.) (1992). *The child as psychologist.* London: Routledge.

Bosacki, S., & Astington, J. W. (1999). Theory of mind in preadolescence: Relations between social understanding and social competence. *Social Development, 8*, 237–255.

Brown, J. R., Donelan-McCall, N., & Dunn, J. (1996). Why talk about mental states? The significance of children's conversations with friends, siblings, and mothers. *Child Development, 67*, 836–849.

Bruner, J. (1990). *Acts of meaning.* Cambridge, MA: Harvard University Press.

Carpendale, J. I., & Chandler, M. J. (1996). On the distinction between false-belief understanding and subscribing to an interpretive theory of mind. *Child Development, 67*, 1686–1706.

Carruthers, P., & Smith, P. K. (Eds.) (1996). *Theories of theories of mind.* Cambridge, England: Cambridge University Press.

Chandler, M. J. (1988). Doubt and developing theories of mind. In J. W. Astington, P. L. Harris, & D. R. Olson (Eds.), *Developing theories of mind* (pp. 387–413). Cambridge, England: Cambridge University Press.

Chandler, M. J., & Carpendale, J. I. M. (1998). Inching toward a mature theory of mind. In M. Ferrari & R. J. Sternberg (Eds.), *Self-awareness: Its nature and development* (pp. 148–190). New York: Guilford Press.

Chandler, M. J., Fritz, A., & Hala, S. (1989). Small-scale deceit: Deception as a marker of two-, three-, and four-year-olds' early theories of mind. *Child Development, 60*, 1263–1277.

Chandler, M. J., & Lalonde, C. (1996). Shifting to an interpretive theory of mind: 5- to 7-year-olds' changing conceptions of mental life. In A. Sameroff & M. Haith (Eds.), *Reason and responsibility: The passage through childhood* (pp. 111–139). Chicago: University of Chicago Press.

Chandler, M. J., Sokol, B. W., & Wainryb, C. (2000). Beliefs about truth and beliefs about rightness. *Child Development, 71*, 91–97.

Chapman, M. (1987). Inner processes and outward criteria: Wittgenstein's importance for psychology. In M. Chapman & R. A. Dixon (Eds.), *Meaning and the growth of understanding: Wittgenstein's significance for developmental psychology* (pp. 103–127). Berlin: Springer-Verlag.

Chapman, M. (1991). The epistemic triangle: Operative and communicative components of cognitive development. In M. Chandler & M. Chapman (Eds.), *Criteria for competence* (pp.209–228). Hillsdale, NJ: Erlbaum.

Chapman, M. (1999). Constructivism and the problem of reality. *Journal of Applied Development Psychology, 20*, 31–43.

Cole, K., & Mitchell, P. (2000). Siblings in the development of executive control and a theory of mind. *British Journal of Developmental Psychology, 18*, 279–295.

Cutting, A. L., & Dunn, J. (1999). Theory of mind, emotion understanding, language, and family background: Individual differences and interrelations. *Child Development, 70*, 853–865.

Davies, M., & Stone, T. (1995). *Mental simulation*. Oxford, England: Blackwell.

de Villiers, J. G., & de Villiers, P. A. (2000). Linguistic determinism and the understanding of false beliefs. In P. Mitchell & K. J. Riggs (Eds.), *Children's reasoning and the mind* (pp. 191–228). Hove, England: Psychology Press.

Dunn, J. (1996). Children's relationships: Bridging the divide between cognitive and social development. *Journal of Child Psychology and Psychiatry, 37*, 507–518.

Dunn, J., Brown, J., Slomkowski, C., Tesla, C., & Youngblade, L. (1991). Young children's understanding of other people's feelings and beliefs: Individual differences and their antecedents. *Child Development, 62*, 1352–1366.

Fernyhough, C. (1996). The dialogic mind: A dialogic approach to the higher mental functions. *New Ideas in Psychology, 14*, 47–62.

Flavell, J. H. (1999). Cognitive development: Children's knowledge about the mind. *Annual Review of Psychology, 50*, 21–45.

Flavell, J. H., Green, F. L., & Flavell, E. R. (1995). Young children's knowledge about thinking. *Monographs of the Society for Research in Child Development, 60* (Serial No. 243).

Flavell, J. H., & Miller, P. H. (1998). Social cognition. In W. Damon (Ed.), D. Kuhn & R. S. Siegler, (Vol. Eds.), *Handbook of child psychology, 5th ed.* (pp. 851–898). New York: Wiley.

Fonagy, P., Redfern, S., & Charman, T. (1997). The relationship between belief-desire reasoning and a projective measure of attachment security (SAT). *British Journal of Developmental Psychology, 15*, 51–61.

Forrester, M. (1992). *The development of young children's social-cognitive skills*. Hove, England: Erlbaum.

Freeman, N. H., & Lacohée, H. (1995) Making explicit 3-year-olds' implicit competence with their own false beliefs. *Cognition, 56*, 31–60.

Freeman, N. H., Lewis, C., & Doherty, M. (1991). Preschoolers' grasp of a desire for knowledge in false-belief reasoning: Practical intelligence and verbal report. *British Journal of Developmental Psychology, 9*, 139–157.

Frye, D. (2000). Theory of mind, domain specificity, and reasoning. In P. Mitchell & K. J. Riggs (Eds.), *Children's reasoning and the mind* (pp. 149–167). Hove, England: Psychology Press.

Frye, D., Zelazo, P. D., & Palfai, T. (1995). Inference and action in early causal reasoning. *Cognitive Development, 10*, 120–131.

German, T. P., & Leslie, A. M. (2000). Attending to and learning about mental states. In P. Mitchell & K. J. Riggs (Eds.), *Children's reasoning and the mind* (pp. 229–252). Hove, England: Psychology Press.

Hacker, P. M. S. (1997). *Wittgenstein: On human nature*. London: Phoenix.

Hala, S. (Ed.) (1997). *The development of social cognition*. Hove, England: Psychology Press.

Hala, S., & Chandler, M. J. (1996). The role of strategic planning in accessing false-belief understanding. *Child Development, 67*, 2948–2966.

Happé, F. G. E. (1995). The role of age and verbal ability in the theory of mind task performance of subjects with autism. *Child Development, 66*, 843–855.

Harris, P. L. (1991). The work of the imagination. In A. Whiten (Ed.), *Natural theories of mind* (pp. 283–304). Oxford, England: Blackwell.

Harris, P. L. (1996). Desires, beliefs, and language. In P. Carruthers & P. K. Smith (Eds.), *Theories of theories of mind* (pp. 200–220). Cambridge, England: Cambridge University Press.

Hobson, R. P. (1993). *Autism and the development of mind*. Hove, England: Erlbaum.

Holmes, H. A., Black, C., & Miller, S. A. (1996). A cross-task comparison of false-belief understanding in a head start population. *Journal of Experimental Child Psychology, 63*, 263–285.

Hughes, C. (1998). Executive function in preschoolers: Links with theory of mind and verbal ability. *British Journal of Developmental Psychology, 16*, 233–253.

Hughes, C., Adlam, A., Happé, F., Taylor, A., Jackson, J., & Caspi, A. (2000). Good test–retest reliability for standard and advanced false-belief tasks across a wide range of abilities. *Journal of Child Psychology and Psychiatry 41*, 483–490.

Jenkins, J. M., & Astington, J. W. (1996). Cognitive factors and family structure associated with theory of mind development in young children. *Developmental Psychology, 32*, 70–78.

Lalonde, C. E., & Chandler, M. J. (1995). False-belief understanding goes to school: On the social-emotional consequences of coming early or late to a first theory of mind. *Cognition and Emotion, 9*, 167–185.

Leslie, A. M. (1987). Pretense and representation: The origins of "theory of mind." *Psychological Review, 94*, 412–426.

Leslie, A. M. (1994). Pretending and believing: Issues in the theory of ToMM. *Cognition, 50*, 211–238.

Lewis, C., Freeman, N. H., Hagestadt, C., & Douglas, H. (1994). Narrative access and production in preschoolers' false-belief reasoning. *Cognitive Development, 9*, 397–424.

Lewis, C., Freeman, N. H., Kyriakidou, C., Maridaki-Kassotiaki, K., & Berridge, D. M. (1996). Social influences on false-belief access: Specific sibling influences or general apprenticeship? *Child Development, 67*, 2930–2947.

Lewis, C., & Mitchell, P. (Eds.) (1994). *Children's early understanding of mind: Origins and development*. Hove, England: Erlbaum.

Lewis, C., & Osborne, A. (1990). Three-year-olds' problems with false belief: Conceptual deficit or linguistic artifact? *Child Development, 61*, 1514–1519.

Mayes, L. C., Klin, A., Tercyak, K. P., Cicchetti, D. V., & Cohen, D. J. (1996). Test–retest reliability for false-belief tests. *Journal of Child Psychology and Psychiatry, 37*, 313–319.

Meins, E. (1997). *Security of attachment and the social development of cognition*. Hove, England: Psychology Press.

Meins, E., & Fernyhough, C. (1999). Linguistic acquisitional style and mentalising development: The role of maternal mind-mindedness. *Cognitive Development, 14*, 363–380.

Mitchell, P., & Lacohée, H. (1991). Children's early understanding of false belief. *Cognition, 39*, 107–127.

Mitchell, P., & Riggs, K. J. (Eds.) (2000). *Children's reasoning and the mind*. Hove, England: Psychology Press.

Montgomery, D. E. (1997). Wittgenstein's private language argument and children's understanding of mind. *Developmental Review, 17*, 291–320.

Moore, C. (1996). Evolution and the modularity of mindreading. *Cognitive Development, 11*, 605–621.

Moore, C., & Dunham, P. (1995). *Joint attention: Its origins and role in development*. Hillsdale, NJ: Erlbaum.

Moore, C., Furrow, D., Chiasson, L., & Patriquin, M. (1994). Developmental relationships between production and comprehension of mental terms. *First Language, 14*, 1–17.

Newton, P., Reddy, V., & Bull, R. (2000). Children's everyday deception and performance on false-belief tasks. *British Journal of Developmental Psychology, 18*, 297–317.

Ozonoff, S., Pennington, B. F., & Rogers, S. J. (1991). Executive function deficits in high-functioning autistic individuals: Relationship to theory of mind. *Journal of Child Psychology and Psychiatry, 32*, 1081–1105.

Perner, J. (1991). *Understanding the representational mind*. Cambridge, MA: MIT Press.

Perner, J. (2000). About + Belief + Counterfactual. In P. Mitchell & K. J. Riggs (Eds.), *Children's reasoning and the mind* (pp. 367–401). Hove, England: Psychology Press.

Perner, J., & Lang, B. (2000). Theory of mind and executive function. In S. Baron-Cohen, H Tager-Flusberg, & D. Cohen (Eds.), *Understanding other minds, 2nd ed.* (pp. 151– 179). Oxford, England: Oxford University Press.

Perner, J., Ruffman, T., & Leekam, S. R. (1994). Theory of mind is contagious: You catch it from your sibs. *Child Development, 65*, 1228–1238.

Peterson, C. C., & Siegal, M. (2000). Insights into theory of mind from deafness and autism. *Mind and Language, 15*, 123–145.

Piaget, J. (1995). *Sociological studies*. London: Routledge (original work published in 1977).

Pillow, B. H. (1991). Children's understanding of biased social cognition. *Developmental Psychology, 27*, 539–551

Premack, D., & Woodruff, G. (1978). Does the chimpanzee have a theory of mind? *Behavioural and Brain Sciences, 4*, 515–526.

Raver, C. C., & Leadbeater, B. J. (1993). The problem of the other in research on theory of mind and social development. *Human Development, 36*, 350–362.

Riggs, K. J., Peterson, D. M., Robinson, E. J., & Mitchell, P. (1998). Are errors in false-belief tasks symptomatic of a broader difficulty with counterfactuality? *Cognitive Development, 13*, 73–91.

Ruffman, T., Perner, J., Naito, M., Parkin, L., & Clements, W. A. (1998). Older (but not younger) siblings facilitate false-belief understanding. *Developmental Psychology, 34*, 161–174.

Ruffman, T., Perner, J., & Parkin, L. (1999). How parenting style affects false-belief understanding. *Social Development, 8*, 395–411.

Russell, J. (1996). *Agency: Its role in mental development*. Hove, England: Erlbaum.

Russell, J. (1999). Cognitive development as an executive process – in part: a homeopathic dose of Piaget. *Developmental Science, 2*, 247–270.

Russell, J., Mauthner, N., Sharpe, S., & Tidswell, T. (1991). The "windows task" as a measure of strategic deception in preschoolers and autistic subjects. *British Journal of Developmental Psychology, 9*, 331–349.

Shantz, C. V. (1983). Social cognition. In J. H. Flavell & E. M. Markman (Eds.), *Handbook of child psychology: Cognitive development* (pp. 495–555). New York: Wiley.

Smith, L. (1996). The social construction of rational understanding. In A. Tryphon & J. Voneche

(Eds.), *Piaget – Vygotsky: The social genesis of thought*. Hove, England: Psychology Press.

Smith, P. K. (1996). Language and the evolution of mind reading. In P. Carruthers & P. K. Smith, (Eds.), *Theories of theories of mind* (pp. 344–354). Cambridge, England: Cambridge University Press.

Sodian, B. (1994). Early deception and the conceptual continuity claim. In C. Lewis & P. Mitchell (Eds.), *Children's early understanding of mind* (pp. 385–401). Hove, England: Erlbaum.

Sutton, J., Smith, P. K., & Swettenham, J. (1999). Social cognition and bullying: Social inadequacy of skilled manipulation? *British Journal of Developmental Psychology, 17*, 435–450.

Symons, D. K., & Clark, S. E. (2000). A longitudinal study of mother–child relationships and theory of mind during the preschool period. *Social Development, 9*, 3–23.

Tomasello, M. (1999). *The cultural origins of human cognition*. Cambridge, MA: Harvard University Press.

Turnbull, W., & Carpendale, J. I. M. (1999). A social pragmatic model of talk: Implications for research on the development of children's social understanding. *Human Development, 42*, 328–355.

Turnbull, W., & Carpendale, J. I. M. (submitted). Talk and social understanding.

Valsiner, J. (1998). The development of the concept of development: Historical and epistemological perspectives. In R. M. Lerner (Vol. Ed.), *Handbook of child psychology, 5th ed.: Vol. 1: Theoretical models of human development* (pp.189–232). New York: Wiley.

Varouxaki, A., Freeman, N. H., Peters, D., & Lewis, C. (1999). Inference neglect and inference denial. *British Journal of Developmental Psychology, 17*, 483–499.

Vinden, P. G. (1996). Junin Quechua children's understanding of mind. *Child Development, 67*, 1701–1716.

Vinden, P. G. (1999). Children's understanding of mind and emotion: a multi-cultural study. *Cognition and Emotion, 13*, 19–48.

Vinden, P. G., & Astington, J. W. (2000). Culture and understanding other minds. In S. Baron-Cohen, H Tager-Flusberg, & D. Cohen (Eds.), *Understanding other minds* (2nd ed.) (pp. 503–519). Oxford, England: Oxford University Press.

Vygotsky, L. (1986). *Thought and language*. Cambridge, MA: MIT Press (original work published 1934).

Watson, A. C., Nixon, C. L., Wilson, A., & Capage, L. (1999). Social interaction skills and theory of mind in young children. *Developmental Psychology, 35*, 386–391.

Wellman, H. M. (1990). *The child's theory of mind*. Cambridge, MA: MIT Press.

Wellman, H. M., Cross, D., & Watson, J. (2001). Meta-analysis of theory of mind development: The truth about false belief. *Child Development, 72*, 655–684.

Wellman, H. M., & Lagattuta, K. H. (2000). Developing understandings of mind. In S. Baron-Cohen, H Tager-Flusberg, & D. Cohen (Eds.), *Understanding other minds (2nd ed.)* (pp. 21–49). Oxford, England: Oxford University Press.

Welsh, M. C., Pennington, B. F., & Grossier, D. B. (1991). A normative-developmental study of executive function: A window on prefrontal function in children. *Developmental Neuropsychology, 7*, 131–149.

Wimmer, H., & Perner, J. (1983). Beliefs about beliefs: Representation and constraining function of wrong beliefs in young children's understanding of deception. *Cognition, 13*, 103–128.

Wittgenstein, L. (1968). *Philosophical investigations* (3rd ed.). Oxford, England: Basil Blackwell (original work published 1953).

Woodfield, A. N. (1996). Which concepts do children use? *Philosophical Papers, 25*, 1–20.

Zelazo, P. D. (2000). Self-reflection and the development of consciously controlled processing. In P. Mitchell & K. J. Riggs (Eds.), *Children's reasoning and the mind* (pp. 169–189). Hove, England: Psychology Press.

Zelazo, P. D., Astington, J. W., & Olson, D. R. (Eds.) (1999). *Developing theories of intention*. Mahwah, NJ: Erlbaum.

20

Children's Interpersonal Skills and Relationships in School Settings: Adaptive Significance and Implications for School-Based Prevention and Intervention Programs

Gary W. Ladd, Eric S. Buhs, and Wendy Troop

Introduction

Schools, and the classrooms they contain, are among the most pervasive socialization contexts in our culture, and potentially one of the most influential for shaping human development over the life span. Of all children between the ages of 5 and 18 in the United States, 9 out of 10 attend school (Coie et al., 1993), and 12% to 30% of these children exhibit moderate to severe adjustment problems in the classroom (e.g., Achenbach & Edelbrock, 1981; Coie et al., 1993). Because early school adjustment problems foreshadow many types of dysfunction over the life cycle (Ladd, 1996; 1999; Parker & Asher, 1987), it is important to understand the processes through which children adapt to school.

Schools are challenging contexts for children by nature and design. These challenges include the instructional features of classrooms, such as didactic small- and large-group instruction, teacher-initiated/monitored learning activities, and programmatic curriculum sequences. At present, much is known about children's cognitive and linguistic skills, and their socioeconomic and ethnic backgrounds as precursors of their adjustment and achieve-

Portions of this article were prepared while the first author was supported by grants 1-RO1MH-49223 and 2-RO1MH-49223 from the National Institutes of Health. Correspondence should be addressed to Gary Ladd, Department of Family and Human Development and Department of Psychology, Arizona State University, Box 87250, Tempe, AZ 85287 (email: gary.ladd@asu.edu).

ment. Less well recognized are the many types of interpersonal challenges that children confront in school. As children enter school, they are typically faced with shifting social ecologies, relationships, and resources. Beyond basic tasks such as relating with classmates and forming ties with teachers, children find that they are under increasing pressure to compare and evaluate themselves, their abilities, and their achievements to those of agemates. Many of these challenges are repeated as children progress through the grades. In each new classroom they must negotiate their needs in dyadic and group settings and re-establish relationships with classmates and teachers. Moreover, it is likely that these challenges are intensified when children change schools or cope with school transitions (see Eccles, Wigfield, & Schiefele, 1998; Ladd, 1996).

Thus, an important task facing educational and developmental researchers is to investigate the role of children's classroom interpersonal skills and relationships as precursors of school adaptation and adjustment. Given the complexity of this phenomenon, there is a need to construct models that will focus the search for interpersonal antecedents, and provide a context for understanding how these factors impact children's school adjustment. It will also be important to consider not only how specific interpersonal factors exert an influence on adjustment, but also which aspects of children's school adjustment are affected by these factors.

Premises examined in this review

Two primary premises are examined in this chapter. First, we contend that, especially among younger children, it is unlikely that cognitive, linguistic, or family factors fully explicate the processes that account for children's school adjustment and progress. Rather, our position is that, in order to obtain a more complete picture of the processes and mechanisms that "attach" children to school and enable them to adapt to challenges within this environment, it is necessary to consider interpersonal factors as well, particularly the adaptive significance of children's interpersonal skills and relationships with classmates and teachers. Second, we contend that the concept of school adjustment has been construed too narrowly in past research, and should be expanded to include other relevant indicators of children's success or maladaptation in this setting. Alternatively, the concept of *school adjustment* is seen as a multidimensional construct that includes children's attitudes toward school, their affect in the classroom, their engagement or participation in the learning environment, and their scholastic progress (see Ladd, 1989, 1996).

Toward this end, a child-by-environment model (cf. Coie et al., 1993) of the interpersonal antecedents of children's school adjustment is presented in Figure 20.1, with paths representing premises about how child attributes, background variables, and interpersonal factors affect each other and, ultimately, children's adjustment to school. Over the years, evidence has been gathered to address each of these pathways, including the link between children's classroom behavior and their relationships with peers and teachers, the link between classroom relationships and school adjustment, and the mediated link from children's behavior through classroom relationships to facets of school adjustment. These three pathways provide a conceptual focus for this review, and an opportunity to evaluate empirical evidence for each premise.

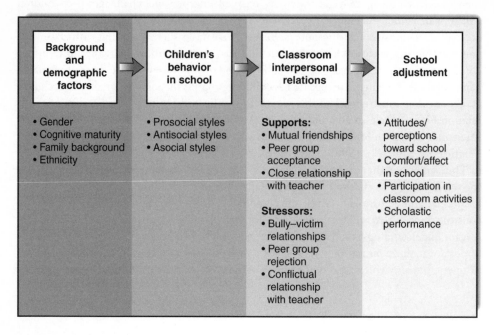

Figure 20.1   Interpersonal model of school adjustment.

Evidence examined in this review

An overarching aim for this chapter is to evaluate evidence that reflects upon the three principal pathways designated within Figure 20.1. Each of these pathways corresponds to one or more premises about children's interpersonal lives in school and how they affect each other and multiple features of their school adjustment. First, we consider evidence bearing on the hypothesis that children's interaction patterns in the classroom influence the types of relationships they form with peers and teachers. Second, we evaluate the tenet that specific features of children's relationships with classmates or teachers facilitate or impede their school adjustment, depending upon the processes (e.g., affirmation, conflict) or instrumental/psychological properties (e.g., stress, support) that children are exposed to in these relationships. Third, we assess empirical support for the premise that the effects of children's interpersonal behaviors on school adjustment are mediated through (or moderated by) the relationships they form with classmates and teachers. Finally, we review evidence from experimental studies in which one or more of the targeted relational variables has been manipulated, and consider the implications of these findings for intervention and prevention programs.

Children's Social Behaviors, Peer Relationships, and School Adjustment

Conceptually, a central premise within the proposed child-by-environment model is that children's adjustment is partly determined by the interface of children's interpersonal behaviors and the surrounding social/school environment (see Ladd, 1996). When applied to peer relations research, a corollary that follows from this model is that children's behavior in classrooms affects the nature of the relationships they develop with classmates and teachers.

Are children's behaviors linked with their relationships in the school context?

Most of the child behaviors that have been examined as correlates or antecedents of classroom relationships can be grouped into three categories, termed *antisocial behaviors* (e.g., aggression), *prosocial behaviors* (e.g., cooperative interaction patterns), and *asocial behaviors*. Investigators have often worked from the premise that antisocial behaviors create high social costs for their interaction partners, and deprive peers of sought-after psychological benefits (e.g. reliable alliance, social support). In contrast, prosocial actions seldom create interpersonal costs and often benefit partners. Children prone to asocial behavior are likely to burden their partners by being unskillful and failing to maintain interactions.

In mapping the relational context of schools, researchers have distinguished between children's dyadic relationships (i.e., friendships, teacher–child relationships; Birch & Ladd, 1996) and group-level constructs such as peer acceptance (see Bukowski & Hoza, 1989). Unlike friendship, peer acceptance is typically defined as how much a child is liked versus disliked by members of his or her classroom peer group. Peer victimization refers to children who are frequently the recipients of peers' aggressive behaviors (see Kochenderfer & Ladd, 1996).

Because longitudinal investigations provide the strongest support for the proposition that children's behaviors affect their relationships, special attention is given to this form of research in the sections that follow. These sections are organized by relationships to consider how different forms of child behavior may be linked with each type of relationship.

Peer acceptance. The behavioral correlates of peer acceptance have received considerable research attention, and a common finding is that aggressive behaviors antecede peer-group rejection (e.g. Coie & Kupersmidt, 1983; Dodge, 1983; Ladd, Price, & Hart, 1988). Recent studies have revealed that some forms of aggression, such as instrumental aggression in boys, predict peer rejection better than others (Coie, Dodge, Terry, & Wright, 1991). Although more common among girls, relational forms of aggression (i.e., attempts to damage another's relationships; Crick, 1996), along with confrontive forms of aggression, predict peer rejection for both boys and girls. These findings support the inference that aggressive behaviors antecede children's acceptance by classmates (although, see Hymel, Wagner, & Butler, 1990), and suggest that there may be gender differences in how aggression is expressed.

In contrast, prosocial behaviors have been shown to antecede peer-group acceptance

(Coie & Kupersmidt, 1983, Dodge, 1983; Ladd et al., 1988). Coie and Kupersmidt (1983) found that boys who asked questions and make positive comments became better liked by peers, and Ladd et al. (1988) found that preschoolers who played cooperatively with peers gained in peer acceptance over a school year.

At present, evidence for the premise that asocial behavior leads to peer rejection appears age-dependent. During early childhood, investigators tend to find that withdrawn children are not rejected by peers (e.g., Ladd & Burgess, 1999). By middle childhood, however, it is more common for investigators to find that asocial behavior is linked with peer rejection, possibly because older classmates tend to judge such behavior as deviant (e.g., Rubin, LeMare, & Lollis, 1990). Other findings suggest that withdrawn children are prone to peer neglect (i.e., receive few liking or disliking nominations from peers) rather than peer rejection (e.g., Dodge, 1983), and early peer isolation has been associated with low peer acceptance in both early and later grade levels (Hymel, Rubin, Rowden, & LeMare, 1990).

In sum, substantial evidence corroborates the premise that children's interpersonal behaviors have a bearing on the status they achieve in peer groups. In general, findings support the inference that children's behaviors play an important role in shaping relationship formation, but may have less effect on peer's sentiments once such reputations are formed (see Hymel, Wagner, & Butler, 1990).

Friendship.   As was the case for peer acceptance, evidence indicates that children's aggressive behavior is inversely related to friendship. Both confrontive and relational forms of aggression have been linked to problematic friendships in boys and girls (Grotpeter & Crick, 1996), and aggressive children appear to have difficulty maintaining their friendships (Parker & Seal, 1996). In contrast, Gottman (1983) found that prosocial skills, such as maintaining connected discourse and managing conflicts adaptively, forecasted children's success at friendship formation. Similarly, Howes (1988) found that toddlers with cooperative play styles were more likely to maintain their friendships, and Berndt and Das (1987) reported that prosocial behavior predicted whether fourth-graders would maintain versus lose friendships over a school year. The relation between asocial behavior and friendship is less clear, although Ladd and Burgess (1999) found that withdrawn children did not differ significantly from either normative or aggressive counterparts in the number of mutual friendships they possessed from kindergarten through second grade. Such findings may be attributable to Rubin and his colleague's (Rubin et al., 1990) contention that asocial activity is normative at younger ages, and not seen as deviant by peers.

Thus, compared to research on peer-group acceptance, less is known about the links between child behaviors and friendship. However, existing evidence is generally consistent with hypotheses about the costs and benefits of aggressive versus prosocial behaviors on relationship formation and maintenance.

Peer victimization.   Some investigators have described bully–victim interactions as a form of relationship because it often involves the same partners and persists over time (see Pierce & Cohen, 1985). Findings point to two distinct subtypes of victims – a passive or nonaggressive type, comprising the majority of victimized children, and a provocative or aggressive type (Olweus, 1994; Perry, Kusel, & Perry, 1988). Schwartz, Dodge, and Coie

(1993) found that, compared to a matched nonvictimized aggressive group, boys who became passive victims exhibited a submissive and incompetent interaction style and became progressively more withdrawn over time. In a study of third through seventh graders, Egan and Perry (1998) found that physical weakness, internalizing problems, and poor social skills all predicted later victimization, especially for children with low self-esteem.

Thus, early evidence supports the notion that children's aggressive and passive behavior, and deficiencies in their social skills, are associated with peer victimization. As of yet, however, longitudinal studies are rare, and the evidence that has accumulated on the linkage between child behavior and peer victimization is primarily of a cross-sectional, correlational nature.

Teacher–child relationships.   Although teacher–child relationships are part of the social ecology of school environments, they have received less attention than children's relationships with classmates. Findings suggest that young children's behaviors in school may affect not only their ties with peers, but also with teachers.

Research on this relationship has been guided by attachment theory, either explicitly (e.g., Howes & Hamilton, 1992; Howes, Hamilton, & Matheson, 1994) or implicitly (e.g., Pianta & Steinberg, 1992). Greater attention has been focused on the correlates of teacher–child relationships than on its antecedents. Early findings (Pianta & Steinberg, 1992) indicated that disruptive child behavior and internalizing/anxious problems correlated negatively with the quality of teacher–child relationships. In a prospective longitudinal study, Birch and Ladd (1998) found that children's antisocial behavior in kindergarten was negatively related to teacher–child closeness and positively related to teacher–child conflict and dependency in first grade. Children's prosocial behaviors correlated positively with their concurrent teacher–child relationships, but were not uniquely predictive of later relationship quality.

In sum, although extant evidence reflects on a limited range of behaviors, relationship features, and developmental periods, it is consistent with the premise that the behaviors children bring to school affect the nature and quality of the relationships they form in this setting. With few exceptions, aggressive and antisocial behaviors have been linked with negative relationship properties, and prosocial behaviors have been linked with positive relationship features. These findings, and especially those for antisocial behaviors, appear to generalize across the types and features of relationships children form at school, including those they have with classmates and teachers. We now turn to the second of the premises embodied in the child by environment model, and consider whether there is evidence to support the contention that children's relationships in school affect their adjustment in this context.

Are children's relationships in the school context associated with their adjustment in this setting?

It has long been assumed that children's adjustment is affected by their relationships with key socializers (see Ladd, 1999), but investigators have only recently investigated this assumption in the school context. Thus far, research has been guided by the premise that children's relationships with classmates and teachers immerse them in interactions (e.g., giving and receiving assistance) that confer specific "provisions" on the participants (e.g., a sense of worth, trust; or their opposites). Because relationships bring different processes to bear upon children and confer different provisions, they vary in adaptive significance for school-related demands (Furman & Robbins, 1985; Ladd, Kochenderfer, & Coleman, 1997). In the next three sections, we consider evidence pertaining to the adaptive value of classroom peer acceptance, friendships, and teacher–child relationships.

Peer acceptance.   A growing corpus of findings links peer acceptance with indicators of later school adjustment. In a critical analysis of this literature, Parker and Asher (1987) found that low peer acceptance was a significant correlate of later school adjustment. Recently, investigators have begun to test hypotheses about the role of peer acceptance on emerging forms of school maladjustment. Early peer rejection – at school entry – has been shown to predict problems such as negative school attitudes, school avoidance, and underachievement during the first year of schooling (Ladd, 1990). Later, in the elementary years, peer acceptance has been linked with loneliness (Parker & Asher, 1993), peer interaction difficulties, lower emotional well-being, and academic deficits (Ladd, et al., 1997; Vandell & Hembree 1994). In other studies, researchers have attempted to distinguish the contributions of peer acceptance from those of other relationships. Ladd and colleagues (Ladd et al., 1997; Ladd, Birch, & Buhs, 1999) found that, even after controlling for other forms of peer and teacher–child relationships, peer rejection predicted children's participation in the classroom which, in turn, was linked to later achievement. In a similar study, Buhs and Ladd (2001) found that children's peer acceptance at school entry predicted changes in classroom participation which, in turn, predicted later academic and emotional adjustment. In general, these results support the premise that peer acceptance promotes social inclusion which, in turn, yields provisions (e.g., sense of belongingness) that enhance interpersonal and scholastic adjustment.

Friendship.   In research on classroom friendships, investigators have often measured children's participation in a close friendship, the number of mutual friends they have in their classrooms, the duration of these relationships, and features that reflect the quality of a friendship (see Ladd, Kochenderfer, & Coleman, 1996). There is growing evidence linking one or more of these facets of friendship to children's school adjustment.

As children enter school, those who have prior friendships and tend to develop new ones are more likely to form favorable school perceptions and do better academically than peers with fewer friends (Ladd, 1990). The processes that typify friends' interactions have also been linked to children's school adjustment. Young children, especially boys who report conflict within their friendships, have been shown to have adjustment difficulties, including lower levels of classroom engagement and participation (Ladd et al., 1996). Ladd et al. also found that when children saw their friendships as offering high levels of validation (support) and aid (assistance) they tended to perceive classrooms as supportive interpersonal environments. Conversely, Parker and Asher (1993) found that third- through fifth-grade children whose friendships lacked supportive features tended to be lonely in school.

Although less well researched, evidence suggests that friendships may not always contribute positively to school adjustment. Berndt, Hawkins, and Jiao (1999), for example, found that fighting and disruptiveness tended to increase if adolescents had stable friendships with peers who exhibited the same problems. While far from being conclusive or exhaustive, these studies suggest that, in addition to peer-group acceptance, the features of children's friendships (e.g., participation, interactional processes, stability, etc.) are potential antecedents of school adjustment across a wide range of ages.

Teacher–child relationships. Research on the links between teacher–child relationships and children's school adjustment has been limited in scope and depth, and constructed largely from an attachment or relationship features perspective. Pianta and Steinberg (1992) found that, among kindergarten children who were at risk for retention, those with positive teacher–child relationships were more likely to advance to first grade and those with conflictual relationships were more often retained. In a longitudinal study, Birch and Ladd (1998) found that kindergartners with conflictual or dependent teacher–child relationships were more likely to develop later adjustment problems, such as delayed academic performance, lower classroom participation, and negative school attitudes. Ladd et al. (1999) also found that qualities of the teacher–child relationship predicted later classroom participation and, indirectly, academic achievement. While these findings have yet to be replicated with older samples and varying demographic groups, available evidence implicates the teacher–child relationship as a potential antecedent of children's school adjustment.

Victimization. A link between peer victimization and school maladjustment has been found in a number of investigations. As illustrations, Boivin, Hymel, and Bukowski (1995) found that grade-schoolers who experienced gains in victimization over a year tended to report higher levels of loneliness. Similarly, at school entrance, higher levels of peer victimization predicted increases in loneliness and school avoidance (Kochenderfer & Ladd, 1996; Ladd et al., 1997), and these difficulties were pronounced for children who were chronically maltreated. These longitudinal findings are corroborated by cross-sectional evidence gathered with diverse age groups around the world. Victims, for example, are more likely than nonvictims to report negative feelings and attitudes toward school and classroom tasks (Boivin & Hymel, 1997; Boulton & Underwood, 1992). Although further investigation is needed, especially across age groups and gender, the bulk of extant evidence conforms to the hypothesis that victimization is a determinant of school-related difficulties.

Do relationships in school mediate the association between children's behavior and school adjustment?

In recent years, researchers have begun to evaluate more complex models than the bivariate ones described above. This progression in thinking is illustrated in Figure 20.1 where classroom behaviors are seen as affecting classroom relationships which, in turn, yield affordances or constraints that impact children's school adjustment. Moreover, reliance on multivariate statistical tools, such as structural equation modeling (SEM), has allowed researchers to conduct more comprehensive tests of alternative paths of influence, including hypothesized direct and/or mediated effects.

Boivin and Hymel (1997) were among the first to examine mediated linkages from children's behavior through peer relationships to adjustment. In a cross-sectional study with 8 to 10 year olds, these investigators found that children's withdrawn and aggressive behavior correlated positively with peer rejection and peer victimization which, in turn, correlated negatively with school loneliness and social dissatisfaction. Ladd et al. (1999) examined a similar set of premises longitudinally with kindergartners and found that even after controlling for demographics/entry factors, there were significant paths from kindergartners' classroom behaviors to both positive and negative features of their teacher and peer relationships, and from these relationships to children's classroom participation and achievement. Also obtained were significant indirect paths that were consistent with the hypothesis that the effects of children's behaviors on their scholastic performance were transmitted through features of their classroom relationships.

Data from these investigations imply that there is a need to broaden the scope of research on the interpersonal antecedents of school adjustment to include multiple aspects of the classroom social environment. Also, because there is growing support for the proposition that children's interpersonal lives in the classroom contribute to their school adjustment, it may be prudent for researchers to experiment with methods that might improve children's interpersonal skills and relationships in this setting. In the sections that follow, evidence relevant to this objective is considered.

Intervention and Prevention Research: Is it Possible to Improve Children's Social Behavior and Relationships in School?

In view of the foregoing findings, it might be argued that children who are not adjusting to school may benefit from learning social skills, becoming accepted by classmates, developing high-quality friendships, and forming close ties with their teachers. Yet, research aimed at improving children's school adjustment is rare because investigators have tended to focus primarily on changing children's behavior (e.g., social skills training) without considering how skill acquisition might affect their success in school. In the balance of this chapter, we consider how experimental interventions could permit tests of hypotheses about the linkages between social skills, classroom relationships, and school adjustment, and whether existing evidence suggests that such manipulations are effective for these purposes.

Interventions to promote social skills or reduce antisocial behaviors

Efforts to promote social competence and improve children's relationships with classmates have a long history. Investigators first used simple procedures such as presenting children with models of prosocial behaviors or arranging for them to receive contingent reinforcement for naturally occurring prosocial behaviors during the school day (see Asher, Renshaw, & Hymel, 1982). As theories implicating social cognition as the basis for competent behavior emerged and received empirical support, investigators began to create interventions to foster social knowledge and problem-solving abilities (e.g., Gesten et al., 1982; Spivak & Shure, 1974). The latest genesis of interventions is more complex and includes components based on social cognitive, motivational, emotional, behavioral, and external reinforcement principles.

Interventions based on one or more of these principles have been used to promote social skills and to reduce antisocial behaviors (Gresham, 1985; Ladd & Mize, 1983; Lochman, White, & Wayland, 1991). Many of the programs built upon social cognitive principles are based on the premise that incompetent social behavior is the result of distortions or deficits in social cognitive processes and knowledge (e.g., see Crick & Dodge, 1994; Ladd & Crick, 1989). Evidence that such programs are effective has begun to accrue. An anger-coping program created by Lochman and colleagues (Lochman, Burch, Curry, & Lampron, 1984; Lochman & Lenhart, 1993) reduced hostile behavior, especially in aggressive males between the ages of 9 and 22, by teaching perspective taking, anger recognition, and social problem-solving skills. Similarly, attribution retraining programs (see Hudley & Graham, 1993) appear to reduce boys' hostile attributions about peers' intentions and reduce antisocial behaviors.

Other successful interventions have been based on the hypothesis that, in addition to changing children's thinking, it is necessary to help children translate interpersonal knowledge into skilled behavior within the context of peer interactions. Coaching programs, as developed within cognitive-social learning theory (see Ladd & Mize, 1983), use instruction (e.g., verbal discussions, modeling), rehearsal, and performance feedback to enhance children's understanding of social principles as well as to facilitate skill acquisition and performance. Evaluations show coaching to be relatively effective at promoting many types of skills with children of differing ages (see Asher, Parker, & Walker, 1996).

Interventions to promote peer relationships

Another aim of experimental interventions has been to improve children's peer relationships (e.g., peer acceptance), and to determine whether changes in relationships stem from skills that children learn during the intervention. In a survey of skill-training interventions, Asher et al. (1996) found that 10 of 14 programs had produced gains in peer acceptance at posttest and/or follow-up. In several studies, the interventions yielded gains in both skill acquisition and peer acceptance (e.g., Bierman, 1986; Bierman, Miller, & Stabb, 1987; Csapo, 1983; Gresham & Nagle, 1980; Ladd, 1981). However, mixed effects have also been reported. In some cases, investigators have found improvements in interpersonal skills but not peer acceptance whereas, in other cases, gains in peer acceptance have been documented in the absence of skill enhancement (see Coie & Koeppl, 1990). These findings underscore the need to examine possible moderators of skill acquisition, design artifacts that might account for improvements in peer acceptance, and processes that affect relationship change.

In contrast, few interventions have been developed to help children form or improve friendships. Typically, children have been taught "general" play or conversational skills as a means of improving peer acceptance. These skills may be relevant to friendship, but success at friendship formation and maintenance may require other, specialized skills such as reciprocity, support, and other ways of being responsive toward friends (see Asher et al.,

1996). Although a few investigators have included "friendship-making skills" in the training curriculum (Gresham & Nagle, 1980; Vaughn & Lancelotta, 1990), friendship has rarely been assessed as an intervention criterion. Exceptions include Oden and Asher (1977) and Gresham and Nagle (1980), who included a best friendship nomination measure in their assessments, but found no evidence of change. Gresham and Nagle (1980), however, did find that children who received general skills training improved on an unlimited friendship nomination measure, suggesting that these children became better acquaintances with classmates (Coie & Koeppl, 1990).

Perhaps the closest approximation of a friendship intervention was conducted by Murphy and Schneider (1994) with fifth graders. Participants chose two same-sex peers with whom "they would like to become better friends" and were coached by adults to communicate liking in their interactions with these peers. Compared to wait-listed controls, the investigators found that trained children received higher liking scores from their "friends" and, in turn, "friends" reported higher liking scores for the trained children as compared to controls. Unfortunately, several limitations interfere with interpretation of the results. For example, children were selected based on peer acceptance rather than friendship criteria, and their prior relationships with training partners was not assessed or controlled. Thus, it remains unclear whether this procedure enhanced the formation of new friendships, improved the quality of existing friendships, or increased level of liking felt between two acquaintances. Clearly, there is a need for intervention research in which friendship skills are taught and friendship is used as a criterion for both selection and improvement.

Interventions aimed at reducing peer victimization suffer from many of the same limitations as programs designed to promote friendship. We know of no interventions for which children have been selected based on assessments of bullying or exposure to peer victimization. Although skills such as coping with teasing have been included in some interventions (e.g., Pepler, King, & Byrd, 1991; Schneider, 1991), researchers seldom specified or evaluated this component of the training. Programs developed to reduce aggression may curtail bullying, but these interventions have usually targeted reactive rather than the proactive forms of aggression that are often associated with bullying (Atlas & Pepler, 1998; Coie, Underwood, & Lochman, 1991; Olweus, 1997). Larger, environmental interventions, such as those conducted by Olweus (1994, 1997), appear to reduce bullying at a schoolwide level, but it is not clear that such programs empower victims or enable them to cope with the effects of peer abuse.

To summarize, the results of experimental interventions provide qualified support for the hypothesis that children can learn skills that improve peer relationships or curtail relationship difficulties. Particularly promising are results indicating that interventions can effect changes in children's interpersonal skills as well as in their acceptance by classroom peers. Far less progress is evident, however, in the development of programs that can assist children in other domains, such as friendship or bully–victim relations.

Interventions to enhance school adjustment

Few, if any, intervention programs have been formulated with the explicit aim of enhancing children's school adjustment. However, investigators who have included school adjustment measures in their assessments sometimes find that interpersonal interventions facilitate children's school performance. Lochman (1985) found that aggressive boys who participated in an anger control program became more task-focused, and Sarason and Sarason (1981) reported that social problem-solving and self-presentation training increased children's school attendance and decreased disciplinary problems. However, whether improvements in school adjustment were attributable to gains in social skills, better classroom relationships, or both, remains unclear. Investigations are needed to determine whether programs designed to enhance social skills and relationships help children adapt to school, and what types of adjustment difficulties respond to this form of treatment. In subsequent sections, we consider whether principles derived from the existing interventions might be adapted for these purposes.

Participant selection. Those who have developed interventions recognize that children experience peer-relationship difficulties for a variety of reasons. Thus, broad selection criteria (e.g., low peer acceptance) tend to identify rather heterogeneous types of children, not all of whom are likely to benefit from a particular type of training. To reduce this heterogeneity, some investigators have narrowed their selection criteria to include only those children who have both relational problems (e.g., low peer acceptance) and related skill deficiencies (e.g., Bierman & Furman, 1984; Bierman et al., 1987; Ladd, 1981; Mize & Ladd, 1990). Others have selected children who manifest specific behavioral problems (e.g., aggressive, withdrawn) and then train skills that are often deficient in children who have these behavioral styles. In general, results show that targeting specific skill deficits enhances the efficacy of interpersonal interventions. For example, Bienert and Schneider (1995) gave aggressive and withdrawn sixth graders deficit-specific training (e.g., aggressive children were trained to reduce hostile acts) or crossover training (e.g., aggressive children were trained in skills best suited for withdrawn children). Results showed that, although crossover training was beneficial, larger gains were achieved when there was isomorphism between children's deficits and the trained skills.

To enhance school adjustment, researchers could intervene with children who manifest interpersonal deficits as well as school adjustment problems. If some children underachieve because they alienate potential collaborators (e.g., classmates and teachers), a skill-based intervention might yield interpersonal gains (better skills and relationships) that mediate improvements in achievement (e.g., through enhanced peer collaboration).

Adapting training content and assessment. To achieve the aim of enhancing classroom relationships as a means of promoting school adjustment, it may be possible to modify existing intervention curricula to include training specific to forming positive relationships with classmates and teachers and, thus, test the premise that better relationships enhance school adjustment. Alternatively, researchers could augment curricula by including other interpersonal skills that are directly related to facets of children's school adjustment (e.g., peer collaboration within learning activities).

Other pathways of influence warrant examination as well, including indirect and mediated effects of skill learning on school adjustment. For example, children who acquire better social problem-solving skills may generalize these skills to academic tasks, and improved skills for peer interaction may foster school adjustment through enhanced self-esteem or generalized self-efficacy beliefs. Also, skills that may be more directly related to children's school adjustment may produce indirect effects through enhanced social relationships. Academic tutoring has been shown to increase peer acceptance (Coie & Krehbiel, 1984), and the reduction of disruptive behavior may generate greater positive regard from peers and teachers. Thus, there may be more to learn about the consequences of helping children develop more adaptive classroom relationships.

Program length.   A common assumption is that intervention effects are magnified by increasing the number of training sessions (Csapo, 1983; Lochman, 1985). However, pragmatic concerns often dictate against this, and little is known about whether simple repetition of the training curriculum/procedures versus extensions/elaborations of a specialized nature (e.g., using later sessions to promote skill generalization) maximize training outcomes.

An alternative is to train children until they reach a performance standard (Csapo, 1983), which has the advantage of ensuring skill mastery. However, this may be more difficult when relationships are designated as intervention criteria. Unlike changes in skilled behavior, which can be observed, indicators of relationship development are less obvious and, therefore, difficult to define and operationalize. Also, repeated relationship assessments are likely to be time consuming, invasive, and subject to reactivity biases. When interventions include skills and relationships as criteria, investigators face the added burden of determining how interventions should proceed when children's skills meet performance standards but features of their relationships have not. Despite these problems, the benefits of mastery standards may outweigh the limitations. Training to criterion serves as a validation check on the experimental manipulation, and evidence that children's relationships have reached a standard is a precondition for establishing that relationship changes are responsible for gains in school adjustment.

Intervention evaluation.   Linking intervention processes with outcome criteria has become an important part of program evaluation in recent years. In addition to examining change on outcome criteria, investigators have been encouraged to assess the change-producing components of interventions (Hops, 1983; Kendall & Braswell, 1985). As an illustration, Bierman and Furman (1984) conducted an intervention with fifth and sixth graders but failed to detect links between trained conversational skills and children's peer acceptance. Further analyses of individual sessions (Bierman, 1986) revealed that children's conversation skills began to correlate with positive peer responses between the sixth and tenth sessions, and these improvements correlated with gains in peer acceptance at follow-up. Careful analyses of changes in skills and relationships will be needed to discern the process by which social competence programs may affect school adjustment.

A number of child characteristics appear to moderate the effectiveness of intervention programs, including initial levels of problem behaviors (Lochman, Lampron, Burch, & Curry, 1985), behavioral style (Schneider, 1992), and children's attributions about social successes and failures (Kendall et al., 1991). Similarly, contextual attributes may moderate whether improvements in interpersonal skills and social relationships lead to better school adjustment. Factors such as teacher beliefs, classroom climate, and academic tracking, or family values, may influence whether improvements in classroom skills or relationships translate into higher levels of school participation and achievement.

In general, it can be argued that evaluations of interventions intended to improve school adjustment should include evidence that children have mastered targeted interpersonal skills, significantly improved their relationships with peers and/or teachers, and become better adapted to the school environment. Ideally, such evidence would be gathered with multisource/multimethod assessments (e.g., self, peer, teacher, observational indices) to control problems with shared method variance and establish convergence on observed treatment gains.

Developmental concerns. There is no clear consensus about when it is best to intervene in children's lives. On the one hand, researchers have shown that problematic peer relationships can influence school adjustment as early as kindergarten (Ladd, 1990; Ladd et al., 1999). Also, it has been argued that younger children may be more willing to participate in interventions, less concerned about why they have been selected, and more facile at changing behavior patterns (Lochman, 1990). In addition, younger children may be less likely to belong to peer groups that support deviance or attempt to subvert behavioral or reputational change (Forehand & Long, 1991).

On the other hand, skills learned at younger ages may not be well suited for the challenges children face at later ages (Bierman & Montimy, 1993), and younger children may not have the competence to profit from certain types of intervention procedures (Weisz, 1997). Furthermore, it may be beneficial to conduct interventions after children have shown a stable pattern of poor school adjustment. Most likely, even though such procedures may be time consuming and costly, intense treatment at early ages followed by continuous "booster treatments" may be the best way to help children at risk for adjustment difficulties (see Lochman, 1990).

Conclusions and Future Directions

Toward an integrated model of the effects of peer relationships on school adjustment

The evidence reviewed in this chapter was largely consistent with our initial premises about the links between children's behavior, classroom relationships, and school adjustment. The proposition that children's behavior plays a causal role in the formation and maintenance of multiple relationships within school broadens our conception of classrooms as complex social ecologies within which children construct a multifaceted relational web. As children navigate the classroom environment, it appears likely that their interactions simultaneously affect multiple types of relationships, including peer relations at the dyadic and group levels, and teacher–child relationships.

It also appears that children's classroom relationships have different features that may make different contributions to school adjustment. Teacher–child relationships tend to be "vertical" in the sense that they afford children less power or control over their interaction partner, whereas peer friendships tend to be more "horizontal" or equitable in this respect. Consistent with this implication are findings indicating that children's relationships with classmates (e.g., friendship, bully–victim, peer-group relations) are differentially linked with various school adjustment criteria (see Ladd et al., 1997, 1999). There is growing evidence to suggest that peer relationships are more directly associated with children's motivational beliefs or emotional adjustment (Boivin & Hymel, 1997; Buhs & Ladd, 2001), whereas teacher–child relationships are more closely tied to achievement (Ladd et al., 1999). In the peer domain, peer-group acceptance more than friendships has emerged as a stronger predictor of children's participation in classroom activities (see Ladd et al., 1999), an aspect of school adaptation that requires involvement with others, and is highly predictive of scholastic achievement.

These findings also illustrate the importance of longitudinal designs and the inclusion of multiple behavioral, relational, and adjustment constructs within the same investigation. In addition to establishing the temporal precedence of predictors and criteria, such designs allow investigators to tease apart the independent (or overlapping) contributions of differing social behaviors to relationship development, and the potential contributions of differing relationships to various facets of children's school adjustment.

Unfortunately, we still know very little about possible gender differences in the links between children's behavior, relationships, and adjustment in the school context. Also, the temporal and causal linkages implied in the proposed model are in need of further elaboration. It is conceivable that children's relationships shape the nature of their interpersonal behaviors, rather than the converse (see Parker & Seal, 1996), and school adjustment problems may alter children's classroom relationships.

Because children's interpersonal skills and relationships are dynamic entities, their associations with school adjustment may change with development

Evidence from correlational and experimental studies supports the premises examined in this review, but much of it comes from investigations with limited temporal purviews, such as the transition to grade school or middle school. Thus, most of these findings illuminate processes that occur in specific developmental periods, but fail to indicate how these linkages may change over the course of children's development. Consider the possibility that children's social needs, skills, and relationships change in form and sophistication as they grow older. To illustrate, the skills that are required to make and keep a friend appear to become more complex and subtle as children grow older (e.g., see Parker & Seal, 1996). Likewise, relationship processes and the provisions they yield are likely to change as children mature, potentially altering their adaptive value. Thus, relationships built around earlier needs and challenges may not supply the provisions children need to adapt to new circumstances. As conditions change, it may be necessary for children to alter their social lives by cultivating new skills and relationships that are more closely associated with environmental demands.

At present, there is a need for both theory and evidence to guide our understanding of developmental progressions in the linkages between children's social skills, peer and teacher–child relationships, and their school adjustment. Toward these ends, child-by-environment models (see Coie et al., 1993) could be elaborated to include descriptive information about the nature of children's interpersonal skills, relationships, and classroom environments (e.g., normative patterns) at different ages, and to generate predictions about how these constructs are interrelated over the course of development.

The extant database could be expanded by gathering correlational and experimental evidence. For example, correlational studies could be conducted to determine whether shifts in environmental demands are accompanied by changes in children's interpersonal skills and relationships, or vice versa. In addition to helping children escape from debilitating forms of relationship (e.g., peer rejection, victimization), experimental studies could be used to ascertain whether children's skills and relationships can be altered so as to provide adaptive resources for age-related environmental tasks, and whether children can be encouraged to develop enduring, multipurpose relationships that are likely to meet their needs over changing environments or developmental periods.

Developing a tripartite model of social competence programs

Until recently, the value of intervention programs has often been justified in terms of potential long-term benefits that may accrue from improved social skills or relationships in childhood, including freedom from later-life dysfunctions such as adult criminality, school failure, and depression (see Parker & Asher, 1987; Kupersmidt, Coie, & Dodge, 1990). This emphasis may have discouraged investigators from gathering evidence on more immediate indicators of children's well-being, including children's perceptions, emotions, and performance in the school environment. Researchers may want to shift their assessment paradigms so as to learn more about their effects on early emerging dysfunction or evolving trajectories as well as distal indicators of adjustment.

The premises and corroborating evidence reviewed in this chapter lend support to the goal of developing tripartite intervention models – that is, programs that enable children to advance in three areas: social competencies (e.g., behavioral skills, social cognitive skills), social relationships (e.g., peer acceptance, friendship, teacher–child relationships), and school adjustment (e.g., academic achievement, loneliness, participation). Interventions that incorporate these objectives may not only promote short-term benefits, such as helping children adapt to the immediate demands of school, but also prevent current difficulties from escalating into reified or cumulative patterns of maladjustment.

Intervention research also advances our understanding of the process by which children's interpersonal skills, social relationships, and school adjustment are interrelated. Investigators often cite findings from intervention studies as evidence that changes in children's interpersonal behaviors influence the way peers regard them. Yet, little is known about how changes in children's behavioral competencies are perceived by peers, or how peers' conceptions of children's social reputations are altered (see Hymel et al., 1990). Much is known about how improvements in behavior are linked to peer acceptance, but the influence of behavioral changes on other relationships, such as friendships and victimization, have not been examined. As larger, integrated models of the interface between social skills, relationships, and adjustment are created, interventions will be useful for examining the process by which skills and relationships affect adjustment. As investigators test more complex, integrated models, it may be possible to design more effective interventions and add to our knowledge about the interface between children's interpersonal and academic worlds.

The task of determining whether existing intervention models are adequate for facilitating children's social behaviors and relationships remains unfinished. Undeniably, advances have been made in our understanding of how to help children learn specific social skills. These advances include recognizing the importance of direct instruction, identification of specific deficits/difficulties, promotion of skills in multiple domains, assessment of the processes underlying behavior and relationship change, and explication of the moderators and mediators of skill acquisition. However, despite improvements in intervention design, curriculum, and evaluation, the current evidence lacks both breadth and depth. This is, in part, reflected in the fact that investigators have limited the focus of their interventions almost entirely to promoting peer acceptance, failed to examine many factors that may influence the effectiveness of interventions (e.g., participants' age, motivation, and gender), and conducted very little research on the utility of particular intervention components (e.g., providing feedback, including nontarget peers).

Clearly, more research is needed to evaluate and refine the effectiveness of interventions that are designed to aid children with peer relationship difficulties. The trend, however, has been to incorporate social competence training programs into larger efforts to ameliorate the difficulties of children who are at risk for psychopathology (e.g., externalizing problems; e.g., Conduct Problems Prevention Group, 1999; Dishion, Andrews, Kavanagh, & Soberman, 1996). These comprehensive programs may be well suited to helping children overcome diverse environmental constraints that may cause early psychopathology. However, it is important that researchers continue to develop a technology that is capable of improving children's interpersonal skills and classroom relationships, and utilize these experimental manipulations as a means of understanding how children's skills and relationships affect their adjustment in major socialization contexts such as school.

References

Achenbach, T. M., & Edelbrock, C. S. (1981). Behavioral problems and competencies reported by parents of normal and disturbed children aged four through sixteen. *Monographs of the Society for Research in Child Development, 46*, 82.

Asher, S. R., Parker, J. G., & Walker, D. L. (1996). Distinguishing friendship from acceptance: Implications for intervention and assessment. In W. M. Bukowski & A. F. Newcomb (Eds.), *The company they keep: Friendship in childhood and adolescence* (pp. 366–405). New York: Cambridge University Press.

Asher, S. R., Renshaw, P. D., & Hymel, S. (1982). Peer relations and the development of social skills. In S. G. Moore & C. R. Cooper (Eds.), *The young child: Reviews of research* (pp. 137–158). Washington, DC: National Association for the Education of Young Children.

Atlas, R. S., & Pepler, D. J. (1998). Observations of bullying in the classroom. *Journal of Educational Research, 92*, 86–99.

Berndt, T. J., & Das, R. (1987). Effects of popularity and friendship on perceptions of the personality and social behavior of peers. *Journal of Early Adolescence, 7*, 429–439.

Berndt, T. J., Hawkins, J. A., & Jiao, Z. (1999). Influences of friends and friendships on adjustment to junior high school. *Merrill-Palmer Quarterly, 45*, 13–41.

Bienert, H., & Schneider, B. H. (1995). Deficit-specific social skills training with peer-nominated aggressive-disruptive and sensitive-isolated preadolescents. *Journal of Clinical Child Psychology,*

24, 287–299.

Bierman, K. L. (1986). Process of change during social skills training with preadolescents and its relation to treatment outcome. *Child Development, 57*, 230–240.

Bierman, K. L., & Furman, W. (1984). The effects of social skills training and peer involvement on the social adjustment of preadolescents. *Child Development, 55*, 151–162.

Bierman, K. L., Miller, C. L., & Stabb, S. D. (1987). Improving the social behavior and peer acceptance of rejected boys: Effects of social skill training with instructions and prohibitions. *Journal of Consulting and Clinical Psychology, 55*, 194–200.

Bierman, K. L., & Montminy, H. P. (1993). Developmental issues in social-skills assessment and intervention with children and adolescents. *Behavior Modification, 17*, 229–254.

Birch, S. H., & Ladd, G. W. (1996). Interpersonal relationships in the school environment and children's early school adjustment: The role of teachers and peers. In J. Juvonen & K. R. Wentzel (Eds.), *Social motivation: Understanding children's school adjustment* (pp. 199–225). New York: Cambridge University Press.

Birch, S. H., & Ladd, G. W. (1998). Children's interpersonal behaviors and the teacher–child relationship. *Developmental Psychology, 34*, 934–946.

Boivin, M., & Hymel, S. (1997). Peer experiences and social self-perceptions: A sequential model. *Developmental Psychology, 33*, 135–145.

Boivin, M., Hymel, S., & Burkowski, W. M. (1995). The roles of social withdrawal, peer rejection, and victimization by peers in predicting loneliness and depressed mood in childhood. *Development and Psychopathology, 7*, 765–785.

Boulton, M. J., & Underwood, K. (1992). Bully/victim problems among middle school children. *British Journal of Educational Psychology, 62*, 73–87.

Buhs, E. S., & Ladd, G. W. (2001). Peer rejection as an antecedent of young children's school adjustment: An examination of mediating processes. *Developmental Psychology, 37*, 550–560.

Bukowski, W. M., & Hoza, B. (1989). Popularity and friendship: Issues in theory, measurement, and outcome. In T. J. Berndt & G. W. Ladd (Eds.), *Peer relationships in child development* (pp. 15–45). New York: Wiley.

Coie, J. D., Dodge, K. A., Terry, R., & Wright, V. (1991). The role of aggression in peer relations: An analysis of aggression episodes in boys' play groups. *Child Development, 62*, 812–826.

Coie, J. D., & Koeppl, G. K. (1990). Adapting intervention to the problems of aggressive and disruptive rejected children. In S. R. Asher & J. D. Coie (Eds.), *Peer rejection in childhood* (pp. 309–337). New York: Cambridge University Press.

Coie, J. D., & Krehbiel, G. (1984). Effects of academic tutoring on the social status of low-achieving, socially rejected children. *Child Development, 55*, 1465–1478.

Coie, J. D., & Kupersmidt, J. B. (1983). A behavioral analysis of emerging social status in boys' groups. *Child Development, 54*, 1400–1416.

Coie, J. D., Underwood, M., & Lochman, J. E. (1991). Programmatic intervention with aggressive children in the school setting. In D. J. Pepler & K. H. Rubin (Eds.), *The development and treatment of childhood aggression* (pp. 389–410). Hillsdale, NJ: Erlbaum.

Coie, J. D., Watt, N. F., West, S. G., Hawkins, J. D., & et al. (1993). The science of prevention: A conceptual framework and some directions for a national research program. *American Psychologist, 48*, 1013–1022.

Conduct Problems Research Group (1999). Initial impact of the Fast Track prevention trial for conduct problems: I. The high-risk sample. *Journal of Consulting and Clinical Psychology, 67*, 631–647.

Crick, N. R. (1996). The role of overt aggression, relational aggression, and prosocial behavior in the prediction of children's future social adjustment. *Child Development, 67*, 2317–2327.

Crick, N. R., & Dodge, K. A. (1994). A review and reformulation of social information-processing mechanisms in children's social adjustment. *Psychological Bulletin, 115*, 74–101.

Csapo, M. (1983). Effectiveness of coaching socially withdrawn/isolated children in specific social skills. *Educational Psychology, 3*, 31–42.

Dishion, T. J., Andrews, D. W., Kavanagh, K., & Soberman, L. H. (1996). Preventive interventions for high-risk youth: The Adolescent Transitions Program. In R.D. Peters, R. J. McMahon et al. (Eds.), *Preventing childhood disorders, substance abuse, and delinquency* (pp. 65–89). Newbury Park, CA: Sage.

Dodge, K. A. (1983). Behavioral antecedents of peer social status. *Child Development, 54*, 1386–1399.

Dodge K. A. (1986). A social information processing model of social competence in children. In M. Perlmutter (Ed.), *The Minnesota Symposium on Child Psychology, 18* (pp. 77–125). Hillsdale: Erlbaum.

Eccles, J. S., Wigfield, A., & Schiefele, U. (1998). Motivation to succeed. In W. Damon & N. Eisenberg (Eds.), *Handbook of child psychology*, 5th Edition, (Vol. 5: pp. 1017–1095). New York: Wiley.

Egan, S. K., & Perry, D. G. (1998). Does low self-regard invite victimization? *Developmental Psychology, 34*, 299–309.

Forehand, R., & Long, N. (1991). Prevention of aggression and other behavior problems in the early adolescent years. In D. J. Pepler & K. H. Rubin (Eds.), *The development and treatment of childhood aggression* (pp. 317–330). Hillsdale, NJ: Erlbaum.

Furman, W., & Robbins, P. (1985). What's the point? Issues in the selection of treatment objectives. In B. Schneider, K. Rubin, & J. Ledingham (Eds.), *Children's relations: Issues in assessment and intervention* (pp. 41–54). New York: Springer-Verlag.

Gesten, E. L. et al. (1982). Training children in social problem-solving competencies: A first and second look. *American Journal of Community Psychology, 10*, 95–115.

Gottman, J. M. (1983). How children become friends. *Monographs of the Society for Research in Child Development, 48* (3, Serial No. 201).

Gresham, F. M. (1985). Utility of cognitive-behavioral procedures for social skills training with children: A critical review. *Journal of Abnormal Child Psychology, 13*, 411–423.

Gresham, F. M., & Nagle, R. J. (1980). Social skills training with children: Responsiveness to modeling and coaching as a function of peer orientation. *Journal of Consulting and Clinical Psychology, 48*, 718–729.

Grotpeter, J. K., & Crick, N. R. (1996). Relational aggression, overt aggression, and friendship. *Child Development, 67*, 2328–2338.

Hops, H. (1983). Children's social competence and skill: Current research practices and future directions. *Behavior Therapy, 14*, 3–18.

Howes, C. (1988). Peer interaction of young children. *Monographs of the Society for Research in Child Development, 53* (1, Serial No. 217).

Howes, C., & Hamilton, C. E. (1992). Children's relationships with caregivers: Mothers and child care teachers. *Child Development, 63*, 859–866.

Howes, C., Hamilton, C. E., & Matheson, C. C. (1994). Children's relationships with peers: Differential associations with aspects of the teacher–child relationship. *Child Development, 65*, 253–263.

Hudley, C., & Graham, S. (1993). An attributional intervention to reduce peer-directed aggression among African-American boys. *Child Development, 64*, 124–138.

Hymel, S., Rubin, K. H., Rowden, L., & LeMare, L. (1990). Children's peer relationships: Longitudinal prediction of internalizing and externalizing problems from middle to late childhood. *Child Development, 61*, 2004–2021.

Hymel, S., Wagner, E., & Butler, L. J. (1990). Reputational bias: View from the peer group. In S.

R. Asher & J. D. Coie (Eds.), *Peer rejection in childhood* (pp. 156–186). New York: Cambridge University Press.

Kendall, P. C., & Braswell, L. (1985). *Cognitive-behavioral therapy for impulsive children*. New York: Guilford Press.

Kendall, P. C., Ronan, K. R., & Epps, J. (1991). Aggression in children/adolescents: Cognitive-behavioral treatment perspectives. In D. J. Pepler & K. H. Rubin (Eds.), *The development and treatment of childhood aggression* (pp. 341–360). Hillsdale, NJ: Erlbaum.

Kochenderfer, B. J., & Ladd, G. W. (1996). Peer victimization: Cause or consequence of school maladjustment? *Child Development, 67*, 1305–1317.

Kupersmidt, J. B., Coie, J. D., & Dodge, K. A. (1990). The role of poor peer relationships in the development of disorder. In S. R. Asher & J. D. Coie (Eds.), *Peer rejection in childhood* (pp. 274–305). New York: Cambridge University Press.

Ladd, G. W. (1981). Effectiveness of a social learning method for enhancing children's social interaction and peer acceptance. *Child Development, 52*, 171–178.

Ladd, G. W. (1989). Children's social competence and social supports: Precursors of early school adjustment? In B. H. Schneider, G. Attili, et al. (Eds.), *Social competence in developmental perspective* (pp. 277–291). Dordrecht, Netherlands: Kluwer.

Ladd, G. W. (1990). Having friends, keeping friends, making friends, and being liked by peers in the classroom: Predictors of children's early school adjustment? *Child Development, 61*, 1081–1100.

Ladd, G. W. (1996). Shifting ecologies during the 5 to 7 year period: Predicting children's adjustment during the transition to grade school. In A. J. Sameroff & M. M. Haith (Eds.), *The five to seven year shift.* (pp. 363–386). Chicago: University of Chicago Press.

Ladd, G. W. (1999). Peer relationships and social competence during early and middle childhood. *Annual Review of Psychology, 50*, 333–359.

Ladd, G. W., Birch, S. H., & Buhs, E. S. (1999). Children's social and scholastic lives in kindergarten: Related spheres of influence? *Child Development, 70*, 1373–1400.

Ladd, G. W., & Burgess, K. B. (1999). Charting the relationship trajectories of aggressive, withdrawn, and aggressive/withdrawn children during early grade school. *Child Development, 70*, 910–929.

Ladd, G. W., & Crick, N. (1989). Probing the psychological environment: Children's cognitions, perceptions, and feelings in the peer culture. In C. Ames & M. Maehr (Eds.), *Advances in motivation and achievement* (pp. 1–44). Greenwich, CT: JAI Press.

Ladd, G. W., Kochenderfer, B. J., & Coleman, C. C. (1996). Friendship quality as a predictor of young children's early school adjustment. *Child Development, 67*, 1103–1118.

Ladd, G. W., Kochenderfer, B. J., & Coleman, C. C. (1997). Classroom peer acceptance, friendship, and victimization: Distinct relational systems that contribute uniquely to children's school adjustment? *Child Development, 68*, 1181–1197.

Ladd, G. W., & Mize, J. (1983). A cognitive-social learning model of social-skill training. *Psychological Review, 90*, 127–157.

Ladd, G. W., Price, J. M., & Hart, C. H. (1988). Predicting preschoolers' peer status from their playground behaviors. *Child Development, 59*, 986–992.

Lochman, J. E. (1985). Effects of different treatment lengths in cognitive behavioral interventions with aggressive boys. *Child Psychiatry and Human Development, 16*, 45–56.

Lochman, J. E. (1990). Modification of childhood aggression. In M. Hersen, R. M. Eisler et al., (Eds.), *Progress in behavior modification* (pp. 47–85). Newbury Park, CA: Sage.

Lochman, J. E., Burch, P. R., Curry, J. F., & Lampron, L. B. (1984). Treatment and generalization effects of cognitive-behavioral and goal-setting interventions with aggressive boys. *Journal of Consulting and Clinical Psychology, 52*, 915–916.

Lochman, J. E., Lampron, L. B., Burch, P. R., & Curry, J. F. (1985). Client characteristics associated with behavior change for treated and untreated aggressive boys. *Journal of Abnormal Child Psychology, 13,* 527–538.

Lochman, J. E., & Lenhart, L. A. (1993). Anger coping intervention for aggressive children: Conceptual models and outcome effects. *Clinical Psychology Review, 13,* 785–805.

Lochman, J. E., White, K. J., & Wayland, K. K. (1991). Cognitive-behavioral assessment and treatment with aggressive children. In P. C. Kendall et al. (Eds.), *Child and adolescent therapy: Cognitive-behavioral procedures* (pp. 25–65). New York: Guilford Press.

Mize, J., & Ladd, G. W. (1990). A cognitive-social learning approach to social skill training with low-status preschool children. *Developmental Psychology, 26,* 388–397.

Murphy, K., & Schneider, B. (1994). Coaching socially rejected early adolescents regarding behaviors used by peers to infer liking: A dyad specific intervention. *Journal of Early Adolescence, 14,* 83–95.

Oden, S., & Asher, S. R. (1977). Coaching children in social skills for friendship making. *Child Development, 48,* 495–506.

Olweus, D. (1994). Annotation: Bullying at school: Basic facts and effects of a school-based intervention program. *Journal of Child Psychology and Psychiatry and Allied Disciplines, 35,* 1171–1190.

Olweus, D. (1997). Tackling peer victimization with a school-based intervention program. In D. P. Fry, K. Bjoerkqvist et al. (Eds.), *Cultural variation in conflict resolution: Alternatives to violence* (pp. 215–231). Mahwah, NJ: Erlbaum.

Parker, J. G., & Asher, S. R. (1987). Peer relations and later personal adjustment: Are low-accepted children at risk? *Psychological Bulletin, 102,* 357–389.

Parker, J. G., & Asher, S. R. (1993). Friendship and friendship quality in middle childhood: Links with peer group acceptance and feelings of loneliness and social dissatisfaction. *Developmental Psychology, 29,* 611–621.

Parker, J. G., & Seal, J. (1996). Forming, losing, renewing, and replacing friendships: Applying temporal parameters to the assessment of children's friendship experiences. *Child Development, 67,* 2248–2268.

Pepler, D. J., King, G., & Byrd, W. (1991). A social-cognitively based social skills training program for aggressive children. In D. J. Pepler & K. H. Rubin (Eds.), *The development and treatment of childhood aggression* (pp. 361–379). Hillsdale, NJ: Erlbaum.

Perry, D. G., Kusel, S. J., & Perry, L. C. (1988). Victims of peer aggression. *Developmental Psychology, 24,* 807–814.

Pianta, R. C., & Steinberg, M. (1992). Teacher–child relationships and the process of adjusting to school. In R. C. Pianta et al., (Eds.), *Beyond the parent: The role of other adults in children's lives. New Directions for Child Development: No. 57* (pp. 61–80). San Francisco: Jossey-Bass.

Pierce, K. A., & Cohen, R. (1985). Aggressors and their victims: Toward a contextual framework for understanding children's aggressor–victim relationships. *Developmental Review, 15,* 292–310.

Rubin, K. H., LeMare, L. J., & Lollis, S. (1990). Social withdrawal in childhood: Developmental pathways to peer rejection. In S. R. Asher & J. D. Coie (Eds.), *Peer rejection in childhood* (pp. 217–249). New York: Cambridge University Press.

Sarason, I. G., & Sarason, B. R. (1981). Teaching cognitive and social skills to high school students. *Journal of Consulting and Clinical Psychology, 49,* 908–918.

Schneider, B. H. (1991). A comparison of skill-building and desensitization strategies for intervention with aggressive children. *Aggressive Behavior, 17,* 301–311.

Schneider, B. H. (1992). Didactic methods for enhancing children's peer relations: A quantitative review. *Clinical Psychology Review, 12,* 363–382.

Schwartz, D., Dodge, K. A., & Coie, J. D. (1993). The emergence of chronic peer victimization in boys' play groups. *Child Development, 64,* 1755–1772.

Spivack, G., & Shure, M. B. (1974). *Social adjustment of young children: A congitive approach to solving real-life problems.* San Francisco: Jossey-Bass.

Vandell, D. L., & Hembree, S. E. (1994). Peer social status and friendship: Independent contributors to children's social and academic adjustment. *Merrill-Palmer Quarterly, 40,* 461–477.

Vaughn, S., & Lancelotta, G. X. (1990). Teaching interpersonal social skills to poorly accepted students: Peer-pairing versus non-peer-pairing. *Journal of School Psychology, 28,* 181–188.

Weisz, J. R. (1997). Effects of interventions for child and adolescent psychological dysfunction: Relevance of context, developmental factors, and individual differences. In S. S. Luthar, J. A. Burack, D. Cicchetti, & J. R. Weisz (Eds.), *Developmental psychopathology: Perspectives on adjustment, risk, and disorder* (pp. 3–22). New York: Cambridge University Press.

Part VII

Play

Children's play is an important part of children's life, taking up a considerable percentage of their time and interest. While it has not always garnered an equivalent interest from developmental researchers, there has now emerged considerable research literature in children's pretend play, and, more recently, in rough-and-tumble play.

Artin Göncü, Michelle B Patt, and Emily Kouba review much of the literature on pretend play. They focus especially on transitions into and out of pretence, for example, via the use of metacommunication and framing, and the kinds of symbolic transformations involved. Age and sex differences are carefully addressed. Social class and cultural differences in the expression of pretend play are fully explored (cf. also Chapter 4 on anthropological perspectives). The authors refer more briefly to the literature on what may be the cognitive functions of pretend play in development, an aspect which is covered more in a chapter by Angeline Lillard on "Pretend play and cognitive development" in the companion *Blackwell Handbook of Cognitive Development*.

Unlike pretend play, rough-and-tumble play shows more continuities with animal play. It is more characteristic of middle childhood, and it is less well liked by adults, especially teachers! Anthony D. Pellegrini describes the nature and developmental trajectory of rough-and-tumble play. He also devotes considerable space to the likely functions of R&T (as it is often abbreviated), which are probably more social than cognitive. Pellegrini argues that the sex differences, similarity to real fighting, and developmental trajectory of R&T support a function linked primarily to assessment and assertion of dominance. The sex differences in R&T and role of hormones are also considered in the chapter on sex differences (Chapter 7).

21

Understanding Young Children's Pretend Play in Context

Artin Göncü, Michelle B. Patt, and Emily Kouba

The discipline of developmental psychology has been ambivalent in its embracing of the study of children's pretend play. This is evident in the inconsistent recognition given to it. The 1983 edition of the *Handbook of Child Psychology* included a review on the description, correlates, and possible developmental consequences of pretend play (Rubin, Fein, & Vandenberg, 1983). However, significant conceptual and methodological advances made in the study of pretend play did not receive coverage in the 1998 edition of the *Handbook*. The Society for Research in Child Development previously included the word "play" as a review panel descriptor in its call for papers, but not in the call for the 2001 conference. The values that underlie this inconsistent practice remain unavailable to us. However, play continues to be a major activity of many children in the world, and researchers continue to publish about it in developmental journals. We therefore welcome the opportunity to organize the knowledge that has emerged since 1983 in the study of pretend play.

The publications on pretend play since 1983 reveal an enormous amount of research effort. Some untangle the cognitive, communicative, and affective developmental processes in pretend play (e.g., Bretherton, 1984; Göncü & Kessel, 1984; Howes, Unger, & Matheson, 1992; Power, 2000; Sawyer, 1997; Singer & Singer, 1990; Stambak & Sinclair, 1993; Sutton-Smith, 1996). Others forcefully bring to our attention that occurrence and frequency of pretend play can best be understood by taking into account the gender, social class, and cultural as well as developmental context of children (e.g., Goldman, 1998; Göncü, 1999;

Göncü was supported by the Spencer Foundation during the writing of this chapter. We acknowledge Anna Beth-Doyle, Jo Ann Farver, and Suzanne Gaskins for comments on an earlier version. Portions of this chapter were presented at the Ankara University Center for Research on Child Culture meeting, "Changing childhood in the world and in Turkey," October, 2000, Ankara, Turkey.

Haight & Miller, 1993; Lancy, 1996; Liss, 1983; Roopnarine, Johnson, & Hooper, 1994). Yet more illustrate the developmental and educational significance of pretend play and discuss ways to promote it (e.g., Göncü & Klein, 2001; Roskos & Christie, 2000).

Here we bring together findings on the pretend play of preschool children, 3 to 6 years of age, covering only research in which children were observed as they engaged in *pretend play*. Studies conducted before 1983 or with children older or younger than preschool age will be referenced only if they shed a particular historical or developmental light. The review focuses on developmental, gender, social class, and cultural differences.

Defining Pretend Play

In the Western world, most adults consider pretend play as a valuable activity with developmental and educational significance, and a commonly accepted definition of pretend play emphasizes this. Pretend play is a pleasurable and intrinsically motivated activity in which participants transform the meaning of objects, identities, situations, and time. However, advances of the last two decades call for an expansion of this definition. Pretend play is an activity framed by metacommunicative messages and it embodies representation of emotionally significant experiences. In what follows, we describe the development of pretend play in the Western world on the basis of this expansive definition. We present research findings on the communicative, transformational, and affective dimensions of pretend play and then move onto the discussion of gender and class and cultural differences in pretend play.

Developmental Context of Pretend Play

Communication

The majority of studies on the development of social pretend play use a combination of Parten's (1932) categories of social participation and Smilansky's (1968) categories of cognitive play (Rubin et al., 1983). Parten's play categories include solitary play, parallel play, associative play, and cooperative play. Smilansky's categories are functional, constructive, and dramatic or pretend play. Of interest are age differences in the frequency with which categories of social participation and pretend play jointly occur. Consistent with Parten's and Smilansky's expectations, preschool-age children spend a good deal of their play time engaging in cooperative-dramatic play whose frequency increases with age (Howes & Matheson, 1992; Pellegrini & Perlmutter, 1989). Findings on solitary and parallel pretend play are less clear, since the frequencies of these categories of play do not change in a predictable pattern with age (Power, 2000).

Recent attempts to understand the emergence of cooperation in social pretend play and to explicate the inconsistency of results on solitary and parallel play lead to three important insights regarding Parten's categories. First, nonsocial play categories may occur as a result of children's preference rather than their inability to engage in social pretend play. Thus, without additional contextual information, the causes of children's play performance cannot be interpreted either as a result of their choice or ability to engage in certain play forms. Second, Parten's categories reveal information about the interactional context of play. However, these categories do not allow us to examine how children negotiate their interaction with one another to construct social play activities. For instance, coding children's play as cooperative indicates the presence of a mutually acceptable plan but such coding leaves open the investigation of how children express and negotiate their ideas with one another regarding having a mutually acceptable plan. Third, Parten's methodology calls for observation of children for a brief period of time. This enables us to categorize the social play of older children accurately, but brief interactive sequences of younger children's social play may be overlooked when we use her categories to describe the predominant play kind in a given observation scan (Fein, Moorin, & Enslein, 1982). In a related vein, unless the relationship between social and solitary play states is taken into account children may appear to engage in solitary play when such solitariness is actually precipitated by an ongoing social play (McLoyd, Warren, & Thomas, 1984).

Much research effort has been devoted to the understanding of the processes by which children make transitions to and from social pretend play and how they maintain it. This led developmental psychologists to draw from anthropology, sociology, and sociolinguistic approaches to children's play. Following Bateson (1955) and Goffman (1974), significant advances have been made in our understanding of the development of how children exchange and negotiate metacommunicative messages that their actions should be interpreted at the representational level rather than at face value. Also, although we did not have a guiding developmental theory two decades ago, a series of theories on the development of children's play communication have emerged (Corsaro, 1985, Göncü, 1993a; Sawyer, 1997).

Research on the framing of social pretend play has addressed two main concerns: first, the development of metacommunication on the basis of molecular units such as utterances, actions, or time sampling; second, using molar units of analyses, and being concerned with event representations.

Among the first group, Howes and her collaborators (Howes, 1985, 1987, 1988; Howes & Matheson, 1992; Howes, Unger, & Matheson, 1992; Howes, Unger, & Seidner, 1989) showed that development of pretend play follows a predictable pattern from infancy to preschool years. A combination of longitudinal and cross-sectional studies revealed that children's complex social pretend play, including adoption of reciprocal and complementary roles such as doctor–patient role play framed by metacommunicative messages, emerges around 3 years of age, reflecting children's developing ability to understand and expand one another's intentions.

McLoyd and her collaborators (McLoyd, Thomas, & Warren, 1984; McLoyd, Warren, & Thomas, 1984) examined preschoolers' pretend play between 3.5 and 5 years. One purpose of this work was to explore the distribution of solitary, dyadic, and triadic states of pretend play and the role of metacommunication in the initiation and maintenance of different forms of social pretend play. Older children were more likely than younger children to engage in interactive forms of pretend play. Also, older children used explicit metacommunication in maintaining their play.

Doyle and her collaborators (Doyle & Connolly, 1989; Doyle, Doehring, Tessier, de

Lorimier, & Shapiro, 1992) examined the transitions to and from social pretend play and its coordination between 4 and 6 years. The most notable finding was that metacommunication in the form of negotiations occurred in conjunction with enactments serving to maintain social pretend play rather than to initiate it. Also, the proportion of time devoted to pretend play did not change from 4 to 6 years although 4 year olds spent more time coordinating their activity than 6 year olds (de Lorimier, Doyle, & Tessier, 1995).

Göncü (1993a, 1993b; Göncü & Kessel, 1984, 1988) examined the initiation, maintenance, and termination of social pretend play in the play of 3 and 4.5 year olds. The purpose here was to explore the distribution of different kinds of metacommunicative statements at these two age levels and also to explore their conversational function and complexity. The distribution of invitations, plans, transformations and their acceptances or rejections by the partners as well as termination statements included the focus of research. Consistent with McLoyd and Doyle's findings, Göncü also found that children at both age levels used metacommunication in maintaining their pretend play rather than in initiating or terminating it. There were no age differences in the frequency of metacommunicative utterances (also see Black, 1992). However, older children were more likely to establish connections between their own and their partners' pretend play ideas. Also, older children were more likely than younger children to express two or more ideas in the same metacommunicative utterance than younger children.

Sawyer (1997) provides the most extensive analyses of 3- to 5-year-old preschool children's construction of social pretend play. Data collected over an 8-month period in a preschool classroom present a complex picture of children's use of metacommunicative messages in ranges varying from implicit to explicit and from about-play to in-play. Consistent with previous qualitative work on children's play actions (Giffen, 1984), Sawyer's correlational analyses showed that children at all ages were likely to use all kinds of messages in negotiating their play frames. However, older children were more likely than younger children to be explicit in negotiating their pretend play frames.

The second line of research addressed developmental differences in event representations and the psychological significance of the events represented in pretend play, using molar units of analyses such as texts (Schwartzman, 1978), action plans (Garvey & Berndt, 1975), or scripts (Nelson & Seidman, 1984) rather than isolated utterances or units of actions. These findings show that children begin to represent events before 3 years of age (cf., Fein, 1981). However, between 3 and 5 years of age, children's pretend scripts become elaborate (de Lorimier et al., 1995; Garvey & Berndt, 1975; Miller & Garvey, 1984; Nelson & Seidman, 1984; Sachs, Goldman, & Chaille, 1984). Also, there is increasing evidence that social pretend play is an expression of events of affective and cultural significance, and such significance can be captured through semiotic analyses (Ariel, 1992; Göncü, 1993a, 1993b; Sawyer, 1996). We return to this issue below in greater detail.

To sum up, the research findings indicate that 3 years of age mark the beginning of shared pretend play (cf., Stambak & Sinclair, 1993). The use of explicit metacommunicative messages increases with age (cf., Lloyd & Goodwin, 1995). Children use metacommunication to maintain their play interaction more than to initiate or terminate it, and to establish coherence and continuity in social pretend play. Finally, there are increases with age in the expansiveness of event representations. These findings should be extended in future work to examine whether or how children's age, events represented in play, and their use of play communication are related to one another. Addressing this question will enable us to describe developmental patterns in children's play performance in an integral fashion as well as help us identify the variability across children's play performances.

Symbolic representation

The most extensively studied feature of pretend play is symbolic representation. Pioneered by Fein's (1975) transformational analysis of pretending, considerable effort was made to understand the development of symbolic representation during infancy. The wealth of knowledge acquired in this arena is documented in several reviews (Fein, 1981; Power, 2000; Rubin et al., 1983). However, research on the development of symbolic representation during the preschool years did not receive as much attention. Recent work has tackled three related questions.

The first was whether or not there are increases with age in the degree of symbolic representations expressed in play. Research addressing this revealed findings consistent with previous ones, that from 3 to 6 years of age social pretend play increases in quantity (Cole & LaVoie, 1985; Connolly & Doyle, 1984) and in complexity (Göncü & Kessel, 1988).

The second question addressed was whether or not there are developmental differences in the mode of transformation, that is, the means by which the signified is represented in pretend play through a signifier. Following the work of Matthews (1977), the mode of transformation in the study of symbolic representation with preschoolers has been categorized as material or ideational. The material mode of transformation refers to the use of an actual object as the signifier. The ideational mode of transformation refers to use of ideas as the signifier without use of objects.

The claim of developmental theories (Piaget, 1962; Vygotksy, 1978) that the material mode of transformations decreases and ideational mode of transformations increases with age generated a considerable amount of research. Both Piaget and Vygotksy believed that infants and toddlers are not able to separate meaning from the concrete environment. Therefore, infants' symbolic transformations are not detached from the physical world. However, with the emergence of semiotic function during preschool years, children become able to use the ideational mode of transformations.

Cole and LaVoie (1985) examined age differences in children's play transformations in a study of 2 to 6 year olds. Basically, the results were in the expected direction; children's use of material transformations decreased and the ideational transformations increased with age. Consistent with these findings, some scholars reported increases with age in the amount of ideational mode of transformations from 5 to 6 years (Doyle, Ceshin, Tessier, & Doehring, 1991; Wall, Pickert, & Gibson, 1990). However, Göncü and Kessel (1984, 1988) and Werebe and Baudonniere (1991) did not find significant differences between 3 and 4.5 year olds in the amount of ideational mode of transformations.

The third question on symbolic transformations was motivated by the thesis that young children's play symbols emerge from their own daily experiences (Piaget, 1962). It was plausible to expect that with increasing age children's symbolic representations would extend from events directly experienced by children to those in which they do not directly participate. For example, it is likely that a toddler will pretend to feed her doll in the adopted role of a mother, whereas a preschool child can adopt the role of a "witch," a role not directly experienced in real life. In support of this, McLoyd, Warren, and Thomas (1984) reported that children's transformations become increasingly distant from their daily experiences from 3.5 to 5 years.

To sum up, with certain exceptions, research indicates that preschoolers' play transformations become increasingly ideational with age. Absence of age differences remains inexplicable due to procedural and sample differences across studies. One profitable way to extend research on symbolic transformations is to examine age differences separately in particular modes of transformations. In work where this kind of analytical strategy was followed, age differences appeared consistently in role play that became increasingly frequent and complex with age (Cole & LaVoie, 1985; McLoyd, Warren, & Thomas, 1984; Wall et al., 1990). A second important issue to address is whether or not developmental differences in transformations appear in the quality of the way in which transformations are expressed. For example, older children may adopt a role and elaborate it in a complex sequence of events when younger children may merely enact the role in isolated sequences of actions. Finally, it would be invaluable to determine if transformations are determined by children's ability or by their choice. It may well be that children prefer material modes of transformations despite their ability to use ideational modes of transformations.

Representation of affect

An aspect of social pretend play receiving increasing research attention during the last decade is that pretend play is an activity of affective significance. This interest emerged from developmental theories stating that pretend play regulates the inner affective life of children. Vygotksy (1978) claimed that children pretend in order to fulfill unrealizable tendencies of real life, and Piaget (1962) and Erickson (1972) stated that children pretend in order to gain mastery over emotionally significant experiences.

Motivated by these theories, researchers have begun to explore the types of affect represented in pretend play and the development of shared representation. Some studies sought to establish whether or not there is an identifiable relation between children's day-to-day experiences and their play representations. For example, Corsaro (1983) observed that a 3-year-old girl tried to recreate her actual experience of viewing her baby brother on a television screen in her pretend play with her peers. Field and Reite (1984) reported that 2 to 5-year-old first-born children pretended that their mothers and newly born siblings were in traffic accidents, expressing their envy, aggression, and anxiety about having siblings. Heath (1983) reported that a 22-month-old child recreated in her play the conversation she had with Heath about having ice cream.

A second set of work has begun to explore the kind of affect being represented in children's play. Some studies explored the relations between children's interpersonal relationships within and outside of pretend play, and illustrated that children's roles and relationships in pretend play are reflections of their relationships in the community in which they live.

Schwartzman (1978) illustrated that the pretend interactions of a kindergarten girl reflected her dominance that she routinely exercised over her peers. Ariel (1992) presented a detailed analysis of two girls' pretend play interactions at ages 4.5 and 5.5 years, illustrating that the girls used pretend play as a way of structuring and regulating their relationship.

Another group of studies also acknowledged the role of pretend play as an interpretive activity. However, interpretation in this case emphasized working through experiences of emotional significance to individual children rather than regulating interpersonal relationships with the play partners. Drawing from psychoanalytic theory, Fein (1989) proposed the first systematic theory and illustrative data on the kinds of issues children work through in their pretend play. According to Fein (1989), children work through five issues that she conceptualized in five bipolar scales: connectedness (i.e., attachment vs. separation); physical well-being (i.e., health vs. body harm);, empowerment (i.e., mastery vs. helplessness); social regulation (i.e., support for social rules vs. defiance); and respect for or aggression against the material world. In her sample of 4- to 5-year-old middle-class children the most frequently expressed issues were connectedness, empowerment, and physical well-being. De Lorimier et al. (1995), using the scheme developed by Fein, added that the expression of psychosocial issues was facilitated as the pretend play communication increased in its coordination. However, the possible developmental changes in these issues and their significance remain to be addressed in future research.

The third set of work provides a theoretical framework for the examination of how representation of affect becomes a shared endeavor in pretend play. Göncü (1993a) argued that with the advent of metacommunicative and transformational competence, children become able to evoke potential scripts for their pretend play around 3 years of age. These proposals are symbolizations of emotionally significant experiences of individual players. A belief among players that they are all familiar with the pretend proposal leads them to engage in negotiations with the purpose of constructing shared pretend play. Agreed-upon proposals get elaborated both within the context of a given activity and with age. From 3 to 5 years of age, children's pretend scripts and the affect represented in them become increasingly varied and elaborate.

To sum up, research on early childhood reflects the daily lives of Western children. Since most children between the ages of 3 and 6 attend school, and are encouraged to engage in play interactions with their peers, most research focused on social pretend play with peers in preschools rather than play at home or in other settings. Also, possibly reflecting the Western world's emphasis on verbal communication, most research focused on children's development of verbal rather than nonverbal behaviors. Research using quantitative analyses of actions and utterances, revealed age differences in children's symbolic transformations and metacommunication.

Gender Context of Pretend Play

Research on the relationship between pretend play and children's gender has traditionally focused on choice of toys and materials and the themes around which pretense is organized (cf., Huston, 1983; Liss, 1983; and Rubin et al., 1983). Current research on gender differences, however, focuses on the interaction between the participants as well as the relation between characteristics of the play environment and gender.

There is no theory that guides the study of gender differences in pretend play. Work on gender segregation provides a general framework for understanding differences between boys' and girls' play (Leaper, 1994; Maccoby, 1990). By examining why preschool children choose to interact in same-sex groupings and the dynamics of those groupings, research on gender segregation brought to our attention the significance of participation and communication in pretend play as a dimension of gender comparison. Below, we first discuss the research findings that emerged in this area and then move on to gender differences in symbolic representations.

Gender differences in participation

Findings on participation in pretend play by preschool age boys and girls have been inconsistent. Some studies with 4- to 6-year-old children revealed that girls engaged in pretend play more than boys. These findings were obtained in semistructured and laboratory settings where the play materials were selected or peer partners were assigned by the researchers (Lindsey, Mize, & Pettit, 1997; Wall et al., 1990; Werebe & Baudonniere, 1991) and during naturalistic observations in children's classrooms (Jones & Glenn, 1991; Weinberger & Starkey, 1994). However, several other researchers found no gender differences in the amount of pretend play in naturalistic classroom settings (Connolly, Doyle, & Ceschin, 1983; Pellegrini & Perlmutter, 1989) and in engaging in an assigned pretend task with siblings at home (Howe, Petrakos, & Rinaldi, 1998) or found that boys pretend more than girls in a play room (Doyle et al., 1991). No clear explanation is possible for the inconsistent findings. However, since the studies did not utilize identical methodologies, aspects of the research design or characteristics of the play settings may have resulted in different findings.

Several researchers addressed how features of play context may be responsible for gender differences in pretend play, reporting inconsistent results. Pellegrini and Perlmutter (1989) found that pretend play for both boys and girls occurred most frequently in the classroom area that contained dramatic play props. In contrast, Howe, Moller, Chambers, and Petrakos (1993) reported that 2 to 5-year-old girls preferred to play in traditional housekeeping centers (e.g., dolls, kitchen, dressing up), while boys preferred novel centers (e.g., pirate ship and hospital). Dodge and Frost (1986) examined play behavior of 5-year-old children in a playroom containing materials for a home, store, and office, finding that while the girls played with all the materials, the boys played mostly in the store, and avoided the more stereotypically feminine home area.

Lloyd and colleagues (Duveen & Lloyd, 1988; Lloyd, Duveen, & Smith, 1988; Lloyd & Smith, 1985) examined whether the specific play materials themselves influenced rates of play during observations of 2- to 4-year old children. In these studies, children were provided with a selection of stereotypically masculine (e.g., trucks and hammers) and stereotypically feminine (e.g., dolls and kitchen toys) materials. Lloyd and colleagues found that for girls, feminine materials were more likely to elicit pretense than were masculine materials, but that there appeared to be no differences for boys.

Neppl and Murray (1997) examined whether or not gender differences in pretend play occur when boys and girls are assigned to play with a masculine toy (pirate ship with figures) and a feminine toy (dollhouse with dolls) rather than playing with toys of their own choosing. Inconsistent with the findings of Lloyd and colleagues, Neppl and Murray reported that both girls and boys in 4 and 5-year-old same- and mixed-sex groups were most likely to engage in pretend play when using toys appropriate for their own gender.

In general, the differences in findings seem to indicate that the design of the play environment, availability of the play materials, and the agency in toy choice seem to be responsible for gender differences observed in participation in pretend play. However, this interpretation remains to be substantiated in future theoretical and empirical work.

Gender differences in interpersonal communication

Gender differences in the communication of pretend play has received increased attention. The two areas addressed are gender differences in use of language forms, and in broader aspects of social interaction such as the complexity, length, and style of children's interactions during play. Sheldon (1992, 1996) examined negotiation strategies of 3 to 5-year-old girl triads. Sheldon identified mitigation (i.e., modifying one's expression to avoid creating offense) as a predominant characteristic of girls' play discourse. Sheldon stated that girls' use of mitigation was similar to those observed of adult females.

Other researchers have found patterns that are not consistent with those of Sheldon. Lloyd and Goodwin (1993) performed naturalistic observations of 4-year-old children playing in their preschool classrooms, finding that overall girls used more directives than boys. However DeHart (1996) failed to note any gender difference when observing 3- and 4-year-old children in home settings, each playing with a sibling whose age was within 2 years of the child's age; the pattern of gender differences in use of mitigation usually reported for peer interactions was not evident in these interactions. These findings suggest that contextual characteristics of the play setting influence children's interactions during play.

Other researchers focusing on contextual characteristics of play have suggested that differences in verbal communication between boys and girls are a function of combination of gender and contextual variables rather than gender itself. Ausch (1994) presented the same and mixed gender dyads with similar masculine and feminine toys and examined their verbal interactions, finding that girls expressed higher levels of confrontational speech when playing with an army themed play set than with a dollhouse, while the level of boys' confrontational speech did not differ with the play materials, suggesting that, at least for girls, characteristics of the play materials may elicit particular interactional styles. Comparing children playing in both mixed- and same-sex dyads, Duveen and Lloyd (1988) found no gender difference in analysis of children's pretend scripts, and found that differences in mean length of utterance were not related to the gender of the speaker, but to the gender of the play partner. These inconsistent findings suggest that a combination of gender and varying social contexts may influence children's discourse during play.

The group of studies concerning interactions found that girls' interactions were generally more sophisticated than boys, in that girls' play was longer, more complex, and had more of a social orientation. Black (1989, 1992) observed that girls had a higher level of coherent discourse and used a style of turn taking in which turns were related to each other interactionally and topically and they suggested topics and roles to others in play. Other research reported similar findings, such as girls engaging in longer episodes of dyadic interaction (Benenson, Apostoleris, & Parnass, 1997), and in more cooperative pretense groups (Neppl & Murray, 1997) than boys. Boys' play was characterized by egocentric speech and rejection of others' ideas (Black, 1992). In general, these findings reflect the gender differences in children's social interaction that have been found both in play and nonplay settings (cf., Huston, 1983).

Gender differences in symbolic representation

Inconsistent results were obtained in research that examined gender differences in material and ideational fantasy. Some studies reported that boys engaged in material fantasy play more than girls (Cole & LaVoie, 1985; Jones & Glenn, 1991) whereas others reported the opposite (Wall et al., 1990). Moreover, in some research girls engaged in different forms of ideational fantasy more than boys (Göncü & Kessel, 1988; Jones & Glenn, 1991) whereas in others no differences were observed between boys and girls (Cole & LaVoie, 1985).

One particular area of inquiry has been gender differences in role adoption. Again, some studies reported that girls adopted pretend roles with significantly greater frequency than boys (Doyle et al., 1991; Jones & Glenn, 1991; McLoyd, Warren, & Thomas, 1984; Wall et al., 1990) while others did not find a gender difference in role play (Cole & LaVoie, 1985; Göncü & Kessel, 1988).

Gender differences have also been examined in the types of roles that boys and girls enact. McLoyd, Warren, and Thomas (1984) examined the distribution of domestic (e.g., mother), occupational (e.g., doctor), fantastic (e.g., Superman) and peripheral roles (i.e., roles that are represented only in terms of actions without explicit identification such as driving). Girls took almost only domestic roles whereas the distribution of different kinds of roles was more even with boys. These findings are consistent with those of Wall et al. (1990) and Connolly et al. (1983) who found that girls often enacted familial roles while boys often enacted character roles.

Some studies examined gender differences in role play in relation to the play objects available for children. Black (1989) found gender differences in the enactment of themes, particularly that girls generated themes elicited by props more than did boys, while boys were more likely to generate themes unrelated to props. Wall et al. (1990) reported that girls incorporated easily animated objects (e.g., horses) more frequently than not easily animated objects (e.g., blocks). The opposite pattern was true for boys.

Finally, consistent with emerging interest in gender differences in the communication of pretending, some researchers began to examine the relation between gender and role play by means of discourse analyses. For example, Sawyer (1996) found that girls used a communicative style of "direct voicing," in which each player acted out a role different from the roles of partners, while boys tended to collectively perform a single play role.

In summary, the existing findings suggest that gender differences may emerge as a function of various contextual features such as the type of play materials, setting, and gender of play partners. However, this interpretation derives from the inconsistency of results rather than the systematic examination of gender within its context. Therefore, future research should address the role of context in the emergence of gender differences.

An additional concern is the lack of naturalistic studies in this area. The majority of the studies involved some sort of intervention or structure imposed by the researcher, such as selection of play materials, and assignment to play partners or groups. Thus, these findings may not reflect play behavior occurring in naturalistic setting without intervention, where children have a wide range of choices, and decide play themes and choose toys independently.

Social Class and Cultural Context of Pretend Play

The work that examined the class and cultural differences in children's pretend play emerged from a concern that children from low-income and non-Western communities may have been misunderstood in the developmental literature. McLoyd's (1982) and Schwartzman's (1978) reviews on class and cultural differences indicated that the studies on class and cultural differences were flawed on methodological grounds. The conclusion that low-income and non-Western children do not play as imaginatively as their middle-income or Western counterparts should be re-examined.

Taking care of the methodological problems alone to properly address class and cultural differences may not be sufficient. Understanding the presence or absence of pretend play requires understanding the economical structure of children's communities and the significance attributed to pretend play. The variations across communities in pretend play can be the result of variations in adults' and children's workload and values about pretend play rather than children's ability to engage in it (Göncü, 1999).

The prevailing belief in this approach is that play is one of the childhood activities that socialize children into their communities' existing system of myths and meanings (Brougere, 2000; Clark, 1995; Goldman, 1998). In order to draw conclusions about children's play behavior, we need to understand the larger community context in which pretend play is embedded. As a result, many scholars have adopted an *emic* approach to understand the opportunities afforded for children's pretend play and its occurrence. This meant going beyond Western theory and research tools. Extensive interviews and observations were conducted to identify unique local definitions, significance, and occurrence of pretend play.

The role of the community structure and adult values as they relate to the occurrence of pretend play has been examined in a number of studies. Below, we first describe the play of children in non-Western village communities, and then move on to the description of children from Western and non-Western urban communities.

Pretend play in village communities

That adults' values about pretend play are closely related to their level of schooling, income level, and sources of income has been shown in a study of toddlers (Göncü, Mistry, &

Mosier, 2000). Caregivers in peasant communities in Rajastan, India and San Pedro, Guatemala, considered adult–child pretend play as either inappropriate for adults or a waste of time due to their workload. Children in these communities engaged in play activities with other children in mixed-age groupings. In contrast, middle to upper middle income parents with numbers of years of schooling in Salt Lake City, USA, and Ankara, Turkey, valued pretend play and pretended with their children, engaging in various forms of verbalizations.

Gaskins (1999) provided an ethnography of Mayan children's activities in a village in the Yucatan. Gaskins stated that three principles of cultural engagement guide the rare manifestation of pretend play in this village. These are the primacy of adult work, importance of parental beliefs about nature and child development, and the independence of child motivation. Based on her observations of 1- to 5-year-old children, Gaskins reported that pretend play occurred rarely in the lives of Mayan children from 1 to 5 years of age. Gaskins states that this is due to the fact that work life occupies a major portion of Mayan adults who do not consider pretend play as a valuable activity of childhood. Also, children themselves are expected to contribute to the work life of the family. Therefore, the caregivers do not make time provisions for pretend play. However, because of their respect for the independence of children's motivation, when children engage in pretend play on their own, parents tolerate this activity. Thus, Gaskins concludes that the relative infrequency of pretend play and its occurrence in the company of other children in this Mayan village is not an indication of children's deficiency to engage in symbolic activity. Rather, it is a consequence of the lack of opportunity and the insignificance attributed to pretend play.

Lancy (1996) illustrated that Kpelle adults in a farming village in Liberia do not serve as children's teachers or make specific efforts to engage in pretend play with their children. However, children from 4 to 11 years pretend in what Lancy calls the "motherground," a village plaza where children can be easily monitored by the adults. Children's pretend play themes are less varied than their Western counterparts and consist of themes of daily life such as pretending to be a blacksmith or a rice farmer.

Goldman (1998) noted that adults did not participate in the social pretend play of children during observations of 4- to 11-year-old Huli children's play in the Southern Highlands Province of Papua New Guinea. Working in a community where adults are subsistence farmers, Goldman stated that through adult activity and adult–child interactions such as metaphors, rhyming, motherese, and proverbs, adults presented themselves as pretend role models to the children. Goldman's naturalistic observations described the communicative and metacommunicative processes by which Huli children constructed pretend play frames and roles just like their Western counterparts. In addition, Goldman observed that Huli children used pretend play as an interpretative activity in which they practiced their understanding of the particular symbols of Huli myth such as "ogre" and "trickster."

Martini (1994) described the play activities of 13 children in the island of "Ua Pou," Marquesas Islands. Children varied in age from 2 to 5 in this stable play group. In the valley where the research took place, men fish and women do house work. Consistent with the studies cited above, Martini also reported that adults did not participate in children's play activity. The observations revealed that children engaged in social pretend play occasionally. Children's pretend play scripts were simple, and repetitious across different play occasions and across different players. According to Martini, keeping pretend simple and repetitious is the result of children's desire not to create situations of conflict and negotiations and to maintain the harmony and hierarchy established in the peer group in their pretend activities.

Bloch (1989) in her description of 2- to 6-year-old children's activities in a village in Senegal noted that Senegalese children engaged in different kinds of play including pretend play as much as their U.S. counterparts. Children's playgrounds were populated by people of different ages but children's play partners were other children rather than adults. Senegalese adults supported children's play but due to their workload they did not engage in play with their children.

In summary, these findings support the expectation that pretend play occurs in the lives of non-Western village children. In village communities where adult workload is overwhelming children serve as play partners for one another.

Pretend play in urban communities

Most work in urban communities was conducted in the United States and such work described the play of middle- to upper-class children. For example, Haight and Miller (1993) examined the development of pretend play of affluent children from European-American households. The data were collected at children's homes from 12 to 48 months of age. The mothers were the primary caregivers and did not work outside of their homes. They had at least college education, and reported that pretend play is an important activity in the development and education of their children. The mothers provided space and toys for children's play. Pretend play occurred mostly with objects, reflecting this community's value about material possessions. Children's play was not limited to their playrooms; they played in the living rooms and in the kitchens.

Consistent with Dunn's (1988) work with middle-class mothers and infants in England, Haight and Miller's findings showed that mothers contributed greatly to the maintenance of pretend play during infancy by asking probing questions and elaborating children's initiations. In addition, in this U.S. community, mothers enthusiastically initiated pretend play at 12 months when half of the children in the sample were not even pretending. After 24 months, mothers and children shared initiations. However, children played with their peers equally as much at 48 months as they did with their mothers. Also, children's pretend play episodes with the peers were the most sustained.

Haight (1999) and her collaborators (Haight, Wang, Fung, Williams, & Mintz, 1999) examined similarities and differences in the play of middle-class Irish-American and Chinese children from 2.5 to 4 years of age. Interviews with parents revealed that parents in both communities considered pretend play as an important activity that contributes to children's development and socialization. Consistent with their reports, parents in both communities engaged in pretend play with their children. However, the way in which parents played with their children differed across the two communities, reflecting the differences in the value they attributed to pretend play. Chinese caregivers considered pretend play as a medium of teaching children culturally accepted forms of conduct, and to do so they adopted a didactic approach and demanded mature behavior from their children, emphasizing social routines in their play. In contrast, Irish-American parents took a "child-centered" approach of meeting their children's needs and supporting their interests, engaging in fantasy play with their children. Irish-American children initiated play with their parents and played with other children more than the Chinese children.

Farver (1999) and her collaborators examined differences in the play of middle-class Korean- and European-American preschool children. Farver, Kim, and Lee's (1995) interviews with mothers revealed that European-American mothers thought of play as a learning experience whereas Korean-American mothers considered play as primarily amusement for children. Their observations indicated that European-American children engaged in social pretend play more than the Korean-American children. In a follow-up study, Farver and Shin (1997) illustrated that the differences in the frequency of social pretend play between the two cultural groups was not due to differences in the ability of children to engage in pretend. Rather, the opportunities provided by children's cultures resulted in the differences in their pretend play. Korean-American children grow up in home and school environments that encourage structured academic work, whereas the European-American children grow up in environments that consider pretend play as an educational opportunity. Thus, European-American children engaged in pretend play more than their Korean-American counterparts during free play but in a controlled experimental setting the differences in the amount of play between the two communities disappeared.

Farver and Shin (1997) also showed that the European-American and Korean-American children differ in their communication of social pretend play. Children in each community communicate with one another in ways that are consistent with their communities' values. Consistent with U.S. values about independence and individualistic orientation towards self, and previous findings (e.g., Garvey, 1990; Göncü & Kessel, 1984), the European-American children were direct and explicit in expressing themselves with their partners. In contrast, Korean-American children's communication reflected their values about interdependence and collective orientation towards self as evidenced in their description of the partners' actions, tag questions, polite requests, and lesser degree of rejection of their partners' ideas than the European-American preschoolers.

Efforts to compare the play of children from different income levels have been rare. Doyle et al. (1991) reported social class differences and concluded that class differences are likely due to cultural rather than cognitive differences associated with income. Tudge, Hogan, Lee, Tammeveski, Meltsas, Kulakova, Snezhkova, & Putnam (1999) examined the distribution of play, work, academic lesson, and conversation activities in day-to-day living of preschool age children with working- and middle-class children in Greensboro (USA), Obninsk (Russia), Tartu (Estonia), and Suwon (Korea). These authors' definition of play included different kinds of play. Therefore, no particular conclusions can be drawn with regard to pretend play. However, it is noteworthy that the most frequently occurring activity was play in all of the communities.

Unfortunately, hardly any effort has been made to describe the play of low-income children since McLoyd's (1982) review. There have been only few efforts to describe the play of low-income African-American (McLoyd et al., 1984; Weinberger & Starkey, 1994) and Puerto-Rican children (Soto & Negron, 1994). These studies provided evidence that low-income children of color also engage in pretend play like their middle-income and European-American counterparts. This information is a valuable contribution to the literature. However, it is limited in that our knowledge of low-income children of color is determined by observational devices developed on the basis of middle-class children's play. A fuller understanding of low-income children's play is possible when we examine these children's activities from their own cultures' points of view. Adopting such an emic approach, Göncü, Tuermer, Jain, and Johnson (1999) reported that low-income European-American, African-American, and Turkish children engage in forms of pretend play such as teasing that have not been observed either conceptually or empirically in the play of middle-class children.

Conclusions

The work of the last two decades on pretend play of preschool children has resulted in important conceptual and empirical advances. Pretend play is a universal activity of childhood with its own definitive features involving symbolic representation of experiences and affect framed by metacommunication. However, variations in pretend play occur as a function of children's social class and cultural background as well as their age and gender. Inquiry into these variations indicate that we need to understand the extent of play opportunities afforded to children before we make judgments about children's ability to engage in pretend play, and make decisions about the need for interventions.

Our efforts to understand variations, especially class and cultural variations, will be productive if we integrate the priorities of Western and cross-cultural research traditions. Western research on play considered largely the microstructures of pretend play (e.g., pretend roles) whereas cross-cultural research on play considered largely the macrostructure of play (e.g., cultural patterns of belief and practice.) If Westerners work on how Western children's culture relates to the internal structure of children's pretend play, and cross-cultural researchers explore in more depth how the environment of play shapes the particular experiences of individual children's play, we will be able to better understand cultural variations in children's pretend play and their sources. We need to conduct research that will simultaneously recognize the cultural structure and the individual instantiation and use of play in all children.

Two tasks qualify as the appropriate beginning points for the immediate future inquiry: The first relates to the most definitive feature of pretend play. We need to explore cultural variations in how children differentiate pretend activity from nonpretend activity. Western experimental research on children's understanding of pretense and their theory of mind shed some empirical light on this issue (e.g., Harris & Kavanaugh, 1993; Lillard, 1996; Woolley, 1997). However, how children's culture and language guide their differentiation of pretend activities from those that are not pretend and how children communicate their differentiations remain unknown.

A second task is to address the contribution of pretend play to children's development and education. Relations have been reported between pretend play and language (Cole & LaVoie, 1985), literacy skills (Roskos & Christie, 2000), story recall (Pellegrini, 1984), and social and affective skills (Connolly & Doyle, 1984; de Lorimier et al., 1995; Doyle & Connolly, 1989; Howes, 1988; Howes & Matheson, 1992; Maguire & Dunn, 1997).

However, it is important to expand examination of these relations to include children's social class, ethnic, and cultural background in an integral fashion so that we have fuller information about whether or how these significant relations exist in different communities.

References

Ariel, S. (1992). Semiotic analysis of children's play: A method for investigating social development. *Merill-Palmer Quarterly, 38*, 119–138.

Ausch, L. (1994). Gender comparisons of young children's social interaction in cooperative play activity. *Sex Roles, 31*, 225–239.

Bateson, G. (1955). A theory of play and fantasy. *Psychiatric Research Reports, 2*, 39–51.

Benenson, J. F., Apostoleris, N. H., & Parnass, J. (1997). Age and sex differences in dyadic and group interaction. *Developmental Psychology, 33*, 538–543.

Black, B. (1989). Interactive pretense: social and symbolic skills in preschool play groups. *Merill-Palmer Quarterly, 35*, 379–397.

Black, B. (1992). Negotiating social pretend play: Communication differences related to social status and sex. *Merril-Palmer Quarterly, 38*, 212–232.

Bloch, M. (1989). Young boys' and girls' play at home and in the community. A cultural–ecological framework. In M. Bloch & A. Pellegrini (Eds.), *The ecological context of children's play* (pp. 120–154). Norwood, NJ: Ablex.

Bretherton, I. (Ed.) (1984). *Symbolic play: The development of social understanding*. New York: Academic Press.

Brougere, G. (2000). Meanings and value of toys for French mothers with children under 7 years old. Paper presented at the meeting of Center for Child Culture, Ankara University, Turkey.

Clark, C. D. (1995). *Flights of fancy, leaps of faith: Children's myths in contemporary America*. Chicago: University of Chicago Press.

Cole, D., & La Voie, J. C. (1985). Fantasy play and related cognitive development in 2- to 6-year-olds. *Developmental Psychology, 21*, 233–240.

Connolly, J. A., & Doyle, A. B. (1984). Relation of social fantasy play to social competence in preschoolers. *Developmental Psychology, 20*, 797–806.

Connolly, J., Doyle, A., & Ceschin, F. (1983). Forms and functions of social fantasy play in preschoolers. In M. B. Liss (Ed.), *Social and cognitive skills: Sex roles and children's play* (pp. 71–92). New York: Academic Press.

Corsaro, W. A. (1983). Script recognition, articulation and expansion in children's role play. *Discourse Processes, 6*, 1–19.

Corsaro, W. (1985). *Friendship and peer culture in the early years*. Norwood, NJ: Ablex.

DeHart, G. B. (1996). Gender and mitigation in 4-year-olds pretend play talk with siblings. *Research on Language and Social Interaction, 29*, 81–96.

de Lorimier, S., Doyle, A., & Tessier, O. (1995). Social coordination during pretend play: Comparisons with nonpretend play and effects on expressive content. *Merrill-Palmer Quarterly, 41*, 497–516.

Dodge, M. K., & Frost, J. L. (1986). Children's dramatic play: Influence of thematic and nonthematic settings. *Childhood Education, 62*, 166–170.

Doyle, A.-B., Ceschin, F., Tessier, O., & Doehring, P. (1991). The relation of age and social class factors in children's social pretend play to cognitive and symbolic ability. *International Journal of Behavioral Development, 14*, 395–410.

Doyle, A.-B., & Connolly, J. (1989). Negotiation and enactment in social pretend play: Relations to social acceptance and social cognition. *Early Childhood Research Quarterly, 4*, 289–302.

Doyle, A.-B., Doehring, P., Tessier, O., de Lorimier, S., & Shapiro, S. (1992). Transitions in children's play: A sequential analysis of states preceding and following social pretense. *Developmental Psychology, 28*, 137–144.

Dunn, J. (1988). *The beginnings of social understanding*. Cambridge, MA: Harvard University Press.

Duveen, G., & Lloyd, B. (1988). Gender as an influence in the development of scripted pretend play. *British Journal of Developmental Psychology, 6*, 89–95.

Erickson, E. (1972). *Play and development*. New York: Norton.

Farver, J. A. M. (1999). Activity setting analysis: A model for examining the role of culture in development. In A. Göncü (Ed.), *Children's engagement in the world: Sociocultural perspectives* (pp. 99–127). New York: Cambridge University Press.

Farver, J., Kim, Y., & Lee, Y. (1995). Cultural differences in Korean- and Anglo-American preschoolers' social interaction and play behavior. *Child Development, 66*, 1089–1099.

Farver, J. M., & Shin, L. (1997). Social pretend play in Korean- and Anglo-American preschoolers. *Child Development, 68*, 544–556.

Fein, G. G. (1975). A transformational analysis of pretending. *Developmental Psychology, 11*, 291–296.

Fein, G. G. (1981). Pretend play: An integrative review. *Child Development, 52*, 1095–1118.

Fein, G. G. (1989). Mind, meaning, and affect: proposals for a theory of pretense. *Developmental Review, 9*, 345–363.

Fein, G. G., Moorin, E. R., & Enslein, J. (1982). Pretense and peer behavior: An intersectoral analysis. *Human Development, 25*, 392–406.

Field, T., & Reite, M. (1984). Children's responses to separation from mother during the birth of another child. *Child Development, 55*, 1308–1316.

Garvey, C. (1990). *Play*. Cambridge, MA: Harvard University Press.

Garvey, C., & Berndt, R. (1975). Organization of pretend play. Paper presented at the annual meeting of the American Psychological Association, Chicago, IL.

Gaskins, S. (1999). Children's daily lives in a Mayan village: A case of culturally constructed roles and activities. In A. Göncü (Ed.), *Children's engagement in the world: Sociocultural perspectives* (pp. 25–61). New York: Cambridge University Press.

Giffen, H. (1984). The coordination of meaning in the creation of a shared make-believe reality. In I. Bretherton, (Ed.), *Symbolic play: The development of social understanding* (pp. 73–100). New York: Academic Press.

Goffman, E. (1974). *Frame analysis: An essay on the organization of experience*. Cambridge: MA: Harvard University Press.

Goldman, L. (1998). *Child's play: Myth, mimesis and make-believe*. New York: Berg.

Göncü, A. (1993a). Development of intersubjectivity in social pretend play. *Human Development, 36*, 185–198.

Göncü, A. (1993b). Development of intersubjectivity in the dyadic play of preschoolers. *Early Childhood Research Quarterly, 8*, 99–116.

Göncü, A. (Ed.) (1999). *Children's engagement in the world: Sociocultural perspectives*. New York: Cambridge University Press.

Göncü, A., & Kessel, F. S. (1984). Children's play: A contextual-functional perspective. In F. S. Kessel & A. Göncü (Eds.), *Analyzing children's play dialogues. New Directions for Child Development* (Vol. 25, pp. 5–22). San Francisco: Jossey-Bass.

Göncü, A., & Kessel, F. S. (1988). Preschoolers' collaborative construction in planning and maintaining imaginative play. *International Journal of Behavioral Development, 11*, 327–344.

Göncü, A., & Klein, E. (Eds.) (2001). *Children in play, story, and school*. New York: Guilford Press.

Göncü, A. Mistry, J., & Mosier, C. (2000). Cultural variations in the play of toddlers. *International Journal of Behavioral Development, 24,* 321–329.

Göncü, A., Tuermer, U., Jain, J., & Johnson, D. (1999). Children's play as cultural activity. In A. Göncü (Ed.), *Children's engagement in the world: Sociocultural perspectives* (pp. 148–170). New York: Cambridge University Press.

Haight , L. W. (1999). The pragmatics of caregiver–child pretending at home: Understanding culturally specific socialization practices. In A. Göncü (Ed.), *Children's engagement in the world: Sociocultural perspectives* (pp. 128–147). New York: Cambridge University Press.

Haight, L. W., & Miller, P. (1993). *Pretending at home: Early development in a sociocultural context.* Albany, NY: State University of New York Press.

Haight, W. L., Wang, X., Fung, H., Williams, K., & Mintz, J. (1999). Universal, developmental, and variable aspects of young children's play: A cross-cultural comparison of pretending at home. *Child Development, 70,* 1477–1488.

Harris, P., & Kavanaugh, R. D. (1993). Young children's understanding of pretense. *Monographs of the Society for Research in Child Development, 58(1), Serial No 231.*

Heath, S. B. (1983). *Ways with words: Language, life, and work in communities and classrooms.* New York: Cambridge University Press.

Howe, N., Moller, L., Chambers, B., & Petrakos, H. (1993). The ecology of dramatic play centers and children's social and cognitive play. *Early Childhood Research Quarterly, 8,* 235–251.

Howe, N., Petrakos, H., & Rinaldi, C. M. (1998). "All the sheeps are dead. He murdered them": Sibling pretense, negotiation, internal state language, and relationship quality. *Child Development, 69,* 182–191.

Howes, C. (1985). Sharing fantasy: Social pretend play in toddlers. *Child Development, 56,* 1253–1258.

Howes, C. (1987). Social competence with peers in young children: Developmental consequences. *Developmental Review, 7,* 252–272.

Howes, C. (1988). Peer interaction of young children. *Monographs of the Society for Research in Child Development, 53,* 1–94.

Howes, C., & Matheson, C. C. (1992). Sequences in the development of competent play with peers: Social and social pretend play. *Developmental Psychology, 28,* 961–974.

Howes, C., Unger, O., & Matheson, C.C. (1992). *The collaborative construction of pretend.* Albany, NY: State University of New York Press.

Howes, C., Unger, O., & Seidner, L.B. (1989). Social pretend play in toddlers: Parallels with social play and social pretend. *Child Development, 60,* 77–84.

Huston, A. C. (1983). Sex-typing. In E. M. Hetherington (Ed.), *Handbook of child psychology, vol. 4* (4th ed., pp. 388–467). New York: Wiley.

Jones, A., & Glenn, S. M. (1991). Gender differences in pretend play in a primary school group. *Early Child Development and Care, 77,* 127–135.

Lancy, D. (1996). *Playing on the mother ground: Cultural routines for children's development.* New York: Guilford Press.

Leaper, C. (Ed.) (1994). *Childhood gender segregation: Causes and consequences (New Directions for Child Development, No. 65).* San Francisco: Jossey Bass.

Lillard, A. S. (1996). Body or mind: Children's categorizing of pretense. *Child Development, 67,* 1717–1734.

Lindsey, E. W., Mize, J., & Pettit, G. S. (1997). Differential play patterns of mothers and fathers of sons and daughters: Implications for children's gender role development. *Sex Roles, 37,* 643–661.

Liss, M. B. (1983). *Social and cognitive skills: Sex roles and children's play.* New York: Academic Press.

Lloyd, B., Duveen, G., & Smith, C. (1988). The social representation of gender and young children's play: A replication. *British Journal of Developmental Psychology, 6,* 83–88.

Lloyd, B., & Goodwin, R. (1993). Girls' and boys' use of directives in pretend play. *Social Development, 2,* 122–130.

Lloyd, B., & Goodwin, R. (1995). Let's pretend: Casting the characters and setting the scene. *Journal of Developmental Psychology, 13,* 261–270.

Lloyd, B., & Smith, C. (1985). The social representation of gender and young children's play. *British Journal of Developmental Psychology, 3,* 65–73.

Maccoby, E. E. (1990). Gender and relationships: A developmental account. *American Psychologist, 45,* 513–520.

Maguire, M. C., & Dunn, J. (1997). Friendship in early childhood, and social understanding. *International Journal of Behavioral Development, 21,* 669–686.

Martini, M. (1994). Peer interactions in Polynesia: A view from the Marquesas. In J. Roopnarine, J. Johnson, & F. Hooper (Eds.), *Children's play in diverse cultures* (pp. 73–103). New York: State University of New York Press.

Matthews, W. S. (1977). Modes of transformation in the initiation of fantasy play. *Developmental Psychology, 13,* 212–216.

McLoyd, V. (1982). Social class differences in sociodramatic play: A critical review. *Developmental Review, 2,* 1–30.

McLoyd, V., Thomas, E. A. C., & Warren, D. (1984). The short-term dynamics of social organization in preschool triads. *Child Development, 55,* 1051–1070.

McLoyd, V., Warren, D., & Thomas, E. A. C. (1984). Anticipatory and fantastic role enactment in preschool triads. *Developmental Psychology, 20,* 807–814.

Miller, P., & Garvey, C. (1984). Mother–baby role play: Its origins in social support. In I. Bretherton, (Ed.), *Symbolic play: The development of social understanding* (pp. 101–130). New York: Academic Press.

Nelson, C., & Seidman, S. (1984). Playing with scripts. In I. Bretherton, (Ed.), *Symbolic play: The development of social understanding* (pp. 45–72). New York: Academic Press.

Neppl, T. K., & Murray, A. D. (1997). Social dominance and play patterns among preschoolers: Gender comparisons. *Sex Roles, 36,* 381–393.

Parten, M. (1932). Social participation among preschool children. *Journal of Abnormal and Social Psychology, 27,* 243–269.

Pellegrini, A. D. (1984). Identifying causal elements in the thematic-fantasy play paradigm. *American Educational Research Journal, 21,* 691–701.

Pellegrini, A. D., & Perlmutter, J. C. (1989). Classroom contextual effects on children's play. *Developmental Psychology, 25,* 289–296.

Piaget, J. (1962). *Play, dreams, and imitation in childhood.* New York: Norton.

Power, T. G. (2000). *Play and exploration in children and animals.* Mahwah, NJ: Erlbaum.

Roopnarine, J., Johnson, J. E., & Hooper, F. (1994). *Children's play in diverse cultures.* New York: State University of New York Press.

Roskos, K., & Christie, J. (2000). *Play and literacy in early childhood: Research from multiple perspectives.* Mahwah, NJ: Erlbaum.

Rubin, K., Fein, G. G., & Vandenberg, B. (1983). Play. In P. Mussen (Series Ed.) & E. M. Hetherington (Vol. Ed.), *Handbook of child psychology* (Vol. 4, 4th ed., pp. 693–774). New York: Wiley.

Sachs, J., Goldman, J., & Chaille, C. (1984). Planning in pretend play: Using language to coordinate narrative development. In A. D. Pellegrini & T. D. Yawkey (Eds.), *The development of oral and written language in social contexts* (pp. 119–128). Norwood: NJ: Ablex.

Sawyer, R. K. (1996). Role voicing, gender, and age in preschool play discourse. *Discourse Processes, 22,* 289–307.

Sawyer, R. K. (1997). *Pretend play as improvisition: Conversation in the preschool classroom.* Mahwah, NJ: Erlbaum.

Schwartzman, H. (1978). *Transformations: The anthropology of children's play.* New York: Plenum.

Singer, D. J., & Singer, J. L. (1990). *The house of make-believe: Children's play and the developing imagination.* Cambridge, MA: Harvard University Press.

Sheldon, A. (1992). Conflict talk: Sociolinguistic challenges to self-assertion and how young girls meet them. *Merrill-Palmer Quarterly, 38*, 95–117.

Sheldon, A. (1996). You can be the baby brother, but you aren't born yet: Preschool girls' negotiation for power and access in pretend play. *Research on Language and Social Interaction, 29*, 57–80.

Smilanksy, S. (1968). *The effects of sociodramatic play on disadvantaged preschool children.* New York: Wiley.

Soto, L. D., & Negron, L. (1994). Mainland Puerto Rican children. In J. Roopnarine, J. E. Johnson, & F. Hooper (Eds.), *Children's play in diverse cultures* (pp. 104–122). New York: State University of New York Press.

Stambak, M., & Sinclair, H. (Eds.) (1993). *Pretend play among 3-year-olds.* Hillsdale, NJ: Erlbaum.

Sutton-Smith, B. (1996). *The ambiguity of play.* Cambridge, MA: Harvard University Press.

Tudge, J., Hogan, D., Lee, S., Tammeveski, P., Meltsas, M., Kulakova, N., Snezhkova, I., & Putnam, S. (1999). Cultural heterogeneity: Parental values and beliefs and their preschoolers' activities in the United States, South Korea, Russia, and Estonia. In A. Göncü (Ed.), *Children's engagement in the world: Sociocultural perspectives* (pp. 62–96). New York: Cambridge University Press.

Vygotsky, L. S. (1978). *Mind in society. The development of higher mental processes.* Cambridge: MA: Harvard University Press.

Wall, S. M., Pickert, S. M., & Gibson, W. B. (1990). Fantasy play in 5- and 6-year-old children. *Journal of Psychology, 123*, 245–256.

Weinberger, L. A., & Starkey, P. (1994). Pretend play by African-American children in head start. *Early Childhood Research Quarterly, 9*, 327–343.

Werebe, M. J. G., & Baudonniere, P. M. (1991). Social pretend play among friends and familiar preschoolers. *International Journal of Behavioral Development, 14*, 411–428.

Woolley, J. D. (1997). Thinking about fantasy: Are children fundamentally different thinkers and believers from adults? *Child Development, 68*, 991–1011.

22

Rough-and-Tumble Play from Childhood through Adolescence: Development and Possible Functions

Anthony D. Pellegrini

In this chapter I will first define a specific form of play, rough-and-tumble (R&T) play, describe how it develops across the life span, and make some inferences about its possible functions.

Defining R&T

Behavioral, consequential, structural, and ecological dimensions

Often R&T is confused with aggression because at some levels they resemble each other. Upon close inspection, however, they are clearly different. In this section I will briefly explicate those differences. Categories of behavior, like aggression and R&T, can be defined along the following dimensions: individual behaviors, consequences, structure, ecology, and developmental trajectories.

Behaviors. Beginning with individual behaviors, numerous factor analytic studies have differentiated R&T and aggression behaviorally (e.g., Blurton Jones, 1972) in the following reliable ways. The assumption here is that behaviors with similar meaning will co-

Work on this chapter was supported by grants from the W T Grant Foundation and the Spencer Foundation. I acknowledge the comments of Peter Smith on an earlier draft.

occur and form a meaningful category. R&T is typically composed of: run, chase, flee, wrestle, open hand hit. Aggression is typified by: closed hand hits, shoves, pushes, and kicks. Also a quite simple, yet reliable, way in which R&T and aggression differ is in terms of expression of affect. Generally, smiles (or a play face) accompany R&T while frowns, or crying, accompany aggression.

Consequences. Classes of behavior can also be differentiated in terms of consequences, or those behaviors immediately following the target behaviors R&T and aggression. As in the case of co-occurring behaviors we assume that behaviors which follow a focal behavior systematically are related to that antecedent in a meaningful way. In many cases we can make assumptions about the meaning, or function of an antecedent behavior based on its consequence. For example, when R&T bouts end, children often stay together and begin cooperative social games (Pellegrini, 1988). Aggression, on the other hand, often leads to one of the participants trying to separate from the other (McGrew, 1972). Thus, R&T may have peer affiliative functions whereas aggression does not.

Structure. The structure of R&T is also different from aggression. By structure I mean the roles that typify each class of behaviors. In R&T youngsters alternate roles, such as chaser and chasee. In some cases, stronger or bigger players "self-handicap" so as to sustain play. For example, an older child may pretend to fall as he is trying escape from a pursuer, thus enabling the younger child to "capture" him. Self-handicapping enables children of different levels of strength and physical prowess to play together. Role alternation is a hallmark of other forms of play, such as dramatic play where children often change, or negotiate, roles repeatedly in the course of an episode. Role alternation seems to play an important part in children's social perspective taking; taking different play roles, both in fantasy (Garvey, 1990) and R&T (Pellegrini, 1993), enables children to take different perspectives. Aggression, on the other hand, is typified by unilateral roles: Aggressors don't switch roles with their victims.

Ecology. Ecologically, R&T tends to occur in spacious areas, such as the outdoors (Smith & Connolly, 1980), and on those parts of playgrounds with soft, grassy surfaces (Pellegrini, 1989b). That R&T is physically vigorous and involves running, falling, and wrestling means that it is more likely to occur in areas supportive of this sort of behavior, compared to more confined areas.

Aggression does not, however, vary according to playground location (Pellegrini, 1989a); it is equally likely to occur anywhere. Among preschoolers, where toys are present, however, aggression is likely to result from children's disputes over objects (Smith & Connolly, 1980).

These differences are empirically verified to the extent that for most children R&T and aggression are not significantly intercorrelated (Blurton Jones, 1972; Fry, 1987; Pellegrini, 1988). Further, aggression and R&T appear to be under the control of different neural and endocrinological systems (Meaney, Stewart, & Beatty, 1985). Additionally, these differences have been observed cross-culturally; for example, among foraging bushmen (Konner, 1972), indigenous Mexican people (Fry, 1987), and in India (Roopnarine, Hooper, Ahmeduzzaman, & Pollack, 1993). As we will see in the next section, R&T leads children into a very positive developmental trajectory; this is not the case for aggression.

The Developmental Trajectory of R&T

The distinction between R&T and aggression is further evidenced by the fact that each has a different developmental trajectory. R&T, like other forms of play (Fagen, 1981), follows an inverted-U developmental curve. Pellegrini and Smith (1998) propose that R&T is the end point on the developmental continuum of physical play which begins with rhythmic stereotypies (which peaks in infancy), moves into exercise play (which peaks during the preschool period), and finally into R&T. Unlike these other forms of physical play, R&T, by definition, has a social dimension.

The earliest cases of R&T are observed between young children and their parents. This is a form of play in which father and sons typically engage (e.g., Parke, Cassidy, Burks, Carson, & Boyum, 1992) and by 4 years of age, it accounts for about 4% of all parent–child behavior (Jacklin, DiPietro, & Maccoby, 1984).

R&T with peers accounts for about 5% of the free play of preschoolers, increases to 10–17% of the play of elementary school children, and declines in middle school to about 5% (Humphreys & Smith, 1984). These figures probably underestimate time spent in R&T, given the bias toward the documenting fantasy play during childhood. That is, in many cases, especially for preschool boys, fantasy and R&T co-occur (Pellegrini & Perlmutter, 1987), and end up being counted as fantasy, not R&T. Clearly more observational work is needed where R&T is examined more carefully in relation to fantasy play.

Sex differences

Males of most primate species engage in R&T more frequently than females (Fagen, 1981; Smith, 1982). This is a very robust finding in the animal and child development literature, being observed cross-culturally in the latter (Pellegrini & Smith, 1998). Differences in initiations of and responses to R&T overtures are crucial in understanding these differences. Males tend to show higher rates of initiations and females higher rates of withdrawals (Meaney et al., 1985). The higher withdrawal rates by females may be due to corresponding differences in response to tactile stimulation of the sort characterizing R&T (Meaney et al., 1985). These differences, in turn, help explain the segregation of boys' and girls' play groups throughout childhood (Maccoby, 1998).

Sex differences in R&T are probably the result of both hormonal and socialization events (Maccoby, 1998), where endogenous and exogenous androgens affect neural organization and behavior. Normal exposure to androgens during fetal development predisposes boys toward physical activity and R&T. Socialization interacts with hormonal events to reinforce these difference (Maccoby, 1998). Starting in infancy, fathers spend more time with sons, compared to daughters (Parke & Suomi, 1981), and when with their sons, may engage in physically vigorous forms of play, including R&T (Carson, Burks, & Parke, 1993; MacDonald & Parke, 1986). Further, girls, compared to boys, are more closely supervised by adults (Fagot, 1994) and they are likely to discourage rough forms of play (Maccoby, 1998).

Individual differences

In most cases R&T does not co-occur with or escalate to aggression (Pellegrini, 1988). Further, young children and adults from a variety of nations (e.g., United States, UK, Italy) are able to reliably distinguish R&T from aggression (Costabile et al., 1991; Pellegrini, 1989b). However, there are individual differences in the expression and perception of R&T. Primary school boys who are sociometrically rejected (i.e., they are disliked by more of their peers than they are liked) and physically aggressive tend to engage in R&T at rates similar to boys of average popularity. The R&T for this first class of boys, however, co-occurs with aggression. That is, rates of aggression and R&T are significantly intercorrelated (Pellegrini, 1988). This may be due to the fact that the R&T of these boys "escalates" into aggression; that is, when an R&T bout ends, aggression follows in one case out of five (Pellegrini, 1988). Further, rejected boys, relative to popular boys, are less accurate in differentiating R&T from aggression (Pellegrini, 1989b). Boys who are aggressive and sociometrically rejected in the primary grades, retain their status as they move into adolescence. In adolescence, however, these boys engage in a particularly rough form of R&T and tend to use R&T to bully their peers (Pellegrini, 1994). While rates of R&T decline markedly for most adolescent boys the R&T of rejected boys remains relatively high and continues to relate to aggression (Pellegrini, 1994).

Children's R&T "escalates" into aggression for at least three different reasons. First, for most children the transition from R&T to aggression may be an "honest mistake" (Fagen, 1981). Mistakes occur, such as one child slipping or accidentally hitting too hard, and can be judged by looking at the expression on the face of the initiator at the instant of the "mistake." A look of surprise probably indicates an accident.

Second, youngsters can exploit the playful tenor of R&T in a more Machiavellian way, by turning R&T into aggressive exploitation; for example, they could hit too hard or not change role. Youngsters may apologize for their "mistakes" when in fact they were intentional. These youngsters seem to deliberately exploit R&T in this way as a way in which to publicly exhibit their dominance over a peer. The occurrence of this sort of behavior in the presence of a crowd or in the presence of high status peers may indicate exploitation. We have also found that when new social groups are forming, youngsters whose dominance status is rising use this strategy with higher ranking individuals, as a way to move up the hierarchy. Youngsters whose status is falling use it only with lower status individuals (Pellegrini, 1995b). In these sorts of cases, individuals are socially sophisticated in their use of aggression; their use of these strategies is related to their ability to take others' points of view (Pellegrini, 1995a).

Third, there are other youngsters whose R&T moves into aggression because they are overly emotional, cannot control themselves, and who might be interpreted as deficient in their interpretation of ambiguous, provocative social information. When presented with R&T, they interpret it as aggressive and respond accordingly.

Functions of R&T

Function is defined, for the purposes of this chapter, in terms of "beneficial consequences" (Hinde, 1980). These consequences can be either immediate or deferred. The dominant view, for much of this century (Groos, 1901), has been that play has deferred benefits; that is, play has been considered practice for adulthood. During the period of extended child-hood, children engage in play to learn and practice those skills necessary to be functioning adult members of society. This view is reflected in both Piaget's (1962) and Vygotsky's (1978) theories of play. This assumption is related to the long-held emphasis among child developmentalists on the importance of early experience and developmental continuity. Bateson's (1976) metaphor for the deferred benefit view of play is "scaffolding"; play functions in skill assembly and then is disassembled when the skill is mastered.

Alternatively, play may be viewed not as an incomplete or imperfect version of adult behavior, but as having immediate benefits during childhood. This "metamorphic" (Bateson, 1976) view posits that play and its consequences are unique to the niche of childhood and that later benefits are not necessary for its explanation. This view is consistent with recent discussions of benefits suggesting that play occurs at specific periods during which development may be modified (Byers & Walker, 1995). Accordingly, the previously discussed age distribution of R&T may be useful in evaluating functional hypotheses.

Social functions of R&T

The distinct functional significance of R&T is suggested by two arguments. The first is the relative and peak frequencies with which it is observed during childhood. R&T peaks during the middle childhood period, when it accounts for about 10% of free-play behavior; it then declines in adolescence, accounting for less than 5%. This peak period co-occurs with the time during which peer relations are becoming increasingly important in chil-dren's lives (Waters & Sroufe, 1983), thus, and as will be discussed below, R&T may be related to learning skills important for peer relations.

The second is an argument by design. R&T is a distinctive form of behavior. It is super-ficially similar to real fighting; however, it is different in many respects and should be regarded as a separate construct. I review here evidence relating R&T to social skills, fight-ing skills, and to dominance functions.

R&T and social skills.   An important dimension of social skill is the ability to encode and decode social signals. Successful encoding and decoding of messages, such as "This is play," is necessary if play is to be initiated and maintained (e.g., Bekoff, 1995). Behaviors that send the message "This is play" are typically exaggerated, compared to more functional counterparts; for example, play fighting, compared to real fighting, might be characterized by open mouth, hunched shoulders and rhythmic movement of the hands.

Research by Parke and colleagues indicates that the ability to encode and decode play signals can originate in socially vigorous play between parents (primarily fathers) and their children (primarily sons), beginning in infancy and continuing throughout childhood (Parke et al., 1992). They found the amount of time spent in vigorous play bouts to be positively related to preschool children's ability to decode emotional expressions. Further, children's expression of emotional states was also related positively to bout length. Involvement in R&T with peers, expressed in terms of proportion of total behavioral output, has also been found to relate to primary school children's ability to decode play signals (Pellegrini, 1988). It may thus be the case that parent–child play provides the groundwork for children's ability to encode and decode emotions, with this ability later being used in physical activity play with peers.

However, there are difficulties with this hypothesis. First, these correlational studies do not establish cause and effect; it is equally plausible that the causal relationship is such that (for example) those children less able to encode/decode emotions are less willing to engage in R&T. Second, and more conclusively, these hypotheses are inconsistent with observed sex differences; encoding and decoding of emotions should be just as important for girls as for boys, and they certainly are no worse at it than boys. Yet, the sex difference in R&T is a well-established finding.

R&T and fighting skills. The most traditional view in the animal and human literature (e.g., Smith, 1982) is that R&T functions to provide safe practice for fighting (and possibly, hunting) skills which will be useful in later life. This hypothesis would be consistent with the strong sex difference observed, if one assumes that fighting (and hunting) skills were and are more characteristically male activities (Boulton & Smith, 1992). It does not predict the age curve for R&T, since "safe" practice for such skills might be especially important in adolescence (when in fact R&T declines). Also, there is little or no direct evidence linking R&T to fighting or hunting skills, in either the animal or human literature (Martin & Caro, 1985). Finally, this hypothesis does not predict the age changes in "cheating" observed in human R&T. Thus, while I do not dismiss this argument – indeed, I suspect it may be a phylogenetically prior function with some remaining relevance for younger children – I review here the argument for dominance functions of R&T, which have not received the same attention but which may yield new insights in the case of human R&T (Pellegrini & Smith, 1998).

R&T and dominance relationships. Dominance is defined as a dyadic, affiliative relationship between individuals, not in terms of one's aggressiveness (Hinde, 1980), though physically aggressive behaviors are often used in the service of dominance. Aggression and affiliative behaviors are correlated with individual's dominance status during childhood (Strayer & Noel, 1986) and adolescence (Pellegrini & Bartini, 2001). Further, dominance hierarchies are generally unique to specific groups and ecologies, the implication being that individuals might have different dominance status in different groups and ecologies (Strayer, 1980). Although explicable in terms of advantage to dominant individuals, dominance hierarchies also mediate group members' access to valued resources and reduce intragroup aggression in many situations (Strayer, 1980). Thus dominance hierarchies benefit individuals (in terms of access to resources and minimized aggression) and the group (in terms of group affiliation).

I postulate that R&T may serve a social function in peer groups, for boys especially, by assisting in the establishing and maintaining of social leadership or dominance relationships. The idea that R&T is related to establishing and maintaining dominance status is consistent with arguments from design. Males often use quasi-agonistic displays (e.g., soft or no contact kicks and punches, light pushes) in the service of dominance. Very similar behaviors are also displayed in R&T, but these behaviors are embedded in a nonserious context: Kicks and punches don't make contact and if they do they are soft; players are smiling; and they often handicap themselves (e.g., let the player on the bottom of a pile get on top).

Symons (1978) was critical of the hypothesis that R&T is related to dominance because of the findings in primate (and child) research on R&T that self-handicapping occurs: Blows are not forceful, and individuals take turns to gain or cede the upper position in wrestling. However, subsequent findings counter this argument in two ways that I review in more detail below. First, children can often evaluate the strength of others from R&T bouts, despite self-handicapping and restraint. Second, in some youngsters (and especially by adolescence), it now appears that subtle or not so subtle forms of "cheating" may occur, demonstrating clearly to opponents and to onlookers, that one participant is in fact stronger (Smith & Boulton, 1990).

This argument is also consistent with the sex differences in R&T. Children establish and maintain dominance in different ways. Girls primarily use verbal, rather than physical, means to gain and keep resources (Charlesworth & Dzur, 1987). Boys, on the other hand, utilize a variety of skills, some of which are related to physical prowess, to regulate access to resources: for example, struggling over access to a toy. Fighting skills, or toughness, when used in conjunction with more affiliative skills is an important dimension of boys' peer-group status and popularity (Pellegrini & Bartini, 2001). It may be the case that dominant individuals reconcile (e.g., shake hands, offer gifts, etc.) after their aggressive acts as a way in which to maintain group harmony (deWaal, 1985). Additionally, leaders may use aggression to stop fights or to help their allies (Strayer & Noel, 1986).

Age trends in R&T also are consistent with this position, if we consider that the immediate preadolescent period is one in which it is important to establish peer-group dominance. At this age, youngsters experience rapid change in body size along with changes in environment, as they move from primary to secondary school. Thus, R&T, along with other agonistic and affiliative strategies is used by boys to establish dominance (Pellegrini & Bartini, 2001).

Observational and interview evidence suggest that R&T may be involved in dominance in two ways, each of which are age related. The first is indirect; R&T may provide a way of assessing the strength of others, so as to decide one's strategy vis-à-vis dominance competition – a form of "ritualized aggression," which leads to real fighting in only certain circumstances. Similarly, children's R&T occurs in symmetrical groups, or children of similar dominance status, and many children say they can determine their own as well as peers' strength from these encounters (Smith, Hunter, Carvalho, & Costabile, 1992). Also with children, R&T occurs between friends (Humphreys & Smith, 1987; Smith & Lewis, 1985) and in groups of 3 to 4 children (Pellegrini, 1993) and this indicates that it is a safe and relatively visible venue to test and exhibit physical strength. That R&T occurs in symmetrical groups and that children can determine peers' strength from these encounters suggests that it can be used in this first, indirect way, to assess strength and prepare for dominance encounters, through the primary school period.

The second way in which R&T may provide the context for establishing or maintaining dominance is more direct. A participant may use an R&T bout to get their partner in a position where they can actually display their superior strength, or assert dominance, for example, by pinning or intimidating a playmate. Indeed, the participant doing this may have lulled their partner into a false sense of security by using the predominantly playful nature of R&T, or have used the self-handicapping and reversal criteria of R&T to get themselves into a "winning" position. Thus, this could be called a "cheating" use of R&T for dominance purposes and was discussed above.

So far as preadolescent children are concerned R&T is not correlated with peer-nominated dominance in that it occurs with partners of similar dominance status (Humphreys & Smith, 1987; Pellegrini, 1993). In most cases, R&T is not exploited for immediate aggressive ends (Pellegrini, 1988). This suggests that R&T may not often be used to establish dominance in this second way, directly, before adolescence.

While R&T and actual fighting remain separate for most children during the primary school years, there are cases, especially involving sociometrically rejected children (Pellegrini, 1988), where R&T and fighting are linked. The ethnographic record provides illustrations. Sluckin's (1981) in-depth study of British 5- to 9-year-old children's behavior and perceptions of their lives in the school playground provides examples of R&T being used to deceive and manipulate peers. Similarly, the work of Oswald and colleagues (1987) in Germany with children aged 6- to 10-years-of-age found instances of hurtfulness in the play of the older children in this age range.

However a clearly different picture emerges in early adolescence. Neill (1976) was the first to suggest that adolescent boys' R&T might be used to establish dominance. His factor analytic study of boys' playground behavior found that R&T and aggression often co-occurred. Neill stated that R&T might be a "means of asserting or maintaining dominance; once a weaker boy has registered distress the bond can be maintained by the fight taking a more playful form, but if he does not do so at the start of the fight, the stronger boy may increase the intensity of the fight until he does" (p. 219). This age change in the function of R&T received some support from Humphreys and Smith (1987). They found that at 11 years, but not at 7 and 9 years, dominance was a factor in partner choice in R&T. When the younger children engaged in R&T they did so in symmetrical groups, or with peers of similar dominance status; for the older children, dominant youngsters initiated R&T with less dominant youngsters, or in asymmetrical groups. This finding would be consistent with stronger children using R&T to exhibit dominance with weaker children.

Results from a study by Pellegrini (1995b) throw further light on this age trend. In a longitudinal study of adolescent boys, he found that asymmetrical choices for R&T were observed during the first year of middle school, but not the second. He also found that during the first year of middle school boys' R&T was correlated with peer-nominated dominance. (Only with sociometrically rejected boys, not popular or average boys, did R&T lead to and relate to aggression, however.) During the second year of middle school R&T continued to relate to dominance status but it did not lead or relate to aggression. These results suggest that R&T is used to establish dominance in early adolescence; and that once established, hierarchies reduce aggression and R&T declines.

In summary, I suggest that the primary function of R&T through the primary years is to provide a way in which boys assess strength of others for dominance purposes; possibly additional to providing practice in fighting skills, for which, however, little direct evidence exists. There is good evidence that in early adolescence (and perhaps earlier for rejected children) R&T functions to actually establish dominance status in boys' peer groups. The contemporaneous correlations between R&T and dominance and R&T and popularity for adolescent boys suggest that R&T is only one behavioral strategy used by boys to gain and maintain status. Finally, I suggest that any benefits for emotional encoding, decoding, or regulation are incidental benefits of R&T, achievable in other ways, rather than functions.

Suggestions for Future Research

As noted above, the study of children's R&T has been limited. Most studies of preschoolers' play, following Piagetian theory, have been concerned primarily with pretend play while less attention is given to functional and constructive play. Given the co-occurrence of R&T and pretend play and the theoretical bias toward studying pretend play, it may have been the case that the occurrence of R& T during the preschool period has been under-reported.

Future research should re-evaluate the place of R&T during the preschool period by considering its pretend and nonpretend dimensions, as well as the play-fighting and chase dimensions. The distinction between chase and play fighting is important for a number of reasons. First, most young children enjoy chasing and fewer, mostly boys, enjoy play fighting (Smith et al., 1992). Second, chasing and play fighting, at least for older children, are statistically independent of each other and have different consequences: play fighting relates to dominance status while chase does not (Pellegrini, 1995b).

Along similar lines, to what degree do play fighting and chasing lead to aggression during the preschool period? That play fighting leads to aggression for sociometrically rejected children during the primary and middle school periods (Pellegrini, 1988, 1994) suggests that the R&T of aggressive/rejected preschoolers might also lead to aggression.

We also need to know the ways in which physically vigorous behavior is used by boys to establish and maintain social leadership in their peer groups. I hypothesize that R&T would be an important predictor of peer leadership, including dominance, especially as they enter new social institutions, such as a new school. From this view, socially competent children may use a variety of agonistic and cooperative strategies to get their way with peers (Vaughn, 1999). Children, however, should not cheat repeatedly at R&T. Where cheating does occur it should be in the presence of a crowd (who can witness the result of cheating). It may be the case that boys initially cheat at R&T by inflicting pain and thereby gaining public notice of their "toughness," then apologize (under the guise of an "honest mistake") and resume another form of play or social interaction. Alternatively, honest mistakes, rather than cheating, may be "punctuated" by subsequent play signals to reinforce the playful intent (Bekoff, 1995).

Differences in sociometric status also may interact in interesting ways with dominance functions of R&T. It appears that sociometrically rejected children are most likely to "cheat" in R&T, and use R&T in overly aggressive ways: By contrast, popular children may be dominant but do not "cheat" so frequently or obviously in their R&T (Boulton & Smith, 1990; Pellegrini, 1988, 1995a). It may be that children are employing different strategies of seeking power. Popular children may do so by demonstrating leadership in ways which may occasionally involve physical strength; rejected children may do so by using R&T and aggression to demonstrate physical dominance over others. If so, R&T may function as one optional strategy for seeking social dominance.

Social skills learned during peer play might include the abilities to detect "cheating" and to regulate physically vigorous play and R&T. Ability to detect cheating could be measured by children's responses to filmed play and aggressive bouts or by observing their responses to instances of cheating. For instance, in response to cheating, targets should terminate the bout and also turn away from the cheater. Direct observation of aggression would be very difficult to collect given their relative infrequency, thus hypothetical situations may be more practical. Use of video and playback procedures (for both participants and nonparticipants) may be useful here.

Lastly, sex differences are important to consider. Researchers should trace the developmental trajectories of boys and girls from infancy through adolescence, observing directly the extent to which children have opportunities for R&T with parents and for play with peers and large motor toys. These observations should be made in conjunction with measures of children's sensitivity to tactile stimulation, for example, do boys and girls respond differently to R&T initiations?

While differential responses to physical stimulation should be related to sex differences in the preference for physical contact play (Meaney et al., 1985), it also may be the case that there are individual differences, associated with factors such as congenital adrenal hyperplasia (CAH) within each sex. Longitudinal observations should be made of CAH and non-CAH girls' and boys' sensitivity to tactile stimulation as well as their R&T with parents and then peers. Early observations of tactile sensitivity and subsequent play with parents should provide information on the specific and interactive contributions of each factor to children's engagement in R&T with peers.

Testing functional hypotheses with cost-benefit analyses

In this chapter I made functional inferences based on the co-occurrence between physical activity play and beneficial consequences in social organization status and social skills. Play may occur at specific ages, which may be sensitive periods in development, and consequently, play may affect these skills.

A complementary approach to the study of function, cost-benefit analyses, has been applied to animal play with results generally supporting the theory (e.g., Martin & Caro, 1985). From an evolutionary perspective, costs associated with play should have corresponding benefits for the individuals of the species in which the play behavior is typically observed. If this were not the case, play would not have been naturally selected for and maintained across the generations. The animal play data generally support the correspondence between costs of play and accrued benefits (Fagen, 1981).

Costs associated with physical activity play can be expressed in terms of time spent playing, calories, or energy expended, during play, or in terms of survivorship where death or injury occurs as a result of play (Martin & Caro, 1985). High costs should be associated with high benefits and low costs could be associated with either high or low benefits. Benefits for play need not be absolutely high but merely greater than associated costs.

Application of a cost-benefit analysis to children's play would be useful on a number of fronts. First, we should empirically test the wide-held assumption that play during childhood is costly; that is, that play consumes a substantial portion of children's time and energy budgets. Second, a description of the time and energy expenditure on physical activity play across childhood would complement the information provided in this review and that provided by Pellegrini and Smith (1998). Functional hypotheses could be evaluated by relating different measures of cost to measures of motor training, cognitive performance, and social organization status and skills during childhood and into adulthood. A necessary first step, however, involves documenting costs associated with physical activity play.

Costs can be documented by measuring the caloric expenditure during play, relative to resting states, across the day (Pellegrini, Horvat, & Huberty, 1998). Documenting play metabolic rate (PMR) involves taking direct measures of energy expenditure, for example, using heart rate monitors and accelerometers, during children's play and during resting states, or resting metabolic rate (RMR). In this way the cost of play, beyond the cost of maintaining a resting state can be gauged. Additionally, these mechanical recording device should be used to document the average daily metabolic rate (ADMR); estimates of ADMR range from 1.5 to 3.0 times RMR (Martin, 1982). Next, the amount of time during the day spent in play (t_p) should be estimated. This can be accomplished by having children or adults recording in diaries the time spent in play. Alternatively, spot sampling can be utilized, where researchers call the homes of children during the day and ask caregivers to report on children's activities. Martin suggest that .05 is a "realistic" estimate of time spent in play across the day. The caloric cost of play can then be derived from the following formula, suggested by Martin (1982): ECP= t_p(PMR –RMR/ADMR).

This sort of analysis has been applied extensively to animals' play (see Martin & Caro, 1985 for a summary) with the results suggesting that physical activity play accounts for 5%–10% of total energy costs. Given this rather low level of cost, we most reasonably would search for immediate, not deferred, benefits in the domains of physical and social skills.

This method to establish the value, or function, of R&T in childhood and adolescence is rather indirect. A more direct method of assessing function is to simply ask youngsters about the meaning and function of R&T. This can be accomplished with questionnaires which ask them questions about R&T in general, or by showing them filmed R&T and aggressive bouts and then asking them questions about those bouts. Variants of both of these procedures have been used widely.

Smith and colleagues have developed and used questionnaire procedures with children in the UK and Italy (Costabile et al., 1991; Smith et al., 1992). Children were asked a series of questions about their perceptions of R&T and aggression; for example, the frequency with which they engage in R&T, the identity of their partners in R&T, and their reasons for engaging in R&T. These studies, like the behavioral studies discussed above, clearly show that children differentiate R&T from aggression and can give reasons supporting their judgments. Generally, children say they engage in R&T, not surprisingly, because it is fun.

The videotape methodology that has been used takes two forms. The more common variant of this procedure has children viewing videotapes of the R&T and aggression of unfamiliar children. Children clearly differentiate R&T from aggression and can give numerous reasons for doing so (Pellegrini, 1989a,b). However, individual differences also crop up here. Rejected children, compared to popular children, are neither very accurate in their discriminations nor do they give as many reasons for their decisions. This difference may be due to the social information-processing deficit described by Dodge (e.g., Dodge & Frame, 1982). Briefly, this argument suggests that rejected children simply do not process ambiguous, provocative interaction (like R&T) accurately. When they see an ambiguous/provocative event (that can be either playful or aggressive) they tend to attribute aggressive intent to it; thus, R&T is seen as aggression.

An explanation for rejected children's poor performance on these discrimination tasks posits that these children, as general "problem children" in school, take on a negative stance when they are being interviewed. As a way in which to project this negative image to the interviewer they label R&T bouts as aggressive (thus the aggressive bias) and minimally comply to requests to give reasons for their responses (thus the low number of attributes given to differentiate R&T from aggression). In short, their responses may have been a way of expressing defiance/noncompliance to an adult in school.

This purposeful, rather than deficient, explanation is consistent with other research showing that rejected boys are also very purposeful in their choice of R&T partners. For a particularly rough variant of R&T, but not other forms of social interaction, rejected boys (who are also considered to be "tough" by their peers) initiate interaction with boys who are weaker than they; these targets are also considered "victims" by their peers. These R&T bouts typically escalate into aggression at a greater than chance probability (Pellegrini, 1994). Thus, "tough" boys may use R&T as a pretext for victimizing less dominant boys. This conclusion is consistent with the view that some aggressive children (bullies) are very good at inferring what their peers are thinking (Sutton, Smith, & Swettenham, 1999).

Another, less commonly used videotape method involves showing children (and their teachers) aggressive and R&T bouts in which they and their classmates were participants (Smith, Smees, Pellegrini, & Menesini, 1993). We showed films to children (individually, not together) who participated in these films on the same day as the bouts and again two weeks later. We also showed the films to the classmates and teachers of these children at the same intervals. We reckoned that asking children to comment on bouts in which they actually participated would provide more direct insight into the meaning of these events. Further, by asking both teachers and children to comment on the events we could contrast their interpretations of the same events. We originally thought that teachers' interpretations would have been inaccurate and at odds with children's, as found by Schafer and Smith (1996).

We found that participants' agreed with each other on the meaning of the event (i.e., whether it was R&T or aggression); this agreement was stable across a 2-week period. To our surprise, however, nonparticipating peers and teachers' agreed with each other, but their interpretations were significantly different from participants.

Participant status, however, may be a proxy for something else. It may be the case that these participants are also friends and have a different sort of relationship than do nonparticipants. We know, for example, that friends tend to engage in R&T with each other, more than with peers who are not friends (Humphreys & Smith, 1987). We also know that friends have a more accurate understanding of each other than do nonfriends (Hartup, 1996). Thus, in our study it may be that our R&T participants agreed with each because they were friends.

These results have very clear implications for both research and educational policy. Researchers should clearly make provision for the differing interpretations of ambiguous provocation events, like R&T, when they interview children. From a policy perspective, these results suggest that in order to understand certain forms of behavior, like aggression and R&T, teachers and school administrators should interview participants and their friends, and not rely on what bystanders say.

Conclusions

I have outlined the ways in which one form of play, R&T, differs from aggression. As part of this exposition I reviewed evidence showing that R&T and aggression had very different developmental histories and, consequentially, had very different impacts on children's social cognitive status. R&T is quite "normal" and actually a "good" form of play for young children, particularly boys. It may be the case that engaging in R&T affords opportunity to practice encoding and decoding social information. Further, the role alternation characteristic of R&T may be an important component in perspective taking. These skills, learned and practiced in R&T during childhood, are then utilized in other forms of reciprocal social interaction, such as cooperative games, during adolescence.

An interesting developmental shift occurs in adolescence. R&T no longer has positive implications for social cognitive development. During this period, R&T is used primarily in the service of social dominance. Thus, this is an interesting case of a set of behaviors serving different functions for different youngsters (i.e., rejected vs. popular) at different periods (i.e., childhood vs. adolescence).

Another important conclusion to be drawn from this work is that not all children seem to need this specific form of play to develop. R&T is a particularly male phenomenon and many boys seem to use it in the service of their social cognitive development. That girls (and some boys) generally do not engage in R&T but also develop into well-functioning social beings is illustrative. Girls use other strategies to become socially competent. That girls engage in social pretence play at high rates, compared to boys, suggests that this form of play, not R&T, is important for their social cognitive development. In short, not all children must travel the same developmental path to competence. Children often take different paths to the same developmental outcome. This sort of behavioral flexibility seems crucial in light of the fact that human children, as a species, are reared in a variety of conditions. In order to flourish in these different niches, children must adopt different strategies. Play has been proffered as one way in which individuals gain this flexibility (Sutton-Smith, 1997). Thus, educators should beware of advice of one "royal road" to anything: There are numerous roads.

References

Bateson, P. P. G. (1976). Rules and reciprocity in behavioural development. In P. P. G. Bateson &. R. A. Hinde (Eds.), *Growing points in ethology* (pp. 401–421). Cambridge, England: Cambridge University Press.

Bekoff, M. (1995). Play signals as punctuation: The structure of social play in canids. *Behaviour, 132*, 419–429.

Blurton Jones, N. G. (1972). Categories of child interaction. In N. G. Blurton Jones (Ed.), *Ethological studies of child behavior* (pp. 97–129). London: Cambridge University Press.

Boulton, M. J., & Smith, P.K. (1992). The social nature of play-fighting and play-chasing: Mechanisms and strategies underlying cooperation and compromise. In J. H. Barkow, L. Cosmides, & J. Tooby (Eds.), *The adapted mind* (pp. 429–444). New York: Oxford University Press.

Byers, J. A., & Walker, C. (1995). Refining the motor training hypothesis for the evolution of play. *American Naturalist, 146*, 25–40.

Carson, J., Burks, V., & Parke, R. (1993). Parent–child physical play: Determinants and consequences. In K. MacDonald (Ed.), *Parent–child play* (pp. 197–220). Albany, NY: State University of New York Press.

Charlesworth, W. R., & Dzur, C. (1987). Sex comparisons of preschoolers' behavior and resource utilization in group problem solving. *Child Development, 58*, 191–200.

Costabile, A., Smith, P. K., Matheson, L., Aston, J., Hunter, T., & Boulton, M. J. (1991). A cross-national comparison of how children distinguish serious and playful fighting. *Developmental Psychology, 27*, 881–887.

deWaal, F. B.M. (1985). The integration of dominance and social bonding in primates. *Quarterly Review of Biology, 61*, 459–479.

Dodge, K., & Frame, C. (1982). Social cognitive deficits and biases in aggressive boys. *Child Development, 53*, 620–635.

Fagen, R. (1981). *Animal play behavior.* New York: Oxford University Press.

Fagot, B. I. (1994). Peer relations and the development of competence in boys and girls. In C. Leaper (Ed.), *Childhood sex segregation: Causes and consequences* (pp. 53–66). San Francisco: Jossey-Bass.

Fry, D. P. (1987). Differences between play fighting and serious fighting among Zapotec children. *Ethology and Sociobiology, 8*, 285–306.

Garvey, C. (1990). *Play.* Cambridge, MA: Harvard University Press.

Groos, K. (1901). *The play of man.* New York: Appleton.

Hartup, W. W. (1996). The company they keep: Friendships and their developmental significance. *Child Development, 67*, 1–13.

Hinde, R. A. (1980). *Ethology.* London: Fontana.

Humphreys, A. P., & Smith, P. K. (1984). Rough-and-tumble play in preschool and playground. In P. K. Smith (Ed.), *Play in animals and humans* (pp. 241–270). Oxford, England: Blackwell.

Humphreys, A. P., & Smith, P. K. (1987). Rough-and-tumble play, friendship, and dominance in school children: Evidence for continuity and change with age. *Child Development, 58*, 201–212.

Jacklin. C. N., DiPietro, J. A., & Maccoby, E. E. (1984). Sex-typing behavior and sex-typing pressure in child/parent interaction. *Archives of Sexual Behavior, 13*, 413–425.

Konner, M. J. (1972). Aspects of the developmental ethology of a foraging people. In N. Blurton Jones (Ed), *Ethological studies of child behaviour* (pp. 285–304). London: Cambridge University Press.

Maccoby, E. E. (1998). *The two sexes.* Cambridge, MA: Harvard University Press.

MacDonald, K., & Parke, R. (1986). Parent–child physical play. *Sex Roles, 15,* 367–378.

Martin, P. (1982). The energy costs of play: Definition and estimation. *Animal Behaviour, 30,* 294–295.

Martin, P., & Caro, T. (1985). On the function of play and its role in behavioral development. In J. Rosenblatt, C. Beer, M. Bushnel, & P. Slater (Eds.), *Advances in the study of behavior, Vol. 15* (pp. 59–103). New York: Academic Press.

McGrew, W. C. (1972). *An ecological study of children's behavior.* New York: Academic Press.

Meaney, M. J., Stewart, J., & Beatty, W. W. (1985). Sex differences in social play. In J. Rosenblatt, C. Beer, M. C. Bushnel, & P. Slater (Eds.), *Advances in the study of behavior, Vol. 15* (pp. 2–58). New York: Academic Press.

Neill, S. R. StJ. (1976). Aggressive and non-aggressive fighting in twelve-to-thirteen year old pre-adolescent boys. *Journal of Child Psychology and Psychiatry, 17,* 213–220.

Oswald, H., Krappmann, L., Chowduri, F., & Salisch, M. (1987). Gaps and bridges: Interactions between girls and boys in elementary schools. *Sociological Studies of Child Development, 2,* 205–223.

Parke, R. D., Cassidy, J., Burks, V., Carson, J., & Boyum, L. (1992). Familial contributions to peer competence among young children: The role of interactive and affective processes. In R. D. Parke & G. Ladd (Eds.), *Family–peer relationships* (pp. 107–134). Hillsdale, NJ: Erlbaum.

Parke, R. D., & Suomi, S. J. (1981). Adult male infant relationships: Human and nonhuman primate evidence. In K. Immelman, G. W. Barlow, L. Petronovitch, & M. Main (Eds.), *Behavioral development* (pp. 700–725). Cambridge, England: Cambridge University Press.

Pellegrini, A. D. (1988). Elementary school children's rough-and-tumble play and social competence. *Developmental Psychology, 24,* 802–806.

Pellegrini, A. D. (1989a). Elementary school children's rough-and-tumble play. *Early Childhood Research Quarterly, 4,* 245–260.

Pellegrini, A. D. (1989b). What is a category? The case of rough-and-tumble play. *Ethology and Sociobiology, 10,* 331–341.

Pellegrini, A. D. (1993). Boys' rough-and tumble play, social competence and group composition. *British Journal of Developmental Psychology, 11,* 237–248.

Pellegrini, A. D. (1994). The rough play of adolescent boys of differing sociometric status. *International Journal of Behavioral Development, 17,* 525–540.

Pellegrini, A. D. (1995a). *School recess and playground behavior.* Albany, NY: State University of New York Press.

Pellegrini, A. D. (1995b). A longitudinal study of boys' rough-and-tumble play and dominance during early adolescence. *Journal of Applied Developmental Psychology, 16,* 77–93.

Pellegrini, A. D., & Bartini, M. (2001). Dominance in early adolescent boys: Affiliative and aggressive dimensions and possible functions. *Merrill-Palmer Quarterly, 47,* 142-163.

Pellegrini, A. D., Horvat, M., & Huberty , P. D. (1998). The relative cost of children's physical activity play. *Animal Behaviour, 55,* 1053–1061.

Pellegrini, A. D., & Perlmutter, J. C. (1987). A re-examination of the Smilansky–Parten matrix of play behavior. *Journal of Research in Childhood Education, 2,* 89–96.

Pellegrini, A. D., & Smith, P. K. (1998). Physical activity play: The nature and function of a neglected aspect of play. *Child Development, 69,* 577–598.

Piaget, J. (1962). *Play, dreams, and imitation in childhood.* New York: Norton.

Roopnarine, J. L., Hooper, F., Ahmeduzzaman, M., & Pollack, B. (1993). Gentle play partners: Mother–child and father–child play in New Delhi, India. In K. MacDonald (Ed.), *Parent–child play* (pp. 287–304). Albany, NY: State University of New York Press.

Schafer, M., & Smith, P. K. (1996). Teachers' perceptions of play fighting and real fighting in primary school. *Educational Research, 38,* 173–181.

Sluckin, A. M. (1981). *Growing up in the playground: The social development of children*. London: Routledge & Kegan Paul.

Smith, P. K. (1982). Does play matter? Functional and evolutionary aspects of animal and human play. *Behavioral and Brain Sciences, 5*, 139–184.

Smith, P. K., & Boulton, M. J. (1990). Rough-and-tumble play, aggression and dominance: Perception and behavior in children's encounters. *Human Development, 33*, 271–282.

Smith, P. K., & Connolly, K. (1980). *The ecology of preschool behavior*. Cambridge, England: Cambridge University Press.

Smith, P. K., Hunter, T., Carvalho, A., & Costabile, A. (1992). Children's perceptions of play-fighting, play-chasing and real fighting: A cross-national interview study. *Social Development, 1*, 211–229.

Smith, P. K., & Lewis, K. (1985). Rough-and-tumble play, fighting, and chasing in nursery school children. *Ethology and Sociobiology, 6*, 175–181.

Smith, P. K., Smees, R., Pellegrini, A. D., & Menesini, E. (1993, July). Play fighting and serious fighting: Perspectives on their relationship. Paper presented at the biennial meetings of the International Society for the Study of Behavioral Development, Recife, Brazil.

Strayer, F. F. (1980). Social ecology of the preschool peer group. In W. A. Collins (Ed.), *The Minnesota symposia on child development, Vol. 13: Development of cognition, affect, and social relations* (pp. 165–196). Hillsdale, NJ: Erlbaum.

Strayer, F. F., & Noel, J. M. (1986). The prosocial and antisocial functions of aggression: An ethological study of triadic conflict among young children. In C. Zahn-Waxler, E. M. Cummings, & R. Iannotti (Eds.), *Altruism and aggression* (pp. 107–131). New York: Academic Press.

Sutton, J., Smith, P. K., & Swettenham, J. (1999). Socially undesirable need not be incompetent: A response to Crick and Dodge. *Social Development, 8*, 132–134.

Sutton-Smith, B. (1997). *The ambiguity of play*. Cambridge, MA: Harvard University Press.

Symons, D. (1978). *Play and aggression: A study of rhesus monkeys*. New York: Columbia University Press.

Vaughn, B. E. (1999). Power is knowledge (and vice versa): A commentary on "Winning some and losing some: A social relations approach to social dominance in toddlers". *Merrill-Palmer Quarterly, 45*, 215–225.

Vygotsky, L. (1978). *Mind in society*. Cambridge, MA: Harvard University Press.

Waters, E., & Sroufe, L. A. (1983). Social competence as a developmental construct. *Developmental Review, 3*, 79–97.

Part VIII

Helping and Moral Reasoning

Recent research has focused on understanding different dimensions of social competence and their unique contributions to psychosocial adjustment (e.g., Chen, Li, Li., Li, & Liu, 2000). In that vein, how children develop altruistic and moral patterns of social behavior has been the subject of conceptual and empirical scrutiny for several decades. The first two chapters synthesize the literature in these areas and chart directions for promising new developments in our understanding of the nature and implications of altruistic and moral constructs. The third chapter helps us step back and consider how societies are characterized by collections of different social, gender, occupational, political, ethnic, and religious groups. Children glean many of their values that can be translated into more or less altruistic and moral behaviors from these societal institutions that are connected to their immediate settings such as family, neighborhood, and school environments (Bronfenbrenner, 1979).

Joan Grusec, Maayan Davidov, and Leah Lundell focus on prosocial behavior (e.g., helping, sharing, comforting). Although children often engage in behaviors that are beneficial to others at a personal cost, caring actions can also stem from self-serving motivations. Grusec and her colleagues examine the phenomenon of prosocial behavior by first delineating the term from altruism. Prosocial behavior may have a variety of motivations while altruistic behavior only comes at some cost to the donor. Having settled that issue, the authors move on to synthesizing the literature on biological underpinnings of prosocial behavior. Empathetic concern is then elaborated as a motivator for prosocial behavior, followed by a careful review of the literature on how parents can promote the internalization of values with specific attention paid to the interaction of nature and nurture. Peers and siblings also play a role. How prosocial behavior increases with age, as well as sex differences in prosocial behavior are explicated. Grusec and colleagues also delineate how prosocial behavior is enacted depending on children's perceived abilities to help and the nature of the situation (e.g., helping someone who is liked rather than disliked). Their chapter concludes with a review of literature on linkages involving social class and culture in the development of prosocial behavior.

Regarding moral development, Charles Helwig and Elliot Turiel begin their chapter by briefly explaining how several disciplines, including philosophy, anthropology, psychology, and sociology have each brought different perspectives to this area of inquiry. The theories of Piaget and Kohlberg are overviewed and then followed by more recent perspectives that separate the moral domain (issues of harm, fairness, and rights) from the social conventional domain (e.g., organizational rules for dress and etiquette). Research indicates that very young children are able to distinguish these domains, but do so in increasingly complex ways over the course of early and middle childhood. How children's actions are actually influenced by their judgments in these domains has been a fruitful field of study. The authors present convincing evidence that how children approach behavioral situations is related to domains of judgment. Of particular interest is the section on culture and social development. How do moral and social conventions vary across Eastern and Western societies? How do religious beliefs affect moral judgments in different cultural settings? These and other issues concerning how children develop concepts of autonomy, rights, and democracy in the context of culture are addressed in illuminating ways.

The discussion of cultural influences by Helwig and Turiel provides a meaningful transition to the final chapter. Martyn Barrett and Eithne Buchanan-Barrow treat readers to a discussion of children's understanding of society. As noted earlier, the way children operate in society is based, in part, on their understanding of societal rules and conventions. Barrett and Buchanan-Barrow examine the most significant societal institutions that touch children beyond the family. How children come to understand the social organization of schools, economics, social class, politics, law, ethnic groups, and nationalities are carefully explicated from a developmental perspective across the early and middle childhood years. In so doing, the authors draw heavily upon Piagetian perspectives when providing stage-based descriptions of children's understandings of societal phenomenon.

References

Bronfenbrenner, U. (1979). *The ecology of human development.* Cambridge, MA: Harvard University Press.

Chen, X., Li, D., Li, Z., Li., B., & Liu, M. (2000). Sociable and prosocial dimensions of social competence: Common and unique contributions to social, academic, and psychological adjustment. *Developmental Psychology, 36,* 302–314.

23

Prosocial and Helping Behavior

Joan E. Grusec, Maayan Davidov, and Leah Lundell

Most people believe they should not harm others. However, beliefs about the extent to which they should engage in actions that will benefit others, particularly if that action is costly to themselves, are less certain. The ambiguity that surrounds helping others, then, is one reason that its study is so interesting. Presumably, parents want to raise children who are caring and concerned, and who will go out of their way to assist others whenever they can. Moreover, children who help others tend to have positive relationships and interactions with their peers (Eisenberg & Fabes, 1998), and people who were prosocial as children are less likely to be antisocial as adults (Hamalaimen & Pulkiinen, 1995). Balanced against these positive outcomes, however, is the fact that help is not always wanted by potential recipients, as well as the possibility that too much devotion to others can be harmful to the self, for example, excessive concern for others may place children at risk for depression (Zahn-Waxler, Cole, & Barrett, 1991). Moreover, agents of socialization appear to have mixed reactions when children show concern for others. Prosocial behavior is often not praised by parents or teachers (Caplan & Hay, 1989; Grusec, 1991) and parents claim they do not encourage it in young children (Rheingold, 1982). It should be noted, however, that ambivalence about prosocial behavior is more characteristic of Anglo-American cultures where social responsibility is less duty-based than in cultures such as the Hindu Indian, where prosocial concern is deemed to be as important as ensuring the achievement of justice (Miller & Bersoff, 1992).

Not all acts that are beneficial to others, of course, have a personal cost. Children can engage in caring actions for self-serving reasons, including gaining a feeling of mastery over the environment, facilitating social interactions, in hope of praise, or in anticipation of future reciprocity. Even caring behavior that is motivated by feelings of empathic arousal can be seen as self-serving if its goal is reduction of the helper's uncomfortable emotional state. The term "prosocial behavior" is used to deal with the fact that it is often difficult to know exactly which of the diverse motivations underlying helpful actions is operating in a given situation. Thus prosocial behavior is defined as any voluntary, intentional action that produces a positive or beneficial outcome for the recipient regardless of whether that action is costly to the donor, neutral in its impact, or beneficial. In this sense it is distinguished from "altruism" which clearly implies that assistance to others came at some cost to the donor.

Actions included in the category of prosocial behavior have been helping, sharing, consideration, concern, and defending. Thus we know a considerable amount about their development and socialization. Greener and Crick (1999), however, recently have pointed out that these behaviors have been somewhat arbitrarily selected by researchers. They asked children aged 8 to 11 years what boys and girls do when they want to be nice to people. The children's responses fell into categories having little overlap with those usually studied. For them, being nice to others included using humor, being friends (e.g., asking about them), avoiding being mean, including them in the play group, ending a conflict, sharing or caring, hanging around with them, and trusting them (e.g., telling them secrets). The most frequently cited exemplars of being nice were, in order, being friends, inclusion in the group, and sharing/caring. Traditionally studied prosocial behaviors – sharing or caring – were deemed more appropriate for peers of the opposite sex, while group inclusion or relationship-centered activities were emphasized more for peers of the same sex. Clearly then, although sharing and caring are salient to children, the most frequently cited instances of nice behavior are not part of the usual definition of prosocial behavior. The reader should keep this limitation in mind in considering the material discussed in this chapter.

Already noted is the fact that prosocial behaviors may have a variety of motivations. Two have been of primary interest to researchers. Each, although not satisfying fully the criteria for altruism, that is, behavior that is costly, still has to with internally-governed behavior. This focus is a reflection of the fact that developmental psychologists who study socialization, although recognizing that much behavior is controlled by the external environment, have tended to look ultimately for conditions that would promote long-lasting acceptance of standards that occurs even when external reward and punishment contingencies are not operative. The first source of internally-governed motivation has to do with feelings of empathy or sympathy that are generated in response to another person's need state and that may promote attempts to modify that state. The second has to do with adherence to a norm because it seems to have been self-generated. Each of these will be discussed below.

Chapter Overview

The core of this chapter deals with the origins of children's prosocial responding in biology, its relation to empathy, and its promotion through socialization experiences, including the impact of peers and siblings. After a brief discussion of sex differences in prosocial responding and its situational determinants we turn to a consideration of prosocial action in the broader social class and cultural context and what discoveries here mean for a more complete understanding of the topic.

Biological Underpinnings of Prosocial Behavior

Evolutionary theorists have addressed the role of biological factors in the development of prosocial behavior, focusing specifically on altruism, or prosocial behavior involving self-sacrifice. The very notion of altruism seems at odds with traditional evolutionary approaches, which stress survival of the fittest and self-preservation strategies. Nevertheless, contemporary sociobiological theories have tried to account for altruism in evolutionary terms, asserting a distinct survival advantage in helping others.

Several mechanisms have been proposed to explain the evolution of altruism. Wynne-Edwards (1962), for example, suggests that natural selection operates at the group level. For a group to survive, individuals must act in ways that help the group as a whole, even if this limits their personal gain. Other models are based on selection operating at the individual level. For example, Hamilton (1964) proposes that genetic fitness depends not only on the survival of individuals' genes but also on those of their genetic relatives. Kin selection can explain altruism in that acts are selected that have the potential to help those who share the same genes survive, even at the risk of endangering the self, with altruism more likely the closer the relationship between donor and recipient. A third explanatory mechanism is Trivers' (1971) notion of reciprocal altruism whereby individuals help others because of the expectation that this will ultimately benefit and enhance their own survival: What drives altruism is the self-serving belief that the beneficiary of the altruistic act will one day reciprocate a similar act.

Evolutionary perspectives point to the universal potential for prosocial behavior. However, there are also individual differences in the innate capacity for prosocial responding. Studies comparing the concordance patterns of adult monozygotic and dyzygotic twins (e.g., Rushton, Fulker, Neale, Nias, & Eysenck, 1986) indicate that approximately 50% of the variance on scales of altruism, empathy, and nurturance can be attributed to genetic influence. Zahn-Waxler, Robinson, and Emde (1992) have reported evidence for the heritability of prosocial acts and empathic concern at 14 and 20 months, although much less than the 50% obtained in twin studies with adults. One explanation for the increasing hereditary influence with age involves the concept of niche picking, or the tendency to select environments that fit with genetic tendencies. Young children's environments are more likely to be selected for them by adults, but as they grow older, they become increasingly more active in choosing their own.

If the tendency to behave prosocially is inherited, what is it that one inherits? One possibility is biologically based temperamental characteristics that are related to empathy. Thus temperamental differences in emotionality and emotion regulation have been implicated in differential empathic and subsequent prosocial responding in children (see Eisenberg & Fabes, 1998). In general, children who are well regulated and low in impulsivity and, accordingly, who are emotionally positive tend to be more prosocial. The relation between negative emotionality, empathy, and prosocial behavior is more complicated and may depend on the intensity and type of negative emotions (e.g., anger or sadness). Further, emotionality may interact with regulation in different ways to affect the incidence of prosocial responding. For example, the tendency to experience negative emotions like sadness or anxiety may be associated with empathic responding for individuals who are well regulated with respect to their emotions but not for those who become overwhelmed by such emotions (Eisenberg, Fabes, Guthrie, & Reiser, 2000).

Clearly, the capacity for prosocial behavior is founded in biology. But prosocial behavior is also strongly influenced by different socialization experiences and, necessarily, the interaction of these experiences with biological givens. We shall turn to a discussion of these experiences, but first we discuss empathy, one of the sources of internally-governed motivation described above, and a source that has received detailed attention.

Empathy and Prosocial Behavior

Empathic concern is an important motivator of prosocial behavior. Both empathy – responding to another's distress with a similar emotion – and sympathy – responding to another's distress with feelings of sadness or concern – are vicarious affective responses that can be experienced in the face of another person's emotion or situation. These uncomfortable responses lead individuals to take even costly action in order to alleviate the other person's need. Although empathy and sympathy are not identical, researchers generally have not distinguished between them.

Early studies examining empathy and prosocial behavior in children failed to show a consistent relationship between the two (Underwood & Moore, 1982). Recent methodological and conceptual advances, however, have enabled researchers to demonstrate a linkage. With respect to methodological advances, early measures involved children reporting their own feelings in response to stories depicting a child experiencing distress (e.g., Feshbach & Roe, 1968). These stories, however, were probably too short to evoke sufficient affect in the child, and the procedure may have created strong demand characteristics to respond in a socially desirable manner. When physiological arousal and facial expression are used to infer empathy, however, the relation with prosocial behavior becomes more compelling (Eisenberg & Miller, 1987). A conceptual advance that led to clearer understanding of the relation between empathy and prosocial behavior involves the distinction between different kinds of vicarious emotional responses. In particular, Batson and his colleagues (see Batson, 1991) have suggested that empathy and sympathy need to be differentiated from personal distress. The former are other-focused emotional reactions whereas the latter is a self-focused response involving such negative emotions as anxiety and feelings of disturbance. While both can lead to prosocial actions, empathy is more likely to do so, given that the primary goal of the individual experiencing it is to increase the other's welfare. In contrast, in the case of personal distress, the individual's primary goal is to relieve his or her own discomfort. In the latter case prosocial behavior occurs only if it is the most cost-effective way of reducing the individual's own distress. If other less costly means exist, for example, escaping from the distress-provoking situation, those alternatives will be preferred and prosocial behavior will not occur.

Considerable research with adults has supported the importance of this distinction (Batson, 1991). Researchers have also obtained similar findings with children (see Eisenberg & Fabes, 1998). In these studies, children typically watch a short film depicting other individuals in a state of distress or need, and their emotional reactions to the film are measured. To distinguish empathy from personal distress children are asked to indicate how they feel by rating adjectives, pointing at line drawings depicting feelings, or simply verbalizing how they feel. Facial expression during the film is also used to make the distinction, with expressions of anxiety and distress indicating personal distress and concerned attention indicating empathy. As well, physiological indices are employed, with heart rate deceleration a marker of other-oriented sympathetic responding and heart rate acceleration and skin conductance reactivity corresponding to a self-focused distress reaction. Following assessment of vicarious emotional reactions, children are given the opportunity to help others at some cost to themselves by, for example, giving up their recess time in the near future to help gather homework materials for injured children, or putting crayons into small boxes for hospitalized children instead of playing with attractive toys. The situation is also structured so that they have the opportunity to escape the emotion-inducing situation, and they are made aware of the fact that no one will know if they have behaved prosocially because the opportunity to do so occurs in private. Overall, a consistent pattern of results has emerged from these studies. In general, the more empathy and sympathy children exhibit in reaction to another's distress, as indicated by self-report and facial and physiological indices, the more they tend to behave prosocially by helping others in need. In contrast, when children respond to another's distress by demonstrating self-focused personal distress, they tend to exhibit less prosocial behavior.

Determinants of empathy and personal distress

Several child characteristics affect emotional responsiveness to the distress of others. One is the ability to take the perspective of others: Chalmers and Townsend (1990), for example, have demonstrated that training in perspective taking increased the self-reported empathy level of maladjusted girls. Temperament, as noted earlier, also plays a role in empathic responding. Children prone to intense and frequent negative emotions tend to exhibit less sympathy and often more personal distress. As well as children who can effectively regulate emotional reactions exhibit more sympathetic responding and sometimes less personal distress than those who have more difficulty with self-regulation (see Eisenberg, Wentzel, & Harris, 1998). Thus it appears that the ability to maintain an optimal level of arousal in response to another's distress is conducive to high empathy and relatively low personal distress, whereas becoming overly aroused leads to high personal distress and low empathy. Finally, the effects of parental characteristics and childrearing practices have been linked to empathic responding. Mothers who are empathic and high on perspective taking and who respond sensitively to their children's needs for comfort have children who are highly empathic (e.g., Eisenberg et al., 1992; Tromsdorff, 1991). Indeed, these maternal characteristics are the hallmark of secure mother–child attachment, with secure attachment associated with greater empathic responding to peers (Kestenbaum, Farber, & Sroufe, 1989) and with more sympathy and fewer distress reactions in response to mothers' enactments of negative emotions (Denham, 1994). With respect to childrearing practices, the use of induction or directing children to consider how their behavior has affected others has also been linked to more child empathy and, consequently, more prosocial behavior (Krevans & Gibbs, 1996).

Of course, the various factors described above may be related to or interact with, one another, although research to date has not focused on such relations. Some possibilities with respect to such interaction, for example, temperament and experience, are discussed in the following section.

Socializing Prosocial Behavior

Promoting internalization of values

Socialization researchers have tried to identify actions by agents of socialization (primarily parents) that will encourage children to adopt a caring orientation that seems to come from within, to be self-generated, or is internalized. Grusec and Goodnow (1994) have suggested that effective internalization of values involves two steps: 1) children's accurate perception of the socialization agent's (usually the parent's) message and 2) acceptance of that message. The first step is accomplished through clear, frequent, and consistent expression of a value in a way that matches the cognitive capacity of the child. The second step is facilitated by three sets of variables. The first set involves the child seeing a value as acceptable or appropriate, that is, parental demands seem reasonable, arguments made to support a position are believable, and the intervention is matched appropriately to the child's temperament and mood state. Parents whose children tend to become aroused in response to other people's expressed emotion, for example, might want to favor arguments for prosocial behavior that focus on the distress of others (cf. Kochanska, 1997a, who has demonstrated an interaction between children's temperament and their responsiveness to reasoning). Grusec, Dix, and Mills (1983) have reported that Anglo-European parents rarely punish children for a failure to share or help: Punishment in this context, then, should be viewed by the child as unfair and would therefore be less likely to promote internalization. The second set of variables affecting acceptance has to do with motivation to accept the message. Facilitating this are such variables as empathic arousal, desire to please the parent, and minimal threats to autonomy. Finally, the child must feel that the action is guided by a norm that has been self-generated.

Relationship variables.   How do parents achieve acceptance of the value of concern for others? One way involves the parent–child relationship. There are at least three aspects of the relationship that have been considered by researchers. First, parents who are warm, that is, who nurture their children and provide noncontingent approval have children who display increased prosocial behavior, although the relation is not always evident (Eisenberg & Fabes, 1998), possibly under conditions where the child has not accurately perceived the prosocial value. Presumably, warm parents increase their children's self-esteem and thereby make them more inclined to assist others (Hoffman, 1970). As well, children may wish to please parents who are nurturant and loving by adopting their values. Second, children who are securely attached have parents who are protective and sensitive to their distress and emotional needs. Not surprisingly, then, they have been shown to be more sympathetic as preschoolers (Waters, Hay, & Richters, 1986) and to display more concern for others at the age of 5 years (Kestenbaum, Farber, & Sroufe, 1989). Finally, parents who are responsive to the reasonable demands and requests of their children have children who are, in turn, more compliant to the requests of their parents (Parpal & Maccoby, 1985) and who score higher on tests of internalization of parental values (Kochanska, 1997b). In this atmosphere of mutual reciprocity child and parent develop shared goals, with the child positively oriented to compliance with the parent's demands.

Parenting practices: Reasoning, modeling, character attributions, and routines.   A second set of socialization variables moves beyond features of the relationship and focuses on parenting practices. Hoffman (1970), for example, argued for the superiority of reasoning, particularly other-oriented reasoning, in promoting prosocial behavior: Reasoning avoids the hostility and oppositional behavior aroused by strong punitive or power assertive interventions used alone (Hart, DeWolf, Wozniak & Burts, 1992), and it promotes the child's empathic capacity. As noted earlier, Krevans and Gibbs (1996) have reported that reasoning that orients children to the impact of their actions on others is associated with prosocial behavior, with empathy playing a mediating role. Other parenting practices include modeling of prosocial actions. Thus children exposed to adults (parents and strangers) who display prosocial behavior are more inclined to be prosocial themselves (Grusec & Lytton, 1988). Character attributions, that is, applying trait labels, as in telling children that they are kind and helpful people, are also effective (Grusec & Redler, 1980). Such labeling (which is effective for 7–8 year olds, but not for 5–6 year olds) presumably leads children to find explanations for their positive behavior in themselves rather than in features of the external environment, and thereby to attribute their actions to a self-generated value. Everyday routines provide another source of internalized values: When socialization agents involve children in activities as a part of the natural course of everyday living strong habits develop, with no feeling of external coercion. Accordingly, in an attempt to evaluate the effectiveness of household work as a way of teaching children a sense of social responsibility, Grusec, Goodnow, and Cohen (1997) found that children who routinely did work around the house that involved benefits to other family members showed greater evidence of general concern for others and prosocial action than those who worked only in response to parental request or who helped with tasks that were of benefit only to themselves. Thus it seems that practice in assisting others that has become routinized may lead to habits of engaging in helpfulness toward others.

Parenting style.   Parenting style also has a role to play in the development of prosocial behavior. Children of parents who are authoritative, that is, firmly controlling but sensitive and responsive to their children's needs, are more prosocial in the home (e.g., Robinson, Zahn-Waxler, & Emde, 1994), at school (e.g., Krevans & Gibbs, 1996), and in a laboratory setting (e.g., Eisenberg, Fabes, & Murphy, 1996). In a recent longitudinal study (Hastings, Zahn-Waxler, Robinson, Usher, & Bridges, 2000) mothers' authoritativeness did not predict children's prosocial behavior at the time of its measurement, but did predict it 2 years later, both at home and at school, even when the child's initial level of concern for others was held constant. Thus the suggestion that authoritative parenting causes prosocial action, rather than the reverse, is further strengthened.

Peers and siblings as socializers

The reciprocal and relatively egalitarian nature of peer and sibling relationships enables, if not compels, the consideration of another's thoughts and feelings. Accordingly, peers and siblings provide, in addition to parents, a source of influence on prosocial development as children learn to respond emotionally to and help each other. Interactions among children provide prosocial opportunities that differ in nature from those that arise from adult–child interactions (Zahn-Waxler, Ianotti, & Chapman, 1982). For example, children are more likely to witness another child (vs. an adult) in distress because a child's distress is often more salient, and thus they will have more opportunities to practice comforting behaviors with peers. Also, children are often in situations that dictate mutual sharing, for example, of toys. Finally, in interactions with adults, children are more likely to be the recipients of aid whereas, in interactions with children, they are equally likely to give and to receive aid. Further, the motivations underlying children's prosocial behavior may differ depending on whether they are interacting with children or adults. For example, young children cite more authority- or punishment-related reasons for complying with an adult's requests, whereas they are more likely to comply with a peer's requests for relational reasons such as friendship (Eisenberg, Lundy, Shell, & Roth, 1985). Consequently, the peer context may be particularly conducive to the learning of other-oriented rather than compliance-oriented prosocial responding.

Experiences with siblings are important in promoting prosocial behavior in part because of differences in age between siblings. Older siblings have more opportunities to practice prosocial behaviors and younger siblings can learn from the behaviors of their older siblings (Brody, Stoneman, MacKinnon, & MacKinnon, 1985; Dunn & Munn, 1986). Whiting and Whiting (1973) have noted the greater frequency of prosocial behavior in cultures where children are assigned the responsibility of taking care of infants. Perhaps, by taking care of younger infants, children learn greater sensitivity to what others are feeling and, further, how to respond to those needs. As well, sibling caregiving is positively related to mature cognitive and emotional perspective-taking skills (Garner, Jones, & Palmer, 1994; Stewart & Marvin, 1984), which contribute to effective and appropriate responding to the distress and needs of younger children. Although the direction of the relationship is unclear (that is, does caregiving promote perspective taking or are children with these skills more likely to care for younger children?) it is plausible that sibling caregiving is an important contributor to the development of perspective taking and thus prosocial responding. The importance of age heterogeneity is further emphasized in Bizman, Yinon, Mivtzari, and Shavit's (1978) finding that children in age-heterogeneous kindergartens display more prosocial behaviors than those in age-homogeneous kindergartens. Age-homogeneous kindergartens, in contrast, lead to more competitive environments in which children might not be as inclined to help each other.

The Development of Prosocial Behavior

Even toddlers are capable of substantial displays of concern for others (Zahn-Waxler, Radke-Yarrow, Wagner, & Chapman, 1992). Indeed, the precursors of empathic responding appear midway through the first year of life as babies cry when they hear others cry – a primitive form of empathy. During the second year of life, as they acquire a concept of person permanence, perceptual role-taking abilities, and a sense of personal identity, young children begin to try to comfort both peers and adults who appear upset (Hay, 1979) and forms of cooperation such as attempts to help with household work emerge (Rheingold, 1982). At this time children also begin to display the precursors of conscience or internalization, with a developing awareness of rules and standards (Kagan, 1981) and an increasing capacity to regulate their own behavior (Kopp, 1982).

A meta-analysis reported by Eisenberg and Fabes (1998) found that, overall, prosocial behavior increases in each age period (infancy, preschool, childhood, and adolescence), although the magnitude of effect sizes depends on a variety of variables including the type of prosocial behavior under investigation, method of data collection, and target of behavior. Nevertheless, although the capacity for prosocial responding may well increase with age, it is clear that children also need to learn a great deal about issues around the appropriateness of its expression. There is a large social psychological literature indicating that help is not always appropriate under all circumstances (e.g., Fisher, Nadler, & Witcher-Alagna, 1982): It threatens the recipient's self-esteem, induces internal attributions for failure (Gross, Wallston, & Piliavin, 1979), and leads to feelings of indebtedness (Greenberg & Shapiro, 1971). Help given to strangers is particularly likely to raise issues of indebtedness and concern about repayment, whereas that given to family members is not (Clark, 1983). These complexities, along with the need not to engage in too much self-sacrifice, provide a challenging learning experience that has yet to receive a great deal of attention in the developmental literature.

Sex Differences in Prosocial Behavior

Although girls are commonly believed to be more prosocial than boys the evidence is in fact equivocal (Radke-Yarrow, Zahn-Waxler, & Chapman, 1983). Eisenberg and Fabes (1998) describe a meta-analysis that found modest sex differences favoring girls. However, these differences appeared to depend on the type of prosocial behavior studied, the methodology employed, and the target of behavior. For example, girls were more likely to be kind or considerate, but not more inclined to share, comfort, or help. Also, girls were more likely to be prosocial when the measure consisted of self or other reports as opposed to direct observation, possibly a reflection of the stereotypes individuals have about how boys and girls should behave rather than reflecting how they actually do behave. Finally, sex differences in favor of girls were more likely when prosocial behavior was directed toward an adult than toward another child, perhaps an indication of greater compliance with adults on the part of girls than boys. Fabes and Eisenberg also reviewed sex differences in empathy and found that girls tended to be more empathic than boys. However, once again, these differences were more pronounced in self-report studies than in observational studies, not appearing when physiological and other, more subtle, measures of empathy were employed.

Some sex differences, however, may be more than artifacts of measurement. Grusec (1987), for example, found that both mothers and fathers rated acts of self-sacrifice, such as donating money to starving children, as more important for girls than boys as well as rated themselves as more pleased when their daughters, rather than their sons, engaged in such actions. Parents also reported that they were more likely to praise girls for self-sacrifice and to criticize or discourage boys for the same actions. These findings support the possibility of differential socialization pressures for boys and girls at least in some areas of prosocial behavior.

Situational Determinants of Prosocial Behavior

Prosocial behavior also depends on a number of characteristics of the helping context. One of these is perceived ability to help. Peterson (1983) found that children whose level of competence was enhanced by training in required helping skills and who were assigned specific responsibility for helping responded by helping more. This finding is complemented by Midlarsky and Hannah's (1985) report that young children, when asked why they had not helped in an emergency situation, reported that they were not sure what to do and feared disapproval. In contrast, adolescents' reasons for not helping reflected concern that the recipient might feel embarrassed or hurt. Related to competence is having an understanding of the need to help. For example, Pearl (1985) found that 4 year olds were more inclined to help in problem situations when both the distress level of the recipient and the cause of distress were made explicit, whereas helping among the older children did not depend on the explicitness of the cues. Thus young children need unambiguous cues that the situation requires intervention and that they have the ability to intervene in ways relevant to the cause of the distress. Children are also more likely to help those who are important in their lives and who they like (e.g., Costin & Jones, 1992), those who are younger and therefore more dependent (Midlarsky & Hannah, 1985), and those they believe do not have control over their own misfortune (Barnett & McMinimy, 1988).

A situational determinant of helping that has received considerable attention is the actor's temporary mood state. Being in a good mood seems to foster prosocial responding in children of all ages, as well as adults (Cialdini, Kenrick, & Baumann, 1982; Isen, 1970; Moore, Underwood, & Rosenhan, 1973). Many explanations have been proposed for this relationship but each to some extent implicates priming processes. A good mood increases the likelihood that other positive thoughts and associations will be generated in response to subsequent events. As a result, individuals in a good mood will view a prosocial opportunity more favorably than those in a neutral or negative mood and will be more inclined to offer assistance (Carlson, Charlin, & Miller, 1988). Findings with respect to negative moods and prosocial behavior are not as consistent and may depend on the age of the helper, with negative moods inhibiting helping in younger children (e.g., Moore et al., 1973) but promoting it in older children (Cialdini et al., 1982). Cialdini et al. suggested that this developmental change results from increasing experiences with adult approval for prosocial behavior which leads these acts to be experienced as secondarily reinforcing. Thus their performance becomes a source of self-gratification and thereby capable of producing a self-generated improvement in mood that can be used to relieve states of sadness. Young children, without this kind of experience, cannot use prosocial action as a way of producing a positive mood. Alternatively, Rosenhan (e.g., Rosenhan, Salovey, Karylowski, & Hargis, 1981) has argued that negative mood enhances helping when the focus of the negative mood is on another person but inhibits it when attention is on the self. He suggests older children and adults have learned to focus their sad thoughts on others which, in turn, arouses empathy and prosocial action. Younger children, on the other hand, may be more inclined to focus sad thoughts on themselves, leading them to be more self-preoccupied and thus less likely to help others.

Prosocial Behavior in its Social Context

Already noted is the fact that most of the research on prosocial development has been conducted in a middle-class, Anglo-European context. In this final section we turn to what is known about it in other social class and cultural contexts. Such attention broadens knowledge of the different cultural manifestations of prosocial action. As well, it allows revision and expansion of the ways it can be conceived of in the middle-class, Anglo-European context about which most is known and from where most of our theory has come.

Social class differences

Studies of social class differences in prosocial behavior have provided mixed findings. Some find that children from lower socioeconomic backgrounds are more prosocial than those from higher socioeconomic backgrounds. Others find they are less prosocial, and yet others that there are no differences (see Eisenberg & Fabes, 1998). The answer to this complexity no doubt lies, as it seems to with other similar complexities in the area, in a consideration of type of prosocial behavior under examination and the processes by which each is socialized, rather than in children's overall prosocial inclinations. For example, children growing up in different classes have different opportunities to help and act prosocially. Thus Call, Mortimer, and Shanahan (1995) found that adolescents from lower income families reported spending more time helping with household chores and taking care of other family members compared to adolescents from higher income families (where such tasks may be done in large part by hired help). In contrast, adolescents from higher income families reported more opportunity to help others in their job setting than did adolescents from lower income families, perhaps due to differences in their job environments or in their attitudes towards their job.

Children are also exposed to different social norms as a function of social class. Class-linked factors such as parents' occupation and sharing and helping arrangements within the family likely convey different norms regarding prosocial behavior, which may in turn be reflected in children's behavior with others. For example, middle-class children shared more candies with peers when they thought their identity would be known to the recipient than in an anonymous condition, while lower-class children either did the opposite or made no differentiation (Dreman & Greenbaum, 1973; Gupta, 1982). This suggests that middle-class children rely more on a norm of social exchange, as opposed to lower class children's greater reliance on norms of communal sharing and mutual aid, characteristics which probably stem from their different experiences at home and in the community.

Cultural differences

The most systematic examination of cultural differences in prosocial behavior has been undertaken by Whiting and Whiting (1973, 1975), whose work we have already mentioned. Observing children between 3 and 11 years of age in six different countries, Whiting and Whiting found that those from Kenya, Mexico, and the Philippines displayed more nurturant behavior (e.g., offering help or support and making responsible suggestions to others) than did those from Okinawa, India, or the United States. The factor that most strongly accounted for these differences in prosocial behavior was assignment of chores to children, particularly the care of infants. Responsibility for chores also explained some of the differences in prosocial behavior observed among the children within each culture. These findings emphasize – now in a cross-cultural context – the importance of everyday routines or practice in the promotion of concern for others (see above). The findings also underline how different aspects of the socioeconomic organization of a culture can limit or expand the opportunities its children have to acquire particular social behaviors. Specifically, the more prosocial cultures were also those in which conditions were such that women's overall workload and contribution to the family's economy were greater, and hence women delegated more responsibility to their children in these cultures (thus providing them with more opportunities to practice prosocial behavior). Interestingly, Whiting and Whiting also studied friendly sociable behavior which, as noted earlier, is closer to the way children rather than researchers have defined prosocial behavior. Here the pattern of relations was different from that found for nurturant behavior, with American children more friendly and Kenyan children less friendly, and with cultures having an independent nuclear family as the modal household structure associated with greater sociability. Thus another feature of cultural organization is highlighted as having an impact on one form or aspect of concern for others.

Socioeconomic organization is frequently associated with differential emphasis of values, and we turn now to a consideration of such emphasis and its impact on differences in prosocial action across cultures.

Cultural values

Cultures that value prosocial behavior, such as those where the help of family members is essential for the family's subsistence, would be expected, of course, to instill higher levels of prosocial tendencies in their children. In other cultures, however, prosocial behavior may contradict other values that receive even greater emphasis. For example, cultures that place great value on personal success may encourage self-enhancing tendencies such as competitiveness and the pursuit of personal academic achievement, because such behaviors can enhance the child's likelihood of future social success. Such a focus on self-enhancement is at least somewhat inconsistent with a focus on helping others (Schwartz, 1994). However, as we shall argue below, the most important difference between cultures in this respect may not lie in the degree to which they each value prosocial behavior, but rather in how they each define it and socialize it.

Individualism and collectivism.   A value dimension that has attracted much research interest is that of individualism versus collectivism. In individualist cultures individuals are seen as independent and autonomous, and their actions as determined by their own inner motivations and dispositions. In collectivist cultures individuals are seen as part of a closely knit social network in which they are interconnected entities, and where their identity is derived from participation in the group and fulfillment of social roles. Individualist cultures (loosely linked to Western countries) value assertion, self-expression, and self-actualization. Collectivist cultures (loosely linked to Asian, African, and Latin American countries) value propriety, fitting in, and harmonious relationships with others (Markus & Kitayama, 1991).

Given this emphasis on harmony and relatedness in collectivist cultures, some researchers have hypothesized that children reared in those cultures would show less aggression and more prosocial behavior compared to children reared in individualist cultures. In general, research has supported the contention regarding aggression (Zahn-Waxler, Friedman, Cole, Mizuta, & Hiruma, 1996). However, the evidence to date has been less persuasive with respect to predictions about prosocial behavior. Although Stevenson (1991) reported greater sharing, comforting, and helping among kindergartners in Japan and Taiwan compared to the United States, the differences were small, and the incidence of prosocial behavior was high in all three cultures. Trommsdorff (1995) found equal levels of empathy and prosocial behavior among Japanese and German 5-year-old girls in their responses to a distressed adult and Zahn-Waxler et al., (1996) report that American preschoolers enacted the same amount of, and in some contexts more, prosocial themes in response to hypothetical social dilemmas compared to Japanese preschoolers. Part of the difficulty here may be that there is heterogeneity of values in any culture, which is possibly greater in some than others. Thus, while Japan may be more likely to be cited as a collectivist culture, it may not be a strong exemplar of the construct.

It is also possible that cultural values reveal themselves not in total amount of prosocial behavior but in other of its aspects, such as which type of prosocial behavior is most valued. Members of individualist cultures seem to evaluate unsolicited or spontaneous prosocial behavior more highly than that which is reciprocal or solicited, while individuals with a collectivist orientation (Hindus and Israelis of Middle-Eastern descent) think equally highly of, or even prefer, reciprocal or solicited prosocial behavior (Jacobsen, 1983; Miller & Bersoff, 1994). These studies suggest cultural differences, then, in conceptions of what constitutes desirable prosocial behavior, with reciprocity and responsiveness to other's needs judged more positively in a culture more strongly characterized by interdependence and compliance with social roles than one more strongly characterized by autonomy and feelings of self-generation.

Different conceptions of what constitutes desirable prosocial behavior are also reflected in cultural differences in socialization. Rather than focusing on techniques that facilitate feelings of self-generation, cultures favoring interdependence and reciprocity emphasize social structure and one's role in it (Schwartz, 1994). Thus authoritative parenting is relatively uncommon among Japanese mothers, with parenting more likely to be either indulgent or strict (Power, Kobayashi-Winata, & Kelly, 1992). Similarly, Stevenson (1991) reports that Japanese and Chinese parents promote interdependence by forming strong affectional bonds with their young children, and making firm demands for adherence to social norms when they grow older. Reliance on the formation of strong parent–child bonds and later strong demands for prosocial behavior may be a better approach for teaching reciprocity and responsiveness than is an approach that emphasizes autonomy and choice.

Different conceptions of prosocial behavior and differences in socialization are reflected in the nature of attributions made for prosocial behavior. Miller (1984) found that although 8- and 11-year-old American and Hindu children do not differ in the kinds of explanations they provide for prosocial (as well as deviant) acts, by the time they reach adulthood Americans make more references to the actor's dispositions (e.g. personality traits) and fewer references to the context (e.g. the actor's social role) compared to Hindu individuals. Again, this suggests that Americans learn to view prosocial behaviors as emanating from inner motives and dispositions, whereas Hindus are socialized to view prosocial behavior as stemming from the social context. There is no reason to think that attributions to personality traits are more likely to promote positive behavior than are attributions to social role demands. Indeed, each should probably be seen as fitting with the particular context in which it occurs. And, as noted above, different socialization practices are required in order to achieve the particular outcome stressed by the culture. One is left to wonder, however, given the increasing inclusion in Western culture of so many people from cultures where autonomy is not so central, whether current emphases on autonomy and self-generation may need to be replaced. Thus, the growing heterogeneity of Western culture challenges researchers to rethink some very basic theoretical issues in the study of socialization.

Conclusion

In this survey we have attempted to demonstrate that, although much is known about children's prosocial behavior, much remains to be learned. It is evident that the multifaceted nature of the construct has led to confusions and vagueness that can only be resolved with greater care in identification of the kind of prosocial action under consideration. As well, increasing information about the meaning and the antecedents of prosocial behavior in a variety of cultural contexts requires questioning of some of the most basic concepts of socialization theory. We have come a considerable distance in our understanding of concern for others, but we still have some distance to go.

References

Barnett, M. A., & McMinimy, V. (1988). Influence of the reason for other's affect on preschoolers' empathy response. *Journal of Genetic Psychology, 149*, 153–162.

Batson, C. D. (1991). *The altruism question: Towards a social-psychological answer.* Hillsdale, NJ: Erlbaum.

Bizman, A., Yinon, Y., Mivtzari, E., & Shavit, R. (1978). Effects of the age structure of the kindergarten on altruistic behavior. *Journal of School Psychology, 16*, 154–160.

Brody, G. H., Stoneman, Z., MacKinnon, C. E., & MacKinnon, R. (1985). Role relationships and behavior between preschool-aged and school-aged sibling pairs. *Developmental Psychology, 21*, 124–129.

Call, K. T., Mortimer, J. T., & Shanahan, M. J. (1995). Helpfulness and the development of competence in adolescence. *Child Development, 66*, 129–138.

Caplan, M. Z., & Hay, D. (1989). Preschoolers' responses to peers' distress and beliefs about bystander intervention. *Journal of Child Psychology and Psychiatry, 30*, 231–242.

Carlson, M., Charlin, V., & Miller, N. (1988). Positive mood and helping behavior: A test of six hypotheses. *Journal of Personality and Social Psychology, 55*, 211–229.

Chalmers, J. B., & Townsend, M. A. R. (1990). The effect of training in social perspective taking on socially maladjusted girls. *Child Development, 61*, 178–190.

Cialdini, R. B., Kenrick, D. T., & Baumann, D. J. (1982). Effects of mood on prosocial behavior in children and adults. In N. Eisenberg (Ed.), *The development of prosocial behavior* (pp. 339–359). New York: Academic Press.

Clark, M. S. (1983). Some implications of close social bonds for help seeking. In B. M. DePaulo, A. Nadler, & J. D. Fisher (Eds.), *New directions in helping: Vol. 2. Help seeking* (pp. 205–233). New York: Academic Press.

Costin, S. E., & Jones, D. C. (1992). Friendship as a facilitator of emotional responsiveness and prosocial interventions among young children. *Developmental Psychology, 28*, 941–947.

Denham, S. A. (1994). Mother–child emotional communication and preschoolers' security of attachment and dependency. *Journal of Genetic Psychology, 155*, 119–121.

Dreman, S. B., & Greenbaum, C. W. (1973). Altruism or reciprocity: Sharing behavior in Israeli kindergarten children. *Child Development, 44*, 61–68.

Dunn, J., & Munn, P. (1986). Siblings and the development of prosocial behavior. *International Journal of Behavior Development, 9*, 265–284.

Eisenberg, N., & Fabes, R. A. (1998). Prosocial development. In. W. Damon (Series Ed.) & N. Eisenberg (Vol. Ed.), *Handbook of child psychology, vol. 3: Social, emotional, and personality development* (5th ed., pp. 701–778). New York: Wiley.

Eisenberg, N., Fabes, R. A., Carlo, G., Troyer, D., Speer, A. L., Karbon, M., & Switzer, G. (1992). The relations of maternal practices and characteristics to children's vicarious emotional responsiveness. *Child Development, 63*, 583–602.

Eisenberg, N., Fabes, R. A., Guthrie, I .K., & Reiser, M. (2000). Dispositional emotionality and regulation: Their role in predicting quality of social functioning. *Journal of Personality and Social Psychology, 78*, 136–157.

Eisenberg, N., Fabes, R. A., & Murphy, B. C. (1996). Parents' reactions to children's negative emotions: Relations to children's social competence and comforting behavior. *Child Development, 67*, 2227–2247.

Eisenberg, N., Lundy, N., Shell, R., & Roth, K. (1985). Children's justifications for their adult and peer-direct compliant (prosocial and nonprosocial) behaviors. *Developmental Psychology, 21*, 325–331.

Eisenberg, N., & Miller, P. (1987). The relation of empathy to prosocial and related behaviors. *Psychological Bulletin, 101*, 91–119.

Eisenberg, N., Wentzel, M., & Harris, J. D. (1998). The role of emotionality and regulation in empathy-related responding. *School Psychology Review, 27*, 506–521.

Feshbach, N. D., & Roe, K. (1968). Empathy in six- and seven-year-olds. *Child Development, 39*, 133–145.

Fischer, J. D., Nadler, A., & Witcher-Alagna, S. (1982). Recipient reactions to aid. *Psychological Bulletin, 91*, 27–54.

Garner, P. W., Jones, D. C., & Palmer, D. J. (1994). Social cognitive correlates of preschool children's sibling caregiving behavior. *Developmental Psychology, 30*, 905–911.

Greenberg, M. S., & Shapiro, S.P. (1971). Indebtedness: An adverse aspect of asking for and receiving help. *Sociometry, 34*, 290–301.

Greener, S., & Crick, N. (1999). Normative beliefs about prosocial behavior in middle childhood: What does it mean to be nice? *Social Development, 8*, 350–363.

Gross, A. E., Wallston, B. S., & Piliavin, I. M. (1979). Reactance, attribution, equity, and the help recipient. *Journal of Applied Social Psychology, 9*, 297–313.

Grusec, J. E. (1987). The socialization of self-sacrifice in boys and girls. In L. Shamgar-Handelman & R. Palomba (Eds.), *Alternative patterns of family life in modern societies* (pp. 265–274). Rome: Instituto di Recherche Sulla Popolazione.

Grusec, J. E. (1991). Socializing concern for others in the home. *Developmental Psychology, 27*, 338–342.

Grusec, J. E., Dix, T., & Mills, R. (1982). The effects of type, severity and victim of children's transgressions on maternal discipline. *Canadian Journal of Behavioural Science, 14*, 276–289.

Grusec, J. E., & Goodnow, J. J. (1994). Impact of parental discipline methods on the child's internalization of values: A reconceptualization of current points of view. *Developmental Psychology, 30*, 4–19.

Grusec, J. E., Goodnow, J. J., & Cohen, L. (1997) Household work and the development of children's concern for others. *Developmental Psychology, 32*, 999–1007.

Grusec, J. E., & Lytton, H. (1988). *Social development: History, theory, and research*. New York: Springer-Verlag.

Grusec, J. E., & Redler, E. (1980). Attribution, reinforcement, and altruism: A developmental analysis. *Developmental Psychology, 16*, 525–534.

Gupta, P. (1982). Altruism or reciprocity: Sharing behavior in Hindu kindergarten children. *Psychological Studies, 27*, 68-73.

Hamalaimen, M., & Pulkiinen, L. (1995). Aggressive and non-prosocial behavior as precursors of criminality. *Studies on Crime and Crime Prevention, 4*, 6–21.

Hamilton, W. D. (1964). The genetic evolution of social behavior. *Journal of Theoretical Biology, 7*, 1–52.

Hart, C. H., DeWolf, M. D., Wozniak, P., & Burts, D. C. (1992). Maternal and paternal disciplinary styles: Relations with preschoolers' playground behavioral orientations and peer status. *Child Development, 63*, 879–892.

Hastings, P. D., Zahn-Waxler, C., Robinson, J., Usher, B., & Bridges, D. (2000). The development of concern for others in children with behavior problems. *Developmental Psychology, 36*, 531–546.

Hay, D. (1979). Cooperative interactions and sharing between very young children and their parents. *Developmental Psychology, 15*, 647–653.

Hoffman, M. L. (1970). Moral development. In P. H. Mussen (Ed.), *Carmichael's manual of child psychology* (Vol. 2, pp. 261–360). New York: Wiley.

Isen, A. M. (1970). Success, failure, attention, and reaction to others: The warm glow of success.

Journal of Personality and Social Psychology, 15, 294–301.

Jacobsen, C. (1983). What it means to be considerate: Differences in normative expectations and their implication. *Israel Social Science Research, 1*, 24–33.

Kagan, J. (1981). *The second year: The emergence of self-awareness.* Cambridge, MA: Harvard University Press.

Kestenbaum, R., Farber, E. A., & Sroufe, L. A. (1989). Individual differences in empathy among preschoolers: Relation to attachment history. *New Directions in Child Development, 44*, 51–64.

Kochanska, G. (1997a). Multiple pathways to conscience for children with different temperaments: From toddlerhood to age 5. *Developmental Psychology, 33*, 228–240.

Kochanska, G. (1997b). Mutually responsive orientation between mothers and their young children: Implications for early socialization. *Child Development, 68*, 94–112.

Kopp, C. B. (1982). Antecedents of self-regulation: A developmental view. *Developmental Psychology, 18*, 199–214.

Krevans, J., & Gibbs, J. C. (1996). Parents' use of inductive discipline: Relations to children's empathy and prosocial behavior. *Child Development, 67*, 3263–3277.

Markus, H. R., & Kitayama, S. (1991). Culture and the self: Implications for cognition, emotion, and motivation. *Psychological Review, 98*, 224–253.

Midlarksy, E., & Hannah, M. E. (1985). Competence, reticence, and helping by children and adolescents. *Developmental Psychology, 21*, 534–541.

Miller, J. G. (1984). Culture and the development of everyday social explanation. *Journal of Personality and Social Psychology, 46*, 961–978.

Miller, J. G., & Bersoff, D. M. (1992). Culture and moral judgment: How are conflicts between justice and interpersonal responsibilities resolved? *Journal of Personality and Social Psychology, 62*, 541–554.

Miller, J. G., & Bersoff, D. M., (1994). Cultural differences in the moral status of reciprocity and the discounting of endogenous motivation. *Personality and Social Psychology Bulletin, 201*, 592–602.

Moore, B. S., Underwood, B., & Rosenhan, D. L. (1973). Affect and altruism. *Developmental Psychology, 8*, 99–104.

Parpal, M., & Maccoby, E. E. (1985). Maternal responsiveness and subsequent child compliance. *Child Development, 56*, 1326–1334.

Pearl, R. (1985). Children's understanding of others' need for help: Effects of problem explicitness and type. *Child Development, 56*, 735–745.

Peterson, L. (1983). Influence of age, task competence, and responsibility focus on children's altruism. *Developmental Psychology, 19*, 141–148.

Power, T. G., Kobayashi-Winata, H., & Kelly, M. L. (1992). Childrearing patterns in Japan and the United States: A cluster analytic study. *International Journal of Behavioral Development, 15*, 185–205.

Radke-Yarrow, M., Zahn-Waxler, C., & Chapman, M. (1983). Children's prosocial dispositions and behavior. In P. Mussen (Series Ed.) & E. M. Hetherington (Vol. Ed.), *Handbook of child psychology, vol. 4: Socialization, personality, and social development* (pp. 469–545). New York: Wiley.

Rheingold, H. (1982). Little children's participation in the work of adults, a nascent prosocial behavior. *Child Development, 53*, 114–125.

Robinson, J. L., Zahn-Waxler, C., & Emde, R. N. (1994). Patterns of development in early empathic behavior: Environmental and child constitutional influences. *Social Development, 3*, 125–145.

Rosenhan, D. L., Salovey, P., Karylowski, J., & Hargis, K. (1981). Emotion and altruism. In J. P. Rushton & R. M. Sorrentino (Eds.), *Altruism and helping behavior: Social, personality, and developmental perspectives* (pp. 233–248). Hillsdale, NJ: Erlbaum.

Rushton, J. P., Fulker, D. W., Neale, M. C., Nias, D. K. B., & Eysenck, H. J. (1986). Altruism and aggression: The heritability of individual differences. *Journal of Personality and Social Psychology, 50,* 1192–1198.

Schwartz, S. H. (1994). Beyond individualism/collectivism: New cultural dimensions of values. In U. Kim, H. C. Triandis, C. Kagitcibasi, S.-C. Choi, & G. Yoon (Eds.), *Individualism and collectivism: Theory, method, and applications* (pp. 85–119). Thousand Oaks, CA: Sage.

Stevenson, H. W. (1991). The development of prosocial behavior in large-scale collective societies: China and Japan. In R. A. Hinde & J. Groebel (Eds.), *Cooperation and prosocial behavior* (pp. 89–105). Cambridge, England: Cambridge University Press.

Stewart, R. B., & Marvin, R. S. (1984). Sibling relations: The role of conceptual perspective taking in the ontogeny of sibling caregiving. *Child Development, 55,* 1322–1332.

Trivers, R. L. (1971). The evolution of reciprocal altruism. *Quarterly Review of Biology, 46,* 35-57.

Trommsdorff, G. (1991). Child-rearing and children's empathy. *Perceptual and Motor Skills, 72,* 387–390.

Trommsdorff, G. (1995). Person-context relations as developmental conditions for empathy and prosocial action: A cross-cultural analysis. In T. A. Kindermann & J. Valsiner (Eds.), *Development of person-context relations* (pp. 113–146). Hillsdale, NJ: Erlbaum.

Underwood, B., & Moore, B. (1982). Perspective-taking and altruism. *Psychological Bulletin, 91,* 143–173.

Waters, E., Hay, D., & Richters, J. (1986). Infant–parent attachment and the origins of prosocial and antisocial behavior. In D. Olweus, J. Block, & M. Radke-Yarrow (Eds.), *Development of antisocial and prosocial behavior: Research, theories, and issues* (pp. 97–125). Orlando, FL: Academic Press.

Whiting, B. B., & Whiting, J. W. M. (1973). Altruistic and egoistic behavior in six cultures. In L. Nader & T. W. Maretzki (Eds.), *Cultural illness and health.* Washington, DC: American Anthropological Association.

Whiting, B. B., & Whiting, J. W. M. (1975). *Children of six cultures: A psycho-cultural analysis.* Cambridge, MA: Harvard University Press.

Wynne-Edwards, V. C. (1962). *Animal dispersion in relation to social behavior.* Edinburgh, Scotland: Oliver & Boyd.

Zahn-Waxler, C., Cole, P., & Barrett, K. (1991). Guilt and empathy: Sex differences and implications for the development of depression. In J. Garber & K.A. Dodge (Eds.), *The development of emotion regulation and dysregulation. Cambridge studies in social and emotional development* (pp. 243–272). New York: Cambridge University Press.

Zahn-Waxler, C., Friedman, R. J., Cole, P. M., Mizuta, I., & Hiruma, N., (1996). Japanese and United States preschool children's responses to conflict and distress. *Child Development, 67,* 2462–2477.

Zahn-Waxler, C., Iannotti, R., & Chapman, M. (1982). Peers and prosocial development. In K. H. Rubin & H. R. Ross (Eds.), *Peer relationships and social skills in childhood* (pp. 133–162). New York: Springer-Verlag.

Zahn-Waxler, C., Radke-Yarrow, M., Wagner, E., & Chapman, M. (1992). Development of concern for others. *Developmental Psychology, 28,* 126–136.

Zahn-Waxler, C., Robinson, J., & Emde, R. N. (1992). The development of empathy in twins. *Developmental Psychology, 28,* 1038–1047.

24

Children's Social and Moral Reasoning

Charles C. Helwig and Elliot Turiel

Introduction

The study of morality has been approached from different perspectives within several disciplines, including philosophy, anthropology, sociology, and psychology. In psychology, proponents of the major theoretical approaches have attempted to explain the acquisition or development of morality. Behavioristic and social learning theorists have proposed that moral development entails a process of acquiring behaviors (Skinner, 1971) or internalizing the standards and values of society so that they are maintained without the necessity of external surveillance (Aronfreed, 1968). Psychoanalytic theorists, too, have presumed that morality comes from the incorporation of societal standards (Freud, 1930). In the psychoanalytic account the process of moral development, as well as the maintenance of morality, is full of conflict and tension for individuals. This is because in acquiring society's moral standards the individual must control strongly felt instinctual drives and needs (through the formation of what Freud referred to as a superego). The emotion of guilt operates so as to maintain control over instincts.

An alternative view on moral development, keeping with a long line of philosophical analyses from Aristotle to Kant and to modern versions (e.g., those of Dworkin, 1977; Gewirth, 1978; Rawls, 1971), is that it involves the construction of judgments about welfare, justice, and rights through children's social interactions. Extensive study of children's moral judgments dates back to the work of Jean Piaget (1932). Piaget's research was extended a number of years later by Lawrence Kohlberg (1981), who was instrumental in drawing attention to the importance of processes of judgment in the moral realm (as well

Preparation of this chapter was supported by a research grant from the Social Sciences and Humanities Research Council of Canada to Charles C. Helwig.

as in stimulating renewed interest in Piaget's research on moral development). Taken together, the research of Piaget and Kohlberg went far in demonstrating that children do not
solely accommodate to societal standards or comply with rules and parental or other social
expectations. Rather, children attempt to understand social relationships, and in the process construct judgments about right and wrong, about how people should act towards each
other.

There is now substantial evidence demonstrating that children form systematic judgments about right and wrong, in the moral sense, that are central to their actions, social
interactions, and development. Piaget and Kohlberg each also described a sequence for the
development of moral judgments in which concepts of justice and rights are not constructed until late childhood or adolescence. Research on a variety of aspects of children's
social and moral judgments conducted over the past two decades has shown, however, that
young children begin to develop moral judgments, distinct from other types or domains of
social judgments. After a brief overview of the ways Piaget and Kohlberg characterized
children's moral judgments, we consider the research on how children form moral judgments that differ from their judgments about the domains of societal convention and
personal jurisdiction. We also consider issues raised by this "domain" approach for development and culture.

The Development of Social and Moral Judgments

The moral thinking of young children was described by both Piaget and Kohlberg as concrete and oriented toward punishment, respect for authority, and the maintenance of existing social rules and laws. Piaget (1932) described moral development as moving from an
orientation characterized by heteronomy, or a strong respect for adult authority and rules,
to an autonomous morality in later childhood in which rules are understood as social
constructions formulated in social relations of cooperation among peers. According to
Piaget, the young child views social rules as fixed and unalterable, and conceptualizes moral
obligation in terms of strict adherence to the rules or commands of adult authorities. A
morality based on adult constraint gives way in later childhood to a morality based on
mutual respect, or cooperation. This progression is facilitated by the older child's cognitive
development from egocentrism to perspectivism, and by a corresponding shift in the child's
social relations from one-way relations of adult constraint to reciprocal relations of mutual
respect among peers.

Similarly, Kohlberg (1981) characterized children's moral reasoning in terms of a punishment and obedience orientation. Kohlberg believed that Piaget mischaracterized the
thinking of the young child as reflecting a reverence for rules; Kohlberg, rather, saw young
children's moral thinking as expressing an expedient concern with obedience to authority
in order to avoid punishment. Nonetheless, Kohlberg likewise saw the young child as
prone to take the perspective of authority in moral judgments and to exhibit a focus on the
concrete consequences of moral acts and disobedience. Based on analyses of children's
reasoning about moral dilemmas, Kohlberg described moral development as moving through
a series of stages, in which morality is defined first in terms of punishment or obedience to

authority, through a conventional level in which individuals take the perspective of the legal system and uphold existing laws (a "law and order" orientation), and finally, in adulthood, a principled level may be reached where individuals develop truly moral abstract principles of justice and rights (an orientation reached only by a minority of adults).

These propositions yield a portrait of young children's moral reasoning as oriented toward authority and characterized by rigid adherence to and respect for, existing social rules, norms, and customs. A substantially different picture of children's moral judgments has emerged from research that examined directly whether children make distinctions between different kinds of social rules and acts. It is a portrait in which children distinguish among social rules in accordance with different domains of social reasoning, and in which they possess conceptions of autonomy, rights, and democracy which sometimes lead them to take a critical perspective on the dictates of authorities and existing social systems. Even young children possess moral concepts that are independent of authority or existing social sanctions or rules, and their moral judgments are *sensitive to both the content of social rules and the context of their application.*

Researchers working within what has come to be known as the "domain approach" have proposed that children's thinking is organized from an early age into the domains of morality and social convention (Turiel, 1983). The *moral domain* pertains to issues of harm, fairness, and rights. The *social conventional* domain comprises behavioral uniformities that serve to coordinate social interactions in social systems (e.g., the organizational rules of the classroom, or uniformities involving matters like dress, etiquette, or titles). Research with children of a variety of ages has shown that they discriminate between moral and social conventional events and reason about them differently (see Turiel, 1998, for a review). Two types of assessments have been employed in the research on children's domain distinctions. The first, termed *criterion judgments*, pertains to the criteria used in making judgments of acts or rules associated with each domain. Criterion judgments include judgments of the generalizability, universality, rule-contingency, and alterability of prohibitions regarding the act. Judgments of moral transgressions (e.g., hitting, stealing) have been found to be generalizable (i.e., wrong across social contexts), non-rule-contingent (i.e., wrong even if there were no rule against it), and rules that pertain to moral acts are seen as unalterable. In contrast, social conventional transgressions (e.g., calling a teacher by his/her first name, eating with one's fingers) are seen as relative to the social context, contingent on the existence of an explicit social rule, and rules regarding social conventions are seen as alterable by authority or social consensus. For example, children judge it acceptable to call a teacher by his or her first name in a school in which there was no rule or social uniformity prohibiting it, and existing rules prohibiting the behavior were seen as alterable if the relevant authorities approved. In contrast, hitting is judged as wrong even if a teacher permitted it, and rules about hitting were not seen as alterable by the commands of those holding authority.

The second type of assessment in the research on morality and convention is children's reasons or justifications for the judgments they make. Reasoning in the moral domain is characterized by references to issues of harm, fairness, and rights. Reasoning in the social conventional domain is characterized by references to rules, authority, social customs, and the coordination of social behavior. The different reasons given by children for moral and social conventional transgressions correspond to their criterion judgments and help account for their differential judgments of generalizability and rule contingency. Because moral events entail acts with intrinsic consequences of harm or unfairness, children's judgments of these acts are independent of social conventional aspects of the social system, such as authority or the presence of explicit social rules. In contrast, social conventions derive their meaning from being embedded within an existing social system with prescribed rules and roles, social hierarchies, or shared symbolic meanings that may be specific to the group. Accordingly, the meaning of a social convention may change along with social agreement or the commands of recognized authorities, and conventions may vary across social systems and across time and place. It has been proposed that different social interactions are associated with each of the domains, by which children construct different types of social judgments (Turiel, 1998). For example, when faced with a moral transgression (e.g., one child pushes another off a swing), children may consider the direct consequences of the act, and arrive at the conclusion that the act is wrong (Turiel, 1983). However, when observing a violation of social convention (e.g., a child calls a teacher by her first name) with no intrinsic consequences of harm or unfairness, children must infer the wrongness of the behavior from features extrinsic to the event. If others (e.g., adult authorities) react to the event as a rule transgression or as part of authority jurisdiction, children will see the act as a violation of social convention.

A large number of studies have yielded evidence that children distinguish morality from convention on these dimensions (see Turiel, 1998, for a review). As a means of conveying how young children make this distinction, we present an example of responses given by a 5-year-old boy. The boy's responses come from a study (Weston & Turiel, 1980) in which children from 5 to 11 years of age were presented with hypothetical stories of preschools in which certain actions are permitted. In one story children are allowed to be without clothes on warm days (a conventional issue). In a second story children are allowed to hit each other (a moral issue). Prior to the presentation of these hypothetical stories, the children had judged both acts as wrong. The first interview excerpt begins with the boy's responses to the question of whether it is alright for a school to allow hitting and the second with his responses as to whether it is alright to allow children to remove their clothes (the excerpts come from Turiel, 1983, p. 62):

> No, it is not okay. (WHY NOT?) Because this is like making other people unhappy. You can hurt them that way. It hurts other people, hurting is not good. (MARK GOES TO PARK SCHOOL. TODAY IN SCHOOL HE WANTS TO SWING BUT HE FINDS THAT ALL THE SWINGS ARE BEING USED BY OTHER CHILDREN. SO HE DECIDES TO HIT ONE OF THE CHILDREN AND TAKE THE SWING. IS IT OKAY FOR MARK TO DO THAT?) No. Because he is hurting someone else.

> Yes, because that is the rule. (WHY CAN THEY HAVE THAT RULE?) If that's what the boss wants to do, he can do that. (HOW COME?) Because he's the boss, he is in charge of the school (BOB GOES TO GROVE SCHOOL. THIS IS A WARM DAY AT GROVE SCHOOL. HE HAS BEEN RUNNING IN THE PLAY AREA OUTSIDE AND HE IS HOT SO HE DECIDES TO TAKE OFF HIS CLOTHES. IS IT OKAY FOR BOB TO DO THAT?) Yes, if he wants to he can because it's the rule.

For this child all rules are not alike and the type of act involved is evaluated in relation to the jurisdiction of the person in authority. With regard to removing one's clothes, the justification of the act and the school policy are based on rules and authority. Although the principal is the "boss and in charge" of the school, it matters in one case but not in the other. This boy's responses provide an example of the general findings of the study (Weston & Turiel, 1980). The majority of children at all ages responded in similar fashion, distinguishing between moral and conventional issues regarding rules and authority.

Research on very young children's ability to distinguish morality and social convention suggests that judgments of these events undergo important development during the preschool years. A set of studies have examined criterion judgments with children from 2 years to 5 years (e.g., Smetana, 1981, 1985; Smetana & Braeges, 1990). Children appear to reliably distinguish basic or prototypical moral and social conventional events by about 4 or 5 years, although not at 2 years. Between these ages, children distinguish the events on some criteria, but not others. For example, during the third year, children apply judgments of generalizability to distinguish moral events from social conventions (with moral events more likely to be judged wrong across social contexts than social conventions). By the end of the third year, they also judge moral transgressions to be independent of rules or authority (Smetana & Braeges, 1990).

Although young children appear to begin to construct a domain of moral judgment by the end of the third year of life, complications in acquiring reliable justification data from very young children have made it difficult to determine the basis of their judgments of generalizability or rule contingency. One possibility, consistent with the domain perspective, is that young children abstract out harm from moral events and use these emerging concepts of harm to guide their moral judgments. Another possibility, however, is that young children may be simply responding to adult patterns of punishment or sanctions (e.g., hitting is punished by adults, therefore it is wrong) rather than using features of actions such as harm in making these judgments. Because moral actions have consequences of harm or unfairness, it is difficult to address this question with normal moral acts such as hitting used in these studies. However, a procedure devised in a study by Zelazo, Helwig, and Lau (1996) gets around this problem. In the study, children were given examples of unusual or "noncanonical" moral events to make judgments about. For example, children were given the fanciful example of an unusual animal, from a far away place, that feels good when it is hit but is hurt when petted. This noncanonical example was contrasted with the "normal" case of an animal that is hurt when hit and that likes to be petted. In the study, 3–5 year olds were asked to judge the actions of agents with harmful or beneficent intentions who performed the actions of hitting or petting on each of these animals. It was found that 3 year olds judged it wrong to inflict harm on either animal, even in the noncanonical case when the action involved petting. Children's moral judgments were not based on a simple association between hitting and punishment, but on an understanding of the harm believed to underlie acts in both normal and noncanonical instances. Three year olds also have been shown to make similar judgments about acts of psychological harm (Helwig, Zelazo, & Wilson, 2001). These results suggest that children develop concepts of harm by 3 years, which they may use to distinguish moral acts from other kinds of social events.

Children also have been found to distinguish morality from authority and legal rules, and to adopt a critical perspective on authority, especially when it conflicts with the demands of morality (Damon, 1977; Laupa, Turiel, & Cowan, 1995). For example, Damon

(1977) found that young children do not accept as legitimate parental commands to engage in acts which violate moral rules, such as commands to steal or to cause harm to another person. Other research explored children's judgments and reasoning about the attributes that give legitimacy to authority, and how children account for the type of act commanded (see Laupa, Turiel, & Cowan, 1995). When reasoning about acts entailing theft or physical harm to persons, 4–6-year-old children give priority to the act itself, rather than the status of the person in a position of authority. For example, commands for children to stop fighting were seen as legitimate whether or not they came from adults or children holding positions of authority. Children also judged commands from a peer (with or without a position of authority in a school) to stop fighting as more legitimate than conflicting commands from an adult authority, such as a teacher. However, with regard to other acts, such as turn taking or interpretations of game rules, children do give priority to adult authority over children or other adults who are not in positions of authority. Children's judgments of obedience in these cases are based on the attributes possessed by authorities, such as their social position in a school or their superior knowledge and experience. Children's reasoning about authority is not based on unilateral respect or an unexamined acceptance of authority injunctions; rather, even young children make subtle discriminations taking into account the type of command given and the attributes that lend legitimacy to individuals in positions of authority.

Children also take a critical perspective on rules and laws when they conflict with the demands of morality – as demonstrated by a recent study (Helwig & Jasiobedzka, 2001). In this study, children (6–11 years) were presented with hypothetical examples of a variety of laws, including socially beneficial laws (e.g., traffic laws or vaccination laws) and laws that involved injustice (e.g., laws discriminating against individuals on the basis of age, income, or eye color). Children were asked to evaluate each law, to judge if it would be legitimate for governments to pass the law, and to judge if it was acceptable to violate the law. In general, children evaluated the socially beneficial laws as more acceptable and legitimate than the unjust laws. Consistent with their law evaluations, children at all ages judged the violation of unjust laws to be more acceptable than the violation of socially beneficial laws. In fact, the majority of children in the youngest age group (6 year olds) judged violations of unjust laws, but not socially beneficial laws, to be acceptable. These findings reveal that even young children consider the content of law and are sensitive to features of laws such as their potential to lead to injustice or harm in making judgments of obedience and law violation.

The Development of Social Thought and Action   Most of the studies considered thus far examined children's judgments regarding different aspects of morality and social convention. This leaves open the question of whether children's actions are related to, or influenced by, their judgments. Within the perspective we have presented it is, indeed, proposed that thought and action are closely related to each other (Piaget, 1932). This does not mean that we can simply predict what people will do from what they say they would do. There are many reasons people may not be able to predict their own actions, including that they cannot necessarily foresee the variety of issues that may come up in particular contexts (Ross & Nisbett, 1991; Turiel & Smetana, 1984). The proposition instead is that people's judgments influence how they approach situations calling for actions, and that actions, in turn, influence the development of their judgments. One feature of this proposition is that children's social interactions influence the development of judgments. A second is that children's judgments are important in how they frame events they experience, and that the different domains of judgments have a bearing on this process.

A number of studies have examined children's social interactions around moral and social conventional events, with children ranging from 2–3 years of age to late childhood, in a variety of contexts such as the home, the school, and the playground. The research has shown that children's social interactions are varied and differentiated according to domains of reasoning (e.g., Much & Shweder, 1978; Nucci & Nucci, 1982a, 1982b; Nucci & Turiel, 1978). Specifically, it has been found that children's responses to moral transgressions (e.g., when one child hits another, fails to share, or takes another child's objects) revolve around communications about the act's effects on others, and attention to the perspectives, needs, and expectations of others. By an early age, children are aware of, and focus on, the consequences of moral actions, including pain and injury and the emotions felt by others. Most of the observational studies have found that young children do not respond as frequently to conventional violations as to moral transgressions. However, adults do respond to violations of social conventions, and their communications generally focus on issues of disorder, the importance of maintaining rules, and obedience to authority, rather than on harmful consequences or the perspectives of others. These findings suggest that the types of events that children experience, as well as the communications they receive or generate during social interactions are distinguished in ways predicted by the domains of social reasoning. The results of these studies are consistent with the proposition that children's domain distinctions are based on early social experiences.

Other research supports the proposition that there is a correspondence between the domains of judgment and how children approach behavioral situations (Turiel, 2000). In this study, observations were made in elementary and junior high schools of spontaneously occurring social interactions entailing moral events (e.g., hitting, fighting, sharing, taking another's goods) and conventional events (e.g., lining up for activities, sitting in assigned seats). Observations were also made of events that combined moral and conventional components (e.g., rules, practices, or authority dictates that entail unfair treatment). Shortly after an event was observed, participants were interviewed to ascertain how they perceived the situations and how they evaluated and judged various aspects of the events. About a month later, the same participants were administered an interview about hypothetical situations describing transgressions comparable to the observed events (a total of 311 participants were administered the two interviews).

The findings on judgments about the hypothetical situations provide a comparison with judgments about the events experienced by the children. As expected, most of the children reasoned about the moral and conventional transgressions depicted in the hypothetical situations in accordance with their domain classification. It was also found that in the events that involved a mixture of components, children were able to separate the moral and conventional components and judge in different ways about each. For the actual events, the majority of children at each age judged that the moral acts would be wrong even if no rule existed, whereas a minority judged that the conventional acts would be wrong under those circumstances. Similarly, a majority judged that evaluations of moral acts were not based on authority expectations, whereas a minority did so for the conventional acts. The findings on justifications provide further evidence that participants were making domain distinctions with regard to the actual events as well. The justifications for the moral evaluations and judgments were mainly based on welfare and justice, and justifications for conventional events were based mainly on tradition, authority, and personal choice. The participants also judged each component of the mixed events differently, reasoning about one on the basis of welfare and justice and the other on the basis of tradition, authority, and social coordination.

Culture and Social Development

The research we have reviewed demonstrates that starting at a young age children form different domains of social judgment. Children make moral judgments based on issues of harm, fairness, and rights, and differentiate morality from social conventions, punishment, and explicit rules. Children do not appear to go through a period of rigid adherence to social rules, and unilateral respect for adult authority, but often adopt a critical perspective in evaluating and judging the legitimacy of rules and authority.

Most of the research discussed thus far was conducted in North America – in Western cultures. It may be, therefore, that the types of judgments found in this research reflect a particular cultural orientation. Our view is that the development of judgments about morality and social conventions stem not from a particular cultural orientation but from children's experiences with others and their ways of making sense of those experiences. It has been argued by some, however, that the distinction between morality and convention stems from a Western cultural construction connected to a general orientation to persons and society (Shweder, Mahapatra, & Miller, 1987). That view is based on the proposition that cultures can be divided, more or less, on their orientations to individualism or collectivism (Triandis, 1996). Western cultures are oriented to the idea of persons as autonomous human agents who are free to belong or not to belong to social systems and groups. Social relationships in Western societies are seen as derivative and arising out of consent and contract between these autonomous individuals. This leads to the idea of conventionality – that some obligations are determined by social contracts or arrangements that individuals willingly enter into. The morality of Western societies can be characterized as rights-based, or one concerned with protecting and fostering the rights of individuals to pursue their activities free from unnecessary external influence.

In collectivistic cultures the person is seen as part of a social network of interdependence and morality is based on duties and maintenance of the social order. Moral duties include what are seen as consensus-based conventions in Western cultures. Shweder et al. (1987) conducted research in India, where supposedly the concept of the self as an autonomous, bounded individual existing free from society but living in society is an alien notion. They proposed that Indians would be likely to treat as moral certain events that Americans would view as conventional or up to the individual's choice, such as matters relating to diet, clothing, and other cultural or religious customs. They conducted a study with Orthodox Hindus (both Brahmans, or upper-class temple priests, and untouchables) from a provincial town in India, as well as with American middle- and upper-middle-class individuals. Participants were presented with a large number of items describing violations of practices and norms. Some were of the type that we would define as moral and conventional. A number of the items they used pertained to content often identified in Western cultures with convention, such as food and dress. These items, however, were also tied to religious practices. Examples of this type are violations of prohibitions against a widow eating fish or wearing bright clothing, or a son eating chicken and getting a haircut the day after his father's death. It was found that although a number of the moral items were judged in similar ways by Indians and Americans, some of the "conventional" ones were judged differently by the two groups. Items like the ones just described pertaining to food and clothing were judged by Indians as serious transgressions and it was thought that the practices were not alterable.

The conclusions drawn by Shweder et al. (1987) about these findings – that what Americans might treat as conventional is treated by Indians as moral – fails to account for a significant aspect of what goes into people's application of their moral judgments. We are referring to their assumptions about reality. As shown by a re-analysis of the items (Turiel, Killen, & Helwig, 1987), assumptions about the "reality" of an after-life and the effects of earthly actions on unobservable entities, such as the soul of a deceased husband, father, or ancestors entered into their moral judgments. As an example, it is believed that if a son were to get a haircut and eat chicken the day after his father's death the father would fail to receive salvation. Although the beliefs about reality varied across cultures (Americans did not believe these practices to result in these kinds of consequences), the moral concern with avoiding inflicting harmful consequences on others appears to be shared. The events interpreted by Shweder et al. (1987) as inherently conventional appear to have been transformed into moral events (having harmful consequences for others) by virtue of the specific beliefs brought to them by Indians. This example shows the importance of considering such beliefs (termed informational or "factual assumptions" in subsequent research on this topic, see Wainryb, 1991) in studying the application of moral judgments.

Other research has confirmed that the moral and social conventional domains are distinguished in India and other cultures. For example, Miller and Bersoff (1992) found that children and adults in India reasoned about school dress codes as social conventions, seeing them as alterable and relative across social contexts, whereas theft was reasoned about as a moral event in the same manner as in the West. It has been found that children and adults in several cultures distinguish morality and social convention, including Indonesia (Carey & Ford, 1983), Nigeria (Hollos, Leis, & Turiel, 1986), Korea (Song, Smetana, & Kim, 1987), Zambia (Zimba, 1994), and Brazil (Nucci, Camino & Sapiro, 1996). Moreover, research in India (Neff, 2001) and in other presumably collectivistic cultures (Wainryb & Turiel, 1994) has shown that persons are often conceptualized as autonomous agents. In particular, people in positions of dominance in the social hierarchy (e.g., as based on social caste or gender) are accorded entitlements to personal choices.

The Development of Concepts of Autonomy, Rights, and Democracy

The development of children's autonomy is an area that has received much attention in recent research. In Piaget's (1932) classic study, autonomy was described mainly as a feature that emerges within children's moral reasoning in later childhood, when children transcend heteronomy and begin to make moral judgments that are independent of authority and existing social rules. As previously noted, however, even young children have been found to distinguish morality from authority and social convention and to identify a moral domain comprising issues of rights, welfare, and fairness. The turn away from describing moral development in terms of a general shift from heteronomy to autonomy has led researchers to refocus their attention on children's reasoning about their own autonomy throughout the age span. Researchers have also taken up the question of how early emerging concepts of autonomy relate to, and inform, more sophisticated moral concepts of individual rights and freedoms.

Research directly examining emerging concepts of autonomy has found that young children identify a domain of personal issues, distinct from the moral and social conventional domains, comprising matters considered to be up to the individual's personal choice and beyond the bounds of legitimate regulation by parents, teachers, and other authorities. For example, American elementary school children have been found to judge issues such as choices about friends, appearance (clothing, hairstyle), and preferences for leisure activities, as up to the child to decide (Nucci, 1981). From the age of 7 onward, participants in Nucci's (1981) study stated that there should not be a rule governing these matters and that they should be up to individual choice. Recent research (Nucci & Smetana, 1996) suggests that the personal domain emerges during the preschool years. Preschoolers (3–4 year olds) have been found to make similar judgments about age-appropriate personal issues. Observations of parent–child interactions show that children are much more likely to challenge parental authority over personal issues than moral or conventional issues. Nucci (1996) provides the following example of a conflict between a parent and a child over what a child is going to wear on the last day of nursery school:

> Mother: Evan, it's your last day of nursery school. Why don't you wear your nursery school sweatshirt?
> Child: I don't want to wear that one.
> Mother: This is the last day of nursery school, that's why we wear it. You want to wear that one?
> Child: Another one.
> Mother: Are you going to get it or should I?
> Child: I will. First I got to get a shirt.
> Mother: [Goes to the child's dresser and starts picking out shirts.] This one? This one? Do you know which one you have in mind? You have to decide, because we have to do car pool. Here, this is a new one.
> Child: No, it's too big.
> Mother: Oh Evan, just wear one, and when you get home, you can pick whatever you want, and I won't even help you. [Child puts on shirt].

The example illustrates a conflict between the parent's assertion of a dress convention (wearing the nursery school sweatshirt on the last day of school) and the child's assertion that it is a matter of personal choice. The example illustrates, first, that the child challenges adult rules when they are perceived to infringe upon the child's sense of autonomy and choice. Second, the adult responds by recognizing the child's agency and autonomy and through negotiation and compromise. Although the child ultimately complies in the immediate instance, the interaction concludes with the mother offering the child autonomy about what to wear after school is over. Nucci (1996) proposes that these kinds of conflicts and negotiations are central to the formation of a sense of autonomy and self, a process that begins very early in life and continues throughout childhood and into adolescence. The negotiations and discussions provoked by these conflicts appear to be important in aiding the child's gradual construction of independence and self-efficacy within an expanding personal domain.

The specific example given above certainly has a middle-class, North American "feel," at least in the particular content invoked and in the granting of autonomy to very young children. Nevertheless, evidence is accumulating that the personal domain is not a specifically North American or Western cultural construction. Nucci, Camino, and Sapiro (1996) examined the judgments of middle- and lower-class children and mothers in cities and rural regions of Brazil. They found that children across social classes and regions differentiated among personal, moral, and social conventional issues in the same way as found in North America. However, there were social class differences in the ages at which personal issues were identified, with middle-class children claiming areas of personal discretion at earlier ages than lower-class children. Similarly, mothers of lower-class children and mothers from rural regions were less likely to grant personal decision-making autonomy to young children. However, by adolescence, these differences disappeared. Both mothers and children tended to grant personal decision making autonomy to adolescents over similar issues, and gave reasons of autonomy, choice, and the development of uniqueness and identity in justifying their judgments.

Studies of social interactions of preschoolers in Japan (e.g., Killen & Sueyoshi, 1995) suggest that the development of autonomy is an important goal even in a culture frequently described as "collectivistic" and promoting group conformity over individual achievement and rights. Killen and Sueyoshi (1995) found that Japanese preschools were hardly "harmonious," as sometimes described. Instead, Japanese preschoolers were involved in a variety of interpersonal conflicts over personal claims, the distribution of resources, and ways of structuring games and other group activities. Teachers preferred a strategy of allowing children to resolve most conflicts among themselves. The interventions of teachers largely took the form of encouraging children to speak up for themselves and to express their desires or to tell others why their actions were wrong. This style differs from the approach to discipline found in many American preschools in which transgressors are sent to "time-out". The Japanese teaching style may be seen as fostering both children's autonomy and independence (in promoting a tendency to speak out and to assert themselves), along with their interdependence, by encouraging them to resolve conflicts among themselves and thus to enhance group cohesion. Another study conducted in Japan (Yamada, 2000) found that mothers of preschoolers do allow their children areas of personal choice in ways not unlike American mothers (Nucci & Smetana, 1996). More research in other cultural settings is needed, to be sure, but the available research suggests that the construction of a personal domain and individual autonomy is not particular to Westerners, and that there may even be similarities across cultures in the sorts of issues judged to be matters of personal choice.

Basic concepts of personal autonomy and individual choice of the kind discussed so far are likely to serve as a foundation for more abstract notions of individual freedom, such as in concepts of civil liberties like freedom of speech and religion (Nucci, 1996). Freedom of speech and religion are important individual and political rights, often associated with modern democratic political systems. Until very recently, it was assumed that concepts of civil liberties and democracy do not develop until adolescence (Gallatin, 1985). This conclusion was based on previous research showing that young children are unable to define basic terms such as democracy, or that they often subordinate individual rights and freedoms to other concerns in certain situations (e.g., in times of war, or when rights conflict with other important social goals). However, research examining children's reasoning about rights and democracy has shown that these concepts have emerged by the early elementary school years, although they are not always applied in the same way as are those of adolescents or adults. For example, research investigating children's and adolescents' reasoning about freedom of speech and religion (Helwig, 1995, 1997, 1998) has found that by 6 years of age, children judge restrictions of these rights by governments or other authorities as wrong and illegitimate. Moreover, young children, as well as older children and adults, view freedom of speech and religion as universal moral rights that should be upheld in all countries. Younger children (6–8 year olds) link these rights mainly to concerns with ensuring personal autonomy and individual self-expression. However, older children (8–11 year olds) and adolescents recognize broader societal, cultural, and democratic aspects to these rights. For example, with age, freedom of speech increasingly was seen as serving interpersonal or societal purposes, such as fostering communication or facilitating the discovery of important innovations that might help to improve society, or as allowing for minorities to express themselves through protest or other democratic means in order to rectify social injustices. Freedom of religion was seen by older children as serving not only individual autonomy and personal expression, but also as ensuring that group and cultural traditions may be preserved and respected.

Developmental differences have been found not only in how young children conceptualize freedom of speech and religion but also in how they apply these concepts. In one study (Helwig, 1997), children were asked whether it would be acceptable for various authorities (e.g., the government, a school principal, or parents) to prohibit adults or children from talking about a forbidden topic (e.g., rock music) or practicing a religion different from that of the authority when the authority disapproves. Consistent with their conceptualization of these rights as grounded in simple personal choice and autonomy, younger children tended not to draw distinctions among different authorities or agents and to view prohibitions on freedom of speech and religion as wrong in equal measure, whether it involved restrictions in the school, the family, or society at large, and whether or not it involved child or adult agents. Younger children focused on personal choice and individual wants and desires (e.g., "It should be up to them; people should be able to do what they want"). Older children (starting at about 11 years of age), adolescents, and adults, however, drew distinctions between children and adults and between different social contexts. For example, many older children and adults saw it as acceptable for parents to prohibit their young (but not adult) children from practicing a religion different from their own. They considered parents' rights to socialize their children as they wish, and children's competence and ability to make choices about matters of religion. Many older children and adults did not see children as competent to decide their own religion, and this decision therefore should be left up to the parents. They did not, however, see it as appropriate for other authorities (e.g., school principals and governments) to make choices about children's religion, nor did they see it as appropriate for parents to decide their grown adult children's religion.

Research focusing on judgments of democratic and other forms of social organization has shown that children prefer democratic over nondemocratic forms of government (Helwig, 1998). Elementary school age children were also asked about whether it would be appropriate for governments of both democratic and nondemocratic types to pass laws restricting the right of a minority to criticize the government. Although at all ages children thought that such laws would be wrong, older children were more likely to consider the type of government in evaluating whether or not such laws were acceptable. Older children were more likely to see such laws as acceptable if passed by a democratic government (e.g., a representative democracy) rather than a nondemocratic government (e.g., a government ruled entirely by the rich). The reasoning of the older children appears to reflect a concern with adhering to and upholding democratic procedures which they judged as fair; younger children, by contrast, simply focused on the decision as restricting individual's personal choice, and thus they failed to draw distinctions among types of governments or to consider how the decision was arrived at.

In a study of children's reasoning about fair procedures for making decisions in groups (Helwig & Kim, 1999), young children were more likely to endorse autonomous or democratic decision-making procedures such as consensus (where everyone must agree on a decision), than decision making based on unilateral adult authority across a variety of decisions made in the peer group, family, and school contexts. Older children, in contrast, drew distinctions about when and for what decisions either consensus or adult authority would be appropriate. For example, older children thought that consensus would be an appropriate way for a class to decide on where to go for a field trip, but not for decisions about the curriculum. Older children reasoned that teachers had more knowledge about curriculum matters than children, and that children would be tempted to compromise their education by choosing "easy" subjects. In contrast, a field trip was seen more as a recreational activity by older children, and thus within the bounds of children's personal choice.

The findings of the research on personal choice, autonomy, and civil liberties show that young children develop notions of personal autonomy, which they use to ground emerging concepts of political and civil rights such as freedom of speech and religion. Interestingly, younger children sometimes seem to overapply their notions of personal choice and autonomy, leading them to assert their autonomy in areas where older children or adults often do not (e.g., as in decisions about religious membership in the family or about curriculum in the school context). The findings, therefore, show a complex pattern where children develop concepts of autonomy at an early age and become increasingly sophisticated with development about the conditions under which autonomy should and should not be asserted. In some cases, this may even lead to situations where children assert or attempt to claim autonomy over areas where it may not be developmentally appropriate for them to exercise it.

Conclusion

The findings of the extensive body of research we have reviewed lead to a picture of children's social and moral development as entailing the construction of distinct domains of judgment through their social interactions. Children distinguish between different types of social rules and construct domains of moral, social conventional, and personal concepts. Children take into account the consequences of actions on others and construct concepts of harm, fairness, and rights, which they use to evaluate individual actions, social rules, and social systems. Neither young children's social judgments nor their social relations can be characterized in unitary terms as reflecting heteronomy or unilateral constraint. Rather, children's social judgments are heterogeneous and differentiated by domain, and their social interactions are characterized by both relations of cooperation and conflict, with peers and authority figures, throughout development. Accounting for the different kinds of social interactions children experience, and the concepts they construct from these experiences, is an important task for an understanding of children's social and moral judgments and behavior.

References

Aronfreed, J. (1968). *Conduct and conscience: The socialization of internalized control over behavior.* New York: Academic Press.

Carey, N., & Ford, M. (1983, August). Domains of social and self-regulation: An Indonesian study. Paper presented at the meeting of the American Psychological Association, Los Angeles.

Damon, W. (1977). *The social world of the child.* San Francisco: Jossey-Bass.

Dworkin, R. (1977). *Taking rights seriously.* Cambridge, MA: Harvard University Press.

Freud, S. (1930). *Civilization and its discontents.* London: Hogarth Press.

Gallatin, J. (1985). *Democracy's children: The development of political thinking in adolescents.* Ann Arbor, MI: Quod.

Gewirth, A. (1978). *Reason and morality.* Chicago: University of Chicago Press.

Helwig, C. C. (1995). Adolescents' and young adults' conceptions of civil liberties: Freedom of speech and religion. *Child Development, 66,* 152-166.

Helwig, C. C. (1997). The role of agent and social context in judgments of freedom of speech and religion. *Child Development, 68,* 484–495.

Helwig, C. C. (1998). Children's conceptions of fair government and freedom of speech. *Child Development, 69,* 518–531.

Helwig, C. C., & Kim, S. (1999). Children's evaluations of decision-making procedures in peer, family, and school contexts. *Child Development, 70,* 502–512.

Helwig, C. C., & Jasiobedzka, U. (2001). The relation between law and morality: Children's reasoning about socially beneficial and unjust laws. *Child Development, 72,* 1382–1393.

Helwig, C. C., Zelazo, P., & Wilson, M. (2001). Children's judgments of psychological harm in normal and noncanonical situations. *Child Development, 72,* 66–81.

Hollos, M., Leis, P. E., & Turiel, E. (1986). Social reasoning in Ijo children and adolescents in Nigerian communities. *Journal of Cross-Cultural Psychology, 17,* 352–374.

Killen, M., & Sueyoshi, L. (1995). Conflict resolution in Japanese social interactions. *Early Education and Development, 6,* 313–330.

Kohlberg, L. (1981). *Essays on moral development: Vol. 1. The philosophy of moral development.* San Francisco: Harper & Row.

Laupa, M., Turiel, E., & Cowan, P. (1995). Obedience to authority in children and adults. In M. Killen & D. Hart (Eds.), *Morality in everyday life: Developmental perspectives* (pp. 131–165). Cambridge, England: Cambridge University Press.

Miller, J. G., & Bersoff, D. M. (1992). Culture and moral judgment: How are conflicts between justice and interpersonal responsibilities resolved? *Journal of Personality & Social Psychology, 62,* 541–554.

Much, N., & Shweder, R. A. (1978). Speaking of rules: The analysis of culture in breach. In W. Damon (Ed.), *New directions for child development: Vol. 2. Moral development* (pp. 19–39). San Francisco: Jossey-Bass.

Neff, K. D. (2001). Judgments of personal autonomy and interpersonal responsibility in the context of Indian spousal relationships: An examination of young people's reasoning in Mysore, India. *British Journal of Developmental Psychology, 19,* 233–257.

Nucci, L. P. (1981). The development of personal issues: A domain distinct from moral or social concepts. *Child Development, 52,* 114–121.

Nucci, L. P. (1996). Morality and the personal sphere of action. In E. Reed, E. Turiel, & T. Brown (Eds.), *Values and knowledge* (pp. 41–60). Hillsdale, NJ: Erlbaum.

Nucci, L. P., Camino, C., & Sapiro, C. (1996). Social class effects on northeastern Brazilian children's conceptions of areas of personal choice and social regulation. *Child Development, 67,* 1223–1242.

Nucci, L. P., & Nucci, M. S. (1982a). Children's responses to moral and social conventional transgressions in free-play settings. *Child Development, 53,* 1337–1342.

Nucci, L. P., & Nucci, M. S. (1982b). Children's social interactions in the context of moral and conventional transgressions. *Child Development, 53,* 403–412.

Nucci, L. P., & Smetana, J. G. (1996). Mothers' concepts of young children's areas of personal freedom. *Child Development, 67,* 1870–1886.

Nucci, L. P., & Turiel, E. (1978). Social interactions and the development of social concepts in preschool children. *Child Development, 49,* 400–407.

Piaget, J. (1932). *The moral judgment of the child.* London: Routledge and Kegan Paul.

Rawls, J. (1971). *A theory of justice.* Cambridge, MA: Harvard University Press.

Ross, L., & Nisbett, R. M. (1991). *The person and the situation: Perspectives on social psychology.* Philadelphia: Temple University Press.

Shweder, R. A., Mahapatra, M., & Miller, J. G. (1987). Culture and moral development. In J. Kagan & S. Lamb (Eds.), *The emergence of morality in young children* (pp. 1–83). Chicago: University of Chicago Press.

Skinner, B. F. (1971). *Beyond freedom and dignity.* New York: Knopf.

Smetana, J. G. (1981). Preschool children's conceptions of moral and social rules. *Child Development, 52,* 1333–1336.

Smetana, J. G. (1985). Preschool children's conceptions of transgressions: Effects of varying moral and conventional domain-related attributes. *Developmental Psychology, 21,* 18–29.

Smetana, J. G., & Braeges, J. L. (1990). The development of toddler's moral and conventional judgments. *Merrill-Palmer Quarterly, 36,* 329–346.

Song, M. J., Smetana, J. G., & Kim, S. Y. (1987). Korean children's conceptions of moral and conventional transgressions. *Developmental Psychology, 23,* 577–582.

Triandis, H. C. (1996). The psychological measurement of cultural syndromes. *American Psychologist, 51,* 407–415.

Turiel, E. (1983). *The development of social knowledge: Morality and convention.* Cambridge, England: Cambridge University Press.

Turiel, E. (1998). The Development of morality. In W. Damon (Series Ed.) & N. Eisenberg (Vol. Ed.), *Handbook of child psychology: Vol. 3. Social, emotional, and personality development* (5th ed., pp. 863–932). New York: Wiley.

Turiel, E. (2000). Judgments and action in practical social situations. Manuscript in preparation, University of California at Berkeley.

Turiel, E., Killen, M., & Helwig, C. C. (1987). Morality: Its structure, functions and vagaries. In J. Kagan & S. Lamb (Eds.), *The emergence of morality in young children* (pp. 155–244). Chicago: University of Chicago Press.

Turiel, E., & Smetana, J. G. (1984). Social knowledge and social action. The coordination of domains. In W. M. Kurtines & J. L. Gewirtz (Eds.), *Morality, moral behavior, and moral development: Basic issues in theory and research* (pp. 261–282). New York: Wiley.

Wainryb, C. (1991). Understanding differences in moral judgments: The role of informational assumptions. *Child Development, 62*, 840–851.

Wainryb, C., & Turiel, E. (1994). Dominance, subordination, and concepts of personal entitlements in cultural contexts. *Child Development, 65*, 1701–1722.

Weston, D. R., & Turiel, E. (1980). Act–rule relations: Children's concepts of social rules. *Developmental Psychology, 16*, 417–424.

Yamada, H. (2000, June). Japanese mothers' concepts of young children's personal domain. Poster presented at the annual meeting of the Jean Piaget Society, Montreal, Canada.

Zelazo, P. D., Helwig, C. C., & Lau, A. (1996). Intention, act, and outcome in behavioral prediction and moral judgment. *Child Development, 67*, 2478–2492.

Zimba, R. F. (1994). The understanding of morality, convention, and personal preference in an African setting: Findings from Zambia. *Journal of Cross-Cultural Psychology, 25*, 369–393.

25

Children's Understanding of Society

Martyn Barrett and Eithne Buchanan-Barrow

Introduction

All children are born into and grow up within particular societies. Each of these societies is a collection of individuals who share common institutions and common economic, political, and legal structures. For the developing child, an important part of the process of growing up is to acquire an understanding of these institutions and structures, so that by the time adulthood is attained, he or she is able to function appropriately within this societal framework.

In addition, all societies contain many different social groups, for example, gender groups, occupational groups, ethnic groups, religious groups, etc. An individual member of a particular society will have multiple group affiliations. Another important task facing the developing child is to learn about these various social groups, to establish a sense of personal identity in relationship to some of the groups which are available, and to internalize those norms, values, representations, and practices appropriate for those social groups to which a sense of personal belonging is established.

This chapter summarizes the research which has been conducted into the development of children's understanding of the institutions and economic, political, and legal systems which characterize the society in which they live, and the development of children's understanding of three large-scale social groupings that characterize most societies: social class, ethnicity, and nationality. (For a more extended discussion of this research literature, see Barrett & Buchanan-Barrow, in press.)

Children's Understanding of the School

The school is one of the most significant societal institutions that children come into contact with beyond the family. The school is a complex institution, with many of its workings, structure, and power patterns invisible and unexplained to the young child, and it presents a considerable interpretative problem. Yet, in order to operate successfully in this system, the child must acquire an understanding of the rules, roles, and power/authority relations that apply within the school.

Children's understanding of the nursery school

Corsaro (1990) studied 3–4-year-old children's adjustment to the system of the nursery school. He found that children first had to acquire an understanding of the social organization of the school, particularly the adult rules. However, once this had been achieved, children made "secondary adjustments" to their shared understanding, in particular by adapting and circumventing the adult-imposed rules in conspiratorial relationships with other children. As Corsaro points out, this second stage in children's thinking, as witnessed by their actions, reveals the existence of a peer culture, which can only be established once children have become cognizant of the authority system of the school.

Understanding of the school in older children

Research with older children has also revealed that children recognize the social system which legitimizes the authority of teachers. Emler, Ohana, and Moscovici (1987) looked at children's understanding of the institutional roles of classroom teacher and headteacher, examining, among other areas, the power of the teachers to make or change rules. Children as young as 7 appeared to understand that teachers' powers, with respect to school regulations, were not unlimited, and that authority was hierarchically distributed. The children's responses suggested that they had grasped the basic fundamentals of the teacher's role.

Variations in the social organization of schools may result in differences in children's thinking in this domain. Ohana (1986) examined children's discourse on rules and responsibilities as a function of the type of school attended. She found that the talk of children from so-described "traditional" schools differed from that of children in "experimental" schools, suggesting they held different understandings of such areas as authority, rule function, and the requirements made by the system on both pupils and staff.

Buchanan-Barrow and Barrett (1996, 1998a, 1998b) examined the thinking of 5–11-year-old primary-school children about the school, probing their understanding of rules, community, self-system interaction, and power, and the links between them. The general picture that emerged suggested that children's thinking begins with a simple and narrow focus on a few central features but, as the children move up through the school, their understanding broadens to include more complex aspects of the school system. The children began by first grasping the role of the headteacher, and even the youngest children understood the position and importance of the headteacher in the school system. Then, around 7–8 years of age, the children began to acknowledge the next layer down in the power hierarchy, that of the teachers. The oldest children suggested that parents have influence in school matters, and also claimed an important role for children. Thus, the oldest children understood the school as a community, in which all members, from headteacher to pupils, had a part to play. Furthermore, the children's developing understanding of each system concept was linked to others, contributing to their overall comprehension of the system of the school.

Conclusion

The picture that emerges in this field is one in which the school-entering child rapidly adapts to the environment of the school, initially learning about the more salient aspects of rules, roles, and power/authority relations. However, children's understanding of some of the more subtle and less visible aspects of the school may take several years to emerge.

Children's Understanding of Economics

Money and economic transactions are omnipresent in the societies within which children live. People carry money around in their pockets and purses; children are given pocket money by their parents; people use their money to buy goods in shops; and adults have jobs that consume many hours of their lives in order to earn money. Children's understanding of these various phenomena has been subject to intense research in recent years.

Children's understanding of money

Understanding of the nature of money is fundamental to all aspects of socioeconomic understanding. Berti and Bombi (1988) examined 3–11-year-old children's understanding of money and work using Piagetian interviewing. They found that 3–4-year-old children have little understanding of money or the origins of money. Ignorant of the link between work and money, very young children believe money is simply obtained from pockets or purses. Between the ages of 5 and 7, children begin to puzzle out connections, as their opportunities to observe the monetary transactions in everyday life increase. Their explanations now reflect this, including such sources of money as the bank, shops, and work. By about 7, children grasp the essential connection with work, and tend to believe that the only way to get money is by working. Finally, by about 10–11 years of age, children understand that it is also possible to inherit money or to obtain money through crime.

The concept of profit also begins to be properly understood by the age of 11, with children recognizing that shopkeepers must charge their customers more than they paid to their suppliers in order to be able to make a living and to pay their employees (Berti &

Bombi, 1988). However, comparing data from Scottish (Jahoda, 1979), English (Furth, 1980), Dutch (Jahoda, 1982), and Zimbabwean children (Jahoda, 1983), Jahoda found a lag in European children in their grasp of the principles of trading, although the stages in their thinking were similar. Using a role-playing situation, Jahoda found that Zimbabwean children display an understanding of profit at around 9, two years before European children. Zimbabwean children's more extensive and relevant experience of trading in their everyday lives may bring about this earlier acquisition of the concept of profit, indicating that cultural context has a role to play in the development of economic understanding.

Children in the United States also appear to acquire an early understanding of economic phenomena. Thompson and Siegler (2000) looked at children's understanding of the causal relations between supply, demand, the price of goods in shops, and the volume of sales (e.g., if something is too expensive, then few people will buy it). They found an understanding of these relations emerging by 7 years of age. They argue that, by this age, the children are constructing a naïve theory of economics, which they use to explain and predict economic phenomena.

Children's understanding of banking

Sociocultural influences in children's economic understanding have also been found in studies of their comprehension of banking transactions. Examinations of children's thinking about interest payments on deposits and loans show that the thinking of Scottish (Jahoda, 1981) and New Zealand (Ng, 1985) children lags behind that of Hong Kong children by about two years (Wong, 1989). Although there are similar stages in their developing thinking about the bank and its activities, Hong Kong children display a comprehension of interest as early as 9 years, as opposed to around 11 years for the other two samples. On the other hand, Japanese (Takahashi & Hatano, 1994) and Black South African (Bonn & Webley, 2000) children show the least mature understanding. Children's development in this domain must be subject to complex influences; while Black South African children have little exposure to banks, this is not the case for Japanese children, who are growing up in a sophisticated economic system and might be expected to display more mature thinking.

Further evidence of the complexities of development in this area comes from a study of the economic thinking of children from 10 countries (Denmark, Finland, France, Poland, Israel, West Germany, Algeria, Yugoslavia, Norway, and Austria) by Leiser, Sevon, and Levy (1990). Differences in the sophistication of the children's thinking about banks did not always reflect the economic standing of their country. For example, while the children of Finland were in the most mature group, the children from the neighboring country of Norway displayed some of the least advanced thinking. Evidently, the development of an understanding of the concepts of banking and interest may be influenced by factors other than the prominence of the banking sector.

Children's understanding of social class

Children are aware of inequalities of wealth at an early age (Jahoda, 1959; Leahy, 1981) but initially at a fairly superficial level. When asked to describe rich or poor people, Jahoda found that 6-year-old children perceive outward differences, mentioning variations in housing, clothing, and lifestyle. Leahy also reported that children aged 6–11 tended to emphasize "peripheral" characteristics (possessions, appearances, and behavior) as opposed to life chances or class differences. Around 6–7, children begin to explain inequalities according to jobs, without reference to income, but by the age of 8, children become aware of the link between social differences and income, and relate the differences in wealth to earnings from work (Berti & Bombi, 1988; Jahoda, 1959). Leahy (1981) also found that there was an increase, with age, in references to the role played by earnings in inequalities of wealth.

Cross-cultural research has revealed variations in children's thinking about social class according to nationality (Leiser et al., 1990). A comparison of Algerian and French children (Roland-Levy, 1990) found that the most prevalent explanation for both poverty and wealth in Algerian children was the personal characteristics of the individual, while for French children poverty was seen as a consequence of the socioeconomic system. Furthermore, while the French children believed that fate played more of a role in being rich than being poor, Algerian children were more likely to attribute being poor to fate. A study of the thinking of Black children in South Africa (Bonn, Earle, Lea, & Webley, 1999) also found differences according to location. Rural children were more likely to say that unemployment was an important cause of poverty and inequality, than children from a semi-urban location. Additionally, rural children had a more fatalistic view of poverty, attributing it to God almost as much as to unemployment. However, Bonn et al. found that age was still a more important factor than social niche. While the social environment may have affected the children's thinking about such concepts as wealth, poverty, inequality, and unemployment, their capacity to formulate causal links between these concepts was more likely to be associated with age than with location.

Evidently, there are culturally based explanations for income inequalities. However, as most research in this area has been conducted from a Piagetian perspective, age is still seen as having the stronger impact, with cultural context playing a more peripheral role by affecting the rate of acquisition. However, there are some findings that suggest that social influences may have a more important part to play in children's acquisition of concepts of inequalities of income (Emler & Dickinson, 1985; Emler, Ohana, & Dickinson, 1990). Emler and Dickinson (1985) found differences associated with socioeconomic class, but notably none with age, in Scottish children's perceptions of wage differentials. For all the occupations under consideration, middle-class children gave higher overall estimates of income and reported a greater spread in incomes, with a much wider division between manual and nonmanual occupations, than working-class children. Furthermore, the explanations offered by the children for wage differentials varied according to socioeconomic class, with middle-class children expressing greater support for income inequality than working-class children. However, while children are developing their thinking about wage differentials, their perceptions of the size of differentials are generally inaccurate. Overall, Dickinson and Emler (1996) argue that children from different socioeconomic backgrounds are developing in very different social worlds, and that this results in varying beliefs about the extent, the causes, and the justifications for economic inequalities in society.

However, a replication of Emler and Dickinson's study with West German children (Burgard, Cheyne, & Jahoda, 1989) failed to find substantial class differences in the children's thinking, while conversely finding differences associated with age. It may be that there is a greater awareness of class differences amongst Scottish children than amongst German children. Or it may be that class differences partly reflect the greater availability of relevant information to middle-class children, thus allowing them to report a more accurate, rather than a more biased, understanding (Jahoda, 1981).

Children as economic actors

Research has examined children's behavior as consumers, investigating their purchasing and saving strategies. Children aged 6–10, tested on their skills as consumers, gave reasonable estimates of the prices of such items as a pencil or a hamburger, and had some understanding of the need to judge prices in terms of the value of the item (Pliner, Freedman, Abramovitch, & Darke, 1996). Other studies have examined children's behavior in play economies using tokens; while very young children have little concept of the value of saving, between the ages of 6–12, children do develop more complex strategies (Sonuga-Barke & Webley, 1993; Webley, Levine, & Lewis, 1991). By about the age of 9, children understand that savings can be used for future expenditure and that savings and expenditure are not separate activities. The 12 year olds displayed an even better grasp of the flows of funds over the course of the study; not only did they save more, but they also used a greater range of strategies to achieve their goals (Webley et al., 1991).

Children may develop good financial strategies from their parents' approach to money. Observations of children's behavior in a make-believe shop revealed that children who are in receipt of regular pocket-money from their parents demonstrate more mature spending strategies than children who were given money unconditionally by their parents (Abramovitch, Freedman, & Pliner, 1991). Abramovitch et al. suggest that the parents who pay their children regular allowances are teaching their children to be responsible with money and that this contributes to their spending behavior.

Conclusion

Much of the research into children's economic socialization has been conducted from a Piagetian perspective, proposing that children's thinking develops according to a universal series of stages which themselves are grounded in the Piagetian stages of development (Berti & Bombi, 1988; Furth, 1980). This approach has drawn criticism because its emphasis on the universality of stages in children's thinking has resulted in the underrating of social and cultural differences (Emler & Dickinson, 1985; Emler, Ohana, & Dickinson, 1990). However, the two approaches are not mutually exclusive. Indeed, the evidence actually suggests that the development of economic thinking proceeds through the child drawing upon both personal economic experience (e.g., dealing with pocket money, experience in trading) and socially provided information (which may be available, e.g., from discourse with parents). As both economic experience and the social provision of information varies according to sociocultural context, it is perhaps inevitable that the child's understanding of economic institutions and phenomena will exhibit sociocultural variation.

Children's Political Understanding

While children's economic understanding has been extensively researched, children's understanding of politics has been a neglected topic in recent years. This may be partly due to the difficulty in finding a productive research perspective. Extensive research in the 1960s and 1970s from within a political socialization perspective, which was favored by political scientists, failed to elucidate developmental mechanisms and processes. Subsequent research from a Piagetian perspective again drew criticism for its emphasis on universality at the expense of contextual variation. However, there are indications that a more productive line of research may be possible using the naïve theory approach as a conceptual framework.

Content of children's political understanding

Some studies have examined children's political thinking by probing their knowledge of specific political institutions and events through open-ended interviewing. Connell (1971) investigated the political understanding of children and adolescents from a Piagetian perspective. Under the age of 7, children revealed *intuitive thinking,* in which political and nonpolitical issues were undifferentiated. From 7–10, children demonstrated *primitive realism,* in which they began to be aware of areas of political interest. Over the age of 10, *the construction of political order,* children began to show a clearer sense of the tasks of government and to see political power as hierarchically and institutionally structured. However, even the older children still lacked much specific understanding. Moore, Lare, and Wagner (1985) also used a Piagetian approach to investigate political understanding of children from kindergarten to fourth grade. They found an increase in the content of children's thinking over these years, but with girls less knowledgeable than boys. Coles (1986) interviewed children in a variety of countries to ascertain their views of political situations in their respective countries. However, while these studies produced a wealth of detail about young children's knowledge of specific political institutions and events, they revealed little of the meanings underlying the children's responses, nor did they reveal much about the influences involved in their formation.

Children's political concepts

In order to examine more fundamental aspects of children's political cognition, Berti (1988) examined the political concepts of 6–15-year-old children. She investigated their understanding of a hypothetical island-society, focusing on such concepts as power, conflict, laws, and community. Using open-ended interviewing, Berti found that the children's responses were grouped into four main areas: (1) collective needs; (2) conflicts; (3) political organization; and (4) laws. The youngest children (under 8) were generally oblivious of conflicts, of the need for organization, or of the function of laws. Children aged 8–9, after some prompting, mentioned *chiefs* who would govern by some sort of *orders*. Children aged 10–11 demonstrated a major advance on the younger children and referred spontaneously to collective needs and political organization. By about 12–13, children volunteered that the whole community was responsible for law making in some sense.

Children's understanding of the state

In an examination of the concept of the state, Berti (1994) investigated children's understanding of such concepts as *state, democracy, law,* and *dominion,* together with a series of public offices and functions, through open-ended interviewing. Children aged 8–9 reported a very simple and loose organization of people, which were under the authority of the chief, but they had little understanding of current political events, nor did they have any sense of a hierarchy of authority beyond the chief. By the age of 10–11, Berti argues that children have some naïve theory of politics. Children now spontaneously offered the word *state* when talking about Yugoslavia, and they also described Europe as a community of states. Furthermore, they displayed a basic grasp of a power hierarchy. However, Berti suggests that their political knowledge was not particularly well organized or accessible, as they still occasionally reverted to less mature responses. Berti postulates that a shift occurs in children's political thinking around the ages of 9–10, as they move from seeing power as generally concentrated in one individual to comprehending that political power is usually hierarchically organized.

Children's understanding of community

Buchanan-Barrow (2000) examined children's understanding of a hypothetical community, using multiple-choice and card-sorting methods to avoid the potential problem of underestimating children's knowledge by relying on their verbal reports. Children aged 5–11 years were given a simple description of the political system of an imaginary island. They then chose a decision maker for each of a series of problems for the islanders. The youngest children tended to choose the highest authority, namely the island Prime Minister, to deal with most of the problems, even the more parochial ones. This supports the view that children develop the concept of the *chief* at an early age, as other studies have suggested (Berti, 1988, 1994; Connell, 1971). However, with age, children began to involve more and lower levels of the hierarchy of authority, spreading the decision-making process to include others, echoing Berti's shift (1994). Finally, the oldest children displayed a belief that all members of the community should be involved in decision making, which would appear to be similar to the views of the oldest children in Berti's earlier study (1988) that all should be involved in law making.

Conclusion

The shift in recent years from the focus on children's political knowledge to investigations of their political concepts (Berti, 1988, 1994; Buchanan-Barrow, 2000) has opened up the possibility of a more fruitful perspective for examining children's political cognition, that of the naïve theory approach (Wellman & Gelman, 1998). These studies suggest that children construct a naïve theory of politics, as they attempt to make sense of systems of power or authority. Children's thinking begins with a simple and narrow focus on the role of a powerful individual, a *chief,* or *prime minister,* exercising absolute power from the highest point in the system. With age, children develop an understanding of the hierarchies of power, as they become cognizant of the parts played at lower levels in the system. Finally, as older children acquire a sense of the community as a whole, their thinking displays a basic grasp of a consent to government, as they propose that all members of a community should be involved in its organization. This "top-down" acquisition of political system understanding echoes children's developing thinking about the school (see above).

Children's Understanding of the Law

Although some findings about children's legal understanding emerge from the studies into children's political cognition, specific research focused on the legal domain has been a fairly recent phenomenon. Interest has been prompted by the increasing levels of participation by children in legal investigations, either as victims in cases of neglect or abuse, or as witnesses to crimes. Research has begun to examine children's perceptions of the legal system, as their legal knowledge may be linked to the effectiveness of their testimony.

Children's legal concepts

Several studies have investigated children's legal concepts. For example, Flin, Stevenson, and Davies (1989) investigated Scottish children's legal vocabulary and knowledge of court proceedings. Children, aged 6–10, responded to 20 common legal terms (e.g., *a law, oath, evidence, trial*), including some legal roles (e.g., *policeman, judge, lawyer, witness*). Overall, children under the age of 10 did not appear to be well informed about the legal system, while the youngest children were only reasonably familiar with four of the terms (*policeman, rule, promise,* and *truth*). Under the age of 8, there was also considerable negativity about the possibility of attending court, which was perhaps prompted by a generally held belief in the younger children that courts were for "bad" people. Similar findings were obtained by Saywitz (1989) and Warren-Leubecker, Tate, Hinton, and Ozbek (1989), who looked at legal understanding in American children aged up to 14 years old. These studies concur in finding considerable limitations in children's understanding of legal concepts below the age of 10.

Children's legal reasoning

Two studies have examined children's legal reasoning, using scenarios. Peterson-Badali, Abramovitch, and Duda (1997) examined 7–12-year-old Canadian children's reasoning about plea bargaining. They found that the majority of children's plea choices were congruent with legal criteria rather than with morality, suggesting that children do have some understanding of the relationship between important legal variables (such as evidence) and plea decisions. However, the younger children (under 10) were generally unable to give an explicit account for their plea choices. In another study by Berti and Ugolini (1998), Italian children (aged 6–14) responded to a crime scenario. They found younger children to be largely ignorant of legal matters. However, there was a major shift around the age of 11, when children demonstrated a more precise knowledge of the court and the role of the judicial system within the wider state system.

Television as a source of children's knowledge of the law

As very few children have direct personal experience of the legal system, one possible source of children's knowledge about the law is television. Children aged 3–7 years old may watch up to 2 hours per week of programs related to crime and legal activities (Huston, Wright, Rice, Kerkman, & St. Peters, 1990), and Saywitz (1989) found that extensive watching of TV programs influences children's legal conceptions. Durkin and his colleagues have conducted a series of studies examining children's understanding of televised crime and police programs (Durkin & Howarth, 1997; Low & Durkin, 1997). Using both spontaneous script generation and picture sequencing of police stories with children aged 5–13, they found that while younger children's thinking was generally limited to the crime and chase scenes, older children's thinking encompassed much more complexity, often including formal legal processes. Younger children also had difficulty differentiating between their own perspective on an event and that of a TV witness, who had not seen the crime committed, suggesting that children might fail to comprehend the problems and limitations with witness testimony in real life. If TV crime and police programs do provide children with their earliest source of legal knowledge, then it is possible that the nonveridical nature of many TV representations could lead children to misunderstand real-life legal processes.

Conclusion

Children's understanding of the law shows considerable developmental change over the course of middle childhood, with the age of 10–11 appearing to be a significant watershed in their understanding. The role that television may play in fostering children's legal understanding serves to re-emphasize a more general point about children's societal understanding: That in knowledge domains in which children have little first-hand personal experience, much of their knowledge may instead be derived from indirect sources such as television, parents or peers.

Children's Understanding of Ethnic Groups

Nowadays, the societies within which children live are rarely homogeneous in terms of their ethnic composition. Instead, most societies contain individuals from a number of different ethnic groups. These ethnic groups may identify themselves, or be identified by others, by all sorts of different criteria or characteristics, including country of origin, religion, culture, language, skin color, etc. The cognitive task facing the child in mastering this system of ethnic categorization is considerable. Investigations into children's understanding of ethnic groups have tended to focus upon three aspects of the developmental process: the development of ethnic awareness; the development of ethnic self-identification; and the development of ethnic attitudes.

The development of ethnic awareness

One method frequently used to study children's ethnic awareness is to show the child pictures or dolls representing people from different ethnic groups, and to ask the child to point to, for example, the White person, the Black person, etc. This method has revealed that even some 3 years olds can identify the ethnicity of Black and White pictures or dolls; amongst 4–5 year olds, 75% of children can identify Black and White ethnicity; and amongst 6–7 year olds, the figure is usually 90% or higher (Clark & Clark, 1947; Williams & Morland, 1976). These figures are typically obtained when the targets are White and Black, and are exhibited by both White and Black children. Other studies have found that White and Chinese-American children acquire the ability to identify Chinese people between 5 and 7 years of age (Fox & Jordan, 1973); White and Native-American children's ability to identify Native-American people continues to develop up to 9 years of age (Rosenthal, 1974); while White and Hispanic-American children's ability to identify Hispanic people continues improving up to 9 or 10 years of age (Rice, Ruiz, & Padilla, 1974).

One problem with these studies is that they only show that children can identify people from different ethnic categories when asked to do so by an experimenter; they do not show whether children spontaneously use these ethnic categories in their own social judgments. Consequently, other methods have been used to see whether children do spontaneously employ ethnic categories. Yee and Brown (1988) presented 3–9-year-old children with pictures of people who differed according to their ethnicity, gender, and age, and asked the children to group them. They found that by 5 years of age, ethnicity was used spontaneously to group the pictures by a third of the children, while by 7 years of age, ethnicity was used by two thirds of them. Davey (1983), who tested 7–10 years olds using a similar method, also found that ethnicity was used spontaneously more frequently than either gender or socioeconomic status.

The development of ethnic self-identification

The standard method used to study ethnic self-identification has again been to show children either pictures or dolls representing people from different ethnic groups, and in this case to ask the child to point to the one which most closely resembles him or her. This method has revealed that, from 3–4 years of age onwards, White children identify with the White person or doll 75% of the time, rising to almost 100% by 6–7 years (Aboud, 1977; Williams & Morland, 1976).

However, a more complicated picture has been found with Black children. Some Black children identify with the Black doll or picture from about 3–4 years of age. However, a large proportion of 3–4-year-old Black children tend to identify with the White person or doll rather than with the Black one. Indeed, in one widely cited study, Clark and Clark (1947) found that over 60% of the 3-year-old Black children identified with a White doll rather a Black one; by 7 years of age, this figure had dropped to 13%. Comparable findings have been obtained with Black children in many other studies (see Aboud, 1988, for a detailed review). Similar trends have been found to occur with Chinese American (Fox & Jordan, 1973) and Hispanic children (Rice et al., 1974): In both cases, half of the children identified with the White person at 4–5 years of age, with identification with the ingroup figure only rising to over 80% by about 7 years of age. Thus, it would appear that majority and minority group children may differ in the development of their ethnic self-identification. Nevertheless, it should be noted that by about 7 years of age, most ethnic minority children do exhibit identification with their own ethnic group.

The development of ethnic attitudes

Children's ethnic attitudes have also been studied using pictures or dolls. However, in this case, the children are asked which one they like the best/least. As far as White majority group children are concerned, they display a consistent preference for the White pictures or dolls from the age of 3–4 years onwards, a preference which often grows in strength between 4 and 7 years of age (Aboud, 1980; Asher & Allen, 1969).

However, once again, a more complicated picture arises in the case of Black minority group children. Firstly, in some of the studies which were conducted before the end of the 1960s, it was found that many young Black children preferred the White dolls or pictures over the Black ones (Asher & Allen, 1969; Clark & Clark, 1947). Furthermore, this preference for the ethnic outgroup was found to peak at about 6–7 years of age, before declining and turning into a pro-Black bias instead. Nevertheless, even in these early studies, not all young Black children were found to exhibit this outgroup preference (Aboud, 1988; Banks, 1976). However, the picture has changed dramatically since the late 1960s. The positive bias toward the majority White outgroup seems to have disappeared in 4–7-year-old Black children in more recent years, with Black children now showing an ingroup bias which is equivalent to that shown by White majority group children (Aboud, 1980; Hraba & Grant, 1970; Vaughan, 1978). In order to explain this change in the pattern of Black children's identity development, Brown (1995) draws attention to the fact that, during the

1960s, Black consciousness political movements appeared in countries such as America and Britain, and these helped to foster a much more positive sense of minority ingroup pride amongst Black people. Brown argues that this more positive group image is probably the source of this change which occurred to the pattern of Black children's ethnic identity development in the late 1960s. So, the current picture is one in which both White majority and Black minority children's positive bias toward their own ingroup strengthens between 4 and 7 years of age.

As far as attitudes toward ethnic outgroups are concerned, these tend to be the inverse of attitudes to the ingroup. Thus, as positive ingroup bias becomes more pronounced between 4 and 7 years of age, negative prejudice against outgroups also becomes more pronounced. A peak in negative prejudice against ethnic outgroups occurs at about 7 years of age. After this, there is typically a decline in both positive feelings about the ingroup and negative feelings about outgroups up until about 11 or 12 years of age (Aboud, 1980, 1988).

Using an adjective attribution task in order to study this latter development trend, Doyle, Beaudet, and Aboud (1988) found that, between 6 and 12 years of age, children shift away from assigning mainly positive attributes to the ingroup and mainly negative attributes to the outgroup at 6 years of age, to assigning both positive and negative attributes to both the ingroup and the outgroup by 12 years of age. Similar developmental trends in the attribution of positive and negative traits to ethnic ingroups and outgroups have been found by Takriti, Buchanan-Barrow, and Barrett (2000) in a study of 5–11-year-old Christian and Muslim children. Thus, the decline in children's prejudice toward ethnic outgroups across the middle years of childhood seems to be associated with the increasing acknowledgement that the members of all ethnic groups can exhibit both good and bad characteristics.

Numerous studies have been conducted into the possible sources of children's ethnic attitudes, with parents and peers being the two main sources that have been examined. These studies are reviewed in detail by Aboud (1988) and Aboud and Doyle (1996). The overall picture which emerges is that, while some studies have found positive correlations between the attitudes of children and those modeled by the socialization agents in their environment (e.g., Branch & Newcombe, 1986), many other studies have failed to find any relationship at all (e.g., Aboud & Doyle, 1996; Davey, 1983; Katz, 1976). In the light of these findings, Aboud and Doyle (1996) conclude that children's ethnic attitudes are not strongly related to either their parents' or their friends' attitudes, and that the widespread assumption that children learn their ethnic attitudes from significant socialization agents is not substantiated by the research.

Conclusion

Children's understanding of, and feelings about, ethnic groups show considerable change between 3 and 12 years of age, with 6–7 years of age appearing to be an important transitional age in the child's development. Because children's ethnic attitudes do not appear to be derived from those which are modeled by either their parents or peers, Aboud (1988) has argued that the development of ethnic attitudes is driven by cognitive-developmental changes rather than by social influences. She postulates that it is changes to the way in which the child is able to conceptualize large-scale social groups which drive the developmental changes in the child's attitudes to ethnic ingroups and outgroups between 3 and 12 years of age, with the onset of concrete operational understanding at 6–7 years of age being the reason why this age is a watershed in the development of children's ethnic attitudes. However, this Piagetian explanation is unconvincing in the light of findings that there is no significant correlation between the development of ethnic attitudes and the development of concrete operations (Doyle & Aboud, 1995), that children are in fact able to exhibit concrete operational abilities in many contexts well before 6–7 years of age (Donaldson, 1978), and that historically the pattern of minority children's ethnic identity development exhibited a significant change in the late 1960s (Brown, 1995), a change which cannot be explained on the basis of Aboud's cognitive-developmental theory. Consequently, this is a domain of development that still stands in need of an appropriate theoretical explanation.

The bulk of the research in this field has focused upon children's judgments concerning those ethnic groups which are distinguished in terms of their physical characteristics such as skin color and physiognomy. Very little research has been conducted into children's awareness of, ability to differentiate between, and attitudes toward, those ethnic groups which are differentiated in terms of their culture, religion, and/or language. Exceptions to this are the studies by Doyle et al. (1988), who studied children's judgments of French-speaking versus English-speaking people, and Takriti et al. (2000), who studied children's judgments of Christian versus Muslim people living in England.

Children's Understanding of Nationality and National Groups

In addition to social class and ethnicity, the societies within which children live today are also structured in terms of nationality. Because the entire land surface of the world, apart from Antarctica, has now been divided up into nation-states, all children nowadays are born within the borders of a particular nation-state, and they have to live their lives in a world which is characterized by the existence of many different national groups. This section describes the research that has been conducted into children's knowledge of, and attitudes to, national groups.

Children's knowledge of their own country and national group

Many studies investigating children's knowledge of their own country and national group have used open-ended interviewing. These studies have shown that, up until about 5 years of age, children often have little knowledge of their own country or national group, and may even be unable to state the name of their own country (Piaget & Weil, 1951). However, from about 5 onwards, children are able to provide the name of their own country, and are able to classify themselves as members of their own national group (Barrett, 2001). Knowledge of emblems such as the national flag, national anthem, national landscapes, national buildings, and salient historical figures also develops from about 5 years of age onwards (Jahoda, 1963b).

Children's geographical knowledge of their own country develops over subsequent years, but this knowledge is error-prone until at least early adolescence (Barrett, 1996; Jahoda, 1963a; Piaget & Weil, 1951). For example, Jahoda (1963a) investigated 6–11-year-old Glaswegian children's knowledge of Scotland. He found that nearly all of the 6 year olds were familiar with the word *Scotland*, but most of the children had a poor understanding of what this word referred to, many of them believing that it was the name of another town or a place outside Glasgow. And even at 10 or 11 years of age, some of the children were still exhibiting these kinds of confusions. Knowledge of national geography correlates with children's degree of identification with their national group (Barrett & Whennell, 1998); thus, in the case of English children, the more geographical knowledge about England and the UK that these children possess, the more English they feel. The causality in this correlational relationship remains unclear, however.

In a study of the attributes which 5–11-year-old children ascribe to the members of their own national group, Barrett, Wilson, and Lyons (1999) found that the younger children were more likely than the older ones to ascribe only positive attributes to their own national group, with older children being more likely to assign a mixture of both positive and negative attributes to the group. Thus, as the children got older, their perceptions of their own national group became less positive overall.

Children's feelings about their own country and national group

Several studies have investigated how children feel about their own country and national group. Adjective attribution tasks or simple rating scales have typically been used and have yielded a mixed set of findings. Some studies found that children do not have a systematic preference for their own country or for members of their own national group until 7 years of age or even later (e.g., Middleton, Tajfel, & Johnson, 1970; Piaget & Weil, 1951). Other studies have suggested that there is a systematic preference for the child's own country from at least 5–6 years of age (e.g., Barrett, 2001; Bennett, Lyons, Sani, & Barrett, 1998; Lambert & Klineberg, 1967). Furthermore, ingroup favoritism is not a universal phenomenon. In particular, children who are members of a negatively evaluated group may not develop a systematic preference for their own group, a finding obtained with both Scottish and non-European Israeli-Jewish children at a time when these two groups were generally perceived to be of a relatively low social and economic status in Britain and Israel, respectively (Tajfel, Jahoda, Nemeth, Rim, & Johnson, 1972).

The importance which children attribute to their national identity, as well as their degree of identification with their national group, increase between 5–6 and 11–12 years of age. However, these general age trends are exhibited to a different extent by children living in different countries, in different regions of the same country, or in different sociolinguistic groups within the same community, apparently as a function of the specific sociocultural situation in which they are growing up (Barrett, in press; Barrett, Riazanova, & Volovikova, 2001).

Children's knowledge of other countries and national groups

Children's ability to name other countries is also very poor before about 5 years of age, and young children have great difficulty in understanding the concept of a foreign country (Piaget & Weil, 1951). Knowledge about other countries begins to develop from about 5, although even at 10 or 11, some children still have very poor geographical knowledge of other countries (Barrett & Farroni, 1996; Jahoda, 1962).

This growth of geographical knowledge is accompanied by the acquisition and elaboration of stereotypes of the people who live in other countries (Barrett & Short, 1992; Lambert & Klineberg, 1967; Piaget & Weil, 1951). The amount of individual variation which is acknowledged to exist around these national stereotypes increases between 5 and 11 years of age (Barrett et al., 1999). Thus, older children are more willing than younger children to admit that there is much variability amongst the people who belong to different national groups.

Children's feelings about other countries and national groups

Children sometimes acquire strong feelings about particular groups of foreign people before they have acquired any concrete knowledge about those groups (Barrett & Short, 1992; Johnson, Middleton, & Tajfel, 1970). In addition, although many children do seem to acquire a systematic preference for their own country and nationality over other countries and nationalities from about 6–7 years of age, it is clear from many studies that children can feel very positively indeed about some national outgroups (Barrett & Short, 1992; Johnson et al., 1970; Lambert & Klineberg, 1967; Middleton et al., 1970).

The relative order of preference for other countries, once it is established (perhaps at 5 or 6 years of age), remains fairly stable and consistent across the remaining childhood years (Barrett & Short, 1992; Johnson et al., 1970). However, the overall degree of liking for all national outgroups tends to increase between 5 and 10 years of age, while after 10 years of age, this general increase in positive regard for other national groups usually levels out (Lambert & Klineberg, 1967).

Conclusion

The overall picture which emerges in this domain is that there is considerable learning about national groups from 5 years of age onwards. From 5 onwards, strong attitudes and affective biases toward the national ingroup and national outgroups are formed. However, even by early adolescence, children still have a great deal more to learn about nations and national groups.

Piaget and Weil (1951) originally proposed that children's thoughts and feelings in this area are determined by their current stage of cognitive development, but Jahoda (1964) showed that this account was inadequate, with many children violating Piaget's proposed developmental-stage sequence. Since that time, much of the research in this field has been descriptive rather than theoretically driven (e.g., Lambert & Klineberg, 1967; Tajfel et al., 1970). More recently, there have been attempts to apply social identity theory and self-categorization theory to children's development in this domain (e.g., Barrett et al., 1999; Bennett et al., 1998), but these attempts have shown that these theories may not be applicable in this context. The naïve theory approach to children's cognitive development (Wellman & Gelman, 1998) has recently been considered as an alternative possible framework for conceptualizing children's development in this domain (Penny, Barrett, & Lyons, 2001), but at the time of writing, the detailed implications of this framework for this domain have not yet been established.

Conclusions

This chapter has reviewed the research literature on children's understanding of society. As we have seen, a substantial proportion of this literature is Piagetian in orientation. Thus, many studies have relied upon open-ended interviewing to gather data, and stage-based descriptions of the development of children's understanding have been put forward, often with the tacit (and sometimes explicit) assumption that the stage sequence is universal, and that influences from the child's sociocultural context are minimal and can only either accelerate or decelerate the rate at which the child progresses through the sequence of stages. In addition, it is often assumed that development proceeds through the child reflecting upon his or her own personal experience, actively constructing his or her own explanations of the observed phenomena using his or her current cognitive capacities and skills.

However, the child does not always have first-hand personal experience of the phenomena or institutions in societal domains (e.g., of teachers' decision making in schools, of profit generation in shops and banks, of procedures in courts of law), and so the child's own personal experience cannot always function as the source of the child's knowledge. Instead, children are heavily reliant upon indirect and socially mediated sources of information for learning about many societal phenomena, with television, parent and peer discourse, and the school curriculum probably being the most important sources of information (Barrett & Buchanan-Barrow, in press). It is for this reason that children's understanding in many different societal domains exhibits variation as a function of the child's sociocultural context (e.g., the school domain, Ohana, 1986; the economic domain, Jahoda, 1983, Leiser et al., 1990; the ethnic domain, Brown, 1995; and the nationality domain, Barrett et al., 2001).

In addition to this increasing acknowledgement of sociocultural variation in the development of children's societal thinking, a second shift which is currently taking place in this field of research is the introduction of the naïve theory approach to children's cognitive development (Barrett & Buchanan-Barrow, in press; Wellman & Gelman, 1998). According to this approach, during the course of development, children construct naïve theories to explain phenomena in particular domains. These theories are specialized for particular types of conceptual content; provide cause-and-effect explanations of the phenomena in that domain; involve hypothetical constructs of unobservable factors or processes; and are subject to change during the course of development. Moreover, these naïve theories are often implicit rather than explicit. Thus, children may not always be able to consciously access and verbalize these theories. As a consequence, Piagetian verbal interviewing is likely to underestimate children's reasoning. Instead, in order to reveal the structure of the child's thinking, the child must be presented with scenarios or stories in which variables are manipulated and about which the child has to make a predictive judgment. In several societal domains, researchers are now beginning to use this alternative to the Piagetian approach (e.g., Thompson & Siegler, 2000, in the economic domain; Berti, 1988, and Buchanan-Barrow, 2000, in the political domain; and Penny et al., 2001, in the nationality domain), and it seems likely that further advances in this field will emerge from the broader application of this post-Piagetian theoretical and methodological approach to the study of children's thinking about society.

References

Aboud, F. (1977). Interest in ethnic information: A cross-cultural developmental study. *Canadian Journal of Behavioural Science, 9,* 134–146.

Aboud, F. (1980). A test of ethnocentrism with young children. *Canadian Journal of Behavioural Science, 12,* 195–209.

Aboud, F. (1988). *Children and prejudice.* Oxford, England: Blackwell.

Aboud, F., & Doyle, A.B. (1996). Parental and peer influences on children's racial attitudes. *International Journal of Intercultural Relations, 20,* 371–383.

Abramovitch, R., Freedman, J., & Pliner, P. (1991). Children and money: Getting an allowance, credit versus cash, and knowledge of pricing. *Journal of Economic Psychology, 12,* 27–45.

Asher, S. R., & Allen, V. L. (1969). Racial preference and social comparison processes. *Journal of Social Issues, 25,* 157–166.

Banks, W. C. (1976). White preference in Blacks: A paradigm in search of a phenomenon. *Psychological Bulletin, 83,* 1179–1186.

Barrett, M. (1996). English children's acquisition of a European identity. In G. Breakwell & E. Lyons (Eds.), *Changing European identities: Social psychological analyses of social change* (pp. 349–369). Oxford, England: Butterworth-Heinemann.

Barrett, M. (2001). The development of national identity: A conceptual analysis and some data from Western European studies. In M. Barrett, T. Riazanova, & M. Volovikova (Eds.), *Development of national, ethnolinguistic, and religious identities in children and adolescents* (pp. 16–58). Moscow, Russia: Institute of Psychology, Russian Academy of Sciences.

Barrett, M. (in press). *Children's beliefs and feelings about nations and national groups.* Hove, England: Psychology Press.

Barrett, M., & Buchanan-Barrow, E. (Eds.) (in press). *Children's understanding of society.* Hove, England: Psychology Press.

Barrett, M., & Farroni, T. (1996). English and Italian children's knowledge of European geography. *British Journal of Developmental Psychology, 14,* 257–273.

Barrett, M., Riazanova, T., & Volovikova, M. (Eds.) (2001). *Development of national, ethnolinguistic and religious identities in children and adolescents.* Moscow, Russia: Institute of Psychology, Russian Academy of Sciences.

Barrett, M., & Short, J. (1992). Images of European people in a group of 5–10-year-old English school children. *British Journal of Developmental Psychology, 10,* 339–363.

Barrett, M., & Whennell, S. (1998). The relationship between national identity and geographical knowledge in English children. Poster presented at XVth Biennial Meeting of ISSBD, Berne, Switzerland.

Barrett, M., Wilson, H., & Lyons, E. (1999). Self-categorization theory and the development of national identity in English children. Poster presented at Biennial Meeting of SRCD, Albuquerque, NM.

Bennett, M., Lyons, E., Sani, F., & Barrett, M. (1998). Children's subjective identification with the group and ingroup favoritism. *Developmental Psychology, 34*, 902–909.

Berti, A. (1988). The development of political understanding in children between 6–15 years old. *Human Relations, 41*, 437–446.

Berti, A. (1994). Children's understanding of the concept of the state. In M. Carretero & J. F. Voss (Eds.), *Cognitive and instructional processes in history and the social sciences* (pp. 49–75). Hillsdale, NJ: Erlbaum.

Berti, A., & Bombi, A. (1988). *The child's construction of economics.* Cambridge, England: Cambridge University Press.

Berti, A. E., & Ugolini, E. (1998). Developing knowledge of the judicial system: A domain-specific approach. *Journal of Genetic Psychology, 159*, 221–236.

Bonn, M., Earle, D., Lea, S., & Webley, P. (1999). South African children's views of wealth, poverty, inequality and unemployment. *Journal of Economic Psychology, 20*, 593–612.

Bonn, M., & Webley, P. (2000). South African children's understanding of money and banking. *British Journal of Developmental Psychology, 18*, 269–278.

Branch, C. W., & Newcombe, N. (1986). Racial attitude development among young Black children as a function of parental attitudes: A longitudinal and cross-sectional study. *Child Development, 57*, 712–721.

Brown, R. (1995). *Prejudice: Its social psychology.* Oxford, England: Blackwell.

Buchanan-Barrow, E. (2000). The development of political cognition: A sense of community. Poster presented at XVIth Biennial Meeting of ISSBD, Beijing, China.

Buchanan-Barrow, E., & Barrett, M. (1996). Primary school children's understanding of the school. *British Journal of Educational Psychology, 66*, 33–46.

Buchanan-Barrow, E., & Barrett, M. (1998a). Children's rule discrimination within the context of the school. *British Journal of Developmental Psychology, 16*, 539–551.

Buchanan-Barrow, E., & Barrett, M. (1998b). Individual differences in children's understanding of the school. *Social Development, 7*, 250–268.

Burgard, P., Cheyne, W. M., & Jahoda, G. (1989). Children's representations of economic inequality: A replication. *British Journal of Developmental Psychology, 7*, 275–287.

Clark, K. B., & Clark, M. P. (1947). Racial identification and preference in Negro children. In T. M. Newcomb & E. L. Hartley (Eds.), *Readings in social psychology* (pp. 169–178). New York: Holt.

Coles, R. (1986). *The political life of children.* Boston: Atlantic Monthly Press.

Connell, R. W. (1971). *The child's construction of politics.* Carlton, Victoria: Melbourne University Press.

Corsaro, W. A. (1990). The underlife of the nursery school: Young children's social representations of adult rules. In G. Duveen & B. Lloyd (Eds.), *Social representations and the development of knowledge* (pp. 11–26). Cambridge, England: Cambridge University Press.

Davey, A. (1983). *Learning to be prejudiced.* London: Edward Arnold.

Dickinson, J., & Emler, N. (1996). Developing ideas about distribution of wealth. In P. Lunt & A. Furnham (Eds.), *Economic socialization* (pp. 47–68). Cheltenham, England: Edward Elgar.

Donaldson, M. (1978). *Children's minds.* London: Fontana.

Doyle, A. B., & Aboud, F. E. (1995). A longitudinal study of White children's racial prejudice as a social-cognitive development. *Merrill-Palmer Quarterly, 41*, 209–228.

Doyle, A. B., Beaudet, J., & Aboud, F. E. (1988). Developmental patterns in the flexibility of children's ethnic attitudes. *Journal of Cross-Cultural Psychology, 19*, 3–18.

Durkin, K., & Howarth, N. (1997). Mugged by the facts? Children's ability to distinguish their own and witnesses' perspectives on televised crime events. *Journal of Applied Developmental Psychology, 18*, 245–256.

Emler, N., & Dickinson, J. (1985). Children's representation of economic inequalities: The effects of social class. *British Journal of Developmental Psychology, 3*, 191–198.

Emler, N., Ohana, J., & Dickinson, J. (1990). Children's representation of social relations. In G. Duveen & B. Lloyd (Eds.), *Social representations and the development of knowledge* (pp. 47–69). Cambridge, England: Cambridge University Press.

Emler, N., Ohana, J., & Moscovici, S. (1987). Children's beliefs about institutional roles: A cross-national study of representations of the teacher's role. *British Journal of Educational Psychology, 57*, 26–37.

Flin, R. H., Stevenson, Y., & Davies, G. M. (1989). Children's knowledge of court proceedings. *British Journal of Psychology, 80*, 285–297.

Fox, D. J., & Jordan, V. D. (1973). Racial preference and identification of Black, American Chinese, and White children. *Genetic Psychology Monographs, 88*, 229–286.

Furth, H. (1980). *The world of grown-ups: Children's conceptions of society*. New York: Elsevier.

Hraba, J., & Grant, G. (1970). Black is beautiful: A re-examination of racial preference and identification. *Journal of Personality and Social Psychology, 16*, 398–402.

Huston, A. C., Wright, J. C., Rice, M. L., Kerkman, D., & St. Peters, M. (1990). Development of television viewing patterns in early childhood: A longitudinal investigation. *Developmental Psychology, 26*, 409–420.

Jahoda, G. (1959). Development of the perception of social differences in children from 6 to 10. *British Journal of Psychology, 50*, 159–177.

Jahoda, G. (1962). Development of Scottish children's ideas and attitudes about other countries. *Journal of Social Psychology, 58*, 91–108.

Jahoda, G. (1963a). The development of children's ideas about country and nationality, Part I: The conceptual framework. *British Journal of Educational Psychology, 33*, 47–60.

Jahoda, G. (1963b). The development of children's ideas about country and nationality, Part II: National symbols and themes. *British Journal of Educational Psychology, 33*, 143–153.

Jahoda, G. (1964). Children's concepts of nationality: A critical study of Piaget's stages. *Child Development, 35*, 1081–1092.

Jahoda, G. (1979). The construction of economic reality by some Glaswegian children. *European Journal of Social Psychology, 9*, 115–127.

Jahoda, G. (1981). The development of thinking about economic institutions: The bank. *Cahiers de Psychologie Cognitive, 1*, 55–73.

Jahoda, G. (1982). The development of ideas about an economic institution: A cross-national replication. *British Journal of Social Psychology, 21*, 337–338.

Jahoda, G. (1983). European "lag" in the development of an economic concept: A study in Zimbabwe. *British Journal of Developmental Psychology, 1*, 113–120.

Johnson, N., Middleton, M., & Tajfel, H. (1970). The relationship between children's preferences for and knowledge about other nations. *British Journal of Social and Clinical Psychology, 9*, 232–240.

Katz, P. A. (1976). The acquisition of racial attitudes in children. In P. A. Katz (Ed.), *Towards the elimination of racism* (pp. 125–153). New York: Pergamon.

Lambert, W. E., & Klineberg, O. (1967). *Children's views of foreign peoples: A cross-national study*. New York: Appleton-Century-Crofts.

Leahy, R. L. (1981). Development of the conception of economic inequality: I. Descriptions and comparisons of rich and poor people. *Child Development, 52,* 523–532.

Leiser, D., Sevon, G., & Levy, D. (1990). Children's economic socialization: Summarizing the cross-cultural comparison of ten countries. *Journal of Economic Psychology, 11,* 591–614.

Low, J., & Durkin, K. (1997). Children's understanding of events and criminal justice processes in police programmes. *Journal of Applied Developmental Psychology, 18,* 179–205.

Middleton, M., Tajfel, H., & Johnson, N. (1970). Cognitive and affective aspects of children's national attitudes. *British Journal of Social and Clinical Psychology, 9,* 122–134.

Moore, S. W., Lare, J., & Wagner, K. A. (1985). *The child's political world: A longitudinal perspective.* New York: Praeger.

Ng, S. (1985). Children's ideas about the bank: A New Zealand replication. *European Journal of Social Psychology, 15,* 121–123.

Ohana, J. (1986). Educational styles and social knowledge. Interim report to CNRS.

Penny, R., Barrett, M., & Lyons, E. (2001). Children's naïve theories of nationality: A study of Scottish and English children's national inclusion criteria. Poster presented at the Xth European Conference on Developmental Psychology, Uppsala, Sweden.

Peterson-Badali, M., Abramovitch, R., & Duda, J. (1997). Young children's legal knowledge and reasoning ability. *Canadian Journal of Criminology, 39,* 145–170.

Piaget, J., & Weil, A. M. (1951). The development in children of the idea of the homeland and of relations to other countries. *International Social Science Journal, 3,* 561–578.

Pliner, P., Freedman, J., Abramovitch, R., & Darke, P. (1996). Children as consumers: In the laboratory and beyond. In P. Lunt & A. Furnham (Eds.), *Economic socialization: The economic beliefs and behaviours of young people* (pp. 35–46). Cheltenham, England: Edward Elgar.

Rice, A. S., Ruiz, R. A., & Padilla, A. M. (1974). Person perception, self-identity, and ethnic group preference in Anglo, Black, and Chicano preschool and third-grade children. *Journal of Cross-Cultural Psychology, 5,* 100–108.

Roland-Levy, C. (1990). A cross-national comparison of Algerian and French children's economic socialization. *Journal of Economic Psychology, 11,* 567–581.

Rosenthal, B. G. (1974). Development of self-identification in relation to attitudes towards the self in the Chippewa Indians. *Genetic Psychology Monographs, 90,* 43–141.

Saywitz, K. J. (1989). Children's conceptions of the legal system: "Court is a place to play basketball." In S. J. Ceci, D. F. Ross, & M. P. Toglia (Eds.), *Perspectives on children's testimony* (pp. 131–157). New York: Springer-Verlag.

Sonuga-Barke, E. J. S., & Webley, P. (1993). *Children's saving: A study in the development of economic behaviour.* Hove, England: Erlbaum.

Tajfel, H., Jahoda, G., Nemeth, C., Rim, Y., & Johnson, N. (1972). The devaluation by children of their own national and ethnic group: two case studies. *British Journal of Social and Clinical Psychology, 11,* 235–243.

Takahashi, K., & Hatano, G. (1994). Understanding of the banking business in Japan: Is economic prosperity accompanied by economic literacy? *British Journal of Developmental Psychology, 12,* 585–590.

Takriti, R., Buchanan-Barrow, E., & Barrett, M. (2000). Children's perceptions of their own and one other religious group. Poster presented at XVIth Biennial Meeting of ISSBD, Beijing, China.

Thompson, D. R., & Siegler, R. S. (2000). Buy low, sell high: The development of an informal theory of economics. *Child Development, 71,* 660–677.

Vaughan, G. M. (1978). Social change and intergroup preferences in New Zealand. *European Journal of Social Psychology, 8,* 297–314.

Warren-Leubecker, A., Tate, C. S., Hinton, I. D., & Ozbek, I. N. (1989). What do children know about the legal system and when do they know it? In S. J. Ceci, D. F. Ross, & M. P. Toglia (Eds.), *Perspectives on children's testimony* (pp. 158–183). New York: Springer-Verlag.

Webley, P., Levine, M., & Lewis, A. (1991). A study in economic psychology: Children's saving in a play economy. *Human Relations, 44*, 127–146.

Wellman, H. M., & Gelman, S. A. (1998). Knowledge acquisition in foundational domains. In W. Damon (Ed.), *Handbook of child psychology, volume 2: Cognition, perception, and language* (pp. 523–573). New York: Wiley.

Williams, J. E., & Morland, J. K. (1976). *Race, color, and the young child.* Chapel Hill, NC: University of North Carolina Press.

Wong, M. (1989). Children's acquisition of economic knowledge: Understanding banking in Hong Kong and USA. In J. Valsiner (Ed.), *Child development in cultural context* (pp. 225–246). Norwood: NJ: Ablex.

Yee, M. D., & Brown, R. J. (1988). *Children's social comparisons.* End of Award Report to ESRC. Canterbury, England: University of Kent.

Part IX

Cooperation, Competition, Aggression, and Bullying

Although, as discussed in the previous section, children can often be helpful and engage in prosocial behavior, so also they can engage in aggressive and bullying behaviors. In fact, cooperative and competitive behaviors can be intimately interwoven. Jacques Richard, Ada Fonzi, Franca Tani, Fulvio Tassi, Giovanni Tomada, and Barry Schneider discuss the possible definitions of both cooperation and competition, and ways in which they can be measured or assessed in childhood. They then overview our knowledge of the developmental origins of, and changes in, these behaviors. Culture is an important influence; Anglo-American children have often been found to be more competitive than other cultural groups. Gender is another important factor. The authors then relate the cooperation/competition construct to developmental outcomes such as performance, motivation, and quality of peer relationships.

There is a very substantial literature on aggressive behavior, reviewed by Marion Underwood. The title of her chapter refers to two very salient issues in the current literature: sex differences and types of aggression. Physical (and to some extent verbal) forms of aggression have long been recognized, and also a prevailing gender difference with boys showing more physical aggression. While this finding is not denied by more recent research, the definition of aggression has come to be expanded, to include more subtle forms of intent to harm others. These other forms have been described as indirect, relational, or social aggression, and social exclusion is an important example. Girls, certainly relative to physical aggression and perhaps absolutely, do experience these latter forms more than boys. Underwood carefully picks her way through these issues, and the evidence for developmental changes. She also reviews a body of research suggesting that both physical aggression, and indirect/relational/social aggression, have negative developmental outcomes. She notes some discordant findings and views here, however; and in adolescence too, there is evidence for some adaptive features of aggression which have been ignored in much research until recently (e.g., Cairns, Cairns, Neckerman, Gest, & Gariepy, 1988; Pellegrini & Bartini, 2001).

Bullying refers to a subset of aggressive behavior – in which a more powerful person or persons repeatedly attack a weaker. As with aggression generally, bullying can take various forms, which have different age and sex profiles. Ken Rigby surveys the research on bullying in childhood, which has grown greatly in volume over the last 10–15 years. He considers the various approaches to studying bullying, and gives examples of both qualitative and quantitative studies. The structural features of bullying, including motivations of the perpetrators, reactions or coping strategies of the victims, and attitudes of the peer group generally, are given detailed consideration. As Rigby indicates, the research is helping to inform school-based interventions to try to reduce this form of behavior, which if continued for long periods can be very damaging to the victims and the school climate generally.

References

Cairns, R. B., Cairns, B. D., Neckerman, H. J., Gest, S. D., & Gariepy, J. L. (1988). Social networks and aggressive behavior: Peer support or peer rejection? *Developmental Psychology, 24,* 815–823.

Pellegrini, A. D., & Bartini, M. (2001). A longitudinal study of bullying, victimization, and peer affiliation during the transition from primary school to middle school. *American Educational Research Journal, 37,* 699–726.

26

Cooperation and Competition

Jacques F. Richard, Ada Fonzi, Franca Tani, Fulvio Tassi, Giovanna Tomada, and Barry H. Schneider

Definitions of Competition and Cooperation

In much of the social-psychological and educational literature, competition is viewed as something harmful that can lead to negative consequences for children's psychosocial development, whereas cooperation is described as competent social behavior that entails many positive consequences (e.g., Foster, 1984). In spite of this common view, children from many cultures are continually encouraged to be competitive in various domains such as school and sports. Many individuals consider competition an important and healthy element in children's development (Roberts, 1992). One possible explanation of such contrasting positions is that there are as many different definitions of competition and cooperation as there are opinions regarding their effects on children.

Competition and cooperation can refer to characteristics of social situations or to the psychological states of the participants in them (Van Avermaet, 1996). For example, a competitive or cooperative structure can be imposed on children playing with a ball. In one instance, there may be strict rules and one child may be required to try to achieve a specific outcome at the expense of another child, as in a tennis match. In another instance, children may be expected to work together to try to reach a common result, as in two children throwing a ball to one another during baseball practice with the aim of developing their throwing skills. The first situation would be described as a competitive situation and the second as cooperative. However, the children involved in the activities may or may not adopt the goals, attitudes, and behaviors that correspond to the apparent external demands of the situation. For example, one of the children in the supposedly cooperative situation (i.e., baseball practice) may try to throw the ball harder than his or her partner in an attempt to be perceived as a better player by the coach. In this example, even though the child was participating in an activity that should elicit cooperative behaviors, his or her goals and behaviors were competitive. To complicate things even further, most situations involving social interactions are not as clearly defined as competitive or cooperative, and many may in fact contain elements of competition *and* cooperation. Perhaps for these reasons, Smith (1996, p. 81) describes competition and cooperation as "often interwoven in intricate ways in their behavioral expression."

Some definitions of competition and cooperation refer to the characteristics of social situations. For instance, Van Avermaet (1996) suggested that the extent to which the *outcomes* of a specific activity are the same for participants A and B vary along a continuum, ranging from complete positive correspondence, which leads to cooperation (i.e., if participant A performs an action that produces a specific result, participant B will obtain the same result) to total negative correspondence, which leads to competition (i.e., if participant A performs an action that brings about a specific result, participant B loses the opportunity to obtain the same result). Most activities would be situated somewhere along the continuum between total competition and total cooperation.

Charlesworth (1996) and other proponents of evolutionary biology propose a definition of competition and cooperation that is based on *resource allocation.* These researchers perceive competition as a strategy adopted to gain a limited resource in which several participants are interested, whereas they view cooperation as a collaborative effort with another to gain a shared resource. Cooperation is even described at times as one possible competitive tactic used to obtain valuable physical, social, or informational resources (Charlesworth, 1996). Thus, the presence of competition or cooperation would be determined by the consequences of social behavior on the allocation of resources. In other words, if two individuals agree to cooperate in order to gain resources, it may be inferred that competition has actually taken place if the resources are not obtained equally by both individuals. For example, two coworkers might decide to cooperate on a common project, but each because of his or her own individual desire of being promoted. If only one of the two receives a promotion, Charlesworth (1996) would argue, their "cooperation" actually constituted a competitive strategy.

Conversely, an example of a definition of competition and cooperation that refers to the psychological state of the participants is one that is based on the *goals* of the participants in social interaction. There is competition when the goals are incompatible and mutually exclusive, and there is cooperation when the goals are compatible and interdependent (Butt, 1987). However, according to some researchers, the idea that all participants cannot reach the same outcomes or accomplish the same goals in a situation may not constitute an adequate definition of competition (e.g., Roberts, 1992). Indeed, in some situations involving competition, the attainment of specific goals by one of the participants does not necessarily prevent the others from attaining some of these goals. In a spelling bee, for instance, Child A might achieve the goals of winning the contest, speaking in front of an audience, and gaining self-confidence, and at the same time, Child B might also attain the goals of speaking in front of an audience and gaining self-confidence. Consequently, Roberts (1992, p. 185) describes competition as "an evaluative system of normative social comparison in which being competent is important."

All of the definitions presented above are based on a unidimensional concept of competition. This unidimensional view may explain why some people perceive competition as either totally healthy or totally unhealthy. Tassi and Schneider (1997) propose a multidimensional definition of competition according to which it is possible to compete for different reasons, which lead to different consequences. They distinguish between *other-referenced* competition (i.e., competing in order to be proven superior to others) and *task-oriented* competition (i.e., competing in order to do well at something). Others have also adopted this multidimensional view of competition. For instance, Griffin-Pierson (1990) makes a distinction between *interpersonal* competition, which she portrays as a desire to do better than others or win, and *goal* competition, which she describes as an endeavor to achieve excellence. Similarly, Ryckman, Libby, van den Borne, Gold, and Lindner (1997) define two types of competitive attitudes: People who exhibit a *personal development* competitive attitude generally try to improve their skills regardless of the outcome, whereas those who manifest a *hypercompetitive* attitude usually possess a strong desire to achieve a specific outcome regardless of the necessary means required. These multidimensional models assume that some form of competition can exist without the desire to outperform another person or obtain a greater share of resources than someone else. Some classic theorists, however, would not use the term "competition" in that way. As Kohn (1992, p. 6) puts it: "Competition is fundamentally an interactive word, like kissing, and it stretches the term beyond usefulness to speak of competing with oneself." Furthermore, according to Sherif (1976), it is possible to compete against a socially shared standard (e.g., trying to run 100 meters faster than the national record), but comparing with oneself (e.g., trying to run 100 meters faster than your previous best) does not constitute competition because there is no social comparison involved.

Methodological Issues in the Study of Cooperation and Competition

Researchers have devised methodologies that either: (a) manipulate the competitive or cooperative nature of specific situations in order to study their effects on children's behaviors; or (b) measure children's individual preferences for competitive or cooperative interaction. There are at least two commonly used methods to manipulate the competitive or cooperative nature of children's games or tasks. The first technique consists of using competitive, cooperative, or individualistic instructions when explaining the objective of the task (e.g., Butler, 1990; Schmidt, Ollendick, & Stanowicz, 1988). For example, Butler (1990, p. 203) gave the following competitive instructions to half the participants in her study: "Try and make the best copy of this drawing. Try and make the best copy in your group. I shall collect your copies to judge who made the best copy," and the following individualistic instructions to the other half: "Try to copy the drawing as closely as you can. I am collecting all the pictures that children copy with stickers."

Another strategy for controlling the competitive or cooperative nature of the activity consists of using cooperative, competitive, or individualistic reward structures (e.g., Hom, Berger, Duncan, Miller, & Blevin, 1994; Newcomb, Brady, & Hartup, 1979). In their study of the effects of reward on intrinsic motivation, Hom et al. (1994) informed children in the cooperative group that the amount of candy they would each receive depended on their team's performance, whereas children in the individualistic group were told that the reward was linked only to their own individual performances.

Children's preferences for cooperative or competitive interaction have been assessed mainly with dyadic games, forced-choice resource allocation measures, and questionnaires. Madsen, Kagan, and colleagues pioneered the use of dyadic games (e.g., Kagan & Madsen, 1971; Madsen, 1971) and forced-choice resource allocation measures (e.g., Kagan & Knight, 1979) in their cross-cultural studies of children's competition and cooperation. The marble-pull game (Madsen, 1971) is the earliest of the dyadic games, and most of the other games are structured according to the same general principles. In the marble-pull game, a plastic cup is placed over a marble on a table. Two strings are attached to each side of the cup. If both children pull on their strings in opposite directions at the same time, the cup separates in two pieces and the marble is released. When this happens, no one collects the marble. If one child pulls toward his or her side and the other releases the string, the cup does not separate and the first child can capture the marble. The game is played over repetitive trials and the marbles obtained by each child are later exchanged for prizes. The only way marbles can be obtained equally is if children cooperate by taking turns.

In forced-choice measures of resource allocation, children are asked to choose between different possible allocations of tokens. The distribution of tokens can either favor themselves, another peer, or neither. Choices favoring oneself are considered competitive, whereas selections privileging another peer, or neither, are considered cooperative. Tokens are also later exchanged for prizes. Dyadic games and resource-allocation measures enable researchers to directly observe children's cooperative/competitive behaviors and preferences. However, this is often done in laboratory settings in the presence of examiners and may not necessarily present an accurate picture of children's behaviors in naturalistic settings with their peers.

Because of this, some researchers assess children's competitive or cooperative preferences by self-report questionnaires (e.g., Engelhard & Monsaas, 1989), and by peer or teacher ratings of competitive and/or cooperative behaviors (e.g., Kerns & Barth, 1995; Tassi & Schneider, 1997). Although self-reports and ratings may offer greater insights into the day-to-day competitive and cooperative behaviors of children with their peers, they do not permit direct observation on the part of the researchers who must rely on the accuracy of the informant. Tassi and Schneider (1997) argue that peer ratings, compared to self-reports, may provide more accurate data on children's competitive and cooperative behaviors.

In spite of their respective limitations, all of those innovative methodologies have assisted researchers in studying the relationships between competition/cooperation in children's behaviors and various relevant variables. The rest of the chapter is devoted to the presumed origins and possible outcomes of children's cooperation and competition.

The Origins of Competition and Cooperation in Children's Behaviors

In this section, we review studies that trace the emergence of competitive and cooperative behaviors in children's interaction.

First manifestations of competitive and cooperative behaviors

According to Piaget (1950), cooperation emerges during the later stages of children's moral development, whereas Vygotsky (1978) maintained that cooperation appears earlier. Their theories have prompted developmental researchers to investigate preschoolers' peer interaction. Verba (1994) observed 1- to 4-year-old children who were engaged in spontaneous joint activity with objects during free play. Verba reported many examples of early cooperation and competition, such as "putting forward ideas that they tried to have their partner adopt, pooling their creative efforts in an atmosphere of good will, taking conflicting stands, and attempting to resolve disagreement (p. 277)."

Reports of early peer cooperation are also found elsewhere. Garnier and Latour (1994) observed 2-, 3-, and 4-year-old children during free play. They assessed *gregariousness*, or the formation of subgroups; the nature of *play*, ranging from no cooperation to high cooperation; and, the degree of interdependence between the members of the subgroups. No differences were found between age groups for all three dimensions of cooperation. There was evidence of cooperation in all age groups which, according to the authors, suggests that cooperation emerges well before the later stages of childhood social development.

There may be important mediating variables that affect the emergence of cooperation in young children. Cauley and Tyler (1989) reported a significant association between preschoolers' self-concepts and their cooperative behaviors as assessed by teacher evaluations and direct observations. Preschoolers with more positive self-concepts were more cooperative than peers with less positive self-concepts. A group of Italian researchers studied the contributions of several intra-individual and contextual factors in promoting cooperative behavior in preschoolers and school-age children. Several processes were found to contribute: capacity for symbolic play, an internal sense of security, and school environments that promote autonomous resolution of conflict with peers. Dogmatism in mothers' child rearing was negatively associated with cooperation (Fonzi, 1991).

Individual differences in cooperative behaviors may also be related to parent–child relationships, which have been found to be associated with children's peer relationships (e.g., Cohn, Patterson, & Christopoulos, 1991). Kerns and Barth (1995) investigated the associations between early parent–child relationships (i.e., attachment) and preschool children's friendly-cooperative behaviors with peers. They found a positive association between security in paternal attachment (as measured by a Q-set sorting task) and teacher ratings of friendly-cooperative behaviors; A similar association was not obtained for maternal attachment. Given the study's cross-sectional design, the researchers were not able to identify causal relationships between the variables. Longitudinal data would be useful in determining, for instance, the implications of early parent–child relationship qualities for subsequent peer cooperation and competition.

Perceived power in parent–child relationships may also be linked to cooperative or competitive behaviors. A study by Bugental and Martorell (1999) showed that 6- to 10-year-old children whose mothers and fathers perceived that they did not have more power than their children demonstrated more verbal competition during competitive and learning activities with their peers than children of parents with high perceived power. Verbal competition was defined as "statements of self praise and friend derogation" (p. 265). Here again, the study would have greatly benefited from a longitudinal design given the bidirectional links between parent–child interactions and peer interactions.

Developmental changes

As stated earlier, social comparison is considered by many to be an inherent feature of competition. Children younger than ages 7 to 9 years may not be able to adequately extract information from social comparison for the purpose of self-evaluation (Ruble, 1983). Children's sensitivity to such information may greatly influence their decisions to pursue competitive or cooperative interactions with their peers. Therefore, there are compelling reasons to expect differences in the manifestation of competitive or cooperative behaviors as children become older.

Research on developmental changes in the display of competitive and cooperative behaviors has produced inconsistent findings. Some studies indicate that competitive behaviors increase as children become older (e.g., Madsen, 1971; McClintock & Nuttin, 1969), whereas other research shows that older children are more cooperative than younger ones (e.g., Handel, 1989; Stingle & Cook, 1985). In McClintock and Nuttin's (1969) study, 8-, 10-, and 12-year-old children played a dyadic game in which maximum rewards went to children who cooperated rather than competed. Children were given neutral instructions that did not specify whether they should compete or cooperate. Although children of all age groups demonstrated more competitive than cooperative behaviors, older children manifested more competitive behaviors than younger ones. Similarly, Stingle and Cook (1985) provided neutral instructions to 5-, 8-, and 11-year-olds who played a dyadic game that rewarded cooperation more than competition. However, in this study, 8- and 11-year-old children showed greater cooperation than 5-year-old children. The game used in Stingle and Cook's (1985) study was more elaborate and seemed to demand greater coordinated effort in order to cooperate than in the McClintock and Nuttin (1969) study. Older children in Stingle and Cook's (1985) study may have been more skillful in coordinating their endeavors, making them appear more cooperative. In any case, further research should attempt to elucidate the links between children's ages and their competitive/cooperative behaviors.

Although research has not yet determined whether older children are more or less competitive/cooperative than younger ones, there may be developmental differences in the way children respond to competitive or cooperative tasks. Older children have been found to be able to adapt to competitive and cooperative tasks by changing their strategies and behaviors according to the competitiveness of the immediate situation (Kagan & Madsen, 1971; Schmidt et al., 1988). In Kagan and Madsen's (1971) study, 9-year-old children competing for prizes under cooperative instructions were less competitive than age-mates who had received individualistic instructions. In contrast, 5-year-old children's competitiveness was not influenced by the experimenter's instructions. Similarly, Schmidt et al.'s (1988) study showed that 11-year-old children playing a game were more competitive under competitive instructions and more cooperative under cooperative instructions, whereas 8-year-old children's competitiveness and cooperativeness were not affected by instructions.

Older children's greater flexibility in the use of competitive or cooperative behaviors may be explained partly by their greater awareness of the social comparison that is involved in competition and their ability to evaluate their own performances more objectively. In one study, 5-, 7-, and 10-year-old children were asked to copy drawings under either individualistic or competitive instructions (Butler, 1990). The drawings were judged by the children themselves and by adult judges. In the competitive condition, younger children tended to overestimate their drawing abilities, whereas older children's appraisals of their own work were equivalent to those of the adult judges. This difference was not observed in the individualistic condition, where older and younger children's evaluations of their own work were approximately equal to the adult ratings. Older children were more objective than the younger ones in their social comparisons with their peers, which may explain why this developmental effect was only observed in the competitive condition. In the individualistic condition, children used the model, rather than their peers' drawings, as their basis for comparison.

Thus, no clear picture has yet emerged from existing research regarding developmental differences in competitive and cooperative behaviors. However, older children seem more adept at coordinating their cooperative or competitive behaviors in order to meet the demands of the situations in which they are placed.

Culture

Given the differences that may exist between various cultures in terms of children's socializing experiences and the social values that are imparted to them, cultural differences in children's cooperative and competitive behaviors may be expected. Most but not all cross-cultural research on children's cooperation and competition reports such differences.

A great number of cross-cultural studies involving Anglo-American, Mexican, and/or Mexican-American children have been conducted by Kagan, Madsen, and their associates (e.g., Kagan & Madsen, 1971; Kagan & Knight, 1979; Madsen, 1971). The methodology used to assess competitive and cooperative preferences in most of those studies consisted of a forced-choice measure of resource allocation; the participants were mostly between ages 5 and 12 years. Their studies have consistently reported more cooperative, and fewer competitive, behaviors among Mexican and Mexican-American children than among their Anglo-American counterparts. Furthermore, Mexican children were found to be more cooperative and less competitive than Mexican-American children (Kagan & Madsen, 1971). Thus, children from a collectivistic culture such as Mexico appear to value cooperation more highly than Anglo-American and even Mexican-American children, both of whom are raised in an individualistic culture that generally values competition. This is further supported by the finding that third-generation Mexican-American children showed a greater preference for competition than their second-generation peers (Kagan & Knight, 1979).

Cross-cultural research comparing American and Chinese children is not as conclusive. Sparkes (1991) studied the cooperative and competitive behaviors of Chinese and American 3- to 5-year-old children. Pairs of same-culture children played an adaptation of Madsen's (1971) marble-pull game. Essentially, each player tried repeatedly to bring a round plastic disc over to his or her side of the board using blocks attached to strings. The disc could only be moved if both children cooperated and decided in advance to which side they would move it. If both children pulled at the same time towards their respective sides on a given trial, the disc would be released and no one would capture it. The disc would then be replaced and the trial would start over. Competition was deemed to have taken place when the children failed to bring the disc to one side on more than 5 occasions throughout 10 trials, whereas cooperation was inferred if they failed to bring the disc to one side on 5 or fewer tries during the 10 trials. Chinese pairs of children demonstrated more competitive behaviors than their American counterparts. This finding is unlike that of Domino (1992) who used a different methodology with older children. In his study, 10- to 12-year-old Chinese and American children's competitive and cooperative preferences were measured using a token-allocation procedure identical to the one used in the previously reported studies by Kagan, Madsen, and their colleagues. In Domino's (1992) experiment, American children gave more competitive and fewer cooperative responses than Chinese children. These conflicting results may be an artifact of the different samples and dissimilar methods used or may reflect a cross-cultural developmental difference given the different ages of the children in both experiments.

In summary, most cross-cultural research on children's competition and cooperation compared Anglo-American children with children from other cultures. In general, Anglo-American children were found to be more competitive, although there is at least one exception (Sparkes, 1991). Unfortunately, all of those studies were conducted in laboratory settings using dyadic games or resource-allocation measures that, as stated previously, may not be indicative of children's day-to-day behaviors with their peers.

Gender differences

In most cultures, the socialization of girls differs from that of boys. This may lead to important differences in cooperation and competition. Boys are frequently described as more competitive and less cooperative than girls (Pepitone, 1980). Strube (1981) conducted a meta-analysis on gender differences in competition across cultures. The analysis included 95 articles published prior to 1978 with children from cultures such as Anglo-American, Mexican/Mexican-American, African American, Israeli, Indian, and Canadian. Results of the meta-analysis showed that boys were significantly more competitive than girls in the Anglo-American, Indian, and Mexican/Mexican-American cultures. Conversely, girls were more competitive than boys in the Israeli culture. Finally, no differences between boys and girls were obtained for the African-American and Canadian cultures. These findings suggest that the common belief that boys are more competitive than girls may be accurate for some, but not all, cultures.

Other studies have investigated gender differences in children's strategies during cooperation and competition. For example, Charlesworth and Dzur (1987) observed 4- and 5-year-old children's behavioral strategies when placed in a situation of scarce resources (i.e., a cartoon viewer that could only be viewed by one child at a time). Children were divided in groups of four same-sex peers. The cooperation of two more children was required in order for one child to view the cartoon: one to press a button that turned on the light and another to turn a crank that set the film in motion. This ingenious set-up permitted the observation of children's strategies in a situation that often produced a combination of competitive and cooperative responses. The researchers found no differences in viewing time between boys and girls, suggesting that both sexes were equally capable of cooperating and competing. However, boys and girls used different strategies to gain access to the viewer: Boys used more physical strategies (e.g., pushing, grasping), whereas girls used more verbal tactics (e.g., requesting, giving commands). In addition, boys displayed more positive affect than girls when competing for the resource. Accordingly, LaFrenière (1999) argued that female–female competition does exist, although it is usually different from that of boys: It is more subtle, less overt, less physical, and not as fun for the competing participants.

Similar studies using mixed-sex groups (e.g., LaFrenière & Charlesworth, 1987) showed that preschool boys obtained more viewing time than girls. The authors proposed that the more subtle, verbal strategies of girls may not be as effective with boys as with other girls, whereas the more direct, physical strategies of boys are efficacious with both sexes. This explanation may account for the common contention that boys usually appear more competitive than girls in naturalistic settings.

In summary, gender differences in children's competition and cooperation seem to vary according to culture. Furthermore, the popular belief that boys are more competitive than girls may be explained by the different strategies used by members of both sexes when competing or cooperating for a resource, and by the presence of greater positive affect when boys compete.

Possible Outcomes of Children's Competition and Cooperation

Being placed in competitive versus cooperative settings, or displaying competitive versus cooperative behaviors, may have different implications. Here we review studies that have addressed the possible outcomes and correlates of children's competition and cooperation. Causal links are difficult to establish given the bidirectionality between competitive/cooperative behaviors and possible outcomes.

Academic, motor, and athletic performance

Franken and Brown (1995) proposed that one of the reasons people like to compete is that it enables them to improve their performance. In his pioneer study of the effects of competition on the performance of cyclists, Triplett (1897) found that cyclists competing against one another recorded faster times than cyclists racing against time. However, a review by Johnson, Maruyama, Johnson, and Nelson (1974) indicated that greater achievement and success occur in cooperative situations than in competitive or individualistic settings.

Mixed results have been found regarding the effects of competition and cooperation on children's academic and motor performance. Engelhard and Monsaas (1989) examined the link between 8-, 10-, and 12-year-old children's self-reported cooperative attitudes and their academic performance. Their results showed that successful students were less cooperative than unsuccessful students and generally preferred working alone. Their findings are not surprising given the competitive and individualistic atmosphere that is frequently found in children's classrooms and it would be very unsubstantiated to conclude that cooperation among children leads to poor academic performances. It is probable that successful students in competitive school environments have learned that it is better to work individually and are being rewarded accordingly. However, a study by Brown and Abrams (1986) revealed that 12-year-old children taking academic tests (i.e., math and English) under cooperative instructions performed better than those who received competitive instructions. Similarly, Johnson and Johnson (1979) reported greater achievement in some academic tasks (e.g., problem solving, knowledge acquisition) from 10-year-old children in cooperative conditions than children in either competitive or individualistic conditions. No significant differences were found between groups on other academic tasks (e.g., knowledge retention).

In another study of academic performance and cooperation, Gillies and Ashman (1998) placed 6- and 8-year-old children into groups of four (i.e., one high ability, one low ability, and two medium ability students) for 6 weeks of either structured cooperative learning or unstructured group learning. Children in the cooperative learning groups received instruction and training in cooperative skills and behaviors, whereas the other children did not receive such training. Results for 8-year-olds indicated that children in the cooperative-learning groups used more advanced cognitive and language strategies, scored higher on an academic test, and showed greater gains in word-reading ability than children in the unstructured learning groups. For 6-year-old children, a significant difference in favor of the cooperative learning groups was obtained only in the use of more advanced cognitive and language strategies. Children's gender may be an important mediating link between competition and academic performance. Johnson and Engelhard (1992) reported that 11- and 12-year-old boys with high academic achievement had a lower preference for competition, whereas high achieving girls had a higher preference for competition.

Other studies have investigated the effect of an arbitrarily chosen competitive or noncompetitive condition on children's motor performance. Butler (1989b) assessed the quality of 5-, 7-, and 10-year-old children's drawings following competitive versus noncompetitive drawing conditions. The pictures of competing children were rated as of lower quality than those of noncompeting children at ages 7 and 10 only. No differences in quality were observed at age 5. According to the author, the findings suggested that the social comparison inherent to competition hindered the performance of the older children in the study, whereas the younger children may not have been aware of, or sensitive to, information obtained by social comparison. Newcomb et al. (1979) paired 6- and 9-year-old children for a block-tower building task. Half of the children were exposed to cooperative and competitive reward systems, whereas the other half was exposed to cooperative and individualistic reward systems. Results showed that performance (i.e., number of successful towers and number of blocks positioned on successful towers) was greater during the cooperative condition. Hom et al. (1994) observed 10-year-old children solving block puzzles under either a cooperative reward structure (i.e., rewards were dependent on the team performance) or an individualistic reward structure (i.e., rewards were based on individual performance). Results showed that children from the cooperative condition solved the puzzles significantly faster than children from the individualistic condition. Conversely, in one study with 10-year-old children, no motor performance differences were obtained for competitive versus noncompetitive task instructions during a cardhouse building activity (Shwalb, Shwalb, & Murata, 1991).

The discrepant findings reported above may result from differences in the nature of the activities in which children took part. Competition and cooperation may have dissimilar effects on children's performance depending, for example, on the degree of difficulty of the task. In support of this hypothesis, Lambert (1989) conducted a study in which 9- to 12-year-old children participated in physical activities of varying levels of difficulty. In the easier activity, children tried to throw darts as accurately as possible toward a specific target. The more difficult activity consisted of a long jump in which children tried to jump as far as they could from a slightly elevated platform. For both activities, children were first placed in a noncompetitive environment (stage 1) followed by a competitive one (stage 2). The dependent variable consisted of the increase of athletic performance between stages 1 and 2. Children's self-reported anxiety level was measured prior to their participation in the activities. Results indicated that children who had reported higher anxiety levels showed a greater increase in performance on the easier activity than children who had indicated lower anxiety levels. However, for the more difficult task, children who had reported lower anxiety levels had greater performance increases than children with higher levels of anxiety. Thus, competition seems to have different implications for children's athletic performance depending on task difficulty and on children's psychological characteristics.

Motivation

According to Deci and Ryan's (1985) cognitive evaluation theory, individuals with higher levels of intrinsic motivation for a specific activity possess greater feelings of competence and self-determination, and generally participate in the activity because they find it to be enjoyable and stimulating. Conversely, their theory posits that individuals who are extrinsically motivated have an external locus of causality for their participation in the activity and an elevated sense of incompetence.

Data from existing research on the implications of cooperation and competition for children's motivation have suggested that cooperation is generally associated with higher levels of intrinsic motivation, whereas higher levels of extrinsic motivation are often related to competition. In Hom et al.'s (1994) study (see previous section), children who solved block puzzles under the cooperative reward structure showed greater post-task intrinsic motivation than children from the individualistic reward structure condition. Intrinsic motivation was defined operationally as the amount of time children spent playing with the blocks in a period during which they were free to choose from various activities. In a similar study, Butler (1989a) observed the intrinsic motivation of preschool, 7-, and 10-year-old children following competitive and noncompetitive art activities (i.e., competitive vs. individualistic instructions). Intrinsic motivation was also defined as the time spent performing the activity during free time. Results showed that 10-year-old children displayed greater intrinsic motivation following the noncompetitive art activities than after the competitive ones. However, no significant differences between groups were observed for the younger children. Once again, the author argues that young children (i.e., before the age of 7) may not have fully attained the capacity to compare their abilities with others and thus their intrinsic interest in the activity would be less affected by a competitive setting.

The competitive or cooperative orientation of children's school programs may also affect their motivation. Benninga et al. (1991) assessed, using self-report measures, 7- to 10-year-old children's motivation for prosocial acts and for academic work using self-report measures. Children from academic programs that encouraged competition reported higher extrinsic and lower intrinsic prosocial motivation than children from academic programs that advocated cooperative learning. However, no differences in academic motivation were found between children from the two types of programs.

Theory and research suggest that children prefer to undertake challenging situations when attempting to show mastery over their environments (e.g., Deci & Ryan, 1985). Consequently, children's preference for situations of competition or cooperation may be influenced by the opportunity provided to demonstrate mastery in challenging tasks. Handel (1989) observed the cooperative responses of 5- to 12-year-old children during a marble-pull dyadic game that produced maximum rewards to children who cooperated; competitive responses in the game always led to few or no rewards. All of the children participated in a simple version of the game (i.e., no challenges were available for children who cooperated) and a complex version of the game (i.e., even the cooperative responses were challenging for the children). Results showed that children displayed significantly more cooperative responses during the complex game than during the simple game.

Thus, existing research shows that cooperation seems to foster children's intrinsic motivation, whereas competition may undermine it, especially with older children. Furthermore, children are more likely to cooperate when given the opportunity to demonstrate competence by cooperating in challenging tasks.

Peer relationships

As stated earlier, many theorists and researchers view cooperation as a joint effort to gain shared resources, whereas they consider competition as an attempt to gain limited resources at the expense of others. Consequently, peer relationships could potentially be enhanced by cooperation and disrupted by competition. In Sherif, Harvey, White, Hood, and Sherif's (1961) extensive study, 11- and 12-year-old boys taking part in summer camps were divided into two groups and observed during intense, intergroup competitive and cooperative conditions. They observed strong negative interpersonal behaviors (e.g., verbal insults, destruction of property) between the two groups during the competitive conditions and reduction of those negative behaviors during subsequent cooperative conditions. However, the negative interpersonal behaviors were especially observed directly following the competitive conditions, during which time experimenters deliberately triggered hostile feelings by setting up situations that frustrated the groups. Nevertheless, their study was instrumental in showing that children's social behaviors can be influenced by competitive and cooperative situations.

Although competitiveness may be related to peer dislike, some studies examining the associations between competition and sociometric status have suggested that this may not always be the case. Defining competition as a multidimensional construct, Tassi and Schneider (1997) measured 8-year-old children's competitive orientations using peer informant measures. Popular children scored significantly higher on task-oriented competition (i.e., competing in order to do well at something) than average children who, in turn, scored significantly higher than rejected children. Conversely, unpopular rejected children scored significantly higher on other-referenced competition (i.e., competing in order to be proven superior to others) than average or popular children. Similar results were also obtained using teacher ratings of competition in a more recent study (Tassi, Schneider, & Richard, 2001). Thus, competition seems to lead to peer rejection only when children try to outdo others when they compete. Here again, gender effects may be important mediators. Steinkamp (1990) reported the relation between preschoolers' competitiveness as rated by teachers and the children's friendship nominations and sociometric status. Boys gave higher sociometric ratings to highly competitive girls, whereas girls gave higher ratings to less competitive boys. No connection between competitiveness and social status emerged for same-sex sociometric nominations.

Some data suggest that participating in cooperative activities can decrease the negative social behaviors manifested by low-accepted and aggressive boys during peer interaction. For example, popular and unpopular (Gelb & Jacobson, 1988) or popular and aggressive (Tryon & Keane, 1991) 9-year-old boys were observed while attempting to join two other children already engaged in competitive or cooperative play. Results of the study by Gelb and Jacobson (1988) showed that the unpopular children were more likely than the popular participants to break rules, disrupt play, and appeal to authority, but only during competitive play. During cooperative play, the unpopular children demonstrated fewer of those negative social behaviors and were more accepted by their peers. In the study by Tryon and Keane (1991), popular children were accepted more readily than aggressive children during competitive play. Popular children also used more socially oriented interventions (e.g., showing agreement or pleasure with one of the group members) than aggressive children when approaching the dyad at play. Differences between groups were much smaller during cooperative play.

Results from Gelb and Jacobson's (1988) study presented in the preceding paragraph suggested that cooperation can have beneficial effects for peer acceptance. This has also been demonstrated elsewhere. Anderson's (1985) study revealed that 10- to 15- year-old learning-disabled boys favorably identified as classmates whom they liked a greater number of their peers following participation in cooperative-learning activities than before the cooperative situation was set up. In a study by Smith, Boulton, and Cowie (1993), 8- and 9-year-old children participated for one year in either cooperative-learning groups in the classroom or traditional-teaching groups. Although no significant differences were observed between the cooperative-learning and the traditional-teaching groups in terms of changes in children's sociometric status, an increase in children's "liking" ratings was noted following participation in the cooperative-learning groups. Thus, participating in cooperative activities may not lead to immediate changes in children's peer status (i.e., a "rejected" child will probably not become "average" or "popular" following cooperation), but may have a more gradual effect on general acceptance among peers. One of the reasons that acceptance may be higher following cooperation is that children seem to manifest more prosocial behaviors, such as asking for and giving reciprocal help, when cooperating (Garaigordobil, Maganto, & Etxeberria, 1996), and more aggressive behaviors when competing (Bay-Hinitz, Peterson, & Quilitch, 1994).

Dorsch and Keane (1994) suggested that competition may have different effects on children's social behaviors depending on their feelings of success during the activity. In their study, peer-rejected and -accepted 8-year-old children played competitive or cooperative computer games with or against a fictitious other child (i.e., each child was told that his or her computer was connected to another machine on which a child of the same age was playing). After failure on competitive games, socially rejected children reported more aggressive social strategies than socially accepted children. A difference in social strategies between the two groups in the Dorsch and Keane (1994) study was not observed following success in competitive games, nor following success or failure in cooperative games. Thus, the negative effects of competition on children's social behaviors were only witnessed following failure on the game.

Competition for resources by friends may have destructive consequences for the equity of the relationship, considered by many (e.g., Walster, Walster, & Berscheid, 1978) as an essential characteristic of friendship. Sullivan (1953) proposed that competition between friends may impede intimacy and lead to a break-up in the relationship.

Janosz and LaFrenière (1991) organized a competitive contest that resulted in a winner and a loser within dyads of preschool friends and nonfriends. Following that contest, dyads were placed in situations of limited resources where only one toy was available for the two members of the dyad. No differences in competitive or cooperative behaviors used to acquire the toy were found between winners and losers of the previous contest. However, dyads of friends demonstrated more cooperative and less competitive behaviors than dyads of nonfriends. Furthermore, winners in friendship dyads were more willing to offer the toy to their partner during subsequent play than winners in nonfriendship dyads. In another study of social interactions in situations of limited resources, Werebe and Baudonnière (1988) observed the play activity of same-sex triads of preschool children consisting of two friends and one familiar peer. The triads were placed in a toy-filled room containing two sets of every type of toy or object. Competition was defined as attempts by one child to acquire an object from another child. Although friends were no more or less competitive than nonfriends, children made significantly more offers to give an object to their friends than to the nonfriends, suggesting a greater desire for cooperation with the friends.

Despite the consistent finding of greater cooperation and less competition between friends than between nonfriends, some competitive children may have many friends. In Steinkamp's (1990) study, reported on the previous page, preschool children perceived as highly competitive by their teachers were named as friends by their classmates more than low-competitive children. One possible explanation for this finding is that children may compete differently with friends than with nonfriends. There is some empirical evidence of this. For example, Fonzi, Schneider, Tani, and Tomada (1997) observed dyads of 8-year-old friends and nonfriends engaged in a car-race competition with clear prestated rules. During the competition, dyads of friends showed greater positive affect and greater adherence to the rules than did dyads of nonfriends.

Ideas for New Research

In many studies reviewed in this chapter, researchers investigated global and diametrical distinctions between competitive and cooperative behaviors. Although such research provided important data, the results of some studies suggest that it may be useful to examine in greater detail the processes by which children compete or cooperate. For example, differences in the processes involved in competitive behavior are reported between girls and boys (Charlesworth & Dzur, 1987); popular and unpopular children (Tassi & Schneider, 1997); and, friends and nonfriends (Fonzi et al., 1997). As part of this focus on process, the goals and motivations involved in competition and cooperation, as embodied in the multidimensional models discussed earlier, need to be examined.

More research is also needed on the mediating role of personal variables (e.g., cognitive, social, emotional) in the emergence and maintenance of competitive and cooperative behaviors. Among the few studies in which such potential mediators have been investigated, findings include greater cooperation in children who show high cognitive flexibility (Bonino & Cattelino, 1999), lower empathy in highly competitive boys (Barnett, Matthews, & Howard, 1979), and greater achievement in competitive situations by children with an internal locus of control (Nowicki, 1982). Further advances in understanding the possible origins and outcomes of children's competition and cooperation will likely stem from process-oriented research tracing the interplay among cognitive, social, and other personal variables that are linked to competitive and cooperative behaviors.

References

Anderson, M. A. (1985). Cooperative group tasks and their relationship to peer acceptance and cooperation. *Journal of Learning Disabilities, 18*, 83–86.

Barnett, M. A., Matthews, K. A., & Howard, J. A. (1979). Relationship between competitiveness and empathy in 6- and 7-year-olds. *Developmental Psychology, 15*, 221–222.

Bay-Hinitz, A. K., Peterson, R. F., & Quilitch, H. R. (1994). Cooperative games: A way to modify aggressive and cooperative behaviors in young children. *Journal of Applied Behavior Analysis, 27*, 435–446.

Benninga, J. S., Tracz, S. M., Sparks, R. K., Solomon, D., Battistich, V., Delucchi, K. L., Sandoval, R., & Stanley, B. (1991). Effects of two contrasting school task and incentive structures on children's social development. *Elementary School Journal, 92*, 149–167.

Bonino, S., & Cattelino, E. (1999). The relationship between cognitive abilities and social abilities in childhood: A research on flexibility in thinking and co-operation with peers. *International Journal of Behavioral Development, 23*, 19–36.

Brown, R., & Abrams, D. (1986). The effects of intergroup similarity and goal interdependence on intergroup attitudes and task performance. *Journal of Experimental Social Psychology, 22*, 78–92.

Bugental, D. B., & Martorell, G. (1999). Competition between friends: The joint influence of the perceived power of self, friends, and parents. *Journal of Family Psychology, 13*, 260–273.

Butler, R. (1989a). Interest in the task and interest in peers' work in competitive and noncompetitive conditions: A developmental study. *Child Development, 60*, 562–570.

Butler, R. (1989b). Mastery versus ability appraisal: A developmental study of children's observations of peers' work. *Child Development, 60,* 1350–1361.

Butler, R. (1990). The effects of mastery and competitive conditions on self-assessment at different ages. *Child Development, 61,* 201–210.

Butt, D. S. (1987). *Psychology of sport: The behavior, motivation, personality, and performance of athletes.* New York: Van Nostrand Reinhold.

Cauley, K., & Tyler, B. (1989). The relationship of self-concept to prosocial behavior in children. *Early Childhood Research Quarterly, 4,* 51–60.

Charlesworth, W. R. (1996). Co-operation and competition: Contributions to an evolutionary and developmental model. *International Journal of Behavioral Development, 19,* 25–39.

Charlesworth, W. R., & Dzur, C. (1987). Gender comparisons of preschoolers' behavior and resource utilization in group problem solving. *Child Development, 58,* 191–200.

Cohn, D. A., Patterson, C. J., & Christopoulos, C. (1991). The family and children's peer relations. *Journal of Social and Personal Relationships, 8,* 315–346.

Deci, E. L., & Ryan, R. M. (1985). *Intrinsic motivation and self-determination in human behavior.* New York: Plenum Press.

Domino, G. (1992). Cooperation and competition in Chinese and American children. *Journal of Cross-Cultural Psychology, 23,* 456–467.

Dorsch, A., & Keane, S. P. (1994). Contextual factors in children's social information processing. *Developmental Psychology, 30,* 611–616.

Engelhard, G., & Monsaas, J. A. (1989). Academic performance, gender, and the cooperative attitudes of third, fifth, and seventh graders. *Journal of Research and Development in Education, 22,* 13–17.

Fonzi, A. (1991). *Cooperare e competere tra bambini* [Cooperation and competition between children]. Florence, Italy: Giunti.

Fonzi, A., Schneider, B. H., Tani, F., & Tomada, G. (1997). Predicting children's friendship status from their dyadic interaction in structured situations of potential conflict. *Child Development, 68,* 496–506.

Foster, W. K. (1984). Cooperation in the game and sport structure of children: One dimension of psychosocial development. *Education, 105,* 201–205.

Franken, R. E., & Brown, D. J. (1995). Why do people like competition? The motivation for winning, putting forth effort, improving one's performance, performing well, being instrumental, and expressing forceful/aggressive behavior. *Personality and Individual Differences, 19,* 175–184.

Garaigordobil, M., Maganto, C., & Etxeberria, J. (1996). Effects of a cooperative game program on socio-affective relations and group cooperation capacity. *European Journal of Psychological Assessment, 12,* 141–152.

Garnier, C., & Latour, A. (1994). Analysis of group process: Cooperation of preschool children. *Canadian Journal of Behavioural Science, 26,* 365–384.

Gelb, R., & Jacobson, J. L. (1988). Popular and unpopular children's interactions during cooperative and competitive peer group activities. *Journal of Abnormal Child Psychology, 16,* 247–261.

Gillies, R. M., & Ashman, A. F. (1998). Behavior and interactions of children in cooperative groups in lower and middle elementary grades. *Journal of Educational Psychology, 4,* 746–757.

Griffin-Pierson, S. (1990). The Competitiveness Questionnaire: A measure of two components of competitiveness. *Measurement and Evaluation in Counseling and Development, 23,* 108–115.

Handel, S. J. (1989). Children's competitive behavior: A challenging alternative. *Current Psychology: Research & Reviews, 8,* 120–129.

Hom, H. L., Berger, M., Duncan, M. K., Miller, A., & Blevin, A. (1994). The effects of cooperative and individualistic reward on intrinsic motivation. *Journal of Genetic Psychology, 155,* 87–97.

Janosz, M., & LaFrenière, P. J. (1991). Affectivité, amitié et compétence sociale chez des garçons d'âge préscolaire en situation de resource limitée [Affectivity, friendship, and social competence among preschool boys in situations of limited resources]. *Enfance, 45*, 59–81.

Johnson, C., & Engelhard, G. (1992). Gender, academic achievement, and preferences for cooperative, and individualistic learning among African-American adolescents. *Journal of Psychology, 126*, 385–392.

Johnson, D. W., Maruyama, G., Johnson, R. T., & Nelson, D. (1974). Effects of cooperative, competitive, and individualistic goal structure on achievement: A meta-analysis. *Review of Educational Research, 44*, 213–240.

Johnson, R. T., & Johnson, D. W. (1979). Type of task and student achievement and attitudes in interpersonal cooperation, competition, and individualization. *Journal of Social Psychology, 108*, 37–48.

Kagan, S., & Knight, G. P. (1979). Cooperation-competition and self-esteem: A case of cultural relativism. *Journal of Cross-Cultural Psychology, 10*, 457–467.

Kagan, S., & Madsen, M. C. (1971). Cooperation and competition of Mexican, Mexican-American, and Anglo-American children of two ages under four instructional sets. *Developmental Psychology, 5*, 32–39.

Kerns, K. A., & Barth, J. M. (1995). Attachment and play: Convergence across components of parent–child relationships and their relations to peer competence. *Journal of Social and Personal Relationships, 12*, 243–260.

Kohn, A. (1992). *No contest: The case against competition*. New York: Houghton Mifflin.

LaFrenière, P. J. (1999, April). Symposium discussion. In J. F. Benenson (Chair), *Are girls as competitive as boys? Gender differences in the dynamics of competition and cooperation*. Symposium conducted at the biennial meeting of the Society for Research in Child Development, Albuquerque, NM.

LaFrenière, P. J., & Charlesworth, W. R. (1987). Effects of friendship and dominance status on preschooler's resource utilization in a cooperative/competitive situation. *International Journal of Behavioral Development, 10*, 345–358.

Lambert, R. (1989). Anxiété et sport [Anxiety and sport]. *Revue Québécoise de Psychologie, 10*, 137–150.

Madsen, M. C. (1971). Developmental and cross-cultural differences in the cooperative and competitive behavior of young children. *Journal of Cross-Cultural Psychology, 2*, 365–371.

McClintock, C. G., & Nuttin, J. M. (1969). Development of competitive game behavior in children across two cultures. *Journal of Experimental Social Psychology, 5*, 203–218.

Newcomb, A. F., Brady, J. E., & Hartup, W. W. (1979). Friendship and incentive condition as determinants of children's task-oriented social behavior. *Child Development, 50*, 878–881.

Nowicki, S. (1982). Competition-cooperation as a mediator of locus of control and achievement. *Journal of Research in Personality, 16*, 157–164.

Pepitone, E. A. (1980). *Children in cooperation and competition*. Lexington, MA: Lexington Books.

Piaget, J. (1950). *Pensée biologique, pensée psychologique et pensée sociologique* [Biological thinking, psychological thinking and sociological thinking]. Paris: Presses Universitaires de France.

Roberts, G. C. (1992). Children in competition: A theoretical perspective and recommendations for practice. In A. Yiannakis & S. L. Greendorfer (Eds.), *Applied sociology of sport* (pp. 179–192). Champaign, IL: Human Kinetics Books.

Ruble, D. N. (1983). The development of social comparison processes and their role in achievement-related self-socialization. In E. T. Higgins, D. N. Ruble, & W. W. Hartup (Eds.), *Social cognition and social development: A socio-cultural perspective* (pp. 134–157). New York: Cambridge University Press.

Ryckman, R. M., Libby, C. R., van den Borne, B., Gold, J. A., & Lindner, M. A. (1997). Values of hypercompetitive and personal development competitive individuals. *Journal of Personality Assessment, 69*, 271–283.

Schmidt, C. R., Ollendick, T. H., & Stanowicz, L. B. (1988). Developmental changes in the influence of assigned goals on cooperation and competition. *Developmental Psychology, 24*, 574–579.

Sherif, C. W. (1976). The social context of competition. In D. Landers (Ed.), *Social problems in athletics* (pp. 18–36). Urbana, IL: University of Illinois Press.

Sherif, M., Harvey, O. J., White, B. J., Hood, W. R., & Sherif, C. W. (1961). *Intergroup conflict and cooperation: The robber's cave experiment.* Norman, OK: University of Oklahoma Institute of Group Relations.

Shwalb, D. W., Shwalb, B. J., & Murata, K. (1991). Individualistic striving and group dynamics of fifth- and eighth-grade Japanese boys. *Journal of Cross-Cultural Psychology, 22*, 347–361.

Smith, P. K. (1996). Strategies of co-operation: A commentary. *International Journal of Behavioral Development, 19*, 81–87.

Smith, P. K., Boulton, M. J., & Cowie, H. (1993). The impact of cooperative group work on ethnic relations in middle school. *School Psychology International, 14*, 21–42.

Sparkes, K. K. (1991). Cooperative and competitive behavior in dyadic game-playing: A comparison of Anglo-American and Chinese children. *Early Child Development and Care, 68*, 37–47.

Steinkamp, M. W. (1990). The social concomitants of competitive and impatient/aggressive components of the Type A behavior pattern in preschool children: Peer responses and teacher utterances in a naturalistic setting. *Journal of Personality and Social Psychology, 59*, 1287–1295.

Stingle, S. F., & Cook, H. (1985). Age and sex differences in the cooperative and noncooperative behavior of pairs of American children. *Journal of Psychology, 119*, 335–345.

Strube, M. J. (1981). Meta-analysis and cross-cultural comparison: sex differences in child competitiveness. *Journal of Cross-Cultural Psychology, 12*, 3–20.

Sullivan, H. S. (1953). *The interpersonal theory of psychiatry.* New York: Norton.

Tassi, F., & Schneider, B. H. (1997). Task-oriented versus other-referenced competition. *Journal of Applied Social Psychology, 27*, 1557–1580.

Tassi, F., Schneider, B. H., & Richard, J. F. (2001). Competitive behavior at school in relation to social competence and incompetence in middle childhood. *International Journal of Social Psychology, 14*, 165-184.

Triplett, N. (1897). The dynamogenic factors in pacemaking and competition. *American Journal of Psychology, 9*, 507–533.

Tryon, A. S., & Keane, S. P. (1991). Popular and aggressive boys' initial social interaction patterns in cooperative and competitive settings. *Journal of Abnormal Child Psychology, 19*, 395–406.

Van Avermaet, E. (1996). Cooperation and competition. In A. S. R. Manstead & M. Hewstone (Eds.), *The Blackwell encyclopedia of social psychology* (pp. 136–141). Cambridge, MA: Blackwell.

Verba, M. (1993). Cooperative formats in pretend play among young children. *Cognition and Instruction, 11*, 265–280.

Verba, M. (1994). The beginnings of collaboration in peer interaction. *Human Development, 37*, 125–139.

Vygotsky, L. S. (1978). *Mind in society: The development of higher psychological processes.* Cambridge, MA: Harvard University Press.

Walster, E., Walster, G., & Berscheid, E. (1978). *Equity: Theory and research.* Boston: Allyn & Bacon.

Werebe, M. J. G., & Baudonnière, P. M. (1988). Friendship among preschool children. *International Journal of Behavioral Development, 11*, 291–304.

27

Sticks and Stones and Social Exclusion: Aggression among Girls and Boys

Marion K. Underwood

Sometimes kids do mean things to other kids, like make faces at them, or not let them be part of their group, or gossip about them. Has anything like this ever happened to you?

"I started hanging with another girl, they didn't like her, they said, "We won't be your friend anymore if you hang with her." (12-year-old girl)

"We were playing a game and some boys got angry and kicked some of us out of the group." (12-year-old boy)

"My best friend and I got in a argument and she just ignored me." (12-year-old girl)

"One boy spread rumors about me...because I had ruined his reputation." (12-year-old boy)

Other times kids do mean things to each other like push them, or hit them, or trip them. Has anything like this ever happened to you?

"Three boys called me a rat and harassed me and hit me with a broom." (12-year-old girl)

"Two girls just walked up and pulled my hair." (11-year-old girl)

"Two days ago my best friend said 'Do my homework,' and I said, 'No,' and he grabbed me by the neck and choked me." (12-year-old boy)

"I was sitting on the bus one day and a boy just came up a hit me for no reason." (12-year-old boy)

from Paquette and Underwood, 1999

Preparation of this chapter was supported by grants from the National Institute of Mental Health and the Timberlawn Psychiatric Research Foundation. Thanks to Julie Paquette for sharing the examples of victimization experiences at the opening of this chapter. Correspondence may be addressed to Marion K. Underwood, School of Human Development, The University of Texas at Dallas, PO Box 830688, M/S GR41, Richardson, TX, 75083. The address for electronic mail is underwd@utdallas.edu.

As these examples of victims' experiences illustrate, children who behave aggressively threaten their peers, disrupt their classrooms, and frustrate parents and teachers who must try to cope with their behavior. Besides being aversive, aggression has been shown to be a fairly stable individual characteristic after about age 10 (Olweus, 1977). Aggressive behavior is related to concurrent peer rejection (Coie & Kupersmidt, 1983), and to academic problems and depressed mood (Capaldi, 1991). Aggression in childhood predicts a number of serious outcomes in later life: school dropout and delinquency (Kupersmidt & Coie, 1990; Parker & Asher, 1987), early sexual activity (Capaldi, Crosby, & Stoolmiller, 1996), adolescent motherhood (Serbin et al., 1998; Underwood, Kupersmidt, & Coie, 1996), and occupational and marital instability during adulthood (Caspi, Elder, & Bem, 1987).

For all of these reasons, a large body of research has addressed the developmental origins of aggression (see Coie & Dodge, 1998, for an overview), as well has how to intervene to reduce and to even prevent aggressive behavior (Conduct Problems Prevention Group, 1992; Kazdin, 1987). This chapter will highlight current research on aggression in children during the preschool (ages 3–5), early school (ages 5–7), and elementary years (ages 5–11), with special attention to gender, culture, and methods for defining and measuring aggression.

Definitions and Subtypes of Aggressive Behavior

Researchers have long struggled with how to define aggressive behavior. Although over 200 definitions of aggression can be found in the psychological literature, most of these share two important features: (a) the behavior is intended to harm the target; and (b) the victim perceives that he or she has been hurt (Harré & Lamb, 1983). Although most previous researchers have interpreted harm to mean physical injury, recently, investigators have suggested that behaviors that hurt others' friendships or social status might also fit these criteria for aggression (Crick & Grotpeter, 1995; Galen & Underwood, 1997).

Other than the general criteria of intent to harm and perceived harm, it has been difficult to specify invariant properties of all aggressive behaviors. In part to cope with contradictory research findings and to describe more precisely the behaviors under study, investigators have proposed numerous different subtypes of aggression (even an incomplete list is too long to repeat here, see Underwood, Galen, & Paquette, 2001). Of all the subtypes proposed, the distinction between reactive and proactive aggression has been particularly useful in that these subtypes seem linked to different developmental antecedents and consequences, as will be discussed in detail later. Reactive aggression is angry and retaliatory, and proactive aggression is dominant aggressive behavior deployed to achieve specific goals. Because one important focus of this chapter is gender, this discussion will also highlight research on subtypes thought to correspond to boys' and girls' aggression: physical versus indirect/relational/social aggression.

Researchers generally agree that boys engage in physical fighting more than girls do (see Coie & Dodge, 1998; Knight, Fabes, & Higgins, 1996), but recently, investigators have argued that defining aggression only as physical harm leaves out more subtle forms of hurtful behaviors that might be more frequent and meaningful among girls. Lagerspetz,

Bjorkqvist, and Peltonen (1988) suggested that girls engage in more indirect aggression, which they defined as "a noxious behavior in which the target person is attacked not physically or directly through verbal intimidation but in a more circuitous way, through social manipulation" (Kaukianinen et al., 1999, p. 83). In 1989, Cairns et al. proposed that girls engage in social aggression, described as "the manipulation of group acceptance through alienation, ostracism, or character defamation" (p. 323). Galen and Underwood (1997) urged expanding this definition, writing, "Social aggression is directed toward damaging another's self-esteem, social status, or both, and may take such direct forms as verbal rejection, negative facial expressions or body movements, or more direct forms such as slanderous rumors or social exclusion" (p. 589). In 1995, Crick and Grotpeter introduced a construct called relational aggression, which they described as "harming others through the purposeful manipulation and damage of their peer relationships" (p. 711).

Because there is considerable overlap among indirect and social and relational aggression and experts disagree as to which construct is most valid, in this chapter, these forms of behavior will be referred to as indirect/relational/social aggression. For each developmental period examined, this chapter will highlight current research on the frequency, functions, and correlates of physical and indirect/relational/social aggression.

The Preschool Years

Physical aggression

Anyone observing children in a preschool classroom would likely see fairly high rates of anger and physical aggression, particularly concerning struggles over objects (Fabes & Eisenberg, 1992). Research suggests that approximately 13% of 3 year olds fight with peers and have tantrums (Crowther, Bond, & Rolf, 1981; Earls, 1980). According to mothers' diaries, physical aggression seems to be highest for 2 year olds, then decreases with age as verbal aggression increases (Goodenough, 1931).

Preschool boys engage in physical aggression more than preschool girls do (Maccoby & Jacklin, 1980), and this difference is evident across different socioeconomic groups (Baumrind, 1971) and cultures (Whiting & Whiting, 1975). In addition to the obvious possibility of biological contributions to gender differences, preschool boys may engage in physical aggression more than girls may for several reasons. Boys become involved in more conflicts (Smith & Green, 1974), boys tend to respond to angry provocation by venting and resistance (Fabes & Eisenberg, 1992), and boys' aggression is more likely than girls' fighting to result in resistance and to elicit like responses from peers, which contributes to the persistence of the aggressive behavior (Fagot & Hagan, 1985). Clearly, even preschool children are influenced by gender stereotypes that make physical aggression more acceptable for males. When preschool children learn to reliably label gender, boys' aggression with peers does not change but girls' aggression drops dramatically (Fagot, Leinbach, & Hagan, 1986).

During the preschool years, high rates of physical aggression are associated with several types of factors. Individual differences in aggressive behavior likely have a genetic

component (Gottesman & Goldsmith, 1994), and may be related to temperamental qualities such as fussiness and inability to be soothed (Bates, Maslin, & Frankel, 1985). High
levels of aggression in preschool children have been shown to be related to punitive and
inconsistent discipline by parents (Campbell, Breaux, Ewing, & Szumowski, 1986) and to
particular types of coercive family processes (Patterson, 1982). Patterson (1982) proposed
that when parents are overwhelmed by the stresses of poverty or marital discord or simply
the demands of parenting challenging children, they become unable to respond sensitively
and positively to desired behaviors, and they become inconsistent in their responses to
negative behavior. A coercive cycle develops in which stressed parents attempt to set limits
or discipline children, these children respond with increasingly noncompliant, negative
behavior, and weary parents give in to such behavior, which reinforces the child's extreme
noncompliance and increases its future likelihood. Preschool children may also learn to
behave aggressively from their siblings (Dunn & Kendrick, 1982), and from exposure to
media violence (see Huston & Wright, 1998, for an overview). Interestingly, research on
nonparental child care suggests that poor quality day care may be associated with high rates
of aggressive behavior with peers for preschool children (Lamb, 1998).

During the preschool period, physical aggression likely declines for several reasons. Children become better able to use language to communicate their needs, and better able to
delay gratification. Peers begin to communicate to one another that physical aggression is
not acceptable, and dominance hierarchies develop that serve to regulate ongoing social
interaction (Strayer & Trudel, 1984). In addition, children become better able to internally regulate emotions, more empathic, and higher on ego-control (see Coie & Dodge,
1998, for a discussion of these developmental changes). Given that during this period
physical aggression decreases and verbal aggression increases, it is interesting to speculate
whether the above factors might actually contribute to the development of indirect/rela-
tional/social aggression.

Indirect/relational/social aggression

Researchers have only begun to investigate indirect/relational/social aggression among preschool children. To date, very little normative information is available about the rates of
these behaviors in preschool classrooms.

In one of the first investigations of relational aggression in young children, Crick, Casas,
and Mosher (1997) developed peer nomination and teacher ratings scales to assess relational aggression in 3–5-year-old children. Relational aggression items included "tells a
peer that he or she won't play with that peer or be that peer's friend unless he or she does
what this child asks" and "when mad at a peer, this child keeps that peer from being in the
play group" (p. 581).

The results indicated that teacher reports showed a moderate relation between relational
and overt aggression for both girls ($r = .73$) and boys ($r = .76$), whereas peer nominations
suggested a weaker relationship ($r = .37$ and .36 for girls and boys, respectively). Teachers
reported that girls were higher than boys on relational aggression and boys were higher
than girls on physical aggression, but the peer nominations showed no gender differences
for either form of aggression. The results indicated that the relation between relational

aggression and psychological adjustment was complex and depended on the gender of the children and the source of the information. For boys, peer nominations of relational aggression were related to peer rejection, but also to peer acceptance as rated by teachers. For girls, relational aggression was related only to peer rejection.

Using similar definitions of aggression, McNeilly-Choque, Hart, Robinson, Nelson, and Olsen (1996) obtained data from multiple informants on 4–5-year-old children's physical aggression, verbal relational aggression, and nonverbal relational aggression. For relational aggression, gender differences depended on the source of the information. Playground observations indicated that girls were more relationally aggressive than boys were, but peer nominations did not show gender differences. Teachers rated girls as higher than boys on verbal relational aggression, but there were no gender differences for nonverbal relational aggression. McNeilly-Choque et al. (1996) found that not all of the preschool children observed engaged in relational aggression: 65% showed no relational aggression, 17% rarely were relationally aggressive, 10% were moderately relationally aggressive, and 7% of children showed high rates of relational aggression. Interestingly, the correlations among the playground observations, teacher ratings, and peer nominations were quite low for relational aggression, suggesting either that children exhibit these behaviors differently in different social contexts, or that these behaviors are difficult to observe or rate accurately.

Researchers have also just begun to investigate biological factors that may relate to indirect/relational/social aggression in young children. Preschool children who are rated by teachers as high on relational aggression show more dramatic elevations in cortisol levels over the course of a day in daycare settings (Dettling, Gunnar, & Donzella, 1999). It also seems sensible that engaging in both relational and overt aggression may be associated with physical characteristics such as body size and physical attractiveness, although research to date has not explored these issues.

Family characteristics may also be related to indirect/relational/social aggression during the preschool years. In a comparison of preschool children in a Head Start and a university-based preschool, McNeilly-Choque et al. (1996) found that teachers rated higher SES children as more relationally aggressive. They suggested that this might be due to higher SES parents using more sophisticated, person-centered forms of socialization, which their children might mimic in hurting others, or to more modeling of snobbishness in affluent homes. McNeilly-Choque et al. (1996) noted that that much more research is needed to confirm these speculations, but little research since has explored the relation between family SES and indirect/relational/social aggression.

In a study of preschool children and families in Russia, Hart et al. (1998) examined whether parenting styles were related to relational aggression (assessed by teaching ratings on items similar to those of Crick et al., 1997). Interestingly, teachers did not report gender differences on relational or on overt aggression. The results indicated that for boys, maternal and paternal responsiveness were related to lower levels of relational aggression. For girls, maternal coercion was related to higher rates of relational aggression. Additional research with other samples is needed to determine the generalizability of these results, but the relations between parenting and relational aggression are intriguing as suggestions of some early origins of this behavior.

The Early School Years

Although early theorists did not label the 5–7 age range as a distinct developmental period, more contemporary researchers have recognized that great developmental advances take place during this period (Sameroff & Haith, 1996). At least in United States culture, this age range includes the transition to organized schooling, which might pose special challenges for children prone to aggression.

Physical aggression

Research suggests that the overall frequency of physical aggression continues to decrease during this age range, although this decline may be largely due to the highly aggressive subgroup becoming less extreme (Ladd & Burgess, 1999). Just as during the preschool years, more highly aggressive children are boys.

During the early school years, individual differences in physical aggression seem related to family factors (SES and parenting) and to how children process social information. Across age ranges, levels of aggression are higher in lower SES groups (see Coie & Dodge, 1998, for a discussion of the complex reasons for this phenomenon). For a kindergarten sample, lower SES predicted higher levels of initial aggression, but lower SES was not related to greater increases in aggression from kindergarten to third grade (McFadyen-Ketchum, Bates, Dodge, & Pettit, 1996).

In this same study, observed maternal coercion and nonaffection were positively related to higher parent ratings of aggression just prior to kindergarten. Maternal coercion and nonaffection predicted increases in aggressive behavior from kindergarten through third grade for boys, but predicted decreases in aggression for girls. McFadyen-Ketchum et al. (1996) interpreted the boys' findings as supporting Patterson's (1982) coercion model, and suggested that because girls are more sensitive and compliant to adult demands, maternal coercion might be more effective in squelching their aggressive behavior. Although this theory awaits empirical confirmation, this result suggests that aggressive boys and girls might respond differently to parental negativity.

Specific types of discipline practices are associated with high levels of physical aggression in this age range. Strassberg, Dodge, Pettit, and Bates. (1994) compared the levels of reactive aggression, proactive aggression, and bullying in the kindergarten children of parents who used no physical discipline, spanking, or violent punishment. The results showed that the highest levels of aggression were associated with parental use of violent discipline, but important differences between the spanking and nonspanking groups were also apparent. Children of mothers who used spanking were observed at school to be higher on reactive and total aggression than children of mothers who used no physical discipline. Children of fathers who used spanking were higher on reactive aggression than those of fathers who used no physical discipline (for boys only, the spanking group was higher than the non-use group on bullying and total aggression). The overall pattern of these results strongly suggests that spanking is associated with high levels of aggression as observed at school. This finding is particularly important given that 90% of parents in the United States report spanking their children (Straus & Gelles, 1986), presumably because they believe that spanking will reduce misbehavior (Holden & Zambarano, 1992).

However, the relation between physical discipline and behavior problems may not be the same for different ethnic groups. For a sample of children followed from kindergarten through third grade, maternal reports of using physical discipline were moderately related to teacher and peer reports of externalizing behaviors for European-American children, but not for African-American children (Deater-Deckard, Dodge, Bates, & Pettit, 1996). Further research is necessary to understand exactly how physical discipline relates to a broad array of parenting behaviors for different ethnic groups, and how particular constellations of family characteristics and parenting behaviors predict aggression.

Perhaps as a result of harsh parenting practices or early stressful events or reinforcement experiences, children who are highly aggressive tend to make particular types of errors in processing social information (Dodge, 1990; Dodge, Bates, & Pettit, 1990). Crick and Dodge (1994) proposed that children come to social interactions with a database of past experiences and biologically determined abilities, but then process social cues in a series of six steps: encoding, interpretation, goal clarification, response generation, response evaluation, and enactment. A large body of research has demonstrated that how children process information at each of these steps relates to social adjustment in important ways, perhaps especially to aggression. A comprehensive summary of social information-processing research is beyond the scope of this chapter (see Crick & Dodge, 1994, for an integrative and thorough review). In short, particular types of aggressive children tend to show specific deficits in social information processing. Children who are high on reactive aggression tend to overattribute hostility in the face of ambiguous cues, and this hostile attribution bias is related to experiencing harsh parental discipline (Dodge, 1990; Weiss, Dodge, Bates, & Pettit, 1992). Children who are high on proactive aggression view the likely outcomes of aggressive behaviors as more positive than other children (Crick & Ladd, 1990), which Dodge (1990) suggested may be due to early experiences of being rewarded for physical aggression.

Children who engage in high rates of aggression during the early school years develop serious difficulties in their relationships with their peers and their teachers. The relation between aggression and peer status depends in part on the particular type of aggressive behavior. For a sample of 5–6 year olds, Price and Dodge (1989) found that observed rates of reactive aggression were associated with peer rejection as measured by teacher ratings, whereas engaging in proactive aggression was related to positive peer status in this age range. In their comparisons of the relationship trajectories of aggressive, withdrawn, and aggressive-withdrawn children, Ladd and Burgess (1999) found that children in the aggressive and the comorbid groups were consistently higher on peer rejection during grades K–2, and had more conflicts with their teachers. Children who were both aggressive and withdrawn reported more loneliness and less social satisfaction than other groups. Together, the weight of the evidence strongly suggests that aggression during the early school years is associated with social and psychological problems.

Indirect/relational/social aggression

Research to date has not investigated the forms and possible developmental consequences of indirect/relational/social aggression during the early school years. Experts agree that during this period, physical aggression declines as verbal aggression increases (see Coie & Dodge, 1998). Bjorkqvist (1994) proposed that as children become more verbally skilled and sophisticated in their social understanding, they become more likely to hurt each other by indirect means, particularly because these more subtle behaviors are less likely to be punished by adults. It seems sensible to expect that predicted increases in indirect/relational/social aggression might be apparent as early as 5–7 years of age. Also during these years, children are experiencing the massive changes in their social ecology as they begin school, as well as moving toward middle childhood, a developmental period in which fitting in with the same-gender peer group is of paramount importance (Gottman & Mettetal, 1986). Empirical research is needed to determine whether indirect/relational/social aggression increases during the early school years, differs for boys and girls, takes both proactive and reactive forms, and is associated with social and academic adjustment.

Middle Childhood

During the later elementary years, children strongly value being accepted by same-sex peer groups and work very hard to maintain emotional control (Gottman & Mettetal, 1986). Children become masters of dissemblance as they learn to cope with conflicting cultural messages about expressing emotions: be honest, but hide your negative feelings if you want people to like you (Saarni & von Salisch, 1993). For these reasons, many children who continue to engage in high rates of aggression during this developmental period are seen as increasingly deviant and disordered.

Physical aggression

Most children become less physically aggressive during the elementary years, but a small number of children continue to start fights (Loeber & Hay, 1993), and at least for boys, engaging in aggression behavior after age 10 is a highly stable trait, as stable as intelligence (Olweus, 1977). Boys continue to be more physically aggressive than girls during this age range (Knight et al., 1996; Maccoby & Jacklin, 1974, 1980).

As mentioned at the opening of this chapter, engaging in physical aggression during middle childhood is associated with poor adjustment in several ways. Although not all aggressive children are socially rejected by peers, about half are (French, 1988). Reactive aggression continues to be strongly associated with peer dislike, and even proactive aggression becomes more strongly associated with rejection in older age groups (Dodge & Coie, 1987). For a sample of sixth-grade boys, aggression was shown to be associated with academic problems and depressed mood (Capaldi, 1991), and for a sample of third- to sixth-grade boys, peer nominations of overt aggression were associated with boys' self-reports of depression (Crick & Grotpeter, 1995).

Interestingly, physical aggression seems related to maladjustment across cultures. In a series of studies conducted in China, physical aggression has been shown to be related to school and social problems (Chen, Rubin, & Li, B., 1995; Chen, Rubin, & Li D., 1997; Chen, Rubin, & Li, Z., 1995). However, in one longitudinal study, there was an unexpected gender difference in the relation between aggressive-disruptive behavior and social adjustment (Chen, Rubin, Li, & Li, 1999). For boys, aggression at ages 8–10 was negatively related to social adjustment 4 years later, but for girls, aggression at ages 8–10 positively predicted social adjustment. The authors explained this finding by pointing out that aggression in girls is less stable, perceived as more deviant, and might take more subtle forms than those that were captured by the measures of physical aggression used here. Future research is needed to explore the fascinating possibility that some types of aggression may be positively related to adjustment for girls in some cultural contexts.

Engaging in high rates of physical aggression during middle childhood appears to be related to some of the same factors as for earlier developmental periods: coming from a low SES family, experiencing harsh discipline, being involved in coercive cycles with parents, and errors in social information processing. In addition, another factor that may strongly influence aggression during the elementary years is exposure to media violence (see Huston & Wright, 1998, for a review of this large and fascinating literature). Meta-analyses combining the findings of the most well-done studies show that the effects of television violence account for about 10% of the variance in children's physical aggression (Wood, Wong, & Chachere, 1991). Some evidence indicates that highly aggressive children are more attracted to violent television (Huesmann & Miller, 1994), which suggests that physically aggressive children who are already at risk for school and social problems might have all of these difficulties exacerbated by more exposure to this widely available environmental agent.

Indirect/relational/social aggression

Most of the research on indirect/relational/social aggression has been conducted with children in the later elementary grades. Hurting others by indirect means such as social exclusion may be particularly powerful during this developmental period in which children strongly value acceptance by the same-gender peer group (Gottman & Mettetal, 1986). Children may seek to hurt each other by damaging what their same-gender groups most value (Crick & Grotpeter, 1995): for boys, physical dominance and for girls, social relationships. Some have even gone as far as to argue that indirect/relational/social aggression in females serves similar functions as physical aggression for males, and that if you consider both indirect/relational and physical aggression, girls are as aggressive as boys are (Bjorkqvist, 1994; Crick et al., 1999).

As intriguing as these theories are, evidence is mixed as to whether there are clear gender differences in indirect/relational/social aggression, and patterns of gender differences seem to depend on the type of measure used. Using peer nomination measures, some studies find clear gender differences for indirect aggression in Scandinavian samples (Lagerspetz et al., 1988) and for relational aggression in Midwestern U.S. samples (Crick, 1996, 1997; Crick & Grotpeter, 1995). However, other studies of U.S. samples using peer nomination items similar to Crick's find no gender differences (e.g., Rys & Bear, 1997), or show that boys are rated higher than girls are on relational aggression (Henington, Hughes, Cavell, & Thompson, 1998). In a study with Italian children, peer reports indicated that boys were higher on relational aggression than girls were (Tomada & Schneider, 1997). Findings from studies using self-report measures are similarly inconsistent. In one study, boys reported engaging in more relational aggression than girls did (Crick & Grotpeter, 1995). Another investigation showed that girls and boys report experiencing similar rates of social aggression (Paquette & Underwood, 1997). Given the lack of consistent findings for gender differences in indirect/relational/social aggression, it seems important to refrain from referring to these behaviors as "female aggression." Although it is likely true that girls engage in relational aggression more than physical aggression, it does not necessarily follow that girls engage in more relational aggression than boys do.

A growing body of evidence suggests that engaging in relational aggression is negatively related to social-psychological adjustment, both concurrently and in short-term longitudinal studies. Children rated by peers as relationally aggressive are disliked by peers, and relationally aggressive girls report greater loneliness and less social satisfaction (Crick & Grotpeter, 1995). For girls, peer ratings of relational aggression predict social rejection 6 months later (Crick, 1996). It is important to note that in both of these studies, relational aggression was related to maladjustment over and above physical aggression (i.e., the predictive relation remained even when levels of physical aggression were statistically controlled).

Given that the above studies all used peer nomination measures of relational aggression, it seems important to consider the possibility that the relation between indirect/relational/social aggression and maladjustment may also depend on the methods used. In a study using peer narrative measures, Xie, Swift, Cairns, and Cairns (2000) found that social aggression in childhood was unrelated to negative outcomes in adolescence.

One study suggests that the aggressive children at most risk for maladjustment are those who engage in gender non-normative forms of aggression: relationally aggressive boys and physically aggressive girls (Crick, 1997). Teachers rated relationally aggressive boys as more maladjusted than relationally aggressive girls, nonrelationally aggressive girls, and nonrelationally aggressive boys. Teachers reported more maladjustment for overtly aggressive girls than for overtly aggressive boys, nonovertly aggressive boys, and nonovertly aggressive girls. These results suggest that the more rare and understudied groups, relationally aggressive boys and overtly aggressive girls, may be perceived as most deviant and perhaps at risk for subsequent psychopathology.

Taken together, the evidence that engaging in indirect/relational/social aggression is related to social-psychological maladjustment makes it imperative that we learn more about the developmental origins of these behaviors. Future research is needed to explore whether higher SES children engage in more relational aggression as McNeilly-Choque et al. (1996) found for preschoolers, and whether particular types of parenting behaviors result in children becoming high on relational aggression. Some evidence suggests that just as for physical aggression, children high on relational aggression may show particular deficits in social information processing. Crick (1995) found that children high on relational aggression were more likely to misattribute hostile intent in scenarios describing relational provocation.

In addition, fully understanding the relation between indirect/relational/social aggression and psychological adjustment will require basic, developmental research to assess whether engaging in these behaviors is indeed rare and related to psychopathology, or more normative and frequent. Interestingly, some studies have suggested that indirect/relational/social aggression may be related to positive social qualities, such as social intelligence (Kaukiainen et al., 1999) and may serve positive developmental functions such as maintaining one's sense of belonging (Paquette & Underwood, 1999) and protecting the integrity of social groups (Leckie, 1999).

Challenges and Future Directions

As rich and interesting as the very large research literature on aggression in childhood has become, important questions remain (see Underwood, Galen, & Paquette, 2001, for a more complete discussion of methodological challenges). One set of questions concerns the fact that aggressive behavior and how it is perceived depends heavily on the social context. To make matters even more complicated, context can have several levels of meaning, such as culture, physical setting, genders or ages or social roles of participants in the interaction, the activity in which they are engaged, and the immediate events leading up to the aggressive event. The few available studies suggest that all of these types of contexts may influence aggressive behavior. In addition to the studies cited above on aggression in different cultures, research suggests that even boys rated by teachers as externalizers only fight in response to particular provocations (such as being teased or threatened, Wright, Zakriski, & Drinkwater, 1999). Particular group dynamics affect rates of physical aggression in experimental play groups (DeRosier, Cillessen, Coie, & Dodge, 1994), and much of the aggression in experimental play groups is exhibited by mutually aggressive dyads who make more hostile attributions about each other's behaviors (Coie et al., 1999).

A second daunting set of challenges is that clarifying the role of context for all forms of aggression will require additional observational research. As many investigators have noted, actually observing aggressive behavior is difficult, especially among older children, because they refrain from aggressing when they know they are being observed (Coie & Dodge, 1998). Crick and Grotpeter (1995) have argued that observing relational aggression is very difficult not only because the behaviors are subtle and difficult to detect, but also because relational aggression takes place in complex sequences over time, and understanding these requires detailed knowledge of all of the participants. Despite these obstacles, Galen and Underwood (1997) have shown that social aggression can be reliably elicited and observed for a small number of girls' laboratory play sessions. Pepler and Craig (1995) reported that reliable coding of indirect aggression was possible using remote audiovisual recording, for which children wear remote microphones and their playground behavior is videotaped from afar using cameras with zoom lenses. Using laboratory methods and new technologies will do much to clarify gender differences, developmental antecedents and consequences of engaging in physical as well as indirect/relational/social aggression.

Finally, additional research is needed on the long-term developmental trajectories of all forms of aggression. A sizable body of research on physical aggression has formed the basis for a developmental model of conduct disorder and a comprehensive prevention program (Conduct Problems Prevention Group, 1992), and this model should serve as a type of standard for research efforts to better understand indirect/relational/social aggression. What are the early developmental origins of indirect/relational/social aggression, how do these behaviors continue to be expressed as children enter adolescence and adulthood, and how do they relate to adjustment in later life? The best answers to these questions might require that researchers move beyond the conceptual frameworks used by researchers studying physical aggression. It might be especially important to consider that indirect/relational/ social aggression may be more qualities of groups than individuals, that these behaviors may occur across more settings because they are so rarely punished, and that these behaviors are more covert and could take place over more extended time scales than physical aggression. Future research should explore whether continuing to engage in indirect/relational/ social aggression into adolescence and adulthood is associated with difficulties with work colleagues, problems in romantic relationships, and ineffective parenting.

References

Bates, J. E., Maslin, C. A., & Frankel, K.A. (1985). Attachment security, mother–child interaction, and temperament as predictors of behavior problem ratings at age three years. In I. I. Bretherton & E. Waters (Eds.), *Growing points of attachment theory and research. Monographs of the Society for Research in Child Development, 50* (1/2. Serial No. 209).

Baumrind, D. (1971). Current patterns of parental authority. *Developmental Psychology, 4*, 1–103.

Bjorkqvist, K. (1994). Sex differences in physical, verbal, and indirect aggression: A review of recent research. *Sex Roles, 30*, 177–188.

Cairns, R. B., Cairns, B. D., Neckerman, H. J., Ferguson, L. L., & Gariepy, J. (1989). Growth and aggression: 1. Childhood to early adolescence. *Developmental Psychology, 25*, 320–330.

Campbell, Breaux, Ewing, & Szumowski (1986). Correlates and prediction of hyperactivity and aggression: A longitudinal study of parent-referred problem preschoolers. *Journal of Abnormal Child Psychology, 14*, 217–234.

Capaldi, D. M. (1991). Co-occurrence of conduct problems and depressive symptoms in early adolescent boys: I. Familial factors and general adjustment at Grade 6. *Development and Psychopathology, 3*, 277–300.

Capaldi, D. M., Crosby, L., & Stoolmiller, M. (1996). Predicting the timing of first sexual intercourse for at-risk adolescent males. *Child Development, 67*, 344–359.

Caspi, A., Elder, G. H., & Bem, D. J. (1987). Moving against the world: Life course patterns of explosive children. *Developmental Psychology, 23*, 308–313.

Chen, X., Rubin, K. H., & Li, B. (1995). Social and school adjustment of shy and aggressive children in China. *Development and Psychopathology, 7*, 337–349.

Chen, X., Rubin, K. H., Li, B. & Li, D. (1999). Adolescent outcomes of social functioning in Chinese children. *International Journal of Behavioral Development, 23*, 199–223.

Chen, X., Rubin, K. H., & Li, D. (1997). Relation between academic achievement and social adjustment: Evidence from Chinese children. *Developmental Psychology, 33*, 518–525.

Chen, X., Rubin, K. H., & Li, Z. (1995). Social functioning and adjustment in Chinese children: A longitudinal study. *Developmental Psychology, 31*, 531–539.

Coie, J. D., Cillessen, A. H. N., Dodge, K. A., Hubbard, J. A., Schwartz, D., Lemerise, E. A., & Bateman, H. (1999). It takes two to fight: A test of relational factors and a method for assessing aggressive dyads. *Developmental Psychology, 35*, 1179–1188.

Coie, J. D., & Dodge, K. A. (1998). Aggression and antisocial behavior. In N. Eisenberg (Ed.), *Handbook of child psychology* (pp. 779–862). New York: Wiley.

Coie, J. D., & Kupersmidt, J. B. (1983). A behavioral analysis of emerging social status in boys' groups. *Child Development, 54*, 1400–1416.

Conduct Problems Prevention Research Group (1992). A developmental and clinical model for the prevention of conduct disorder: The FAST Track Program. *Development and Psychopathology, 4*, 509–527.

Crick, N. R. (1995). Relational aggression: The role of intent attributions, feelings of distress, and provocation type. *Development and Psychopathology, 7*, 313–322.

Crick, N. R. (1996). The role of overt aggression, relational aggression, and prosocial behavior in the prediction of children's future social adjustment. *Child Development, 67*, 2317–2327.

Crick, N. R. (1997). Engagement in gender normative versus gender nonnormative forms of aggression: Links to social-psychological adjustment. *Developmental Psychology, 33*, 610–617.

Crick, N. R., Casas, J. F., & Mosher, M. (1997). Relational and overt aggression in preschool. *Developmental Psychology, 33*, 589–600.

Crick, N. R., & Dodge, K. A. (1994). A review and reformulation of social-information mechanisms in children's social adjustment. *Psychological Bulletin, 115*, 74–101.

Crick, N. R., & Grotpeter, J. K. (1995). Relational aggression, gender, and social-psychological adjustment. *Child Development, 66*, 710–722.

Crick, N. R., & Grotpeter, J. K. (1996). Children's treatment by peers: Victims of relational and overt aggression. *Development and Psychopathology, 8*, 367–380.

Crick, N. R., & Ladd, G. W. (1990). Children's perceptions of the outcomes of aggressive strategies: Do the ends justify being mean? *Developmental Psychology, 26*, 612–620.

Crick, N. R., Wellman, N. E., Casas, J. F., O'Brien, M. A., Nelson, D. A., Grotpeter, J. K., & Markon, K. (1999). Childhood aggression and gender: A new look at an old problem. In D. Bernstein, (Ed.), *Nebraska Symposium on Motivation*. Lincoln, NE: University of Nebraska Press.

Crowther, J. K., Bond, L. A., & Rolf, J. E. (1981). The incidence, prevalence, and severity of behavior disorders among preschool-aged children in day care. *Journal of Abnormal Child Psychology, 9*, 23–42.

Deater-Deckard, K., Dodge, K. A., Bates, J. E., & Pettit, G. S. (1996). Physical discipline among African-American and European-American mothers: Links to children's externalizing behaviors. *Developmental Psychology, 32*, 1065–1072.

DeRosier, M. E., Cillessen, A. H. N., Coie, J. D., & Dodge, K. A. (1994). Group social context and children's aggressive behavior. *Child Development, 65*, 1068–1079.

Dettling, A. C., Gunnar, M. R., & Donzella, B. (1999). Cortisol levels of young children in full-day childcare centers: Relations with age and temperament. *Psychoneuroimmunology, 24*, 519–536.

Dodge, K. A. (1990). The structure and function of reactive and proactive aggression. In D. Pepler & K. H. Rubin (Eds.), *The development and treatment of childhood aggression* (pp. 201–218). Hillsdale, NJ: Erlbaum.

Dodge, K. A., Bates, J. E., & Pettit, G. S. (1990). Mechanisms in the cycle of violence. *Science, 250*, 1678–1683.

Dodge, K. A., & Coie, J. D. (1987). Social information processing factors in reactive and proactive aggression in children's peer groups. *Journal of Personality and Social Psychology, 53*, 1146–1158.

Dunn, J., & Kendrick, C. (1982). *Siblings*. Cambridge, MA: Harvard University Press.

Earls, F. (1980). The prevalence of behavior problems in 3-year-old children. *Archives of General Psychiatry, 37,* 1153–1159.

Fabes, R. A., & Eisenberg, N. (1992). Young children's coping with interpersonal anger. *Child Development, 63,* 116–128.

Fagot, B. I., & Hagan, R. (1985). Aggression in toddlers: Responses to the assertive acts of boys and girls. *Sex Roles, 12,* 341–351.

Fagot, B. I., Leinbach, M. D., & Hagan, R. (1986). Gender labeling and the adoption of sex-typed behaviors. *Developmental Psychology, 22,* 440–443.

French, D. C. (1988). Heterogeneity of peer-rejected boys: Aggressive and non-aggressive subtypes. *Child Development, 59,* 976–985.

Galen, B. R., & Underwood, M. K. (1997). A developmental investigation of social aggression among children. *Developmental Psychology, 33,* 589–600.

Goodenough, F. L. (1931). *Anger in young children.* Minneapolis, MN: University of Minnesota Press.

Gottesman, I. I., & Goldsmith, H. H. (1994). Developmental psychopathology of antisocial behavior: Inserting genes into its ontogenesis and epigenesis. In C. A. Nelson (Ed.), *Threats to optimal development: Integrating biological, psychological, and social risk factors* (pp.69–104). Hillsdale, NJ: Erlbaum.

Gottman, J., & Mettetal, G. (1986). Speculations about social and affective development: Friendship and acquaintanceship through adolescence. In J. M. Gottman & J. G. Parker (Eds.), *Conversations with friends: Speculations on affective development* (pp. 192–237). New York: Cambridge University Press.

Harré, R., & Lamb, R. (1983). *The encyclopedic dictionary of psychology.* Oxford, England: Basil Blackwell.

Hart, C. H., Nelson, D. A., Robinson, C. C., Olsen, S. F., & McNeilly-Choque, M. K. (1998). Overt and relational aggression in Russian nursery-school-age children: Parenting style and marital linkages. *Developmental Psychology, 34,* 687–697.

Henington, C., Hughes, J. N., Cavell, T. A., & Thompson, B. (1998). The role of relational aggression in identifying boys and girls. *Journal of School Psychology, 36,* 457–477.

Holden, G. W., & Zambarano, R. J. (1992). The origins of parenting: Transmission of beliefs about physical punishment. In I. E. Siegel, A. V. McGillicuddy, & J. J. Goodenow (Eds.), *Parental belief systems: The psychological consequences for children* (2nd ed., pp. 143–174). Hillsdale, NJ: Erlbaum.

Huesmann, L. R., & Miller, L. S. (1994). Long-term effects of repeated exposure to media violence in childhood. In L. R. Huesmann (Ed.), *Aggressive behavior: Current perspectives* (pp. 153–186). New York: Plenum.

Huston, A. C., & Wright, J. C. (1998). Mass media and children's development. In I. E. Sigel & K. A. Renninger (Eds.), *Handbook of child psychology* (pp. 999–1058). New York: Wiley.

Kaukiainen, A., Bjorkqvist, K., Lagerspetz, K., Osterman, K., Salmivalli, C., Rothberg, S., & Ahlbo, A. (1999). The relationships between social intelligence, empathy, and three types of aggression. *Aggressive Behavior, 25,* 81–89.

Kazdin, A. E. (1987). Treatment of antisocial behavior in children: Current status and future directions. *Psychological Bulletin, 102,* 187–203.

Knight, G. P., Fabes, R. A., & Higgins, D. A. (1996). Concerns about drawing inferences from meta-analyses: An example in the study of gender differences in aggression. *Psychological Bulletin, 119,* 410–421.

Kupersmidt, J. B., & Coie, J. D. (1990). Preadolescent peer status, aggression, and school adjustment as predictors of externalizing problems in adolescence. *Child Development, 61,* 1350–1362.

Ladd, G. W., & Burgess, K. B. (1999). Charting the relationship trajectories of aggressive, with-drawn, and aggressive/withdrawn children during early grade school. *Child Development, 70*, 910–929.

Lagerspetz, K. M. J., Bjorkqvist, K., & Peltonen, T. (1988). Is indirect aggression typical of females? Gender differences in aggressiveness in 11- to 12-year-old children. *Aggressive Behavior, 14*, 403–414.

Lamb, M. E. (1998). Nonparental care: Context, quality, correlates, and consequences. In I. E. Sigel & K. A. Renninger (Eds.), *Handbook of child psychology* (pp. 73–134). New York: Wiley.

Leckie, B. A. (April, 1999). Girls' perceptions of two subtypes of aggression: Are there differences and does sociometric status play a mediating role? In D. S. J. Hawker & N. H. Bartlett (Co-Chairs). *Subtypes of peer aggression and victimization: Current issues and controversies*. Sympo-sium presented at the Biennial Meeting of the Society for Research in Child Development, Albuquerque, New Mexico.

Loeber, R., & Hay, D. F. (1993). Developmental approaches to aggression and conduct problems. In M. Rutter & D. F. Hay (Eds.), *Development through life: A handbook for clinicians* (pp. 488–516). Oxford, England: Blackwell.

Maccoby, E. E., & Jacklin, C. N. (1974). *The psychology of gender differences*. Stanford, CA: Stanford University Press.

Maccoby, E. E., & Jacklin, C. N. (1980). Sex differences in aggression: A rejoinder and reprise. *Child Development, 51*, 964–980.

McFadyen-Ketchum, S. A., Bates, J. E., Dodge, K. A., & Pettit, G. S. (1996). Patterns of change in early childhood aggressive-disruptive behavior: Gender differences in predictions from early coercive and affectionate mother–child interactions. *Child Development, 67*, 2417–2433.

McNeilly-Choque, M. K., Hart, C. H., Robinson, C. C., Nelson, L. J., & Olsen, S. F. (1996). Overt and relational aggression on the playground: Correspondence among different inform-ants. *Journal of Research in Childhood Education, 11*, 47–67.

Olweus, D. (1977). Aggression and peer acceptance in adolescent boys: Two short-term longitudi-nal studies of ratings. *Child Development, 48*, 1303–1313.

Paquette, J. A., & Underwood, M. K. (1999). Young adolescents' experiences of peer victimization: Gender differences in accounts of social and physical aggression. *Merrill-Palmer Quarterly, 45*, 233–258.

Parker, J. G., & Asher, S. R. (1987). Peer relations and later personal adjustment: Are low accepted children at risk? *Psychological Bulletin, 102*, 357–389.

Patterson, G. R. (1982). *Coercive family process*. Eugene, OR: Castalia.

Pepler, D. J., & Craig, W. M. (1995). A peek behind the fence: Naturalistic observations of aggres-sive children with remote audiovisual recording. *Developmental Psychology, 31*, 357–389.

Price, J. M., & Dodge, K. A. (1989). Reactive and proactive aggression in childhood: Relations to peer status and social context dimensions. *Journal of Abnormal Child Psychology, 17*, 455–471.

Rys, G. S., & Bear, G. G. (1997). Relational aggression and peer relations: Gender and develop-mental issues. *Merrill-Palmer Quarterly, 43*, 87–106.

Saarni, C., & von Salisch, M. (1993). The socialization of emotional dissemblance. In M. Lewis & C. Saarni, (Eds.), *Lying and deception in everyday life* (pp. 106–125). New York: Guilford Press.

Sameroff, A. J., & Haith, M. (1996). *The five to seven year shift: The age of reason and social responsi-bility*. Chicago: University of Chicago Press.

Serbin, L. A., Cooperman, J. M., Peters, P. L., Lehoux, P. M., Stack, D. M., & Schwartzman, A. E. (1998). Intergenerational transfer of psychosocial risk in women with childhood histories of aggression, withdrawal, or aggression and withdrawal. *Developmental Psychology, 34*, 1246–1262.

Smith, P. K., & Green, M. (1974). Aggressive behavior in English nurseries and playgroups: Sex differences and response of adults. *Child Development, 45*, 211–214.

Straus, M., & Gelles, R. J. (1986). Societal change and change in family violence from 1975 to 1985 as revealed by two national surveys. *Journal of Marriage and the Family, 48*, 465–479.

Strassberg, Z., Dodge, K. A., Pettit, G. S., & Bates, J. E. (1994). Spanking in the home and children's subsequent aggression toward kindergarten peers. *Development and Psychopathology, 6*, 445–461.

Strayer, F. F., & Trudel, M. (1984). Developmental changes in the nature and function of social dominance among young children. *Ethnology and sociobiology, 5*, 279–295.

Tomada, G., & Schneider, B. H. (1997). Relational aggression, gender, and peer acceptance: Invariance across culture, stability over time, and concordance among informants. *Developmental Psychology, 33*, 601–609.

Underwood, M. K., Galen, B. R., & Paquette, J. A. (2001). Top ten methodological challenges for understanding gender and aggression: Why can't we all just get along? *Social Development, 10*, 248–267.

Underwood, M. K., Kupersmidt, J. B., & Coie, J. D. (1996). Childhood peer sociometric status and aggression as predictors of adolescent childbearing. *Journal of Research on Adolescence, 6*, 201–223.

Weiss, B., Dodge, K. A., Bates, J. E., & Pettit, G. S. (1992). Some consequences of early harsh discipline: Child aggression and a maladaptive social information style. *Child Development, 63*, 1321–1335.

Whiting, B. B., & Whiting, J. W. M. (1975). *Children of six cultures: A psychocultural analysis.* Cambridge, MA: Harvard University Press.

Wood, W., Wong, F. Y., & Cachere, G. (1991). Effects of media violence on viewers' aggression in unconstrained social interaction. *Psychological Bulletin, 109*, 371–383.

Wright, J. C., Zakriski, A. L., & Drinkwater, M. (1999). Developmental psychopathology and the patterning of behavior and environment: Distinctive situational and behavioral signatures of internalizing, externalizing, and mixed-syndrome children. *Journal of Consulting and Clinical Psychology, 67*, 95–107.

Xie, H., Swift, D. J., Cairns, B. D., & Cairns, R. B. (April, 2000). Aggressive behaviors in interaction and in prediction: A developmental examination of aggressive strategies in interpersonal conflicts. Paper presented at the Biennial Meeting of the Society for Research in Adolescence, Chicago, IL.

28

Bullying in Childhood

Ken Rigby

Introduction

Bullying among children has long been acknowledged as commonplace, especially in school settings, as is evident from accounts of bullying among English school boys by Thomas Hughes (1857) in *Tom Brown's Schooldays*. In many respects the situation at school for many children has not changed over the last 150 years (see Rigby, 1997a). What has changed, however, is the degree of attention being paid to the issue of school bullying, both in the press and in educational and research journals.

The impetus for the upsurge in interest in bullying came through the work of the Swedish psychologist, Dan Olweus, beginning in the 1970s. His work, originally focusing on the nature and prevalence of bullying between schoolboys in Scandinavia, stimulated similar research elsewhere, in the 1980s in Britain and other parts of Europe, then more widely in Australia and North America. It is now evident from the recently published book on national perspectives on bullying (Smith et al., 1999), that bullying among children, both boys and girls, is an issue of worldwide interest.

Over the last 10 years data has been steadily accumulating about bullying across age groups from early childhood to late adolescence. In this review I examine the prevalence nature and effects of bullying as experienced by children under 12 years of age, principally in school settings.

The problem of definition

As is common in new areas of study, there has been, and continues to be, a diversity of views as to how bullying can most usefully be defined. An early formulation focused only on the desire or intention of the bully to hurt another person; for example, one popular definition was "the wilful, conscious desire to hurt another and put him/her under stress" (Tattum & Tattum, 1992). This definition, however, proved unsatisfactory to more behaviorally inclined researchers such as Olweus (1993) who saw bullying as essentially "negative" behavior, not merely a desire to hurt which may or may not be expressed. It also became clear that "bullying" needed to be distinguished from aggression in general. Hence, more recently, writers in this area have generally emphasized that bullying can only occur when there is imbalance of power between aggressor and victim (Farrington, 1993; Olweus, 1993; Rigby, 1996; Smith & Sharp 1994). There is still some dispute as to whether one should limit the term "bullying" to a sequence of negative actions, that is, repeated aggression, as Olweus has suggested, or to accept (as in common usage) that the term can sometimes be used to describe a one-off experience, as Randall (1996) has argued.

Smith and Sharp (1994) have provided what is arguably the most comprehensive and parsimonious definition of bullying as "the systematic abuse of power." By including the term "abuse" in the definition, one is forced to consider what in a given situation is the proper or appropriate use of power. This would appear to depend upon prevailing norms and cultural mores and these may differ from place to place and from time to time. A school prefect in a nineteenth-century English boarding school could chastise his fag for not cleaning his boots without being accused of bullying him. Not so today. A degree of cultural relativity must be accepted in examinations of what constitutes bullying.

Methods of Investigation

Self-report questionnaire

This is by far the most commonly used method for investigating the prevalence of bullying and other aspects of the phenomenon. Probably the most frequently used instrument of this kind is that developed by Olweus and subsequently modified for an English language version (Smith & Sharp, 1994). Another widely used self-report questionnaire is the Peer Relations Questionnaire or PRQ (Rigby & Slee, 1993a), which has been used with over 40,000 schoolchildren in Australasia and in other English-speaking countries.

These and similar questionnaires typically provide a definition of bullying with illustrations in terms easily understood by children. Versions have been developed which are mainly pictorial and suitable (with teacher assistance) for children in the early years of primary school (Smith & Levan, 1995: given in Sharp, 1999). It is typically emphasized that a power imbalance is an essential part of the definition; for example, by asserting that "it is not bullying when students of the same strength or power have the occasional fight or quarrel." In order to maximize reliability, such questionnaires are answered anonymously.

The question is sometimes raised as to whether student respondents are apt to confuse bullying (in which there is an imbalance of power) with aggression generally. This may sometimes occur, despite the emphasis provided, but it is notable that when students are asked to make drawings to illustrate bullying they typically depict a smaller figure being attacked by a larger person or group of persons (see Rigby, 1996).

A further problem is that bullying is frequently construed by children (and others, too!)

as physical in nature. It is therefore necessary to provide examples of other, psychological forms of bullying, such as that conveyed through verbal abuse and exclusion. Self-report questionnaires typically enable respondents to indicate which of the various means of bullying have been applied to them over a stipulated time period and how often.

The peer nomination method

This approach involves respondents identifying students in their class who are involved in bully/victim interactions. It has been used in a variety of studies (e.g., Perry, Kusel, & Perry, 1988; Rigby & Slee, 1999). It has the important advantage of drawing upon the judgments of a number of students who have been able to observe their peers over a period of time. Where a high consensus emerges that a student is acting as a "bully" or a "victim" (in ways that are specified) it can be taken that the information is reliable. A problem with this approach is that it is seen by some educational and research bodies as unethical, on the grounds that respondents may be placed in an invidious position in reporting negatively upon their peers. Nevertheless, the approach is widely used, and may be justified as long as respondents are given the option of not making judgments of their peers' behavior if they dislike doing so. A further related issue concerns the use to which such data might be put. It is wise to make it clear that the results would be available in confidence to the researchers only and not accessible by school authorities.

Interviews

Interviewing children about bullying is sometimes undertaken, for example, in studies by Rigby and Slee (1990) and Williams, Chambers, Logan, and Robinson (1996). This option has some advantages. One can ensure, through further clarification, that the respondent understands the question being asked (as opposed to misreading or misinterpreting a written question); one can assess the extent to which the respondent is genuinely and sincerely engaged in the exercise; and, most important of all, one can obtain information from children who could not read a written questionnaire. The difficulty remains, however, that respondents may be loath to provide information about themselves when it reflects on them being aggressive (and culpable), or victimized by others (and thereby reveals weaknesses they would like to hide).

Teacher reports

A convenient way of obtaining data in children's bullying behavior is to ask class teachers to rate the behavior of each child (see Crick, Casas, & Mosher, 1997). For children in primary schools in which teachers see a great deal of children in their class this is a viable option. Where there are several teachers who have observed a child's behavior, inter-rater reliability can be usefully assessed. In secondary schools in which students are normally taught by a wide range of instructors, data from teacher assessments of behavior are far less reliable. Further, we know that most bullying takes place not in the classroom where the teacher can often see it, but rather at recess or on the way to and from school when the teacher is not present. This approach should therefore be confined to obtaining information about younger children under relatively close supervision from teachers and in circumstances when other approaches, for example, the anonymous questionnaire, are not practicable.

Phone-ins

A further source of data on bullying in childhood comes from records of children's calls to public services that provide opportunities for children to share their problems with a counselor and receive brief counseling or advice. Kids Help Line in Australia provides one such service (see http://203.37.145.243/INFO7/contents.htm). Although data collected in this way is extensive (some 6,000 children phoned in about bullying in 1999) this method inevitably elicits calls predominantly from older children who are more able to use the service.

Direct observational methods

This approach has a strong appeal because it circumvents the problem of obtaining socially desirable verbal responses to (possibly) misunderstood questions. It can also be carried out in a naturalistic setting, for instance in school playgrounds at recess times. It may nevertheless be difficult to observe the behavior of interest unobtrusively, especially at close quarters. To some extent, this difficulty may be overcome by making use of video and audio recordings, as was undertaken in observations of bullying behavior between Canadian primary school children (Craig & Pepler, 1995; Pepler & Craig, 1995). This involved setting up a video camera overlooking the playground. During filming each child in the study wore a small remote microphone and pocket-sized transmitter. The remote microphone picked up not only the "target's" speech but also that of those around him or her. The children were instructed to play as they normally did during lunch and recess.

This method has provided much data in a form that can be carefully and minutely coded and interpreted at a later stage. However, one must still reckon with the artificiality of children having to carry recording devices in the knowledge that what they say and do could be accessed by researchers. Also this research method may be considered by some ethical bodies as too intrusive. Its chief value appears to lie in enabling researchers to identify a range of bullying behaviors in a naturalistic setting, and more especially how children respond (or more often fail to respond) to bullying episodes that are taking place around them.

Bullying in Early Childhood

Bullying behavior can often be observed between very young children, for example between siblings in a family context. This is distinct from "conflict" which may arise over a struggle for possession of a prized toy and cease when the issue of ownership has been resolved. When an older and more powerful child persistently seeks to hurt a weaker sibling, this can legitimately be called bullying. Yet systematic studies of such behavior in the family context are notably lacking and for an examination of bullying in early childhood we must turn to studies conducted in preschool and kindergarten settings. Even here, compared with studies undertaken in primary and secondary schools, there have been relatively few systematic inquiries. To some extent this may be due to the difficulties of obtaining reliable data from the self-reports of the young children, especially through the use of questionnaires, which constitute the most widely used method of generating data on bullying and are more appropriately answered by older, more literate children. For younger children alternative and time-consuming methods are needed, such as one-to-one interviews with children and with teachers, and the use of direct observational methods.

Qualitative research

Qualitative research may be illustrated by a study based mainly upon direct observations of children's interpersonal behavior undertaken at four early childhood centers in Canberra, Australia in 1994 (Main, 1999). Some 98 hours of nonparticipant observation focused on the behavior of infants (6 weeks to 18 months), toddlers (18 months to 3 years) and preschoolers (3 years to 5 years). In addition 20 hours of semistructured interviews were conducted with 17 staff members of the selected child care organizations. Main reported that in all the subgroups (infants, toddlers, and preschoolers) a relatively few children were responsible for initiating aggressive actions which included pushing, biting, and hitting. Altogether 1,441 violent incidents were observed. In many cases a clear imbalance of power was apparent. For example:

> Tom is running around poking many children. He has a texta lid on his finger, and smiles as he pokes the children hard with it. He comes over to the observer and pokes her with his finger and says, "Do you want to see my powerful finger?" (The Observer responds that she is not interested because he had poked her with it.) He runs off and continues to poke children with it. A little later, when the children have moved inside, he grabs Rob and pushes his face hard into a pillow and holds him down. Rob is very distressed. A member of staff suggests that Tom does some hammering. Tom replies, "No! I don't have to!"

Main suggests that in general the children's aggressive behavior could not be explained as deriving from an "inability to share," and that the support that many early childhood educators give to the "principles of free play" with minimal intervention from teachers actually encourages bullying behavior in young children (see also Davies, 1997).

In many cases the motivation for acts of bullying appeared to be "for fun."

> A preschool boy throws a sandpit spade at a toddler girl as she comes out of the toddler's room. He misses and laughs with the other boys sitting with him. Then he grabs a sandpit spade from her and hits her hard on the body with it.

Not uncommonly, the observed behavior included a variety of bullying acts: aggressive gestures, physical attack, and verbal abuse.

> Jim (a preschool boy) goes over to the corner where Sal is playing with a group of girls on a pile of pillows. He growls at them, putting his face very close to theirs and grimacing. They scream and grab the pillows around them. Jim tells them to share the pillows. He then lies down on the pillows and the girls say "We had them first." Jim does not respond and the girls move away, going back only to retrieve their shoes. Jim then moves from the pillows and gets a piece of string. He grabs Sybi and puts the string around her neck, pulling it around her neck. Sybi cries. A member of staff comes over and tells him to play with Ian. He turns to Sybi and says "Cry baby." Jim then goes over to Melanie and, smiling, pulls her hair.

Although this research does not provide detailed statistical data on the incidence of bullying among preschool children, it clearly demonstrates its nature and prevalence.

Quantitative research

Much quantitative research has focused upon students who are frequently the targets of aggression from peers, but are not necessarily being bullied in the sense of being victimized by those more powerful than themselves. They may simply be more often involved in fights or quarrels. Hence results from studies that do not make a distinction between bullying (where there is an imbalance of power) and peer aggression (where no such imbalance may be present) arguably need to be differentiated.

A study of peer victimization in early childhood that fits into the broader category of peer aggression is that of Kochenderfer and Ladd (1996). They interviewed 200 students attending kindergarten (105 males and 95 females) at the beginning of their school year. The mean age of these children was 5.5 years. They were asked to say whether any of the children in their class had done any of the following things to them, and, if so, how often another student had: (i) picked on them; (ii) hit them; (iii) said mean things to them; (iv) said bad things about them to other kids at school. Responses were scored as 1 "never", 2 "sometimes", and 3 "a lot". The internal consistency of this measure (alpha = .74), suggests that children at this age who were repeatedly targeted tended to be treated negatively in a number of different ways. In short, there appears to be support for the generality of their concept of peer victimization.

Taking the view that a victimized child is one who is *repeatedly* treated badly, the criterion for identifying "victims" was scoring above the midpoint on the scale. Some 20.5% were identified in this way. The authors claim a significant level of agreement between children identified as victims in this way and the judgments of teachers based upon direct observations. Further, they claim that this estimate of the extent of peer victimization in U.S. kindergartens is, in fact, not very different from that reported by Olweus (1993) for Norwegian second-grade students among whom some 17% reported being victims of school bullying. Here, then, is a suggestion that the "victimized" children in the study by Kochenderfer and Ladd are in the same category as those reported as being bullied in the sense employed by Olweus.

Kochenderfer and Ladd also examined the question of whether at this age children identified as victims continued to be victims of peer aggression. They report that there were some 8% of respondents who were identified as victims on the basis of self-reports 6 months later. This suggests that a small minority of children had over this period continued to be "victims." Almost twice as many initial victims no longer met the criterion of repeatedly victimized.

Somewhat similar research with young children has been conducted in a series of studies by Crick and others. Again these authors did not differentiate between "peer aggression" and "bullying." However, they have examined an aspect of aggression of interest to research into bullying, one generally seen as prevalent more especially among senior students, namely, relational aggression. In a study by Crick, Casas, and Mosher (1997) with children ($N = 65$) between 3 to 5 years, it was reported that relational kinds of bullying were evident among boys and girls, but more commonly among girls, and could be differentiated from other forms of aggressive behavior. To identify different kinds of aggressive behavior teachers were asked to rate children in their class according to how often they acted in various aggressive ways with their peers. Ways assumed to be "relational" included: (i) tells others not to play with or be a peer's friend; (ii) tries to get others to dislike a peer; and (iii) when mad at a peer, keeps that peer away from being in the peer group. Analysis confirmed that ratings on these and similar items were loaded on a different factor from that associated with verbal and physical overt forms of aggression. At the same time, scale scores based on "relational" items correlated highly ($r = >.7$) with scale scores for other nonrelational items, suggesting that children whose aggression is expressed in a relational manner tend to be aggressive in other ways. Similar findings were reported using data derived from peer ratings.

In a further study by Crick, Casas, and Ku (1999) a focus was on children in the same age range who were continually victimized by others. Again teacher ratings constituted the main method of acquiring relevant data. For example, teachers were asked to identify children who "get pushed and shoved" (overt victimization) and those who "get left out when someone is mad with him/her" (relational victimization). Again, using factor analyses, the researchers were able to show that being victimized relationally could be differentiated from overt forms. Crick et al. also provided results that suggest that being victimized at this age is relatively stable over a 1-month interval. For relational bullying the test–retest correlation was moderately high ($r = .63$); for physical victimization, lower but still significant ($r = .37$). This appears to conflict with the finding reported by Kochenderfer and Ladd who reported low levels of stability for peer victimization. These differences may be due to Kochenderfer and Ladd using children's self-report data as opposed to teacher ratings, and assessing stability over a 6-month period rather than over 1 month.

In the study by Crick et al. (1999) it was also possible to examine the correlations between acting aggressively and being victimized by peers. Correlations between physical aggressiveness and being physically victimized were moderately strong: .65 for boys and .65 for girls. Corresponding correlations for relational aggression and victimization were .45 and .58. These results appear to be at variance with results obtained from research in which bullying behavior (implying an imbalance of power) has been specifically studied. For example, Rigby and Slee (1993b) reported correlations for older students between reliable scales assessing bullying others and being victimized by others that were not significantly different from zero. It is possible that among very young students the more severely victimized children do tend to engage more in aggressive behavior toward others, as the correlations provided by Crick et al. suggest, and that with increasing maturity they become more submissive. However, a more likely explanation for the differences lies in the different ways in which being victimized or being an aggressor is conceptualized; that is, as occurring in situations in which one party cannot defend itself adequately due to a power imbalance (the bullying situation), or as occurring whenever there is peer aggression more generally. Until studies are conducted which clearly differentiate between bullying and peer aggression more generally this important question will not be resolved.

Bullying in Later Childhood

Estimates of the incidence and nature of bullying and related attitudes can be assessed more reliably by questionnaire among older students. Further, the bulk of research with older children has been based upon a conceptualization of bullying that identifies bullying as occurring only where there is an imbalance of power.

Peer victimization

There is general agreement that the incidence of reported victimization declines with age. This appears to be the case from the earliest years of school to the end of secondary schooling. The decline is evident in the period between 8 and 11 years, as illustrated in the data (see Table 28.1) for a large sample of Australian schoolchildren ($N = 3440$). These data were collected over a 4-year period using the PRQ (Rigby & Slee, 1993a). The criterion for "being bullied" was reporting being bullied at least once a week during the current year of schooling.

Evidence for the near ubiquity of this trend among children between the ages of 7 and 11 is included in a paper by Smith, Madsen, and Moody (1999). They cite figures from

Table 28.1   Percentages of Students Reporting being Bullied Weekly in Australian Schools (Ns range from 176 to 803)

	Ages in years			
	8	*9*	*10*	*11*
Boys	48.0	30.7	24.3	22.5
Girls	33.3	32.9	26.1	20.8

large-scale studies undertaken by Olweus (1993) in Norway and in Sweden; by Whitney and Smith (1993) in England; by Rigby (1996, 1997c) in Australia; and by O'Moore, Kirkham, and Smith (1997) in Ireland. In each case for both boys and girls a steady decline is evident over these years. This is despite the fact that somewhat different criteria were used by the researchers to define "being bullied"; for instance, Olweus has used, on occasions, "now and then"; Rigby, "at least once a week." However, in one American study which obtained data using peer nominations, no evidence of a decline in peer victimization was found for children between the ages of 8 and 12 years (Perry, Kusel, & Perry, 1988).

Below the age of 8 years the PRQ and similar questionnaires have limited value as a means of assessing the incidence of peer victimization. Smith, Madsen, and Moody (1999) have argued it is likely that bullying may be conceived in a somewhat different way according to the maturity of the respondent, and results for groups varying widely in age may not be strictly comparable. It is possible that 8 year olds see bullying in a somewhat different way from 11 year olds. Further research is needed to address this possibility.

The content of peer victimization

In assessing the incidence of peer victimization some studies have sought to examine specific kinds of aggressive acts to which victims in different age groups may be subjected. Typically, studies have differentiated between being a victim of physical, verbal, and relational aggression. Results using the PRQ in Australia include measures using such indices. Their relative frequency according to age and gender groups is given in Table 28.2. For each of the indices of victimization there is over the age range of 8 to 11 a trend towards a lower incidence of occurrence. The proportions of students reporting being victimized to not being victimized for each of the ways of being victimized and for each sex group differ significantly ($p < .05$ by chi square).

Table 28.2   Percentages of Students Reporting Peer Victimization of Different Kinds (Ns range from 172 to 765)

	Ages in years			
	8	*9*	*10*	*11*
Being called hurtful names				
Boys	65.1	58.5	53.8	51.8
Girls	58.2	61.9	53.2	53.0
Being left out of things				
Boys	54.3	45.1	37.7	33.9
Girls	58.2	52.2	50.5	45.3
Being hit or kicked				
Boys	66.7	54.1	43.0	34.0
Girls	43.4	39.9	29.5	22.9

Table 28.3   Percentages of Students Reporting Bullying Others More Than "Once or Twice" During the Year (Ns range from 176 to 803)

	Ages in years			
	8	*9*	*10*	*11*
Boys				
As an individual	13.6	11.3	10.5	10.0
As a group member	12.5	12.2	9.3	9.7
Girls				
As an individual	3.0	5.8	6.3	6.5
As a group member	2.5	4.9	4.1	4.5

Perpetrators of Bullying

Among children between 8 and 11 years there is little evidence of a change in the tendency to bully others. The figures for Australian students completing the PRQ (given in Table 28.3) indicate that within groups of boys and also within groups of girls the proportions of self-reported bullies, both individually and in groups do not change from year to year. This finding is consistent with research reported elsewhere (e.g., Olweus, 1993).

The differences between the proportions of students in the different age groups are small and nonsignificant (for each of the comparisons by chi square, $p > .05$). From this it would appear that the tendency to engage in bullying others is relatively stable between the ages of 8 to 11 years, whether perpetrated by individuals or as members of a group; and as a boy or as a girl.

Reactions to Being Bullied

Little attention has been paid to how students react emotionally to being bullied. In a study with Australian students, again using the PRQ, respondents were asked to say how they generally reacted to being bullied by another student. Results are given in Table 28.4 for those students who admitted that they had been bullied at least once at school, that is, approximately 50% of students of each sex.

Among boys the proportions of kinds of reactions differed significantly according to age group (chi square 29.6, $p < .001$). The percentages of boys claiming that they were "not bothered" by it increased steadily from 33.1% at 8 years to 52.3% at 11 years. Somewhat similar results have been reported for English school children who with increasing age were less likely to cry when they were bullied and more likely to ignore the bullying (Smith & Shu, 2000). We may speculate as to whether the bullying experienced by boys at age 8 is more severe than that at age 11; or alternatively whether boys become more resilient (or

Table 28.4   Percentages of Students Reporting Having Reacted to Bullying in Different Ways (*N*s range from 146 to 587)

	Ages in years			
	8	9	10	11
Boys				
Not bothered	33.1	40.9	44.1	52.3
Angry	34.7	39.3	36.3	29.8
Sad	32.0	19.8	19.6	17.8
Girls				
Not bothered	30.8	31.3	30.0	33.7
Angry	19.2	23.0	20.9	26.1
Sad	50.0	47.7	49.1	40.2

perhaps more prone to adopt a macho attitude) with increasing years. Among girls, age proved to be unrelated to reaction tendencies (chi square 8.6, $p > .05$).

Numerous studies have recently been carried out on the effects of bullying on the well-being and health of children. Most of these are correlational in design, and establish that primary school children who are frequently victimized are more likely to have low self-esteem (Boulton & Smith, 1994; Mynard & Joseph, 1997) and to suffer psychological distress such as depression (Slee, 1995) and not sleeping well, headaches, and bed-wetting (Williams, Chambers, Logan, & Robinson, 1996). In addition, several longitudinal studies have established that peer victimization commonly leads to a loss in self-esteem (Egan & Perry, 1998) and social maladjustment, as indicated by increased loneliness and absenteeism from school (Ladd, Kochenderfer, & Coleman, 1997).

Reported Reasons for Bullying

According to Boulton and Underwood (1992), the most common reason given by children is that victims provoke bullying, a view more frequently expressed by bullies. An Australian study canvassed seven possible reasons (derived from prior discussions with children in this age group) that students might give if they did bully a peer. Respondents could answer "yes" or "no" in relation to each proposed reason. Approximately 16% of respondents omitted to respond to one or more of these questions. Responses of children aged 8 to 11 years who did answer are given in Table 28.5.

The order of frequency of endorsing reasons was similar for boys and girls. (There is one exception – boys placed "for fun" higher than did girls; girls placed "because others were doing it" higher.) In endorsing the main two reasons, it appears that respondents were (as in the earlier study by Boulton & Underwood) looking for justification and perhaps choosing

Table 28.5   Percentages of Students Between the Ages of 8 and 11 Years Indicating That if They Bullied Someone it Would be for Specified Reasons (Ns range from 1535 to 1770)

Reason	Boys	Girls
Because they annoyed me	68.2	60.7
To get even	64.0	46.0
For fun	16.0	10.0
Because others were doing it	14.0	13.3
Because they were wimps	11.3	7.0
To show how tough one is	11.3	7.0
To get things or money from them	6.1	4.2

the least socially undesirable options. At the same time, substantial numbers of respondents acknowledged they could bully others for fun, because others were doing so, because they saw some peers as deserving to be bullied because they were "wimps," and in order to impress others with their toughness. Relatively few saw bullying as a means they might employ for extortionary purposes. Significant age trends ($p < .001$) for both boys and girls were evident for two of the reasons: with increasing age students were more inclined to justify their bullying along the lines that "they had annoyed me" and "to get even."

Attitudes to Victims of Bullying

Attitudes to victims were examined by Rigby and Slee (1991), using a reliable 20-item scale (alpha = .78) assessing provictim attitude. Sample items were: "It's a good thing to help children who can't defend themselves" and "I wouldn't be friends with kids who let themselves be pushed around" (reverse scored). Scores for 314 boys and 353 girls between the ages of 8 and 15 indicated that most students were generally supportive of victims: for example, some 80.9% agreed with the statement: "I like it when someone stands up for kids who are bullied." This result showing a clear majority support for victims was subsequently replicated in England with final year primary school children of around 11 years (Randall, 1995). In the Australian study for both boys and girls there was a significant decline in support for victims between 8 and 11 years. Consistent with this finding in Italy, Fonzi et al. (1999) have reported a trend toward less help being given by peers to victims up until middle school, which begins in Italy at age 11. These results are in some ways counter-intuitive. One might expect that with an increase in the capacity for empathy with increasing maturity (see Damon, 1983) support for victims would gradually increase rather than decrease.

Another index relating to children's attitudes to bullying is that of a readiness to talk with other students about the issue. The Australian study included this question: "Would you be interested in talking about the problem of bullying at school with other students to see what can be done about stopping it?". The results provide a contrast between the

Table 28.6   Percentages of Students Responding According to their Interest in Talking with Others about Stopping Bullying (Ns range from 174 to 770)

	Ages in years			
	8	9	10	11
Boys				
In favor	51.7	47.2	43.3	34.2
Unsure	32.2	31.9	36.2	40.9
Against	16.1	20.9	20.5	24.9
Girls				
In favor	50.3	51.4	51.8	49.5
Unsure	39.6	39.0	37.4	37.8
Against	10.2	9.6	10.8	12.7

readiness to talk about bullying among the younger students in primary school and the older ones at secondary school. For instance, among 8 year olds some 51.7% of boys and 50.3% of girls wanted to talk; among 15 year olds the corresponding figures were 21.6% and 33.3%. Results for the age range 8–11 years are given in Table 28.6.

The trend towards fewer students being in favor of, and more being against, talking about bullying in class is evident for boys (chi square was 30.3, $p < .001$). Among girls the proportions for the three responses to the question are not significantly different (chi square = 2.7, $p > .05$). It would seem that although at no stage are more than 25% of boys or girls against talking about it in class, there is an increasing reluctance among boys in particular to engage in such talking. This result parallels the finding that there is a lessening of support for victims over this period, again notably among boys, and may in fact reflect a growing lack of sympathy with the plight of victims, and possible apprehension about what talk about bullying may reveal about themselves.

Transition from Primary to Secondary School

Changes in the prevalence of peer victimization may be affected not only by increasing age, but also by changes in the nature of the schooling. For example, children in some countries and in some localities transfer around the age of 11 or 12 years from a primary school where they are among the oldest children in the school to a secondary school where they are among the youngest. Because younger children are more vulnerable to attack one would expect the incidence of reported victimization to rise after entering the school catering for predominantly older students. This is what was found in Australian schools (Rigby, 1997b). In an analysis of students attending coeducational schools only, the reported incidence of weekly victimization was traced for Australian students attending Year 4 to Year 12 (approximately 8 to 16 years). Analyses were conducted separately for students who transfer

Table 28.7   Percentages of Students Reporting being Bullied Weekly According to Year of Schooling (Ns range from 40 to 1025)

	4	*5*	*6*	*7*	*8*	*9*	*10*	*11*	*12*
				Year of schooling					
Students starting Year 7									
Boys	31.3	30.6	17.4	28.0	25.1	22.3	14.9	12.1	4.6
Girls	36.4	21.2	18.2	23.1	19.6	14.6	11.2	8.4	6.9
Students starting Year 8									
Boys	30.0	22.4	23.3	17.0	24.9	23.5	15.1	9.7	3.1
Girls	28.0	21.1	17.9	9.8	19.6	11.4	10.2	5.4	3.4

Note. Students starting secondary school in Year 7 were drawn from 4 primary and 18 secondary schools; those starting in Year 8 were drawn from 14 primary and 17 secondary schools.

to secondary school in Year 7 (in the States of Tasmania, Victoria, New South Wales, and Australian Capital Territory) and for those who transfer in Year 8 (in the States of South Australia, Queensland, Western Australia, and Northern Territory). Rates of reported victimization are given in Table 28.7.

These results indicate that reported victimization in coeducational primary schools declines gradually between Years 4 to 6 in States in which the students are normally transferred to a secondary school for their Year 7 schooling, and then increases before reducing again in later years. For students in other States where transfer to secondary school occurs in Year 8, the decline in the incidence of reported peer victimization continues for another year, before rising when these students enter secondary school, again decreasing later.

What is clear from these data is that in the Australian context the level of reported victimization around the ages of 11 and 12 years is dependent in part on whether the student has entered secondary school. If the incidence of victimization were determined only by chronological age one would expect a simple linear trend, not increases in peer victimization when a child changed schools. Clearly in accounting for peer victimization at a given age one must take into account social situation and organizational structure.

Gender Differences

Studies of gender differences in overall peer victimization have produced mixed results. Data for children under the age of 12 years from England (Whitney & Smith, 1993), the United States (Perry, Kusel, & Perry, 1988) and Australia (see Table 28.1), suggest that there is little or no sex difference between the extent of peer victimization. On the other hand, in some countries, for example, Norway (Olweus, 1993), Portugal (Almeida, 1999), and Germany (Losel & Bliesener, 1999), significantly higher levels of peer victimization have been reported for boys.

The similarities in overall victimization may mask differences in the kinds of bullying to which boys and girls are subjected. Table 28.2 shows that among Australian children for each of the age groups boys are more likely to be the targets of physical bullying, while girls are more likely to report "being left out of things," which is one of the relational forms of bullying that researchers such as Crick et al. (1997) have reported as occurring more often to girls, even at preschool age.

Whilst boys and girls under 12 appear to be victimized by peers equally often, there have been numerous reports that boys are more likely than girls to engage in bullying behavior (see Olweus, 1993; Rigby, 1998; Whitney & Smith, 1993). Table 28.3 shows that whilst boys and girls seem equally likely to bully in groups as to bully individually, the percentages of boys reporting bullying others as group members and as individuals is approximately twice as great as for girls. In part this may be explained by noting that boys bully members of the opposite sex far more than girls do (Rigby, 1998). It may also be the case that boys tend to see the practice of bullying others in a more positive light than girls do, and are more likely to want to report doing so. Although data bearing on this matter derive from responses to anonymous questionnaires, they may still be affected by considerations of social desirability, which influence boys and girls differently.

Less well researched are the reactions of boys and girls to being bullied at school. In general, girls report being "bothered" more by it. From Table 28.4, among 11 year olds who had been bullied some 52.3% reported that they were "not bothered" by it, compared with 33.7% of girls. When children are bothered, girls are more likely than boys to say they felt "sad"; boys are more likely to say they felt "angry." It is noteworthy that the tendency among boys to report not being bothered increases with age, arguably because they are being more and more socialized into a culture that expects boys to be tough, "macho," and to deny hurt. Among girls the data suggest that there is no such tendency.

A further difference relates to attitudes toward bullying and also to normative influences on children to engage in bullying others. Significant differences between boys and girls in the age range of 9–10 years have been reported indicating that girls were: (i) more supportive of victims; (ii) less probully; (iii) pressured to bully less by significant others, namely close friends, mother, father, or teachers; and (iv) believed they were less able to bully than boys. Girls also were more likely to report that they would feel "ashamed of themselves" if they bullied someone (Rigby, 1997c). Not surprisingly (see Table 28.6) girls were more interested than boys in talking in groups to discover a way to stop bullying.

Nevertheless the reasons boys and girls give for bullying (if they were to bully) are remarkably similar in relative importance. For both sexes the "revenge motive" appears to be paramount (see Table 28.5), and although it is socially more desirable to give such a reason than to admit to extortion or a desire to upset "a wimp," it is striking that both boys and girls tend to justify their bullying behavior in similar ways – or, alternatively, provide similar rationalizations for what they are doing. The gender difference in the ranking of "bullying for fun," with boys seeing bullying more often as a source of enjoyment, may reflect a more insensitive view of bullying on the part of boys.

Race and Ethnicity

Sometimes children are victimized because they are racially or ethnically different from the majority of other students. Those of non-White ethnic origin in one study conducted in England were found to have experienced more racist name-calling than other children of the same age and gender (Boulton, 1995). However, in that study, "bullying in general" was also reported as taking place predominantly between members of the same racial group (British Asian or British non-Asian). A report from Germany indicated that children of non-German extraction were no more likely to be targeted as victims of peer bullying than others (Losel & Bliesener, 1999). Evidence of ethnic group members attracting greater than average overall bullying has been provided by the Kids Help Line in Australia who claim that calls from children of ethnic background on matters of bullying are some 30% greater than others. However, in an Australian study by Rigby (unpublished) utilizing data from the PRQ, quite different results were found. Some 891 children (25% of all respondents in this age group) reported that their family was of ethnic origin other than White Australian. Among these "ethnic" students, 29.2% of boys and 27.2% of girls reported that they had been bullied at school at least once a week. This was only slightly (nonsignificantly) more than other students. (The reported incidence of weekly victimization of White Australian students was 26% for boys and for girls.) However, an examination of reported victimization by specific ethnic group membership did show one significant difference. Among the 34 male Aboriginal respondents in the sample, 18 (53%) reported being bullied weekly. This was significantly greater ($p < .05$) than that reported by other students from "ethnic families", which included children who identified their families as Italian, Greek, Polish, and Vietnamese. Although the sample of Aboriginal children is small and of questionable representativeness, the finding is consistent with many anecdotal accounts of discrimination experienced by Aboriginal children from peers in Australia.

Social Class

The relationship between children's involvement in bully/victim problems and the socioeconomic status of their parents has been studied with mixed results. In a study conducted in schools in and around Sheffield, England, a largely industrial area, it was found that involvement in bully/victim problems was significantly more likely to occur in schools in relatively disadvantaged places (Whitney & Smith, 1993). In Scotland, Mellor (1999) found that children of parents with professional and managerial jobs were less likely to be bullied, whilst those whose parents had skilled manual jobs were more likely to be victims and also more likely to be bullies! Research conducted in the Netherlands suggests that bullying is more common among children from socially disadvantaged and inner city areas (Junger-Tas, 1999). As against these findings, Olweus (1993) claimed that among boys attending Swedish schools bullying was unrelated to social class as indicated by indices of parent income level and length of parent education. In neither Spain nor Portugal, was bullying found to be related to social class (Almeida, 1999; Ortega & Mora-Mechan, 1999).

Thus, whether social class is a factor in bullying among children appears to vary between countries. Given what has been reported about the parenting styles of parents of different social classes (Newson & Newson, 1976), with lower-class parents being more inclined to use – and arguably model – physical violence, it seems possible that the mode of bullying, rather than the totality of bullying, may be worth examining as a variable in future studies.

The Effectiveness of Interventions to Reduce Bullying

There is now considerable evidence that bullying in schools can be reduced through the use of whole-school antibullying policies and practices (Eslea & Smith, 1998; Olweus, 1993). However, apart from the report by Olweus on the national campaign to reduce peer victimization in Norway for which a 50% reduction in bullying was claimed, the reductions following interventions have been modest in size and not always significant. Many methods of intervention are currently being canvassed, such as the use of peer counseling and training in conflict resolution skills for all students; but few have been carefully evaluated. An exception is the Method of Shared Concern (Pikas, 1989; Smith & Sharp, 1994): a counseling approach which has been reported as largely successful in preventing the repetition of bullying by perpetrators of group bullying. Further studies to evaluate interventions are clearly needed.

Conclusions

Bullying in schools, as distinct from conflict or aggression in general between children, has over the last 10 years become an important area of study cross-nationally. We now know that bullying is prevalent in early childhood, is perpetrated more by boys, and tends to reduce somewhat as children progress through primary school. It produces considerable distress and psychological harm to the minority of children who are frequently victimized by their peers. Verbal forms of bullying are most prevalent and equally experienced by boys and girls; physical bullying is more commonly perpetrated and experienced by boys; relational bullying by girls. Reactions to bullying tend to differ between the sexes, with boys being more inclined to deny its effect upon them. Motives for bullying may vary widely and include a wish to get even, a means of amusement, acquiescence to peer pressure, extortion, and a desire to appear tough. As well as developmental changes that can affect the incidence of bullying for a given age group, one should recognize as factors the school environment, the social disadvantage of families, and the ethnic mix in some communities. Interventions to reduce bullying are increasingly being developed, proposed, and implemented but as yet with modest success.

References

Almeida, A. M. T. D. (1999). Portugal. In P. K. Smith et al. (Eds.), *The nature of school bullying* (pp. 174–186). London: Routledge.

Boulton, M. J. (1995). Patterns of bully/victim problems in mixed race groups of children. *Social Development, 4*, 277–293.

Boulton, M. J., & Smith, P. K. (1994). Bully/victim problems in middle school children: Stability, self-perceived competence, peer perception and peer acceptance. *British Journal of Developmental Psychology, 12*, 315–329.

Boulton, M. J., & Underwood, K. (1992). Bully/victim problems among middle school children. *British Journal of Educational Psychology, 62*, 73–87.

Craig, W. M., & Pepler, D. J. (1995). Peer processes on bullying and victimization: an observational study. *Exceptionality Education Canada, 5*, 81–95.

Crick, N. R., Casas, J. F., & Ku, H. (1999). Relational and physical forms of peer victimization in preschool. *Developmental Psychology, 35*, 376–385.

Crick, N. R., Casas, J. F., & Mosher, M. (1997). Relational and overt aggression in preschool. *Developmental Psychology, 33*, 579–588.

Damon, W. (1983). *Social and personality development.* New York: Norton.

Davies, M. (1997). The teachers' role in outdoor play: Preschool teachers' beliefs and practices. *Australian Research in Early Childhood Education, 6*, 10–20.

Egan, S. K., & Perry, D. G. (1998). Does low self-regard invite victimization? *Developmental Psychology, 34*, 299–309.

Eslea, M., & Smith, P. K. (1998). The long-term effectiveness of anti-bullying work in primary schools. *Education Research, 2*, 203–218.

Farrington, D. P., (1993). Understanding and preventing bullying. In M. Tonry & N. Morris (Eds.), *Crime and justice, Vol. 17* (pp. 381–459). Chicago: University of Chicago Press.

Fonzi, A., Genta. M. L., Menesini, E., Bacchini, D., Bonino, S., & Costabile, A. (1999). Italy. In P. K. Smith et al. (Eds.), *The nature of school bullying* (pp. 140–156). London: Routledge.

Hughes, T. (1968, first published, 1857). *Tom Brown's School Days.* New York: Airmont.

Junger-Tas, J. (1999). The Netherlands. In P. K. Smith et al. (Eds.), *The nature of school bullying* (pp. 205–223). London: Routledge.

Kochenderfer, B. J., & Ladd, G. W. (1996). Peer victimization: Cause or consequence of school maladjustment. *Child Development, 67*, 1305–1310.

Ladd, G. W., Kochenderfer, B. J., & Coleman, C. C. (1997). Classroom peer acceptance, friendship and victimization: Distinct relational systems that contribute uniquely to children's social adjustment? *Child Development, 68*, 1181–1197.

Losel, F., & Bliesener, T. (1999). Germany. In P. K. Smith et al. (Eds.), *The nature of school bullying* (pp. 224–249). London: Routledge.

Main, M. (1999). Children's perception of violence in early childhood. Paper presented at the Children and Crime: Victims' and Offenders' Conference. Australian Institute of Criminology, Brisbane, 17–18 June.

Mellor, A. (1999). Scotland. In P. K. Smith et al. (Eds.), *The nature of school bullying* (pp. 91–111). London: Routledge.

Mynard, H., & Joseph, S. (1997). Bully/victim problems and their association with Eysenck's personality dimensions in 8 to 13 year olds. *British Journal of Educational Psychology, 66*, 447–456.

Newson, J., & Newson, E. (1976). *Seven years old in the home environment.* London: Penguin.

Olweus, D. (1993). *Bullying at school.* Cambridge, MA: Blackwell.

O'Moore, M., Kirkham, C., & Smith, M. (1997). Bullying behaviour in Irish schools: A nation-wide study. *Irish Journal of Psychology, 18*, 141–169.

Ortega, R., & Mora-Mechan, J. A. (1999). Spain. In P. K. Smith et al. (Eds.), *The nature of school bullying* (pp.157–173). London: Routledge.

Perry, D. G., Kusel, S. J., & Perry, L. C. (1988). Victims of peer aggression. *Developmental Psychology, 24*, 807–814.

Pepler, D. J. & Craig, W. M. (1995). A peek behind the fence: Observations of playground interactions with video camera and remote microphones. *Developmental Psychology, 31*, 548–533.

Perry, D. G., Kusel, S. J., & Perry, L. C. (1988) Victims of peer aggression. *Developmental Psychology, 24*, 807–814.

Pikas, A. (1989). The Common Concern Method for the treatment of mobbing. In E. Munthe & E. Roland (Eds.), *Bullying: An international perspective* (pp. 91–104). London: David Fulton.

Randall, P. (1995). A factor study of attitudes of children to bullying in a high risk area. *Educational Psychology in Practice, 11*, 22–27.

Randall, P. (1996). *A community approach to bullying*. Stoke on Trent, England: Trentham.

Rigby, K. (1996). *Bullying in schools – and what to do about it*. Melbourne, Australia: ACER.

Rigby, K. (1997a). Reflections on *Tom Brown's Schooldays* and the problem of bullying today. *Australian Journal of Social Science, 4*, 85–96.

Rigby, K. (1997b). *Manual for the Peer Relations Questionnaire (PRQ)*. Point Lonsdale, Victoria, Australia: The Professional Reading Guide.

Rigby, K. (1997c). Attitudes and beliefs about bullying among Australian school children. *Irish Journal of Psychology, 18*, 202–220.

Rigby, K. (1998). Gender and bullying in schools. In P. T. Slee & K. Rigby (Eds.), *Children's peer relations*. London: Routledge.

Rigby, K., & Slee, P. T. (1990). Victims and bullies in school communities. *Journal of the Australasian Society of Victimology, 1*, 23–28.

Rigby, K., & Slee, P. T. (1991). Bullying among Australian school children: Reported behaviour and attitudes to victims. *Journal of Social Psychology, 131*, 615–627.

Rigby, K., & Slee, P. T. (1993a). The Peer Relations Questionnaire. Adelaide, Australia: University of South Australia. (Subsequently in 1997: Point Lonsdale, Victoria, Australia: *The Professional Reading Guide*.)

Rigby, K., & Slee, P. T. (1993b). Dimensions of interpersonal relation among Australian children and implications for psychological well-being. *Journal of Social Psychology, 133*, 33–42.

Rigby, K., & Slee, P. T. (1999). Suicidal ideation among adolescent school children, involvement in bully/victim problems and perceived low social support. *Suicide and Life-Threatening Behavior, 29*, 119–130.

Sharp, S. (1999). *Bullying behaviour in schools. Psychology in Education Portfolio*. Windsor, England: NFER-NELSON.

Slee, P. T. (1995). Peer victimization and its relationship to depression among Australian primary school students. *Personality and Individual Differences, 18*, 57–62.

Smith, P. K., & Levan, S. (1995). Perceptions and experiences of bullying in younger pupils. *British Journal of Educational Psychology, 65*, 489–500.

Smith, P. K., Madsen, K. C., & Moody, J. C. (1999). What causes the age decline in reports of being bullied at school? Towards a developmental analysis of risks of being bullied. *Educational Research, 3*, 267–285.

Smith, P. K., Morita, J., Junger-Tas, D., Olweus, D., Catalalano, R., & Slee, P. T. (1999). *The nature of school bullying: A cross-national perspective*. London: Routledge.

Smith, P. K., & Sharp, S. (Eds.) (1994). *School bullying insights and perspectives*. London: Routledge.

Smith, P. K., & Shu, S. (2000). What good schools can do about bullying: Findings from a survey in English schools after a decade of research and action. *Childhood, 7,* 193–212.

Tattum, D., & Tattum, E. (1992). *Social education and personal development.* London: David Fulton.

Whitney, I., & Smith, P. K. (1993). A survey of the nature and extent of bullying in junior/middle and secondary schools. *Educational Research, 35,* 3–25.

Williams, K., Chambers, M., Logan, S., & Robinson, D. (1996). Association of common health symptoms with bullying in primary school children. *British Medical Journal, 313,* 17–19.

Part X

Children with Special Needs

The concluding section of this *Handbook* is devoted to the increasingly important topic of children with special needs. Karen Diamond reminds us that approximately 10% of the world's population has disabilities that can interfere with social functioning. Depending on how disability is defined, this percentage can vary dramatically according to country or state policies and practices (sometimes between 30–70%). No matter how the statistics are derived, the number of children with disabilities is large. Many of these children are unable to participate in social activities on the level of their typically developing peers.

How well do children with mild to severe disabilities adjust to the peer group? Do certain types of classroom structures (e.g., inclusive) promote higher levels of peer interaction for children with disabilities than others? How can parents, teachers, and other adults provide supporting opportunities for social interactions? Diamond discusses these and many other questions in the context of describing how deficits in cognitive processes (e.g., mental retardation) and emotion regulation (e.g., autism) increase the probability of peer interaction difficulties. However, environmental factors that include adult coaching, attitudes towards involving children with disabilities in peer interaction, and opportunities for associating with peers can serve to mediate linkages between cognitive and emotional regulation deficits and the development of social competencies. She also explains how disabilities that do not affect cognition or emotion regulation (e.g., physical disabilities, chronic illness such as asthma or cancer, blindness) likely result in different, but lesser challenges for peer group interaction. Future research that fosters an understanding of which social context characteristics are most important for facilitating social abilities in children with disabilities as well as discovering how typically developing children may benefit from interacting with peers with disabilities are pointed to as exciting new directions for study.

Bonnie Brinton and Martin Fujiki have pioneered research in a new area of social development research that focuses on children with specific language impairment (SLI). They also cover profound hearing loss in their chapter. It is fitting that this volume ends with a synthesis of their work as it takes readers to the beginning of scholarly inquiry in an area where little was known just a few short years ago. They begin with a discussion of how profound hearing loss develops and some of the challenges that it poses for family communication and peer group interaction. The extant research literature on why profound hearing loss is often associated with children not being integrated into the fabric of peer group interaction is reviewed. From there, the authors focus on different profiles of linguistic strengths and weaknesses that children with specific language impairments bring to social interaction. It is estimated that 7% of children suffer from this disorder that stems from relatively unknown causes. The research of Brinton and Fujiki clearly highlights the importance of functional communication skills in socially competent behavior (see Hart, Newell, & Olsen, in press). They have documented how some children with SLI have difficulty entering ongoing conversations, negotiating, collaborating, and making joint decisions. Children with SLI are also prone to be more anxious and wary with peers, and suffer from deficits in language abilities that are detrimental to friendship formation and maintenance functions. Future research in this area will focus on effective and efficient ways to simultaneously facilitate language and social skill development so that children with SLI will be better able to function in socially competent ways.

References

Hart, C. H., Newell, L. D., & Olsen, S. F. (in press). Parenting skills and social/communicative competence in childhood. In J. O. Greene & B. R. Burleson (Eds.), *Handbook of communication and social interaction skill.* Mahwah, NJ: Erlbaum.

29

The Development of Social Competence in Children with Disabilities

Karen E. Diamond

The World Health Organization estimates that 10% of the world's population has some type of disability that interferes with full participation in the community in which the individual lives (WHO, 1999). However, definitions of disability are "moving targets" that change across communities and cultures. While individuals with more severe disabilities or identified syndromes are likely to be identified as disabled in many communities, this is less often the case for those with less severe disabilities. It is not surprising to find that children who are identified as having "mild" disabilities in Western schools are unlikely to be identified as disabled in other groups (Harry, Rueda, & Kalyanpur, 1999).

Over the past several decades in the United States, there has been an increasing emphasis on including children with disabilities in activities and environments designed primarily for children without disabilities. Opportunities that children with disabilities have to participate in activities with their typically developing peers can be very different, even within a single country. For instance, in a recent report, the proportion of elementary age children with disabilities enrolled in regular education classes in the United States ranged between 30–70%, with variations related to state policies and practices (U.S. Dept. of Education, 1997). Bochner and Pieterse (1996) reported that at least half of children with Down syndrome born in the 1970s in New South Wales, Australia, received education in primary schools designed for typically developing children, while almost all children with Down syndrome born during the same time period in South Wales, Great Britain, were enrolled in self-contained special education schools.

Normalized life experiences for children with disabilities have different meanings within

The author wishes to thank Dr. William LeFurgy for his helpful comments on earlier drafts of this chapter.

different cultures, and cultural expectations for success vary widely. Ideas of equity in opportunity and treatment reflect distinctly Western cultural values (Harry et al., 1999). Many families expect that a child with a significant disability will be cared for by family members throughout his or her life. In these families, the critical issues for a child's social development may be quite different than for families whose goal is to have their child with disabilities participate in school, work, and community activities.

If children are to successfully participate in school and community settings with peers, developing age-appropriate social behaviors is an important challenge. There is consistent evidence that children with disabilities display lower levels of social competence than typically developing peers. Peer relationship problems have been reported for children with learning disabilities (Juvonen & Bear, 1992), communication disorders and mild mental retardation (Guralnick, Connor, Hammond, Gottman, & Kinnish, 1996), and sensory disabilities (Erwin, 1993), as well as for children with significant mental, physical, and behavioral disabilities (Staub, Schwartz, Gallucci, & Peck, 1994) and chronic health problems (Wallander & Varni, 1998). For all of these children, problems with peer relationships become especially evident as children's activities become less structured (e.g., recess or lunch at school).

Because independent living is an important value in Western societies, much of the research on social relationships between children with disabilities and their typically developing age-mates has taken place in European countries or the United States. This research forms the basis for this chapter. The framework for discussing social development is a distinctly Western one. In addition, some disabilities that will be discussed in this chapter (especially learning disabilities and mild mental retardation) are unknown in many groups. The social stigma surrounding a child's identification as a "slow learner" is uniquely Western.

Contextual Variables

Contextual variables are related to social competence for children with disabilities. In recent research, Guralnick and his colleagues (1996) found that preschool children with mild disabilities displayed more frequent social interaction and higher levels of social play when they were in a play group with typically developing children than when they participated in a specialized group that included only children with disabilities. Bronson and her colleagues found that preschool children with disabilities displayed clear benefits in the quality of their social interactions with peers when they were enrolled in classrooms that were most similar (in terms of class size, teacher:child ratio, activity choices, and with a small proportion of children with identified disabilities) to early childhood settings designed for children without disabilities. Children in more inclusive settings engaged in more and higher levels of peer interaction and were more independent and less controlled by adults. Relationships between classroom structure and social competence remained significant even after accounting for the child's intellectual abilities (Bronson, Hauser-Cram & Warfield, 1997; Hauser-Cram, Bronson, & Upshur, 1993). Similar results have been reported for older children, and for children with more severe disabilities (Fryxell & Kennedy, 1995).

Developmental Perspectives on Peer-Related Social Competence for Children with Disabilities

The extent to which children with disabilities grow up to live independently (or semi-independently) as adults depends to a considerable extent on their ability to engage in appropriate social interactions with others. Dodge and his colleagues have suggested that children's social strategies are governed by underlying social-cognitive processes, including encoding relevant social cues, interpreting these cues correctly, generating a variety of responses, evaluating each response, and enacting the selected response (Crick & Dodge, 1994; Dodge, Pettit, McClaskey, & Brown, 1986). Guralnick (1999) adapted this model for children with disabilities, postulating that the social-cognitive skills described by Dodge and his colleagues are built upon foundation processes of emotion regulation and shared understanding. These foundation processes, along with social-cognitive processes, are nested within *higher order* processes that "represent the over-arching social task recognition, monitoring, and goal maintaining (planning) features that characterize socially competent functioning" (Guralnick, 1999, p. 22). Thus, foundation processes of emotion regulation and shared understanding, social information-processing variables, and higher order processes determine the social strategies that a child uses in an interaction. If any of these processes are adversely affected by characteristics of the individual (e.g., cognitive deficits) or of the environment (e.g., environmental factors that make emotion regulation more difficult), less competent social strategies may result. Because these processes are closely linked, significant peer interaction deficits may result when there are even relatively small discrepancies from expected developmental levels (Guralnick, 1999).

Qualities of the social environment also contribute to the development of socially competent behavior (Diamond & Innes, 2001; Guralnick, 1999). One would hypothesize that children who have opportunities to practice social skills within supportive peer social networks are likely to demonstrate more social competence than children without these experiences. An important component of supportive peer networks includes the adults who support children's development of age-appropriate social interaction strategies. Teachers provide support when they arrange the physical environment to allow interactions to occur and use child-directed learning strategies in their teaching (Staub et al., 1994). Parents of children with and without disabilities play an important role in fostering children's peer social network by arranging play opportunities outside of the school classroom (e.g., Block & Malloy, 1998; Ladd & Hart, 1992). Finally, the attitudes of others (including attitudes of peers and adults) play a role in supporting opportunities for social interactions (Helmstetter, Peck, & Giangreco, 1994; Okagaki, Diamond, Kontos, & Hestenes, 1998).

What does this suggest about social development of children with disabilities? First, disabilities that are associated with deficits in cognitive processes (such as mental retardation) or emotion regulation (for example, autism) increase the likelihood that a child will have significant difficulties in peer interaction. In addition, this model suggests that environmental factors mediate the influence of cognitive and emotional regulation deficits on the development of socially competent behaviors. These environmental factors include opportunities to participate in a broad range of social networks, the role played by adults in helping children develop appropriate social interaction strategies, and attitudes toward the participation of children with disabilities in peer activities. Finally, this model implies that disabilities that do not affect cognition or emotion regulation (e.g., physical disabilities or blindness) are likely to have different, lesser impacts on children's development of age-appropriate social relationships.

What Do We Know about the Social Development of Children with Disabilities?

Research in inclusive play groups has consistently demonstrated that children with disabilities are included in social interactions with their peers much less than are children without disabilities, with social play less sophisticated than that of typically developing peers (Guralnick & Neville, 1997). Despite lower overall rates of interaction, interactions between children with disabilities and their typically developing peers have been reported to occur quite often in preschool and elementary school settings (Guralnick et al., 1996). Although varying with the type of disability, the majority of children with disabilities who participate in programs with their typically developing peers are reported to have at least one mutual friend (Buysse, 1993). These results suggest that children with disabilities are included in some activities with typically developing peers. At the same time, because children with disabilities participate in social play less often and in less sophisticated ways, their social experiences are likely to be different from those of typically developing children. The sections that follow focus on research that has examined the social development of children with specific types of disabilities.

Disabilities that affect cognition

Children with mild mental retardation or learning disabilities.　In the United States, children with learning problems related to low levels of school achievement without other obvious disabilities are typically identified as having either a learning disability or mild mental retardation. There is substantial evidence that children with learning disabilities, mild mental retardation, and low ability are not clinically different groups. Gresham and MacMillan (1997) argue that "blurring of these formerly distinct groups makes much of the research on differences in social competence and affective characteristics [of children with these disabilities] uninterpretable" (p. 403). Thus, they suggest that research on the social skills of children with mild disabilities (i.e., students with mild mental retardation, specific learning disabilities, and low ability) should be aggregated. This is the approach that is taken in this chapter.

Research on the social competence of young children with mild mental retardation conducted by Guralnick and his colleagues has used a planned play group methodology to study the development of young children's social relationships. Results have been consistent in describing children with mild disabilities as less preferred playmates than their peers (e.g., Guralnick et al., 1996), with peer interaction difficulties associated with deficits in communication skills (a higher order process), as well as difficulties using appropriate interaction strategies (i.e., deficits in social information processing) which may, or may not, be related to deficits in communication and cognition (Guralnick, 1999). The importance of communication skills for social interaction is supported in many studies in which typically developing children were more successful in their social bids than were children with communication disorders (Guralnick et al., 1996; Hartas & Donahue, 1997).

Recently, Kravetz, Faust, Lipshitz, and Shalhav (1999) found some support for the hypothesis that difficulties in interpersonal understanding contribute to social behavior problems in preadolescent children with learning disabilities. Deficits in generating alternative solutions to social problems have been reported in studies of adolescents with learning disabilities (e.g., Hartas & Donahue, 1997). Leffert and Siperstein (1996) found that 10–13-year-old children with mild mental retardation were similar to typically developing peers in accurately interpreting hostile intentions in peer conflict situations, and varying their choice of social strategy based on the situational context. Unlike typically developing children, children with mental retardation encoded benign intention cues with significantly greater accuracy than they interpreted them. In the procedure used in this study, both hostile and benign intention cues were associated with negative outcomes. The authors suggest that children's difficulties interpreting benign cues were related to underlying cognitive difficulties reconciling situations in which there was a conflict between intention (benign) and outcome (negative). Thus, mild deficits in social understanding also appear to be related to difficulties in peer interaction with these deficits appearing as early as preschool.

Although children with mild cognitive disabilities display significant deficits in peer interaction, the developmental processes that underlie peer-related social competence may be substantially similar to those described for children without disabilities. Guralnick and Hammond (1999) found similar sequential play patterns for typically developing preschool children and children with disabilities that were consistent regardless of the setting in which children were observed (inclusive class with typically developing peers or self-contained special education class). Siperstein and Leffert (1997) found that children with mental retardation who displayed sociable behaviors gained greater acceptance from their peers without disabilities in inclusive settings, while children who displayed sensitive-isolated behaviors were more likely to be rejected.

There is considerable evidence that preschool and elementary-age children and adolescents with mild cognitive disabilities are less popular and more likely to be rejected and neglected than their peers without disabilities when sociometric assessments are used (e.g., Diamond, LeFurgy, & Blass, 1993; Ochoa & Palmer, 1995; Taylor, Asher, & Williams, 1987). Results are somewhat different when the focus becomes that of mutual friendships. Juvonen and Bear (1992) reported that third graders with learning disabilities in inclusive elementary classes reported similar levels of mutual friendship and acceptance by classmates as did their classmates without disabilities, while Vaughn and Elbaum (1999) reported that students with learning disabilities were similar to their classmates without disabilities in their reports of the number and quality of their friendships. These results are consistent with Bukowski and Hoza's (1989) suggestion that having friends and being well accepted are distinctly different.

Research on the social development of children with learning disabilities and mild mental retardation points to the important relationship between communication skills and social initiations with peers. Deficits in foundation processes (specifically mutual understanding of roles, rules, and expectations governing social behavior) and in social-cognitive processes (especially interpreting social cues) may account for some of the delays in social development reported for children with mild cognitive disabilities. Although children with mild mental retardation and learning disabilities are less popular than their normally developing peers, they may be similar to children without disabilities in the number of best friends and in the quality of their friendships.

Children with Down syndrome.   As a group, children with Down syndrome show greater expressive than receptive language delays, especially as they advance in mental age. Cognitive performance is also delayed, with IQ scores often diminishing (and mental age scores increasing) as children grow older (Rynders & Horrobin, 1990). Using the model of social competence described earlier, one would expect to find that such deficits in cognitive and language abilities (higher order variables) would be associated with difficulties in many social-cognitive processes, including encoding and accurately interpreting cues, and generating and enacting social strategies. Sigman and Ruskin (1999) have reported, however, that delays in language skills were not associated with comparable delays in nonverbal communication or play skills for children with Down syndrome. In addition, they found that preschool children with Down syndrome were responsive to adults' displays of emotion, and regularly initiated social interactions with adults. The frequency of early social interactions with adults was associated with peer involvement in later childhood. Classroom and playground observations suggested that peers accepted more than 70% of the social play initiations of children with Down syndrome. Similarly, children with Down syndrome accepted a significant majority (73%) of peer play initiations (Sigman & Ruskin, 1999). These results suggest that although children with Down syndrome have significantly delayed cognitive abilities and expressive language skills, nonverbal abilities, especially social and emotional responsiveness, may play an important role in the development of social competence.

A substantial number of children with Down syndrome are reported to have best friends, including friends who are typically developing (Sigman & Ruskin, 1999). In a recent study in Great Britain, Begley (1999) found that 8–16-year-old children with Down syndrome had generally positive perceptions of their acceptance by peers, with children in mainstream schools reporting more positive self-perceptions than children enrolled in self-contained special education schools. Bochner and Pieterse (1996) reported that slightly more than one third of the teenagers with Down syndrome they studied in New South Wales participated in inclusive social activities with typically developing peers (e.g., Girl Guides), while approximately half participated in a club or activity designed specifically for adolescents with disabilities (e.g., Special Olympics). Many teenagers with Down syndrome also spent much of their social lives with their families, a result that has also been reported for adolescents with Down syndrome in the United States (Putnam, Pueschel, & Gorder-Holman, 1988).

Greater sociableness in children with Down syndrome, compared to children of the same mental age, is a common finding (Kasari & Hodapp, 1996). Children with Down syndrome appear interested in others, even during infancy, and this general social responsiveness continues into adulthood. It has been suggested that the higher levels of social and emotional responsiveness seen in children with Down syndrome, compared to children with other syndromes, may lead to higher levels of social competence. Although adolescents with Down syndrome appear to spend more of their leisure time alone than do their peers without disabilities, recent research suggests that these children have positive perceptions of their acceptance by peers.

Children and adolescents with Down syndrome have cognitive and communication delays that are typically associated with deficits in many of the social information-processing components of socially competent behaviors. Research suggests that children with Down syndrome may be especially adept at emotion regulation; children with Down syndrome generally appear socially interested and responsive and show relatively few negative behaviors. Thus, motivation to participate in social interactions, along with a "more sociable style" (Kasari & Hodapp, 1996, p. 6) may mediate the effects of cognitive and communication deficits on social competence.

Children with severe mental retardation and multiple disabilities.   When children with severe disabilities are enrolled in self-contained special education classrooms with peers who also have severe disabilities, opportunities for peer interactions are severely limited by the nature of each child's disability. There is evidence, however, that significant social benefits accrue to children with severe disabilities from their planned participation in general education settings with classmates without disabilities (Fryxell & Kennedy, 1995). Hanline (1993) found that preschool children with severe disabilities had numerous opportunities for peer social interactions in an inclusive summer program, and Kennedy and his colleagues have reported that elementary and middle-school students with severe disabilities who were enrolled in general education classes had more social contacts with typically developing peers, received and provided higher levels of social support, and had larger and more durable friendship networks than students in self-contained special education classrooms (Kennedy, Shukla, & Fryxell, 1997). It is important to note that the students they observed were enrolled in schools in which inclusion efforts were planned on a building-wide basis. Hughes and her colleagues reported different results when they observed social behaviors of students with moderate to severe mental retardation and their typically developing peers in a high school lunchroom. (Students with disabilities participated in lunch and nonacademic classes, but spent most of their day in special education classes.) Few social interactions occurred over 3 months of observation. The authors suggest that a lack of shared classroom experiences may have played an important role in limiting interactions (Hughes et al., 1999).

For children with severe disabilities, some competencies appear more important than others in the development of interactions with peers. Responsiveness to others and motivation to engage in interactions are positively associated with the development of social relationships for children with severe disabilities, while limitations in physical mobility, often associated with severe mental retardation, reduce opportunities to participate in activities with peers (Grenot-Scheyer, 1994; Strain, 1985). Interactions between children with severe disabilities and their typically developing peers are usually not symmetrical: the typically developing peer often directs the interaction and/or provides assistance, while the child with a severe disability is a more passive recipient.

Although much research on the social development of children with mental retardation has resulted in identification of specific deficits, children with mental retardation may have more strategy capabilities than are often identified (cf. Bray, Saarnio, & Hawk, 1994). Many children and adolescents with mild, as well as more severe, mental retardation participate in social relationships with peers, with some children participating in peer group activities in ways similar to age-mates without disabilities.

Not surprisingly, the significant deficits in cognition and communication that are found in individuals with severe disabilities are related to deficits in many of the social-cognitive processes that underlie socially competent behavior. Children with severe disabilities who are more responsive to peers' initiations and motivated to engage in social interactions demonstrate higher levels of social competence, with opportunities to participate in settings with normally developing peers related to more competent social interactions for children with severe disabilities.

Disabilities related to behavior/affect regulation

Children with autistic spectrum disorders.   Children with autism and related disorders (e.g., Asperger syndrome, Pervasive Developmental Disorder) show consistent, pervasive impairments in social interactions and communication that are manifested in the first three years of life (Sigman & Ruskin, 1999). Defining features of autism include social and communicative deficits and repeated stereotyped behaviors, with the key diagnostic behaviors those that reflect social development (Volkmar & Lord, 1998). Current estimates suggest that autism occurs in as many as 1 in 1,000 children, with the rate of autism spectrum disorders approaching 1% of the school age population (Kadesjö, Gillberg, & Hagberg, 1999; Sponheim & Skjeldal, 1998). Mental retardation is present in approximately 75% of individuals with autism, with the frequency of children's stereotyped behaviors increasing with more severe retardation (Volkmar & Lord, 1998). Not surprisingly, nonretarded autistic children display higher levels of social behavior than mentally retarded autistic children (Lord, 1993).

Descriptions of the social development of children with autism point to deficits in the development of basic interpersonal skills during infancy. These include failure to make eye contact and to use gaze to regulate interaction, as well as failure to engage in early social games, such as peek-a-boo (Volkmar, 1993). Although social skills change as children develop, social responsivity remains a source of difficulty.

There is also evidence of deficits in emotion regulation that are related to social competence in children with autistic spectrum disorders. Yirmiya, Kasari, Sigman, and Mundy (1989) found that children with autism showed significantly more facial expressions of negative affect than did children of the same mental age who had mental retardation or were typically developing. They suggested that the effect on the interactive partner may have been significant because the negative expressions were so unexpected.

There is evidence that social deficits in autism may be associated with specific deficits related to theory-of-mind skills, especially deficits in shared attention and understanding of others' intentions and desires (Phillips, Baron-Cohen, & Rutter, 1998). Just as work with typically developing children provides evidence that children's understanding of others' mental states has important implications for social development and communication (Astington & Jenkins, 1995), so, too, does this appear to be important in the social development of young children with autism. Children with autism appear to have most difficulty with tasks that require nonverbal joint attention skills (Mundy & Crowson, 1997), with impairments in joint attention more severe for social than nonsocial stimuli (Dawson, Meltzoff, Osterling, Rinaldi, & Brown, 1998). Mundy and Crowson (1997) have also suggested that children's joint attention bids may provide a measure of motivation to communicate (see also Yirmiya, Pilowsky, Solomonica-Levi, & Shulman, 1999). Dawson and her colleagues recently proposed, however, that deficits in joint attention may be a result of a more basic failure to attend to social stimuli, with deficits in social orienting behaviors occurring earlier in development than deficits in shared attention (Dawson et al., 1998). Bauminger and Kasari (2000) also provide evidence that children with autism lack an understanding of the affective components of social relationships.

Because autism is associated with significant impairments in social interaction, most children with autism are educated in self-contained special education classrooms. These settings provide few opportunities for social interaction. However, typically developing peers may play important roles in facilitating social interactions for children with autism. For example, O'Neill and Lord (as cited in Lord, 1993) reported that autistic children with normally developing siblings were more likely to produce spontaneous peer-directed language in their classrooms, suggesting that social experiences with siblings or peers may play a role in preparing children for interactions in other settings. Roeyers (1996) found that children with autism who had regular opportunities to interact with their typically developing peers made significant gains in social skills (especially the frequency of social initiations) when compared to matched children without this experience. Lee and Odom (1996) found a decrease in stereotypic behaviors for two children with autism associated with increased opportunities for social interaction with typically developing peers. When Sigman and Ruskin (1999) observed school-age children with autism and Down syndrome in their classrooms and on the school playground, they found that children with autism were as likely as children with other disabilities to receive initiations from typically developing peers, but were less likely than others to accept social bids. In addition, children with autism were significantly less likely to initiate interactions with typically developing peers than were children with Down syndrome. In fact, nearly half of the school-age children with autism in this study never initiated any interaction with a peer. These results are similar to those of Lord and Magill-Evans (1995), who found that autistic children and adolescents produced significantly fewer initiations to peers than did children with language disorders or typically developing children.

In sum, research on the social development of children with autistic spectrum disorders suggests that deficits in attention to faces (and, subsequently, joint attention) and orientation to social stimuli are early characteristics of children with autism. These difficulties are thought to result from an underlying disorder in interpersonal perception and communication which interferes with the child's ability to experience others as individuals who are important in the social environment. Thus, in the model of social competence discussed earlier, children with autistic spectrum disorders show deficits in foundation processes (including both emotion regulation and social understanding) and in social information processing which are critical for the development of socially competent behavior.

Physical and sensory disabilities

Children with chronic illness and physical disabilities.   Chronic illnesses lead to regular hospitalization or interfere with children's ability to function in their typical environment. Illnesses or physical disabilities that fall in this category include asthma, diabetes, cancer, and hemiplegia. Epidemiological studies suggest that between 10–20% of children in Western-developed countries have a chronic disorder, although only about 10% of children in this group have severe conditions. While each of these illnesses or disabilities is medically unique, their effects on children's social experiences are similar (Wallander & Varni, 1998).

Children with chronic disorders appear vulnerable to peer relationship problems, with the risk increasing for illnesses or disabilities that involve the central nervous system or motor skills (Wallander & Varni, 1998). Children with chronic illnesses may be at risk for peer relationship difficulties because opportunities for social interaction are limited by absenteeism from school, physical limitations, and parents' concerns (Zbikowski & Cohen, 1998). Based on the model of social development that was described earlier, it is reasonable to hypothesize that physical disabilities and chronic illnesses are likely to influence the development of children's social relationships when they interfere with opportunities to participate in supportive peer social networks.

Asthma is the most common chronic illness of childhood in Western countries; the 1990–1992 National Health Survey reported that 6.1% of U.S. children under 18 had asthma (Collins, 1997). Because asthma often limits children's physical activity, and requires long-term use of medications and regular medical care including hospitalization, this illness provides a model for examining the role of chronic illness in the development of children's social competence. In a study of 8–13-year-old children, Graetz and Schute (1995) found no significant differences in the peer relationships of children with asthma compared to healthy peers. Children with more frequent hospitalizations, however, were perceived as more sensitive and isolated, were less preferred as playmates, and reported themselves to be lonelier than their peers. Zbikowski and Cohen (1998) found no significant differences on measures of social acceptance or popularity for elementary age children with asthma when compared with their healthy peers. Older children with asthma (10–12 year olds) were not significantly different from their healthy age-mates on the number of mutual friendship nominations or parent-rated measures of social competence. In contrast, parents rated younger children with asthma (6–9 year olds) as less socially competent. Younger children with asthma had significantly fewer mutual friendship nominations than either children without asthma or older children with asthma. The authors suggested that differences between younger and older children with asthma may reflect increased restrictions on social activities of younger children. If parents of older children with asthma are more comfortable with their child's illness, children may have social opportunities that are similar to those of their healthy peers. In addition, older children with asthma may have developed a variety of coping strategies that are not available to younger children. These results are similar to those reported by Noll and his colleagues who found few differences from healthy peers on teacher-rated measures of social adjustment or acceptance for children with cancer or sickle cell disease (Noll, Ris, Davies, Bukowski, & Koontz, 1992).

Reduced opportunities to participate in social activities put children with chronic illness at greater risk for social isolation. Overall, however, the social development and competence of children with chronic illnesses does not appear to be substantially different from that of their healthy peers. Results are more equivocal for children with physical disabilities. In studies examining the social adjustment of a cohort of children with hemiplegia enrolled in mainstream primary schools in London, Yude and Goodman (1999) found that 9–11-year-old children with hemiplegia were less popular, more likely to be rejected, had fewer friends, and were more often victimized than were their classmates without disabilities (although approximately one third of the children with hemiplegia had no apparent peer relationship difficulties). Not surprisingly, children attributed their social difficulties to physical factors. Even when motor difficulties were mild, children with hemiplegia were often marginalized within the school environment. Although this type of exclusion clearly put these children at risk for problems in social relationships, the most powerful predictors of peer relationship problems when children were 9–11 years old were teachers' reports of conduct problems and/or hyperactivity, together with low IQ, measured soon after school entry (age 6 or 7). Yude and Goodman (1999) suggested that at least some of the peer relationship problems faced by children with hemiplegia may be related to significant neurological deficits that affect learning and behavior. These results are similar to those of Zurmohle and his colleagues who found that children with spina bifida were at increased risk for social adjustment problems. Interestingly, they found that children with spina bifida who attended a school for children with disabilities, even though it was "an IQ-appropriate setting" had a higher rate of social adjustment problems than children with spina bifida who were enrolled in mainstream schools (Zurmohle, Homann, Schroeter, Rothgerber, Hommel, & Ermert, 1998). Thus, the results of these studies suggest that both child-specific factors (especially learning and behavior problems) and factors in the social environment are related to social development and social adjustment of children with mild physical disabilities.

Children with visual impairments.   Vision impairments that are severe enough to significantly interfere with children's daily activities are relatively rare. Some children with visual impairments have no useful vision while other children have partial vision but require assistance with daily activities. Globally, the prevalence of severe visual impairments (the child is legally or totally blind) is slightly less than 1 of every 1,000 children (WHO, 1999).

In the model of social competence described earlier, the ability to encode and interpret social cues is a critical component of socially competent behavior. Many of the skills that are essential for effectively encoding and interpreting social cues are nonverbal and are based on the ability to observe and interpret the behaviors of others (Rosenblum, 1997). Self-monitoring, another component of socially competent behavior, also requires encoding and interpreting both verbal and nonverbal responses to one's own behaviors (Erwin, 1993). Children who have significant visual impairments may experience difficulties in social relationships because they are unaware of subtle social cues that provide information about others' feelings, and because they may not know how others respond to their own behaviors. In addition, shared understanding of play activities, social rules, and social conventions are components of socially competent behavior that can be affected by a child's inability to observe social interactions and play (McAlpine & Moore, 1995),

There is relatively little research on the social development of children with visual impairments (Warren, 1994), in part because this is an uncommon disability and recruitment of study participants is challenging. In the majority of studies that are discussed below, substantial numbers of participants with visual impairments had additional disabilities that made social interaction even more problematic.

Several studies examining the social development of children and adolescents with visual impairments describe lower rates of social interaction with peers, more frequent interactions with adults, and more participation in solitary activities than are typical for same-age peers without disabilities (Skellenger, Rosenblum, & Jager, 1997). Children with some useful vision (i.e., children who were visual learners) typically engaged in significantly more interaction with peers than did children who were blind (i.e., tactile learners), although rates of interaction were lower than found for children without disabilities.

In a recent study, Hatton and her colleagues found that preschool children with visual function of 20/800 or worse performed at lower levels on personal-social tasks than children with vision function in the range of 20/70 to 20/500 (Hatton, Bailey, Burchinal, & Ferrell, 1997). They suggested that functional vision of 20/500 or better may be the level necessary for making eye contact and recognizing nonverbal social cues, both of which facilitate responsive interactions with others.

Finally, visual impairments may make it difficult for a child to participate in some activities with peers. For example, many sports require visual skills such as throwing or hitting a ball. It is hardly surprising that young children with visual impairments have reported that their inability to participate in activities such as these interferes with the development of social relationships with sighted peers (MacCuspie, cited in Rosenblum, 1997).

If a child's play partner provides information about the social environment in ways that are accessible to the child with a visual impairment (e.g., by providing verbal cues), it makes it somewhat easier for the child to participate in the social activity (Sacks, 1992). In order for this to occur, however, the child's partner needs to understand the importance of providing additional information and support. This is a task that is developmentally difficult for many children, without specific intervention from adults. Thus, it is hardly surprising that typically developing children often think that it takes an extra effort to be friends with a child with a visual impairment (MacCuspie, cited in Rosenblum, 1997).

These results suggest that children and adolescents with visual impairments are more isolated from peer interaction, have more frequent contacts with adults, and participate in more solitary activity than do their sighted peers. Functional vision that is sufficient for making eye contact and recognizing nonverbal social cues appears to be associated with higher rates of interactions with peers. Children with visual impairments whose vision is not sufficient for recognizing nonverbal behaviors typically have deficits in encoding social cues, as well as in monitoring their own behaviors and interpreting others' responses to them, that interfere with socially competent behavior.

Future directions

There is ample evidence that children with cognitive delays have social skills that are delayed when compared with typically developing peers. The model of social competence in children with disabilities, described by Guralnick (1999), suggests that deficits in cognitive skills will be associated with deficits in other areas important for social development, including shared understanding of social situations, and encoding and responding to social stimuli. Evidence from studies of children with autistic spectrum disorders, in particular, points to the important role of theory-of-mind skills (including joint attention and understanding of others' intentions and desires) in the development of social understanding.

The results of recent studies suggest that characteristics of the social setting, including the availability of typically developing peers as play partners and support from adults, are important in the development of children's social skills. More frequent interactions, and higher levels of social skills, have been reported for preschool, elementary school, and high school students with disabilities when they participate in activities that include peers without disabilities. Greater social benefits may result when the environment is most similar to that found for children without disabilities. These results suggest that although children with disabilities have delayed social skills, the development of these skills can be enhanced for many children when they participate in activities with typically developing peers, and are supported in their interactions by parents and teachers. Research is only beginning to examine the role of adults and peers, as well as child and setting characteristics, in the social development of children with disabilities.

Models of social competence, such as those proposed by Dodge and his colleagues (Crick & Dodge, 1994; Dodge et al., 1986) and Guralnick (1999) provide a beginning point to understand the ways in which disability interferes with children's participation in social settings. Research that examines specific cognitive processes, such as the work on theory-of-mind skills in children with autism or role understanding in children with mild mental retardation/learning disabilities, are beginning steps toward understanding the ways in which child specific competencies affect social relationships. Understanding which characteristics of the social context are important in supporting social interactions of children with disabilities is also an important focus of research. Finally, there is evidence that typically developing children may reap benefits from interactions with peers with disabilities (Diamond & Innes, 2001). Research that examines the ways in which these interactions foster the development of socially desirable characteristics (such as altruism) in children without disabilities provides an important focus for future research.

References

Astington, J. W., & Jenkins, J. M. (1995). Theory of mind development and social understanding. *Cognition and Emotion, 9*, 151–165.

Bauminger, N., & Kasari, C. (2000). Loneliness and friendship in high-functioning children with autism. *Child Development, 71*, 447–456.

Begley, A. (1999). The self-perceptions of pupils with Down syndrome in relation to their academic competence, physical competence and social acceptance. *International Journal of Disability, Development and Education, 46*, 515–529.

Block, M. E., & Malloy, M. (1998). Attitudes on inclusion of a player with disabilities in a regular softball league. *Mental Retardation, 36*, 137–144.

Bochner, S., & Pieterse, M. (1996). Teenagers with Down syndrome in a time of changing policies and practices: Progress of students who were born between 1971 and 1978. *International Journal of Disability, Development and Education, 43*, 75–95.

Bray, N. W., Saarnio, D. A., & Hawk, L.W. (1994). Context for understanding intellectual and developmental difficulties in strategy competencies. *American Journal on Mental Retardation, 99*, 44–49.

Bronson, M. B., Hauser-Cram, P., & Warfield, M. E. (1997). Classrooms matter: Relations between the classroom environment and the social and mastery behavior of five-year-old children with disabilities. *Journal of Applied Developmental Psychology, 18*, 331–348.

Bukowski, W., & Hoza, B. (1989). Popularity and friendship: Issues in theory, measurement, and outcome. In T. J. Berndt & G. W. Ladd (Eds.), *Peer relationships in child development* (pp. 15–45). New York: Wiley.

Buysse, V. (1993). Friendships of preschoolers with disabilities in community-based child care settings. *Journal of Early Intervention, 17*, 380–395.

Collins, J. G. (1997). Prevalence of selected chronic conditions: United States, 1990–1992. National Center for Health Statistics. *Vital Health Statistics, 10* (194).

Crick, N. R., & Dodge, K. A. (1994). A review and reformulation of social information-processing mechanisms in children's social adjustment. *Psychological Bulletin, 115*, 74–101.

Dawson, G., Meltzoff, A. N., Osterling, J., Rinaldi, J., & Brown, E. (1998). Children with autism fail to orient to naturally occurring social stimuli. *Journal of Autism and Developmental Disorders, 28*, 479–485.

Diamond, K., & Innes, F. K. (2001). The origins of young children's attitudes toward peers with disabilities. In M. J. Guralnick (Ed.), *Early childhood inclusion: Focus on change* (pp. 159–178). Baltimore: Paul H. Brookes.

Diamond, K., LeFurgy, W., & Blass, S. (1993). Attitudes of typical preschool children toward their peers with disabilities: A year-long study in four integrated classrooms. *Journal of Genetic Psychology, 154*, 215–222.

Dodge, K. A., Pettit, G. S., McClaskey, C. L., & Brown, M. M. (1986). Social competence in children. *Monographs of the Society for Research in Child Development, 44* (2, Serial No. 213).

Erwin, E. J. (1993). Social participation of young children with visual impairments in specialized and integrated environments. *Journal of Visual Impairment and Blindness, 87*, 138–142.

Fryxell, D., & Kennedy, C. H. (1995). Placement along the continuum of services and its impact on students' social relationships. *Journal of the Association for Persons with Severe Handicaps, 20*, 259–269.

Graetz, B., & Shute, R. (1995). Assessment of peer relationships in children with asthma. *Journal of Pediatric Psychology, 20*, 205–216.

Grenot-Scheyer, M. (1994). The nature of interactions between students with severe disability and their friends and acquaintances without disabilities. *Journal of the Association for Persons with Severe Handicaps, 19*, 253–262.

Gresham, F. M., & MacMillan, D. L. (1997). Social competence and affective characteristics of students with mild disabilities. *Review of Educational Research, 67*, 377–415.

Guralnick, M. J. (1999). Family and child influences on the peer-related social competence of young children with developmental delays. *Mental Retardation and Developmental Disabilities Research Reviews, 5*, 21–29.

Guralnick, M. J., Connor, R. T., Hammond, M. A., Gottman, J. M., & Kinnish, K. (1996). The peer relations of preschool children with communication disorders. *Child Development, 67,* 471–489.

Guralnick, M. J., & Hammond, M. A. (1999). Sequential analysis of the social play of young children with mild developmental delays. *Journal of Early Intervention, 22,* 243–256.

Guralnick, M. J., & Neville, B. (1997). Designing early intervention programs to promote children's social competence. In M. J. Guralnick (Ed.), *The effectiveness of early intervention* (pp. 579–610). Baltimore: Paul H. Brookes.

Hanline, M. F. (1993). Inclusion of preschoolers with profound disabilities: An analysis of children's interactions. *Journal of the Association for People with Severe Handicaps, 18,* 28–35.

Harry, B., Rueda, R., & Kalyanpur, M. (1999). Cultural reciprocity in sociocultural perspective: Adapting the normalization principle for family collaboration. *Exceptional Children, 66,* 123–136.

Hartas, D., & Donahue, M. L. (1997). Conversational and social problem-solving skills in adolescents with learning disabilities. *Learning Disabilities Research and Practice, 12,* 213–220.

Hatton, D. D., Bailey, D. B., Burchinal, M. R, & Ferrell, K. A. (1997). Developmental growth curves of preschool children with vision impairments. *Child Development, 68,* 788–806.

Hauser-Cram, P., Bronson, M. B., & Upshur, C. (1993). The effects of the classroom environment on the social and mastery behavior of preschool children with disabilities. *Early Childhood Research Quarterly, 8,* 479–497.

Helmstetter, E., Peck, C. A., & Giangreco, M. F. (1994). Outcomes of interactions with peers with moderate or severe disabilities: A statewide survey of high school students. *Journal of the Association for Persons with Severe Handicaps, 19,* 263–276.

Hughes, C., Rodi, M. S., Lorden, S. W., Pitkin, S. E., Derer, K. R., Hwang, B., & Cai, X. (1999). Social interactions of high school students with mental retardation and their general education peers. *American Journal on Mental Retardation, 104,* 533–544.

Juvonen, J., & Bear, G. (1992). Social adjustment of children with and without learning disabilities in integrated classrooms. *Journal of Educational Psychology, 84,* 322–330.

Kadesjö, B., Gillberg, C., & Hagberg, B. (1999). Autism and Asperger Syndrome in 7-year-old children: A population study. *Journal of Autism and Developmental Disorders, 29,* 327–331.

Kasari, C., & Hodapp, R. M. (1996). Is Down syndrome different? Evidence from social and family studies. *Down Syndrome Quarterly, 1,* 1–8.

Kennedy, C. H., Shukla, S., & Fryxell, D. (1997). Comparing the effects of educational placement on the social relationships of intermediate school students with severe disabilities. *Exceptional Children, 64,* 31–47.

Kravetz, S., Faust, M., Lipshitz, S., & Shalhav, S. (1999). LD, interpersonal understanding and social behavior in the classroom. *Journal of Learning Disabilities, 32,* 248–255.

Ladd, G. W., & Hart, C. H. (1992). Creating informal play opportunities: Are parents' and preschoolers' initiations related to children's competence with peers? *Developmental Psychology, 28,* 1179–1187.

Lee, S., & Odom, S.L. (1996). The relationship between stereotypic behavior and peer social interaction for children with severe disabilities. *Journal of the Association for Persons with Severe Handicaps, 21,* 88–95.

Leffert, J. S., & Siperstein, G. N. (1996). Assessment of social-cognitive processes in children with mental retardation. *American Journal on Mental Retardation, 100,* 441–455.

Lord, C. (1993). The complexity of social behavior in autism. In S. Baron-Cohen, H. Tager-Flusberg, & D. Cohen (Eds.), *Understanding other minds: Perspectives from autism* (pp. 292–316). New York: Oxford University Press.

Lord, C., & Magill-Evans, J. (1995). Peer interactions of autistic children and adolescents. *Development and Psychopathology, 7,* 611–626.

McAlpine, L. M., & Moore, C. L. (1995). The development of social understanding in children with visual impairments. *Journal of Visual Impairment and Blindness, 89,* 349–358.

Mundy, P., & Crowson, M. (1997). Joint attention and early social communication: Implications for research on intervention with autism. *Journal of Autism and Developmental Disorders, 27,* 653–676.

Noll, R. B., Ris, M. D., Davies, W. H., Bukowski, W. M., & Koontz, K. (1992). Social interactions between children with cancer or sickle cell disease and their peers: Teacher ratings. *Journal of Developmental and Behavioral Pediatrics, 13,* 187–193.

Ochoa, S. H., & Palmer, D. J. (1995). Comparison of the peer status of Mexican-American students with learning disabilities and non-disabled low-achieving students. *Learning Disability Quarterly, 18,* 57–63.

Okagaki, L., Diamond, K., Kontos, S., & Hestenes, L. (1998). Correlates of young children's interactions with classmates with disabilities. *Early Childhood Research Quarterly, 13,* 67–86.

Phillips, W., Baron-Cohen, S., & Rutter, M. (1998). Understanding intention in normal development and autism *British Journal of Developmental Psychology, 16,* 337–348.

Putnam, J. W., Pueschel, S. M., & Gorder-Holman, J. (1988). Community activities of youths and adults with Down syndrome. *British Journal of Mental Subnormality, 34,* 47–53.

Roeyers, H. (1996). The influence of nonhandicapped peers on the social interactions of children with a pervasive developmental disorder. *Journal of Autism and Developmental Disorders, 26,* 303–320.

Rosenblum, L. P. (1997). Adolescents with visual impairments who have best friends: A pilot study. *Journal of Visual Impairment and Blindness, 91,* 224–235.

Rynders, J. E., & Horrobin, J. M. (1990). Always trainable? Never educable? Updating educational expectations concerning children with Down syndrome. *American Journal on Mental Retardation, 95,* 77–83.

Sacks, S. Z. (1992). The social development of visually impaired children: A theoretical perspective. In S. Z. Sacks, L. S. Kekelis, & R. J. Gaylord-Ross (Eds.), *The development of social skills by blind and visually impaired students* (pp. 3–12). New York: American Foundation for the Blind.

Sigman, M., & Ruskin, E. (1999). Continuity and change in the social competence of children with autism, Down syndrome, and developmental delay. *Monographs of the Society for Research in Child Development, 64* (1, Serial No. 256).

Siperstein, G. N., & Leffert, J. S. (1997). Comparison of socially accepted and rejected children with mental retardation. *American Journal on Mental Retardation, 101,* 339–351.

Skellenger, A. C., Rosenblum, L. P., & Jager, B. K. (1997). Behaviors of preschoolers with visual impairments in indoor play settings. *Journal of Visual Impairment and Blindness, 91,* 519–530.

Sponheim, E., & Skjeldal, O. (1998). Autism and related disorders: Epidemiological findings in a Norwegian study using ICD-10 diagnostic criteria. *Journal of Autism and Developmental Disorders, 28,* 217–227.

Staub, D., Schwartz, I. S., Gallucci, C., & Peck, C. A. (1994). Four portraits of friendship at an inclusive school. *Journal of the Association for Persons with Severe Handicaps, 19,* 314–326.

Strain, P. S. (1985). Social and nonsocial determinants of acceptability in handicapped preschool children. *Topics in Early Childhood Special Education, 4,* 47–58.

Taylor, A. R., Asher, S. R., & Williams, G. A. (1987). The social adaptation of mainstreamed mildly retarded children. *Child Development, 58,* 1321–1334.

U.S. Department of Education (1997). *Nineteenth annual report to Congress on the implementation of the Individuals with Disabilities Education Act.* Washington, DC.

Vaughn, S., & Elbaum, B. (1999). The self-concept and friendships of students with learning disabilities: A developmental perspective. In R. Gallimore, L. P. Bernheimer, D. L. MacMillan, D. L. Speece, & S. Vaughn (Eds.), *Developmental perspectives on children with high-incidence disabilities* (pp. 81–107). Mahwah, NJ: Erlbaum.

Volkmar, F. R. (1993). Social development in autism. In S. Baron-Cohen, H. Tager-Flusberg, & D. Cohen (Eds.), *Understanding other minds: Perspectives from autism* (pp. 40–55). New York: Oxford University Press.

Volkmar, F. R., & Lord, C. (1998). Diagnosis and definition of autism and other pervasive developmental disorders. In F. Volkmar (Ed.), *Autism and pervasive developmental disorders* (pp. 1–25). New York: Cambridge University Press.

Wallander, J. L., & Varni, J. W. (1998). Effects of pediatric chronic physical disorders on child and family adjustment. *Journal of Child Psychology and Psychiatry, 39,* 29–46.

Warren, D. W. (1994). Blindness and children: An individual differences approach. New York: Cambridge University Press.

World Health Organization (1999). *WHO Statistical Information System.* Geneva, Switzerland.

Yirmiya, N., Kasari, C., Sigman, M., & Mundy, P. (1989). Facial expression of affect in autistic, mentally retarded and normal children. *Journal of Child Psychology and Psychiatry, 30,* 725–735.

Yirmiya, N., Pilowsky, T., Solomonica-Levi, D., & Shulman, C. (1999). Gaze behavior and theory of mind abilities in individuals with autism, Down syndrome, and mental retardation of unknown etiology. *Journal of Autism & Developmental Disorders, 29,* 333–341.

Yude, C., & Goodman, R. (1999). Peer problems of 9- to 11-year-old children with hemiplegia in mainstream schools. Can these be predicted? *Developmental Medicine and Child Neurology, 41,* 4–8.

Zbikowski, S. M., & Cohen, R. (1998). Parent and peer evaluations of the social competence of children with mild asthma. *Journal of Applied Developmental Psychology, 19,* 249–265.

Zurmohle, U. M., Homann, T., Schroeter, C., Rothgerber, H., Hommel, G., & Ermert, J. A. (1998). Psychosocial adjustment of children with spina bifida. *Journal of Child Neurology, 13,* 64–70.

30

Social Development in Children with Specific Language Impairment and Profound Hearing Loss

Bonnie Brinton and Martin Fujiki

Steven's Story

Steven is a 6-year-old boy. He lives in a middle-class home with his parents and two older siblings. Shortly after he was born, neonatal hearing screening suggested Steven was at-risk. Subsequent testing confirmed he had a bilateral, profound hearing loss. Steven was fit with hearing aids when he was 6 months old, and has worn aids ever since. Steven's mother enrolled in an early intervention program soon after the diagnosis was made. This program stressed total communication (signing combined with spoken language). Steven's mother began to learn sign language, but this proved more difficult for the rest of the family. Steven met developmental milestones as expected with the exception of delayed communication skills. Although Steven learned signs quickly (he produced his first signs at 10 months), his spoken language developed much more slowly. Last year when he began kindergarten, psychological testing revealed that Steven's nonverbal IQ was within normal limits.

With his hearing aids, Steven can hear loud environmental noises and can tell if people around him are talking. He cannot discriminate speech well, however. Steven attends a first-grade classroom that contains both hearing children and children with hearing impairment. The class stresses total communication.

Steven communicates fairly well with his mother using a combination of signs, gestures, and some spoken language. Since his speech production is largely unintelligible, he communicates with other family members using gestures and facial expressions. He sometimes plays games such as basketball and chase with his older siblings and neighborhood children, but they tend to exclude him from many activities. At school, Steven has two reciprocal friends in his class, both of whom also have hearing impairment. At recess and lunch, Steven tends to congregate with other children who have hearing impairment. He prefers interacting in dyads rather than in groups of peers.

David's Story

David is a 6-year-old boy. He lives in a middle-class family with his parents and two older siblings. David's parents reported that his developmental history was quite typical except for the fact he did not learn to talk as expected. David did not produce his first word until he was 20 months old, and then learned new words slowly. He did not seem to understand when his parents gave him verbal directions. By the time he was 3 years old, his parents were concerned that he might not be able to hear, so they arranged for an audiological evaluation. All hearing measures were within normal limits, and David's parents pursued additional psychological and language evaluation. Testing indicated David's nonverbal IQ score was within age-level expectations, but language measures revealed delays of 2 or more years in his ability to produce and understand spoken language. David was enrolled in a special preschool at age 4.

David's parents find it difficult to communicate with him. They tend to ask him series of questions, which he does not always answer. David sometimes plays games or rides bikes with his siblings and the neighborhood children, but he is rarely invited to anyone's house to play and does not have any close friends.

David attends a regular first-grade class. A speech-language pathologist and a resource teacher come into his classroom twice a week to work with him in a small group on reading and math. David has difficulty following directions in class, responding to questions, and joining in class discussions.

As is the case in his neighborhood, David has no reciprocal friends in his class. At recess, he tends to wander around unoccupied or to drift from one playgroup to another. He is usually one of the last to be chosen for class teams. When he is grouped with other children for class assignments, he tends to watch others work rather than participate.

Language and Social Competence

Steven and David share a common challenge; they both have difficulty using language to communicate effectively within their communities. Because of the close relationship between language and social behavior, it is likely that any disability affecting one may impact the other. For Steven and David, there is a high probability that their language problems will have social ramifications. It is not the case, however, that there is a simple causal relationship between language impairment and social deficits. That is, it cannot be assumed that language difficulties always lead to social problems in a predictable fashion. Rather, language and social development are intertwined in complex ways. To understand the social challenges and needs of children with language problems, it is first necessary to consider the nature of specific language deficits and how they impact a child's social interactions. For example, Steven and David both have disabilities that undermine their ability to acquire and use spoken language. Both children also have difficulty interacting with their classmates. Although these observable outcomes are similar, the nature of each child's disability is unique. Steven has a sensory deficit that makes much of the spoken language that surrounds him inaccessible. He is unable to use the mode of communication used by his parents, family, and most of his community. It is important to note, however, that Steven seems to be able to acquire language much more readily if it is made accessible to him through the visual modality. He learns signs quickly when he is exposed to them in interaction. It is fair to speculate that if Steven had been born into a family fluent in American Sign Language (ASL), he would have acquired ASL as expected and would now communicate freely within a signing community. David, on the other hand, has an auditory system that is intact; he can hear the language around him without difficulty. He cannot process all of the language he hears, however. David frequently does not comprehend enough of the words and syntactic structures that he hears to appreciate the speaker's intent. He struggles to formulate and produce sentences; his production is labored, difficult, and immature. David's language impairment would be evident in almost all environments where language production and comprehension are important (e.g., the classroom).

In this chapter, we discuss two groups of children who demonstrate language problems; those with profound hearing loss (such as Steven) and those with specific language impairment (SLI) (such as David). For both we consider how language impairment has the potential to disrupt social interaction with lasting consequences for affected children and their families. As a part of each discussion we review the nature of parent–child interactions and educational contexts. Both are of basic importance to social outcomes and must be taken into account as we discuss the social competence of these groups of children.

Profound Hearing Loss

Overview

There are many degrees and types of hearing loss. The term "profound hearing loss" is used to describe a loss exceeding 70 dB HL (Northern & Downs, 1991). Some classification systems are more stringent, however, and specify a loss exceeding 90 dB (Clark, 1981). Unless indicated otherwise, a profound loss is assumed to be bilateral. The term "deaf" is sometimes used in reference to children with hearing loss so profound that it is impossible to rely on hearing in order to acquire language (Diefendorf, 1996). A profound loss may be present at birth (congenital) or may be acquired. Some types of profound loss are progressive and become more pronounced over time. Dependable prevalence data are difficult to obtain, however, it is often reported that approximately one child in a thousand is born with a profound hearing loss. Data from several large prevalence studies indicate the actual figure is somewhat lower (Mauk & Behrens, 1993).

Profound hearing loss stems from involvement of the inner ear or a combination of inner ear and middle ear pathologies. Many causal agents can result in profound hearing loss. For example, certain bacterial and viral diseases can attack the hearing mechanism. A number of drugs are ototoxic, and their use can cause irreversible damage to the inner ear. Some congenital syndromes involve malformations of the middle and/or inner ear, which may result in profound hearing loss.

Arnos, Israel, Devnos, and Wilson (1996) note that over half of profound hearing losses are genetic in origin. That does not mean, however, that over half of the children with profound loss are born to parents who also have profound loss. In fact, over 90% of children with profound hearing loss have hearing parents (Northcott, 1981). Congenital profound hearing loss is usually permanent, although recent developments in both cochlear and brainstem implants offer exciting possibilities for treatment. Cochlear implants have enhanced the sensory systems of many children but these implants are not usually recommended for children under 1 year of age. As of this writing, brainstem implants have not yet been approved by the FDA for children under 12 years of age.

As Steven's case illustrates, the fact that children with profound hearing loss do not learn to produce or comprehend spoken language easily does not mean they cannot acquire language at all. Children with profound hearing loss who are born to deaf parents may grow up in a deaf culture rich with a language (ASL) that is accessible to them. Just as importantly, these children belong to a deaf community that does not view profound hearing loss as a disability but as a cultural characteristic. From this perspective, Steven has a "handicap" only in the context of his hearing community and the value that community places upon typical hearing. Although his current social world is largely composed of hearing individuals who must make accommodations for his hearing loss, Steven may one day affiliate with a deaf community where his hearing loss does not single him out as different or present a barrier to interpersonal interaction, acceptance, or belonging (Maxwell, Poeppelmeyer, & Polich, 1999). At age 6, however, Steven lives primarily in a hearing world. His spoken language skills are limited, and his difficulty communicating is associated with social challenges.

Early parent–child interactions

It is important to qualify comments on parent–child interactions by recognizing that some children with profound hearing loss have associated disabilities that significantly impact development. These problems cannot help but influence parent–child interaction. For purposes of this discussion, we focus on those children with profound hearing loss who have relatively typical intellectual and physical abilities.

Regardless of the cause of their profound hearing loss, children who are born to hearing parents are basically cut off from the primary medium of communication utilized by their families – spoken language. Even with amplification these children are usually unable to hear well enough to differentiate different speech sounds (although children with cochlear implants may do better in this regard than children with traditional hearing aids). Thus, even for those children like Steven whose hearing loss is not complicated by other factors, the communicative and social environment they experience from birth is qualitatively different compared with that of hearing children. Early parent–child interactions may differ, especially if the hearing loss has not been identified. Parents may interpret their child's failure to react to spoken input as nonresponsive and may alter or reduce their interaction with their child (Marschark, 1993). An infant with a profound hearing loss cannot hear her mother when out of view and cannot anticipate her return unless the mother provides tactile or visual cues (Manfredi, 1993). The nature of early social interactions may differ because these children do not engage in vocal play in the same way as hearing infants (Manfredi, 1993). Early social interactions between hearing parents and children with profound hearing loss depend on parents' ability to establish reciprocal interactions with their infants. On a basic level, parents of children who cannot hear spoken input must present compelling visual input in order to engage their infants' attention to their communicative message (Lederberg, 1993). At the same time, parents must carefully gear their input to their children's needs. For example, too much physical input may overwhelm an infant and interfere with the ability to learn from the interaction (MacTurk, Meadow-Orlans, Koester, & Spencer, 1993). It is not always a simple matter for parents to find a medium of communication that they can share with their children. This medium may involve a level of facial expression, gesture, or sign that may not be altogether comfortable for hearing parents. This complicates social-play exchanges that might otherwise occur naturally and spontaneously.

Education

As infants with profound hearing loss develop, their social interactions are influenced by the communication they share with their families and peers. In turn, their communication systems are, to a large extent, determined by their educational experience. In the past, educational approaches for children with hearing loss were the subject of intense and extended controversy. Proponents of oral approaches advocated educating children to enable them to function in a hearing world by relying on residual hearing, speech reading, and speaking. Proponents of manual approaches felt that spoken language competence was an unrealistic goal and stressed signing systems. Total communication approaches that included both signing and spoken language were viewed by some as a compromise, but the controversy lived on. To complicate matters, there were several different signing systems used in educating children with profound loss. ASL is a language with its own syntax and vocabulary, but several other signing systems mix ASL signs with English syntax and usage (see Bernstein-Ratner, 2001, for a brief overview).

In recent years, increasing emphasis has been placed on early intervention to provide children with profound hearing loss with the opportunity to develop a rich language system to permit the communication necessary to develop and maintain personal relationships as well as to learn academic content (Northern & Downs, 1991). For children with profound loss, some type of signing system is often indicated. This means, of course, that hearing parents and family have the best chance of communicating their child with profound loss if they are familiar with the signing system the child uses. As in Steven's family, this is not always the case.

Social competence

The research on the social competence of children with profound hearing loss has been complicated by a myriad of factors that influence social development. For example, children with profound hearing loss demonstrate varying levels of language development, a wide range of communicative opportunities within the home, and different opportunities to interact with peers who share the same language system. These variables have not been systematically controlled across research studies, and research outcomes must be evaluated with these factors in mind.

Spencer and Deyo (1993) suggested that there are at least two groups of children with profound hearing loss (deaf) who could be expected to show distinct patterns of social development. These groups consist of (a) children who develop language typically and have typical early parent–child interactions and (b) children who have difficulty acquiring language and have "difficult, relatively nonreciprocal interactions with parents" (Spencer & Deyo, 1993, p. 71). These authors noted that these groups are usually, but not always, configured based on the hearing status of the parents. Spencer and Deyo summarized a number of studies that suggested that deaf children born to deaf parents "tend as a group to have more positive socioemotional characteristics, better language development, and higher academic performance than deaf children with hearing parents" (p. 70).

Additional research is needed to confirm the existence and describe the development of different groups of children with profound hearing loss. More longitudinal studies are needed to compare the social development and friendship formation of children of deaf parents with those of children with hearing parents. We do not yet fully understand the relative influence of many important factors on social competence. We do, however, understand that children with profound hearing loss experience certain challenges in social interactions.

The fact that children with profound loss often use some system of signing to communicate means that their mode of communication will differ from that of many of their peers. This may, in part, explain the fact that children with hearing loss are not easily integrated into the social fabric of the regular classroom. As Lee and Antia (1992) note, ensuring physical proximity among children with hearing loss and their hearing peers does not guarantee that these children will interact. In fact, providing casual contact is not sufficient to foster acceptance or friendship (Antia & Kreimeyer, 1996). In integrated classrooms, children with hearing loss tend to segregate themselves and hearing children often avoid them (Bench, 1992; Minett, Clark & Wilson, 1994; Spencer, Koester, & Meadow-Orlans, 1994).

Children with hearing loss in integrated settings tend to be rejected by their peers more often than are hearing children. For example, Cappelli, Daniels, Durieux-Smith, McGrath, and Neuss (1995) found that 30% of the elementary school aged children with hearing loss they studied were rejected by their peers. Additionally, these children were aware of their rejection.

Loeb and Sarigiani (1986) studied children and adolescents with hearing loss and compared them to hearing peers as well as to peers with visual impairments. Teachers perceived the students with hearing loss as being more shy and having lower self-esteem than the other groups, and the students with hearing loss perceived themselves as more shy and less popular. Not all studies using teacher report have demonstrated social or behavioral difficulties in children with hearing loss, however (MacLean, 1983). Still, parents often complain of the difficulty their children with hearing loss experience in interacting with others and establishing friendships (Davis, Elfenbein, Schum, & Bentler, 1986).

Even though children with profound hearing loss are not always accepted or included in classroom activities in integrated or mainstreamed settings, in the long run, these children may function better socially than do children with hearing loss who are educated in isolated or institutional settings. For example, Aplin (1987) found that 12-year-old children with hearing loss who attended regular schools showed better levels of social and emotional adjustment than did their peers who attended special schools. Similarly Cartledge, Cochran, and Paul (1996) reported that adolescents who attended regular schools rated their own social competence higher than did peers in a residential school setting.

Language proficiency is extremely important to peer interaction. Children with profound hearing loss who have more developed language systems tend to interact more often with peers than do children with more limited language ability (Spencer, Koester, & Meadow-Orlans, 1994). There are indications that language proficiency is related to the mode of language to which children are exposed. That is, children with profound hearing loss who communicate using at least some signing may acquire language more easily than those who must depend only on spoken language. This greater facility with language can also promote positive social interaction. For example, Cornelius and Hornett (1990) reported that kindergartners with hearing loss in classes where instruction included signs and spoken instruction engaged in more social play and produced fewer physically aggressive acts toward each other than did children in oral classes, where instruction was carried out primarily through spoken language.

The contexts in which children interact present different language demands for children with profound hearing loss. For example, Lederberg (1991, 1993) noted that children with profound loss may participate in dyadic play using limited language, but they have difficulty in groups because group play demands a higher level of language ability. Difficulty interacting in groups may persist throughout life. Adults with hearing loss have also reported that they are uncomfortable talking with groups of hearing peers because of the increased demands of watching multiple speakers in order to utilize visual cues (Maxwell et al., 1999).

As important as language ability is to social interaction, it is not the only factor that determines social functioning in children with profound hearing loss. For example, children form peer relationships based on many factors. To illustrate, Lederberg (1991) observed 3- to 5-year-old children with hearing loss in outdoor play at school. Forty-two percent of children in dyads who formed long-term friendships (identified according to mutual responsiveness and time spent playing together) had different levels of language ability. Children seemed to choose each other as playmates according to factors such as gender and age. Drawing from this study and earlier work, Lederberg (1991) concluded that "linguistic competence was found to affect only a very narrow area of deaf children's peer relations" (p. 58).

Summary: Profound hearing loss

It is difficult to generalize about the social functioning of children with profound hearing loss. Unfortunately, research has not fully described the social expectations and developmental patterns of children within deaf or hearing communities. Although it is obvious that hearing loss can affect language and social growth, it is less clear how hearing loss interacts with other factors to influence the development of individual children. The early social environment of a child with hearing loss depends on the parents' ability to engage that child's attention and provide highly salient language and social input that the child can process. Parents who sign fluently may find this a natural task, but hearing parents may be more dependent upon early intervention programs to assist them. The choice of communication modality (signing, speech, or a combination) that families adopt is another factor that influences social development. Children in families and educational programs that incorporate signing may develop language more readily. Enhanced language development is one important factor that facilitates interaction with peers.

Children with profound hearing loss who grow up in hearing communities are at risk for social isolation. Children born to parents who belong to a deaf community may grow up in a signing environment that values hearing loss as a cultural characteristic. These children may function well socially within their minority community, but may never feel quite "at home" in the hearing world. Some children, especially those who do not learn sign language and acquire limited spoken language, may never feel totally included in either the deaf or the hearing world.

Specific Language Impairment

Overview

In the case description presented earlier, David did not acquire language typically despite the fact that his hearing was intact. In addition, David's difficulty with language could not be attributed to more generalized cognitive deficits, obvious neurological problems, or environmental deprivation. The term "specific language impairment" (SLI) is currently used to describe David's difficulty (Leonard, 1998). A number of other terms overlap partially or completely with SLI, including learning disability, developmental language disability, developmental language disorder, and language-learning impairment (Nelson, 1998). Although the term SLI suggests a specific disability, children who are identified with SLI form a heterogeneous group. Two individuals diagnosed with SLI may have very different profiles of linguistic strengths and weaknesses. Despite this variability, it can be said that children with SLI demonstrate a variety of problems with comprehension and expression of language. These may include difficulty learning vocabulary, syntax, and morphological structures. Additionally, children with SLI may struggle in social conversation and most have difficulty producing and understanding narratives. Children with SLI tend to produce spoken language that is limited, labored, and immature. SLI persists as children grow up, although the manifestations of the disorder change (Bashir, 1989). For example, a 4 year old with SLI might produce short utterances with various grammatical structures missing or modified (e.g., "Him baby. Him not eat candy"). At 12 years of age, that same child might have a command of basic syntax and morphology but might struggle producing a fluent narrative that is coherent enough to describe a simple event. As might be expected, difficulty with language translates into social and academic problems that are particularly evident in tasks involving listening, speaking, reading, and writing (Fey, Catts, & Larrivee, 1995).

SLI is a relatively common disability. Tomblin et al. (1997), using strict diagnostic standards, found a prevalence rate of 7% in a sample of over 7,000 kindergartners. SLI is more prevalent in boys than in girls, and recent study has focused on familial aggregations of SLI. The cause of SLI is not well understood. There has been a great deal of discussion regarding etiology, but a definitive explanation of causal factors remains elusive (see Bishop, 1997; Leonard, 1998 for discussion).

Unlike children with profound hearing loss, there is no context in which children with SLI will find both a viable alternative to spoken language and membership in a cultural community that does not view language impairment as handicapping. A child with profound hearing loss who is fluent in ASL may interact freely with other members of the deaf culture. For a child with SLI growing up in a society that values verbal ability, there is no equivalent community.

Parent–child interactions

Thanks to recent advances in audiological assessment procedures, Steven's hearing loss was identified in his infancy, and his parents were referred to an early intervention program. David's SLI was not identified until he was a preschooler. Unfortunately, the most obvious manifestations of SLI are not evident until children reach the age where they would be expected to start talking. This makes SLI difficult, if not impossible, to identify in infancy. Since there is considerable variation in the times at which typical children reach language milestones, it can be difficult to distinguish children who are normal "late talkers" from children who have language impairment in the early stages of acquisition (for discussion see Leonard, 1998; Paul, 2000). It might be speculated that children with SLI, like children with hearing loss, experience early interactions with their caretakers somewhat differently than do typically developing children. Just how different the experience is from the child's perspective, however, is not clear. Infants with SLI can hear the sounds that inform them of the caretaker's presence when not in sight. Likewise, they have access to vocal and sound play input from their parents. As they mature, however, they may have difficulty making sense of the language they hear, and they are slow at acquiring the lexical and syntactic characteristics of language.

As children with SLI become preschoolers, the interactions they have with their caretakers may differ from those experienced by typical children. Although most research has focused on the influence of parental input on the acquisition of language structure, some studies have addressed the social nature of parent–child interactions. The results of this research are equivocal. It is evident, however, that many parents modify their input in order to communicate with their children who are less skilled conversational partners (see Leonard, 1998 for review). It is likely that these modifications shape parent–child social interactions in important ways that are not yet fully understood.

Education

As previously noted, children with SLI can be expected to have academic problems. One reason for this is that these children are at a great disadvantage in the classroom where rules, routines, and instruction are largely carried out via language. A number of special service delivery models have been employed to support these children in academic work and to facilitate their language growth. Some children with SLI are placed in small, self-contained classrooms for children with language problems. These classrooms are generally located within regular elementary schools, and the children with SLI may share recess time or specific classes with typically developing children. Other children with SLI attend regular classrooms and are pulled out periodically for small group or individual sessions with a speech-language pathologist and/or learning specialist. Some children, like David, attend regular classrooms, and speech-language pathologists and other special service providers team with the classroom teacher to provide services within the curriculum of the classroom. For a child with SLI, opportunities for social interaction with peers may vary greatly depending on educational placement.

Little work has been done to compare the social behaviors of children with SLI in various types of school placements. It can be said, however, that children with SLI frequently have social difficulty in school settings. The work of researchers who have described the social problems of these children is reviewed in the next section.

Social competence

Since language skills are often critical to successful social interaction, it might be expected that children with SLI would be at risk for social difficulty. Investigations conducted over the past decade suggest that the most common manifestations of social difficulty in elementary school children with SLI are withdrawal and weak sociable behaviors. For example, Fujiki, Brinton, and Todd (1996) found that teachers rated 8- to 12-year-old children with SLI as having more behavior problems and poorer social skills than their typically developing peers using the teacher version of the *Social Skills Ratings System* (Gresham & Elliott, 1990). Although specific item analyses were not conducted, it was noted that the main behavioral differences were evident in subscales assessing hyperactivity and internalizing behaviors, and differences in social skills were evident in subscales assessing cooperation and assertion.

Redmond and Rice (1998) employed the *Child Behavior Checklist* (Achenbach, 1991a) and the *Teacher Report Form* (Achenbach, 1991b) to measure parent and teacher perceptions of the social functioning of children with SLI and typically developing peers when they were 6 and 7 years of age. Teachers rated children with SLI as having more social, internalizing, and attention problems than their typical peers. Parent reports for children with SLI and typically developing children did not differ. That is, teachers reported social difficulties at school that parents evidently did not perceive at home. It was also of note that the teacher ratings for individual children were not stable over time.

Fujiki, Brinton, Morgan, and Hart (1999) used the *Teacher Behavior Rating Scale* (Hart & Robinson, 1996) with teachers of 5–8 and 10–13-year-old children with SLI and their typically developing peers. Teachers reported that children with SLI demonstrated higher levels of reticent behavior than did typical children, and boys with SLI demonstrated higher levels of solitary-active withdrawal than any of the other groups. In addition, children with SLI were rated below their peers on the impulse control/likeability and prosocial behavior subscales.

Researchers have also directly observed the social interactions of children with SLI. These data have mirrored those obtained from teacher report. Children with SLI may become isolated from their peers as early as preschool. For example, Rice, Sell, and Hadley (1991) found that unlike their typical matches, children with SLI in a preschool classroom preferred adults as conversational partners over peers. Hadley and Rice (1991) found that these same preschool children did not respond well to their peers' conversational bids and were, in turn, often ignored by their peers. Guralnick, Conner, Hammond, Gottman, and Kinnish (1996) observed 4- and 5-year-old children with language impairment in play-groups over a 2-week period. These researchers found that children with language problems were less well integrated into groups than were typically developing peers.

Patterns of isolation in group interactions appear to continue as children progress through the elementary school years. Fujiki, Brinton, Robinson, and Watson (1997) observed interactions of 8- to 12-year-old children with SLI as they talked together in a toy selection task. They found that when placed in a group with two typically developing peers, children with SLI became marginal participants, talking less, and being talked to less than their typical peers. In addition, Brinton, Fujiki, Spencer, and Robinson (1997) found that the inability to participate using spoken language did not fully account for the failure of these children to become part of group interactions. The children with SLI were not easily integrated into nonverbal aspects of group activity either. The children with SLI did not compensate for their difficulty in talking by contributing collaborative or cooperative action to the group activity.

The difficulty children with SLI experience in classroom and small group interactions also seems to extend to less structured contexts. Children with SLI are often isolated at recess, moving from playgroup to playgroup or spending a lot of time doing little or nothing. For example, Fujiki, Brinton, Isaacson, and Summers (2001) observed first- to fifth-grade children with language difficulties at recess. Typical children spent significantly more time in peer interaction, whereas children with language impairment spent significantly more time exhibiting withdrawn behaviors. In particular, several children with language impairment showed high amounts of reticence and solitary-active withdrawal.

The loneliness that many children with SLI experience (Fujiki et al., 1996) probably reflects the difficulty these children experience with many social tasks. For example, children with SLI have difficulty gaining access to ongoing play activities (Brinton et al., 1997; Craig & Washington, 1993). They seem to lack the assertiveness or the strategies to join in group activity. Once they gain access to an activity, they may not know how to respond to bids from their conversational partners such as questions or comments (Fujiki & Brinton,

1991; Hadley & Rice, 1991). Children with SLI may be at a loss when they need to reach mutual decisions, negotiate courses of action, or resolve conflicts with their peers (Brinton, Fujiki, & McKee, 1998; Grove, Conti-Ramsden, & Donlan, 1993; Stevens & Bliss, 1995). They may also have difficulty collaborating with their peers in cooperative work groups (Brinton, Fujiki, & Higbee, 1998; Brinton, Fujiki, Montague, & Hanton, 2000).

Peer relations

The isolation children with SLI often experience at school and the difficulty they have with classroom social tasks could be expected to affect the way they are viewed by their peers. Few studies have investigated peer acceptance of children with SLI, but those that have suggest that children with SLI are not perceived as very desirable playmates by their peers as early as preschool (Gertner, Rice, & Hadley,1994). Fujiki, Brinton, Hart, and Fitzgerald (1999) found considerable variability in acceptance of elementary school children with SLI. For example, one first grader with SLI was among the most popular children in her class and another was the least popular. For these elementary school children, a measure of reciprocal friendship was more telling than the measure of peer acceptance, however. Most of the children with SLI had no reciprocal friends in their classes. In fact, they were not named as a friend by anyone. It may have been the case that these children had reciprocal friends in other classes or in their neighborhoods who could soften the effects of having no friends in class. It is more likely, however, that their difficulty establishing and maintaining peer relationships extended beyond the schoolyard. This idea was supported by Fujiki et al. (1996), who found that children with SLI reported fewer peer contacts in play activities outside of school than did typically developing children.

Summary: Specific language impairment

Because SLI is not identified until the age that children would be expected to begin to produce spoken language, it is difficult to speculate on the early social development of infants with SLI. It is likely that language plays a different role in the early social interactions of babies with SLI, but research has not described the nature of that role.

By the time they reach preschool, however, children with SLI are at risk for social difficulties. These problems have been documented in children through the elementary school years. Children with SLI tend to show patterns of isolation characterized by reticence and exclusion. They have difficulty establishing and maintaining friendships with peers. Difficulty forming friendships may be attributed, at least in part, to the struggles children with SLI experience with tasks that are important in the social world of the classroom. Difficulty entering ongoing interactions, responding to bids in conversation, negotiating differences, and collaborating on tasks may work against their integration into the social fabric of the classroom. Some special service delivery models may inadvertently contribute to the isolation of children with SLI. Placements into self-contained classes may distance children with SLI from most of their peers, and intermittent removal from class for language intervention may make children with SLI feel disoriented and removed from class activities.

Conclusions

Children with profound hearing loss and children with SLI share a common challenge in social development. Their ability to communicate with others is seriously undermined by their difficulty acquiring spoken language. Frequently, children with hearing loss or SLI must learn to establish and maintain relationships when they cannot easily share their ideas, their thoughts, or their feelings with others. They must somehow make sense of events without understanding much of the language that shapes the interactions within those events. In addition, caretakers and parents frequently use language-based activities to expose children to their social community and to teach them how to behave within it. For example, consider the prominence of language in activities such as conversing at the dinner table, negotiating bedtime, settling a sibling dispute, or sharing a favorite book. Children who do not have full access to the language through which these activities are conducted may miss important information concerning how their parents view the world and what their parents expect of them. Similarly, children with weak language abilities are at a disadvantage in academic and social settings at school.

Because language ability is such an important factor in social competence, it is tempting to conclude that language deficits lead directly and predictably to social problems. The relationship between the language and social competence is strong, but it is neither simple nor direct. Language impairment does not guarantee social problems, nor does the degree of language impairment always predict the severity of social deficits. Language ability is one important factor in the development of social behavior, but the interaction of impaired language with other cognitive, social, and behavioral processes is complex and may vary from child to child.

The case studies of Steven and David illustrate how profound hearing loss and SLI are associated with somewhat different social challenges. Because of his profound hearing loss, Steven's strongest language modality is visual (signing). He has limited social interaction with his family members and peers who do not sign. He does have two reciprocal friends who also sign in his class, however, and a small group of children with whom he eats lunch and plays at recess. The fact that Steven has been able to interact with peers and make friends in contexts where he can communicate bodes well for his future social development. Although Steven may always be isolated from many people in the hearing world, he may also eventually affiliate with the deaf community where, depending on his signing fluency, he may enjoy unfettered communication (Maxwell et al., 1999). Within the context of this minority culture, Steven may function well socially.

For David, the outlook is different. Although intervention is helpful and essential, manifestations of David's language impairment are likely to persist into adulthood. Although there may be contexts in which his language impairment will not be a handicap, there will be no equivalent to the deaf community for David. Also, it is important to remember that David's social difficulties are evident even in situations that require little language. As a child, David's social difficulty is intertwined with, but cannot be entirely attributed to, his language impairment. The social problems that are associated with his language impairment may persist as he matures. In fact, a recent longitudinal study by Howlin, Mawhood, and Rutter (2000) paints a bleak picture of the social adjustment of some young men with SLI.

For children with profound hearing loss and SLI, educational programs have wisely targeted language development as a major objective. It has become clear, however, that increased educational emphasis on social functioning is warranted. We are looking for more effective, efficient ways to facilitate language and social skill simultaneously. It is time to help Steven bridge the gap between the hearing and deaf communities and to bring David in from the outskirts of social interaction.

References

Achenbach, T. M. (1991a). *Manual for the Child Behavior Checklist/4–18*. Burlington, VT: University of Vermont Press.

Achenbach, T. M. (1991b). *Manual for the Teacher Report Form*. Burlington, VT: University of Vermont Press.

Antia, S. D., & Kreimeyer, K. H. (1996). Social interaction and acceptance of deaf or hard-of-hearing children and their peers: A comparison of social-skills and familiarity-based interventions. *The Volta Review, 98*, 157–180.

Aplin, D. Y. (1987). Social and emotional adjustment of hearing-impaired children in ordinary and special schools. *Educational Research, 29*, 56–64.

Arnos, K. S., Israel, J., Devlin, L., & Wilson, M. P. (1996). Genetic aspects of hearing loss in childhood. In F. N. Martin & J. G. Clark (Eds.), *Hearing care for children* (pp. 20–44). Needham Heights, MA: Allyn & Bacon.

Bashir, A. S. (1989). Language intervention and the curriculum. *Seminars in Speech and Language, 10*, 181–191.

Bench, J. R. (1992). *Communication skills in hearing-impaired children*. San Diego, CA: Singular.

Bernstein Ratner, N. (2001). Atypical language development. In J. Berko-Gleason (Ed.), *The development of language (5th ed.)*. (pp. 347–408). Needham Heights, MA: Allyn & Bacon.

Bishop, D. V. M. (1997). *Uncommon understanding: Development and disorders of language comprehension in children*. Hove, England: Taylor & Francis.

Brinton, B., & Fujiki, M. (1999). Social interactional behaviors of children with specific language impairment. *Topics in Language Disorders, 19*, 49–69.

Brinton, B., Fujiki, M., & Higbee, L. (1998). Participation in cooperative learning activities by children with specific language impairment. *Journal of Speech, Language, and Hearing Research, 41*, 1193–1206.

Brinton, B., Fujiki, M., & McKee, L. (1998). The negotiation skills of children with specific language impairment. *Journal of Speech, Language, and Hearing Research, 41*, 927–940.

Brinton, B., Fujiki, M., Montague, E. C., & Hanton, J. L. (2000). Children with language impairment in cooperative work rroups: A pilot study. *Language, Speech, and Hearing Services in Schools, 31*, 252–264.

Brinton, B., Fujiki, M., Spencer, J. C., & Robinson, L. A. (1997). The ability of children with specific language impairment to access and participate in an ongoing interaction. *Journal of Speech, Language, and Hearing Research, 40*, 1011–1025.

Cappelli, M., Daniels, T., Durieux-Smith, A., McGrath, P. J., & Neuss, D. (1995). Social development of children with hearing impairments who are integrated into general education classrooms. *The Volta Review, 97*, 197–208.

Cartledge, G., Cochran, L., & Paul, P. (1996). Social skill self-assessments by adolescents with hearing impairment in residential and public schools. *Remedial and Special Education, 17*, 30–36.

Clark, J. G. (1981). Uses and abuses of hearing loss classification. *ASHA, 23,* 493–500.

Cornelius, G., & Hornett, D. (1990). The play behavior of hearing-impaired kindergarten children. *American Annals of the Deaf, 135,* 316–321.

Craig, H. K., & Washington, J. A. (1993). The access behaviors of children with specific language impairment. *Journal of Speech and Hearing Research, 36,* 322–336.

Davis, J. A., Elfenbein, J., Schum, R., & Bentler, R. A. (1986). Effects of mild and moderate hearing impairments on language, educational, and psychosocial behavior of children. *Journal of Speech and Hearing Disorders, 51,* 53–62.

Diefendorf, A. O. (1996). Hearing loss and its effects. In F. N. Martin & J. G. Clark (Eds.), *Hearing care for children* (pp. 3–19). Needham Heights, MA: Allyn & Bacon.

Fey, M. E., Catts, H. W., & Larrivee, L. S. (1995). Preparing preschoolers for the academic and social challenges of school. In M. E. Fey, J. Windsor, & S. F. Warren (Eds.), *Language intervention: Preschool through the elementary years* (pp. 3–37). Baltimore: Paul H. Brookes.

Fujiki, M., & Brinton, B. (1991). The verbal noncommunicator: A case study. *Language, Speech and Hearing Services in Schools, 22,* 322–333.

Fujiki, M., Brinton, B., Hart, C. H., & Fitzgerald, A. (1999). Peer acceptance and friendship in children with specific language impairment. *Topics in Language Disorders, 19,* 34–48.

Fujiki, M., Brinton, B., Isaacson, T., & Summers, C. (2001). Social behaviors of children with language impairment on the playground. *Language, Speech, and Hearing Services in Schools, 32,* 101–113.

Fujiki, M., Brinton, B., Morgan, M., & Hart, C. H. (1999). Withdrawn and sociable behavior of children with specific language impairment. *Language, Speech, and Hearing Services in Schools, 30,* 183–195.

Fujiki, M., Brinton, B., Robinson, L., & Watson, V. (1997). The ability of children with specific language impairment to participate in a group decision task. *Journal of Children's Communication Development, 18,* 1–10.

Fujiki, M., Brinton, B., & Todd, C.M. (1996). Social skills of children with specific language impairment. *Language, Speech, and Hearing Services in Schools, 27,* 195–202.

Gertner, B. L., Rice, M. L., & Hadley, P. A. (1994). Influence of communicative competence on peer preferences in a preschool classroom. *Journal of Speech and Hearing Research, 37,* 913–923.

Gresham, F. M., & Elliott, S. N. (1990). *Social Skills Rating System–Teacher Form.* Circle Pines, MN: American Guidance Service.

Grove, J., Conti-Ramsden, G., & Donlan, C.(1993). Conversational interaction and decision-making in children with specific language impairment. *European Journal of Disorders of Communication, 28,* 141–152.

Guralnick, M. J., Conner, R. T., Hammond, M. A., Gottman, J. M., & Kinnish, K. (1996). The peer relations of preschool children with communication disorders. *Child Development, 67,* 471–489.

Hadley, P. A., & Rice, M. L. (1991). Conversational responsiveness of speech- and language-impaired preschoolers. *Journal of Speech and Hearing Research, 34,* 1308–1317.

Hart, C. H., & Robinson, C. C. (1996). *Teacher Behavior Rating Scale.* Unpublished teacher questionnaire.

Howlin, P., Mawhood, L., & Rutter, M. (2000). Autism and developmental receptive language disorder – A comparative follow-up in early adult life. II: Social, behavioural, and psychiatric outcomes. *Journal of Child Psychology and Psychiatry. 14,* 561–578.

Lee, C., & Antia, S. (1992). A sociological approach to the social integration of hearing-impaired and normally hearing students. *The Volta Review, 95,* 425–434.

Lederberg, A. R. (1991). Social interaction among deaf preschoolers: The effects of language ability and age. *American Annals of the Deaf, 136,* 53–59.

Lederberg, A. R. (1993). The impact of deafness on mother–child and peer relationships. In M. Marschark & M. D. Clark (Eds.), *Psychological Perspectives on Deafness* (pp. 65–91). Hillsdale, NJ: Erlbaum.

Leonard, L. B. (1998). *Children with specific language impairment.* Cambridge, MA: MIT Press.

Loeb, R., & Sarigiani, P. (1986). The impact of hearing impairment on self-perceptions of children. *The Volta Review, 88,* 89–100.

MacLean, G. (1983). Teacher ratings of behavior in hearing-impaired, orally taught, mainstreamed children. *Journal of the American Academy of Child Psychiatry, 22,* 217–220.

MacTurk, R. H., Meadow-Orlans, K. P., Koester, L. S., & Spencer, P. E. (1993). Social support, motivation, language, and interaction: A longitudinal study of mothers and deaf infants. *American Annals of the Deaf, 138,* 19–25.

Manfredi, M. M. (1993). The emotional development of deaf children. In M. Marschark & D. Clark (Eds.), *Psychological perspectives on deafness* (pp. 49–63). Hillsdale, NJ: Erlbaum.

Marschark, M. (1993). Origins and interactions in the social, cognitive, and language development of young children. In M. Marschark & D. Clark (Eds.), *Psychological perspectives on deafness* (pp. 7–26). Hillsdale, NJ: Erlbaum.

Mauk, G. W., & Behrens, T. R. (1993). Historical, political, and technological context associated with early identification of hearing loss. *Seminars in Hearing, 14,* 1–17.

Maxwell, M., Poeppelmeyer, D., & Polich, L. (1999). Deaf members and nonmembers: The creation of culture through communication practices. In D. Kovarsky, J. F. Duchan, & M. Maxwell (Eds.), *Constructing (in)competence: Disabling evaluations in clinical and social interaction* (pp. 125–148). Mahwah, NJ: Erlbaum.

Minett, A., Clark, K., & Wilson, G. (1994). Play behavior and communication between deaf and hard of hearing children and their hearing peers in an integrated preschool. *American Annals of the Deaf, 139,* 420–429.

Nelson, N. W. (1998). *Childhood language disorders in context: Infancy through adolescence (2nd ed.).* Needham Heights, MA: Allyn & Bacon.

Northcott, W. (1981). Freedom through speech: Every child's right. *Volta Review, 83,* 162–181.

Northern, J. L., & Downs, M. P. (1991). *Hearing in children (4th ed.).* Baltimore: Williams & Wilkins.

Paul, R. (2000). Predicting outcomes of early expressive language delay: Ethical implications. In D. V. M. Bishop & L. B. Leonard (Eds.), *Speech and language impairments in children: Causes, characteristics, intervention and outcome* (pp. 195–209). Philadelphia: Taylor & Francis.

Redmond, S. M., & Rice, M. L. (1998). The socioemotional behaviors of children with SLI: Social adaptation or social deviance? *Journal of Speech, Language, and Hearing Research, 41,* 688–700.

Rice, M. L., Sell, M. A., & Hadley, P. A. (1991). Social interaction of speech and language impaired children. *Journal of Speech and Hearing Research, 34,* 1299–1307.

Spencer, P. E., & Deyo, D. A., (1993). Cognitive and social aspects of deaf children's play. In M. Marschark & M. Diane Clark (Eds.), *Psychological perspectives on deafness* (pp. 65–91). Hillsdale, NJ: Erlbaum.

Spencer, P., Koester, L. S., & Meadow-Orlans, K. (1994). Communicative interactions of deaf and hearing children in a day care center: An exploratory study. *American Annals of the Deaf, 139,* 512–518.

Stevens, L. J., & Bliss, L. S. (1995). Conflict resolution abilities of children with specific language impairment and children with normal language. *Journal of Speech and Hearing Research, 38,* 599–611.

Tomblin, J. B., Records, N. L., Buckwalter, P., Zhang, X., Smith, E., & O'Brien, M. (1997). Prevalence of specific language impairment in kindergarten children. *Journal of Speech Language Hearing Research, 40,* 1245–1260.

Subject Index

aberrant behavior 287

abilities: behavioral 45; cognitive 35, 45, 47; concrete operational 504; determined by biology 539; domain-specific 50; intellectual 572, 591; mental 53; physical 591; social 47; verbal 49–50

Aboriginals 564

absenteeism 277, 559, 580

abstraction 81

abuse 244, 294, 499, 550; verbal 551, 554

academic difficulties 276, 277

acceptance: barrier 591; cultural mannerism of 89; group 535; maternal 103; of parental authority 213; social 33, 358, 365, 366, 580; see also peer acceptance

accommodation 82, 363

accuracy 230, 291, 299, 523, 575; perception 365, 366, 367, 368, 369

achievement: academic 297, 400, 401, 469, 524; educational 90; encouragement 103; ethnic 81; low 275; school 246, 406, 574

acquaintances 293

acquiescence 138

acting-out behavior 190, 276, 277

actions: collaborative or cooperative 598; correspondence between ideas and 69;

hostile 288, 292; negative 550; prosocial 228, 458; social 139, 480–2; structural re-organization of 10; undesirable 106

activities 50, 61, 98, 149, 428, 515–16, 578, 582; after-school 164; antisocial 163; channeled in safe and productive ways 100; children with disabilities 574; children with severe mental retardation 577; choice or timing of 213; classroom 344, 594; collective 86; common-ground 308; daily 581; exclusion from many 588; family 245; formal 164; group 485; high level 100, 102, 109; intrinsic interest in 526; joint 519; legal 500; leisure 484; other-sex 130; participation in 72; peer group 578; physical 131, 440, 443, 580; restrictions on 216; rule-governed, participation in 332; sensorimotor and dramatic 330; sex-typed 128; shared 120; social 163, 580, 581; social interaction mostly driven by 288; solitary 582; structured 69; symbolic 429

adaptability 98, 102; family 195

adaptation 13, 521; evolutionary 55; family 69; social 158, 162, 294, 299

adaptiveness/adaptedness 44–5, 49, 50, 54, 308

addictive behaviors 296

helplessness 424
hemiplegia 580, 581
heredity 34, 157
heritability 29, 33, 45–6, 98, 459; defined 28; for
    warmth 34; greater for aggressive problems
    31; increases 35; moderate 30, 32
heroic roles 119
hierarchy 50, 55, 56, 90, 441, 493; dominance
    443, 536; established in peer group 430;
    power 498; social 478, 483
Hindus 457, 469, 470; Orthodox 482–3
Hispanic-Americans 233, 501, 502
hitting 479
holistic view 79
HOME (Home Observation for Measurement of
    the Environment) 34
homeostasis 68, 82
homicide 49
Hominids 44–5, 47
homophilous pools 291
homosexuality 247
Hong Kong 494
"honorship" 103
horizontal relationships 210
hormones 95, 440; androgenic 126, 127; gonadal
    123; "masculinizing" 124; testicular 122
hospitalization 461, 580
hostility 169, 212, 288, 292, 316, 362–3, 539,
    543; mother–partner 227; preschool 315;
    reasoning avoids 463; sibling 224, 226, 227,
    228; toward strangers 55
household chores 467
household structure 248
housekeeping 66
HPA (hypothalamic-pituitary-adrenocortical)
    333, 334–5
HRAF (Human Relations Area Files) 63
Huli children 429
human development 123
humiliation 330
hunter-gatherers/hunting 45, 48, 63
hurt 319, 321, 330, 479, 537, 549, 553; denial of
    563
hurtfulness 445
hyperactivity 110, 581; *see also* ADHD
hypersensitivity 340
hypothalamus 333
hypotheses 443, 525; functional 442; stage-
    related 10; testing 447–50

I-C (individualism-collectivism) construct
73–4
ID (intentionality detector) module 52
idealization 189, 241
ideals 241; cherished 242; cultural 253
ideas 69, 193; structuralist 5
identification 245; national group 505; same-sex
    parent 253; self, ethnic 501, 502
identity 286, 485; development 502; educational
    86; emergent 84; ethnic 138, 503, 504;
    national 505; personal 465; problems 245;
    sexual 247, 253; social 84; *see also* gender
    identity
Ifaluk 62
illegitimate children 245–6, 247
illness 158, 233
imagination 378
imitation 49; reinforced 9; same-sex parents 129
immaturity 186; adaptive value of 49; extended
    period of 47; friends 297; metacognition 50;
    social 330
impoverished children 383
imprinting in animals 182
imprisonment 168
impulse regulation 148–9
impulsivity 251, 459; toddler 109
inadequacy 84, 212; adolescent siblings 229;
    social 339
inappropriate behavior 287
incentives 344
inclusion 308, 577
inclusive fitness 51, 55, 182–3
income: high 141; indices of 564; inequalities
    495; low(er) 145, 147, 168–9, 428, 431,
    432, 467; maternal employment 230;
    middle 168–9, 431
incompetence 229
inconsistency 34, 184
inculcation 85
indebtedness and repayment 465
independence 63, 73, 74, 209, 485; age-
    appropriate 6; lack of parental
    encouragement of 336–7; motivation 429;
    values about 431
India 64, 65, 429, 439, 468, 482–3, 522; play
    time with peers of own sex 121
indices acceptance 267, 270, 276; attachment-
    related 186–8, 191–2; attraction 266;
    behavioral and facial 361; childcare quality
    148; liking/disliking 270; observational 407;
    parent income level 564; physiological 461;
    rejection 267, 276; sociometric 267; status

Author Index